NEW GUINEA
PAPUAN SUBREGION

*Outline map of the Papuan Subregion
showing principal geographical features
of interest to the ornithologist, together
with a number of modern fixes (towns
and villages) and an up-to-date river
system.*

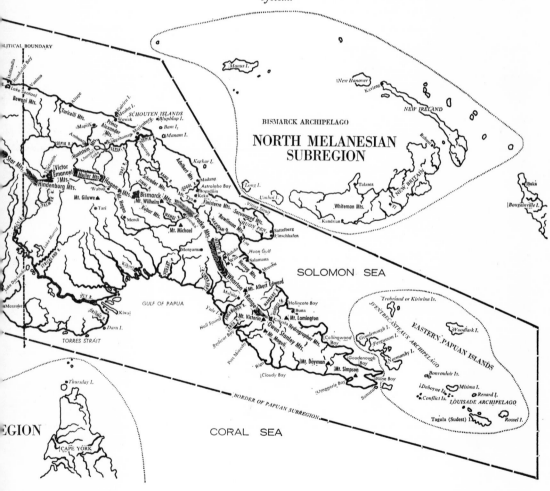

THE WORLD NATURALIST

Birds of Paradise and Bower Birds

THE WORLD NATURALIST / Editor : Richard Carrington

IN MEMORIAM

While the manuscript of this volume was in the

editor's hands, E. Thomas Gilliard, in his 53rd year,

died of a heart attack in New York, 26 January 1965

Birds of Paradise and Bower Birds

E. Thomas Gilliard

Late Curator of Birds
The American Museum of Natural History, New York

Weidenfeld and Nicolson
5 Winsley Street London W1

SBN 297 17030 9

Phototypeset by BAS Printers Limited
Wallop, Hampshire

Printed offset in Great Britain by
Ebenezer Baylis & Son Limited

Contents

Illustrations in the text

All species illustrations in the text are taken either from Sharpe's (1891–8) monograph of the birds of paradise and bower birds, illustrated by J. Gould, W. Hart and J. G. Keulemans, or from Elliot's (1873) monograph of the birds of paradise (including bower birds), illustrated by J. Wolf and J. Smit.

Maps

Plates

All photographs were made by the author unless otherwise stated in the caption.

Foreword

EVERY ornithologist and birdwatcher has his favourite group of birds, whether they be nightingales or storks, hummingbirds or penguins. Frankly, my own are the birds of paradise and bower birds. If they do not rank as high in world-wide popularity as they deserve it is only because so little is known about them, living as they do in inaccessible places, New Guinea and (with a few exceptions) the remoter parts of Australia. For in their ornamentation and courtship behaviour birds of paradise are not surpassed in the whole class of Aves.

The mountain wilderness of New Guinea, the centre of their distribution, is about as remote a place as is still left on this globe. It is no wonder then that our knowledge of these birds has lagged far behind that of any other group. Only a handful of people have ever been able to admire their beauty and bizarre displays outside museums and zoos. The variety of colour, form and courtship displays borders the incredible. Where else in nature is there anything like the 'flags' of the King of Saxony Bird of Paradise or the plumes of *Paradisaea*? Where else is there such a variety of bird-made structures as among the bowers of the New Guinea bower birds?

From the days of Wallace and Beccari on, every ornithologist who ever visited the Papuan region fell in love with these birds and could not say enough about their beauty and bizarreness. Yet these early ornithologists were far too busy with meeting the objectives set for their expeditions, with accumulating their collections and preserving them under the most adverse conditions, to be able to devote the necessary time to detailed life history studies. As it was, we had better descriptions of the display of birds of paradise based on observations of birds living in zoos than on such observed in the wild. Austin Rand was the only naturalist before World War II to add materially to information accumulated by the pioneers in the last century.

It was on one of his earlier expeditions to New Guinea that E. Thomas Gilliard fell under the spell of these birds. As it turned out he was the right man at the right time to fill a gaping void in the ornithological literature. At first he was primarily interested in obtaining as informative a pictorial report of these birds as possible. Yet, watching the birds from the photographer's blind he realised the unexcelled opportunity for keeping an accurate record of all he was observing, and before he knew it he had become the world's leading expert on these birds. He kept watching them hour after hour through torrential downpours, undismayed by insects, heat or cold. Though often living in the most remote mountains, many of the species, particularly the gardener bower birds are unbelievably shy. Only he who has patience and dedicated determination will succeed in making a worthwhile contribution to our knowledge.

When Tom, after his return, began to compare his own notes with the extraordinarily scattered information in the literature, a book manuscript developed almost spontaneously. Tom realised clearly what was needed. It was not only to place on paper his own original discoveries, important and pioneering though they were, but also to bring together the already existing information, hitherto hopelessly scattered in scores of obscure publications of many languages. To produce a volume that could serve as the starting point for all further research on birds of paradise and bower birds, that was his ambition and in this he succeeded admirably. But he did more than that. By bringing all this information together, by advertising, so to speak, the awe-inspiring diversity of form and habit among these two families of birds, he is enabling the ethologist and the evolutionist to include these birds within their sphere of interest.

Bower birds and birds of paradise raise difficult questions, questions that penetrate to the very foundation of our biological theories. How can natural selection favour, one might almost say permit, the evolution of such conspicuously bizarre plumes and displays? How can it permit such 'absurd exaggerations', as one is almost tempted to call them? How can it happen that apparently closely related species and genera differ so drastically in their habits and colorations? Is there merit in Gilliard's theory that sexual dimorphism is reduced in the species with more advanced bower structures? What convergent similarities are there between birds of paradise and other birds with conspicuous displays such as grouse, ruffs, manakins, hummingbirds, etc.?

Thinking about bower birds and birds of paradise can lead us to ask rather disturbing questions. Hutchinson some time ago started to open the door to this subject. What about the sense of aesthetic values among these birds? What about utilisation of leisure time? We have been raised to shudder even at the thought of asking such 'anthropomorphic' questions. Yet the organic world is full of convergence. Do we reject it as 'ichthyomorphic' when someone compares certain properties of porpoises and whales with those of fish? Is is 'myrmecomorphic' if we compare the social structure of termite colonies with that of ant colonies? To me it seems completely legitimate to compare similar phenomena in the organic world even when man is involved. Indeed such a comparative approach is likely to lead to more meaningful results than a study of the human situation as if it were a *Ding an sich*.

Tom Gilliard was fully aware of the many gaps in our information and the inevitable shortcomings of his pioneering effort. We must be grateful to him to have had the courage to complete his manuscript in the full awareness of these shortcomings. He knew that nothing is ever perfect, but the best way to achieve advance is to expose it to constructive criticism. Most importantly, there is little doubt that the availability of this volume will encourage many biologists to take up the study of these birds, indeed to go to New Guinea and Australia and search them out in their native haunts. There is every reason to believe that the publication of Gilliard's *Birds of Paradise and Bower Birds* will be the starting point of a new era in their exploration.

Tom Gilliard did not live to see this volume go to press. It would seem proper therefore to use this opportunity to say a few things about him and his achievements. E. Thomas Gilliard was born in York, Pa., on 23 November 1912. When seven years old he went to live in Ruxton, Maryland, to stay with his mother's sister Thérèse Waelchli, where he attended the small progressive school she had started, the spirit of which left an indelible impression on his entire outlook on life. It was this aunt who was responsible for his freedom of spirit and utter belief in himself and it was she who raised him to believe that he was capable of doing anything under the sun, whether to build his own summer cottage in the Pocono Mountains of Pennsylvania or to connect up a newly-invented electronic gadget with his movie camera. It was this ability to use his hands and be inventive which was part of the secret of his success as photographer, documented in this volume and in his many contributions to the *National Geographic Magazine*.

As a teenager he was an ardent bird-watcher and, as was then customary, egg-collector. The more adventure was mixed in with it, like climbing a seabird cliff or up to a hawk's nest on a tall tree, the better he liked it. This spirit of adventure never left him. In his last year at school he suffered a severe eye injury (detatched retina) in a lacrosse game and was unable to attend school during his Junior year. In spite of this, by working doubly hard in his Senior year he succeeded in graduating with his class. He was awarded a scholarship by Cornell University's Telluride Association and attended their Deep Springs School in California for less than a year before he was forced to leave because of additional injury to his eye. In 1932 he came to the American Museum of Natural History in New York as a volunteer on a $14 a week allowance from his aunt. Thus began in 1932 his association with the American Museum of Natural History where nine months later he was employed as an assistant and after passing through the entire scale of promotions, reached the rank of full Curator in 1963.

I still remember the very day when Tom turned up at the Museum asking whether he could help in the Bird Department. He was at once everyone's favourite owing to his enthusiasm and boyish charm. In both of these characteristics he did not change a bit to the last day of his life. Frank M. Chapman, at that time chairman of the Department, took an instant liking to Tom and was responsible for his further development in these early years. He took him to Barro Colorado, Panama to serve as his assistant in 1936 and 1937 (the two expeditions that proved to be Dr Chapman's last). It is here where Tom acquired his love for the tropics, the scene of so many of his later triumphs. His earlier interest had been the northern seabirds and in 1934 he led an expedition to the Gaspé Peninsula in Quebec to observe the breeding habits of oceanic birds, and in 1936 with Samuel K. George III he went to Funk Island off Newfoundland, the last known American breeding colony of the extinct Great Auk, where they excavated some 6000 bones of this species, including one complete skeleton.

From 1936 on Tom specialised in the birds of South America where he served as ornithologist of the Phelps Venezuelan Expedition to Mount Auyan-tepui and was the first to penetrate the

Macarena chain, an isolated range east of the Colombian Andes. His publications on the collections brought back from these expeditions now belong to the classical literature of South America.

World War II first took him to the interior of Brazil and later to New Guinea and the Philippines. Although he returned to South America several times more in the post-war years, his war experiences had awakened in him a great fascination with the bird life of the eastern tropics. In 1947 he led an expedition to the Zambales Mountains of Luzon, Philippines, and in 1949 he undertook the first of five expeditions to New Guinea. Here he filled in one blank spot on the ornithological map of this island after the other. The discovery of new species and subspecies was his main objective during the earlier trips, but the study of bird behaviour eventually usurped an ever greater share of his interest and attention. His third interest, bird photography, fitted perfectly well with his behaviour studies. Thus it was natural that bower birds and birds of paradise, being both photogenic and fascinating in their behaviour, should eventually dominate his interests. His last trip, to western New Guinea, in 1964, took place only a few months prior to his unexpected death on 26 January 1965 due to a sudden heart attack.

What makes Tom Gilliard so unforgettable was his extraordinary enthusiasm. Natural history is fortunate to be able to attract in each generation such enthusiasts. Will Beebe and Frank Chapman were others. He loved the unspoiled wilderness, he loved colour and beauty, he loved adventure, and he loved his fellow man. He never said an unkind or unpleasant thing about anyone and, when praise was due, Tom gave it more spontaneously and unstintingly than anyone else. It was this warmth of heart and consideration for others that made him also a model father of his three children and a model husband. His wife, a talented artist and writer, was the ideal companion for this explorer naturalist. She accompanied him on several of his most daring and strenuous expeditions and always contributed more than her share to their success.

Tom in many ways seemed so lighthearted, so full of fun, sometimes so casual, that one needed to know him well to realise how single-minded he was in purpose and how dedicated to his life work. His capacity for work was quite unbelievable. He lectured, he wrote popular articles for *Natural History* and the *National Geographic Magazine*, he processed and edited his rich photographic harvest and he produced a steady stream of scientific publications. His

Living Birds of the World entailed an enormous amount of hard work and so did his *Handbook of New Guinea Birds*, written in collaboration with Austin L.Rand, and the present volume. All this was done in the face of troubles that would have discouraged anyone else. His injured eye continued to give him trouble and, after several hospital stays and operations, he finally totally lost sight in it. Ever since the war (indeed already during his South American trips) he suffered from malaria and had to take increasingly toxic treatments to knock out the symptoms (he apparently never got rid of the infection itself). Yet neither eye trouble nor malaria kept him from starting still another expedition and exposing himself to all the incredible hardships of climbing the precipitous mountains of New Guinea and New Britain and suffering through the unspeakable weather of those places. And when he came back from such a trip he would not rest a minute, but plunged right into the working out of the material, the sorting of his photographs, the editing of his films and the preparations for the next trip. There was never a minute when he did not have an exciting new plan. After his last malaria treatments he developed severe heart symptoms but it wasn't Tom's nature to retire to the sidelines. He plunged right back into his usual active life, the only life he knew. Even though he was only fifty-two when he died he had filled these years with more activity than most octogenarians. He has left behind a solid body of achievement and an indelible imprint on the minds and hearts of his countless friends.

ERNST MAYR
Director, Museum of Comparative
Zoology, Harvard University.

Introduction

IT IS perhaps not too much to say that paradise birds are the most beautiful of all living creatures and that, short of man himself, bower birds are the most bizarre. Seafarers of old when they first encountered the glorious birds of paradise took them to be wanderers from a celestial paradise; and in 1872 the first naturalist to encounter a skilfully constructed bower complete with its mysterious garden and attractive furnishings, attributed it to the inventiveness of man.

Sixty-five years later a British ornithologist wrote (Stonor, 1937) that even today '. . . the display grounds of bower birds are one of the strangest and least understood phenomena in nature.' And a professor of zoology at Yale only a decade ago agreed with him (Hutchinson, 1952): '. . . some of the bower birds exhibit behavior of a kind which in its complexity and refinement is unique in the nonhuman part of the animal kingdom.' He added: 'The extraordinary display activities . . . are exhibited by birds of a group in which other species, the birds of paradise, are celebrated for the extreme beauty of their epigamic structure and the elaborateness of their ceremonial dances. The bower bird's behavior is . . . no less extraordinary, if in a quite different way.' Then Professor Hutchinson concluded with a question which cut to the heart of the mystery: 'Why,' he asked, 'should this have happened twice over in such different ways among these exotic relatives of the crow?'

What manner of creatures are these to have inspired such a wealth of superstition and scientific wonder? Fourteen years and six New Guinea expeditions ago I resolved to try to unmask some of the mysteries surrounding these fascinating, elusive birds. What little I have been able to discover is recorded within the covers of this book.

Birds of paradise are best known for their extraordinary courtship plumage (skirts, whips, capes, lace-like feathers, twisted enamel-like wires, erectile expandable fans, sabre-shaped tails, patches of mirror-like iridescent plumage) and other ornaments (jade and opal coloured mouths; naked, garishly painted areas of skin, sometimes of great relative size; nut-like and leaf-like wattles; etc.) which develop in the males two to five years after hatching. Birds of paradise are famous also for their strange and beautiful dance movements which frequently make the males appear startling and grotesque and more ornament-like than bird-like. Some species dance in trees, charging and then posturing stiffly with their long lace-like cascades of plumage; some hang in shimmering, pendulous masses beneath limbs. Other species dance on vertical shafts in columns of sky light which they let in through the roof of the forest by laboriously stripping away the leaves. Other males dance on low vines or on the ground, alternately freezing then spinning with their circular feather skirting extended ballerina-like.

All of the highly ornamented species breed polygynously, that is they breed without forming pair bonds, but instead by mating with as many females as they can attract by means of their extraordinary plumes, movements and call notes. In such species the male plays no part whatever in the duties of nesting. Often in the plumed species the males live apart from the females in bachelor clans, with each clan maintaining breeding stations which have nothing whatever to do with feeding or nesting. And in these plumed species the males and females are usually so different in appearance they can easily be mistaken for different species. But in a number of birds of paradise the plumage is rather starling-like and there is very little difference in dress between the sexes. These rather drably coloured species all appear to be monogamous in their breeding behaviour, or at least the male mates with a single female at a time and then assists her in the tasks connected with nest building, rearing and protection of the young.

Bower birds appear at first glance to be quite unlike birds of paradise. Almost all are relatively drab, short-plumed birds, best known as the only birds in the world which build and decorate elaborate terrestrial dance pavilions. These pavilions apparently serve in place of the bright plumage found in their near relatives, the birds of paradise. The bowers take a number of architectural forms ranging from mats, avenued chambers, carefully planted lawns, stick towers, to tepee-roofed huts, and all are decorated with odd and colourful forest jewellery such as bright flowers, chips of amber-coloured resin, iridescent insect skeletons, stones and many kinds of colourful berries and shells; also ornaments of many sorts pilfered from man.

Most adult male bower birds display in and around their colourful bowers, each of which is privately built and owned. Apparently bower birds mate with as many females as they can attract to their individual bachelor bowers. And as in the birds of paradise, the bower-building polygynous species play no part whatever in the duties of nesting.

In some bower birds the males have bright head plumes and sometimes bright body plumage, but as a general rule the better 'architects' and 'artists' are the species with the least ornamental feathering; that is to say there seems to be an inverse ratio between the development of the bower and the development of the courtship plumage. This seems to be correlated with the possibility that the more advanced birds use the bower rather than the nuptial plumage in the optical stimulation of the female.

But again (as in some of the birds of paradise), in some of the species of bower birds the male and the female are boldly or brightly coloured – jade green, gold and so on – and in these species no bower structure is built and the courtship display apparently always takes place in trees. Also, most importantly, in the tree-displaying species pair bonds are formed and monogamy is practiced with the male assisting his mate in the duties of nesting.

In addition to the phenomenon of bower building, which is unique, some species of bower birds are world famous for their ability to mix and apply paint to the walls of their colourful bowers. An almost unbelievable refinement to their extraordinary painting abilities is their use of a tool, a brush-like tool, to apply the specially mixed pigments.

The bower birds and birds of paradise may be said to form a slightly forked branch in the highest part of the tree of avian evolution. One twig of the fork represents the birds of paradise with their extreme modifications of plumage, the other twig represents the bower birds with their extreme modifications of behaviour. The bird of paradise twig is composed of a group of forty-two species of starling-to crow-sized birds which occurs in Australia, New Guinea and the Moluccan Islands; the bower bird twig is composed of a group of eighteen species of thrush- to small crow-sized birds limited to Australia and New Guinea.

For generations ornithologists believed the birds of paradise and the bower birds to be closely related to the crows and jays – the Corvidae – but in 1963 Walter Bock announced the discovery of cranial characters which linked the bird of paradise–bower bird group very closely to the starlings. At first glance this seems strange; but one has only to examine the many spectacular species of starlings that occur in the Old World, chiefly in the tropics of Africa, India, Malaya and the Australian region, to see that the family Sturnidae is composed of stocks which have an extraordinary capacity for evolutionary divergence, both in the direction of glittering colouration and in the direction of exaggerated plumage. Another capacity of the starling stock is to be seen in the elaborate domed nests which are constructed by many of the species: in short, in their capacity for architectural achievements, and this may be correlated with bower building.

In Chapter 6 (p. 40), I put forward a hypothesis which I believe explains the extraordinary developments found in bower birds. In his theory of sexual selection, Charles Darwin (1871) recognised the operation of two main forces: (a) selection exerted through rival males, resulting in the development of special weapons such as antlers; (b) selection dependent on the sexual preferences of females, resulting in the development of male ornamentation in the form of colourful plumage, wattles and so on. This theory adequately explains many of the evolutionary developments found in birds of paradise. But in the case of bower birds, I suggest that a third force exists: this comes into play through the transference of sexual signals from the physical features of the male to the objects used by him in his courtship displays.

This third force develops on very rare occasions. It is so potentially powerful that it can penetrate the barriers of counter-selective forces imposed by natural selection and may carry an animal into an entirely new adaptive zone. It is probably responsible for house building and tool using in bower birds – and, indeed, in Man himself.

Acknowledgments

A GREAT many people, both directly and indirectly, play a part in the writing of a volume such as this. Had the author lived he would have wished to express his gratitude to all of those who in any way contributed to the final product and in particular to thank the following individuals.

His wife, Margaret, accompanied him to some of the wildest parts of New Guinea and worked unceasingly to make each expedition a success. Since the author's death she has actively helped with the many problems that have arisen regarding this volume and has given much encouragement and advice.

Especial thanks are due to Dr Walter Bock whose anatomical studies on birds of paradise and bower birds have contributed largely to our knowledge of the relationships among these birds; to Dr Ralph Bulmer whose own field notes were generously turned over to the author for his use and who went over the manuscript with Gilliard in New Guinea in 1964; to Mr James C. Greenway, Jr who read the manuscript and offered many helpful suggestions; to Dr Ernst Mayr whose own studies in the field and in the museum have placed him in the top rank of students of these birds and who most generously consented to write the foreword; to Dr Austin L. Rand, another of the leading authorities on birds of paradise and bower birds, who helped the author greatly and who has done much to make the present volume possible, and with whom Gilliard completed a handbook of New Guinea birds shortly before his death; and to Dr Erwin Stresemann, the dean of world ornithologists and for more than half a century a leading authority on this group of birds, who encouraged the author and then had the great kindness to read and check the manuscript.

Others who have helped in various ways have been the Government authorities in New Guinea, in particular Sir Donald Cleland,

Administrator of Papua and the Territory of New Guinea (now retired), and the many patrol officers in the hinterlands of the island who have provided much assistance over the years. Numerous non-Government people in Australia and New Guinea have also helped. The following must be singled out for special thanks: Sir Edward Hallstrom; Mr Fred Shaw Mayer, veteran New Guinea naturalist and aviculturist; Captain Neptune Blood; and Mr Arnold McGill. The Indonesian Government representatives, including Dr S. Somadikarta of the Museum Zoologicum Bogoriense, were most co-operative and helpful during work in West Irian in 1964. Mrs Mary LeCroy has carried out many tasks involved in the writing of this volume and in seeing it through the press; Mr Richard Carrington and numerous others at Weidenfeld and Nicolson have provided encouragement and help; Mrs Margaret Hanson and Miss Marlis Kistner very ably prepared the manuscript for publication.

Financial support for the author's many expeditions has come from a number of sources. The Sanford family, through Dr Leonard C. Sanford and then through his sons William and James, gave much encouragement and support. The National Geographic Society, through its past presidents Gilbert Grosvenor and Melville Grosvenor, provided funds and valuable help on many expeditions. The backing of the authorities at The American Museum of Natural History and of the Explorers Club was always generously given and most appreciated. A grant from the Frank M. Chapman Memorial Fund, through The Natural History Press, made publication possible.

There are probably many others whom the author would have wished to thank. To them we can only apologize, and hope that they understand that Tom Gilliard appreciated most deeply the assistance they gave him.

The American Museum of Natural History,   DEAN AMADON
New York

Part One

Chapter One

The Biogeography of
New Guinea

WEST, north, and east of New Guinea the sea bottom falls away precipitously; but to the south, in a broad region known as the Sahul Shelf between New Guinea and Australia, the sea is shallow – thirty feet in the narrows. It is so shallow that, geologically speaking, the two land masses may be said to form a single sharply isolated subcontinent; this isolation has persisted since the beginning of the Tertiary period, about sixty million years ago. The deep seas surrounding this great subcontinent are wide and sparsely studded with islands, except to the west; here, somewhat crowded together between the western Papuan Islands and the main islands of Indonesia, lie Celebes, the Moluccas and associated smaller islands. Farther to the west and to the south, the sea again becomes shallow as a result of a great marine peninsula, the Sunda Shelf, which, geologically speaking, is a borderland of Asia. This peninsula supports the great islands of Sumatra, Java, and Borneo and the bulk of the smaller islands which today comprise the country of Indonesia. But shallow or deep, the over-water distance between the Australo–Papuan region and the tip of the Asiatic mainland exceeds 2000 miles.

The island of New Guinea is 1490 miles long by 410 miles in greatest breadth, with an area of 312,000 square miles. It is thus the second largest island in the world after Greenland (827,000 square miles). Incidentally, the New Guinea region breaks down as follows: Papua, 87,786 square miles; Mandated Territory, 69,700 square miles; Irian Barat (formerly Netherlands New Guinea), 154,514 square miles. The island lies just south of the equator between latitude 0° 19′ S. and 10° 43′ S., longitude 130° 45′ E. and 150° 48′ E., and is separated from Australia by a shallow, island-studded strait ninety-five miles in width. Its chief feature is a massive cordillera running from one end of the island to the other;

this mountain system represents the eastern extremity of the great arc of 'fold mountains' which extend through the Himalayas and Malaya into the Pacific (Carey, 1938). The New Guinea cordillera culminates in the snow-covered peaks of Mt Carstensz (16,500 feet) in west New Guinea. In the Nassau and Oranje ranges of west New Guinea and in the Star Mountains of central New Guinea there are many 15,000-foot peaks, for example Mount Idenburg (15,800 feet), Mt Wilhelmina (15,500 feet), Mt Juliana (15,200 feet). In eastern New Guinea there are also some high peaks such as Mt Wilhelm (15,400 feet) and Mt Victoria (13,400 feet). The island's main cordillera '. . . represents an axis of tertiary and mesozoic mountain-building situated in a zone of crustal weakness separating the relatively stable Australian continental mass from the Pacific Ocean' (Anon., 1962: 11).

Irregular and jagged in profile, with only a few passes crossing it through notches as low as 5500 feet above sea level, this cordillera forms an almost impassable barrier between the biological communities of the tropical and subtropical regions which occur for more than 1000 miles along each of its sides. Only at the ends of the wall, and in a gap in the isthmus south of Geelvink Bay, can the tropical species make their way around the great barrier wall. This is a situation which is highly interesting to the biologist because of its evolutionary effects on the flora and fauna. For example, in walking through one of the passes in the wall – the Baiyer–Wahgi pass for example – the biologist finds very different races of the same species living hardly a mile apart on each side of the pass. This phenomenon is particularly striking in the genus *Paradisaea*, in which the great flank plumes of the males are blood red on one side (south) of the pass and orange-yellow on the other.

In many places the cordillera, which is geologically very young, consists of a complex system of nearly parallel ranges each often very different in character, separated by high-floored, intermontane valleys. Some of the valleys are small, some are large; a few remain almost inaccessible and are populated by pockets of men who are just emerging from the Stone Age. Others are lovely, cool oases populated by both native and European planters.

The cordillera varies in width from about twenty-five miles to 200 miles. At its edges it usually falls away steeply in deeply incised, heavily eroded slopes, even precipices, to rolling plains covered with dripping rain forest. On the main body of the island,

2

outlying mountains often protrude from the cordillera or rise from the plains nearby. These are largely encircled with sediments and gravels of Pleistocene or Recent age.

Because the ranges were thrust upward relatively recently, perhaps as recently as two million years ago, they still exhibit much evidence of the rapid carving wrought by water and mountain slides – characters of 'young' mountains. A feature of these young mountains is the unsettled condition of the structures upon which they stand.

It is worth taking into consideration before one embarks for New Guinea, that this island is in one of the most unstable parts of the globe. Earth tremors occur so frequently that one soon learns to mistrust the land and its gelatinous base, and to take precautions against seismic waves.

Volcanic activity is confined almost entirely to a belt of small islands fringing the northern coast, some of which rise like classic cones more than 4000 feet above the sea. Their vulcanism is of the explosive type, with the volcanoes occasionally blowing up with the abruptness and strength of an atomic bomb.

Much of the structure of the main ranges consists of folded limestone overlying the basic rocks, and with extinct volcanic craters here and there, attesting to the massive disturbances which occurred when the central cordillera was elevated in relatively recent time from the depths of the sea. The 'youth' of the range is confirmed by marine limestone caps of Late Pliocene age on many of the high ranges, including the Carstensz Toppen with its halo of permanent ice.

To the north and south of the main ranges occur a number of very large rivers which wind in ox-bow loops, for long distances through broad alluvial plains. Sometimes they flow hundreds of miles to drop less than 100 feet towards the sea. These jungle rivers have everything that the imaginative dreamer might expect: endless mangrove swamps, swarms of crocodiles, bands of nomadic headhunters, fast war canoes, water lilies six feet tall – but that is another subject.

At their mouths the rivers are usually bordered with casuarinas and mangroves, just behind begin swamps pock-marked with lagoons and overgrown with aquatic plants. Here one finds teeming masses of waterfowl. Much of the river basins consist of vast fields of cane grasses, some species of which reach sixteen feet in height, and, in this setting, islands of swamp forest occur. On higher

3

ground one finds dense tropical rain forest heavily coiffured with arboreal gardens of orchids and intermeshed with endless vines and creepers. The latter are garnished with screaming cockatoos, flying foxes, and huge honking hornbills.

The largest river, the Fly, forms a zoogeographical barrier to many species of tropical plants and animals living on the southern watershed. At the tip of its broad mouth it is thirty miles wide; inland, at its main stream, it narrows to ten miles, and thereafter this waterway, which ranks among the great rivers of the world, remains tidal (with dangerous bores) for 150 miles. Its seasonal rise is thirty feet and it is navigable at all seasons for at least 500 miles.

Nearly all the rivers of the south coast are navigable for at least short distances, and nearly all of them have wide mouths. It is believed that this is because the whole south coastline is subsiding. By contrast on the north coast, even the greatest rivers are virtually non-tidal, have no bores, and are often not, or hardly, navigable; also, they are usually quite narrow and shallow. This the geologist interprets as being due to the elevating of the coast above the sea. He believes that, although the whole island of New Guinea is settling like a floundering boat, it is listing as it settles. In the listing the north coast tends to rise somewhat above sea level while the south coast dips deeply under it.

None of the rivers of the north coast are effective as zoogeographical barriers. The largest is the Sepik; although some 700 miles long, with a seasonal rise of twenty-six feet and unusual in that it is navigable during high water for a distance of some 530 miles, it is only a mile wide at its mouth. The second largest, the Mamberamo, a 500-mile-long river, is navigable to a point 105 miles above its mouth. There it becomes constricted and tortured, causing fast water and seasonally is made very dangerous by rising some forty-six feet.

All of the large rivers of the northern watershed help to drain a 1000-mile-long trough of structural origin which (with part of Geelvink Bay and MacCluer Gulf) is known to geologists as the Central Depression. It separates the main cordillera from a series of ranges called the North Coastal Ranges. Some of the Arfak, Saruwaged and Finisterre peaks reach 13,000 feet, the rest of the northern mountains range between 5000 and 8000 feet or less. Next to the central cordillera this depression is the most important zoogeographical barrier on the mainland of New Guinea. The

4

fauna of the mountains lying north of the depression is often very different from that of the mountains lying to the south of it. This is particularly evident in the birds of paradise; for example, the two species of Six Wired Bird of Paradise, Wahnes' Six Wired (*Parotia wahnesi*) and Lawes' Six Wired (*P. lawesi*) found on either side are of the sort that one would expect to find on moderately isolated oceanic islands, not on mountains situated twelve miles apart across a narrow valley! The same degree of speciation is found between the Stephanie (*Astrapia stephaniae*) and Rothschild's Bird of Paradise (*A. rothschildi*). Thus it seems that the Central Depression has, and is still playing an important part in the speciation of many lines of New Guinea animals.

A geographical feature which played a vital part in multiplication of species was a now vanished island in southern New Guinea. Zeuner (1942) notes that south-central New Guinea was an island separated from the main New Guinea land mass in the Pleistocene before the last (Würm) glaciation (see also Koopman, 1957).

A number of highland lakes play minor but significant roles in the biogeography of New Guinea. Among these are Wissel Lakes, Anggi Lakes, Lake Tamur, and Lake Habbema. Some, including the highest, Habbema Lake, situated 12,000 feet above sea level, are inhabited by unique races or even species of birds, mammals and plants.

In the lowlands many large lakes, such as the beautiful Lake Chambri, 180 miles up the Sepik River, and lakes Murray and Daviumbu, hidden in the vast swamplands of the lower Fly River basin, constitute ecological centres of major importance. The largest is Lake Rombebai near the delta of the Mamberamo River with an area of some sixty square miles.

The Climate

In general, the climate of New Guinea is divisible into two seasons, a 'dry season' which occurs from May to November, and a 'wet season' from October to April. The 'dry season', however, is relatively wet, with rain falling frequently. Many, if not most of the birds of paradise – indeed, most of the birds of the island – have their peak display periods during the dry season and their peak nesting periods in the early part of the wet season. These seasons are controlled by two major wind systems, which predominate during eight months of the year, (a) the *Southeast Trades* which operate from June to October ('winter') and (b) the *Northwest Monsoon* which operates in the reverse direction from December to March ('summer'). Both wind systems convey much moisture to the island but the amount of precipitation in any one spot is regulated by the height and the position of the land in relation to the wind.

The rainfall varies locally from fifty-five inches to more than 300 inches per annum. The temperature, like the rainfall, is regulated by the height and position of the land and the strength and direction of the rain-laden winds. Temperatures at sea level rise as high as 95° F. and rarely fall below 70° F. In the mid-mountain valleys the range is from about 50° to 80°. As a general rule the temperature drops 3° F. for every 1000 feet of altitude. Night ice frequently forms at 11,000 feet and permanent snow line occurs at 15,345 feet on Mt Carstensz. Incidentally the present snow-covered area of Mt Carstensz is given as eighty square miles (Reiner, 1960).

Annual changes in climate (in the absence of any definitive changes in day-length) probably operate as the 'triggering' mechanisms responsible for regulating the often rather precise breeding cycles of New Guinea birds. Some other seasonal changes which may assist in the regulation of the breeding cycles are (a) a slight average temperature difference between the 'winter' and the 'summer' seasons of about 3° F.; (b) a slight decrease in average cloud cover and increase in sunlight during the dry or summer period; (c) a slight increase in day length amounting to about half an hour in the extreme times of sunrise and sunset during the course of the year. However, the most powerful 'triggering' device, I believe, is rainfall and its secondary effects. Seasonal fluctuations in rainfall cause seasonal fluctuations in plant and animal foods, and probably it will be found that New Guinea birds have synchronised their breeding cycles to these fluctuations so as to bring forth their young at the season when they have the best chance of surviving.

Vegetational Zones

New Guinea supports a rich assortment of botanical communities, all of which are predominantly Asiatic in origin. The most widespread type of vegetation is the tropical rain forest, but the zone in which most species of birds of paradise and bower birds are found, is the mid-mountain forest. An interesting formation of very limited distribution is the grassland, in which no birds of paradise and only a few bower birds are found. Grassland turns up here and there on the coastal plain, in small areas of the mid mountains and near the summits of the largest ranges. It is nowhere much of a factor in the distribution of animal life except in the coastal regions adjacent to Australia, for example, in the district of Australian flora around Port Moresby, in the Daru-Merauke region, and on the Bomberai Peninsula. Also worthy of mention are the grassfields of the Vogelkop south of the Tamrau Range, some sizeable fields around Lake Sentani in the Sukarnapura (formerly Hollandia) region, and long belts in the bottomlands of the central depression.

One suspects the workings of primitive man whenever the enormous forests of New Guinea are broken and replaced with grass. He is undoubtedly responsible for the bulk of the destruction that has occurred in the mid mountains, for example, in the Goroka, Wahgi, Baiyer, Telefomin and Balim Valleys; but he is usually not responsible for the alpine grasslands that occur above the tree line on all the great mountains.

Immediately above the tropical rain forest, which extends upwards from sea level to about 4500 feet, is the mid-mountain oak forest (this formation extends upward to about 7500 feet); then comes the beech forest (up to about 10,200 feet); and finally the subalpine forest up to the tree line at about 11–12,000 feet. A label beside the Snow Mountain habitat group in the American Museum of Natural History gives this telegraphic description of the zones: 'Going up from sea level one passes through belts of oak, beech to pines, tree blueberries, rhododendrons and alpine tundra and finally to everlasting snow.' Each of these vegetational formations interdigitates with others so that its upper and lower limits are areas of gradual transition. Each supports a distinctive biological community which is immediately recognisable by reason of its special bird of paradise calls, its specialised plants, and its specialised animals.

Altitudinal Zones

Zonalised biological communities are very obvious to the ornithologist with a flair for mountain scaling. As he climbs he will exchange the generally wide-ranging 'fluid' tropical plants and animal species for more localised species with a tolerance for colder temperatures and less sunlight (due to increasing cloud and mist cover).

He leaves behind the wide-ranging tropical species that encircle the great island in the lowlands just as if he were climbing from the ocean on to an island at sea. If the island happens to be isolated from the main chain of mountains, or if it is a spur or knob that is more or less cut off from the main range, he will not infrequently discover species on 'his' island which occur nowhere else in the world.

In birds the transition will be gradual to heights of about 5000 feet, but as the climber passes that elevation a sharp break seems to occur. There he will leave behind all the bird species that he has known in the lowlands. After passing that point he will find an entirely new assortment of species that again change gradually with altitude. This abrupt break in the altitudinal zonation of birds has never been satisfactorily explained. Stresemann (1923), among others, has called attention to this phenomenon.

Some of the factors which may bear on the problem of altitudinal zonation may be correlated with temperature changes that occurred during the Pleistocene Epoch. The last period of maximum glaciation in New Guinea probably occurred only about 10,000 years ago. Geologists have found evidence of a number of ancient glaciers on the island. For example, it is known that one extended downwards to 10,900 feet on Mt Wilhelm (Reiner, 1960), and another descended to 6000 feet on Carstensz Toppen (Dozy, 1938).

It thus seems probable that a number of major ecological shifts have occurred hand in hand with the temperature changes which caused these glaciations on the equatorial island of New Guinea. Just how pronounced these shifts must have been is suggested by comparing the altitudinal zones of vegetation as they exist today with a reconstruction of the formations which probably existed 10,000 years ago, when in places the ice extended down to 6000 feet.

In this connection it is important to note that geologists believe that the physiography of the ranges from which hung these glacier tongues has not changed appreciably in the last 10,000 years. It therefore follows that the mountain forests of that cold period must have been compressed into a much narrower altitudinal belt. This forested zone probably extended upwards from about sea level only to about 6–8000 feet. Today by contrast unbroken forests extend upwards to about 11,000 feet. Doubtless the rapid postglacial increase in forests was accompanied by great changes in the distribution of animal life.

Another point of biogeographical importance is that hand in hand with the compression of the forests during this recent period of glacial maxima, another mechanism was brought into play. This occurred in connection with the lowering of the oceans by some 300 feet due to the storing of sea water in the continental ice shields. The lowered water level enabled the tropical forests to expand far out into the shallows of what is now the ocean bottom, probably linking New Guinea and Australia with a vegetational belt through which faunal interchanges could take place. As will be shown later, there is much evidence in the distribution of both birds and mammals that such interchanges occurred rather freely. Another effect may be the avian altitudinal zones mentioned by Stresemann and Rand, namely, the division of New Guinea birds into two primary groups, (a) forms of the lowlands and lower mountain slopes, and (b) forms of the upper mountain zone. Intrinsic differences in variability between the two groups may be the fundamental reason for this division: the bird species which today live appreciably above the Pleistocene tree line (6–8000 feet) may be 'plastic' species with a capacity for pronounced genetic variation, whereas the species which have not moved upwards to take advantage of the 'new' mountain niches may be non-plastic 'old' species.

Whatever the reasons for the striking differences between the bird life of the lowlands and the mountains of New Guinea, a biologist visiting the island will encounter two different worlds, the fluid, far-reaching one of the lowlands and the restricted one of the highlands. The latter he will find when he steps from his aircraft in any of the many mid-mountain valleys, formerly so inaccessible and now so easily reached by air from the coast.

c

Chapter Two

The Origin of Animal Stocks

WITH the geological, physiographical, climatological and vegetational resumé outlined in Chapter One as a background, the stage is set for a brief look into the mystery of the origins of the New Guinea–Australia animal stocks. How and when did these stocks first reach the area, and from where did they come? For possible answers to these questions I have leaned heavily on G. G. Simpson (1961), E. Mayr (1953) and A. Keast (1961). Some 566 species of land and fresh water birds occur on the ancient island of New Guinea. What are the factors responsible for the radiation there of such a galaxy of species, especially such as we find among the birds of paradise and bower birds? How frequently was the island colonised? How old must the colonising stocks be for so many to have reached the level of endemic genera and some even the level of endemic families? What is the phylogeny of the birds of paradise and bower birds, and did they arise as a group on New Guinea itself? These are difficult questions, but we must attempt to answer them in the course of this book.

Authorities agree that the ancestors of both the flying and non-flying Australo–Papuan animals are of Asiatic origin. They also agree that these stocks reached the Australo–Papuan region by island-hopping through the East Indies and not by way of former land bridges. As to the chronology of their emigrations, the earliest arrivals were the ancestors of the well-nigh unbelievable egg-laying mammals, the spiny anteaters (of Australia and New Guinea) and the duck-billed platypus (of Australia and Tasmania), which probably reached Australia in the Jurassic or late Triassic (Simpson, 1961). Incidentally, Simpson thinks it very likely that the ancestors of these animals evolved into monotremes (Monotremata) after their arrival in the Australian region and that this amazing branch of egg-laying, hair-clad animals never occurred outside the Australian region.

Later waves of land animals arriving during the late Mesozoic or earliest Cenozoic, again by island-hopping down the East Indies chain fron Asia, formed the second of five successful animal colonisations of the Australian region. The second wave brought the ancestors of the marsupials. This stock radiated widely in Australia and then spread through New Guinea, thence to the Moluccan and Celebes islands and to some of the islands of Micronesia. This was an important wave, as evidenced by the fact that today four families of marsupials with a total of twenty-one genera are known. In fact, the marsupials constitute the most important group of animals in the non-flying biological community of New Guinea.

The third colonisation of the Australo–Papuan region – according to Simpson – occurred from the early Tertiary onward when flying mammals began a series of invasions from Asia, speciating along the way as they island-hopped down the East Indies chain to New Guinea. There they underwent major differentiations before radiating south to Australia. The pattern of colonisation, speciation, and counter-migration of flying mammals may be rather similar to that which affected the bird stocks.

Like the flying mammals, birds must have encountered much less difficulty than non-flying animals in negotiating the numerous ecological and geographical barriers of the East Indies. Simpson estimates that bats crossed through the barriers thirty or more times. Birds crossed them often enough to establish the root stocks for the fifty-six families of land and fresh water birds now found in the Australo–Papuan region. This number becomes more significant when it is compared with the number of families of birds found today in the much larger region of origin, the Ethiopian–Oriental–Malayan region, in which some eighty families of comparable stocks occur.

Among the fifty-six Australo–Papuan families are twelve uniquely distinctive ones, together with forty-four which are widely distributed in other parts of the world. Darlington (1957), in his valuable contribution on the geographical distribution of animals, cites the following bird families as being 'nearly or quite' Australo–Papuan in origin, and he notes that this group of endemics is larger than that of any other continental faunal region except the Neotropical: cassowaries (3 species), emus (2 species), megapodes (10 species), owlet frogmouths (8 species), lyre birds (2 species), scrub birds (2 species), flowerpeckers (54 species), honeyeaters (159 species), bell magpies (4 species), bower birds (18 species), and birds of paradise (42 species).

The richness of this avifauna is best illustrated by comparing it with that of the other major zoogeographical sectors of the world. The Australian zoologist Allen Keast (1961), who recently completed a survey of avian speciation on the Australian continent, found that there are 906 species of land and fresh water birds breeding in the Australo–Papuan region, whereas only about 750 species are known from all of North America north of Mexico, and only about 1100 are known from the entire Palearctic region, (i.e. all of Europe and North Africa together with most of Asia north of the Indian lowlands). By way of further comparison, in Africa south of the Sahara about 1750 species are known, and in the ornithologically richest part of the world, tropical America, about 2500 are known.

Keast's most interesting observation is that the 906 Australo–Papuan species are distributed as follows: 566 in the New Guinea region and only 531 in Australia, although the latter is geographically ten times greater in size. Another surprising discovery is that only 191 species are shared between the two sub-regions of Australia and New Guinea, despite their close geographical relationships.

Applying this form of analysis to the superfamily of birds of paradise and bower birds, we find that of the sixty known species from the Australo–Papuan region, forty-seven are endemic to the New Guinea region[1], four are shared with Australia and only nine are endemic to Australia.

The twelve unique or nearly unique Australo–Papuan bird families contain a total of 318 species. Three of these families, the emus, lyre birds, and scrub birds, with a total of only six species, are exclusively Australian, and they probably evolved to the level of distinct families in Australia. None of the endemic families is exclusively Papuan. It is likely that birds of paradise and bower birds evolved to the level of a distinct family in the forests of New Guinea and then spread to Australia.

It is particularly interesting that a large proportion of the 906 land and fresh water bird species known from the Australo–Papuan

---

[1] The two endemics (*Lycocorax* and *Semioptera*) found in the northern Moluccas are considered to be peripheral elements belonging to the Papuan subregion (Mayr, 1953).

region should belong to a few endemic passerine land bird families whose age is apparently so great that their relationships are obscured. Examples are the flowerpeckers, the honeyeaters and the birds of paradise which have a combined total of 256 species, or 28·1 per cent of the entire Australo–Papuan complement of land and fresh water birds. With regard to the total endemism found in this region, Keast (1961) found that 369 of the 906 species (or 41 per cent) are species belonging to endemic families or subfamilies.

Unlike the early arrival passerines, the later arrivals did not find a wealth of open niches into which to radiate. Instead they had to overcome both the long island hopping journey and then the stiff competition involved in winning niches in an area already well filled with birds.

Today the species which have resulted from relatively few ancient colonisations (and their subsequent radiations) encompass the entire island from the depths of the tropical swamps to the alpine grasslands capping its greatest ranges. They form a marvellously rich avifauna in terms of species, but one which is not rich in terms of families. The main endemic elements are the bower birds, the birds of paradise, the megapodes, the owlet-nightjars, the flowerpeckers and the honeyeaters. The paradise and bower bird assemblage almost certainly underwent its chief differentiation in the ancient forests of New Guinea before radiating to Australia, where some of the ancestral bower birds became adapted for life in grasslands, then re-radiated to New Guinea.

Mixed with these old Australo–Papuan endemic species are a fair number of other groups, themselves old, but widespread in the world. For example the rails, the babblers, the parrots, the hornbills and the pigeons. Also present are larks, swallows, drongos, Old World warblers, flycatchers and thrushes, also a few sunbirds, starlings and weaverbirds, all families which have their centres of abundance and usually their origins in Asia or Africa.

Despite this confusion of bird life, the naturalist will not be long in the forests of New Guinea before he will note the almost mysterious absence of certain major groups of birds. Not present for example are the trogons (which like the parrots are nearly universal in the tropical forests of the Old and the New World); missing too, are the woodpeckers, a family which is virtually cosmopolitan in the woodlands of the world other than those of the Australo–Papuan region. The absence of these birds has given the New Guinea region a unique personality. For example, the place normally occupied by woodpeckers is taken up by tiny stiff-tailed parrots found nowhere else in the world. These parrots have been modified to exploit niches left vacant by the absence of woodpeckers.

Equally mysteriously missing from the biological community of New Guinea and of course Australia, are the arboreal primates, the monkeys, which occur almost throughout the tropical rain forests of the world. Had they reached New Guinea they would have found their niches already occupied by prehensile-tailed arboreal mammals of another much older sort, namely the phalangers, a group of marsupials which superficially resemble monkeys. Their absence (plus the absence of many other forest-living Asiatic groups of animals) from the ancient forests of New Guinea indicates that this island and Australia were never connected with Asia.

These then are some of the characteristics of the biological community of the ancient isolated continental island known as the Australo–Papuan region, a community in which the most interesting elements are the endemic families and subfamilies of birds, the honeyeaters, the bell magpies, the butcher birds, the piping crows, the magpie larks, the flowerpeckers, the megapodes, the honeyeaters, the owlet-nightjars and most fascinating of all, the birds featured in this work, the bower birds and the birds of paradise.

Chapter Three

Discovery of the Home of the Bird of Paradise

PORTUGUESE treasure hunters using Goa as a base – they established Goa in India in 1498 – were the first to carry out extensive explorations of the islands of the Malay Archipelago. By 1521 they had established a permanent post on Amboina in the Moluccas and their ships bearing nutmegs, cloves, and other spices began sailing regularly to Portugal. At this period the prestige and power of Portugal was high and her vessels ranged widely over the oceans of the world. One ship in 1511 with the commanders Antionio d'Abreu and Francisco Serrano on board, was the first to sight the island of New Guinea. However, the first man to set foot ashore was probably the Portuguese Governor of Ternate, de Menenez, who was forced by adverse winds to take shelter 'for a season' in the northern part of the Vogelkop, western New Guinea.

This event took place around the year 1512, and it seems highly likely that during the period of the Governor's visit, if he did not know it before, he discovered that New Guinea was the true home of the valuable plumed birds of paradise. However, there is nothing in his record to indicate this. In fact years after the Governor's enforced sojourn on the Vogelkop, Captain El Cano was told (at Tidore Island a few miles from Ternate) that the plumed birds were wanderers from paradise! I suspect that the people who told El Cano this tale on 8 November 1521, were intentionally concealing the source of the feathers which were then more valuable than gold. In this connection, it is probably significant that the plumes given to Captain El Cano were those of the Lesser Bird of Paradise, the species which occurs along the coasts of the Vogelkop where the Governor had been blown ashore. Going a step further, I also suspect that the Governor's 'accidental' visit to the Vogelkop was a subterfuge to permit plume-hunting and that perhaps a goodly portion of the early Portuguese explorations in the south-west Pacific were for the purpose of finding and collecting the feathers.

Be that as it may, the Portuguese and Malay traders soon had to share their secret with the Spaniard Alvaro Saavedra Ceron, who landed at a New Guinea island which he named *'isla del oro'* (Gold Island). This was probably Japen Island, one of the islands of Geelvink Bay, where the golden-plumed Lesser Bird of Paradise also abounds. Ceron reported that the 'naked black people', with whom he stayed a month in 1528, called their island Hamey and that they were already well acquainted with iron tools.

Shortly afterwards, in 1545, came another Spaniard, Ortiz de Retes, in the *San Juan,* who went ashore just to the east of the mouth of the Mamberamo River. There amongst natives who reminded him of the people he had encountered earlier in African Guinea, he planted the Spanish flag. He named his discovery 'Nueva Guinea' and took possession of this *tierra incognito* on behalf of Spain. Thus the great island was named. In 1606 Luis Vaes de Torres sailed through the shallow strait which bears his name. In 1623 Jan Carstensz, sailing off the south-western coast sighted the snow-clad range which bore his name until 1964, when the peak was renamed Sukarnatop. In 1660 the Dutch East Indies Company took over from the Spanish, who had suffered a series of reverses and, in 1678 the Dutch flag was first flown in New Guinea.

In 1750 the Dutch East India Company came on hard times and soon thereafter Prince Nuku, pretender to the throne of Tidore, undertook warfare against the Dutch in New Guinea. In 1793 the British established a fort at Dore on the Vogelkop; but in less than three years they abandoned it after the Papuans attacked and captured a number of their men and sold them into slavery. In 1828 the second New Guinea fort – Fort du Bus – was established, at Lobo, Triton Bay, in south-western New Guinea; but after eight years the British abandoned this one too as a result of malaria and other tropical diseases. Therefore in 1855, when the first missionaries, Ottow and Geissler, set up a little mission station on a small offshore island at Dore, they were the only Europeans living in New Guinea.

In 1883, things began to change: the British flag was unfurled at Port Moresby when the Australians staked their claim to Papua. In 1884 the Germans took possession of most of the land on the northern watershed of the eastern half of New Guinea. By treaty with the Australians on 16 May 1895, the Dutch took all land in New Guinea west of the 141st meridian of east longitude. They soon began sending out expeditions to establish order among some of the tens of thousands of savages living in what was then called Netherlands New Guinea. This was a difficult period because most of the aborigines living at any distance from the sea-coast were still collecting heads and dining on their foes. In 1910, Hollandia (now Sukarnapura) became the official seat of the Dutch Government and remained so until 1 October 1962, when the interim United Nations commission took over from the Dutch. In 1963 the Indonesians took over from the Interim Commission and the name of the former Netherlands New Guinea was changed to Irian Barat.

About 1930, a wave of Dutch settlers had arrived to take up residence chiefly in the Hollandia (now Sukarnapura) region and at Manokwari. However, it was not until 1938 that Dutch settlers began moving into the interior to settle in a few spots, such as around the lovely, cool Wissel Lakes discovered in a high rift valley shortly before by a government patrol.

In the eastern portions of New Guinea, settlers were almost as slow in moving away from the coastal lowlands. With the exception of the rugged, inhospitable Edie Creek region in the Herzog Mountains, where large quantities of gold had been discovered in 1927, virtually no white man lived inland except along the edges of a few tropical rivers. In fact it was not until 8 March 1933, that the Michael Leahy expedition laid to rest the widely held theory that the interior of New Guinea consisted entirely of rough, uninhabitable mountains and gorges. On that memorable day a bush pilot named L. Grabowski, a Major Harrison and the three Leahy brothers, Michael, Jim and Dan, flew over the 'backbone' of the island to see what lay in the vast unknown southern watershed. Immediately after crossing the dividing ranges they flew out over a great valley, the floor of which had an average height of 5000 feet above sea level. This valley, the Wahgi Valley, twenty miles wide and nearly 100 miles long, contained a large patchwork of gardens somewhat resembling (from the air) the farmlands of Belgium. To everyone's great surprise, the expedition found that the inhabitants of this valley – some 100,000 of them – were still living in a Stone Age culture completely cut off from the outside world.

This epic discovery, which was featured throughout the world, soon drew hordes of gold prospectors and carpetbaggers to New

Guinea. The young Errol Flynn, then a genuine hell-for-leather soldier of fortune, was counted among them, as were many veterans of the Alaska and California gold fields. Almost hand in hand with this invasion came the missionaries. One of the earliest was Father William Ross, a Catholic from New York State, who soon set up a mission near the spot where the Leahy expedition had found a placer gold mine in the 'land that time forgot', as the Wahgi Valley has been called.

The Wahgi natives, who at first had been friendly, soon took action to halt the influx of strangers. In a series of fleeting attacks they murdered six white men, two of them missionaries. With this development, the government at Port Moresby closed the valley to further exploration but permitted the original discoverers and Father Ross to stay in the area. The Leahy brothers built a station at a little placer mine they had discovered at Ewunga Creek near Mount Hagen. They got along well with the local natives and during World War II enlisted their aid in the building of a number of emergency landing fields in the Wahgi and adjacent valleys. After World War II the first cattlemen and planters were permitted to move into the highlands of eastern New Guinea.

In the two decades since the eastern highlands were opened for settlement hundreds of hardy men, women and children – Australians, New Zealanders, Europeans and a few Americans – have taken up land and built homesteads there. Their chief investment has been in coffee and tea plantations. Now the area has several sizeable towns, dozens of little airfields and many hundreds of miles of roadway. Stone-capped roads thread through the valleys and link the picturesque plantations with the northern coasts. These rapid changes have led to many fascinating and a few unfortunate collisions between the Stone Age and the Twentieth Century in the Wahgi Valley.

Other interior valleys with large native populations have frequently been harder to 'enlighten'. They lie mostly in the central and western parts of the island. Their owners, also usually friendly when first contacted, generally become reticent to accept the blessings of the Twentieth Century.

Although widely scattered, the natives who dwell in the high mountains, particularly those of the main ranges, usually bear striking similarities of appearance, habits and language. Almost all of the mountain tribes until recently were adept at the art of performing stealthy murder, and many of them resort to fierce ambushes to defend their mountain refuges. This form of defence usually takes place in intermediate zones called 'death lines'. Such lines are always a source of danger or at least of inconvenience, to the outsider who seeks to march any distance through the 'uncontrolled' regions of New Guinea.

In the Balim Valley of western New Guinea many bitterly contested 'death lines' dividing clan lands persist to this day. Some are so fiercely defended against intrusion of any sort that missionaries and government officers resident in the valley dare not enter certain parts of it. And in the vast swamp forests of south-western New Guinea, where headhunting still flourishes, braves still sleep with the skull of an enemy for a pillow and walk about with totem skulls dangling from their necks. In this area where the native lives pretty much as he did 5000 to 15,000 years ago, a young man must still take a human life before he can be admitted to the status of manhood.

Called Papuans after *papua*, the Malay word for 'curly haired', the New Guinea aborigine is a mixture of very old stocks which are quite distinct from the light-skinned, frail, short-statured peoples of Indonesia, who represent a branch of the Mongoloid or yellow race. The Papuan probably represents a mixture of Australoid and Melanesian or Oceanic peoples. Papuans are characterised by '. . . a lanky long-limbed body, dark skin, and a narrow and angular face, with thin lips and a long nose, the latter often full-fleshed and hooked at the tip. The body is hairy, the face frequently bearded, and the head hair frizzy' (Kennedy 1943).

In the high, refuge-like valleys of the interior occur isolated pockets of men who are hold-overs from prehistoric colonisations of the island. These people, the Negritos or Pygmies, who are often referred to as the 'big pygmies', are of uncertain origin, but probably preceded all other immigrants to the island. Although seemingly frail and dwarf-like, they are often dangerous.

Along the eastern and northern coast live peoples who are best described as water-loving Papuans. Mostly they dwell over lakes and protected coastal waters, and employ sea-going canoes in which they make month-long expeditions to and from their chief hunting grounds. These Papuans are probably much like the 'Pacific Vikings' who made prehistoric invasions of New Guinea, subsequent to those of the Negritos.

In the lowland swamps of the south-western portions of the island, in areas adjacent to Australia, the 'purest' and fiercest Papuan stock is found today. This relict stock appears to retain a lot of the old Australoid and dark, heavy Melanesian characteristics of the earliest invaders. In this area the explorer who cuts a trail from the shore into the mountains finds himself climbing backwards through history. Once he leaves the coast with its predominantly trading–fishing–canal cultures and ascends into the highlands of the Snow, Star, Hindenburg, Hagen or Kubor ranges, he encounters aborigines who live by a combination of taro-sweet potato farming and by hunting. Many are semi-nomadic in that periodically, sometimes for two to three months at a time, they become wandering hunters. They gather fruit, nuts, and hunt game in the deepest forests, even in the seemingly inaccessible forests crowning the higher mountains and in the grasslands above the treeline.

Chapter Four

The Era of Commercial
Plume-hunting

ALL OF the plumed birds of paradise and the majority of the bower birds live in New Guinea, many of them in areas which until a short while ago, were dangerous or even inaccessible except to primitive Stone Age hunters. Nevertheless, long ago, probably before the Christian Era, the gorgeous feathers of one or two species of birds of paradise drifted mysteriously via Malaysia to western Asia and perhaps to eastern Europe. These lovely plumes, coming from beyond the borders of the known world, stirred deep emotions in the people who beheld them.

It is not hard to understand why ancient man valued paradise plumes so highly. Even today the filmy beauty of paradise feathers outstrips the finest of our spun metals, the most resplendent of our plastics and iridescent fabrics, and even the most intricate of our laces. Primitive man must have set out in search of this treasure with the same blind daring that later men called up in their nearly suicidal quests for gold.

About the year 1600, bird of paradise skins began arriving rather regularly in Europe, where they were much sought after for the private collections of the nobility and persons with scientific interests. These specimens were sometimes accompanied by fairly precise information as to their points of origin. It was from such specimens that, in 1605, the great naturalist Charles de L'Écluse (= Carolus Clusius) of the University of Leiden was able to provide accurate descriptions of both the Greater and the Lesser Birds of Paradise and to announce rightly that the former lived in the 'Aru Islands', and the latter in the 'Papuan Islands near Gilolo Island'. Stresemann (1954) noted that this is apparently the first published reference to Papua in the historical literature of the birds of paradise. L'Écluse's (1605) exact wording is '. . . *insular papuae, insulae Gilolo vicinae*'.

As more and more information filtered through to Europe, scientifically minded people began to dream of visiting the islands where these magnificent creatures lived. One such was Willughby (1676) who, in the seventeenth century, pleaded that on-the-spot observations of the habits of birds of paradise and the uses they made of their extraordinary feathering would be of utmost interest. But many years were to pass before this was to happen.

One of the earliest to describe birds of paradise was an extraordinary naturalist, George Eberhard Rumpf (Rumphius) who continued his work even after becoming blind. He lived for some forty years (1660 to 1700) in the Moluccas on the little island of Amboina and described in all six or seven species of plumed birds of paradise. By a quirk of fate, the Rumphius journals disappeared. Of this terrible loss Stresemann (1954) wrote: '. . . all of these studies would have perished if the Dutch preacher François Valentinjn had not obtained his records and included them in his *Oud en Nieuw Oost-Indien*, a compilation published in 1726. (It is true he neglected to give the source of his information)'. Species known to have been described by Rumphius were the Greater, the Lesser, the King, the Vogelkop Astrapia, the Giant Sickle-bill, the Twelve-wired Bird of Paradise and the Glossy-mantled Manucode.

But, as Stresemann wrote, still the years rolled by and no naturalists went to the true home of the birds of paradise. All that was known concerning these extraordinary birds, now famous in Europe for more than 200 years, was from the lips of native collectors. Just why this was so is not clear because the island could be visited. For example the Englishman Thomas Forrest visited Waigeu Island, Dorey in the Vogelkop and Misol Island, and then in 1784 he baited the stay-at-home naturalists with this immortal sentence in his book *The Breadfruit Tree*: 'Birds of Paradise glisten like the seldom glimpsed denizens of an Asiatic harem who are clad in gold of many hues and dipped in the purple of dawn.'

The first naturalist to see birds of paradise in the wild was a Frenchman, Réné P. Lesson. He arrived at Dorey on board the French corvette 'La Coquille,' already half way round the world on her famous cruise of discovery. During the two weeks that Lesson spent at Dorey in 1824, he personally observed and collected two species of birds of paradise, the Lesser and the King, and he discovered two additional species, the Trumpet Bird and the Glossy-mantled Manucode. Of his first observations of a living bird of paradise, he wrote: 'The view of the first Bird of Paradise was overwhelming. The gun remained idle in my hand for I was too astonished to shoot. It was in the virgin forest surrounding the harbour of Dorey. As I slipped carefully along the wild pig's trails through this dusky thicket, a Paradisaea suddenly flew in graceful curves over my head. It was like a meteor whose body, cutting through the air, leaves a long trail of light. With the ornamental plumes pressing against its flanks, this bird resembles an ornament dropped from the curls of a gouri and floating idly in the layer of air that encircles our planet's crust.'

The second naturalist to see birds of paradise in the wild was Alfred Russel Wallace, who, of course, is best remembered as the co-originator of the theory of evolution with Charles Darwin. He made some fascinating observations and discoveries in the Moluccas, where he discovered Wallace's Standard Wing; in the Aru Islands, where he observed the courtship displays of the Greater Bird of Paradise; and in the western Papuan islands and Vogelkop, where he observed the Red Bird, the Lesser and probably the King Bird of Paradise. The report which this brave and brilliant Englishman left behind of his travels in the Malay Archipelago during eight years (1854–1862) is a classic to which we shall refer many times in this book.

Hundreds of naturalists[1] and thousands of plume-hunters have explored the wilds of New Guinea for birds of paradise in the 140 years that have elapsed since Lesson's visit. For the most part, the discoveries of the naturalists are well documented. Not so the discoveries of the plume collectors, which consisted mostly of skins purchased from Papuans and at best vaguely labelled. However, such specimens often found their way into museums, and into the literature, because professional ornithologists habitually picked over each incoming collection of paradise plumes almost as soon as they reached the millinery markets of Paris, Amsterdam and London. Thus it came about that many of the greatest rarities were described from specimens whose geographical origin was obscure or unknown. The rediscovery of such species in the wilds of New Guinea has long presented a formidable challenge to naturalists.

Chinese and Arab traders made early contact with the natives of western Papua. In exchange for paradise plumes they bartered salt,

[1] See Appendix II.

tools, trinkets and some opium. At length the practice of plume-hunting spread eastward and southward over the island but early records of this traffic are lacking. Plume-taking was intensified in 1873 and 1874 when New Guinea was finally divided between Holland, Germany and England.

From the writings of Captain John Moresby (1875), who happened to pass this way in 1873 on an exploring expedition, we can reconstruct some of the colourful sidelights of the plume industry as it operated a century ago along the north-west coast of New Guinea.

On 27 May [1873] we had reached [Threshold Bay near] the western extreme of New Guinea . . . we anchored off a delicious little cove of this large open bay, before a large village . . . The inhabitants are pure Malays, descendants of those who have driven the aboriginal inhabitants back into the interior, and now hold their own by the use of firearms. The Rajah of Salwatti, who is supreme ruler at this extreme of New Guinea, came off to visit us on the following day in a large prahu, rowed by about twenty men, and ornamented with various banners, and an enormous Dutch ensign . . . We went to quarters and showed him the power and range of our great guns, which seemed to astonish him not a little: and he then exchanged gifts with me, presenting me with some live cassowaries, a tree kangaroo, and some beautiful bird of paradise skins, which I returned with a regulation sword, giving him also a quantity of tea and sugar, which he said was the greatest luxury he could have. He then took his leave with much ceremony, and landed at the village, where the prahu was hauled above high-water mark, and we thought we had done with him; but no, the Rajah doffed his robe of state, and launching in a small canoe, with two men to paddle, came off to the ship as a trader of bird skins. Very keen bargains he drove, coaxing fowling-pieces, powder, shot and pistols from the officers for his skins . . .

In south-east New Guinea (in Australian hands since 4 April 1883, when the Union Jack was hoisted at Port Moresby), plume collecting continued haltingly for many years but never reached large proportions. For a while the Blue Bird of Paradise (which was discovered some 55–65 miles inland from Port Moresby by Karl Hunstein in 1884) brought 20 pounds sterling in Port Moresby and skins of the Raggiana averaged a pound each. At Bootless Bay near Port Moresby, Archibald Whitbourne told me in 1948 that the Blue Bird of Paradise required a great deal of time and effort to collect because it lived so far back in the interior and because even in its home territory the plumed males were very uncommon. The

Raggiana, however, he said he had collected in fair numbers. Each year it was his custom to arm a team of natives with shotguns and to go with them into the forest to hunt birds of paradise. In good years he would bring out 600 to 700 male Raggianas. For these he generally received one pound sterling per skin.

In north-eastern New Guinea the Germans were better organised and plume-collecting was more efficient. Their collecting had begun some years before Germany proclaimed this area Kaiser Wilhelmsland by raising the German flag at Astrolabe Bay on 16 November 1884. In 1885 the German Trading and Plantation Company (later to be renamed the New Guinea Company) was issued an extraordinary charter by the German Kaiser, which made it the sovereign power of north-eastern New Guinea and the Bismarck Archipelago. Soon thereafter North German Lloyd steamers began visiting this new territory four times a year. They would call at Madang or Stephansort (Bogadjim) from Singapore to deliver and pick up cargo. Large on the ships' registers were paradise plumes, chiefly the plumes of the Augusta Victoria, the Lesser and the Emperor of Germany birds of paradise.

So bad was the health problem in Kaiser Wilhelmsland that the Germans sought relief by moving the seat of the government. In 1892 it was transferred from Finsch Harbour, where many men had perished, to Stephansort on Astrolabe Bay. But the new location proved even more unhealthy than the old one. In 1899 the seat of government was moved completely away from New Guinea to the island of New Britain. Tales of suffering and death intermixed with outrages of every sort from simple murder to cannibal orgies and headhunting fill the record of this unhappy period. But despite great odds, the German régime made progress and in the end, when in 1916 they lost their Papuan holdings as a result of World War I, they left behind a valuable legacy in the form of well laid-out plantations. They also left a number of methodical scientific reports and detailed maps which have been of considerable help to those who have followed in search of Papuan treasures.

For many years the chief treasure was bird of paradise plumage and it is surprising how important this source of income was in the opening up of the country. During the seven-year wait between the planting and the harvesting of the first paying crop of copra, many of the pioneers counted heavily on the funds they obtained by plume-hunting. Some oldtimers have told me that the birds provided just

D

about the only source of ready money available in those days.

Adolph Batze of Lae, New Guinea, an old friend of mine and one of the pioneer planters who got his start through paradise plume-hunting, was probably rather typical of this long dead era. With his father and two brothers, Arthur and Karl, he reached New Guinea from Germany in 1906. Each hunting season the four men 'went bush' and in good years each of the Batzes got several hundred skins and in prime years each got up to 700 skins. The shooting, which was rigidly controlled by the German Government, was restricted to the months of June through August. All of the paradise plumes had to be sold to the government.

The weapons used for plume-hunting were chiefly shotguns (12 gauge, 16 gauge, and 410 gauge). These could be rented from the New Guinea Company together with ammunition and a grubstake, just as in prospecting enterprises. Arsenical soap was used for the preparing of the commercial skins. There was no trapping or use of bird lime and none of the species was taken alive. On a good day Adolf would get fifty to sixty males of the Augusta Victoria Bird of Paradise and several of the King Bird of Paradise. Of the former, he frequently came on clusters of trees in which 'as many as twelve males displayed'. The King Bird of Paradise he claimed to have seen 'hanging upside down' in its solitary display tree. This bird, he said, had a call phrase which was almost exactly like that of the Augusta Victoria but higher, more musical, and more whistle-like.

As regards values, Adolf told me that of the birds of paradise collected in his area (the King, the Raggiana, the Stephanie, the Magnificent, the Augusta Victoria, the Blue, the Emperor of Germany and the Lesser), the Blue Bird of Paradise 'from way up behind Morobe' was by far the most valuable. It was, he said, worth forty pounds sterling! Next in value were the Stephanie and the Raggiana, after which came the King and the Augusta Victoria. The Germans, he added, imposed a high duty on each skin that was exported. When I asked Adolf for an estimate of the number of skins exported from Kaiser Wilhelmsland in a good year he said that the number was probably in the tens of thousands. All plume-hunting ceased in 1914 with the onset of World War I and the annual plume cropping was never resumed.

However, the Papuans continued to kill a few birds for a few years longer. As late as 1916 according to my old friend 'Kasser' (George) Townsend, a famous pioneer government officer in the

Sepik District, some skins were sold to commercial interests. He remembered 'discovering too late' several footlockers filled with paradise plumes that had somehow accompanied his long overland patrol in 1916 from Wewak across the Dutch border to Hollandia. He was of the opinion that these plumes were about the last commercial plumes to be taken out of Kaiser Wilhelmsland (now the Mandated Territory of New Guinea).

To understand the importance of the plume industry to the economy of the country, one has only to read the official record of the early exports from Merauke (Anon, 1920) which consisted chiefly of copra and bird of paradise skins.

At Merauke there was no plume-hunting by Europeans; instead it was done almost entirely by the local inhabitants. This was because the Tugeri tribes of that area were fierce hunters of human heads as well as excellent hunters of birds of paradise.

Figures of the chief exports from Merauke for the years 1913 to 1915 indicate that paradise plumes constituted the second most important resource in south New Guinea. In west New Guinea, however, plumes were undoubtedly the most important resource, witness the official records published in 1910 by the plume industry (Downham, 1910) which state '. . . the total export of skins of the birds of paradise (chiefly the lesser bird of paradise) has for the past twenty years regularly represented between 25,000 and 30,000 birds.' These plumes came from the west New Guinea lowlands, chiefly from the Vogelkop and the north coast as far east as Humboldt Bay.

In the Foreign Office report we also read that 'Chinese traders visit these two ports and others in Dutch New Guinea and purchase the birds from Chinese storekeepers at the coast towns, who buy from the native chiefs. The Chinese storekeepers pay for the birds in kind, and fix their own prices. They have been engaged in the trade in Geelvink Bay for more than two centuries, supplying the demand for bird of paradise plumes in China . . .'

Paradise plumes were also an important resource of the Aru Islands, where for centuries the natives had cropped the Greater Bird of Paradise – we hear of this industry in Alfred Russel Wallace's description (1869: 485) of almost a century ago:

The trade carried on at Dobbo [Aru Islands] is very considerable. This year there were fifteen large praus from Macassar, and perhaps a hundred small boats from Ceram, Goram, and Ké . . . The largest and most bulky items are pearl-shell and tripang, or 'bêche-de-mer,' with smaller quantities of tortoiseshell, edible birds' nests, pearls, ornamental woods, timber, and birds of paradise.

Not long after Wallace's time, Australian plume-collectors began visiting the Aru Islands in quest of paradise plumes, as witness Captain John Moresby's account (1876):

On 18 January [1873] we took up our old anchorage off Somerset [Cape York] ... Whilst here we fell in with a lonely waif of society, named [J.] Cockerill, who has betaken himself to live in a tiny vessel of about eight tons, and accompanied only by his son and two natives, cruises about these seas as a naturalist, and seems to be happy enough in his own way. His boat was laden with specimens of beautiful birds; and from the Aru Islands, 500 miles west of Somerset, which he had just left, he had brought some boxes full of the Great Bird of Paradise, and the still more exquisite King Bird of Paradise, of which he kindly gave me a specimen . . . .

It is evident that in the wilder regions the 'unspoiled' Papuan with only his ingenuity and primitive tools, was able to collect even the most elusive of the birds of paradise. This we learn from the reports of many men including the great zoological collector, Albert S. Meek (1913), a Queenslander who left Australia in the mid-nineties to collect for twenty years in Papua:

The natives ... are very clever at snaring birds, adopting many different methods for different kinds .... To snare Bower Birds and Birds of Paradise the natives search for the playground of the bird, and then set a snare of a loop of native twine in which the bird gets entangled. In other cases birds of paradise are caught by a loop which is left on the bough of the tree and connected with a long piece of twine to the hunter, who is concealed in the brush nearby. When the bird steps within the loop the hunter pulls the snare.

Meek then wrote of his expedition to the Owen Stanley Mountains in February, 1905:

In two days near Owgarra I recollect that 47 male Birds of Paradise were brought to me. All arrived alive, tied by the leg with twine to sticks. There were seven or eight different species comprised in these.

The following quotation from A. E. Pratt (1906), referring to observations which he made at Yule Island in 1903, is further confirmation of the Papuan's hunting abilities which began ages before the plumes became popular in Europe:

... the most splendid of all the articles of the Papuan costume is the feather headdress, 16 feet high, which forms the center point of attraction when it occurs in a tribal dance. The ornament is extremely rare, and is always an heirloom, for it has taken generations to complete. It is a wonderful, fantastic device of feathers, built upon a light framework. The bird of paradise and the Goura Pigeon are laid under tribute for its construction, and the feathers of the different species of the same bird, are kept carefully apart, and are arranged in rows according to their natural color. A few lines of Birds of Paradise, a few lines of Goura Pigeon, then a few lines of another species of Bird of Paradise, and so on. The whole contrivance is most fantastic, and looks really impressive in the weird light of the torches as the dancers, decorated with flowing bunches of grasses behind, proceed with their revel.

With the development of a world wide market for paradise plumes, the Papuan sometimes found himself enjoying a measure of wealth that he had never known before. In the 1920 report of the British Foreign office referred to earlier (Anon., 1920: 29), there appears this remark:

The sale of birds of paradise has brought wealth to the natives and in some districts they are even becoming too lazy to catch the fish which abound in all the seas, or to make sago, which they are now importing from the Moluccas.

Chapter Five

Conservation and Poaching Today

IN 1928 and 1929, Ernst Mayr, Agassiz Professor of Zoology at Harvard University and world authority on the birds of New Guinea, conducted a remarkable series of ornithological expeditions to New Guinea for Lord Rothschild of the Tring Museum, Leonard C. Sanford of the American Museum of Natural History and Erwin Stresemann of the Berlin Museum. He succeeded in surveying the birds of the Vogelkop, the Wandammen Mountains, the Cyclops Mountains, the Saruwaged Mountains and the Herzog Mountains – in short he made a comprehensive sweep of the coastal ranges of nearly all of northern New Guinea. Therefore from first hand experience and as a trained biologist, he knew what he was talking about when he wrote that although the number of bird of paradise skins exported from New Guinea was appalling, none of the species seemed to have suffered any permanent harm. Mayr noted that around 10,000 skins of plumed birds of paradise were exported from German New Guinea annually up till the onset of World War I. He wrote that in 1913 no less than 30,000 were offered for sale in London auctions alone, and that in a single shipment in 1912, a British firm received 28,300 skins.

Counting skins from the Aru Islands, Merauke, Fak Fak, Sorong, the western Papuan islands, Manokwari and Hollandia, plus all of the less important outlets in British New Guinea and Kaiser Wilhelmsland, the total number of skins shipped in a peak year may well have exceeded the figure of 80,000 skins given by Mayr.

The economic importance of this traffic in paradise plumes was thus very great. With so much money involved one wonders how conservationists finally managed to halt it. Their success is especially surprising because many hard-pressed settlers leaned heavily on the plume revenues and there was a general feeling among the New Guinea residents of the inexhaustibility of the birds.

The manner in which conservationists mustered their power and finally succeeded in halting this formidable industry is of much interest. Already aware and shocked by the 'sudden' extinction of certain famous birds in other parts of the world, the Passenger Pigeon, for example, which had once occurred in seemingly countless numbers, public sentiment was easily aroused. First, the conservationists undertook a highly publicised programme to halt the most nauseous form of plume taking, the stripping of aigrette plumes from backs of adult herons during the breeding season, a practice which not only killed the adults but left the young to perish in the nest. Next, they sought to halt the killing of incredible numbers of hummingbirds and birds of paradise for their plumes. The conservationists refused to listen to any measures short of a complete world-wide ban on plume taking. Soon, any woman caught wearing plumes was viewed with disdain. The merchants, by way of rebuttal asked the eminent New Guinea naturalist, A. E. Pratt to draw up a detailed report of the effects of plume collecting on birds of paradise. He concluded his report by writing that 'so long as New Guinea remains undeveloped, and its development, under most favourable conditions, must be a matter of centuries, paradise birds will thrive, because the conditions under which they are killed preserve both the young males and the females.'

A few years back I flew 1000 miles along the northern coast of New Guinea a few days after flying across the deforested, over-populated subcontinent of south-east Asia. The contrast in what I saw was staggering. I found myself gazing hour after hour in admiration and disbelief at New Guinea's 'endless' forests. Only rarely could I see a trace of the workings of man. One has to see it to believe it. By way of analogy I should say that if a football field represented the forests of New Guinea as they stood on the day that man first arrived, then a postage stamp cut into slivers and scattered over the field would represent the total amount of forest that man has altered or obliterated since his arrival.

It is, of course, largely because of this vast refuge of forest that Pratt and Mayr were convinced that plume taking had done no permanent harm. Another factor explained why in 1928, so shortly after plume taking had been halted, Mayr found the most heavily hunted of the species '... displaying right in the outskirt ...' of Hollandia, a town which was long the centre of the plume industry.

31

The answer is that the plumed species practice a form of court-ship behaviour in which only a relatively few fully adult males of each generation are needed for the species to survive and the only birds having any commercial value are the fully adult males. As explained in more detail elsewhere in this work, in this form of behaviour, no pair bond develops between the sexes and the males take no part in the duties of nesting or in the rearing of the young. Yet another reason for the resilience of these birds is that the males do not acquire their commercially valuable adult plumage until they are four or five years old. And finally (see Delacour, 1963: 232) subadult males still in largely female dress can serve the females if for some reason the fully adult males are not present.

In 1910 a bill prohibiting the sale or exchange of paradise plumes, promoted by Percy Alden, MP, and signed by six members includ-ing J.Ramsay MacDonald, was passed by the British Parliament. Soon other countries followed with similar bans. The result is that since 1924 no birds of paradise have been legally collected for commercial purposes anywhere in New Guinea.

Captain Jean Delacour, who had the great kindness to read the section of my book devoted to plume-hunting and conservation, called it to my attention that an American, William T.Hornaday, was the key person responsible for putting across the legislation which eventually resulted in the outlawing of plume taking through-out the world. Through Hornaday's crusading efforts plume taking was banned in the United States in 1913; soon thereafter Canada, England, Holland and France followed suit. Hornaday (1931) writes of his part in these developments as follows:

The American campaign for the stoppage of the importation of the plumage of the birds of the world into the United States came to a victorious finish in July 1913, in the Wilson Tariff Act. In due course of time, though not in that year, Canada, England, the Straits Settlements, and Australia handsomely extended the victory.

In October 1913, the desirability of attacking the bird-of-paradise plume industry at its source, in New Guinea and the Aru Islands, became strongly evident. The 'Paradise plume', then eagerly sought in all civilized lands except the United States, seemed likely to exterminate some of the most beautiful birds of the world. Holland, a wild-life-loving nation, held the key to the Paradise situation. *If Holland would stop the commercial killing of birds of paradise, the lid would be on.* And of course she did.

As Delacour stated, it all started with Hornaday, and who else would know better than this great ornithologist and conservationist who has devoted so much of his life to the preservation of wild life.

As far as I know, there has been remarkably little poaching of birds of paradise in the areas that I am familiar with: the Owen Stanley Mountains, the mountains fringing the Wahgi Valley, the forests around Madang, Lae, the Adelbert Mountains, the Sepik country, Telefomin and Wewak. To be specific, in the Port Moresby region of south-east New Guinea there is little illegal shooting of birds of paradise even in fertile areas like the Lower Brown River forests and the woodlands bordering the Laloki River where the city hunters frequently go for a day of 'sport'. Farther back in the foothills of the Owen Stanley Mountains (Koitaki, Ilolo, Goldie River gorge, Uberi, Ioribawa) the same holds true. Throughout these areas the Papuans have largely ceased hunting these birds for their plumes. Consequently until recently at least, it was fairly easy to observe the males of the most colourful lowland species, the red-plumed Raggiana which, if poaching were prevalent, would be the first species to suffer. Other species such as the Twelve-wired, the King, the Blue, the Six-wired, and the Superb Birds of Paradise, live in less accessible areas and are much less vulnerable to poaching.

In the more accessible Markham River region of north-eastern New Guinea the Augusta Victoria Bird of Paradise, the only plumed species which was ever heavily hunted in that region, is still killed in some numbers by Chinese and Papuan hunters and the gold-orange plumes are still occasionally offered for secret sale in the native markets. However, no serious damage has resulted from this small illicit traffic and the species remains abundant.

Even relatively large-scale hunting by the mountain-living Papuans has had no effect on the survival of any of the species. Take the Wahgi Valley, for example. When this beautiful valley was discovered by the Leahy brothers in 1933, it was already an area of open farmlands and grass some 20 miles wide and 60 miles long, with only scattered patches of secondary forest. The removal of the forest had, of course, reduced the numbers of certain species of birds of paradise in this valley. For example, the Blue Bird of Paradise, which happens to be firmly 'rooted' in the original forest between about 4500 and 6300 feet, has been largely extirpated by the removal of the forests. When I worked in the valley in 1950 and 1952, I was dismayed to find it living only in little lobes of forest

33

which protruded down from the unbroken forests above. The birds occupied remnants of the original mid-mountain forests which had once filled the entire valley and were actually 'trapped' against the ceiling of their range, squeezed to death between the up-creeping grasslands of the pioneer fringe and the upper mountain forests which they were unable to tolerate. The Blue Bird of Paradise is not in any way threatened as a species, but its extirpation in this relatively tiny valley must be lamented because it is one of the few readily accessible spots where these birds can be seen. With their passing from the valley a valuable natural resource for naturalists and tourists will be lost. Elsewhere in the vast range of this species, from the mountains behind Tari in central New Guinea to the mountains of south-eastern New Guinea, it usually takes a small-scale expedition to reach the forests in which the Blue Bird of Paradise lives. Its inaccessibility, of course, was the chief reason for its great value during the era of commercial plume collecting.

Another species which should be protected in the Wahgi Valley is the very beautiful red-plumed Raggiana which is cropped by native hunters in fairly large numbers in most of the south water-shed valleys of eastern New Guinea. In the Wahgi I almost despaired in my attempts to photograph this species in the wild because of the Papuan hunting pressure. To my great surprise, in this region I discovered that the Papuans recognise and honour the ownership of individual wild males. They are able to do this because the adult males display on private perches in certain trees and virtually all of the trees they select in this valley are privately-owned, many of the trees, mostly casuarinas, being planted for firewood or as graveyard or fairground decorations. Thus the Papuan owner of the display tree containing the limb on which a wild male habitually displays is acknowledged as the 'owner' of the bird and he jealously guards his bird and watches its development.

As an aid to collecting, little blinds of grass, vines, and leaves are constructed in the tree and left there for the birds to become accustomed to. When the 'owner' thinks it time to collect his prize, he climbs into the blind before dawn and shoots his bird from concealment, usually with a three-pronged arrow.

The Papuan crops the adult males of many species of birds of paradise pretty regularly either in his own way or with the illegal help of shoot boys carrying government permits and mission-owned shotguns. A decade ago this cropping made no difference in terms of the survival of the species. In recent years, however, the highland Papuans have been encouraged to gather annually to dance in immense numbers at Goroka and at Mount Hagen. At such times great emphasis is placed on costuming and an almost incredible number of bird of paradise plumes are displayed by the tribesmen as they compete with each other. This great New Guinea spectacle, which is usually staged for visiting dignitaries, may be affecting the local populations of birds of paradise, for there are practically no limits to which the natives will not go to obtain the beautiful male raiment.

This fact was first driven home to me in 1950, at 9500 feet on the south shoulder of Mount Wilhelm, when I came on the display tree of the Princess Stephanie Bird of Paradise – a tree so tall it overshadowed the rest of the original mountain forest. It stood on a steep slope and to my amazement I found that Chimbu natives had long since installed an elaborate ladder with which they could ascend the trunk to a small house that they had erected about 100 feet above ground in the tree's crown. I learned from my guides that Chimbu bird of paradise hunters would ascend Mt Wilhelm from their houses 2000 to 5000 feet below and then climb the precarious ladder to the arboreal hut. From there they would shoot arrows at the resplendent long-tailed male Stephanie which they said frequented this special tree. Obviously the tree was a well established display stage for this wide-ranging mountain-loving species, a species which remains little known to ornithologists. The natives, however, must know it well for many thousands of its twin tail plumes are worn by the men of the Wahgi Valley.

The killing of such large numbers of adult males of the unique mid-mountain species thus contributes to the rarity of birds which should be an important natural resource of New Guinea. As it is now, the visitor can rarely see the resplendent males, except on the heads of Papuans. He will, however, find the females and young males of most species common. In the red Raggiana, the young males resemble the females but often can be distinguished by their partially developed tail wires, iridescent throats and short flank plumes which they wear for a period of years before acquiring the adult plumage. Such young males are extremely active in the peripheries of the clan arenas and sometimes, when a dominant long-plumed adult male leaves his private dancing perch to feed, a young male will sneak in to dance on the absent owner's stage.

35

The young males, largely still dressed as females, actively seek mates and are doubtless responsible for some matings in the wild. That male Raggianas still garbed like females are able to breed successfully with adult females was proven in New Guinea on 10 November 1962 when Shaw Mayer and Delacour discovered a nest with young in a Nondugl aviary. No adult males had ever been kept in this aviary (see Delacour, 1963: 232).

The apparent rarity of the adult males is, however, only partly due to hunting pressure. It is also due to the fact that generally the males tend to keep apart from the females in special breeding areas which are often difficult to find.

The King of Saxony Bird of Paradise is one of the most highly coveted and valuable of all of the plumed species and probably the most difficult of all for the native to collect. This species has occipital plumes of great length which resemble blue plastic cut-outs, not feathers; these are so outlandish that when in 1894 the great ornithologist Bowdler Sharpe, Keeper of Birds at the British Museum read A.B. Meyer's description of this bird, it is said that he exploded with words to the effect that anyone could tell at a glance that this so-called new discovery was an artifact.

The Wahgi natives wear the pair of amazing head plumes in their noses. They pierce the nasal septum and place a plume in each nostril. The glistening blue flags extend sideways from the head and then are bent upwards to join on the Papuan's forehead; thus they form a vivid facial frame, robin's egg blue in colour.

The King of Saxony lives in a narrow altitudinal belt of the cloud forest 5000 to 8000 feet above sea level. In this belt the clans dance in isolated ill-defined groups usually very high up in the fog-dimmed canopy. During the course of my general collecting in five ranges inhabited by this species, I always found the females and young males to be common. On the other hand the adult males were always uncommon except locally in their special display areas. With such a distribution it would be easy to blame the rarity of the males on the plume hunters; but I found the same imbalance in the Victor Emanuel and Hindenburg mountains, where very little if any plume-hunting occurs. Indeed, although the females and young males were abundant in both areas, I found the adult males relatively more common in the forests ringing the Wahgi Valley where the males have been heavily hunted for centuries. To illustrate, in the Kubor Mountains I encountered three groups (one in 1950 and two in 1952) of males (five to ten miles apart) in each of which three to seven males were found displaying on private perches. Each male owned a main display perch within auditory range of the other males. On Mount Hagen I found another such group and on the northern slopes of the Wahgi Divide Mountains I found yet another one. All of these groups were shown to me by native plume hunters who prize their knowledge of the display locations.

I shall never forget discovering how the Wahgi native hunts this elusive bird of the highest forest limbs. I was stalking birds in the mountains behind Nondugl in 1950 and had pulled out my double-barrelled shotgun when suddenly I heard a grunt in a faggot of brush at my feet. To my intense chagrin a Papuan then crawled from the faggot into the sights of my shotgun. He was furious and it turned out that the fellow was after the same quarry as I, an adult male King of Saxony which we had both seen from afar as it danced on a spire of the mountain rain forest. Both of us had climbed a very steep mountain to a point seventy to ninety feet above the foot of a display tree in which the bird perched. Both of us were thus as close to the bird as we could get. From this position I had planned to use my shotgun. The Papuan, however, was using another technique. He had dammed up a small trickle of water to make a foot-wide puddle on the mountain side. The water dripped from a funnelled leaf into the puddle, making a steady splash sound. A sloping stick perch had been placed just above the water and the vegetation above the pool had been removed to allow the King of Saxony a clear view of the inviting little spot. A few feet distant from the pool, the Papuan hunter had erected a blind which looked, as I said, like a faggot of sticks. In this the hunter had been lying in wait with his bow and arrow set but not taut. The arrow, which was four-pronged, stuck out of the faggot and was cradled in a crotch and aimed at the pool. It seemed to have been adjusted to hit any spot in or around the pool, and I suppose that any animals that might have been attracted to the Papuan's water trap would have been acceptable. However, from the location of this trap it was clearly designed to lure the *kisaba*, the King of Saxony Bird of Paradise, whose display limb was about twenty-five feet higher than the pool and perhaps eighty feet distant.

One wonders how frequently during his lifetime the average Papuan hunter is able to kill or capture this elusive prize. One thing certain is that the Saxony plumes become native heirlooms and many of the older men living in the Wahgi region possess a set. Once I saw a man wearing four sets!

The Superb Bird of Paradise is another much coveted species which is still common in the Wahgi region, but I have no knowledge of how it is collected. This species lives in an altitudinal belt that is usually slightly below the one occupied by the King of Saxony. The expandable breast plate of the male is often worn on the head by men and young women. These treasures are preserved with great care and probably for very long periods of time. They are stored in plugged bamboo tubes in tinder-dry places in the smoke blackened rafters of low dwelling houses. Every few years special 'sing-sings' are staged and the plumes may then be carried long distances. At the dance the Papuan will spend hours 'dressing', then suddenly he will burst forth under a shimmering crown fit for an emperor. Sometimes the crown contains the plumes of a dozen or more males of half a dozen species and when fifty or so men get together in a dance, the swaying plumage makes them appear to be on fire.

Seeing such gatherings the newcomer is apt to conclude that birds of paradise are threatened and that the Papuans should be prohibited from killing them for purposes of personal adornment. I disagree because it is simply not true that any species of bird of paradise is even remotely threatened by the Papuan's ancient hunting practice and love of feather adornment. This is proven by the fact that the most popular species in the Wahgi region, the Raggiana, the Lesser, the Stephanie, the Superb, the Mountain Sickle-bill and the King of Saxony, remain common species in the forests ringing the Wahgi Valley where a great concentration of feather-loving men dwell.

The other species of paradise birds which one encounters in the native headdresses of the Wahgi region are less valuable in the native economy and therefore are not in any sort of danger. I found that the less prized species include the Macgregor's Bower Bird, in which the gold crest of the male is stripped off and worn as a flat ornament; the orange red body plumage of the Sickle-crested Bird of Paradise which is dried flat and worn on the forehead; and the King Bird of Paradise with its glittering green tail medallions which are worn in the feather crown. Only rarely is the Blue Bird of Paradise seen, probably because its forested home in the Wahgi region has been largely converted to grasslands.

In conclusion, my thoughts regarding the protection needed to preserve birds of paradise in New Guinea is very much different from what I expected it would be when I began my studies some fourteen years ago. Then I thought that the only way to preserve these gorgeous birds was to prohibit all killing for purposes of commerce or native adornment. Now I feel that arena birds such as birds of paradise have 'built-in' mechanisms which operate to protect the species. I thus feel that no harm can befall any of the birds of paradise by permitting the local inhabitants to hunt the birds in their time-honoured ways for the purpose of their own personal adornment. In addition since we know that the annual killing of more than 80,000 males – and these were mostly of three species – did not threaten any of the birds of paradise, I would strongly advocate that small numbers of live birds be collected each year for the zoos of the world, to be used for educational purposes.

Chapter Six

The Evolution of Birds of Paradise and Bower Birds with a Suggested Sequence of Genera

THE THOUGHTS and ideas I have expressed below (and which have guided me in my classification) concerning the phylogeny of birds of paradise and bower birds are based in large degree on ethological evidence, particularly on evidence derived from a comparative study of their courtship and nesting systems; but I also weighed rather heavily the comparative morphology of (a) the female, (b) the egg, (c) the nest, (d) the bower, and (e) the adult male. The differences noted by Bock (1963) between the cranial anatomy of the true birds of paradise and the true bower birds (but which appear to be 'bridged' in some of the birds of paradise) I suspect are due to adaptive divergences that are correlated with the more terrestrial life of bower birds (see below).

1. It seems likely that the paradise and bower bird group is derived from a single colonisation of New Guinea. This phyletic line is probably very old and it is almost certainly Asiatic or African in origin. Bock (1963) suggests that the ancestral stock was starling-like. The founding stock probably reached New Guinea directly by hopping (and speciating) down the East Indian islands (possibly blown by occasional hurricanes) rather than indirectly by way of Australia (See Simpson's analysis of the possible origin of volant New Guinea mammals: Chapter Two). The ancestors of the Paradisaeidae were doubtless forest loving, arboreal birds whose reproductive processes were patterned on monogamy (pairing behaviour) as is practised by virtually all forest loving birds (and by more than ninety-eight per cent of all living birds: see Chapter Seven).

2. Finding many open niches in the vast forests of New Guinea, the founding stock diverged in many directions. During this adaptive radiation a segment of the stock developed in a manner that is rare

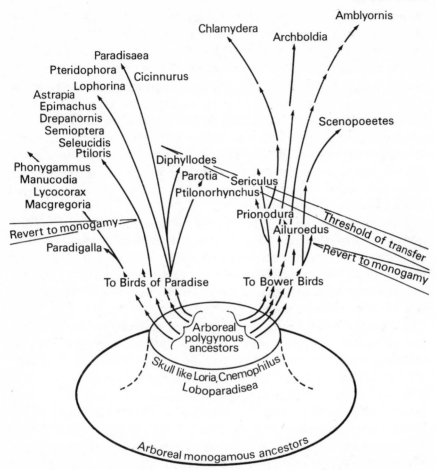

Figure 6.1 Relationship of birds of paradise and bower birds, shown diagrammatically by a dendrogram.

in birds. In response to unknown factors it entered a new adaptive zone by adopting arboreal polygynous behaviour of the 'arena' (rather than the harem) type. In arena behaviour no pair bond is formed between the sexes (see Chapter Seven), the males live apart from the females, often in clans, during prolonged breeding seasons and each male seeks to acquire as many mates as he can attract to his private display stage within the clan arena. This type of mating system is rare in birds and unknown in forest birds except for some of the New World manakins and cotingas.

3. The adoption of this rare breeding system apparently triggered a surge of evolutionary activity which brought on the extraordinary

changes in behaviour and morphology for which birds of paradise and bower birds are justly famous. The forces set loose were apparently of the sort envisioned by R. A. Fisher (1929): 'In species so situated that the reproductive success of one sex depends greatly upon winning the favour of the other, as appears evidently to be the case with many polygamous birds, sexual selection will itself act by increasing the intensity of the preference to which it is due, with the consequence that both the feature preferred and the intensity of the preference will be augmented together with ever-increasing velocity, causing a great and rapid evolution of certain conspicuous characters, until the process can be arrested by the direct or indirect effects of Natural Selection.'

4. I found that the rapidly evolved polygynous 'genera' resulting from such hypothetical runaway surges of evolution usually behave somewhat like a semispecies in that they exclude each other ecologically; but the primary pressures of exclusion apparently involve the breeding grounds (the arenas), which they defend vigorously, and not the feeding grounds, as in semispecies.

5. Another effect of this runaway surge of evolution is the retention of fertility between very different appearing genera and the production of relatively large numbers of intergeneric hybrids. This may indicate that much of the radiation is recent.

6. For reasons still unclear the exclusion pressures of (4) may lead to the generic 'tiering' or 'layering' of the arenas that I found in the higher forests of New Guinea.

7. A probable consequence of the exclusion pressures of (4) is that some polygynous lines were turned away from the rapidly developing arena evolution to eddy back to the slower pair-bond behaviour. Such 'turn-backs' presumably escaped the pressures of (4) and were able to live side by side with other polygynous species. This may be the history of *Manucodia*: Bock in his studies of cranial morphology found that it has the advanced skull of *Paradisaea*, but judging from its external morphology *Manucodia* appears to be a primitive type. The same applies to its breeding behaviour which Rand found is of the pair-bond type. To sum up, in view of its advanced skull and primitive breeding behaviour Bock believes that this species may have secondarily taken up this monogamous behaviour. I think it likely that Bock is correct and that the exclusion pressures of (4) may be the mechanism which brought about this shift.

8. An almost certain consequence of the exclusion pressures of (4) is that some polygynous lines were (and are now being) displaced downward to the forest floor. Those descending at the present time are two lines of paradise birds: *Diphyllodes* and *Parotia*. Those that reached the ground at different periods in the past are (a) the tower builders, (b) the court clearers, (c) the mat makers and (d) the avenue builders, all of which are commonly thrown together to form what I consider to be the synthetic family Ptilonorhynchidae.

9. The origin of bower making in each of these lines of polygynous paradise birds, I think, came about as follows: As with males engaging in arena behaviour in trees, each semi-terrestrially or terrestrially displaying male continued to stake out and defend a private display space, the positioning of which apparently dictated his breeding rights within his clan. And as in the arboreal arenas the males continued to spend much time idly waiting in their terrestrial spaces. As a consequence of boredom, nervousness, or as displacement activities for nest building (Marshall, 1954) in emancipated males, the waiting birds often picked at nearby leaves, twigs, moss, etc., just as their ancestors had done in trees. In trees, however, these items after being pulled loose with the bill were (and are: see *Paradisaea minor*, p. 234) dropped, so that their removal caused only slight alterations of the arboreal display space. But on the ground these activities, together with wing blasting from repeated landings and take-offs, soon caused pronounced alterations of the terrestrial display space. After a time quite by accident the courts thus cleared, and the repetitious cleaning activities (the shifting of sticks, leaves, berries, snail shells, insects, etc.) became incorporated in the terrestrial courtship ceremonies and from these beginnings the habit of bower building developed convergently in several lines of birds of paradise.

10. The first ground courts were probably very similar to those constructed by *Parotia* and *Diphyllodes* today; namely, they were simple courts located just beneath sapling and vine perches which still were important as arboreal components of the display. It is probable that such courts were rather widely spaced in the forest much like the spacing of the original tree courts. It is also probable that when the courts were shifted to the ground visual interactions between clan members were sharply curtailed. A result of this curtailment was probably the rapid development of strong vocal (especially ventriloquial) powers; another result was probably that

the clan members began shifting their courts closer together. These are some of my reasons for thinking that the concentration of ground courts may reflect the length of time that the various lines have been adjusting to the ground niche. For example, in *Diphyllodes* and *Parotia* the ground courts of individual males are so widely spaced in the forest that the males often appear to be solitary. Since these genera are clearly arboreal bird of paradise-like there seems little doubt that they are only now just reaching the ground. On the other hand, the courts of *Amblyornis* are somewhat clustered and closer together and, from a study of the morphology of these birds and of their bowers, it is obvious that *Amblyornis* has been displaying on the ground for a relatively long time. A group which, I believe, has been a ground displayer for a still longer time is the bower builder *Archboldia* in which groups of males place their private courts in concentrations (arenas) in widely isolated places in the forest, more or less after the pattern of certain manakins and the Cock-of-the-Rock.

11. Further to (9), the two main evolutionary steps by which tree displaying birds of paradise shifted (a) to terrestrial display and (b) to bower building, I think, were as follows:

Step (a): Individual males began clearing ground courts on the forest floor under their private arboreal display perches. The arboreal display perches were situated low on vertical trees or low on horizontal vines.

Step (b): Individual males began clearing ground courts around small piles of debris which they had assembled accidentally (probably by dropping from a favourite arboreal display perch).

12. Further to (11), the types of terrestrial bowers known today and their probable lines of origin are as follows:

The Amblyornis *type*. Ground courts are cleared in deep forest (and covered with tree moss) around columnar piles of sticks that in turn are intermeshed horizontally around slender vertical saplings. Individual males build, own and defend such courts and they apparently display terrestrially on the moss around a vestige of the former main display perch – the vertical sapling trunk.

In the early stages of the development of this bower (see Step b, above) the sticks were picked up by the court clearer after they had fallen from trees overhead. In later stages (and now) the male gathers the sticks in the crown of the mist forest. Such twigs are often partly sheathed with pale green epiphytic moss. Probably formerly this living moss fell or was pulled from the collections of sticks and in time it grew into a carpet covering the cleared ground encircling the stick tower. Today the moss has become a component of display and the male bower builder gathers it in the crown of the forest and 'plants' it around the stick column.

This is the form of the bower in three species of *Amblyornis* and somewhat the form in *Prionodura*. It evolved, I strongly suspect, in a stock which once displayed on vertical sapling trunks near the forest floor somewhat as *Diphyllodes* does today.

The Scenopoeetes *type.* Ground courts are cleared (usually amongst thin forest floor saplings), kept meticulously clean, and constantly refurbished with a covering of ornamental leaves. Individual males build, own and defend such courts and display terrestrially on them. The male maintains a low singing perch usually in a sapling very near the court. This perch may be a vestige of the arboreal display perch. This is the form of the bower in the single species of *Scenopoeetes*. It may be traceable to a stock which formerly displayed on vertical saplings close to the forest floor.

The Archboldia *type.* Ground spaces are covered with mats of leaves and a few twigs, and decorated and ringed with various colourful and shapely objects. Individual males build, own and defend such courts and display terrestrially on the mats. No vestige of an arboreal display perch remains. This is the form of the bower in the lone species of *Archboldia*. It may be traceable to a stock which once displayed on horizontal vines near the forest floor as in the four species of *Parotia*.

The walled type. Ground spaces are covered with horizontally intermeshed mats of sticks (in which sticks and grasses are inserted vertically to form walled passages) and decorated and surrounded with colourful objects. This is the form of the bower in *Ptilono-rhynchus*, *Sericulus* and *Chlamydera*, genera which build in the forest, forest edge and in pure grasslands. Individual males build, own and defend such courts and display around and on the horizontal mats. Mating takes place on the mats. No vestige of a relict arboreal display perch remains. However an occasional bower in *Chlamydera lauterbachi* has the end walls gracefully curved far around and almost encircling a short central avenue. This 'aberrant' construction I suspect is a vestigial character of circular construction around tree shafts.

13. The above types of bower construction seem to have been derived from at least two differently behaving 'lines' of paradise birds, (a) vertical pole dancers and (b) horizontal vine dancers. This suggests that the bower building birds are derived from a number of distinct lines (I think at least three) of tree displaying birds of paradise and that the development of ground displays (and bower building) should not be regarded as an indication of intergeneric relationship. In short I consider the Ptilonorhynchidae to be probably polyphyletic in origin and therefore invalid as a taxonomic family.

14. The lines of polygynous paradise birds which because of (4) and (6) shifted their arenas downward to 'slide' under other genera apparently continued to exclude each other in the terrestrial niche. Today the exclusion process affects all but the most widely differentiated genera, and consequently in the bower builders congeneric overlap is virtually unknown. A probable consequence of this exclusion process is that some lines of bower birds may have been turned back from bower building to arboreal non-bower building behaviour. I suspect that some of the genera which appear to bridge the differences between typical birds of paradise and typical bower birds (see above), and which are the most difficult to analyse, developed in this manner. Examples are *Loria* which has the stocky shape and the voice (even the surprising ventriloquism) of a bower bird, and *Loboparadisea* in which the immature (but not the adult female) resembles the female of *Amblyornis subalaris* to a remarkable degree. Another example is *Cnemophilus* in which the female is bower bird-like in shape. Further complicating the picture, some of the possible 'turn-backs', (but not *Cnemophilus* and *Loria*) may have eddied all the way back to pair-bond behaviour as a result of the exclusion pressures of arena behaviour. As pointed out above, species that secondarily adopt monogamous behaviour can presumably live side by side with the arena species without competing. For example a close relative of the polygynous bower-builder *Scenopoeetes*, namely the cat bird *Ailuroedus* in which pairs are formed and both sexes care for the young, may have such a history. Bock (1963) noted that *Ailuroedus* is not primitive. In calling this to my attention he expressed the thought that *Ailuroedus* might have adopted pairing behaviour secondarily. I think he may very well be correct.

15. One of the most interesting aspects of bower birds is, I think,

that some few of the ground displaying polygynous species collided with and then successfully by-passed the powerful counter-selective forces (see 4) described by Fisher. They did this I think when their secondary sexual characters were transferred to objects (see Chapter Seven). These hypothetical transfers occurred bit by bit as first one object associated with court clearing and then another and another was incorporated into courtship behaviour.

16. I believe the process of externalisation that operated through the transfer of sexual signals from morphological characters to sexually significant objects was (a) responsible for the development of the cluster of sexual objects commonly called the bower and (b) largely responsible for the pronounced secondary morphological changes (mostly convergent simplifications of the phenotypes resulting from loss of sexual plumage) that are correlated with bower development.

17. In my view it is necessary to apply exceptionally broad taxonomic principles in classifying polygynous arena birds if one is to show clearly their presumed phylogeny. This is because the rapid evolution and the relative superficiality of their wide phenotypic divergence (which becomes even wider through the phenomenon of transfer) masks their true affinities to a very much greater extent than in monogamous birds.

Suggested Taxonomic Sequence of the Birds of Paradise and Bower Birds[1]

Family PARADISAEIDAE
Genus   *Macgregoria*
            Lycocorax
            Manucodia
            Phonygammus
            Ptiloris
            Semioptera
            Seleucidis
            Paradigalla

[1] This arrangement reflects the author's own conclusions regarding the relationships between the genera of birds of paradise and bower birds and was written subsequent to the species accounts of chapters 9 and 10. The arrangement in these chapters follows Mayr (*in* Peters, 1962), except as stated on p. 61. In the following list the bower birds are considered to be polyphyletic and therefore the family Ptilonorhynchidae is invalid as a taxonomic unit (see p. 43).—Ed.

Drepanornis
Epimachus
Astrapia
Lophorina
Parotia
Pteridophora
Cicinnurus
Diphyllodes
Paradisaea
Cnemophilus
Loria
Loboparadisea
Ailuroedus
Scenopoeetes
Archboldia
Amblyornis
Prionodura
Sericulus
Ptilonorhynchus
Chlamydera

Chapter Seven

The Evolution of Bower-Building in Birds

A NINETEENTH CENTURY naturalist once suggested that just as mammals are commonly divided into two groups – man and the lower forms – all birds should be split into two categories: bower birds and other birds. Anyone who has observed the behaviour of these remarkable creatures of Australia and New Guinea and examined their artifacts can understand this and sympathise with Dr Odoardo Beccari, the first naturalist to discover a bower, for thinking it the product of human artistry and invention.

As we have already seen, the males of some species build elaborate walled bowers of sticks and decorate them with bright objects and even with paint. Others construct towers up to nine feet high, some with tepee-like roofs and internal chambers, on circular lawns that they tend carefully and embellish with golden resins, garishly coloured berries, iridescent insect skeletons and fresh flowers that are replaced as they wither. Today we know that the bowers are stages set by the males on which to perform intricate routines of sexual display and to mate with the females of their species. However displays still pose many mysteries – so many that Professor G. Evelyn Hutchinson of Yale University wrote: it constitutes behaviour that '. . . in its complexity and refinement is unique in the nonhuman part of the animal kingdom'.

The student of evolution inevitably asks how such extremely specialised behaviour came about. The answer, I suspect, can be unmasked if one steps back to survey all the birds with behavioural affinities to the bower birds, that is, those birds that practice the pattern of courtship behaviour known as arena behaviour. There are only eighteen species called bower birds, but there are in all some eighty-five species that have been described as arena birds. This is still a small proportion – about one per cent – of the avian species of the world. But arena birds are a world-wide assemblage including species in such disparate families as sandpipers, grouse, bustards, blackbirds, small tropical manakins and the bizarrely beautiful birds of paradise.

It has fallen to my lot to be able to make comparative ethological investigations of many of these species both in New Guinea and South America. As a result of these studies I have reached some conclusions that seem to be new. One is that arena behaviour, wherever it appears, probably has a common origin and that its development represents evolutionary advancement in the species employing it. Once set in motion, I think, it has a predictable evolution leading rather quickly to the development of the highly specialised combinations of structure and behaviour found in all the far-flung arena species. The bower birds are at the pinnacle of arena evolution. They have gone a step beyond the most richly ornamented arena birds, substituting fancy houses and jewellery for colourful plumage. The step they have taken, I will attempt to show below, can only be taken by means of an hitherto unrecognised mechanism in the process of sexual selection.

Arena behaviour was defined by the ornithologist and student of evolution Ernst Mayr (1935) as a pattern of territorial behaviour in which the males establish a mating station that has no connection with feeding or nesting. I would add that it is a rather rare form of courtship behaviour involving a group of males usually living in an organised band on or about a traditional mating space: the arena. Each arena is composed of a number of courts, the private display territories of individual males. To establish their right to a territory the males go through ritualistic combat routines, fighting, charging, displaying their plumage or brandishing twigs, singing or producing 'mechanical' sounds. Once territories are established there is little fighting for mates because the females do the choosing. The sexes live apart for long periods of the year and are often so dissimilarly dressed as to look like different species. Since there is no true pair bond, the males play no part whatever in building or defending the nest or in rearing the young.

This advanced courtship pattern is in sharp contrast to the less advanced behaviour of the other ninety-nine per cent of the world's birds. For them the central event is the establishment of a pair bond between a male and a female, with the pair proceeding to share the work of raising the young. (The word 'advanced' is not intended to imply a value judgement on the state of matrimony.

50

Ornithologists simply assume that pair-bonding and work-sharing habits represent the less advanced evolutionary condition in birds because these habits are so nearly universal.) The pair-bond pattern is found regularly not only in the phylogenetically recent passerine (perching) order of songbirds, which is at the present time the most numerous and highly differentiated avian group, but also in the older non-passerine birds; it is a 'conservative' behavioural pattern that has resisted modification. Yet the breakthrough to arena behaviour seems to occur, apparently at random, just about anywhere in the world and at scattered points on the family tree of birds.

The characteristics that define arena behaviour and argue for its common origin and line of evolution emerge from the study of a fairly large number of arena birds. The pattern is most evident when the arena is small, as in the case of the Ruff, a sandpiper of northern Europe and Asia whose behaviour has been described in detail by the British ornithologist C.R. Stonor (1940). The males and females apparently live apart except for a few minutes in the breeding season. Each spring the males gather in isolated clans, each of which populates a small, grassy hillock in rolling meadowland. After a period of fighting and display among themselves the males learn to recognise one another as individuals, and arrange themselves on the mound in a social order that presumably remains fairly fixed throughout the breeding season. Each male's territory is a private court about two feet in diameter that he defends vigorously against other males. The clan waits day after day for the visits of occasional females in search of mates. When one appears, the males go to their courts and assume strangely stiff postures, extending the colourful plumage of their neck ruffs. Displaying in this manner they reminded Stonor of a bed of flowers. The female wanders through this cluster and pecks at the neck feathers of the bird she prefers. Mating occurs immediately – whereupon the rejected males immediately collapse on their courts as if in a fainting spell.

Arena behaviour of a similar sort but on a larger scale is practised by the Sage Grouse and Prairie Chicken of North America. The grouse's arena may be half a mile long and 200 yards wide, with 400 males within its boundaries, each standing twenty-five to forty feet apart on its private court. The zoologist John W. Scott (1942) was able to study the breeding hierarchy in a clan of these grouse.

He found that the great majority of matings went to four 'master' and a few 'submaster' cocks with courts located along the centre line of the long, narrow arena. Of 114 observed matings involving males whose place in the hierarchy had been determined, seventy-four per cent went to the four master cocks. Only after these birds had become satiated did thirteen per cent of the matings go to the submasters, and the few remaining matings went to scattered owners of peripheral courts. These and other observations make it clear that arena matings are not random: the coordinated clan activities that serve to establish the territorial hierarchy, and thus the breeding rights, are of primary evolutionary importance.

Some years ago (Gilliard, 1962) on an expedition to South America I studied arena behaviour in a very different bird, a cotinga called Cock-of-the-Rock (*Rupicola rupicola*). I found a clan of these brilliant orange birds, which wear a great semicircular crest resembling that of a Roman helmet, in the Kanuku Mountains of British Guiana. The males held and defended an arena some forty by eighty feet in extent including about forty small courts – cleared areas on the ground under saplings and vines that provided convenient perches. For 20 consecutive days I watched three members of the clan, readily recognisable as individuals, that held adjacent courts in one part of the arena. I was struck by the silence and deliberateness of movement that characterised their behaviour on the courts; it was reminiscent of the behaviour of a pair-bonded male at its nest. During the period of observation females visited the arena several times. Whenever a female arrived, the three males, if they were not already on the ground, would fall almost like stones from their perches to their courts. There, with bodies flattened and heads tilted so that the crests were silhouetted against the bare ground, they would posture stiffly for many minutes. Again there was a resemblance to the attitude of a male attending a nest. The three birds jealously defended from one another their own courts and a cone-shaped space about them. But when a wandering nonclan male visited them, they would fly up and attack him as a team with violent chasing displays, wing-buffeting, strange cries and whinnying sounds.

As we have seen earlier, the twenty-four species of birds of paradise in which arena behaviour is known vary widely in physical characteristics and in the details of their displays. Some clear courts on or near the ground, some inhabit the middle levels of tropical forests and some display high in the treetops. In many of them the arena is so large that it has not usually been considered an arena at all. The distances between the individual courts can mislead one into believing that each male is operating in solitude, but this is almost certainly not the case. Apparently these species have 'exploded' arenas; the birds' calls and mechanisms for the production of other sounds are always highly developed and powerful, so that the males can interact in spite of their seeming isolation. Strong evidence in favour of the exploded-arena hypothesis is the fact that in many of these species the courts have been found to be concentrated in certain areas of the forest year after year.

I have studied two of the species that clear courts on or near the ground beneath low branches, vines and saplings: the Magnificent Bird of Paradise (*Diphyllodes magnificus*) and Queen Carola's Bird of Paradise (*Parotia carolae*). For both species the court is the property of a single male that remains in attendance many hours a day, probably for several months a year. Austin L. Rand of the Field Museum of Natural History, Chicago, has described how the Magnificent Bird of Paradise spends countless hours trimming away the forest leaves above its court, thereby enabling a shaft of sky light to enhance the bird's iridescent colouring. Similar but less well developed court-clearing is practised by other arena birds. In an arena of blue-backed manakins on Tobago in the West Indies I saw that much of the foliage had been cut around the arboreal courts. Frank M. Chapman (1935) of The American Museum of Natural History studied clans of Gould's manakins located miles apart in Panama that had made many small, patelike clearings in 200-foot-long strips of the rain-forest floor. The Cock-of-the-Rock clears its court with violent wing thrashing, whereas most other arena birds use their bills for this purpose. However it is done, the court of many arena birds is swept clean of fallen debris if it is terrestrial, and stripped of many leaves and twigs if it is arboreal.

It seems not too big a step from the court-clearers to such elementary bower-builders as Archbold's Bower Bird (*Archboldia papuensis*). These are clearly arena birds: the males and females apparently live apart most of the year. The males spend the breeding season on or close to table-sized stages on the ground in high mountain forests of New Guinea. Each stage is owned and defended by a single male who carpets it with ferns, decorates it with shafts of bamboos, piles of resin, beetle skeletons, snail shells and lumps of charcoal. Each is within audible range of other stagetending males. On one slope of Mount Hagen I found five stages (Mayr and Gilliard, 1954; Gilliard, 1959a) concentrated in a zone about two miles in diameter, and my native hunters reported others I did not see. Although the species seemed rather common, a number of expeditions failed to find any of these birds elsewhere on Mount Hagen; however, a similar group was discovered on another mountain some fifteen to twenty miles away. In my opinion each of these groups represents a clan, and its gathering place is the clan's arena. The males within each clan maintain contact with one another by uttering mighty whistles and harsh, rasping notes, and it seems likely that all know when a female is in the arena and act in concert as many other arena birds do.

I watched one male receiving a visit from a female. As soon as the female arrived near the court the male dropped to its colourful stage and began to act in a manner resembling that of a young bird begging food. With its wings outstretched and its tail spread, it crawled tortuously toward the female, which perched at the edge of the court and kept moving around its periphery. The male held its head up like a turtle, made gasping movements with its bill and kept up a deep, penetrating 'churr' song. In spite of the vigour of this display the ceremony was apparently not consummated by mating. After twenty-two minutes something disturbed the birds and the female flew off. Soon the male began rearranging the piles of ornaments and resumed its long, solitary wait.

Another New Guinea bower bird with an exploded arena is the extraordinary Gardener Bower Bird (*Amblyornis*). A male of this genus builds its bower by piling sticks against a sapling on the floor of a mountain rain forest and clearing a mossy saucer around the tower. Some species build large towers with roofs and internal chambers and decorate the moss court with snail shells, insect and spider silk and fresh flowers changed daily for months on end. Others build only a small roof and use fewer ornaments, and still others merely maintain a clearing around a modest tower of intertwined sticks.

Some years ago I noticed that there is an inverse ratio in the three known *Amblyornis* species between the complexity of the bower and the plumage of the male bird (the three females are virtually indistinguishable). In the species *A. macgregoriae*, which builds the simple bower, the adult male wears a long golden-orange crest.

54

In *A. subalaris*, which builds the somewhat more complex bower, the male wears a shorter crest. And in the aptly named species *A. inornatus*, which builds the most elaborate bower (with a broad roof overhanging a court decorated with berries, shells and piles of flowers), the male wears no crest and is virtually indistinguishable from any of the females!

I believe that the forces of sexual selection in these birds have been transferred from morphological characteristics – the male plumage – to external objects and that this 'transferral effect' (see Gilliard, 1956) may be the key factor in the evolution of the more complex bower birds. This would explain the extraordinary development and proliferation of the bowers and their ornaments: these objects have in effect become externalised bundles of secondary sexual characteristics that are psychologically but not physically connected with the males. The transfer also has an important morphological effect: once colourful plumage is rendered unimportant, natural selection operates in the direction of protective colouration and the male tends more and more to resemble the female.

Further evidence of this sort came from observations of Lauterbach's Bower Bird (*Chlamydera lauterbachi*), a grassland and forest-edge species of New Guinea. In an area several miles in diameter I once found sixteen bowers of this 'avenue-building' species hundreds to many thousands of feet apart (see Mayr and Gilliard, 1954). One bower I examined contained almost 1000 pale pebbles weighing nearly ten pounds. More than 3000 sticks and 1000 hairlike strands of grass had gone into the four-walled structure. The sticks were interlocked to form a rigid structure and the grass was used to line the vertical walls facing the inner court. Three times during the many days I watched, a female entered a bower. The male became highly excited and began to dance. The female jumped quickly within the walls and then stood still and alert. Almost as soon as she was in the bower the male picked up with its bill a marble-sized red berry, held it high and displayed it to the female much as it would have displayed its bright crest feathers – if it had had any. *C. lauterbachi*, like *A. inornatus*, is the most advanced builder of its genus. It is also a species in which the male and female cannot be told apart except by dissection. The transferral effect seems to be operating in this case too.

It appears that once the female has selected a bower-owner she stays for several days. (This has also been reported in some other arena birds, such as the Argus Pheasant: see Beebe, 1926). These stays may be responsible for the assumption made by many investigators that there is a pair bond in bower birds. Pair-bonding cannot be proved or disproved except by marking and observing females; my investigations indicate that at least most of the bower-building bower birds are polygynous, with exploded arenas like those of their close relatives, the birds of paradise.

One further observation bearing on the transferral effect should be mentioned. In the Finisterre Mountains of New Guinea I watched and filmed the courtship behaviour of the Fawn-breasted Bower Bird (*Chlamydera cerviniventris*), in which both sexes are an identical drab brown. When a female entered the two-walled avenue bower and squatted on the floor, the male immediately approached. On the ground several feet from the bower the male suddenly appeared to be overcome by a spasm. Its head seemed to turn involuntarily away from the female again and again. Finally the bird appeared to regain control, seized a sprig of green berries in its bill, faced the female and waved the berries up and down as it slowly approached the bower. I saw several more such visits by a female, and each time the male went through the curious twisting motions that presented the back of its head to the female.

Later, watching the films I had made of these movements, a thought occurred that the head-screwing might constitute crest display – except for the fact that *C. cerviniventris* has no crest! But many males closely related to this species do have glittering violet-to-pink crests at the nape of the neck and the Australian ornithologist John Warham (1957) has described how they twist their necks to display the crest to a female in the bower. I concluded (Gilliard, 1959) that the head-twisting of *C. cerviniventris* is a relict movement dating from the time when the species had such a crest. With the later incorporation of the berries as ornaments in the courtship ceremony, I postulated, the crest became unimportant. Since it was now simply a liability in terms of protective colouration, it was lost through natural selection – but the movement associated with it persists. This I consider a strong second line of evidence for the transferral effect.

Again it must be emphasised that the courtship behaviour of this species and probably that of all other ground-displaying bower birds, even though complicated and camouflaged by refinements of ornamentation and stick architecture, follows the basic pattern of arena behaviour the world around. It is the behaviour of a clan of males interacting in an arena, each on its own territory and competing with the other males for itinerant females. Many arena species clear courts and some do it more effectively than others; some build stages or erect walls, towers or houses. All these actions seem to be levels of refinement of the same basic behaviour.

Is the history of the bower, then, the same as the history of the arena bird's court? I think so. Arena behaviour, I suggest, can develop fortuitously at any period in the history of any bird group as a result of a shift in the work load shared by a pair-bonded male and female. The division of labour in nest construction and the care and rearing of the young varies from species to species. In extreme cases the males may be completely released from all nesting duties – perhaps because natural selection favours a stock in which brightly coloured males stay away from the nest. Emancipated from the pair bond, the males can live apart from the females in bachelor clans. Now sexual selection can operate freely, tending in the direction of brighter plumage and more complex display behaviour that will attract more females.

The next step, from elementary arena behaviour to bower-building, may not be so great as it seems at first. I have pointed out that most arena birds clear some sort of display space for themselves. In the species that have come down from the trees to the ground, such as the Cock-of-the-Rock and some birds of paradise, the males spend much of their time clearing away twigs and leaves and perhaps berries, stones and shells, if there are any about. A. J. Marshall (1956) of Monash University in Australia and Erwin Stresemann of the Zoologisches Museum, Berlin, have speculated that the handling of these objects may accidentally have become incorporated in and important to the courtship ceremony for which the court is maintained, and so have led to bower-building. I think it likely that both court-clearing and bower-building are deeply rooted in the nesting impulses of the male birds. Nest-building and the actions associated with it by each species constitute fixed behavioural patterns that are not easily abandoned and are more likely to be diverted into new directions. Other investigators have noted actions in arena birds, and particularly in bower birds, that reminded them of nesting behaviour. V. G. L. van Someren (*in* Armstrong, 1947) remarked some years ago that in shaping its court the male of the weaverbird species known as Jackson's Dancing Whydah 'creates recesses resembling the early stages of a nest, butting into the grass and smoothing it down with his breast'. Armstrong (loc. cit.) commented in his classic book on bird behaviour that 'this performance would seem to be due to the survival of the nest-building impulse'.

Marshall, a leading student of the bower birds, has called attention to many activities he believes stem from displaced nesting habits. Certainly as one looks at a New Guinea stick bower, particularly that of Lauterbach's Bower Bird, one cannot but feel it is some sort of monstrous nest. The wall of sticks, the lining of grass, even the way the male places egg-sized berries or pebbles near the centre of the basket-like structure – all suggest aspects of nest-building that still survive in males that have had no nesting responsibilities for tens of thousands of years and probably much longer. In other bower birds and arena birds this impression of a physical nest is, to be sure, not so vivid. But, as noted in the case of the Cock-of-the Rock, I have often been impressed by the male's strangely quiet and attentive manner when it visits its court or bower, a manner that reminds an ornithologist of a parent bird arriving at its nest.

I would define arena behaviour as courtship behaviour reshaped by emancipated males to include their nondiscardable nesting tendencies. I would further suggest that bower behaviour has developed in certain arena birds under the influence of natural and sexual selection, that some of the ground-clearing arena birds are even now on the way to becoming builders of bowers, and that the dully dressed bower birds that build the most complex and ornamented structures are at the leading edge of avian evolution.

This hypothesis does not in itself explain the great variety and variability of bowers or the complexities of behaviour and plumage in arena birds, all of which seem to imply that these birds are evolving at an accelerated rate compared with other birds. The biological advantage of arena behaviour may be closely linked to this factor. Because of promiscuous polygyny a few males in each generation are enough to propagate a species. Losses by predation can be very acute (and indeed must be in the case of terrestrially displaying males), and both natural and sexual selection can operate more severely than usual.

An indication that some such process may be at work is the fact that 'intergeneric hybrids', although extremely rare in all animals, are rather more common in arena birds. Since a species – a limb-tip on the avian tree of evolution – is identified as such by its 'reproductive isolation' from the other limb-tips, it is difficult to explain even one case of interfertility between genera, the main limbs of the tree. Yet in our collection at The American Museum of Natural History we have no less than eleven adult male intergeneric hybrid offspring of the Magnificent Bird of Paradise (*Diphyllodes magnificus*) and the King Bird of Paradise (*Cicinnurus regius*), two 'genera' which no taxonomist in his wildest dreams would consider 'lumping' into one. The number of hybrids occurring between these birds leads me to suspect that *Diphyllodes* and *Cicinnurus* may not be nearly so distantly related as their structures seem to indicate and that their evolution has been very rapid and very recent. Is there perhaps a correlation between such birds and the many varieties of domestic dogs, in the case of which man has acted as the agent of rapid selection and has bred such different but interfertile forms ('genera') as the Pekinese and the Great Dane?

Keeping to firmer ground, it is safe to say that the highly specialised combinations of structure and behaviour seen in arena birds argue most eloquently that these birds are evolving at a faster rate than most birds and that this accelerated evolution is due to their behaviour. One has only to consider the magnificent plumage of the Argus Pheasant, the great inflatable bibs of the Bustard, the radiant orange paraphernalia of the Cock-of-the-Rock and the lacy plumage of the birds of paradise to be seized by the notion that some rapidly operating mechanism is directing the evolution of these birds. The same holds true for the even more wonderful arena birds called bower birds, with their houses and ornamental gardens and their courtship displays that replace plumage with glittering natural jewellery.

But to sum up, my hypothesis that accelerated evolution associated with arena behaviour may be of basic importance in avian evolution goes beyond the mere question of rapid evolution of the secondary sexual characters themselves, which was the chief consideration of earlier proponents of the theory of sexual selection (Charles Darwin, 1871; R. A. Fisher, 1929; Julian Huxley, 1938).

My principal points are (a) that bower birds, at least many of them, practice arena behaviour, *not* pair-bond behaviour as generally thought, and this, I hypothesised, is the key factor that made possible the development of the extraordinary ornamented bowers

59

('bundles of externalised secondary sexual characters'), and (b) that the development of this ornamental bower made possible the hypothesised secondary loss of sexual plumage once the forces of sexual selection had been transferred from colourful feathers to colourful objects.

The biological advantage conferred through polygynous behaviour in arena birds is, I think, a fundamental one. It operates through the combined effects of polygyny and transfer noted above, but the threshold at which it becomes operative is reached by way of the simpler forms of polygyny. To explain: Darwin's theory of sexual selection has two main elements (see Fisher, 1929): (a) a selection exerted through rival males that results in the selection of special weapons (antlers and so forth), and (b) a selection exerted through females as a consequence of their sexual preferences that results in the development of certain physical features in males (plumage, wattles and so on). This second force, I believe, is the key one operating in all arena birds below the level of the bower birds.

On rare occasions near peaks of development in the evolution of polygynous animals, I believe, these two forces are reinforced by a third one that is released by the transfer of sexual signals from the physical features of the male to the objects used by the male in his courtship displays. At first the effects are disarmingly subtle, but I think this force is so potentially powerful it can open a pathway through the almost impenetrable maze of barriers (counterselective forces) imposed by natural selection. It does this, I think, by allowing for the externalisation and proliferation of sexual signals [objects which can also be used as weapons] and thus unshackling an evolving animal from the inhibiting effects of direct counterselection. This process of externalisation through transfer, I think, is accompanied by bursts of evolutionary activity of such intensity they sometimes carry an animal into an entirely new adaptive zone. In my opinion this process, with polygyny as the boosting force, is the fundamental one responsible for the evolution of the house building, tool using bower birds.

I also think that this mechanism played a fundamental part in the evolution of hominids but that in the hominids (with their clasping fore extremities) it was (and is) able to operate much more effectively than in birds.

Part Two

Chapter Eight

Introduction: Birds of Paradise and Bower Birds

INTRODUCTION. It is very possible that all of the species of this fascinating superfamily have now been uncovered. The last new species of bird of paradise to be discovered – the Ribbon-tailed Astrapia – was found in 1938 in the Mandated Territory of New Guinea, and the last new species of bower bird – Archbold's Bower Bird – was turned up in the heart of the Snow Mountains of West New Guinea in 1939.

Today the inventory of birds of paradise and bower birds stands at sixty species. We know of forty-two species of birds of paradise: two are exclusively Australian and two are shared with New Guinea; thirty-six occur exclusively in New Guinea, and two are exclusively Moluccan. In the bower birds we know of eighteen species: six are exclusively Australian, two are shared with New Guinea and ten are exclusively from New Guinea.

I have described the general characters of these extraordinary birds in the introduction to this volume. In a following section immediately ahead of the species biographies, I have provided brief technical keys (generic synopses) which are patterned after the keys in the *Handbook of New Guinea Birds* (Rand and Gilliard, 1967).

In this work I have followed the arrangement of species advocated by Ernst Mayr in his most recent revision of these birds (*in* Peters, 1962). The only exceptions are (a) that I have transposed the bower bird and the bird of paradise groups, and (b) I have elevated one population of bower birds and two populations of birds of paradise to the status of full species. My reasons for so doing are stated in the species biographies.[1]

I have republished below Sharpe's list of all of the birds of

---

[1] For the author's suggested sequence of genera, see chapter 6, p. 47. (Ed.)

paradise and bower birds that were known to him when he compiled his monograph of these birds (1891–98). Of course I have removed from his list all of the species which today are considered to be hybrids. Immediately after the Sharpe list I have listed all of the species that have been discovered since Sharpe's time. From a study of the two lists it becomes abundantly clear that the possibility of making new discoveries in these groups is now remote. Only six species have turned up in the nearly three quarters of a century since Sharpe's time and none have been uncovered in the last quarter century despite some rather extensive searching.

At the end of the species lists I have inserted a table containing all of the known bird of paradise and bower bird hybrids together with some of Stresemann's remarks concerning his discovery that many of the 'rare birds of paradise' are hybrids. Finally I have appended some remarks concerning my belief that some few of the 'hybrids' are probably 'lost' species which still await discovery.

Species of Birds of Paradise and Bower Birds known to Bowdler Sharpe

Family PARADISAEIDAE

Loria loriae
Loboparadisea sericea
Cnemophilus macgregorii
Macgregoria pulchra
Lycocorax pyrrhopterus
Manucodia ater
Manucodia jobiensis
Manucodia chalybatus
Manucodia comrii
Phonygammus keraudrenii
Ptiloris paradiseus
Ptiloris victoriae
Ptiloris magnificus
Semioptera wallacei
Seleucidis melanoleuca
Paradigalla carunculata
Drepanornis albertisi
Drepanornis bruijnii
Epimachus fastosus

Epimachus meyeri
Astrapia nigra
Astrapia splendidissima
Astrapia stephaniae
Lophorina superba
Parotia sefilata
Parotia carolae
Parotia lawesi
Pteridophora alberti
Cicinnurus regius
Diphyllodes magnificus
Diphyllodes respublica
Paradisaea apoda
Paradisaea raggiana
Paradisaea minor
Paradisaea decora
Paradisaea rubra
Paradisaea guilielmi
Paradisaea rudolphi

Family PTILONORHYNCHIDAE

Ailuroedus buccoides	*Prionodura newtoniana*
Ailuroedus crassirostris	*Sericulus aureus*
Ailuroedus melanotis	*Sericulus chrysocephalus*
Scenopoeetes dentirostris	*Ptilonorhynchus violaceus*
Amblyornis flavifrons	*Chlamydera maculata*
Amblyornis macgregoriae	*Chlamydera nuchalis*
Amblyornis subalaris	*Chlamydera cerviniventris*
Amblyornis inornatus	*Chlamydera lauterbachi*

Species of Birds of Paradise and Bower Birds which have been discovered since Bowdler Sharpe's time

1906: *Astrapia rothschildi*	1928: *Sericulus bakeri*
1906: *Parotia wahnesi*	1938: *Astrapia mayeri*
1911: *Paradigalla brevicauda*	1939: *Archboldia papuensis*

Hybrid Birds of Paradise and Bower Birds.

It is generally believed that about eighteen 'rare birds of paradise' and one 'rare' bower bird are of hybrid origin. Most of these became known to science through specimens which turned up amongst the tens of thousands of market skins that formerly were offered for sale each year in Ternate, Amsterdam, Paris and London. For a long while these 'rare' species were the objects of intense search in New Guinea, but in 1930 after many expeditions had failed to discover any of the species Erwin Stresemann (1930) made a surprising discovery. He tells it as follows (1954): 'When (Ernst Mayr) was no more fortunate (in finding the "lost" species) than his predecessors, I decided in 1930 to examine all "suspicious" species of Birds of Paradise to see whether they might prove to be generic or specific hybrids. I reached the surprising conclusion that no less than 18 species and 8 genera should be removed from the list of "normal" Birds of Paradise because they were hybrids. Time has proved that I was right.'

But has time proved that Stresemann is right in all of his determinations? The final answer to this question I feel cannot be given until New Guinea has been fully explored. Many of the hybrids involve high altitude species, and many high areas of New Guinea,

63

although visited in former times by Papuan plume collectors, have never been visited by ornithologists. Therefore, it is my belief that some of the birds which are now classified as hybrids are actually 'lost' species that still await discovery even as does the Yellow-fronted Gardener Bower Bird (*Amblyornis flavifrons*). This bower bird, which is known from a few trade skins which turned up in Paris before the turn of the century, is a species of the high mountain forests. When the ecological 'island' on which it lives is discovered I strongly suspect that certain other rarities (and even some undiscovered species) will be found living side by side with it, and one or more of these may prove to be the 'rare birds of paradise' now considered hybrids.

The following is a list of all of the species which are thought to be of hybrid origin. I have included the original technical names so that the older literature may be deciphered. This list is taken largely from Rand and Gilliard (Handbook of New Guinea Birds, 1967). For technical details see Stresemann (1930) and Mayr (*in* Peters, 1963).

Hybrid Birds of Paradise and Bower Birds

Intergeneric Hybrids

1 *Astrapimachus ellioti; (Astrapia × Epimachus)*
2 *Pseudastrapia lobata; (Epimachus × Paradigalla)*
3 *Loborhamphus ptilorhis; (Paradigalla × Parotia)*
4 *Parotia duivenbodei; (Lophorina × Parotia)*
5 *Loborhamphus nobilis; (Lophorina × Paradigalla)*
6 *Lamprothorax wilhelminae; (Diphyllodes × Lophorina)*
7 *Paryphephorus duivenbodei; (Craspedophora × Lophorina)*
8 *Heteroptilorhis mantoui;(Craspedophora × Seleucides)*
9 *Janthothorax mirabilis; (Paradisaea × Seleucides)*
10 *Janthothorax bensbachi; (Craspedophora × Paradisaea)*
11 *Neoparadisea ruysi; (Diphyllodes × Paradisaea)*
12 *Cicinnurus lyrogyrus; (Cicinnurus × Diphyllodes)*
13 *Rhipidornis gulielmitertii; (Cicinnurus × Diphyllodes)*
14 *Ptilonorhynchus rawnsleyi; (Ptilonorhynchus × Sericulus)*

Intrageneric Hybrids

15 *Paradisaea maria; (Paradisaea raggiana × P. guilielmi)*
16 *Paradisaea duivenbodei; (Paradisaea minor × P. guilielmi)*

17 *Paradisaea mixta; (Paradisaea minor × P. raggiana)*
18 *Paradisaea apoda luptoni; (Paradisaea apoda × P. raggiana)*
19 *Paradisaea bloodi; (Paradisaea rudolphi × P. raggiana)*

Synopsis of Genera of Birds of Paradise

1 *Loria* One species; length $8\frac{3}{4}$ inches; bill shorter than head; tail rounded. Sexes different: male black with iridescent patches on secondaries and lores. Female olive and somewhat bower bird like. (New Guinea mountains.) See page 81.

2 *Loboparadisea* One species; length $6\frac{3}{4}$ inches; bill shorter than head. Sexes different: male unique in having greenish wattles covering base of maxilla; male brown with silky yellow underparts. Adult female unique in being like adult male but paler. Juvenals brown above with pale streaked underparts, and resembling the adult female of *Amblyornis subalaris*. (New Guinea mountains.) See page 83.

3 *Cnemophilus* One species; length $9\frac{3}{4}$ inches; bill shorter than head; tail shorter than wing; unique in having erectile crest plumes. Sexes different: male orange red to yellow above and blackish below. Female brownish olive and rather bower bird like. (New Guinea mountains.) See page 86.

4 *Macgregoria* One species; 13 to 15 inches; bill nearly straight; sexes nearly alike: generally velvet black with orange in wings and with large orange lappet wattles surrounding the rear half of eye. (New Guinea mountains.) See page 91.

5 *Lycocorax* One species; length 14 to 17 inches; bill nearly straight and stout; sexes nearly alike: crow-like without special ornamentation. (Moluccan Islands.) See page 93.

6 *Manucodia* Four species; length 12 to $17\frac{1}{2}$ inches; bill nearly straight and stout; sexes nearly alike except trachea often looped in male: plumage black glossed purple to green and often crinkled. (New Guinea region.) See page 95.

7 *Phonygammus* One species; length 10 to $12\frac{1}{2}$ inches; much

65

like *Manucodia* but with 'horn-like' tufts on head and lanceolate feathers on neck; adult male with a large coiled trachea. (Australia and New Guinea region.) See page 104.

8 *Ptiloris* Three species; length 8¾ to 13 inches; bill slightly curved and longer than head; central rectrices shortest. Sexes different: male black with iridescent patches on crown, throat, breast and central rectrices. Female brown to pale grey with dark barring below. (Australia and New Guinea.) See page 108.

9 *Semioptera* One species; length 10 inches; bill slightly curved and equal in length to head; (tail shorter than wing); central rectrices shortest. Sexes different: male brown with iridescence on crown (subobsolete) and breast and unique in having two pairs of long erectile white plumes on bend of wing. Female brown without ornamental feathering. (Moluccan Islands.) See page 121.

10 *Seleucidis* One species; length 12 to 13½ inches; bill slightly curved and one-and-one-half times length of head; tail short and square. Sexes different: male black and yellow with yellow flank plumes terminating in wire-like tips (six on each side) that bend forward. Female brown with a dark head and pale grey with black barring below. (New Guinea lowlands.) See page 126.

11 *Paradigalla* Two species; 8½ to 15 inches; bill slightly longer than head; sexes black and nearly alike (but plumage of male suffused with bronze), forecrown naked; unique in having yellow wattles at base of maxilla and blue wattles at basal sides of mandible. (New Guinea mountains.) See page 131.

12 *Drepanornis* Two species; 13½ to 14 inches; bill very long, slender and sickle-shaped; base of bill and stripe on side of head naked. Sexes different: male greyish below with elongated feather tufts on breast and flanks; female barred below. See page 134.

13 *Epimachus* Two species; length 39 to 44 inches; bill sickle shaped and long somewhat as in *Drepanornis* but much heavier; tail long and graduated. Sexes different: male generally black with long glossy tipped feathers on sides of breast; female brownish above and barred below. (New Guinea mountains.) See page 137.

14 *Astrapia* Five species; length 15 to 46 inches; bill slender, slightly curved and about equal to length of head; tail long to very long and step-like with the longest rectrices six to sixteen times longer than shortest. Sexes different: male above generally blackish suffused with green or purple; head, neck and breast iridescent greenish, side of neck and upper breast copper; underparts blackish (or oil green) tail black, the plumes a) often broad with purple iridescence above, or b) black with white bases or c) with white on inner two thirds of central rectrices, or d) with immensely elongated white central rectrices. Female smaller, more brownish, without white in tail and with barred underparts. (New Guinea mountains.) See page 146.

15 *Lophorina* One species; length 8½ to 10 inches; bill about equal to length of head; tail shorter than wing; sexes different: male with an enormous erectile cape of feathers springing from nape; crown, breast and central rectrices glossy. Female brownish with pale dark barred underparts. (New Guinea mountains.) See page 163.

16 *Parotia* Four species; length 9½ to 17½ inches; bill about equal to length of head; tail short and rounded (to long and graduated in one species). Sexes different: male black (one species black with white flanks) with an erectile crest (black, copper or white), iridescent patches on nape and breast and unique in having three long 'flag' tipped 'wires' springing from tufts, one on each side of the nape. Female brownish often with a blackish head and pale barred underparts. (New Guinea mountains.) See page 170.

17 *Pteridophora* One species; length 8 to 9 inches; bill straight and less than length of head; tail short and square. Sexes different: male black to yellow below with a single immense blue flanged quill two to three times the length of the body springing from each side of nape. Female grey above and whitish with blackish barring below. (New Guinea mountains.) See page 184.

18 *Cicinnurus* One species; length 5 to 6½ inches (without central tail feathers); bill equal to length of head. Sexes different: male unique in having thread-like tail wires equal in length to body and terminating in iridescent coin-like tips; male red with a white

abdomen. Female brown to grey with dark barring below. (New Guinea region.) See page 192.

19 *Diphyllodes* Two species; length 6½ to 7½ inches (without central tail feathers); bill straight and about equal to length of head. Sexes different: male unique in having two very long tail plumes which are feathered only on the outer side of the shafts; male with yellow collar, red back and patches of iridescence on throat and breast. Female olive to pale brown with blackish barring below. (New Guinea region.) See page 201.

20 *Paradisaea* Seven species; length 11½ to 18 inches (without central tail wires); bill nearly straight and about equal to length of head. Sexes different: male with the central rectrices greatly elongated and usually wire-like or ribbon-like, but in one species the shafts have narrow feather vanes; male with massive filmy-tipped feather tufts (red, orange, yellow, white or blue) on sides of breast. Females smaller and lacking flank tufts and tail wires. (New Guinea region.) See page 214.

Synopsis of Genera of Bower Birds

1 *Ailuroedus* Three species; length 10 to 13 inches; bill bulky, straight and nearly length of head. Sexes similar except females with crown paler. Adults: upperparts bright green boldly patterned with black; underparts pale brown to ochraceous. (Australia and New Guinea.) See page 258.

2 *Scenopoeetes* One species; length 10½ inches; bill straight, stocky, deeply notched (and nearly length of head). Sexes similar: adults brownish olive with bold striping on underparts. (Australia.) See page 273.

3 *Archboldia* One species; length 12 to 15 inches; bill straight and nearly length of head. Sexes different: male generally black with a slightly forked tail and with a gold crest (or uniform dusky grey in one subspecies?). Female blackish or dusky greyish with pale brown to buff marks on wings. (New Guinea mountains.) See page 281.

4 *Amblyornis* Four species; length 8½ to 10½ inches; bill straight and shorter than head; tail slightly rounded except in one species (*A. flavifrons*) it is slightly forked. Sexes different: male generally

68

rust-brown with a large orange-red to yellow crest (except one species, *A. inornatus,* is crestless). Female like male but lacking crest. (New Guinea mountains.) See page 294.

5 *Prionodura* One species; length 9 to $9\frac{1}{2}$ inches; bill nearly straight (and shorter than head). Sexes different: male bright olive with yellow on head, neck, tail and with yellow underparts. Female dull olive with grey underparts (and very similar in appearance to females of *Amblyornis*). (Australian mountains.) See page 318.

6 *Sericulus* Three species; length $9\frac{1}{2}$ to $10\frac{1}{2}$ inches; bill nearly straight and about equal to head. Sexes different: males with much bright yellow, orange and red plumage and with an erectile cape collar. Female: upper parts brown, underparts olive to grey with a dark scaled pattern, or pale yellowish. (Australia and New Guinea.) See page 325.

7 *Ptilonorhynchus* One species; length 11 to $12\frac{1}{2}$ inches; bill straight and stocky (and about length of head). Sexes different: male black glossed purple. Female greyish green tinged blue. (Australian forests.) See page 344.

8 *Chlamydera* Four species; length $10\frac{1}{2}$ to 15 inches; bill nearly straight and two-thirds length of head. Sexes different in two species: male greyish brown to yellowish brown with a scaled or spotted appearance below and with an iridescent violet pink nuchal crest; the females in these two species occasionally have the bright crests. Males and females in two species lack the bright crest and are generally grey brown to olive brown washed with ochraceous. (Australia and New Guinea.) See page 354.

Synopsis of Paradise and Bower Bird Displays and Nesting Systems

In the following pages I have adopted the style used by Snow (1963) in his splendid synopsis of Manakin displays, but I have added nest and egg morphology to the synopsis.

1 *Loria* (dimorphic)
Organisation: Unknown but with males spaced widely through mountain forest.

Special display perch: A horizontal limb high in a tree at the edge of a small forest clearing or gorge.

Display: Unknown, but much shifting of position in a small area of limb where the male sits and emits highly ventriloquial 'tolling' calls for long periods day after day.

Breeding system: Unknown.

Nest: Unknown.

2 *Loboparadisea* (dimorphic)
Organisation: Unknown.
Special display perch: Unknown.
Display: Unknown.
Breeding system: Unknown.
Nest: Unknown.

3 *Cnemophilus* (dimorphic)
Organisation: Unknown.
Special display perch: Unknown.
Display: Unknown.
Breeding system: Unknown.
Nest: Domed. Egg: (Presumably white with brownish black spots and grey patches: 31·5 × 20 mm.).

4 *Macgregoria* (monomorphic)
Organisation: Two or more adults in alpine forests (tree tops to undergrowth).
Special display perch: Apparently none.
Display: Chasing (hopping, gliding, flying) in pairs or three-somes to accompaniment of wing rustling sounds and loud sharp calls.
Breeding system: Monogamy with the female building nest, male accompanying mate and both sexes feeding young.
Nest: A bulky cup. Egg: Earthy pink sparsely spotted with brown; 39 × 27·5 mm.

5 *Lycocorax* (monomorphic)
Organisation: Unknown.
Special display perch: Unknown.
Display: Unknown but this species is reported to be a rapidly moving, restless one which makes rustling, whirring noises

I Sickle-crested Bird of Paradise (*Cnemophilus macgregorii*). Sub-adult male and female plumaged birds.

II Brown Sickle-billed Bird of Paradise (*Epimachus meyeri*). Adult female.

III Splendid Astrapia Bird of Paradise (*Astrapia splendidissima*). Adult female.

IV Greater Bird of Paradise (*Paradisaea apoda*). Male displaying.

v Archbold's Bower Bird (*Archboldia papuensis*). Male of eastern sub-species
A. p. sanfordi. (From a painting by George Sutton)

vi Vogelkop Gardener Bower Bird (*Amblyornis inornatus*). Male at bower.

VII Golden Regent Bower Bird
(*Sericulus aureus*). Male at bower.

VIII Lauterbach's Bower Bird (*Chlamydera
l. lauterbachi*). Male displaying to female
of the same species in a bower of another
species, *Chlamydera cerviniventris*.

IX Wahgi Valley native with feather headdress in which flank plumes of Count Raggi'
Bird of Paradise (*Paradisaea raggiana*)
predominate. An expanded shield of the
Superb Bird of Paradise (*Lophorina superba*)
is seen over the forehead, and occipital
plumes of the King of Saxony Bird of
Paradise (*Pteridophora alberti*) have
been inserted in the pierced nasal septum.

in flight and emits monotonous 'barking' notes.

Breeding system: Unknown but monogamy is presumed.
Nest: A large cup. Egg: Pinkish-stone with irregular streaks
and hair-lines; 37 × 26 mm.

6 *Manucodia* (monomorphic)
Organisation: Apparently a solitary male displays to female in
forest canopy.
Special display perch: Unknown but male displays in crown of
forest.
Display: Preening, feather flexing, shaking, some chasing
accompanied by loud wing rustling and perhaps by moaning
cries or deep 'chug' notes.
Breeding system: Monogamy, with apparently the female
incubating alone. Male remains in vicinity of nest and assists
in brooding and feeding young.
Nest: Deep cup cradled or suspended in fork of branch. Egg:
Pale with brown spots and streaks; 24–30 × 32–45 mm.
(4 species).

7 *Phonygammus* (monomorphic)
Organisation: A solitary male displays to female.
Special display perch: Apparently a horizontal exposed forest
branch fairly high up.
Display: Male depresses body then spreads wings and gives
harsh call. Female flies into forest and male chases. These
two events are repeated several times.
Breeding system: Apparently monogamy with both male and
female taking part in nest duties.
Nest: Open shallow cup in forked branch. Egg: Pale pinkish
purple smudged and streaked with brown; 35·5 × 24 mm.

8 *Ptiloris* (dimorphic)
Organisation: Small groups of males display high in tree,
presumably in traditional display areas.
Special display perch: Often horizontal thick limbs or vines in
open spot in mountain forest occupied by solitary owners.
Display: Head thrown back, bill pointed upward, wings
elevated close together over back or extended; whirling,

swaying or fluttering on horizontal or hanging vine; chasing; wing rustling in flight; loud calls precede display.

Breeding system: Polygyny.

Nest: Shallow bowl often ornamented with snake skin. Egg: Reddish with darker streaks and smudges; 32–34 × 23–25 mm. (3 species).

9   *Semioptera* (dimorphic)

Organisation: Large groups of males assemble together in traditional display areas.

Special display perches: 20 to 30 feet up in a concentration of thin saplings with a few very large trees nearby.

Display: Chasing, fluttering, swaying, whirling, to the accompaniment of rasping notes and sharp calls. Breast plumage elevated vertically, wing flags alternately elevated and depressed.

Breeding system: Polygyny with the males probably living in clans apart from females.

Nest: Nest and eggs apparently undiscovered.

10   *Seleucidis* (dimorphic)

Organisation: Unknown but probably small widely spaced groups of males gather together in the breeding season.

Special display perch: A high exposed branch in swamp forest.

Display: Breastplate extended, body plumage compressed, flank plumes expanded; male whirls around vertical branch; wings fluttered to accompaniment of sharp notes.

Breeding system: Unknown but probably polygyny; nest-building and care of young are the responsibility of the female alone.

Nest: Shallow cup. Egg: Cream coloured with longitudinal darker streaks; 40·7 × 26·5 mm.

11   *Paradigalla* (somewhat dimorphic)

Organisation: Unknown.

Special display perch: Unknown.

Display: Unknown. Call note: a melodic *hui*.

Breeding system: Unknown.

Nest: Collected (see Rothschild, *et. al.*, 1913: 104) but

apparently undescribed.

12 *Drepanornis* (dimorphic)
Organisation: Unknown.

Special display perch: Unknown.
Display: Unknown.
Breeding system: Unknown.
Nest: Flat structure on horizontal branch in a fork. Egg: Pale
with spots and streaks; 39 × 25 mm.

13 *Epimachus* (dimorphic)
Organisation: Males spaced far apart in traditional display
trees.
Special display perch: Bare branch high up in hill forest.
Display: Shield and tail spreading, body jerking, body flatten-
ing, mouth opened; loud call followed by steep dive toward
ground and sailing flight back up to same limb; pneumatic
rattling (one species), whistled 'whick' (one species).
Breeding system: Polygyny.
Nest: A cup of living moss in crotch of a small tree. Egg:
Cinnamon colour with brownish streaks and spots; 40 ×
27·5 mm.

14 *Astrapia* (dimorphic)
Organisation: Unknown, but probably with the males gathering
in groups in traditional display trees.
Special display perch: Unknown but probably of the arena
type in the crown of mountain forest.
Display: Unknown but possibly with the individual males
posted on private perches and indulging in wing clapping
over the back (see *Astrapia stephaniae*); tail switching.
Breeding system: Polygyny.
Nest: Open shallow saucer of living vines. Egg: Pinkish cinnamon with brown blotches; 37 × 28·5 mm.

15 *Lophorina* (dimorphic)
Organisation: Unknown, but probably with the males spaced
far apart in traditional display trees.
Special display perch: Unknown, but probably high in middle

part of ridge and forest edge trees.

Display: Unknown in wild; probably with breast plate widely expanded, nape cape widely expanded and elevated, and accompanied by a *chr chr* rasping like steam escaping.

Breeding system: Polygyny.

Nest: Dry leaves, roots and twiglets, shape unknown. Egg: Buff marked with brownish; 32 × 22·4 mm.

16 *Parotia* (dimorphic)

Organisation: Males spaced far apart (and seemingly solitary) in traditional display spaces in the substrata of mountain forest.

Special display perch: A bramble of horizontal vines close to a cleared court on floor of thick forest where main dance takes place in semi-silence.

Display: Shrill and hoarse cries from low vines; on ground plumage expanded, flank plumes umbrella-like; crest raised; head bent forward; swaying, jerking; short hops; tail spreading; posturing; tail bent to side; head swayed and flag tipped wires rotated; at end of display a shrill cry.

Breeding system: Polygyny.

Nest: Apparently saucer-shaped of vines. Egg: Vinaceous red with dark rufous patches and spots; 33 × 24 mm.

17 *Pteridophora* (dimorphic)

Organisation: Males are spaced very far apart (and seemingly solitary) in exploded clans in top of mountain forest.

Special display perch: A thin dead limb projecting above the forest crown, sometimes a high thin limb with leaves; sometimes with several secondary display limbs (or vines) nearby.

Display: Much head switching, pulsating of back plumes, elevating of long head plumes, puffing of plumage, twisting on perch; accompanied by low hissing notes with mouth held open; back plumage expanded; wing fanning, neck puffing, much head turning; occasional gurgling, hissing; head thrusting (causing long plumes to whip in and out); in presence of female: bouncing, deep bowing toward female; an occasional hissing note followed by an explosive note, *Kissss-saa-BAH*, that carries long distances.

Breeding system: Polygyny, with the male living apart from

the female in widely spaced 'exploded' clans.

Nest: Nest and eggs are unknown.

18 *Cicinnurus* (dimorphic)

Organisation: The males spaced very far apart in exploded clans in sub-canopy of tropical rain forest.

Special display perch: A thin limb or vine under a thick concentration of arboreal vegetation (such as an 'umbrella' of mistletoe) in a very tall thickly vined tree.

Display: Swaying, squatting, shaking, switch hopping up vertical vine, puffing of plumage; pulsating breast fans; probably a towering flight over display tree; mouth opened; tail raising; inverted displaying with wings open and walking under limb; whistles and bugles like *Paradisaea* but higher in pitch, a deep rasping note, an insect buzzing sound.

Breeding system: Polygyny.

Nest: In cavity in small forest tree. Egg: Creamy white with dark brown streaks; 27·5 × 21 mm.

19 *Diphyllodes* (dimorphic)

Organisation: The males are spaced very far apart in substrata of hill and mountain forest in traditional display areas.

Special display perch: On the thin vertical trunk of a sapling close above a cleared ground court 8–20 feet in diameter.

Display: Stretching, pulsating of breast shield, hanging back on vertical perch close to ground and directing flattened breast plumage upward (at approaching female) like mirror, cape elevated, tail at right angles to body, switch climbing of sapling. Calls: harsh 'police whistle' notes, also hoarse notes which carry far.

Breeding system: Polygyny, with the males living apart from females for many months of year.

Nest: A cup. Egg: Yellowish cream with light brown and grey longitudinal marks; 29·8 × 22·0–24·0 mm.

20 *Paradisaea* (dimorphic)

Organisation: Medium to large groups of males clustered loosely or tightly together in certain traditional areas in the tropical rain and mid-mountain forest, forest edge or in small islands of trees in grasslands.

Special display perch: Each male wins a private perch in the middle tier limbs or high in the forest.

Display: Elaborate displays with flank plumes expanded or elevated; much charging and much bugled calling; some calls and display synchronised very closely; in presence of female, males retire to their private perches and display (inverted or upright) is apt to become static; much quivering, wing waving, wing clapping, posturing.

Breeding system: Polygyny. The displays enable males to find and establish their breeding rights within the clan or arena to which itinerant females comes to be fertilised.

Nest: A cup. Egg: pale with longitudinal markings; 33–39·4 × 23–27·4 mm (six species).

21   *Ailuroedus* (monomorphic)

Organisation: Male usually solitary in shrubbery or in dense substage of mountain forest.

Special display perch: Unknown but males appear to defend a territory in substage of forest.

Display: Chasing; jumping upward in slender trees; wing rustling; head jerked upward, then depressed to accompaniment of rasping notes; other sounds, scratching notes, cat-like meows, hissing.

Breeding system: Monogamy, with both the male and female performing distraction displays at the nest.

Nest: A bulky cup. Egg: Clear rich cream colour; 39–45 × 26–31 mm. (three species).

22   *Scenopoeetes* (monomorphic)

Organisation: Males spaced fairly far apart in forest substage in traditional areas.

Special display perch: A private singing perch near or close above a cleared ground court amongst thin saplings which is decorated with large leaves laid upside down and a few snail shells.

Display: Head bobbing from side to side, beak gaping, feathers of breast loosened, wings flicked out, erratic hops, snatching of leaf and holding for minutes in bill. Sounds made on and near bower: 'hissing, mechanical whirring, soft whistling.

Breeding system: Polygyny.

Nest: Frail dish-shaped structure. Egg: Creamy brown; 40·4–44·2 × 27·0–29·4 mm.

23 *Archboldia* (dimorphic)

Organisation: Males spaced fairly far apart in traditional areas in forest substage.

Special display perch: A waiting perch (or several) about 10–20 feet up near a ground court which has been decorated with ferns, snail shells, insect skeletons, resin chips and slender yellowish vines.

Display: Male in presence of female flattens itself on fern mat and crawls (with short pauses to make short hops) for up to 22 minutes, always toward female who moves around edge of fern stage. Male carries a small stick crosswise in bill; display is accompanied by churring and rasping sounds, which are highly ventriloquial in nature.

Breeding system: Polygyny.

Nest: Unknown.

24 *Amblyornis* (three dimorphic, on monomorphic)

Organisation: Each adult male spaced out moderately close together, sometimes fairly far apart, in a traditional courtship area.

Special display perch: A waiting perch (or several) 15–30 feet up near ground court which is a moss covered, saucer-like, stage around a sapling ringed with sticks. In two species, at a height of several feet the tower is covered with sloping sticks forming a tepee roof up to five feet in diameter. In two species the moss stage is decorated with little piles of flowers; red, blue and yellow fruit; and some charcoal and mushrooms. In one it has no roof and few stage ornaments.

Display: Voice (highly ventriloquial and imitative of all sorts of forest sounds; delivered from moss saucer), crackling, rasping, wavering whistles; an extraordinary song delivered in trees; sounds given with the neck stretched toward tower; bill probing moss of tower base; hopping side to side, head moving side to side; and female close at hand at edge of saucer and also singing.

Breeding system: Polygyny.

Nest: Fairly deep firm cup. Egg: Yellowish white; 40 × 29 mm.

25 *Prionodura* (dimorphic)

Organisation: In groups, with each adult male maintaining a private court and bower within a traditional courtship area of considerable size.

Special display perch: A stick or vine intermeshed with the stick tower or towers forming the bower structure on which the male spends most of his time. The tower may be up to 7 feet tall, may be surrounded by a cluster of small towers apparently all belonging to one male; it may be decorated with moss and flowers and berries.

Display: Male sits for long period in trees over bower; often gives pulsing insect sounds, chattering, hissing, harsh chattering croaks; in visiting bower he usually carries a stick or flower; some displays are hovering displays at bower, head jerking from side to side, wing fluttering.

Breeding system: Polygyny.

Nest: Fairly deep in tree cavity, strong cup. Egg: Pale cream colour; 36–37 × 25–26 mm.

26 *Sericulus* (dimorphic)

Organisation: Unknown, one species at least has probably discarded bower building.

Special display perch: Unknown.

Display: Unknown but in two species a walled bower is sometimes built.

Breeding system: Unknown.

Nest: Fragile saucer. Egg: Pale grey streaked with black; 34·3–40 × 22·8–27·9 mm.

27 *Ptilonorhynchus* (dimorphic)

Organisation: In groups with each mature male maintaining a private court and bower within a traditional courtship area.

Special display perch: A mat of sticks with two parallel stick walls, painted and highly decorated, and maintained by one male.

Display: Male spends much time at bower; makes crackling, churring, gear clashing notes; dances with tail elevated, prances, leaps over bower, eyes bulge, bill points to ground.

Female enters avenue, crouches; copulation occurs there.

Breeding system: Polygyny, but apparently the female remains with a male for some days.

Nest: Open shallow saucer. Eggs: Dark cream spotted with cinnamon brown and underlying purplish grey spots; 40·5 × 27·5 mm.

28 *Chlamydera* (two dimorphic, two monomorphic)

Organisation: In widely spaced groups with each mature male building and maintaining a private bower within a traditional courtship area.

Special display perch: A mat of sticks with two parallel stick walls (sometimes four walls), highly decorated, and defended by one male.

Display: Male spends much time at bower; cat-like calls, explosive sounds, hissing, ticking, rhythmic mechanical noises, much vocal mimicry; crouching; beak opening; wings up; much holding and shaking of objects in bill; jerky erratic leaping; expanding of nape crest (in two species); tail cocking; wing drooping; circling of bower on the run. Mating takes place in or near bower.

Breeding system: Polygyny, perhaps with the female remaining with male for a period of several days.

Nest: Bulky, shallow cup. Egg: Pale with hairlike to spotlike markings of brown or blackish; 34–45 × 25–30 mm. (4 species).

Chapter Nine

Birds of Paradise

Birds of Paradise: Species List

Family PARADISAEIDAE

Subfamily CNEMOPHILINAE

Loria loriae

Loboparadisea sericea

Cnemophilus macgregorii

Subfamily PARADISAEINAE

Macgregoria pulchra

Lycocorax pyrrhopterus

Manucodia ater

Manucodia jobiensis

Manucodia chalybatus

Manucodia comrii

Phonygammus keraudrenii

Ptiloris paradiseus

Ptiloris victoriae

Ptiloris magnificus

Semioptera wallacei

Seleucidis melanoleuca

Paradigalla carunculata

Paradigalla brevicauda

Drepanornis albertisi

Drepanornis bruijnii

Epimachus fastosus

Epimachus meyeri

Astrapia nigra

Astrapia splendidissima

Astrapia mayeri

Astrapia stephaniae

Astrapia rothschildi

Lophorina superba

Parotia wahnesi

Parotia sefilata

Parotia carolae

Parotia lawesi

Pteridophora alberti

Cicinnurus regius

Diphyllodes magnificus

Diphyllodes respublica

Paradisaea apoda

Paradisaea raggiana

Paradisaea minor

Paradisaea decora

Paradisaea rubra

Paradisaea guilielmi

Paradisaea rudolphi

Loria's Bird of Paradise

Loria loriae Salvadori
Male $8\frac{3}{4}$ in.

Range: Mountains throughout New Guinea, except apparently the Vogelkop and Huon peninsulas. From 5000 to 9000 feet, but very uncommon below 6000 feet. (See Map 9.9, page 209.)

Adult Male: A thrush-like velvet black bird with yellow gape wattles and small areas of iridescence on forehead and wings. In more detail, bill short and widely split, with narrow, pale yellow gape wattles; plumage generally velvet blue black except fore half of crown, nasal plumes, lores, patch over eye, and inner four secondaries metallic blue-green (to violet purple in one subspecies); underparts duller. Iris blackish brown; bill black; feet greyish black; gape wattles and inner surfaces of mouth cream yellow. Wing 97–106; tail 68–80; culmen from base 25; tarsus 38 mm.

Adult Female: Very different from adult male. Uniform yellowish olive with faint dusky edges especially on crown, back, and upper breast; wings and tail dark olive brown with some ochraceous brown edges; underparts paler, especially abdomen. Iris greyish black; feet greenish. Wing 98–106; tail 67–82; culmen from base 24; tarsus 38 mm.

Immature: First year plumage much like adult female. Male intermediate plumage: like adult female but with some iridescence on forehead and scattered black feathers on head and breast.

Remarks: This interesting species was discovered by Lamberto Loria in the Moroka District of the Owen Stanley Mountains. I found it fairly common to common at higher elevations in the forests of the Bismarck, Kubor, and Hagen ranges. Its calls are powerful, highly ventriloquial bell-like tolls repeated at moderately long intervals. On Mt Hagen (8500 feet) in July, 1950, I heard the elusive tolling periodically for several days near my camp before I discovered that the source was close at hand. It was an adult male calling and displaying from a limb about 70 feet high and projecting from the side of a very large tree. This tree was in the edge of a wall of forest fringing a small cleared area in original forest. The display limb where the cock habitually perched was about an inch in diameter and nearly horizontal. Each afternoon the powerful notes of the male would ring through the forest. I watched often from my skinning tent and noted that the male moved about a lot in an area of several cubic feet, but I failed to watch this male closely, a matter which I have long regretted, because I have never encountered another displaying male.

The ventriloquistic quality of the voice of Loria's Bird of Paradise is apparently unique among the birds of paradise but fairly similar to many of the bower birds.

Stein (1936) reported 'Except for one screaming cry, which a male uttered as it flew away, I found that the birds were always quiet. Usually they were close to the ground and they have a preference like thrushes for the rather large branches covered with moss along which they hop. Pairs were never encountered. Males in nuptial plumage were always alone. Females frequently were seen although they were also encountered in groups of up to ten, eating in fruit bushes close to the ground.'

Subspecies: Three quite similar races are recognised:

1 *L. l. inexpectata* Junge, 1939, *Nova Guinea*, (N.S.), vol. 3, p. 77; type locality Bijenkorf, Oranje Mountains. Known from Weyland, Nassau, Oranje, Hindenburg and Victor Emanuel mountains. In this race the iridescent portions of the inner secondaries are blue green.

2 *L. l. loriae* Salvadori, 1894 (May), *Ann. Mus. Civ. Genova,* ser. 2, vol. 14, p. 151; type locality Moroka, Owen Stanley Mountains. Known from the mountains of south-eastern New Guinea (including the Herzog Mountains). It differs from *inexpectata* by having the inner secondaries blue green edged with purple.

3 *L. l. amethystina* Stresemann, 1934, *Orn. Monatsb.,* vol. 42, p. 144; type locality Schraderberg, Sepik Mountains. Known only from Schraderberg and the east central highlands (Bismarck, Wahgi Divide, Kubor, Hagen, and Giluwe? mountains). This race

differs from all others by having the iridescent surfaces of the inner secondaries solid violet purple.

Wattle-billed Bird of Paradise

Loboparadisea sericea Rothschild
Male $6\frac{3}{4}$ in.

Range: Mountains of the trunk of New Guinea, from 3200 to 6200 feet. (See Map 9.1, page 85.)

Adult Male: A starling-sized dark brown bird with yellow rump and yellow underparts; unique in having thick yellow lappet wattles covering the basal third of the maxilla. In more detail, upper back dark rufous brown (amber brown in one race) washed with gold (greenish amber in one race); lower back and rump pale silky yellow; sides of head and neck like back; underparts silky yellow; wings and tail mostly chestnut brown with somewhat darker tips; tibia and upper tail coverts chestnut brown. Iris brown; bill black; nasal lappet wattles yellow to sea green. Wing 88–96; tail 51–56; culmen from base 17–19; tarsus 29 mm.

Adult Female: Rather like adult male but without wattles and upperparts dark olive brown; head and nape paler with indistinct dusky scalloping; lower back and rump dark brown with variable amounts of pale silky yellow tipping; underparts dull yellow with indistinct brown markings, particularly on sides. Wing 95–97; tail 56–60 mm.

Immature: Very different from adults. First year plumage: upperparts dark olive brown without yellow; underparts warm fuscus with some dark edging on feathers of breast, giving a suggestion of striping; lower abdomen with a patch of pale grey (in this plumage the immature is rather similar to the adult female of *Amblyornis subalaris*); no trace of nasal lappets. Second year plumage in both sexes like adult female, but the second year male with partially developed nasal lappets.

Remarks: Although locally not uncommon in west New Guinea, the Wattle-billed Bird of Paradise is a rare and little-known species in eastern New Guinea. Mayr (1930: 147) collected five adult males and Stevens (*in* Greenway, 1935: 89) collected one in the Herzog Mountains (at Wau, 3800 feet). Only one specimen appears to have been taken in the east central highlands, despite the extensive surveys that have been conducted in this region during the past decade. The specimen, a male taken by Captain N.B.Blood on the northern slopes of the Wahgi Divide at 6000 feet, is intermediate in colouration and size between the two races listed below. In the Telefomin highlands I obtained only a single specimen, an immature. On Mt Goliath in the Snow Mountains Meek in 1911 obtained two females, but early in 1913 the Wollaston Expedition obtained a series of six males, females and young. Farther west, various collectors have obtained examples in the Weyland Mountains (the Pratt brothers obtained two males; Shaw Mayer got a male and a female; and G. Stein got a series of five males and three females). Thus it seems that the species is far less rare in the west than in the east.

Georg Stein (1936: 23) is the only naturalist who appears to have observed this bird in the wild. He wrote that it was frequently met with in the Weyland Mountains between altitudes of 3200 and 4800 feet, but that one specimen was collected at 5500 feet. 'The birds are always quiet and never high in the air. Usually they are comfortably eating in berry bushes in the underbrush. Here they are found in small groups of up to ten. Otherwise always alone. The birds are calm and meditative. Either you see them hopping slowly from twig to twig or sitting still and digesting. The daily activities of all birds of paradise, which are essentially fruit-eaters, seem with the exception of the brooding period to follow the same course. In the grey morning light they are most active if one can judge from their calls. A short time later they begin to rest and then one can find them eating in the fruit trees. They then fly to a resting place where they await digestion. This must proceed very rapidly because during the course of the day a considerable quantity of nourishment which is low in calories is required. Birds which have been shot always have a stomach full of fruit. Eating and digesting seem to be the prime activities of the birds. During the late afternoon, about 5:00, I found them for the last time in their fruit trees.'

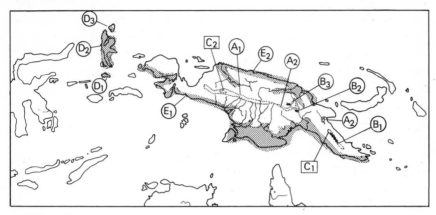

Map 9.1   *Loboparadisea* etc.

Loboparadisea sericea (A) 3200–6200 feet
 Loboparadisea sericea sericea (A1)
 Loboparadisea sericea aurora (A2)
Cnemophilus macgregorii (B) 7600–11,200 feet
 Cnemophilus macgregorii macgregorii (B1)
 Cnemophilus macgregorii kuboriensis (B2)
 Cnemophilus macgregorii sanguineus (B3)
Macgregoria pulchra (C) 8900–12,800 feet
 Macgregoria pulchra pulchra (C1)
 Macgregoria pulchra carolinae (C2)
Lycocorax pyrrhopterus (D) sea level to 5200 feet
 Lycocorax pyrrhopterus obiensis (D1)
 Lycocorax pyrrhopterus pyrrhopterus (D2)
 Lycocorax pyrrhopterus morotensis (D3)
Seleucidis melanoleuca (E) near sea level
 Seleucidis melanoleuca melanoleuca (E1)
 Seleucidis melanoleuca auripennis (E2)

In 1964, Ralph Bulmer, working in the Schrader Mountains, got two immatures. He writes (personal communication) that

85

the natives say it is fairly common '. . . in the forest edge, bush fallow and forest from 6500 feet up to 8500 feet where one was shot by a native hunter in my presence, in substage bushes right on the crest.'

Nesting: Stein wrote that '. . . it may be worthy of mention that the Papuans of the high mountains state that *Loboparadisea* builds an open moss nest which is said to be rather low in the foliage and to contain one egg. I give this information with mental reservations. However, the people certainly knew a great deal and also admitted gaps in their knowledge. They said, for example, that they knew nothing about the reproduction of the common *Parotia* or of *Epimachus, Lophorina,* or *Astrapia.* . . .'

Subspecies: Two fairly well marked ones are recognised:

1 *L. s. sericea* Rothschild, 1896, *Bull. Brit. Orn. Club,* Vol. 6, p. 16. Type locality 'Dutch New Guinea' [type in The American Museum of Natural History, henceforth abbreviated to AMNH, no. 679048]. Known from Weyland, Nassau (Utakwa River), Oranje (Mount Goliath), and Victor Emanuel mountains. Upperparts reddish brown; crown dark brown; underparts bright silky yellow; wing male 88–93; tail, male, 51–54 mm.

2 *L. s. aurora* Mayr, 1930, *Orn. Monatsb.,* vol. 38, p. 147. Type locality Dawong, Herzog Mountains. Range: Herzog Mountains and mountains of the Jimmi River region, Central Highlands. This race differs from *sericea* by having the upperparts much brighter, more yellowish brown, the crown more greenish, less brownish; underparts pallid yellow; wing male 96; tail male 56 mm.

   Bock (1963) found that *Loboparadisea* is virtually identical in skull characters with *Loria* and *Cnemophilus.* A knowledge of the nest form (domed or cup-shaped) and egg markings (striped, spotted, or solid white) is eagerly awaited.

   This species is unique among the birds of paradise in that the female is nearly as brightly coloured as the male and the immatures are very differently dressed from the adult female.

Sickle-crested Bird of Paradise

Cnemophilus macgregorii De Vis.
Male: 9¾ in.

Range: Mountains of eastern and south-eastern New Guinea
From 7600 to 11,200 feet. (See Map 9.1, page 85.)

Adult Male: An orange or yellow thrush-sized stocky bird with
blackish underparts and a small, curved forecrest unique in birds of
paradise. In more detail, upper
back orange red, brightest on
head and neck, becoming dull
ochraceous cinnamon on rest of
upperparts (or upper back pale
orange yellow, shading to
yellowish orange with some red
on crown in one subspecies);
crest composed of from four to
six short, curved plumes, reddish
brown to fuscus; underparts,
including throat and sides of
head below eyes and under wing
coverts, blackish brown. Iris
dark brown, bill and feet brownish black. Wing 106–15; tail
86–97; exposed culmen 22;
tarsus 42 mm.

Adult Female: Very different from adult male. Generally dark
brownish olive with obscure dusky scalloping on head and upper
back; lower back and wings more fuscus olive; underparts pale
olive brown washed with buff on abdomen; crest plumes olive and
much reduced in length. Wing 106–13; tail 88–97 mm.

Remarks: This very curious species is named in honour of its
discoverer, Sir William Macgregor, pioneer administrator of Papua,
who found it on Mt Knutsford at 11,000 feet in 1889. On this
expedition, one of his many ventures into the Owen Stanley
Mountains, he was accompanied by George Belford, Karl Kowald,
and P. A. Goodwin.

The Sickle-crested Bird of Paradise was long thought to be an
aberrant bower bird, but an intensive search by the writer in 1950
in the Bismarck, Kubor, and Hagen mountains failed to reveal its
bower. Subsequent searches by Loke Wan Tho and Fred Shaw
Mayer in 1952 and Gyldenstolpe in 1951 (1955: 144) also failed to

H

turn up the bower, but Loke Wan Tho and Shaw Mayer found and photographed its nest on Mt Hagen (Loke Wan Tho, 1957: 105). Theirs was an important discovery, for the nest was of a type unknown in bower birds or birds of paradise.

Mayr (in Mayr and Gilliard, 1954: 362) was the first to show that, anatomically, *Cnemophilus* is a bird of paradise. Bock (1963: 195) added greatly to our knowledge of the phylogeny of this family through his studies of skull anatomy. He showed why *Cnemophilus* was closely related to two other aberrant birds of paradise, *Loboparadisea* and *Loria*. Bock then set up the subfamily Cnemophilinae for these three genera, all of which may prove to build domed nests.

It is peculiar how snarled the historical record can become and how science can suffer because of it. For example, a great part-native collector, A. S. Anthony (see Appendix 2, p. 447) actually collected the nest and egg of *Cnemophilus* at 11,000 feet in south-eastern New Guinea in 1898. However, since both the nest and the egg were so different from anything known in the birds of paradise and bower birds, Ernst Hartert (1910: 487) disallowed the record. His exact words were: 'The egg, however, is so utterly unlike any eggs of Paradisaeidae hitherto known, exactly looking like an Oriole's egg, and the thick, soft nest differs so much from all nests of Paradisaeidae which we know, that we do not believe this nest and egg are exactly identified.'

Shane Parker of the British Museum who examined the egg but not the nest, wrote to me that he agrees with Hartert. However, in 1964, in London, I examined the egg myself and although its markings are different from those of the true birds of paradise, it has the general size and shape of a paradise bird egg. Considering the very atypical nest built by *Cnemophilus* (see Loke Wan Tho's photographs) and the fact that many bower birds lay pure white eggs, I think it very likely that the egg and nest in question are correctly identified. Another point is that A. S. Anthony found more nests and eggs of birds of paradise than any man who ever lived and I am sure that it took strong evidence to convince him that this was in fact a bird of paradise egg.

The Hon. Walter Rothschild (1898: 26) described the nest which Anthony had taken on Mt Knutsford, Owen Stanley Mountains, altitude 11,000 feet, as follows: 'The nest is a well built structure about 90 mm. high, 150–80 mm. wide, and with an inside cup of from 75–85 mm. diameter and a depth of about 53 mm. in the middle. The walls of the nest consisted chiefly of green moss, interwoven with ferns and rootlets, and it was lined with skeletonised leaves and some feathers of *Casuarius*. The single egg – unfortunately damaged – had a very fine shell, was elongate–ovate in shape, white, with an irregular ring of brownish-black spots near the larger end and a few such spots all over, and with some underlying grey patches. It measured about 31·5 × 20 mm. in breadth.'

To correct the record it is important to note that Loke Wan Tho's photograph of *Cnemophilus* at its nest was erroneously identified as *Loria loriae* and so published by Count Gyldenstolpe (1955: pl. XI); also that R.W. Sims (1956: 426) published Loke Wan Tho's observations of the actions of *Cnemophilus* at the nest under the wrong species.

Nesting: Loke's observations and photographs were made near Tomba, Mt Hagen, at an altitude of about 8500 feet. Loke (in Sims, 1956: 426), described the nest as follows: 'A domed nest with an exceptionally wide round opening was built about twelve feet up in a decayed tree-stump in the forest. It was deep-set in living moss and built of green ferns and moss with a lining of fern stalks. There was one juvenile in the nest (25 September). Its head and breast were a smoke-grey and the wings a darker grey; the gape and the inside of the mouth were white in colour. While the nest was being watched during the early part of one morning the female returned about every ten to fifteen minutes to feed the young and called with a soft 'wark, wark' each time she approached. The food was regurgitated and appeared to consist of large berries and plum-coloured fruits. A short while after being fed the young bird expelled the fruit stones from its crop, they were ejected with a force sufficient to shoot them out through the mouth of the nest. Faecal capsules were also ejected occasionally from the nest, but generally the female assisted with nest sanitation. When the nest was examined a few days later it was deserted and contained faeces and fruit stones.'

Rand found the species fairly common but shy on Mt Tafa and Murray Pass. It kept to the lower part of the forest and was 'often found in the tangled ground cover where the male with its striking inverted colour pattern was difficult to see. It fed on small fruits of shrubs and low second-storey trees of the forest, and when feeding sometimes could be closely approached.' The species, Rand noted, 'has a variety of calls, a low harsh, hissing call, a loud clicking call repeated a number of times and a loud call that I can only describe as being similar to the sound of two timbers being rubbed together under considerable stress. The last call was startling in quality, and its author was long a puzzle to me.'

The writer found the males much less common than the females in the Hagen, Wahgi Divide and Kubor Mountains. The highest specimen taken was a male seen on a perch fifteen feet up in a dripping wet moss-festooned forest at 11,000 feet. The bird was in a gully crammed with stunted rhododendron forest. The forest formed a lobe which projected above the tree line into the alpine grassland crowning Mt Hagen. The rarity of this species except at high altitudes is demonstrated by the following records.

On Mt Hagen in 1955 and 1956 Bulmer got only one example, a specimen collected by a native at 10,000 feet. However, most of Bulmer's collecting was done between 4000 and 7000 feet. On the other hand, we got twenty specimens on this mountain where we collected almost exclusively between 8000 and 12,000 feet. One was taken at 8500 feet in the mid-limbs of an open ridge forest almost immediately above the bower of *Archboldia papuensis*.

At Miramar, near Goroka, the skin of a male was found in the headdress of a native who claimed to have shot the bird in the Kraetke Mountains. This specimen appeared to have considerably paler upperparts than birds taken in the Wahgi Highlands and if not faded may represent an unknown race.

Subspecies: Two rather similar ones and a third very distinct:

1   *C. m. macgregorii* De Vis, 1890 (Feb. 22), *Ann. Rep. Brit. New Guinea*, 1888–89, p. 62. Type locality Mt Musgrave, Owen Stanley Mountains. Known only from the mountains of south-eastern New Guinea from Mt Knutsford west to the Wharton Range. Upperparts chiefly yellow to cinnamon yellow.

2   *C. m. sanguineus* Iredale, 1948, *Australian Zoologist*, II, p. 162. Type locality Kumdi, Mt Hagen district. Known only from Mt Hagen. Like *macgregorii* but with upperparts orange-red.

3   *C. m. kuboriensis* Mayr and Gilliard, 1954, *Bull. Amer. Mus. Nat. Hist.*, 103, p. 361 [type in AMNH, no. 748584]. Type locality Mt Orata, Kubor Mountains. Known only from Kubor Mountains.

Very like *sanguineus* but upperparts paler, less saturated with red, and underparts more blackish, less brownish black.

Macgregor's Bird of Paradise

Macgregoria pulchra De Vis
Male 13–15 in.

Range: Mountains of west and south-east New Guinea; from about 8900 feet to 12,800 feet. (See Map 9.1, page 85.)

Adult Male: A jay-sized black bird with large orange 'ear' wattles and ochraceous wing quills. In more detail, generally velvet black with massive orange wattles encircling eye and covering the whole of ear-covert region; the wattles are narrow in front of eye and very broad and lappet-like above and behind it; primaries cinnamon ochraceous with black tips. Iris red to dark reddish brown; bill black; feet bluish grey. Wing 197–206; tail 135–157; exposed culmen 25; tarsus 63 mm.

Adult Female: Smaller, wing 162–186; tail 119–148 mm.

Juvenal: Dusky black.

Remarks: Macgregor's Bird of Paradise is reported to be a common inhabitant of the podocarpus forests crowning the high ranges on each end of the trunk of New Guinea. It was discovered by Sir William Macgregor in May 1896, during his expedition from the Mambare to the Vanupa River in company with his zoological collector A. Guilianetti. Its food is tree fruits and the species is generally encountered in pairs or in small bands.

Breeding Behaviour: Rand, who has collected this hard-to-reach species in its remote homes at both ends of New Guinea, made important studies of its ecology, courtship, and nesting behaviour (Rand, 1940). Its display, he found, usually involved two (but sometimes several) birds which chased each other in a small area of forest near tree line '. . . one bird followed the other one, hopping through the tree tops, thus travelling considerable distances rapidly on foot and flying with a great rustling noise across the open spaces back and forth through the forest. Sometimes when descending across an open space the birds glided, with fully extended wings, the air whistling past the widely separated tips of the primaries, making a loud ripping 'zing'. Sometimes, in the midst of the chase, the birds give a sharp, not very loud 'chic chic chic chic' or 'chick-chick chick-chick' call, but for the most part the noise is mechanical. Frequently the birds descended into the undergrowth and the chase continued there . . .'

Rand found that a strong pair bond developed between the female and her mate. This was indicated by the fact that although only the female built the nest, her mate accompanied her back and forth as she gathered the nest material. Rand also discovered that the female did all the incubating of the eggs, brooding for periods of some 15 minutes, then absenting herself from the nest for 10 minutes or so. During her period on the eggs the male remained in the vicinity of the nest, and when the female left she was some-times accompanied by her mate. Both sexes fed the young with the male making more trips to the nest with food.

Nesting: Rand found a nest with one egg, 14 August 1938, at Lake Habbema, Snow Mountains, 11,000 feet. It was a bulky cup of herbaceous stems and coarse moss placed about 50 feet up in an especially large podocarpus tree. The nest cup was firmly lined with slender stems and a few small leaves. The exterior measurements were 190 × 240 and the interior 90 × 130 mm. The egg, which was ovate, slightly glossy, earthy pink in colour and sparsely spotted with brown, measured 39 × 27·5 mm.

Subspecies: Two, which appear to differ only in size:

1   M. p. pulchra De Vis, 1897, *Ibis,* p. 251, pl. 7. Type locality Mt Scratchley, south-eastern New Guinea. Known only from Mt Scratchley, Mt Victoria, Mt Batchelor, Murray Pass and Mt Albert Edward, south-eastern New Guinea, between the altitudes of 8900 and 11,900 feet. This is a large form: male wing 206 mm.; tail 161 mm.

2   *M. p. carolinae* Junge, 1939, *Nova Guinea* (N.S.), vol. 3, p. 82. Type locality Oranje Mountains. Known only from the Oranje or Snow mountains between the altitudes of 9300 and 12,800 feet. This form is smaller than *pulchra:* male wing 188–200; tail 162–179 mm.

Taxonomy: Bock (1963) in his studies of the skull anatomy of the bird of paradise-bower bird complex, found three sharply separated skull forms; *Paradisaea, Loria,* and *Ptilonorhynchus;* whereas earlier students, including Pycraft and Stonor, had distinguished but two forms, *Paradisaea* and *Ptilonorhynchus. Macgregoria,* Bock found, was the only genus in the complex which did not fall readily into one of the three groups. This puzzling species, he wrote, is of great taxonomic interest because while it has many characters in common with *Loria,* it also possesses a few characters in common with *Paradisaea.* Bock concluded that its characters were so contradictory that it was impossible for him to determine its exact relationship.

Addendum: In the Telefomin highlands, Macgregor's Bird of Paradise appeared to be known to a few old men as a bird of the highest mountain forests. Their name for it is *Kondimkait.* This intermediate population has never been collected.

Paradise or Silky Crow

Lycocorax pyrrhopterus (Bonaparte)
Male 14–17 in.

Range: Moluccan Archipelago. From sea level to 5200 feet. (See Map 9.1, page 85.)

Adult Male: Crow-like with soft, dusky, somewhat lustrous plumage. In more detail, generally dusky brown to blackish, glossed slightly with oil green and with a silky texture, wings dull fuscus with paler edges; inner edges of remiges tinged buff to white; tail deep bluish black. Iris deep crimson; bill and feet black. Wing 194–215 (subspecies); tail 137–140; culmen from base 47–51; tarsus 41–47 mm.

Adult Female: Similar but somewhat smaller (wing 186–205).

Remarks: Bernstein (1864): from translation in Iredale, 1950: 150), apparently the first to observe this species in the wild (Morotai Island), wrote: 'Like the other species of the genus, it inhabits the thick woods and is rarely seen outside of them. It generally lives in trees of moderate height, especially where they stand close together, in the tops of which it hides closely, so that, though often heard, it is a very difficult bird to see. It is most easily observed if the hunter places himself in the early morning near some tree on the fruit of which the bird comes to feed. But even then the greatest attention must be maintained, as the bird does

not come flying in like a Pigeon, but glides quietly from the top of one tree to the summit of another, lights for an instant on some fruit-bearing bough, is seen for a second on the outer branches, and then dives into the thickest of the foliage. In all its ways of life there is very little [that is] Crow-like, and it seems to feed exclusively on the fruit of trees. Its cry is a short, interrupted, monotonous "wuhk" or "wunk", which is especially heard in the morning and evening. My hunters fancied that the note had some similarity to the ringing bark of a dog, and called the bird *"Burung andjing!"* or "Dog-bird".' More recently Gerd Heinrich (1956: 31) reported the species to be a fairly common, shy inhabitant of the mangrove edge and hill forests up to about 3700 feet on Halmahera and Gamkonora islands, and up to about 5200 feet on Batjan Island. It is a very restless species which moves rapidly from tree to tree in the forest shadows making a rushing, whirring noise as it flies. Its voice, Heinrich writes, is a monosyllabic, off-pitch cry which, from a distance, sounds like a short, hoarse dog bark. Its other calls are audible only close at hand. One is an alarm note not unlike that of *Centropus celebensis*. Heinrich found that the fruit of the Pinang Palm is the chief food of this species.

Nesting: Shaw Mayer (Parker, 1963 : 127) collected two nests each with one egg, 24 December 1929, at Patani on Halmahera

Island. Parker described one of the nests as 'large and basin-shaped, built of roots and moss, and lined with soft woodchips.' This nest was placed about 23 feet up in the forest (according to the original label). It held a single fresh egg which Parker described as of a pinkish-stone ground colour, marked all over in an irregular pattern with sparsely distributed lines of violet, brown and hair-streaks of pale lilac, measurements 37 × 26·3 mm. The egg from the second nest measured 35·2 × 25 mm.

Nehrkorn (1910: 356) describes an egg from Obi as pink with a labyrinth of black hairlines, as they are frequently seen in eggs of *Emberiza citrinella*, and gives its measurements as 41 × 29 mm. (see Hartert, 1910:491).

Subspecies: Three well differentiated ones:

1 *L. p. obiensis* Bernstein, 1864, *Journ. f. Orn.*, vol. 12, p. 410. Type Obi Island. Known only from Obi Island. Like *pyrrhopterus* but darker, more glossy blackish and with the concealed basal halves of primaries with only a trace of white; male wing 198–214 mm.

2 *L. p. pyrrhopterus* (Bonaparte) 1851, *Consp. Av.*, 1 (1850), p. 384. Type locality Gilolo. Known only from the northern Moluccas: Batjan and Halmahera islands. Generally blackish with concealed basal halves of primaries ochraceous; wing male 194–201 mm.

3 *L. p. morotensis* Schlegel, 1863, *Ibis*, p. 119. Type locality 'Mortag.' Known only from northern Moluccas: Morotai and Rau islands. Similar to *pyrrhopterus* but paler, more brownish, and with concealed basal halves of primaries whitish; wing male 205–215 mm.

Evolution and Taxonomy: See remarks under *Manucodia ater*.

Glossy-mantled Manucode

Manucodia ater (Lesson)
Male 13½–16 in.

Range: New Guinea, western Papuan islands, islands of Geelvink Bay and islands of south-eastern New Guinea. From sea level to about 3000 feet. (See Map 9.2, page 98.)

Adult Male: A stout-billed jay- to thrush-sized black bird glossed purple, green, and blue. In more detail, head feathering short and somewhat stubbly; feathering of the neck and upper breast somewhat elongated and pointed; feathering of the under- parts with dull edges suggestive of scalloping. Generally glossed oil green, violet and pinkish violet especially upperparts. Iris orange to red; bill and feet black. Wing 159–208 (subspecies); tail 123–180; culmen 21–32; tarsus 37·5–52 mm.

Adult Female: Similar but somewhat smaller: wing 155–199 mm.

Immature: Dull black.

Remarks: Rand's observations of the Glossy-mantled Manucode are of primary interest and comprehensive: he wrote (1938: 1–2) 'At Lake Daviumbu in August and September this was a common forest species feeding in fruiting trees and spending most of its time in the lower parts of the forest canopy, and the tops of the lower trees. It was frequently found in pairs and was not especially wary. When nervous, these birds give a quick little flit to their tail and have a deep "chug" call repeated a number of times, apparently expressing alarm or annoyance. A call commonly heard at this camp, and which I think was given by this bird was a drawn out, whistled call, and is probably similar to the "long drawn moaning cry" recorded for *M. jobiensis* by Claude Grant. . . . In addition I have heard a low chattering call given at the nest. . . . In flight these birds have the heavy, silken rustling of wings common to many Birds of Paradise.

'On September 22, I was watching a *Manucodia* feeding in a seventy-foot fruiting tree in the forest. Another came into the tree and was at once chased some distance, both birds disappearing from sight through the forest. Trying to locate the birds again I saw one, apparently adult, sitting in the top of a tree twenty yards from the fruiting tree. It sat there quietly some time, preening its feathers. Then another came flying through the forest to perch there below it. The first bird began to shake its slightly spread wings and tail and hopped down near the new arrival. The second bird flew to another branch ten feet away followed by the first bird. The latter again shook its wings and tail and erected its body feathers for a moment. Then both flew off through the forest. Possibly this is part of the display of this species.'

Nesting: Rand found two nests 20 to 25 feet up in 30 to 35 foot trees.

The Glossy-mantled Manucode usually places its nest on a lateral bough in thickly leafed trees growing in the semi-open rain and flood plain forests. The nest is a cup of solidly coiled vines and sticks, with a lining of blackish tendrils. In the flooring of the nest cup are a few dead leaves and bits of rotten wood. The nests found by Rand (12 and 21 September 1936), measured, externally, 250 × 140 mm. deep, and 130 × 100 mm., internally.

A nest which I found on 2 January 1954 was situated in a thickly leafed wild mango tree with its crown reaching to the middle storey of tropical rain forest. It contained one egg which measured 24 × 35 mm., whereas the eggs discovered by Rand in the southern drainage of New Guinea measured 25·7 × 39 and 26·8 × 39·2 mm., and an egg collected by Heinrich Kühn in the Aru Islands measured 27·5 × 41 mm. Rand found that the incubation period is more than 14 and less than 18 days, and that apparently the female alone incubates. However, the male remains in the vicinity of the nest and, later, assists in brooding and in feeding the young. The young, he noted, are hatched naked without a trace of down and are blackish in colour.

Subspecies: Three races are recognised. One is well differentiated, and two are very similar and have been the subject of considerable taxonomic interest because they contain geographical populations which intergrade into each other very smoothly; but at the ends of the clines (colour and size) are found morphological extremes which are so distinct they might easily be taken for distinct species (see Mayr, 1941; Rand, 1942; Junge, 1939; Gilliard, 1956; and Mayr, *in* Peters, 1962).

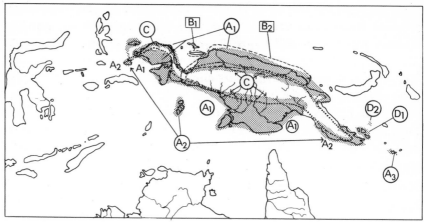

Map 9.2 *Manucodia*

Manucodia ater (A) sea level to 3000 feet
  Manucodia ater ater (A1)
  Manucodia ater subalter (A2)
  Manucodia ater alter (A3)
Manucodia jobiensis (B) lowlands to
  1600 feet
  Manucodia jobiensis jobiensis (B1)
  Manucodia jobiensis rubiensis (B2)

Manucodia chalybatus (C) 1900 to
  5500 feet
Manucodia comrii (D) lowlands
  Manucodia comrii comrii (D1)
  Manucodia comrii trobriandi (D2)

Note that *ater* extends up to only 3000 feet, while *chalybatus* extends from 1900 to 5500 feet, and thus extends farther up in the mountains and thus inland where *ater* does not occur.

1 *M. a. ater* (Lesson), 1830, *Voy. Coquille, Zool.*, p. 638. Type locality Dorey, north-western New Guinea. Range: Vogelkop eastward in the north to about the Huon Gulf and eastward in the south to about the Purari River. Very variable but averaging smaller (wing, tail, bill, and tarsus) than insular and southeastern peninsular populations and with a strong tendency toward oil green plumage in adults. Male wing 159–185; tail 123–164; exposed culmen 21–27; tarsus 37–43 mm.

2 *M. a. subalter* Rothschild and Hartert, 1929, *Bull. Brit. Orn. Club,* vol. 49, p. 110 [type in AMNH no. 677266]. Type locality Dobbo, Aru Islands. Known from western Papuan islands (Misol, Salawati, Batanta, Gemen, Gebe, Waigeu); Aru Islands; southeastern New Guinea westward in the southern lowlands to about

98

the Purari River and west in the northern lowlands to about the Kumusi River (also some coastal islets: Yule, Maibu, Samarai and Sariba). Much like *ater* but averaging larger to distinctly larger and with the populations averaging much more purple and violet (blue occurs in all races) and with oil green colouration rare in adults. Male wing 182–208; tail 150–180; culmen 25–29 mm.

3   *M. a. alter* Rothschild and Hartert, 1903, *Novit. Zool.*, vol. 10, p. 84 [type in AMNH no. 677282]. Type locality Sudest Island. Known only from Sudest Island. Bill much larger than in any other subspecies and flanks and abdomen distinctly more violet. Male wing 197–206; tail 166–180; exposed culmen 32 mm.

Evolution: Bock (1963) in his analysis of skull morphology found that the skull of *Manucodia* (and *Phonygammus*) shows typical Paradisaea features and he includes it with the true birds of paradise. Bock is emphatic in pointing out that *Manucodia* (together with *Lycocorax* and *Phonygammus*), although usually considered the most primitive of the birds of paradise (p. 54), *does not* [italics mine] have a generalised skull and, indeed, has 'all of the Paradisaea features. . . .' He concludes very tentatively that these birds may be specialised offshoots of the 'primitive ancestral Paradisaeinae which have split off the main line before the acquisition of the specialised courtship habits.'

Bock observes further that *Manucodia*, *Lycocorax*, and *Phonygammus* have been usually considered '. . . representatives of the ancestral stock of the entire group of birds of paradise because of their plain colouration and normal avian courtship and breeding habits,' whereas his studies suggest '. . . that the plain plumage and normal courtship and breeding habits may be secondarily primitive.'

This is a revolutionary idea, and at first glance one which seems quite wrong. However, I have found some evidence which suggests that arena behaviour, even when it involves ground display and the clearing of ground courts, may sometimes be secondarily discarded in favour of pair-bond behaviour. Some 98% of the world's birds practise the primitive pair-bond behaviour, whereas the pattern of courtship and the breeding behaviour apparently employed by all of the plumed birds of paradise is polygynous, or 'arena behaviour.' This rare form of behaviour thus involves an evolutionary advance beyond the level of the primitive pair-bond behaviour. Its adoption is almost invariably accompanied by relatively great morphological (massive, colourful plumage, for example) and behavioural changes; but these changes immediately call into operation powerful counter-selective forces (increased predator pressures, for example) and it may very well be that one result of this counter-selection is to turn back some of the arena species from polygynous behaviour to pairing behaviour.

Jobi Manucode

Manucodia jobiensis Salvadori
Male 12–14¼ in.

Range: Japen Island and the trunk of New Guinea from Geelvink Bay south to the Setekwa and Mimika rivers and east to Astrolabe Bay and the upper Ramu River. Lowlands to about 1600 feet. (See Map 9.2, page 98.)

Adult Male: A jay-sized, glossy, greenish blue black species; similar to the Crinkle-collared Manucode (*M. chalybatus*) but with the short feathers of the neck and upper breast usually only lightly crinkled and steel bluish, not tinged metallic yellow green. In more detail, plumage, especially upper breast and back, obscurely barred subterminally with black; stubby, crisped feathering of head and neck glossed greenish or purplish. Iris orange red; bill and feet black. Wing 168–179; tail 127–142; exposed culmen 38; tarsus 39 mm.

Adult Female: Somewhat smaller (wing 154–173 mm.) with a yellow iris.

Juvenal: (a) Dull sooty black; (b) intermediate plumage, wing and tail somewhat glossy.

Remarks: The Jobi Manucode holds particular fascination for the biologist for while there is no doubt that it is a perfectly good biological species, it is often nearly indistinguishable from *M. chalybatus*. Apparently the isolating mechanisms between these morphologically similar species are almost entirely behavioural (probably chiefly vocal) since these 'twin' species live side by side (are sympatric) over much of their range.

Claude Grant (*in* Ogilvie-Grant, 1915: 9) found this bird to be the most common manucode inhabiting the forest of southwestern

New Guinea (in the neighbourhood of the Mimika and Setekwa rivers). He described its call as a long-drawn moaning cry. Its food is chiefly tree fruits.

Nesting: Grant described its nest as a deep cup-shaped structure composed of roots, creepers, and leaves. One that he found 28 December 1910, was suspended between two horizontal branches eight feet up. It contained two eggs which were short oval in shape, and pale pinkish spotted with small dark Vandyke brown dots and larger oblong lavender-grey spots, chiefly in a wreath around the larger end. Measurements 32 × 24·5; 31·5 × 24 mm.

Subspecies: Two nearly similar ones:

1 *M. j. jobiensis* Salvadori, 1876, *Ann. Mus. Civ. Genova,* vol. 7, Japen Island. Known only from Japen Island, Geelvink Bay. Male wing 177–179; tail 132–142 mm.

2 *M. j. rubiensis* Meyer, 1885, *Zeitschr. Ges. Orn.,* vol. 2, p. 374. Type locality Rubi, Geelvink Bay. Range: From head of Geelvink Bay (Rubi, Siriwo, Waropen) south to the Setekwa River, eastward to Astrolabe Bay and the upper Ramu River. Similar to *jobiensis* but smaller: wing male 168–174; tail 127–133 mm.

Crinkle-collared Manucode

Manucodia chalybatus (Pennant)
Male 12¾–14¼ in.
[1781, *Spec. Faun. Ind.,* in Forster's *Indian Zool.,* p. 40. Type locality (based on Daubenton, *Pl. Enlum., pl.* 634) 'New Guinea,' restricted to Arfak Mountains.]

Range: Misol and all New Guinea. From about 1900 feet to about 5500 feet; occasionally down to sea level. (See Map 9.2, page 98.)

Adult Male: A jay-sized glossy greenish blue black species; similar to the Jobi Manucode *(M. jobiensis)* but with the neck and upper breast tinged metallic yellow green and heavily crinkled. In more detail, crown, back, flight quills, sides, and abdomen metallic purple, with much of the dorsal plumage obscurely barred velvet black; feathering of crown compressed and velvety; hind neck, chin, and sides of head glossed steel blue green. Iris reddish brown, bill and feet black. Wing 165–189; tail 138–150; exposed culmen 40; tarsus 40 mm.

Adult Female: Smaller, wing 160–172 mm.

Juvenal: Dull black.

Remarks: The monotypic Crinkle-collared Manucode is apparently fairly common between about 2000 and 5500 feet and very uncommon to rare elsewhere. Bulmer's record of a pair collected at their nest (see below) indicates that this species, like the Glossy-backed Manucode, employs the less advanced pair-bond behaviour which is so widespread in birds but so rare in birds of paradise.

Nesting: Hartert (1910: 490) writes that the nest of this species hangs in a branch fork like an *Oriolus* nest and is constructed of brown wiry stalks intermingled with leaves and is lined with finer stalks and fibres. The eggs, of which he examined three received from Carl Wahnes (from 'German New Guinea'), are creamy white, rather roundish, with brown and purplish grey markings. They measured 35·1 × 26·7, and 36·7 × 26·7 mm. In the Baiyer region of Mt Hagen, Bulmer on 22 September 1955, shot a male 'at its nest' (containing two newly hatched young) and then he collected its 'mate.' On 4 January 1956, he obtained a chick from another nest (4500 feet) in the same area.

Curl-crested Manucode

Manucodia comrii Sclater
Male 17½ in.

Range: Eastern Papuan islands: D'Entrecasteaux and Trobriand archipelagos. (See Map 9.2, page 98.)

Adult Male: A curl-crested, crow-sized black bird, glossed purple, blue, and oil green, with a boat-shaped, curled, twisted tail. In more detail, generally black; crown with a mat of short, curled feathers glossed purple; neck and upper breast finely crinkled and glossed oil green; rest of ventral plumage rippled and sub-terminally barred with dull black; rest of dorsal plumage glossed steel green to purple; exposed surfaces of wings and tail glossed pinkish purple; central tail quills twisted and recurved. Iris dull red; bill and feet black. Wing 219–248; tail 154–183; exposed culmen 55; tarsus 57 mm.

Adult Female: Smaller, wing 209–228 mm.

Remarks: In 1959 Shaw Mayer informed me that the Curl-crested Manucode is abundant on Fergusson Island and that he found it nesting within 100 feet of the coast. Miss Ann Chowning told me (in conversation 5 April 1963) that the plumes of this ornate manucode are frequently used in native ceremonies in the Trobriand Islands.

Nesting: Rothschild and Hartert (1896: 234) reported that A. S. Meek found a nest and eggs in the Trobriands: 'The nest hangs in the fork of a branch, the upper margin being in equal height with the branch, just as an oriole's [*Oriolus*] nest hangs. It is fastened with thin twigs of a convolvulus-like plant. The bottom is very thick, and outside [it is] ornamented with large, thick leaves, and in the middle of the bottom layer are a good many pieces of rotten wood . . . . The eggs are of a pale buffy salmon-colour, one clutch with a more greyish tint, shaped like crow's eggs, marked with underlying pale cinereus and pale purplish brown patches, and with dark brown or rufous brown blotches.' Hartert (1910: 490) gave the measurements of two eggs [Meek found two sets of two in March] as 29 × 43 and 30·5 × 45·5 mm.

Subspecies: Two, differing only in size:

1 *M. c. comrii* Sclater, 1876, *Proc. Zool. Soc. London,* p. 459, pl. 42. Type locality 'Huon Gulf,' error for Fergusson Island. Known only from the D'Entrecasteaux Archipelago (Fergusson, Goodenough, and Normanby islands). Male wing 241–248; tail 175–183 mm.

2   *M. c. trobriandi* Mayr, 1936, *Amer. Mus. Novit.*, no. 869, p. 3 [type in AMNH no. 224342]. Type locality Kaileuna, Trobriand Islands. Known only from the Trobriand Islands (Kiriwina and Kaileuna islands). Like *comrii* but smaller: male wing 219–231; tail 154–168 mm.

Trumpet Bird

Phonygammus keraudrenii (Lesson and Garnot)
Male 10 to 12½ in.

Range: New Guinea lowlands occasionally up to 6000 feet; the Aru and D'Entrecasteaux archipelagos, and northeastern Australia. (See Map 9.3, page 107.)

Adult Male: A starling- to thrush-sized blackish species glossed oil green, blue, and violet purple, with elongated plumes formed into horn-like head tufts. In more detail, mantle generally glossy steel green to bluish or purplish violet; head and neck glossed steel green to steel blue; occipital tufts much elongated and lanceolate; throat and neck plumes oil green to purplish (one subspecies), ranging from long to very long and narrow and pointed; wings and tail violet blue to purple, sometimes steel green; rest of plumage mostly oil green to purplish green (to pinkish purple in one sub-species); undersides of wing and tail blackish. Iris orange red; bill and feet black. Wing 155–188; tail 111–135; exposed culmen 27–34; tarsus 38–41 mm.

Adult Female: Smaller, wing 147–182 mm.; iris orange. Young, iris brown.

Juvenal: A nestling (Rand, Lake Daviumbu) had the wings and tail glossed steel blue.

Remarks: The Trumpet Bird is one of the two species of birds of paradise that are shared by

Australia and New Guinea. It is named for its powerful call notes which, in the male, are produced in a long, winding trachea that extends over the furcula and then is coiled over the muscles of the breast.

In Australia, Banfield (*in* Iredale, 1950: 158) described the call as a loud, rich note which frequently resembles its native name, *Calloo-calloo*. He wrote that this species is remarkably shy, very rarely venturing out of the seclusion of the thickest jungle. On the other hand, Thorpe (*in* Iredale, 1950:158), also writing of Australian birds, found the Trumpet Bird '. . . plentiful in the dense bushes close to Somerset. Usually they are met with in pairs, high up in the fruit and berry-bearing trees, and frequently in company with other species. The males utter a very loud and deep guttural note, unlike that of any other bird I am acquainted with, and it astonished me that a comparatively small bird could make so much noise. In the trees they are very active in their movements, and on the appearance of an intruder evince more curiosity than timidity. I have frequently shot them by trying to imitate their notes, or by making a strange noise, when they would hop down from branch to branch in an inquisitive kind of way, as if trying to ascertain its source. The bird is particularly fond of the fruit of a certain species of fig; but the stomachs of those I examined contained insects, as well as fruits and berries of various kinds.'

In New Guinea, Rand (1942a) reported the Trumpet Bird as fairly common in the rain forest near the mouth of the Fly River where he encountered it singly or in pairs from the substage to the top of the forest. He recorded one of its calls as a loud squawk rather like *Mino dumonti*. Another of its calls was a slightly prolonged harsh call emitted during display.

Breeding Behaviour: Concerning displays, Rand wrote (1938): 'On 12 December I heard one of these birds [see above], and saw one, then another, fly to a large, horizontal exposed branch thirty feet up. They were male and female, judging by their difference in size. They perched a foot or so apart, the male turned toward the female and depressed the fore part of its body so that it was more or less parallel to the branch on which they sat. The male then slightly raised and spread its wings, erected its body feathers and gave a single loud, slightly prolonged harsh call, relaxing its feathers and folding its wings as it did so. Then the male moved toward the female which flew fifty yards into the forest where the performance was repeated. Apparently the chasing and display continued for some moments, though due to the density of the foliage and frequent movements of the birds, I could catch only an occasional glimpse of them. Apparently this display was given solely for the benefit of the female. The above is evidently the mating display of this species, and from this and the fact that the species is frequently, perhaps usually, found in pairs, one may perhaps conclude that this bird is monogamous and that both male and female take part in the nest duties, as in *Manucodia*. This conclusion is in accord with the observations on the Queensland race.'

Nesting: According to Australian records (Cayley: 1959) the nest is an open, shallow cup of vines usually placed high (up to 70 feet) in a forked branch. Two oval, pale pinkish purple eggs are laid. These are streaked and smudged with brown, purple, and grey. A set of two eggs collected by A. S. Anthony at 6000 feet in the Owen Stanley Mountains measured 35·5 × 24 and 35·3 × 23·8 mm. Hartert (1910: 490) described them as pale pink, spotted all over with brownish red surface patches and violet grey.

Subspecies: Eight well marked races are known:

1 *P. k. keraudrenii* (Lesson and Garnot), 1826, *Bull. Sci. Nat.* (Férussae), vol. 8, p. 110. Type locality Dorey, Vogelkop. Range west New Guinea: Vogelkop, Onin Peninsula, and Weyland Mountains. This is a small (male wing 157–165 mm.), generally steel greenish blue form, with purplish wings and tail.

2 *P. k. jamesii* Sharpe, 1877, *Cat. Birds Brit. Mus.*, vol. 3, p. 181. Type locality Aleya, Hall Sound, south-eastern New Guinea. Known from Aru Islands, southern New Guinea (from the Mimika River in the west, east to Hall Sound). Like *keraudrenii* but larger (male wing 158–169 mm.) and with longer head tufts.

3 *P. k. purpureo-violaceus* Meyer, 1885, *Zeitschr. ges. Orn.*, vol. 2, p. 375, pl. 15. Type locality Astrolabe Mountains. Known only from the mountains (2250 to 5800 feet) of south-eastern New Guinea. Like *keraudrenii* but back purplish violet not steel green.

4 *P. k. mayri* Greenway, 1942, *Proc. New England Zool. Club.* vol. 19, p. 51. Type locality Wau, Morobe District. Known only from

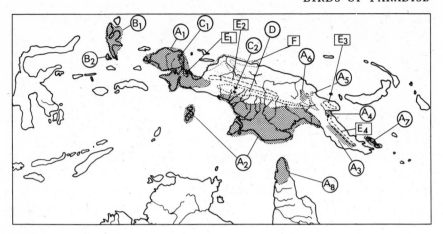

Map 9.3 *Phonygammus keraudrenii,* etc.

Phonygammus keraudrenii (A) Lowlands to 6000 feet
   Phonygammus keraudrenii keraudrenii (A1)
   Phonygammus keraudrenii jamesii (A2)
   Phonygammus keraudrenii purpureo-violaceus (A3)
   Phonygammus keraudrenii mayri (A4)
   Phonygammus keraudrenii adelberti (A5)
   Phonygammus keraudrenii neumanni (A6)
   Phonygammus keraudrenii hunsteini (A7)
   Phonygammus keraudrenii gouldi (A8)
Semioptera wallacei (B)
   Semioptera wallacei halmaherae (B1)
   Semioptera wallacei wallacei (B2)
Paradigalla carunculata (C) 4800–7000 feet
   Paradigalla carunculata carunculata (C1)
   Paradigalla carunculata intermedia (C2)
Paradigalla brevicauda (D) 5500–7800 feet
Drepanornis albertisii (E) 2200–7200 feet
   Drepanornis albertisii albertisii (E1)
   Drepanornis albertisii inversus (E2)
   Drepanornis albertisii geisleri (E3)
   Drepanornis albertisii cervinicauda (E4)
Drepanornis bruijnii (F)

the Morobe District, north-eastern New Guinea. Like *purpureo-violaceus* but with a higher wing-tail index.

5 *P. k. adelberti* Gilliard and LeCroy, 1967, *Bull. Amer. Mus. Nat. Hist.*, vol. 138, p. 72 [Type in AMNH no. 791016]. Type locality Nawawu, Adelbert Mountains. Known only from the Adelbert Mountains, northern New Guinea. Like *keraudrenii* but with the wings and tail green not blue to purple.

6 *P. k. neumanni* Reichenow, 1918, *Journ. f. Orn.*, vol. 66, p. 438. Type locality Lordberg. Known from Lordberg (4600 feet), Sepik Mountains and Jimmi and Baiyer river regions. Like *keraudrenii* but with the lower back, rump, wings and tail dark bluish violet not greenish.

7 *P. k. hunsteini* Sharpe, 1882, *Journ. Linn. Soc. London*, Zool., vol. 16, p. 442. Type locality 'East Cape, New Guinea,' error for Normanby Island. Known only from D'Entrecasteaux Archipelago (Fergusson, Goodenough, and Normanby Islands). Like *keraudrenii* but back dark bluish purple not steel green and with the head tufts longer, more greenish, less bluish.

8 *P. k. gouldi* (Gray), 1859, *Proc. Zool. Soc. London*, note, p. 158 (fig. Gould, *Suppl.*, pl. 9). Type locality Cape York. Known only from Northern Queensland, Australia. Like *keraudrenii* but generally more steel green, less purplish, especially on the wings.

Taxonomy: Despite the elaborateness of the plumage and the highly developed trachea in the male, there is general agreement that *Phonygammus* is very closely related to *Manucodia*.

Addendum: The matter having come up several times, I must mention an apparent error in the literature of this bird. W. J. C. Frost (*in* Rothschild, 1930: 9) apparently erroneously reported that this species lays its eggs in the nests of *Paradisaea apoda* (in the Aru Islands), and that it has the mannerisms of an avian parasite.

Paradise Rifle Bird

Ptiloris paradiseus Swainson
Male 10¾ in.

[1825 (Jan.), *Zool. Journ.*, vol. 1 (4), p. 481. No type locality (= northern New South Wales)].

Range: Eastern Australia: The upper Hunter River area of New South Wales north to the Rockhampton region of central Queensland. (See Map 9.4, page 110.)

Adult Male: (Very similar to *Ptiloris victoriae* but much larger.) A curve-billed, short-tailed black bird with iridescent green on the crown, throat, and central rectrices. In more detail, upperparts, including wings and tail, velvet black with a pinkish purple iridescence; tail with the somewhat shorter central pair of rectrices metallic blue green on upper surface; forehead, crown, and nape with broad iridescent tips forming a metallic shield; nasal plumes, lores, sides of head (enclosing eye), sides of neck, cheeks, and chin black glossed purple; central throat, neck, and upper breast metallic oil green, the plumage formed into a shield which, at sides of breast, is slightly elongated and erectile; upper breast like back; lower breast black with narrow, iridescent oil green edges; lower

breast, sides, and abdomen strongly glossed oil green; rest of underparts, including under wing and under tail coverts, black. Iris brown; bill and feet black; wing 155–159; tail 94–99; exposed culmen 46; tarsus 35 mm.

Adult Female: Nearly similar to *P. victoriae* above, but underparts buffy white with heavier, broader dark markings. Upperparts olive-brown; wings blackish brown with exposed edges chestnut; tail olive brown; top and sides of head dark olive brown with narrow whitish streaks; a broad whitish superciliary streak; throat and sides of lower head to upper neck whitish washed with buff; underparts, including under wing and under tail coverts, ochraceous buff with bold black bars. Iris brown; bill and feet black; wing 140–151; tail 87–95; exposed culmen 53; tarsus 37 mm.

Remarks: Tom Iredale, in an excellent historical survey of this species (1950: 21), the most southerly of all the birds of paradise, reports that the first appearance of the name 'riflebird' is apparently in Barron Field's *Glossary of the most common objects of Natural History in New South Wales*, published in London in 1825, in which the name is introduced without explanation. Newton (1899: 789), however, noted that the name of this handsome bird was based on its resemblance to the uniforms of riflemen in the British army ' . . . while in its long and projecting hypochondriac plumes and short

Map 9.4 *Ptiloris*

Ptiloris paradiseus (A)

Ptiloris victoriae (B)

Ptiloris magnificus (C)

    Ptiloris magnificus magnificus (C1)

    Ptiloris magnificus intercedens (C2)

    Ptiloris magnificus alberti (C3)

tail a further likeness might be traced to the hanging pelisse and the jacket formerly worn by the members of these corps.' The Paradise Rifle Bird is now rare (McGill, 1960: 50) in New South Wales where it is found throughout the coastal and adjacent hill rain forests to as far south as Wallis Lake. Strange (*in* Iredale, 1950: 27) wrote that: 'The principal resort of the Rifle Bird is among the large cedar [forests] that skirt the mountains and creeks of the Manning, Hastings, Macleay, Bellenger, Clarence and Richmond Rivers . . . .'

Food: Insects, obtained mostly under the bark or in crevices in the trunks of trees, also fruits and berries. Newton (1899: 790) reported that this species gets its food '. . . by thrusting its somewhat long bill under the loose bark on the boles or boughs of trees, along the latter of which it runs swiftly, or by searching for it on the ground beneath.'

Voice: A greatly prolonged note sounding like *jass,* also a mechanical rustling made with the wings, resembling the shaking of stiff silk.

Breeding Behaviour: Strange (*op. cit.*) noted that during the breeding season the male is easily found: 'At that time of the year, as soon as the sun's rays gild the tops of the trees, up goes the Rifle Bird from the thickets below to the higher branches of the pines (*Araucaria macleayana*) which there abound. It always affects a situation where three or four of these trees occur about two hundred yards apart, and there the morning is spent in short flights from tree to tree, in sunning and preening its feathers, and in uttering its song each time it leaves one tree for another. The sound emitted resembles a prolonged utterance of the word 'Jass,' by which this bird is known to the natives of the Richmond River. In passing from tree to tree, it also makes an extraordinary noise resembling the shaking of a piece of new, stiff silk. After 10 a.m. it descends lower down, and then mostly resorts to the thick limb of a cedar tree (*Cedrela australis*), and there continues to utter its cry of 'Jass' at intervals of two minutes' duration; at this time, owing to the thickness of the limb and the closeness with which this bird keeps to it, it is very difficult of detection; wait with patience, however, and you will soon see him, with wings extended, and his head thrown on his back, whirling round and round, first one way

111

and then another.' Cayley (1959: 14) in writing of this performance says simply that it 'displays in an extraordinary manner, usually selecting for his performance a bare horizontal limb of a tree at the edge of the [forest], or overlooking a gorge.'

Nesting: Nest: a shallow bowl of thin vines and dead leaves, lined with fine fibres and twigs and often ornamented with snake skins. The usual nest location is in a mass of vines high up (sometimes ninety feet up) in a thickly formed tree. Eggs: two, reddish cream, spotted and longitudinally streaked with chestnut, purple, and grey. Measurements: 32·8–35·0 × 22·9–24·9 mm. (Schönwetter, 1944: 17). Nesting season: October to December.

Taxonomy: Bock (1963: 122) includes the genus *Ptiloris* in the true birds of paradise, *Paradisaeinae,* as the fourth of eight generic groups that may be established on the basis of subtle similarities in skull structure.

Mayr (1962: 187) 'lumps' *Craspedophora* (a genus long maintained because in the males the flank plumes are elongated) in the genus *Ptiloris.* The females of the two are extremely similar and in skull morphology they are identical (Bock, 1963).

The race *P. p. queenslandica* Mathews, 1923, *Austral. Avian Rec.,* Vol. 5, p. 42, is taxonomically invalid.

Queen Victoria Rifle Bird

Ptiloris victoriae Gould
Male 8¾ in.
[1850 (between January and June), *Proc. Zool. Soc. London,* 1849, p. 111, pl. 12. Type locality Barnard Island, north Queensland.]

Range: Australia. North Queensland in the Cairns district. (See Map 9.4, page 110.)

Adult Male: Much like *P. paradiseus* but smaller. A curve-billed, short-tailed black species with iridescent green crown, throat, and central rectrices. In more detail, crown and nape with scale-like plumes glossed blue green; rest of upperparts velvet black tinged pinkish purple to deep purple; tail black glossed purple on edges, except central pair of rectrices solid iridescent oil green to blue green (and shorter than others); lower throat to upper breast iridescent oil green; upper throat, sides of head, sides of neck, and upper breast black tinged metallic purple; lower breast and abdomen blackish tipped dark green. Iris Vandyke brown; bill and feet black. Wing 133–140; tail 78–81; exposed culmen 36; tarsus 34 mm.

Adult Female: Very different from adult male. Much like female of *P. paradiseus* but smaller and paler above, more grey, less brown, and underparts more ochraceous, less whitish and less heavily marked with brown. Upperparts generally brownish grey; the crown and nape with narrow buff shaft streaking and the wings with some narrow cinnamon margins; a streak from lores over eye to nape, also throat and neck below buffy; sides of throat with narrow dark streaks; rest of underparts ochraceous with sparse and variable amounts of dusky barring and spotting. Iris dark hazel; bill and feet black. Wing 118–131; tail 74–80; exposed culmen 40; tarsus 32 mm.

Immature: First year plumage much like adult female. Male intermediate plumage like adult female but with a few iridescent green feathers on forehead and lower breast.

Remarks: The Queen Victoria Rifle Bird was discovered more than a century ago by John Gould's collector, John Macgillivray, in north-east Australia. Macgillivray wrote (1852: 23): 'On one of the Barnard Isles (No. III in lat. 17° 43′ S.), which is covered with dense brush, I found Queen Victoria's Rifle Bird in considerable abundance. Females and young males were common, but rather shy; however, by sitting down and quietly watching in some favourite locality, one or more would soon alight on a limb or branch, run along it with great celerity, stop abruptly every now and then to thrust its beak under the loose bark in search of insects, and then fly off as suddenly as it had arrived. Occasionally I have seen one anxiously watching me from behind a branch, its head

113

and neck only being visible. At this time (June) the young males were very pugnacious, and upon one occasion three of them were so intent upon their quarrel that they allowed me to approach sufficiently near to kill them all with a single charge of dust shot. The adult males were comparatively rare, always solitary, and very shy. I never saw them upon the trees, but only in the thick bushes and masses of climbing plants beneath them; on detecting the vicinity of man they immediately shuffled off among the branches towards the opposite side of the thicket, and flew off for a short distance. I did not observe them to utter any call or cry; this, however, may have arisen from my attention not having been so much directed to them as to the females and young males, which I was more anxious to procure, the very different style of their colouring having led me to believe that they were a new species of *Pomatostomus* (Australian Babbler).'

Later (1887–9), E. T. Cairn and Robert Grant found the species very common on the Atherton Tableland and in 1943–5 Bourke and Austin found it still plentiful on this tableland (see below). Cairn and Grant (1890) wrote that it was most abundant on the tablelands amidst 'the dense and luxuriant tropical vegetation, in which palms, ferns, orchid-covered trees and vines flourish.' They noted that 'each male seems to have a special haunt of its own, and when another of his own sex and species encroaches or trespasses on his domain, they chase one another here and there through the foliage. The male delights in swinging and fluttering on some rope-like vine extending across a creek, or hanging from tree to tree, especially in a spot where the sun's rays filter through the canopy of leaves overhead. He is extremely active when searching for food among the bark of trees, staghorn, bird nest, and other ferns, arboreal orchids, and other epiphytes. One can hear, in the early morning, the harsh, rasping-like note uttered at intervals by this species; but being difficult to imitate, great caution must be used in approaching them. The flight of the male is short but rapid; sometimes when one is seated in the scrub the well-known rustle of the wings is heard as he flies quickly past. This noise, which resembles in sound the rustling of a lady's silk dress close by, is produced by the movement of the wing-feathers, and is confined to the males. One morning, when following a pebbly creek, I entered a small glade almost clear of trees, on the other side of which was part of a dead tree, almost denuded of its branches. On this tree I observed three or four birds, and from their strange and peculiar actions I concluded it was to me an unknown species. Trying to get within shooting range, I disturbed them, and they quickly darted into the scrub. Early next morning, under cover of the scrub, I approached the tree from the opposite side, and managed to get close to it unobserved. Peering through the foliage, I was delighted to find the birds on the same branch as I saw them the previous day, and having a good view of them, soon discovered they were Queen Victoria's Riflebirds; one a fully plumaged adult male, the others females or young males, and evidently a pair of adults accompanied by their young. The brilliantly-plumaged male was spreading his wings in such a manner that the primary feathers of each wing were brought close together right over his head; added to this there were the gorgeous metallic golden green-tipped plumes of his body spread out in circular form around his breast. The bill was pointed upwards, showing to advantage the resplendent green scale-like feathers of the throat, and giving the bird the appearance of a living jewel. All the time he was swaying his body backwards and forwards, and twisting and turning his head with seeming delight. The other birds kept hopping around him with outspread wings, evidently taking great pleasure in his actions, and occasionally like him uttering their loud and somewhat discordant note.'

Food: Bourke and Austin (1947 : 112) observed small parties digging grubs and other insects from rotten logs and stumps and searching nooks and crannies in the bark of forest trees. This bird gathers animal food from beneath scales of bark which it pries loose with its bill. It obtains food by climbing tree trunks and steep limbs with great agility. It also eats forest fruits.

Voice: Loud, gasping *yaas* uttered every few minutes from special displaying limbs (Bourke and Austin, 1947 : 113).

Breeding Behaviour: 'The display . . . is easy to observe when a "stage" has been discovered, as the birds use the same spot day after day' (Bourke and Austin, 1947). These observers report that '. . . each adult male seems to have sole rights to all the vantage points in an area of some five acres or more. Typical stages are bare horizontal limbs amongst the upper branches . . . or the tops of large stumps.'

Display: 'On several occasions' wrote Bourke and Austin (*op. cit.:* 113) 'we were able to spend periods of an hour or more observing single fully-plumaged males. They spent their time moving from one stage to another, uttering their loud gasping "yaas" every few minutes, and following what appeared to be a routine – first a visit to a "stage", a rest for a few moments during which the bird called loudly as though challenging other males, or possibly calling to the females, then a full display performance, followed by a rest for perhaps five minutes, after which he commenced feeding. A quarter of an hour later, or even less time, would find him back on one of his "stages," ready to display again.'

The following highly interesting display was witnessed several times by Bourke and Austin (*op. cit.:* 113): 'What appeared to be a female, but was possibly an immature male, was observed displaying on top of a twenty foot stump. [This bird] was joined by a second bird, in full plumage, and the pair went through the performance together. The birds faced one another with breasts almost touching, the drab bird slowly stretched and raised [its] wings to a horizontal position, swept them slightly forward, and then relaxed. This action was repeated by each bird in turn, with increasing tempo, until one wondered how they avoided wing clashes. As the speed of the wing movements increased, the birds crouched until their breasts seemed to touch the stump, while their heads were thrown further and further back, and bills opened wider and wider. Finally when both birds were lying almost flat, with heads at a seemingly impossible angle, and quivering furiously all over, the tails were spread, the wings were thrown forward until they met in front of the breasts, and were then rocked up and down and sideways.

'The performance stopped abruptly, the actors rested quietly for several minutes, and then repeated the whole act, after which the second bird flew away, and the first remained perched quietly on the stump.' Bourke and Austin added (*op. cit.:* 113) that they '. . . have seen pairs perform the whole display four times with a short rest between each act. Usually one act occupies about a minute, and the rests may extend to 10 minutes or more, during which time the birds sit quietly facing one another.'

Nesting: The nest is constructed of twigs, vines, rootlets, and leaves, and very often is decorated with a snakeskin. It is usually placed in a small tree, often a pine, 5 to 15 feet up. Two eggs are laid (measurements: 33 × 23·2 and 34·8 × 22·9 mm., A.S.

Meek), usually in October to December. These are reddish flesh colour with longitudinal streaks and a few smudges reddish, brownish, purplish to dark greyish in colour.

P. p. dyotti Mathews, 1915, *Austral. Avian Rec.,* vol 2, p. 133, is an invalid race.

Magnificent Rifle Bird

Ptiloris magnificus (Vieillot)
Male 13 in.

Range: Widespread in New Guinea and north-eastern Australia; sea level to about 4000 feet. (See Map 9.4, page 110.)

Adult Male: A curve-billed, short-tailed black species with a glossy green crown, throat, upper breast, and central rectrices. Much like *P. magnificus* and *victoria* but differing from both by having the glossy green breast and throat patch much more extensive (extending upward to chin) and the upper breast burnished bronze green not velvet black. In more detail, upperparts and sides of head velvety black with violet purple reflections; crown and nape metallic oil green; wings and tail black with traces of metallic blue; central pair of rectrices iridescent greenish blue; midline of chin, throat, and breast metallic blue green (the feathers at sides of the breast forming an erectile fan);  a narrow pectoral band bronze green with traces of ruby red; rest of underparts and elongated hair-like flank plumes black (suffused with greenish or pinkish purple in two races). Iris dark brown; bill black; feet dark slate to black; gape grass green; inside of mouth greenish yellow; wing 179–193; tail 97–103; exposed culmen 50–57; tarsus 42 mm.

Adult Female: Very different from adult male. Upperparts ochraceous to brown; a narrow whitish streak over eye; sides of head from lores to ears dusky brown; a narrow submalar streak dark brown; underparts, including wing linings, dull white with profuse blackish brown barring except on throat; inner edges of flight quills and tail cinnamon chestnut. Iris dark grey brown; bill black; gape green; feet dark grey; inside of mouth pale greenish yellow; wing 140–159; tail 92–103; exposed culmen 40; tarsus 37–42 mm.

Juvenal: The nestling has the plumage soft with the dark bars of the breast and belly sooty brown and more widely spaced than in the adult female.

Immature: First year plumage much like the adult female. Male intermediate plumage or stage of dress: like adult male but rectrices (except central pair), some outer and inner primaries and alula as in female.

Remarks: The Magnificent Rifle Bird has the distinction of being one of the two species of birds of paradise which is shared by both New Guinea and Australia. In New Guinea it is generally uncommon in the lowlands and fairly common in the lower hill and mountain forests but it is always a difficult species to observe. In the Adelbert Mountains in tall original forest at about 3400 feet, I found a male in its display tree in late March, 1959. From the shrill calls he delivered for many days running, always from the same spot high up and concealed from my view, I concluded that the tree was the chief display court of this one male. I did not hear any others calling in the distance. The display tree was one of the largest on the hill. It was about ninety feet tall and heavily draped from base to crown with vines and other epiphytic plants. The solitary male had its singing (and display?) perch about 60–70 feet up. From there it periodically emitted an explosive rasping cry.

Hunstein (*in* Iredale, 1950: 30) noted that the species in southeastern New Guinea has a different call from that of the Australian Rifle Bird and is shy and difficult to find in its favourite habitat which, he states, is mostly in the mountains where it frequents trees with plenty of vines and creepers on them. Goodwin also found the Magnificent Rifle Bird very shy and elusive in the Owen Stanley Mountains where he met with it between 2000 and 3000 feet above sea level.

C. H. B. Grant (1915: 11) in south-western New Guinea '... found the species most plentiful inland and along the mountain slopes. The adult males are much more wary than the females or immature birds, and the jungles resound with their clear whistles, consisting of two long-drawn notes, one ascending, the other descending.' John Macgillivray, the discoverer of this species in Australia, wrote: 'This fine Rifle-bird inhabits the densest of the brushes in the neighbourhood of Cape York. The natives are familiar with it under the name of "Jagoonya"; the Darnley Islanders also recognised a skin shown them, and described it to be a native of Dowde, on the south coast of New Guinea, near Bristow Island. Its cry is very striking; upon being imitated by man, which may be easily done, the male bird will answer; it consists of a loud whistle resembling "wheeoo" repeated three times and ending abruptly in a note like "who-o-o." Both sexes utter the same note, but that of the male is much the loudest. The old males were generally seen about the tops of the highest trees, where, if undisturbed, they would remain long enough to utter their loud cry two or three times at intervals of from two to five minutes. If a female be near, the male frequently perches on a conspicuous dead twig in a crouching attitude, rapidly opening and closing his wings, the feathers of which, by their peculiar form and texture produce a loud rustling noise, which in the comparative stillness of these solitudes may be heard at a distance of a hundred yards, and may be faintly imitated by moving the feathers of a dried skin. The full-plumaged males are much more shy than the females or immature birds. . . . From the shyness of this Rifle-bird, it is difficult to catch more than a passing glimpse of it in the dense brushes which it inhabits; I once, however, saw a female running up the trunk of a tree like a creeper, and its stomach was afterwards found to be filled with insects only, chiefly ants; while the stomach of a male, shot about the same time, contained merely a few small, round berries, the fruit of a tall tree, the botanical name of which is unknown to me.'

Displays in Captivity: Crandall and Leister (1937), who observed a male which displayed in captivity (on a sloping branch to a stuffed female), noted two forms of display, one short and one long: the first was usually preceded by a few abrupt, jerky movements of the head and neck. 'With this slight warning the wings are then thrown slightly forward and opened wide, to the fullest extent. Simul-

K

taneously, the neck is extended and the head moved to one side and brought to rest just behind the bend of the outstretched wing. The head is then moved from side to side, first in a period of about two seconds, but immediately and regularly increased in speed until brought to an abrupt stop in the middle after about a dozen movements. This is a remarkably rhythmic performance and the last few movements are executed with such rapidity that it is practically impossible to determine their extent. As the head movements cease the wings are folded and the display ended.' In the long form, at '. . . the start of the display the wings are usually opened so abruptly as to produce a rustling "plop." As the head is being moved from one side to the other the bird rises on its perch and slightly elevates (thereby relaxing) the extended wings. Simultaneously, as the head reaches the opposite side, the body is lowered on the perch and the wings are snapped back to their full-extended position. This again produces a sharp, rustling which is, of course, repeated with every similar movement of the wings throughout the performance. All of these movements are repeated in unison, again and again. The wings-extended-head-to-the-side position is held rigidly for about three seconds. The time of movements then decreases to about three-quarters of a second and is maintained to the end of the display. During the longest and most regularly-executed of the displays observed the head was moved from side to side thirty-five times, punctuated, in perfect rhythm, by the rustling snap of the extended wings. No two displays were exactly alike, for they all varied by changing the regular, rhythmic beat of these coordinated movements. Action may be slowed down for a few seconds, then speeded up to the original beat.' Crandall and Leister also noted that between display periods the male frequently uttered his loud call notes, and also a pleasing low pitched version of the same. During the display, however, they noted no vocal sounds and, surprisingly, the mouth was never opened to show its bright internal colouration.

Nesting: The Magnificent Rifle Bird in Australia constructs a scanty cup-shaped nest of vines, tendrils, and dead leaves and lines it with vines and plant fibres. The nest is placed 7 to 40 feet up, usually in a pandanus palm in dense forest. In New Guinea a nest (with two eggs) found by C. Wahnes (Hartert, 1910: 488) was a deep cup composed of thin wire-like fibres surrounded by large dry leaves.

In Australia and New Guinea the usual set is two eggs. The eggs collected by Wahnes were cream coloured and longitudinally marked with brown and pale grey. They measure 34·4 × 23·6 and 33·3 × 23·2 mm.

Subspecies: Three fairly well marked races:

1 *P. m. magnificus* (Vieillot), 1819, *Nov. Dict. Hist. Nat.*, nouv. ed., vol. 28, p. 167. Type locality 'Nouvelle Guinée', restricted to Dorey, Vogelkop. Known from western New Guinea, from the Vogelkop eastward in the north to the Sepik River, and eastward in the south to the Fly River. In this race the lower breast and abdomen are weakly suffused with dark pinkish purple.

2 *P. m. intercedens* Sharpe, 1882, *Journ. Linn. Soc. London, Zool.*, vol. 16, p. 444. Type locality Milne Bay and East Cape. Known from easternmost New Guinea westward in the south to Hall Sound and westward in the north to Astrolabe Bay. This race differs from *magnificus* by having the lower breast and abdomen with a much brighter suffusion of pinkish purple.

3 *P. m. alberti* Elliot, 1871, *Proc. Zool. Soc. London*, p. 583. Type locality 'Cape York.' Known only from northern Queensland, Australia, in the Cape York and Claudie River district. The race differs from *magnificus* by having the lower breast and abdomen chiefly dusky black with the purple subobsolete.

Wallace's Standard Wing

Semioptera wallacei Gould
Male 10 in.

Range: The Moluccan islands of Halmahera and Batjan (See Map 9.3, page 107.)

Adult Male: A pale brown bird with a large iridescent oil green breast shield and two pairs of long white flag plumes springing from the bend of the wing. In more detail, upperparts dark earth brown with a fugitive pinkish purple iridescence; wings and tail above faded canvas brown with ivory shafts (and with the central pair of rectrices somewhat shorter than remainder); wing quills greyish white on outer vanes; on outer edge of bend of wing, two extra-ordinary narrow spatula-shaped whitish plumes (up to 160 mm.

in length); crown and nape greyish lilac to purple, iridescent in certain lights; a medium large nasal tuft covering basal two-thirds of maxilla pale ochraceous; sides of head and neck, also back of neck, brown with a faint violet iridescence; chin faded canvas brown; lower cheeks and throat faded canvas brown tipped with variable amounts of iridescent green; central throat, neck, and upper breast with a vivid iridescent oil to emerald green shield suffused with gold in certain lights; shield greatly elongated on sides of breast; breast dusky canvas brown scalloped irregularly with iridescent green: lower breast and sides canvas brown glossed oil green; rest of underparts canvas brown; wings and tail below pale brownish grey. Iris deep olive; bill horny olive; feet orange. Wing 152–157; tail 75–85; culmen from base 33; tarsus 43 mm.

Adult Female: Much like adult male but lacking long plumes and green iridescence. Generally canvas brown with a faint lilac iridescence on upperparts; tuft at base of maxilla, sides of head and throat paler, more buffy. Iris deep brown; bill purplish grey with a brown base; feet orange ochraceous. Wing 144–149; tail 82–90; culmen from posterior edge of nostril 32; tarsus 41 mm.

Remarks: In 1926, Walter Goodfellow observed and collected five live specimens of Wallace's Standard Wing near Patani in the southeast sector of Halmahera. He wrote (1927: 59) that this bird, the '*Burong Plet*,' is very difficult to find and very few of the Halmahera people are familiar with it, since it lives in the uninhabited interior of the island. For weeks Goodfellow searched in vain for it '. . . till all my shoe leather was worn through on the sharp outcrop of coral which one encounters everywhere. My body also ached with rheumatism all over, through being constantly wet, and sometimes sleeping out all night in the rain. By the beginning of the third week I think I had abandoned all hope of ever getting Wallace's Standard Wing; then one night a man came to me mysteriously, and said he knew a place where they abounded. How many did I want, and what would I pay for them? etc., etc. All this sounded too good to be true, especially as he was not willing to take me along with him. Then another week, and still no further news. The weather was very wet and stormy. Real southeast monsoon. I had just one week left before the boat was due to call for me. . . . Then the man . . . turned up again. He said the birds were still there, but he could not catch them, so came to enlist my help. I arranged to go with him early the next morning, and he insisted that we must start before daylight, so that the villagers should not see the way we went. Before daybreak we were off. . . . After . . . perhaps three hours . . . we came to a stunted kind of jungle. A few enormous trees grew here and there, but the majority were saplings of 30 or 40 feet high, straight, and with few branches, and these quite short; very little undergrowth, in some places none at all. Perhaps after being disappointed so many times, my surprise may be imagined when I saw in comparatively low trees at the very least thirty Wallace's Birds. I really could hardly believe my eyes, and out of all this number possibly not more than two females, or birds in brown plumage. The others seemed to be all fully adult males. My guide had certainly done his best to catch them. He must have put up scores of limed twigs, some being long tapering bamboos 20 or more feet long, with lime on the extreme ends. This bird-lime is made out of the sap of the breadfruit-tree, and in the Aru Islands I have myself caught *apodas* with it. In the present case I think it had been badly prepared, as he said birds had repeatedly settled on it and were not held. The birds were all constantly on the move, flying backwards and forwards from tree to tree with a great fluttering of their wings, and at times hanging in all sorts of positions from the slender branches, some turning round and round like a cartwheel, and all the time making a variety of squawks and calls. . . . Although we were plainly visible, the birds were not in the least alarmed at our presence; in fact, some came lower down to look at us, and one or two came within 15 feet.'

Food: Goodfellow continues: 'Neither then nor on subsequent visits could I find any fruit-trees in the neighbourhood, and I never did find out what they live on. Of course, it would have been easy enough to have shot one to see what it had in its stomach, but this would have frightened them away, the very last thing I wanted to do. Wallace . . . says "They seem to feed principally on fruit, but probably take insects occasionally." My experience now is that they are *very* insectivorous, and certainly prefer green-coloured insects, with a pronounced partiality for the large soft-bodied grasshoppers, nearly 5 or 6 inches long, which live on the branches of the coco-nut palms. It was a lesson in anatomy to watch the expert way they dissected these insects, and also the large tropical cockroaches. These preferences were, of course, noted in the early days of their captivity. They naturally change later.'

Ornamental Plumes: Goodfellow wrote 'I saw some . . . birds with their green breast shields elevated, not horizontally, but perpendicularly, so that the head only is seen looking through at the deep V-shaped base of green feathers. At this time the long shoulder plumes stand out at right angles below the shield. These whitish plumes are constantly raised and depressed. The short scalelike feathers on the top of the head, which are silvery purple, also seem to undulate with a curious effect. Of course, this I only noticed in captivity, as it requires a certain position of the head to show it off, otherwise this colour effect is not even suspected.'

Courtship Behaviour: Goodfellow continues: 'As I have before said, I was always looking for their dancing places in the jungle, but I now feel certain that these low trees formed a dancing place, and what I saw there, the display, otherwise why did they frequent it more than any other spot, for it certainly was not their feeding ground? I spent the remainder of the first day at this place and noticed that at midday all the birds disappeared. A few, I believe, remained in the dense top of one of the great trees near by, and came out again for a short time later in the afternoon. It did not take me long to note that certain trees were more frequented than others, so the next day we started to put up the nets. The trees were far too slender to allow of anyone but a very light person climbing them, so I sent my Indian boy up. As he was arranging the first net, one bird came within 3 yards of him to watch the proceedings and as soon as the boy came down it went and shook the net with its bill. I was standing at the base of the tree and at once gave it a shake, when the bird flew *right into the net,* so I got my first Wallace. . . . It was so inextricably entangled, the whole net had to be taken down with the bird in it. As the boy was coming down with it its screams brought all the other birds around, and I am sure if I had then had all the other nets up my scoop would have been a large one. This habit of coming to a companion in distress is not, of course, peculiar to Paradise Birds, but I have many times seen plume hunters in the Aru Islands and in New Guinea take advantage of this and *deliberately* wound a bird and keep it tied up out of sight under a dancing tree for its cries to attract the other birds, so that they could more easily shoot them.'

Goodfellow noted that '. . . during rain or dull weather no birds came out at all. This further convinces me that I had found a real dancing place; but with one ray of sunshine, birds suddenly appeared from somewhere, and at such times during the remainder of the week, we managed to secure four more birds, three males and one female.'

A. R. Wallace's description of this species written immediately after he discovered it on the island of Batjan in 1858, is a classic in the history of the birds of paradise; it is also an excellent description of the extraordinary ornamentation of this bird '. . . just as I got home, I overtook Ali returning from shooting, with some birds hanging from his belt. He seemed much pleased, and said, "Look here, Sir, what a curious bird," holding out what at first completely puzzled me. I saw a bird with a mass of splendid green feathers on its breast, elongated into two glittering tufts; but what I could not understand was a pair of long white feathers, which stuck straight out from each shoulder. Ali assured me that the bird stuck them out this way itself, when fluttering its wings, and that they had remained so without his touching them. On lifting the wing coverts these feathers are seen to arise from two tubular horny sheaths, which diverge from near the point of junction of the carpal bones. The *Semioptera* frequents the lower branches of the virgin forests, and is almost constantly in motion. It flies from branch to branch, and clings to the twigs and even to the vertical smooth trunks almost as easily as a Woodpecker. It continually utters a harsh croaking cry, something between that of *Paradisea apoda* and the more musical cry of *Cicinnurus regius*. The males, at short intervals, open and flutter their wings, erect the long shoulder feathers, and expand the elegant shields on each side of the breast. Like the Birds of Paradise, the females and young birds far outnumber the fully plumaged birds, which renders it probable that the extraordinary accessory plumes are not fully developed until the third or fourth year. The bird seems to feed principally upon fruit, but it probably takes insects occasionally.'

Nesting: Apparently the nest and eggs remain undiscovered.

Subspecies: Two nearly similar ones:

1 *S. w. halmaherae* Salvadori, 1881, *Orn. Papuasia Mol.,* vol. 2, p. 573. Type locality Halmahera. Known only from Halmahera Island. Crown and nape with rich iridescent pinkish blue purple reflection.

2 *S. w. wallacei* Gould, 1859, *Birds Australia Suppl.,* pl. 11 and text. Type locality Batjan. Known only from Batjan Island. This race is like *halmaherae* but the crown is much paler, more greyish lilac.

Ethology: From Goodfellow's description of the congregations of adult males in certain areas of the forest it seems certain that the pattern of breeding behaviour employed by this species is of the arena type (see p. 41) with the males living in clans apart from the females.

Twelve-wired Bird of Paradise

Seleucidis melanoleuca (Daudin)
Male 12½ to 13½ in.

Range: Salawati Island and New Guinea except the north-eastern portion from the Markham River valley to about Collingwood Bay; lowland forests. (See Map 9.1., page 85.)

Adult Male: A long-billed velvet black species with yellow abdomen and elongated yellow side plumes tipped on each side with six long wire-like prolongations. In more detail, back and lesser upper wing coverts velvet black glossed oil green; rest of wing coverts and flight quills black glossed pinkish purple; head all around with short velvety black feathering, purplish above, tinged greenish below; neck and upper breast velvet black tinged dusky green; feathers of upper breast long, erectile, and broadly edged iridescent emerald green (forming in display an emerald-rimmed pectoral shield); rest of underparts lemon yellow (fading to white in the dried skin); on each side of breast a tuft of very long ornamental plumes with ivory shafts; on each side six of the ornamental plumes are furnished with blackish wire-like prolongations (up to 300 mm. long) that bend sharply forward along the body; wing linings black. Iris vermilion; bill black; feet flesh yellow; inside of mouth aqua green; bare area behind eye bronze black to black; wing 163–178; tail 64–74; exposed culmen 64; tarsus 41 mm.

Adult Female: Very different from adult male. Top half of head to upper back black; rest of mantle chiefly chestnut brown; primaries with much dark inner edging; underparts generally buffy grey finely barred dusky brown; throat palest with barring subobsolete; under wing coverts buffy ochraceous with chestnut barring; inner edges of wing quills and tail below ochraceous chestnut. Iris red; bill black; feet flesh colour. Female wing 152–163; tail 97–110; exposed culmen 57; tarsus 40 mm.

Remarks: The Twelve-wired Bird of Paradise is confined to lowland forests near the sea and along the edges of lowland rivers and lakes. It was an uncommon species in the two areas where I have seen it in the wild (the lower Brown River near Port Moresby and the middle Sepik River region). Its favourite haunts are in sago and pandanus forests growing amongst tall swamp trees. Near Kanganaman village on the Sepik River I found it breeding and observed the female about ten times as it came to the nest. About two miles down the river near Kararau village, I heard males calling from a clump of big, forest-edge trees. C. H. B. Grant wrote that the males are both wary and scarce and that they frequent taller trees, often in parties of three or four. He recorded the call as a long-drawn *oou* ending in two sharp, loud *wah wah* notes. He noted that the flight is swift and graceful, the wings producing a curious *wish wish* like those of *Ptiloris magnificus*.

Wallace, writing of the Salawati Island population, reported that the Twelve-wired Bird of Paradise frequents flowering trees, especially sago palms and pandanus, sucking the flowers and moving rapidly from tree to tree.

Breeding Behaviour: Sten Bergman (1957:19) observed the Twelve-wired Bird of Paradise displaying in the wild in November near Sworof village, Salawati Island, where the species is called *palengo*. One display area was on a dead branch some eighty feet up in an especially large tree. The first display began at 6.15 a.m. and lasted ten minutes. A single male occupied the lofty perch. A day later the male arrived at the same perch at 6.20 a.m. and displayed intermittently until 6.43 a.m. Again the male displayed alone on its perch. The next morning Bergman visited another display tree and succeeded in observing a male as it received a visit from a female. Bergman wrote (*op. cit.:* 20): 'For some 150 yards we had to walk on the mangrove roots to avoid sinking into the mud, then we came to some bushes on relatively dry ground and there we hid. Some thirty yards away was a tree with a withered branch at its top. The branch rose almost vertically out of the green of the tree and was sixty-five feet from the ground.

'As we landed we had heard a palengo call several times, and at 6.18 one flew up onto this dead branch, but flew off again at once. Three minutes later two of them, a cock and a hen, flew on to the dead branch, but they too flew off again at once. Possibly they had seen one or other of us. Suddenly they alighted on another top branch, it too some thirty yards from me, and the cock began clambering up and down in the same way as I had seen them do on the two previous occasions. The hen came and climbed until she was right under the cock, which now was in complete ecstasy. The two crept round the tree-top. The cock's breastplate was extended, and they both twirled round the top branch several times.

'The cock repeatedly prodded at the hen with its beak. The hen was then above it. I could hear a hissing sound as they were climbing about most eagerly. All at once, when the hen was on top of the branch, the cock flew up and on top of her and mated her. The two then flew off and disappeared. It was then 6.30, but they were not far away, for we could distinctly hear the cock calling.

'At 6.40 the cock returned to the first dead branch. Then two hens appeared. The display continued in the same way as before with the birds in full ecstasy; there was no mating on this occasion, however; and it all came to an end shortly before seven when we returned to our camp.'

L. S. Crandall (1937a and b), who kept a male for nearly twenty-three years in the New York Zoological Park, described its display in captivity. The male, he observed, required seven years to complete the transition from immature to fully adult plumage. He wrote (1937a: 194): 'the bird was observed with his body held parallel to the perch. The green breast plate was widely extended, while the yellow feathers of the lower breast and abdomen were tightly compressed, forming a strong contrast. The short flank plumes were slightly spread in the perpendicular plane, barely extending above and below the body line. With wings tightly closed, the bird leaped sideways to the trunk of the perch, seized it with its powerful feet and turned slowly round it. He frequently repeated a sharp, metallic, single note, opening his mouth widely for each call, showing the bright green interior. When the turn had been completed, the bird leaped back to the branch from which he had started. With the body again stiffy horizontal, breast plate still extended, abdominal feathers still compressed and plumes slightly expanded, the wings were rapidly opened and closed ten or twelve times. The usual rustling sound made by the wings in flight was not detected. The normal position was then assumed. On another occasion the bird spiralled slowly down the trunk of the perch, head downward, instead of going directly around it.'

The peculiar wires for which the species is named were not mentioned by Crandall because they had been broken by cage life. Later, however, they grew in successfully and Crandall was able to discover their position in the display. He found that when '. . . the bird is perching normally the wires extend outward and slightly downward without strict regard to order. In display, with the feathers of the abdomen tightly compressed and the flank plumes slightly expanded . . . there appears to be a muscular pull or tension which causes the wires to rotate slightly. This rotation has the effect of bringing the wires into set alignment . . . in the horizontal plane . . . . In the delicate central pair, the direction is almost entirely downward and forward. This leaves the twelve wires, approximately evenly spaced, extending forward, around, and beneath the bird's body, none rising higher than its level.'

Nesting: The nest which I found in February (see pl. 2b) was a shallow cup of pandanus bark strippings and vines on a scant foundation of sticks and leaves, and was lined with rootlets and plant fibres (measurements: inside 90 × 35; outside 200 × 90 mm.). It was ten feet up in a pandanus palm growing in swampy riverine forest, containing many limbum and some sago palms, also a scattering of tall trees. The nest tree was 150 feet inland from the north bank of the Sepik River at a point about 195 miles above its mouth. The egg, found 22 February 1954, contained a large embryo. It was cream coloured, with longitudinal rufous and greyish streaks concentrated chiefly about the larger end. It measured 40·7 × 26·5 mm.

(On 13 January the same female had begun another nest 12 feet up in a limbum palm. That nest was located about 50 feet from the river in the forest edge, over dry ground.) Males were never seen or heard anywhere near the nests. The female was very shy and secretive; she habitually approached her second nest by flying in deep shadows near the forest floor. When about five feet from the palm, she would fly steeply upward and then land on the level tops of the curving, spine-edged pandanus leaves. The nest was very hard to see from below. It was carefully hidden amongst the leaf bases. Moments after landing, the female would jump to the nest, seem to examine it, and then settle down on the egg with much turning, shuffling, and adjusting of her body. One such arrival I filmed; also, I made a number of still photographs in colour of the female on this nest, one of which was published in the *National Geographic Magazine* (Gilliard, 1955: 468).

A. S. Anthony in 1905 told Colin Simson (1907: 385) that he found the nest of this species and that it contained one egg. This is probably the nest and egg that Rothschild (1899: 13) reported receiving.

Subspecies: Two very similar races differing only in size:

1 *S. m. melanoleuca* (Daudin), 1800, *Traité Orn.*, vol. 2, p. 278. Type locality 'Waigiou,' in error for Salawati or the Vogelkop. Known from Salawati and all of New Guinea except the north coast. Male wing 177–178; tail 70–74 mm. Female wing 157–163; tail 97–110 mm.

2 *S. m. auripennis* Schlüter, 1911, *Falco*, vol. 7, p. 2 [type in AMNH, no. 677823]. Type locality Dallmannshafen (= Wewak), German New Guinea. Known only from northern New Guinea from the Mamberamo River to Astrolabe Bay and the Ramu River.

This race is somewhat smaller: male wing 163–167; tail 64–68 mm. Female wing 152–155; tail 97 mm.

Long-tailed Paradigalla

Paradigalla carunculata Lesson
Male 14–15 in.

Range: Arfak and western Snow mountains between 4800 and 7000 feet. (See Map 9.3, page 107.)

Adult Male: A jay-sized black bird with a moderately long to long wedge-shaped tail (subspecies), naked forehead, glossy crown and large yellow wattles in front of eyes. In more detail, generally black to velvet black, reflecting deep bronze in certain lights, particularly in upperparts and exterior edges of the wings and tail; crown and nape scale-like with glossy deep blue to oil green feathers; sides of head and throat blue black with some glossiness; wattles in front of eye at base of maxilla lemon yellow to yellowish green with some reddish colour on outer edges or clear lemon yellow (subspecies); wattles at basal sides of lower mandible violet blue and yellow orange to orange red beneath or clear lemon yellow (subspecies). Wing 153–195 (subspecies); tail 110–169; exposed culmen 29; tarsus 50 mm.

Adult Female: Like male but generally duller, more blackish and smaller (including wattles); wing 160 mm.

Remarks: The Long-tailed Paradigalla is apparently an elusive species of the mountain forests. Its nest and eggs seem never to have been found and apparently the only observations of the bird in the wild are those of Odoardo Beccari who wrote: 'As to *Paradigalla,* I shot one from my hut, whilst it was eating the small fleshy fruits of an *Urtica.* It likes to sit on the tops of dead and leafless trees, like the *Mino dumontii.* The finest ornaments of this bird are the wattles, which in the dried skin lose all their beauty.

131

The upper ones, which are attached one on each side of the forehead, are of a yellowish green colour; those at the base of the lower mandible are blue, and have a small patch of orange red beneath. The arfaks call the *Paradigalla* "Happoa".'

In 1960 Ripley (1964) collected an adult male in the Ilaga Valley, western Snow Mountains, which confirmed Ogilvie-Grant's description of *intermedia* '. . . and demonstrates that in fact two species, *carunculata* and *brevicauda* are represented in the central highlands.'

Subspecies: Two (after Ripley, 1964):

1 *P. c. carunculata* Lesson, 1835, *Hist. Nat. Ois. Parad.*, p. 242. Type locality Arfak Mountains. Known only from the Arfak Mountains. Male wing 170–195, tail 120–169 mm. Wattles: upper set yellowish green, lower set blue with a small area orange red basally.

2 *P. c. intermedia* Ogilvie-Grant, 1913, *Bull. Brit. Orn. Club.*, vol. 31, p. 105. Type locality Utakwa River, Nassau Range. Known from Utakwa River region and the Ilaga Valley, Nassau Mountains. Male wing 153–157, tail 110 mm. and wedge shaped. Wattles clear lemon yellow, both above and below, iris dark brown, bill and feet black.

Bock (1963: 122) places *Paradigalla* between the *Ptiloris* group (*Ptiloris, Semioptera,* and *Seleucidis*) and the *Drepanornis* group (*Drepanornis* and *Epimachus*) but he warns that the skull anatomy does not supply good evidence and therefore the affinities of the groups should be based on other data. Such data are a knowledge of nest and egg morphology and the patterns of parental care employed by this species. Unfortunately, none of this is yet known in this elusive species.

Short-tailed Paradigalla

Paradigalla brevicauda Rothschild and Hartert
Male 8½ to 9 in.
[1911, *Novit. Zool.*, vol. 18, p. 159 (type in AMNH, no. 678355). Type locality Mt Goliath, West New Guinea.]

Range: Mountains of the trunk of New Guinea (Weyland, Nassau, Oranje, and Victor Emanuel mountains, Mt Giluwe, Mt Hagen,

Bismarck and Schrader mountains) between 5500 and 7800 feet. (See Map 9.3., page 107.)

Adult Male: A stocky, black, slender-billed bird with a glossy cap and large erectile wattles in front of eyes. In more detail, generally black, faintly bronzed on upperparts, forebreast, and throat; exposed margins of secondaries and upper wing coverts narrowly iridescent bronze green; crown and nape with scale-like glossy blue green plumage. Iris blackish brown; bill black; feet dark grey; wattles at base of maxilla in front of eye bright yellow tinged green at bases; wattle at basal sides of mandible bright ultramarine blue on upper aspect and yellow beneath; inside of mouth bluish aqua. Wing 152–160; tail 45–63; exposed culmen 32; tarsus 47 mm.

Adult Female: Closely similar to the male but body plumage more dead black, less bronzed and wattles reduced in size. Wing 147–162; tail 48–63 mm.

Immature: Like adult female but with the tail much longer (up to 95 mm.).

Remarks: The Short-tailed Paradigalla is fairly common in the forest and forest edge of the Wahgi region and uncommon in the Victor Emanuel Mountains where I encountered it only in pure forest. Bulmer (MS no. 1) collected six specimens on the north flank of Mt Hagen between 6000 and 6900 feet. The Schoddes (personal communication) collected a male at 7000 feet on Mt Giluwe, and Stein (1936: 23) observed this species in the Weyland Mountains above 5700 feet, '. . . usually in the crowns of the highest isolated old forest trees in which they hop around in the moss layers of the twigs and forked branches.' Stein recorded the song as a melodic *hüi.* The food of the Short-tailed Paradigalla is chiefly vegetable matter, mainly seeds and small fruits (Bulmer).

Nesting: On 12 January 1956, Mt Hagen, 6000 feet, Bulmer obtained an adult from a native who said he had trapped it on its nest in a bush near gardens. The nest was said to contain one egg which was broken at the time of the trapping. The adult was a female with ova measuring 12 × 7 mm. According to Ogilvie-Grant (1915) the Wollaston–Kloss expedition secured a nest with one nestling '. . . the latter having the wattles on the sides of the face almost as well developed as in the nearly adult male,' but no further description of these specimens seems to be available.

Black-billed Sickle-billed Bird of Paradise

Drepanornis albertisii (Sclater)
Male 14 in.

Range: Widespread in mountainous regions of New Guinea between the altitudes of about 2000 and 7200 feet. (See Map 9.3, page 107.)

Adult Male: A chestnut-tailed, small-headed bird with a very long, slender, curved bill. In more detail, upperparts generally dark rufous brown becoming chestnut to pale ochraceous on rump to tail; sides of head with naked blue streaks extending forward to orbital region; loral region with two small dark iridescent spots; one at base of maxilla steel blue green, and one near front of eye horn-like and violet rose; underside of head black glossed green; underparts sooty brown tinged with purple and with concealed bases on abdomen white; a black band across lower breast glossed purple; at each side of neck a dusky erectile fan tuft (with plumes up to 2½ in. long), tipped with greenish gold; at each side  of breast a dusky, erectile fan tuft (with plumes up to 4 in. long) broadly tipped with amethystine purple; wings below grey brown with ochraceous inner edges. Iris brown; bill black; feet grey. Wing 147–156; tail 125–137; exposed culmen 70–75; tarsus 36 mm.

Adult Female: Upperparts as in male, but iridescent plumage of head replaced by dark brown; no fan tufts; underparts buffy to pale ochraceous with fine irregular barring, strongest on upper breast and with the throat nearly solid dusky brown with fine buff shaft streaks. Wing 142–147; tail 122–126 mm.

Remarks: Despite its wide range very little is known concerning this bird in the field. It seems always to be an elusive species of the mountain forest where it keeps to the topmost branches of the highest trees (Goodwin in Sharpe, 1895, part IV). No one seems to have observed its method of feeding with its remarkably long, curved bull; but a specimen autopsied by Shaw Mayer in the Finisterre Mountains had eaten grasshopper-like insects. Stein (1936: 26) described its call as a series of notes rather like the Green Woodpecker of Europe *üe üe üe üe* which, when repeated, attracted the bird.

Nesting: Ramsay described the nest and egg as follows (Sharpe, 1895, part IV): 'The nest is a thin, rather flat structure, built between a horizontal bough in a fork of a thin branch; it has a slight depression about an inch deep, a network of wire rootlets is stretched across the fork, and the nest proper built on them; it is composed of wiry grasses of a light reddish brown colour, the platform being of black wiry roots .... The egg [which measures 39 × 25 mm.] is of a light dull cream colour, with a reddish tinge, spotted all over with oblong dashes of reddish brown and light purplish grey, closer on the thick end.'

Subspecies: Four rather similar races are known:

1 *D. a. albertisii* (Sclater), 1873 (June), *Nature*, vol. 8, p. 151, and 1873, *Proc. Zool. Soc. London*, p. 558, pl. 47. Type locality Hatam, Arfak Mountains. Range western New Guinea in the Arfak and Wandammen mountains. In this race the upperparts are dark fuscus, the rump and tail are strongly saturated with chestnut brown and the underparts are dusky grey brown.

2 *D. a. inversus* Rothschild, 1936, *Mitt. Zool. Mus. Berlin*, vol. 21, p. 188 [type in AMNH, no. 302362]. Type locality Mt Kunupi, Weyland Mountains. Range: northern slopes of the central ranges from the Weyland to the Sepik mountains at Lordberg. Like *albertisii* but with the upperparts, especially the rump and tail, much paler, more ochraceous brown.

3 *D. a. geisleri* Meyer, 1893, *Abh. Ber. Mus. Dresden*, vol. 4 (1892–3), no. 3, p. 15. Type locality Sattelberg, Huon Peninsula. Known only from the mountains of the Huon Peninsula (Saruwaged, etc.). Like *albertisii* but with the upperparts, especially the rump and tail much paler more ochraceous brown.

4 *D. a. cervinicauda* Sclater, 1883, *Proc. Zool. Soc. London*, p. 578.

L

Type locality 'vicinity of Port Moresby.' Known only from the mountains of south-eastern New Guinea (including the Herzog Mountains). Much like *inversus* but with the rump and tail darker more chestnut, less ochraceous.

Taxonomy: Bock (1963: 122) in his studies of skull anatomy found that *Drepanornis* is very similar to *Paradisaea*. He places this genus (together with *Epimachus*) in a group between *Paradigalla* and *Astrapia*.

White-billed Sickle-billed Bird of Paradise

Drepanornis bruijnii Oustalet
Male 13½ in.
[*Drepanornis Bruijnii* Oustalet, 1880, *Ann. Sci. Nat.*, ser. 6, vol. 9, art. 5, p. 1 and 1880, *Bull. Assoc. Sci. France*, p. 172. Type locality 'coast of Geelvink Bay between 136° 30' and 137° of longitude.']

Range: Known only from the lowland forests of north-western New Guinea, west as far as Waropen on the south-east coast of Geelvink Bay and the Mamberamo basin and east as far as the Tami River 12 miles east of Humboldt Bay. (See Map 9.3, page 107.)

Adult Male: Much like *Drepanornis albertisii* but bill pale, not black, and sides of head largely bare. In more detail, upperparts dark rufous brown becoming rust brown on wings and rump and chestnut on tail; forehead (on midline) and sides of head naked and blue (?) in colour; crown with short blackish feathering glossed pinkish to greenish; side of throat below eye with a large black spot glossed purple; otherwise sides of head and throat blackish glossed oil green on throat and upper breast; sides of lower neck with extensile fan-like tufts glossed oil green at

base and black at tips; with a shorter course of feathers tipped iridescent ruby pink to gold; a second pair of fan-like tufts at sides of upper breast with iridescent violet pink to opalescent green tips; breast and abdomen grey; lesser under wing coverts dark brown; greater coverts, inner edges of remiges and under sides of tail pale ochraceous. Iris brown; bill pale bone brown; naked areas of head greyish brown to purplish brown; feet brown sometimes with a purplish cast. Wing 153–160; tail 109–115; culmen from nostril 66; tarsus 34 mm.

Adult Female: Like male on upperparts, wing, and tail but with the glossy black plumage of the head replaced with dark brown. Underparts very different from male; without feather tufts and generally buffy ochraceous with narrow dark brown barring, especially on breast. Wing 145–151; tail 106–110; culmen from nostril 61; tarsus 32 mm.

Immature: First year plumage much like adult female. Male intermediate plumage like adult male but with the abdomen and sides barred and coloured as in adult female.

Remarks: Apparently this species is very local in the vicinity of rivers near the coast. Specimens with the testes generally enlarged were collected by Mayr in the Humboldt Bay region (native name *Yokwa*) in August and October. Ripley (1964) recently described the call notes of the male as '. . . a loud, not unmusical series of descending whistles reminiscent of the rifle bird's call. From this start came a series of descending whistles, repeated over again, several at a time. In between these extremely loud calls, this male as it moved about in the tree, made several gruff, churring notes rather like a typical *Paradisaea*.'

Black Sickle-billed Bird of Paradise

Epimachus fastosus (Hermann)
Male length 44 in.

Range: The midmountain regions of the trunk of New Guinea and the Vogelkop from about 4200 to 7700 feet. (See Map 9.6, page 166.)

Adult Male: A jay-sized black bird with a relatively huge saber-shaped tail, a long, curved bill and with large erectile fans on sides of breast. In more detail, upperparts jet black tinged with metallic violet; a large area on back and rump glossy blue green; crown with short glossy oil green to blue green plumes; sides of head glossed blue green with some purple tinging; wings and immensely long graduated tail black, the latter strongly glossed above with iridescent purple blue; chin to lower neck blackish tinged with metallic greenish purple; remaining underparts brownish black to dull black; very large erectile fan tufts, one on each side of the upper breast, blackish burnished with some green and with broad mirror-like violet tipping; immediately behind a second larger erectile velvet black fan, forming a background (in display) for the glittering frontal tuft; a similar set of large fan tufts (with black plumes up to 250 mm. long) on each side of lower breast. Iris red to reddish orange; bill black; feet pale blue with blackish toes; postocular bare areas black; inside of mouth egg yellow. Wing 186–222; tail 657–827; culmen from nostril 63; tarsus 53 mm.

Adult Female: Very different from male, without ornamental plumage. Crown dark chestnut, rest of upperparts dull olive brown becoming rusty brown on tail and with chestnut outer edges on wing quills; sides of head and neck, also forebreast to throat blackish brown; rest of underparts greyish with narrow black barring. Wing 153–182; tail 255–270; culmen from nostril 65; tarsus 48 mm.

Juvenal: Like adult female but plumage very soft and somewhat more brownish, less deeply saturated with black; dorsal plumage somewhat brighter.

Immature: First year plumage much like adult female. Male intermediate plumages: (a) like adult female but with the head and neck as in adult male (but retaining a few rufous feathers on crown), some glossy blue black margins on primaries and tail; (b) like adult female but with head and forebody below (including ornamental fans) as in adult male, back with some dark plumes, wings and very long tail with some plumes glossy black or streaked boldly with glossy black; (c) like adult male but with scapulars, some primaries, and secondaries, some shorter rectrices and central abdomen as in adult female.

Remarks: The Black Sickle-billed Bird of Paradise is the largest of the Paradisaeidae. Judging from the many tail plumes of males that I saw in the feather headdresses of Wahgi Valley men in 1950 and 1952, I am tempted to believe that this species is not uncommon in the midmountain forests of that region. However, I failed to collect a single specimen in the southern watersheds of the Kubor, Bismarck, and Hagen mountains, where I collected assiduously for many months. In fact, my only specimen was shot in the northern watershed of Mt Hagen where I collected but briefly. Bulmer, working in the northern watershed region of Mt Hagen, found six specimens in the forest edge and in the forest proper between 6000 and 7000 feet. But somewhat farther west in the south watershed the Schoddes obtained four specimens between 6600 and 7000 feet on Mt Giluwe in 1961.

In the Hindenburg Mountains (north watershed) at 5800 feet I encountered an adult male which called day after day apparently always from one spot not far inside the forest bordering a small clearing in which I had my tent. I failed to find its perch, which was high up in the forest. From there at long intervals throughout the daylight hours it would suddenly burst forth with powerful, liquid, whip-like notes which carried about half a mile and were by all odds the most penetrating sounds to be heard in the forests at that altitude.

Ripley (1957: 207) fared better. He observed the display of this species in late March in the Tamrau Mountains of the Vogelkop: 'A male was sitting very high up on the bare branch of a huge dammer, *Agathis* sp., in a display posture. The pectoral shields were spread out and upwards like two raised arms. The tail was partially spread showing the shorter, outer feathers. A brownish bird, presumably a female, was sitting near on a lower branch. Suddenly the male called, a loud penetrating whistle sounding like the syllable "whick." Then, so rapidly that I could not see the pectoral shield retracted, he turned and dived straight downwards off the branch towards the ground, perhaps a hundred feet below . . . at the bottom of the dive, the male came out with spread wings and sailed back up again to the same branch almost as if on the rebound . . . .'

Nesting: Nest unknown. Ralph Bulmer collected a female with large eggs in its oviduct on 5 February 1955, at about 6000 feet in forests bordering native gardens in Baiyer Valley, north flank of Mt Hagen. A fledgling several weeks out of the nest was collected by A. S. Meek on Mt Goliath, Oranje Mountains, 17 February 1911.

Food: Odoardo Beccari, writing of Vogelkop birds, noted that the Black Sickle-billed Bird of Paradise fed on fruits of certain Pandanaceae, and especially on those of the Freycinetiae, which are epiphytic on the trunks of trees. In three stomachs examined on Mt Hagen, Bulmer found seeds in one, purple fruits in one, and orange brown fruit pulp in one.

Subspecies: Three fairly similar races are known:

1 *E. f. fastosus* (Hermann), 1783, *Tab. aff. Anim.*, p. 194 (based on *Pl. Enlum.*, pls. 638–639). Type locality New Guinea, restricted to the Arfak Mountains by Hartert. Known only from the Arfak and Tamrau mountains of the Vogelkop from 5200 to 7700 feet. This race is generally brownish black with a short wing. Male wing 193–198 mm.

2 *E. f. atratus* (Rothschild and Hartert), 1911, *Novit. Zool.*, vol. 18, p. 160 [type in AMNH, no. 677957]. Type locality Mt Goliath, Oranje Mountains. Known from the west ranges of the trunk of New Guinea (Wandammen, Wondiwoi, Weyland, Nassau, and Oranje mountains). Like *fastosus* but less brownish, more blackish below. Male wing 186–205 mm.

3 *E. f. stresemanni* Hartert, 1930, *Novit. Zool.*, vol. 36, p. 34 [type in AMNH, no. 677964]. Type locality Schraderberg, Sepik Mountains. Known from the east and central ranges of the trunk of New Guinea (Schrader, Hagen, Bismarck, Hindenburg mountains). Like *fastosus* but larger. Male wing 204–222 mm.

Taxonomy: Bock (1963), on the basis of similarities in cranial anatomy, places *Epimachus* and *Drepanornis* in a close-knit group. His observations confirm those of earlier specialists who, on the basis of external morphology, generally reached the same conclusions.

Brown Sickle-billed Bird of Paradise

Epimachus meyeri Finsch
Male 39 in.

Range: Mountains of the trunk and south-eastern peninsula of New Guinea; 5400 to 10,000 feet. (See Map 9.6, page 166.)

Adult Male: A jay-sized dark brown and black bird, very similar to *Epimachus fastosus*, with a very long pointed tail and a long curved bill. In more detail, upperparts black tinged with metallic violet; a large area of back and rump glossy oil green with a bluish cast; crown velvety with short glossy oil green to blue green plumes; wings blackish; chin to upper neck blackish suffused with iridescent bronze purple; sides of head to sides of throat iridescent blue green; rest of underparts dull olive brown suffused with purple at sides; wings and tail black, the latter very long, graduated and strongly glossed above with pale greenish blue; very large erectile fan-tufts on sides of upper breast dark brownish to black burnished with pinkish purple and broadly tipped with iridescent violet  blue; immediately behind the preceding tuft a longer set of fan-tufts sooty black; a similar double set of large fan-tufts (with plumes up to 195 mm.) on each side of lower breast. Iris pale blue; bill and feet black; edges of mouth yellowish green; inside of mouth yellow. Male wing 171–191; tail 520–785; culmen 70; tarsus 53 mm.

Adult Female: Very different from male. Entire crown to hind neck chestnut brown; rest of upperparts dull rust to dull olive brown; base of maxilla, lores and sides of head enclosing eye and ear brownish black; throat blackish brown; underparts buff profusely barred black. Iris bluish white; bill black; mouth yellowish green; feet black. Wing 146–173; tail 225–370; culmen 68; tarsus 47 mm.

Juvenal: Nestling like adult female but mantle brighter, more rust coloured; plumage generally soft and fluffy, especially on abdomen.

Immature: First year plumage much like adult female. Male intermediate plumages: (a) like adult female but crown darker chestnut brown, a narrow margin at base of maxilla, lores, eye ring, chin to central throat iridescent black as in adult male; (b) like adult female but head (including sides and throat), hind neck, centre line of back (with the glossy greenish blue plumes), rump, many rectrices (including the four central plumes) as in adult male; also with the brown dorsal plumage suffused with much black and with the wing quills and upper wing coverts largely black; (c) like adult male but with scapulars, some secondaries, some neck feathering, sides of breast, and entire lower abdomen as in adult female.

Remarks: The Brown Sickle-billed Bird of Paradise is a rather common to very common species of the tall mountain forests. Its immensely elongated, saber-shaped central tail plumes are prized for human ornamentation in the Wahgi region where, during large 'sing sings,' one can often see hundreds of such plumes.

In the mountains bounding the Wahgi Valley two species occur, a black one, *Epimachus fastosus,* and a brown one, *E. meyeri,* whereas to the eastward only the latter occurs. In areas where the two species are found they tend to displace each other altitudinally. Captain N. B. Blood (*in* Iredale, 1950: 92) was the first to note this. He found the Brown Sickle-billed Bird of Paradise at 7850 feet on Mt Hagen and the Black Sickle-billed species at 5500 feet on the same mountain. In 1950 between 8000 and 9500 feet on Mt Hagen I found the brown species to be abundant but my only record of the black species was of a single bird shot at 4000 (?) feet where we rarely collected. The same situation obtained in the Hindenburg Mountains where the brown species was found only above 7000 feet and the black species only below 6000 feet (Gilliard and LeCroy,

1961 : 65). However, in south-eastern New Guinea where only the brown species occurs it ranges down to 5500 feet.

General Habits: The call of the Brown Sickle-billed Bird of Paradise is a sudden loud clatter sounding very much like a pneumatic hammer. On Mt Hagen above 8000 feet this is the most distinctive call to be heard. In 1956, in July, while closely observing Archbold's Bower Bird over a period of several days, I heard the triphammer burst of the Brown Sickle-bill many times. For example, on 14 July, at 8500 feet, this bird called first at 6.48 a.m. – a single short 'burst' of sound. Thereafter until 8.57 a.m. I recorded the call exactly twenty times, twice as single 'bursts,' 17 times as double bursts, and once as a double set of two bursts. The last was deeper than usual and sounded somewhat muted like an air hammer enclosed in a building. These calls were delivered, I believe, by one male as he waited in and very close to his display tree (which I did not see). After a silence of many minutes this male suddenly became very loud, delivering in three minutes' time ten powerful 'air hammer' calls after which much wing thrashing over a period of about a minute was heard from the direction of the display tree.

One male which I observed in July, 1950, on Mt Hagen was flexing its semi-closed wings as it delivered the powerful rattle. It was perched about 40 feet up in a thickly limbed tree (near the trunk) growing at 8500 feet. It remained on its nearly level perch until disturbed, a matter of at least 10 minutes.

Food: Once in the Kubor and once in the Hagen mountains I observed the Brown Sickle-bill as it searched for food in the middle portions of a large tree in deep forest. It jumped along mossy limbs near the trunk of the trees. The Mt Hagen bird worked up the trunk and its nearby limbs beginning about 15 feet from the ground. Shaw Mayer (*in* Sims, 1956: 423) found berries, grasshoppers, other insects and various other fruits in specimens that he autopsied on Mt Hagen and Mt Wilhelm. The writer found hard green fruits in the mouth of one specimen and Rand noted a specimen with stomach contents consisting of 80 per cent *Elaeocarpus* fruit and 20 per cent insects. Another of Rand's specimens had eaten 'large insects.'

Courtship Behaviour: The powerful sounds noted above are doubtless important components of the courtship displays in this species. They always seem to emanate from solitary males who remain for long periods in special trees. It seems most likely that such males are in auditory contact with other males scattered through the forest, and that the males are not positioned at random, but in large arenas.

Crandall's description (1932: 82) of a male displaying in captivity probably gives us a valid picture of the displays which take place in the wild. He wrote that the male first gave its rattling call and then '. . . turned his body so that the breast was directed upward, his feet retaining their original position on the perch. The breast feathers were spread as widely as possible (which was not very much in the immature bird), lapping over the tightly closed wings. The tail was partly spread. This position was held stiffly for about ten seconds; the bird then moved rapidly about the cage, returned to the original spot and repeated the display.'

After the male had acquired adult plumage, Crandall wrote, it displayed like the immature male, but the display was more complicated: 'Standing normally on the perch, the bird expanded the feathers of the breast, taking some time to arrange the short decorative flank plumes, which extended outward, forming a fringe around the sides. He then gave his rattling call and turned the breast upward . . . the breast feathers now spread to their fullest extent, the bird's body appearing flattened. The short feathers of the upper breast turned upward about the head, circling the throat so closely that the iridescent black of the face and throat became very conspicuous. The wings were closely folded and the tail was slightly spread, though not vibrating or moving. The beak was closed.'

Crandall observed a second form of display in the adult male: 'In this phase, the bird sits in the normal position, ostensibly preening the loosely extended breast feathers and pectoral shields. Suddenly, without calling, the body is drawn erect, with tail very slightly opened, wings tightly closed. The breast feathers, encircled by the decorative flank plumes, are widely spread. The pectoral shields are thrown straight upward, so that they extend far above the head, wrapping it closely. At the upper extremity, the shields are narrow and compressed; at their bases they broaden gradually, to pick up the line of the spread breast feathers. The beak is widely opened, to show the bright yellow lining of the mouth. This position is usually held rigidly for about five seconds . . . . Sometimes, when in this frozen attitude, with the feet firmly grasping the perch . . . the bird rotates his body in a series of short jerks, pausing for several seconds at the end of each, until it is at right angles with the axis of the perch. He then jerks slowly in the opposite direction until he has again come to a right angle with the perch facing the other way. This movement may be continued for from two to five minutes.'

Nesting: A nest with one well incubated egg brought into my camp on 21 April 1950, had been collected by a native at about 8000 feet in the Kubor Mountains behind Kup. The nest was a cup of stringy living moss and slender vines attached to slender crotch limbs of a small tree which grew in the substage of the mountain forest. The nest was lined with slender rootlets and a few skeletonised leaves. It measured, externally, 175 × 100 deep; internally 95 × 45 mm. The single egg was oval, cinnamon in colour with bold brown, grey, and reddish brown longitudinal streaks (mostly on the larger end) and with a sprinkling of small brown and lavender spots. The egg measured 40 × 27·5 mm. Also I obtained a nest with one nestling (see above) about ready to fledge on 14 July 1950, on Mt Hagen at about 8500 feet.

Subspecies: Four rather similar races are known:

1 *E. m. meyeri* Finsch, 1885, *Zeitschr. Ges. Orn.,* vol. 2, p. 380. Type locality Hufeisengebirge, south-eastern New Guinea. Known from south-eastern New Guinea and westward as far as Mt Misim in the Herzog Mountains. Flank plumes pale brown; culmen 70 mm.

2 *E. m. bloodi* Mayr and Gilliard, 1951, *Amer. Mus. Novit.,* no. 1524, p. 10 [type in AMNH, no. 348211]. Type locality Mt Hagen. Known from the central highlands (Giluwe, Hagen, Kubor, Wahgi Divide and Bismarck mountains). Like *meyeri,* with the flank plumes grey.

3 *E. m. albicans* (van Oort), 1915, *Zool. Meded.,* Leiden, vol. 1, p. 228. Type locality Treub Mountains. Known from central New Guinea (Oranje, Hindenburg, and Victor Emanuel mountains). Like *meyeri* but with the flank plumes whitish.

4 *E. m. megarhynchus* Mayr and Gilliard, 1951, *Amer. Mus. Novit.,* no. 1524, p. 10 [type AMNH, no. 677998]. Type locality Gebroeders Mountains. Known only from the Weyland Mountains. Like *meyeri* but bill longer; culmen 80 mm.

Evolutionary Conclusions: From the meager ethological information now available it seems likely that the display patterns of both species of *Epimachus* are of the arena type.

Ecological evidence (see above) suggests that the two species occupy similar niches and that they are ecological competitors in all areas in which they come into contact. Thus they tend to exclude each other altitudinally but with some overlap and with the brown species tending to be better adapted to conditions at higher altitudes. No hybrids are known. The chief isolating mechanisms operating between these very similar-appearing species are probably their very different call notes (a) the machine-gun clatter of the brown species and (b) the melodious, liquid whip sound of the black species.

Arfak Astrapia Bird of Paradise

Astrapia nigra (Gmelin)
Male 29–31½ in.
[*Paradisea nigra* Gmelin, 1788, *Syst. Av.*, vol. 1, pt. 1, p. 401. Type locality 'Oceanic Islands,' restricted to Arfak Mountains.]

Range: Known only from the Arfak Mountains from 5400 to 7100 feet. (See Map 9.5, page 150.)

Adult Male: A green-bellied, jay-sized black bird with a slender black bill, a very long, broad tail (up to 23½ in.) and much iridescence. In more detail, upperparts blackish burnished with purple and bronze; crown, nape and sides of neck blackish glossed with blue and purple; nape with an erectile fan-tuft of long iridescent green broad tipped feathers; sides of nape and neck with long velvet black feathers; wings and tail black tinged purple violet; side of head with a vivid pinkish copper line from eye along neck to shoulders then across breast to form a broad copper band;

146

chin and throat blackish tinged purple blue; lower throat and upper breast black; lower breast and abdomen oil green with some glossy blue green tipping forming a line on sides; sides of body and under tail coverts sooty black. Iris dark brown; bill black; feet grey brown. Wing 178–184; tail 515–563; central pair of tail plumes 65 mm. broad; culmen from nostril 25; tarsus 43 mm.

Adult Female: Very different from male. Generally brownish; head and fore part of body blackish brown faintly glossed purple; rest of underparts dusky brown narrowly barred with buff; wing quills above with narrow rufous edges, below with ochraceous inner edges; tail brownish; iris brown; bill and feet black. Wing 155–165; tail 312–325; culmen from nostril 25; tarsus 43 mm.

Immature: First year plumage much like adult female. Male intermediate plumage like adult female but upperparts generally blackish brown and with the exposed edges of the wing quills solid blackish brown without rufous edging; underparts generally blackish without barring or with traces of barring on lower abdomen.

Remarks: The dazzling beauty of this bird was best expressed by the great French ornithologist F. Levaillant, who, after studying specimens in Sir Joseph Bank's collection '. . . rendered homage . . . with the appropriate name "*L'Incomparable*" ' (Stresemann, 1954). But despite its great beauty the Arfak Astrapia still remains little known in life. Its home was discovered in 1872 by Odoardo Beccari in the high forests of the Vogelkop. It lives, Beccari said, only on the highest and most difficult peaks of the Arfak Mountains, and males in adult plumage are rare, perhaps because they take some years to develop this plumage. Beccari noted that the Arfak Astrapia feeds on the fruits of certain Pandanaceae, especially those of the Freycinetiae. He wrote that the neck feathers are erectile and expand into a magnificent collar around the head.

Taxonomy: The five species of *Astrapia* form a closely knit superspecies which all recent authorities place immediately above the *Epimachus* group.

Splendid Astrapia Bird of Paradise

Astrapia splendidissima Rothschild
Male 15–18 in.

Range: Weyland, Nassau, and Snow mountains eastward to the Hindenburg and Victor Emanuel mountains. Found between 5800 and 10,000 feet, rarely up to 11,000 feet. (See Map 9.5, page 150.)

Adult Male: A green-bellied jay-sized black bird with a slender black bill, a long black and white tail (up to 10 in. long) and with much green, gold, and purple iridescence. In more detail, back blackish suffused with iridescent pinkish purple, becoming blackish on rump and upper tail coverts; head with short stubbly plumes bronze green; neck with a cape-like collar extending to back and glossy green; hind and sides of neck tinged purple; a glossy reddish copper stripe from under eye to sides of breast thence joining on upper breast; abdomen oil green with glossy green tips forming a line along sides; rest of underparts blackish; wings blackish; tail blackish brown, the central pair of rectrices white (with ivory white shafts) on basal two-thirds; the two rectrices adjoining central pair with some white on basal halves. Iris dark brown to blackish; bill black; inside of mouth pale yellow tinged aqua; feet silvery blue grey. Wing 130–142; tail 193–245; culmen from nostril 25; tarsus 40 mm.

Adult Female: Very different from male. Generally brownish black above, darkest (with a dull greenish gloss) on head and neck; neck and upper breast blackish brown; rest of underparts buffy to ochraceous profusely barred blackish; the central pair of rectrices with broad white bases, the next pair with some white; under wing coverts like abdomen but with rufous tipping. Iris grey brown; bill black; feet lead grey. Wing 129–138; tail 191–248; culmen from nostril 25; tarsus 40 mm.

Juvenal: Nestling like adult female but plumage very soft and fluffy.

148

Immature: Like adult female but crown and hind neck deep chestnut brown. Male intermediate plumages: (a) like adult female but underparts appearing darker due to somewhat narrower light barring; (b) like adult female but central throat and central crown from line between eyes glossy green; hind neck and upper back with scattered green and ruby-coloured iridescent feathers; (c) like adult male but lower breast to under tail coverts much as in adult female (but with some patches of sea-green feathering).

Remarks: In the Snow Mountains this species is uncommon from 5800 to 6800 feet, common from 7000 to 9000 feet, uncommon at 10,300 feet and rare at 10,900 feet (Rand, 1942b: 496). The writer found that the adult male of the Splendid Astrapia, if not rare, is an extremely difficult bird to find. In the Hindenburg Mountains in 1954 (Gilliard and LeCroy, 1961: 67) 250 man-hours of hunting were required to bring down two adult males and during that time fewer than ten males were observed, yet females and young males were fairly common at all elevations surveyed above 6500 feet. This situation has nothing whatever to do with plume hunting since this species is rarely hunted by the local inhabitants. In the Victor Emanuel Mountains where four adult males were collected during 150 man-hours of hunting, the writer had the good fortune to observe an adult male and then collect it on 11 May 1954. In manner typical of the males, it was solitary and it moved methodically through the heavily moss-covered limbs and trunks of the forest, never staying long in one spot. I watched it working along moss-covered limblets, flying down to lower limbs, to scan their mossy surfaces as if apparently searching for insect food. I was in the shadows of a very steep-walled, mist-enshrouded forest. The male flew to a limb 15 feet up close to the trunk of a large, steeply sloping tree trunk. It then jumped to the trunk and ascended its upper side until I shot it. The trunk was moss-covered on its upper surface. The male moved upward rather slowly over the moss. The stomach of this male contained many coral-coloured pandanus seeds averaging 11 mm. long, which I recognised as belonging to a palm found frequently above 6000 feet which grows to a height of about 40 feet.

Of 15 specimens autopsied by the Archbold Expedition in the Snow Mountains (Rand, 1942b: 197), 12 stomachs contained fruit, one a lizard, one a frog, and two contained insect remains.

Nesting: A nestling was collected on 4 November 1938, at 7000 feet in the Mt Wilhelmina region (Archbold Expedition). The nest and egg apparently remain undiscovered.

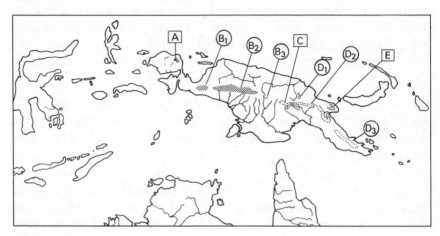

Map 9.5 *Astrapia*

Astrapia nigra (A) 5400 to 7100 feet

Astrapia splendidissima (B) 5800 to 10,000 feet

　Astrapia splendidissima splendidissima (B1)

　Astrapia splendidissima helios (B2)

　Astrapia splendidissima elliottsmithi (B3)

Astrapia mayeri (C) 7800 to 10,800 feet

Astrapia stephaniae (D) 5000 to 9500 feet

　Astrapia stephaniae feminina (D1)

　Astrapia stephaniae ducalis (D2)

　Astrapia stephaniae stephaniae (D3)

Astrapia rothschildi (E) 4800–7500 feet

Subspecies: Three rather similar subspecies are known:

1　*A. s. splendidissima* Rothschild, 1895, *Novit. Zool.,* vol. 2, p. 59, pl. 5 [type in AMNH, no. 678036]. Type locality 'probably Charles-Louis Mountains,' type came almost certainly from the Weyland Mountains. Known only from the Weyland Mountains eastward to the Wissel Lake district. Back pinkish purple, tail short with relatively small spatula-shaped tips.

2　*A. s. helios* Mayr, 1936, *Amer. Mus. Novit.,* no. 869, p. 3 [type in AMNH, no. 448981]. Type locality Mt Goliath, Oranje

Mountains. Known only from the Oranje and Nassau mountains and from the mountains of the upper Mamberamo River. Like *splendidissima* but larger and with a longer tail.

3 *A. s. elliottsmithi* Gilliard, 1961, *Amer. Mus. Novit.*, no. 2031, p. 3 [type in AMNH, no. 648726]. Type locality Mt Ifal, alt. 7200 feet, Victor Emanuel Mountains. Known only from the Hindenburg and Victor Emanuel mountains. Like *splendidissima* but back darker, more plum purple and tail longer with larger spatula-shaped tips.

Behaviour: It is most probable that the Splendid Astrapia is an arena bird with the adult males living apart from the females and young males.

Ribbon-tailed Bird of Paradise

Astrapia mayeri Stonor
Male 42–46 in.
[*Astrapia mayeri*, Stonor, 1939, (Feb.), *Bull. Brit. Orn. Club*, vol. 59, p. 57. Type locality 'Eighty to a hundred miles west of Mt Hagen [Station]' [= Mt Hagen].

Range: Mt Hagen and Mt Giluwe west along the main cordillera to the mountains of the Wabag and Strickland region; from 7800 to 10,800 feet. (See Map 9.5, page 150.)

Adult Male: A jay-sized black bird with a small black bill, much iridescence on fore body and with a very long (up to 38 inches) slender white tail. In more detail, upperparts velvet black suffused with bronze green in certain lights; a large pom-pom (nasal tuft) concealing basal half of bill; crown, sides of head, throat and upper breast iridescent yellow green tinged purple on throat and upper breast; ear coverts, sides and back of head glossed violet purple; upper breast with a broad black band suffused bronze followed by a narrow iridescent copper red band; breast black with much copper red; lower breast and abdomen black glossed slightly oil green; under tail and under wing coverts black tinged purple; wing quills blackish brown; rectrices blackish (and pointed) except central pair about 97 per cent white with narrow black tips (and very narrow and excessively elongated in relation to rest). Iris dark brown; bill black; feet dark grey; mouth pale greenish yellow. Wing 172–180;

M

tail 857–995; culmen from nostril 18; culmen from nasal tuft 10; tarsus 45 mm.

Adult Female: Very different from male. Crown and nape dull iridescent green; upperparts blackish tinged brown on rump and tinged dark blue on upper back; head and neck all around blackish glossed greenish blue; chin, throat, and upper breast blackish somewhat glossed blue; breast and abdomen buffy brown to rufous, rather heavily barred with black; wings and tail, except central rectrices, dark brown; central pair of rectrices sometimes solid dark brown but usually with variable amounts of white (on basal two-thirds) and often with dark shafts and dark fringing enclosing the elongated white areas; under wing coverts dark brown tipped rufous. Iris dark brown; bill black; feet dark grey; wing 153–160; tail 284–351; culmen from nostril 18; tarsus 40 mm.

Juvenal: Like adult female but plumage very soft and fluffy. Upperparts black with a faint greenish cast; underparts to upper breast brownish black; rest of breast and abdomen buffy with blackish bars.

Immature: (See Mayr and Gilliard, 1952: 5). First year plumage much like adult female. Male intermediate plumages: (a) like adult female but lower flanks, abdomen, and under tail coverts blackish with weak buff to brown barring; not light buff to rufous, heavily barred with black; under wing coverts solid blackish brown; not dark brown with strong buff to rufous tips; (b) Like adult female but upperparts more highly glossed, more pinkish purple (but not deeply bronzed black as in the adult male); sides of head and throat brighter oil to yellow green; sides of neck and a broad area of upper breast blackish strongly suffused with purplish blue; lower breast and abdomen dusky with few traces of barring; central rectrices usually broadly striped with white on both vanes but in this character highly variable and probably strongly influenced by age (less than 10 per cent have central pairs of rectrices solid brown; 50 per cent have tail less than half white; about 40 per cent have tails between 50 and 80 per cent white). The fully adult plumage probably requires four to five years to develop.

Remarks: The Ribbon-tailed Bird of Paradise, or Shaw Mayer's Bird of Paradise, as the describer named it (Stonor, 1939), probably will go down in history not only as the last but as one of the most wonderful species of this extraordinary family to be discovered. One of the most fascinating aspects of this discovery is that the species was named and its relationships defined to a fine degree of accuracy from a mere few feathers! The species is named for a great field naturalist and New Guinea explorer, Fred Shaw Mayer, who for some 30 years had lived and collected in the interior of the great island. The discovery is documented in the following letter (*op. cit.*) which Shaw Mayer wrote to Sims on 16 December 1938:

'I am sending you two tail-feathers of a new Bird of Paradise (*Astrapia?*). Briefly the history of the white-tailed bird; the first mention of a new Bird of Paradise, is in the late J. G. Hide's book "Papuan Wonderland" published 1936; on p. 106: "As I stood in the branches of this tree gazing at the rock and heather-covered summit of the peaks in front of me, I noticed pairs of an interesting species of paradise birds flitting through moss-covered branches of the trees around me. The males had two long ivory-white feathers as a tail, with which they made flicking noises as they trailed the plumes after them through the air. I did not know the species, so for the information of our ornithological department, I instructed one of the police to shoot a male bird, remove the tail-feathers, and carefully pack them away." On this expedition Mr Hides was accompanied by Mr O'Malley, a patrol officer. In December, of last year I met Mr O'Malley and questioned him about the birds.

'He remembered them quite well, and described the bird as being black in some lights and showing colours in others. Very true of the *Astrapias*. I was able to show him my live Princess Stephanie's (*A. stephaniae*), and he agreed they were very like these birds, only the body was a little smaller and, of course, had the two long white tail-feathers. He could not tell me what happened to the two feathers they brought back. He said the beak was short and not long like that of my live *Epimachus*. In May of this year I had a long talk with the Fox brothers, two New Guinea miners, who also made a remarkable journey of some hundreds of miles through the wild country west of Mt Hagen.

'They remembered meeting the white-tails well, some eighty to a hundred miles west of Mt Hagen. The natives of that part wore the tail-feathers in their hair.

'The Fox brothers memories were better, as they thought these feathers had a black tip. They described the bird much as O'Malley did, and remarked about the flicking of the tail-feathers. They brought nothing back, but thought one of their boys might have saved a feather or two from a native's head. However, nothing turned up.

'In the middle of last August I was given by a missionary the two tail-feathers I am sending you. They were taken out of the hair on the head of a Mt Hagen native. The bird is *not* found though in the Mt Hagen district, but about eighty to a hundred miles west of it. It was a very great joy to see the feathers. I was surprised to find them so narrow . . . . I give the feathers to the Museum quite freely.'

Stonor lost no time in publishing his findings and it was well he did because the same month Roy Kinghorn of the Australian Museum received a whole specimen (which he named *macnicolli* in honour of the Administrator of Papua-Territory of New Guinea). Kinghorn's type was one of three birds collected by Taylor and Black on their epic journey from Mt Hagen to Telefomin and return. The birds were obtained, Taylor wrote, '. . . in the forested range of the main cordillera west and north-west of Mt Hagen between longitude 143 degrees 30 minutes east and 142 degrees 30 minutes east on both sides of the Strickland (Fly, Yuat, Sepik) watershed . . . . The species appears to be confined to altitudes between 8000 and 10,000 feet above sea level, and is more numerous at 9,000 feet than at any other height.'

From 1 to 28 July 1950, I worked from camps located between 8400 and 11,200 feet on the south slopes of Mt Hagen. During this period much effort was made to study and collect the Ribbon-tail. The species was found in tall original forests from about 7800 feet to about 10,000 feet. Generally, it was quite common as it is on Mt Giluwe where, in 1961, the Schoddes obtained 18 skins between 8000 and 10,000 feet.

The natives of the Tomba area (south watershed) of Mt Hagen call the male *Kugo* and the female *Togi*. One male in fully adult plumage that I watched for several minutes as it fed 40 to 50 feet from me had a large round pom-pom which nearly matched the size and colour of large soft tree buds upon which it fed. The male moved about slowly as it fed, leaning down steeply to get at the buds so that at times its great white tail kited out of control over its head, or it dragged the tail like a narrow train through outer limblets and vines in searching for food. It kept mostly to the short, vine-covered middle limbs of a very tall tree growing in the edge of an open forest glade in which I stood. Once it flew over the little clearing to another tree where it continued feeding in silence. Its action in leaving the tree was beautiful and I immediately sketched it in my journal. It had been feeding amongst short limblets, flowers, and vines near the main trunk some 40 feet up, when suddenly it dived out in a deep arc, its white tail streaming behind it like a wake. Not until it was 10 to 20 feet on its way did it open its wings and then arc out and upward to a nearby tree in the forest edge where it landed in the middle limbs.

Watching through glasses, I saw it turn its head sharply and often to meet the partly opened green buds head on. It picked gently at the buds as though to open them.

Food: Four specimens from between 9000 and 10,000 feet autopsied by Bulmer had seeds in their stomachs, and Shaw Mayer found that some of his specimens from Mt Giluwe and Mt Hagen had eaten 'fruits and green berries' (Sims, 1956: 425).

Breeding Behaviour: In March, 1952, at the Taronga Zoological Park, Sydney, Australia, I was watching an adult male when it suddenly emitted a raucous *grrrow, grr, grr*. This bird was perched about two feet from an adult female. It next stood sidewise as though looking at the ground with one eye, at the same time it let its wings droop, then held them over the back. Suddenly it flew forcefully from perch to perch (six feet), thumping the cross bars with its feet, then pausing to flick its tail like an angry cat. The whole performance was shortlived, it took place in hot sunlight at 3 p.m. (Mayr and Gilliard, 1954: 358).

At 10 a.m., 27 July 1950, at about 9000 feet on the south flank of Mt Hagen I watched a solitary adult male as it basked in sunlight in the uppermost limbs of a large tree in tall open mountain forest. During the ten or more minutes of observation (during which I made telephoto shots of it) this individual preened almost continuously, paying much attention to the grooming of its rump and tail. In so doing it often moved the spectacular white tail far to the side or even obliquely forward (Mayr and Gilliard, 1952: 11).

Nesting: The writer purchased five nests from natives in the Hagen Mountains. One, received 11 July 1950, contained a live nestling, about eight days old (see above). This nest, which externally measures 10 in. in diameter by 4 in. deep, is dish-shaped. It is composed mostly of thin arboreal rootlets and vines, with a few fragments of thick leaves mixed in. Many of the vines were coiled spring-like and some were alive and decorated with small green leaves.

Hybridisation: '*Astrachia barnesi*' of Iredale (1948: 162) from the Mt Hagen district is a hybrid between *A. mayeri* and *A. stephaniae* (Mayr and Gilliard, 1952: 9). A narrow zone in which these species hybridise rather freely was discovered at Yanka on the east slopes of the main Hagen Range by Shaw Mayer. See annotations under *A. stephaniae* for details.

Taxonomy: Stonor (1939) and Mayr and Gilliard (1952) are agreed that although *A. mayeri* and *A. stephaniae* hybridise rather freely in one narrow zone of contact, both are good biological species and not 'glorified subspecies.' For one reason, *A. mayeri* differs from all other Astrapias by having the tail very narrow and pointed, and the tail of much greater length and of different proportions. For another reason, the two types hybridise rather than intergrade in the zone of overlap; and for still another reason, the two appear to live side by side, one above the other, on Mt Giluwe without appreciable hybridisation.

Princess Stephanie Bird of Paradise

Astrapia stephaniae (Finsch)
Male 30-33 in.

Range: South-eastern New Guinea westward to the north-eastern slopes of Mt Hagen (where it slightly overlaps and hybridises with *A. mayeri*); and to Mt Giluwe (where it lives side by side with *A. mayeri*); from 5000 to 9500 feet.

Adult Male: A jay-sized black bird with a black bill, much green, purple and copper iridescence on forebody, and with a very long, broad tail. In more detail, upperparts black, somewhat glossed oil green; forehead and lores glossy yellow green; crown and nape iridescent green tinged violet; sides of head to hind neck glossed purple; sides of head about eye, throat, neck and upper breast iridescent yellowish green tinged blue; a broad pectoral band black with bronze reflections, followed by a glittering reddish copper band; lower breast and abdomen dark copper brown to blackish with some indistinct oil green barring; sides of body, under tail coverts, wings and tail black; central rectrices very broad and long but rather evenly graduated in relation to rest with bright iridescent pinkish purple reflections in certain lights and with white shafts on basal halves (and sometimes with narrow white feather bases). Iris dark brown; bill black; feet bluish grey; mouth pale green. Wing 165–169; tail 639–655; culmen from nostril 22; culmen from nasal tuft 22; tarsus 44 mm.

Adult Female: Very different from male: upperparts black to dusky brown on lower back; head and forebody below black, slightly glossed with dull green; rest of underparts buffy ochraceous with black bars; wings and tail blackish brown. Iris brownish grey; bill black; feet dark slate. Wing 152–155; tail 332–364; culmen from nostril 23; tarsus 42 mm.

Juvenal: Plumage very soft and fluffy. Upperparts black with a faint bluish cast; underparts to upper breast brownish black; rest of underparts buffy with blackish barring. Iris brownish grey; bill black; feet dark bluish grey.

Immature: First year plumage much like adult female. Male intermediate plumages: (a) like adult female but forehead, crown, and chin glossed yellow green; (b) like adult female but entire head, throat, and upper breast iridescent as in adult male.

Remarks: This beautiful bird of paradise, discovered in 1884 by Carl Hunstein on Horseshoe Mountain in the Owen Stanley Mountains, was named for the Crown Princess of Austria. In the mountains where it was discovered it is difficult to find, chiefly because of the rough terrain, but in the Wahgi Highlands it is very common between 5500 and 8000 feet. It is easily observed in the forests bordering the valley and the long pairs of central tail plumes of the male are highly valued articles of native adornment. At Katumbag village in the Kubor Mountains at 5600 feet in June 1952, I found that of 54 Papuans participating in a small 'sing

sing' dance, 26 wore the elongated twin tail plumes of the adult male Princess Stephanie Bird of Paradise. One man wore four sets and many had two sets. The plumes were always worn like giant stick-pins standing straight up from the head.

General Habits: In the Wahgi Highlands and probably throughout the range of this species females and young males are fairly common and are met with singly or in small parties. The mature males are, however, very uncommon. Since this is precisely the situation which I encountered in *A. splendidissima,* a species which is under no pressure whatsoever from local feather hunters, I strongly suspect that the males live away from the females and young males during much of the year, perhaps in organised clans which congregate in certain highland areas. The following observations reinforce this hypothesis.

On Mt Wilhelm at 9500 feet in mid-June, 1950, native hunters showed me a dance tree in which many males were said to have been killed by certain Chimbu Valley natives who 'owned' the tree (see Mayr and Gilliard, 1954, pl. 28, 2, for a photograph of this tree). The tree, an especially tall, straight-shafted one, growing to a height of about 100 feet in mountain forest averaging 75 feet in height, held a house-like 'blind' in its upper limbs. This structure, which was not new, was reached by means of a permanent ladder which had been constructed with a considerable skill and care. It is possible that a clan of males used this remote tree as their principal display arena and that it is by the use of 'hunting stands' such as this that the bow and arrow hunters are able to collect so many adult males of a species which European hunters armed with shot-guns find very hard to collect.

Voice: A male in captivity uttered fairly shrill *quee quee* notes; a female gave an occasional weak, cat-like *meow*. In flight the male makes a rustling sound.

Ecology, Food, Movements: For these points I shall refer to observations which I made on the north-east flank of Mt Hagen at 8000 feet, at 4 p.m. on 13 May 1952 (Mayr and Gilliard, 1954: 357).

'A male with a long black tail was seen moving about in the crown limbs of a rain forest tree heavily decorated with arboreal plants and moss. The junior author watched this bird for 20 minutes from a position of equal height on a neighbouring ridge.

The bird hopped agilely about, flew twice to trees 40 to 50 yards away only to return quickly. It seemed to prefer large horizontal or gently pitched limbs. On these it worked its way along the mossy tops, dragging the giant tail like a train. Often it bent down and worked its head as though excavating in the moss. It nudged the green covering forward or pulled it back with the bill. Several times as it dug it backed up, causing the outer foot of the two long tail feathers to drop like a pendulum from the side of the limb. Once it flew to a near-by tree and ate small green fruits growing in the canopy. To get to these it crawled almost cat-like on the tiny outer limbs bearing the fruit.'

In five specimens from Mt Hagen collected between 6600 and 8000 feet, Bulmer (MS₂) found seeds in the stomach of one, fruit and seeds in two, vegetable matter and seeds in one and insects in one. Shaw Mayer (*in* Sims, 1956: 425) observed this species apparently '. . . hunting for insects in the moss covering the branches of the trees; one bird was seen to swallow what was probably a spider.'

Breeding Behaviour: The male, which I observed on Mt Hagen after feeding '. . . flew to a horizontal limb 50 feet up and well under the canopy. It perched across the limb with its tail hanging in a wide inverted V. The bird then displayed by lifting the wings in a most peculiar manner as though stretching, so that the primaries were held up at right angles to the body and the wrists were held in a touching position over the back. The head was pulled down in a crook. This position was held for at least three seconds. The bird, which was solitary (and silent) then flew off.'

Nesting: Apparently the only record of the nest is the following which I find in Bulmer's manuscript (MS₂):

'Specimen 219 [♀, ova cluster 11 mm. long. Ambulama?, 8000 feet?, north slopes of Mt Hagen] was shot at the nest on 7th October, 1955 by my shoot boy. The nest, which he brought back, was a thick shallow structure of large leaves and creeper, lined with root fibres. External dimensions 7½″ diameter by 3½″ deep. Internal dimensions 4½″ diameter by 1¾″ deep. The single egg was dropped and lost when the nest was taken, so I did not see it.'

The only specimen of an egg that I find recorded is a single egg collected by A.S.Anthony in the Owen Stanley Mountains at about 8000 feet. Hartert (1910: 488) describes it as 'smooth, glossy, light brown, with deep longitudinal dashes from the thick end downwards, a few spots on the thick end, and paler brownish red spots.' Measurements 36·5 × 25·4 mm.

I collected nestlings from natives on Mt Hagen at 7500 feet (14 May 1952) and on Mt Wilhelm at 9000 feet (7 June 1950).

Subspecies: Three quite similar races are recognised:

1   *A. s. feminina* Neumann, 1922, *Ver. Orn. Ges. Bayern,* vol. 15, p. 236. Type locality Schraderberg. Known only from the Schrader Mountains. Differs from *stephaniae* and from *ducalis* by having underparts more rufous, less buffy.

2   *A. s. ducalis* Mayr, 1931, *Mitt. Zool. Mus. Berlin,* vol. 17, p. 711. Type locality Dawong, Herzog Mountains. Known from Giluwe, Hagen, Wahgi Divide, Kubor, Bismarck and Herzog mountains. Wing female 145–151 (av. 146) mm.

3   *A. s. stephaniae* (Finsch and Meyer), 1885, *Zeitschr. Ges. Orn.,* vol. 2, p. 378. Type locality Hufeisengebirge. Known only from the Owen Stanley range of south-eastern New Guinea. Like *ducalis* but larger, female wing 147–156 (av. 151) mm.

Hybrids: In 1952 I visited an area on the north-eastern flank of Mt Hagen where this species and *Astrapia mayeri* hybridise. The majority of specimens that I encountered near my camp at 7500 feet closely resembled *A. stephaniae* but many of the adult males showed traces (longer tail) of hybridisation with *A. mayeri,* the species found at higher elevations above my camp and exclusively on the south side of Mt Hagen. One male with a very long tail (839 mm.) had the tail broadly streaked and partially margined with white. As Shaw Mayer pointed out (*in* Sims, 1956: 425) the 'overlapping areas (between *A. stephaniae* and *A. mayeri*) where hybridization takes place are small . . . .'

In 1951 Shaw Mayer found both species on Mt Giluwe, *A. stephaniae* at 8500 feet and *A. mayeri* at 9000 feet. This discovery was repeated in 1961 when the Schoddes also got both species on Mt Giluwe, the first at 7000 feet, the latter at 8000 to 10,000 feet. Thus, Mt Hagen and Mt Giluwe are the only known areas in New Guinea which support two species of *Astrapia.* In May 1964 the author ascended Mt Kominjim in the Schrader Mountains to 8500 feet in quest of the unknown male of *feminina.* The unusual glossiness of the five females collected in 1912 on Schraderberg had led him to suspect that the unknown male of *feminina* was the Ribbon-tail. He found only dark astrapias which clearly belonged to the species *A. stephaniae*. Since he failed to find females which had the glossiness of Bürgers' specimens, there remains the strong possibility that two *Astrapia* species occur in the Schrader Mountains as on Mt Hagen and Mt Giluwe.

Huon Astrapia Bird of Paradise

Astrapia rothschildi Foerster
Male 25–27 in.
[*Astrapia rothschildi* Foerster, 1906, *Two New Birds of Paradise*, p. 2 (type in AMNH, no. 678080). Type locality Rawlinson Mountains.]

Range: Known only from the Rawlinson and Saruwaged mountains of the Huon Peninsula, from 4800 to 7500 feet. (See Map 9.5, page 150.)

Adult Male: A green-bellied, jay-sized black bird with a slender bill, much green, purple, and copper iridescence on the fore body, and with a long, very broad, plumed tail. In more detail, back black glossed oil green, becoming dead blackish on rump and upper tail coverts; top of head stubbly with a dull blue gloss; nape reddish copper; hind neck to upper back iridescent pinkish purple with iridescent green subterminal barring; the plumes elongated and formed into a cape which extends to the upper back; chin to upper breast black glossed slightly with blue; a gleaming copper bronze pectoral band; lower breast and abdomen oil green with some glossy tips forming a line on sides; rest of underparts blackish; wings and tail black glossed pinkish purple especially tail which is very broad and long. Iris dark; bill black; feet greyish brown. Wing 182–191; tail 422–461; culmen from nostril 26; tarsus 45 mm.

Adult Female: Very different from male. Upperparts dark brown; entire head and fore body below blackish brown; rest of underparts blackish with narrow whitish barring; wing and tail dark brown. Wing 159–167; tail 256–260; culmen from nostril 23; tarsus 40 mm.

Immature: Much like adult female. Male intermediate plumages:

like adult female but larger (wing 175, tail 283 mm.) and with forehead, lores and chin glossed blue green, and with abdomen barring much reduced.

General Remarks: Although it is more than a half century since Carl Wahnes discovered the home grounds of this remarkably beautiful species in the mountains behind Sattelberg, we still know virtually nothing of its habits in the wild. However, Crandall (1932) recorded its voice and observed its display in captivity. Its voice is a jay-like *kak*, which seemed to be used as either a call or an alarm note.

Breeding Behaviour: Crandall observed two types of display in the New York Zoological Gardens. In one, the bird stood erect on its perch with the tail canted forward and somewhat spread. At the same time it (a) spread and flattened its blue breast shield so that its golden copperish edges glowed, (b) expanded laterally the green feathers of its breast. In this position it froze silently for about ten seconds. Sometimes it spread and rapidly closed the lateral tail feathers as it postured.

In the second form of display observed by Crandall, the male tipped backward under the perch, the body nearly horizontal and upside down, but with both the head and the tail directed upward. While in this position it spread the feathers of the breast shield and the abdomen, also the ear coverts which now opened to form a nape ruff. While so positioned the wings were held tight to the body and the feathers of the back were extended laterally over them; the tail was first upright and widely expanded, then rapidly opened and closed. Crandall noted that this display lasted 10 to 15 seconds and was repeated at four- to five-minute intervals in silence.

Nesting: I can find no record of the nest but Rothschild obtained an egg which is pinkish cinnamon with pale brown blotches at the larger end, has a number of grey longitudinal streaks over the entire surface, but with a concentration of larger darker ones only at centre; measurements 37 × 28·5 mm.

Evolution and Taxonomy: It is perhaps significant that in *Astrapia* the most widely separated species, *A. nigra* of the Vogelkop Peninsula in the west and *A. rothschildi* of the Huon Peninsula in the east, are morphologically the most similar. This resemblance, which involves both feather structure and colour pattern (chiefly the broad tail and the distribution of the oil green coloration) is the result, I think, of true relationship and not character convergence.

Superb Bird of Paradise

Lophorina superba (Pennant)
Males 8½ to 10 in.

Range: Mid-mountains virtually throughout New Guinea; from 4200 to 7300 feet, occasionally down to 3200 feet. (See Map 9.6, page 166.)

Adult Male: A thrush-sized glossy-crowned black bird with an enormous cape of feathers springing from the hind crown and a large iridescent chest shield. In more detail, generally dull black but with the central pair of rectrices velvet black glossed violet purple; an immense erectile cape (with plumes up to 130 mm. long) covering the back like an umbrella, springing mostly from tufts on each side of the hind head; the cape which is velvet black with bronze reflections is normally carried folded over the back. A tuft of feathers at base of maxilla, forehead, lores and chin glossed purplish; crown iridescent oil green; upper breast with a large erectile iridescent oil green shield (in certain lights reflecting purple); rest of bird  dull black. Iris blackish; bill and feet black; interior of mouth lime yellow. Wing 126–145; tail 85–103; bill from base 25; tarsus 33 mm.

Adult Female: Very different from male and of two distinct types: upperparts deep reddish brown (to greyish brown in one type); top and sides of head and neck black with traces of pale tipping over eye (to dark brown broadly spotted with white on forehead, also on sides of head under eye, and with broad whitish superciliary streaks

163

extending backward over ears and joining to form a broad whitish patch on the hind neck in one type); wings and tail dark brown with chestnut outer edges. Underparts including under wing coverts grey often tinged with buff and with narrow blackish bars. Iris dark brown; bill black; feet dark grey; mouth pale greenish yellow. Wing 110–129; tail 76–103; bill 28–31; tarsus 28–32 mm.

Juvenal: Like adult female but dark crown barred with ochraceous and hind and sides of neck ochraceous; plumage generally very soft, especially on lower parts.

Immature: First year plumage much like adult female. Male intermediate plumages or stages of dress: (a) like adult female but light feathers of forehead, superciliaries, and sides of throat much reduced in area and dark areas of head more extensive and more blackish; (b) like (a) but with some iridescent feathering on fore crown and upper breast; (c) like adult female but with the head all around (including all of superciliary area) dark brownish black; some wing quills and wing coverts dull black; sides of upper breast, flanks, rump, and upper tail coverts dull black; (d) like adult female but crown iridescent and breast with a moderately large iridescent shield.

Remarks: The Superb Bird of Paradise is yet another species which, although constantly hunted for its feathers (see pl. IX), seems to be just as numerous in regions such as the Wahgi Valley where it is heavily hunted as in areas such as Telefomin and the Owen Stanley Mountains where it is little hunted. In the Wahgi–Baiyer–Giluwe regions, for example, it remains common despite the intense pressure of plume hunting. This was my observation in 1950 and also Gyldenstolpe's observation in 1951 (1955a: 132). And in 1955–1956 Bulmer (MS3. 22) found it not uncommon in dense second growth near forest edge, in forest edge and forest, between 5000 and 6000 feet, and the Schoddes (MS) found it apparently fairly common on Mt Giluwe (5900 to 7000 feet) in 1961. Females and young males are most common in the forest edges and isolated patches of secondary forest, also in strip forests bordering grassland streams but the species also occurs in the crown of the original forest. In the Wahgi Valley the writer observed birds in female plumage feeding on yellow figs in the middle and upper limbs of the original forest and also in clumps of second growth in native gardens hundreds of yards from the forest edge. Adult males are much harder to observe and they appear to be much less common, but they too can occasionally be seen – as I have seen them – in slender trees of native gardens as low as six feet above the ground. However, for the most part, the males always seem to be solitary and they usually keep to the high trees of the forest and forest edge, and particularly to partition forests with many original trees among the second growth.

Breeding Behaviour: Stein (1936:24) writing of Weyland Mountain birds noted that the male calls while sitting high up and hidden in the top of a tree. Its cries are hoarse and very loud, he noted, and sound like *chr chr* or *krr krr*. I recorded this call in the Wahgi region as a drawn-out series of rasping notes sounding somewhat like escaping steam and sounding somewhat like the call of *Pteridophora*. Bergman wrote that the call in the Vogelkop region is *mjat, mjat,* repeated continuously.

One of Stein's hunters stated that he shot a male during its dance which occurred in a low tree. While hunting in company with a native shoot boy on 30 July 1950, I was shown an adult male which was perching in a small, exposed tree on the edge of a native garden at about 5700 feet. Behind it some 20 feet distant was a high wall of original and second-growth forest. The male sat about four to five feet up on a nearly horizontal small limb a foot from the thin trunk. It remained on this perch for several minutes as we approached it through the garden and then shot it. Possibly this male was on its display perch. However, in the middle Wahgi Valley near Kup, in an area several miles long, I was shown three dancing trees, each of which was said to be the property of a single male. One was at 5000 feet, one at 5600 feet, and one was at 7250 feet. The last was definitely occupied by a solitary adult male whose sharp insect buzzing, rasping notes could be heard periodically as it called from the tree – a tall open tree in the midst of an old forest clearing now cluttered with low second growth, at the top of a long semi-deforested hill. The calls of this male could be heard from the blind at 7300 feet in which we spent much time observing *Pterido-phora*. My preliminary observations indicated that the two genera replace each other altitudinally, with *Lophorina* always occuring at least a few hundred feet below *Pteridophora*.

Crandall described the display of this species in captivity: The

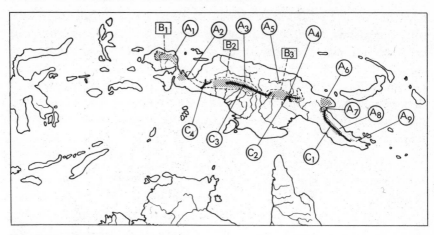

Map 9.6 *Lophorina* and *Epimachus*

Lophorina superba (A) 3200–7250 feet
  Lophorina superba superba (A1)
  Lophorina superba niedda (A2)
  Lophorina superba feminina (A3)
  Lophorina superba addenda (A4)
  Lophorina superba pseudoparotia (A5)
  Lophorina superba latipennis (A6)
  Lophorina superba connectens (A7)
  Lophorina superba minor (A8)
  Lophorina superba sphinx (A9)
Epimachus fastosus (B) 4200–7700 feet
  Epimachus fastosus fastosus (B1)
  Epimachus fastosus atratus (B2)
  Epimachus fastosus stresemanni (B3)
Epimachus meyeri (C) 5400–10,000 feet
  Epimachus meyeri meyeri (C1)
  Epimachus meyeri bloodi (C2)
  Epimachus meyeri albicans (C3)
  Epimachus meyeri megarhynchus (C4)

male '. . . crouches low on his perch, partly spreading his wings and expanding his breast-plate to the utmost. At the same time he erects the cape so that it stands out about his head in a tremendous ruff, the longer feathers at the sides almost meeting in front. He then begins a clumsy sort of dance, slightly ludicrous but still fascinating and filled with a wild, exotic beauty.'

Nesting: The prodigious collector A. S. Anthony collected the only known nest and eggs in the Owen Stanley Mountains in 1895–1896 at an altitude of about 5000 feet. Hartert (1910: 487) described these: 'The nest consists of dry and partially decayed leaves, dry twigs and rootlets. The two eggs sent differ from each other. The one is brownish buff, longitudinally splashed and marked with pale brownish grey, and some apparently deeper lying, pale brown markings. This egg measures 32 × 22·4 mm. The other one is more cream colour, with rufous spots and longitudinal markings, and underlying pale bluish grey longitudinal splashes and spots, as well as with some brown points and dots. It measures 31·8 × 20·6 mm.' A nestling collected by a native was purchased by me on 9 April 1954, in the Hindenburg Mountains.

Subspecies: Nine races are recognised on the basis of characters found in the female:

1 *L. s. superba* (Pennant), 1781, *Spec. Faun. Ind.,* in Forster's *Indian Zool.,* p. 40 (based on Daubenton, *Pl. Enlum.,* pl. 632). Type locality New Guinea, restricted to the Arfak Mountains. Known only from the Arfak and Tamrau mountains of the Vogelkop. Head to side of throat virtually solid black in female; underparts grey tinged faintly buff, and barred with blackish brown.

2 *L. s. niedda* Mayr, 1930, *Orn. Monatsb.,* vol. 38, p. 179. Type locality Wondiwoi, Wandammen Mountains. Known only from Mt Wondiwoi, Wandammen district. Female like *superba* but underparts darker, more ochraceous.

3 *L. s. feminina* Ogilvie-Grant, 1915, *Ibis,* Jubilee Suppl. No. 2, p. 27. Type locality Utakwa River, Nassau Range. Known from the Weyland and Doormanpaad mountains east through the Nassau and Oranje mountains. Head to sides of throat very different from the above: crown profusely tipped buff to white; forehead and superciliaries broadly white joining on nape; sides of lower head to sides of throat mostly greyish; dark postocular stripe profusely streaked with light shafting; underparts pale ochraceous.

4 *L. s. addenda* Iredale, 1948, *Australian Zoologist,* vol. 2, p. 162. Type locality Mt Hagen. Known from the (?) Hindenburg, (?) Victor Emanuel, (?) Giluwe, Hagen, Kubor mountains and the Wahgi Spur of the Bismarck Mountains. Female as in *feminina* but

crown, nape, and postocular stripe more solid blackish; underparts paler, less ochraceous.

5 *L. s. pseudoparotia* Stresemann, 1934, *Orn. Monatsb.*, vol. 42, p. 144. Type locality Hunsteinspitze. Known only from the Hunstein Mountains of the middle Sepik Valley. Similar to *feminina* but with the back browner and the crown browner, more nearly the same colour as the back.

6 *L. s. latipennis* Rothschild, 1907, *Bull. Brit. Orn. Club*, vol. 19, p. 92 [type in AMNH, no. 678271]. Type locality Rawlinson Mountains. Known from the mountains of the Huon Peninsula. Rather close to *addenda* but with the abdomen and under tail coverts somewhat paler.

7 *L. s. connectens* Mayr, 1930, *Orn. Monatsb.*, vol. 38, p. 180. Type locality Dawong, Herzog Mountains. Known only from the Herzog Mountains. Very similar to *latipennis,* but upperparts browner.

8 *L. s. minor* Ramsay, 1885, *Proc. Linn. Soc. New South Wales,* vol. 10, p. 242. Type locality Astrolabe Mountains. Known from the mountains of southeast New Guinea (Rothschild's *lehunti* from Mekeo, S.E. New Guinea, is invalid). Like *addenda* but female with throat somewhat more blackish due to reduction of white tipping; superciliaries narrower and upperparts more warm brown, less greyish brown.

9 *L. s. sphinx* Neumann, 1932, *Orn. Monatsb.*, vol. 40, p. 121. Origin of type unknown. Range unknown (Mayr, *in* Peters, 1962: 194 writes 'possibly the mountains at the extreme south-east of New Guinea'). More reddish brown on upperparts than *minor*. Eyestripe less extensive and forehead and neck without white flecks (but the type may be an immature male).

Taxonomy: There is general agreement among systematists that *Lophorina* is closely allied to *Astrapia* (two species of which have cape-like occipital plumes) as well as to *Parotia* in which the occipital plumes (the 'flags'), crown, and chest shields indicate fundamental similarities. Morphological similarities between the females of *Parotia* and *Lophorina* are much greater than between *Astrapia* and *Lophorina*.

Evolution: Because of its wide horizontal range and the intermediate position of its vertical range, *Lophorina* probably interacts
with more genera of plumed birds of paradise than any of the other
plumed birds. It is free from possible interactions with only *Seleucidis,
Cicinnurus* and *Ptiloris*. Its altitudinal range, in many areas, overlaps
that of *Diphyllodes, Epimachus, Astrapia,* and *Pteridophora*.

Lophorina is therefore an ideal genus with which to test Sibley's
hypothesis that sympatry (overlapping) in species which practice
polygyny (in which the sexes meet only for rapid mating without
prior association and pairing) requires the development of highly
exaggerated species-specific signals (plumage). In certain vegetational formations such as that of the mid-mountain forests, Sibley's
hypothesis seems correct. Sometimes in such areas three or four
genera do indeed plainly overlap. For example, in a single square
mile of forest it is sometimes possible to find *Parotia* displaying on
or near the ground, *Lophorina* displaying on middle limbs, and
Pteridophora displaying on the pinnacle limbs of the forest. The
genera are not actually in the same tree, but their courtship calls
overlap. Since the females of these genera are all rather similar
in their external morphology, it does seem that in the absence of
pair-bond behaviour (and the opportunity it offers before mating
for the correction of mistakes in species recognition), the females
might indeed be attracted to and be accepted by the wrong males
in the absence of vivid isolating mechanisms.

Sibley's idea has much merit, but I believe it is but a secondary
force behind the development of the extraordinary plumage and
patterns of behaviour found in the birds of paradise, bower birds,
and the many other birds that practise arena behaviour. The
primary force, I believe, is due to accelerated evolution resulting
from polygynous behaviour. When this pattern of behaviour takes
over from the less specialised pair-bond type, great changes in
morphology and behaviour are apt to occur rapidly whether the
species is sympatric (as in *Lophorina* and its relatives) or allopatric
(as in the Ruff, the Cock-of-the-Rock, the Argus Pheasant, or, for
that matter, such widely allopatric species as Wallace's Standard
Wing among the birds of paradise, and in many of the bower birds).
Mayr (in Mayr and Jennings, 1952: 15) in his remarks on speciation in bower birds seems to take a similar view: 'As in other
groups of birds in which the males have special displays, there
seems to be a rapid differentiation of genera. Of the ten genera now

recognised in the family, no fewer than seven are monotypic . . . '.

Wahnes' Six-wired Bird of Paradise

Parotia wahnesi Rothschild
Male 16 to 17½ in.
[*Parotia wahnesi* Rothschild, 1906, *Two New Birds of Paradise*, p. 2 (type in AMNH, no. 678233). Type locality Rawlinson Mountains.]

Range: Known only from the mountains of the Huon Peninsula, from 3800 to 5500 feet. (See Map 9.7, page 179.)

Adult Male: A jay-sized long-tailed black bird with six flag-tipped head wires, and iridescent head and breast plumage. In more detail, generally black, velvety above with an erectile forehead tuft iridescent gold; a narrow nape patch iridescent violet blue; on each side of crown behind eye a tuft of three erectile wire-like plumes (up to 143 mm. long) with paddle-shaped tips. Upper breast and lower neck with large iridescent yellowish green (in some lights pinkish purple or sea green) shield; rest of underparts black; black washed purple on throat and neck and appearing somewhat shiny on lower breast and elongated flank feathers (with plumes up to 110 mm.). Wing 156–163; tail 192–218; culmen from nostril 16; tarsus 49 mm.

Adult Female: Very different from male. All of head and upper half of neck blackish with a narrow whitish streak behind eye and a broad whitish streak from bill under eye to ear; throat whitish edged with black; rest of upperparts chestnut to dark brown narrowly barred with black on fore back and sides of neck; underparts paler with narrow blackish barring. Wing 145–147; tail 164–166; culmen from nostril 18; tarsus 48 mm.

Immature Male: First year plumage like female then in successive plumages acquiring the elaborate head and neck plumage of the adult male (also black feathering at bend of wing) but otherwise retaining the dress of the female.

General Remarks: Although Carl Wahnes discovered this beautiful, long-tailed species in 1906 in the Rawlinson Mountains, it remains little known in the wild state.

Breeding Behaviour: Crandall (1940: 257–259) described the display of the male in captivity: 'When about to display on the ground, the [male] stands with its body in a horizontal position, with the wings held closed but high, in order to clear the slightly loosened flank feathers. The tail is turned sideways, usually to the left. The bird feigns picking at the ground, then suddenly throws the body forward and downward with the head turned under the breast, so that its crown is nearly parallel with the ground. The tail now becomes the centre of attraction, for it is thrown straight upward, behind the crouching body. While all else remains immobile, the graduated lateral feathers are now rapidly opened and closed, the central pair remaining fixed. After this fan-like effect has been obtained perhaps five or six times, the bird suddenly drops the tail and throws its body into an upright position. Simultaneously, the long feathers of the back and flanks are raised to form the "umbrella" well known in other forms of *Parotia*, and the head plumes are thrown far forwards, three on each side of the crown. The brilliant breast plate is noticeably flat and lies between a slight extension of the feathers of the upper neck and the erected flank and breast plumes. With the head now extended to its greatest possible height, the bird turns it rapidly from side to side, causing the tabs on the plumes to rotate in the typical manner. Several mincing, short steps are now taken along the ground, usually to the right. After moving perhaps a foot in this manner, the bird suddenly becomes immobile except for the neck, which is rapidly moved from side to side, between the head and the breast plate. The display usually ends with this maneuver. During the upright form of the display, the tail takes a negligible part and may turn to either side or even drag on the ground.' Crandall also describes an arboreal display which is very similar to that performed on the ground except that it begins with the male moving about on horizontal perches with its tail held to one side and its body stiffly horizontal.

Evolution: The tail of *Parotia wahnesi* is long and graduated and strikingly like that of the astrapias, whereas all other *Parotia* species have the tail short and rather blunt. Not only is the tail of *P. wahnesi* uniquely long but Crandall (*op. cit.*: 259) noted that in display it is fanned in a similar manner to that of *Astrapia rothschildi*. This is very interesting because *P. wahnesi* is a ground-displaying bird, while *A. rothschildi* is a tree-displaying species.

171

Since display in trees probably preceded display on the ground in this family it follows that the parotias are evolutionally more advanced in their courtship behaviour than their close relatives, the astrapias. It also follows that *P. wahnesi*, which still possesses a tail of the type best used in trees, is probably the least advanced of the parotias. Support for this hypothesis – that the tail becomes short in species which shift their displays from trees to ground – is seen in the fact that all of the ground-displaying birds of paradise (including the other parotias) have fairly short to very short tails.

Taxonomy: Because of similarities in structure (chiefly the tail) and in display (see above) to *Astrapia*, I believe that *Parotia wahnesi* is the most primitive of the parotias. I have therefore shifted it downward to a position just above the astrapias.

Arfak Six-wired Bird of Paradise

Parotia sefilata (Pennant)
Male 12 in.
[*Paradisea sefilata* Pennant, 1781, *Spec. Faun. Ind.*, in Forster's *Indian Zool.*, p. 40. Type locality New Guinea, restricted to the Arfak Mountains.]

Range: The Arfak and Tamrau mountains of the Vogelkop and the Wandammen mountains near the head of Geelvink Bay; from 3500 to 5800 feet. (See Map 9.7, page 179.)

Adult Male: A jay-sized black bird with six flag-tipped head wires, a long white-tipped fore crest and iridescent nape and breast plumage. In more detail, generally black, velvety above, with an erectile silvery white forehead tuft; a narrow nape patch iridescent green to violet; on each side of crown behind eye a tuft of three long erectile, wire-like shafts (up to 180 mm. long) with paddle-shaped black tips. Upper breast to lower neck with a highly reflective feather shield iridescent golden green (in some lights pinkish purple); rest of underparts including elongated plumes at sides of breast black with a slight gloss. Iris china blue with an outer ring yellow; bill black; feet greyish black; mouth chartreuse yellow. Wing 164–168; tail 128–134; exposed culmen 16; tarsus 53 mm.

Adult Female: Very different from male. Top and sides of head and neck blackish brown with a broad line from gape to neck grey flecked with black; rest of upperparts dark rufous brown; wings blackish brown with exposed edges rufous; tail dark rufous brown; underparts, wing linings and axillaries grey to pale ochraceous narrowly barred blackish; inner edges of flight quills ochraceous. Iris deep bright blue with an outer ring greenish white; bill black; feet grey. Wing 148–151; tail 124–126; exposed culmen 17; tarsus 49 mm.

Immature: First year plumage like adult female but with inner edges of the flight quills generally solid blackish brown, not ochraceous. Male intermediate plumages and stages of dress: (a) like adult female but top and sides of head and neck uniform blackish brown; nape with a few iridescent purplish blue tipped feathers; flight quills above narrowly margined and streaked with velvet black; (b) like (a) but with chin and throat nearly solid black; a few iridescent copper red plumes on upper breast; a few black plumes on sides; (c) like (a) but with the fore crest silvery white; head wires present but short; upperparts, except scapulars, and fore half of underparts as in adult male.

Remarks: The Arfak Six-wire is a common species in the Tamrau (Ripley) and Arfak regions and quite common in the Wondiwoi Mountains of the Wandammen Peninsula (Mayr, *in* Hartert, 1930: 31).

Food: Two specimens in The American Museum from Mt Wondiwoi collected in mid-September by Shaw Mayer, had eaten fruits. D'Albertis (*in* Iredale, 1950 :39) wrote, 'It feeds upon various kinds of fruits, more especially on a species of fig . . . at other times . . . on a small kind of nutmeg.'

Breeding Behaviour: Two adult males (in The American Museum) with much enlarged gonads and one male in immature plumage were shot in mid-September as they perched in their bowers (Shaw Mayer).

Count D'Albertis' account (*op. cit.*) of this species was an important early contribution: 'My observations were made in the natural haunts of these elegant birds, from numerous specimens both living and dead. These birds are found in the north of New Guinea. I met with them about thirty miles from the coast, at an elevation of 3,600 feet . . . near Mount Arfak. I have never found the adult male in company with the females or young birds, but always in the thickest parts of the forests.' D'Albertis then noted that he generally found the females and young males at lower elevations. He recorded the voice as a very noisy *Gnaad-gnaad*, and the native Arfak name as *Coran-a*.

Ripley (*in* Mayr and de Schauensee, 1939: 136), who found the species common in the Tamrau Mountains, observed several dancing grounds at 5000 feet. He wrote: 'These consisted of cleared rings on the ground about five feet in diameter. These areas were apparently jealously guarded and frequently cleared of falling twigs or leaves.' From concealment Ripley observed a male descend to a dance ground and he noted that the bird's ' . . . route from branch to branch seemed to be done with a trained precision as if his course were definitely circumscribed. This proved to be the case, for, on the branches [Ripley] saw that each one was sharply scored in one place with marks of hundreds of claws, so that the growing end of each of these branches looked definitely stunted.'

Recently Sten Bergman (1957: 186–199) observed the courtship behaviour in the wilds of the Arfak Mountains. Later he saw it again in great detail in his laboratory in Sweden. Near Bivak in October he found several terrestrial dancing areas. Each was less than a yard in diameter and irregular in shape with some horizontal branches about two feet above it. At one of these Bergman often observed an adult male removing fallen debris from the surface of the ground. When approaching the bower the male emitted shrill notes and its wings rustled the air. At 4 p.m. on 8 August, the male uttered a hoarse cry from one of its horizontal perches, then flew to the ground. Soon it ruffled its tail feathers, raised its head and extended its neck; the body now seemed to widen and the long flank plumes were expanded from the sides of the body. The silver white feathers of the fore crown were raised and directed forward and, at the same time, the long velvet body plumes were erected like a circular ballet skirt. In the open position they completely covered the wings. The head was now bent forward, then swayed to the right and left in jerky movements. The male now danced back and forth and in half circles, then suddenly it folded its plumage, flew up to a branch and twice uttered a shrill cry before returning to the dance ground to continue cleaning it of leaves. In captivity Bergman noted that young males still in female plumage displayed in a similar manner except that they were more vigorous, dancing up to fifty times a day and often making little hops straight up into the air. He noted also that the adult captive male hopped to the lowest branches in the cage 'when it feels the desire to dance' and then flapped the wings and spread the tail before hopping to the ground. When it jumps to the ground it stands motionless 'as though frozen' for a few seconds with the head and the beak directed upwards and the body stretched upwards alertly. Later he directs his head toward the ground and his 'rear' is pointed upward and this position is then held for about a second. Next the male slowly raises its head and lowers its rear and in this position the dance plumes encircling the body are extended outwards to form an almost perfect circle. During this performance the tail is bent to one side out of the way. In dancing the male shifts forward and backward in half circles, at the same time swaying the head to right and left so that the flag-tipped wires bob about. This dance sometimes becomes very jerky. At other times the male hops about with outspread plumage. Always when the dance is over the male utters a shrill cry, then he usually flies up to a low branch in the cage and there spreads and retracts the tail feathers. He next hops about before again returning to the dance stage on the bottom of the cage. In returning to the court after a period of display the male is nervous and alert.

Nesting: The nest and egg of this species are apparently unknown.

Evolution and Behaviour: The behaviour of the male on and near its dance ground is in certain respects remarkably similar to that of many other arena birds, for example the Cock-of-the-Rock, in which the male freezes for a few seconds immediately after jumping to its ground court. Quite possibly the males of this species interact together in a kind of 'exploded' arena (see p. 53) with each male owning and maintaining a separate court within a given territory, but this remains to be proven.

Queen Carola's Six-wired Bird of Paradise

Parotia carolae Meyer
Male 9⅓ in.

Range: Mountains of the trunk of New Guinea from the Weyland to the Victor Emanuel mountains; 3800 to 6000 feet. (See Map 9.7, page 179.)

Adult Male: A thrush-sized black bird with six flag-tipped head wires, white and gold crest, iridescent nape and upper breast and white flank plumes. In more detail, generally black, velvety tinged bronze above; an erectile fore crest black, tipped silvery white, followed by gold-tipped crest feathers (which fold backwards into a dish-shaped skull); a narrow nape patch iridescent green to purple; on each side of crown behind eye a tuft of three long erectile wire-shafted plumes (up to 131 mm. long) with paddle-shaped black tips; lores golden brown or black (subspecies); eye ring golden brown, deep brown or solid black (subspecies); lower sides of head and throat buffy to blackish brown (subspecies); lower throat whitish to buff with chestnut tipping (subspecies); upper breast with  an extensive iridescent shield pinkish violet to lilac, in certain lights reflecting green to gold; some flank plumes (up to 128 mm. long) pure white, some dark brown; rest of underparts brownish black. Iris lemon yellow with a narrow inner ring of tan; bill and feet black; mouth greenish yellow. Male wing 146–164; tail 72–86; exposed culmen 18; tarsus 51 mm.

Adult Female: Very different from male. Upperparts generally grey brown to brown; a line from forehead over eye to nape whitish; a broad line behind eye brown; a broad indistinct line from gape to side of neck whitish; sides of throat greyish brown; throat greyish; exposed edges of wing quills chestnut; under wing coverts and inner edges of wing quills ochraceous, the former with some dark barring;

rest of underparts pale ochraceous with narrow dark barring. Iris lemon yellow; bill black; feet dark brown; mouth lemon yellow. Wing 131–149; tail 86–95; exposed culmen 22; tarsus 49 mm.

Immature: First year plumage much like adult female. Male intermediate plumages or stages of dress: (a) like adult female but a dark spot over lores glossed bronze; (b) like adult female but fore half of head and chin as in adult male; (c) like adult female but head to back of neck (including the six wires) as in adult male; (d) like (c) but fore half of body, wings (except some lesser coverts and secondaries) and feet black; (e) like adult male but central back, scapulars, some secondaries, lower breast and abdomen as in adult female; (f) like adult male but abdomen as in adult female.

Remarks: Very little is known about this bird in the wild. My only record is of a male seen at 5500 feet which came to investigate a disturbance near its bower. It moved deliberately 12 to 20 feet up in the forest and resembled a jay in its movements. The species seems to be generally scarce and of local distribution in the mid-mountain forests. In the Telefomin region I observed two bowers, apparently the first to be described. One of the bower owners was captured. This bird proved remarkable because it seemed constantly to change its facial expression. This was due to the skull top being dish-shaped, with ample room for the bird to retract and largely conceal its brilliant golden crest. This male, even when perching quietly, often slightly pulsated its crest up and down and at the same time moved its chin and throat 'whiskers.' It also would flex its flag-tipped crown wires and, although these were not exactly a part of the 'facial expression', they added much to the changing appearance whenever the male moved its head.

Voice: The call of this bird has been recorded by C.H.B. Grant as *prat, prat*.

Food: Tree fruits and berries.

Breeding Behaviour: (Also some observations concerning native trapping and ecology). Walking north-east from Telefomin Valley (4800 feet) in the Victor Emanuel Mountains, on 23 March 1954, we departed from the grassy clearing on a gradually ascending trail. We passed through narrow clearings spotted with clumps of rhododendron, bearing huge, aromatic white flowers, and small trees, then entered a cavernous forest (with crown averaging seventy feet) which presented a solid wall as we approached it. We ascended to 5500 feet, crossing one small stream, then at the base of a steep slope (rising to the north) we turned left off the trail into the forest. Large patches of second growth appeared here and there. Many dead trees rose like masts above the younger stands of second growth which averaged about thirty feet in height. The substage of this new forest was very thick and confused.

While in this habitat Ininsip's actions suddenly indicated that the *Dul* was in the vicinity. Parting the bushes, I saw a kind of 'telephone booth' blind built of dried palm leaves. Beyond it, hardly six feet from the blind, I saw the *Dul*'s dance ground or bower. It was a cleared patch of fairly level ground surmounted by a kind of 'jungle gym' of dead sticks, vines, and saplings. Several of the larger dead limbs formed nearly horizontal perches up to two inches in diameter and 2 to 4 feet above the cleared area. The most prominent perch (a dead limb) was $3\frac{1}{2}$ feet up and 2 inches in diameter. It was over the middle of the clearing and had been stripped of its bark and moss and was buff coloured and worn from use. Below it the ground had been cleared of fallen debris. However, it was covered with a kind of brownish grey mossy growth which was so short it reminded me of wet burlap. All about were droppings containing many red and yellow seeds. In places the clearing was heavily splattered with these colours. The cleared area was 6–8 feet in diameter, roughly round, and was only slightly inclined downward to the west. Some 10 to 15 feet away a large dead tree rose to sixty feet, but directly over the dance ground the canopy of leaves was thick and only about 30–40 feet high.

The native blind had been built so that its arrow porthole was about six feet away from the main display perch. This blind had been in position for many days judging by the wilted condition of the leaves used in its construction. From an examination of the blind it was evident that the hunter positions his bow and arrow, and himself stands in the firing position within the narrow structure. Probably his four-pronged bird-catching arrow protrudes three or four feet from the front of the blind.

I failed to catch sight of the male on its dance ground. Then to my intense disappointment several days later a wounded male was brought to my camp by a stranger. It developed that it was 'my' bird. It had been stunned by a blunt arrow blow on the chest. It soon recovered but could not fly very well and within a few weeks it became quite tame. By day it lived in a bower-like heavily shaded structure of bushes and trees which we made for it in the centre of a large clearing of grass. It remained there in the shadows guarded by native boys.

Before leaving Telefomin we took this male back to its original bower and, with a team of boys encircling the playground, I liberated the *Dul*. It immediately hopped around to investigate, tried various perches, and in a few minutes expanded its white flank plumes (these are normally concealed) and began to preen them while standing on one of the central perches. It now switched its head and wires, examined the ground and seemed most content. During this period I made stroboscopic spotlight pictures and several close-ups showing the male in what I am reasonably certain is a normal attitude on its own display ground.

After nearly an hour at the bower it began to rain. The bird was

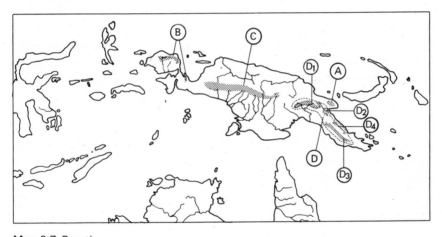

Map 9.7 *Parotia*

Parotia wahnesi (A) 3800 to 5500 feet	*Parotia lawesi exhibita* (D1)
Parotia sefilata (B) 3500 to 5800 feet	*Parotia lawesi fuscior* (D2)
Parotia carolae (C) 3800 to 6000 feet	*Parotia lawesi lawesi* (D3)
Parotia lawesi (D) 3200 to 7500 feet	*Parotia lawesi helenae* (D4)

then recaptured and in June 1954, I sent it to the Honolulu Zoo. There Director Paul Breeze provided it with a large private cage near cages containing *Diphyllodes magnificus, Paradisaea rudolphi, P. rubra, P. minor, Cicinnurus regius,* and one or two additional species of Paradisaeidae. In May 1959, when I saw my *Dul* in Honolulu, it was displaying rather statically on the ground under a bush, and in 1962 a friend reported it healthy and displaying by perching on the ground under the same bush. [In 1968 Mrs Gilliard reported it still healthy and still displaying under the same bush.]

A series of three photographs in colour of this male on its bower (made under the controlled conditions described above) were published in the *National Geographic Magazine* for October 1955, page 479 (see pl. 9).

Subspecies: Six fairly well differentiated races are known:

1 *P. c. carolae* Meyer, 1894, *Bull. Brit. Orn. Club,* vol. 4, p. 6. Type locality 'Amberno River' (but apparently from the Weyland Mountains). Known from the Weyland Mountains and the Wissel Lake region. Upperparts blackish; chin and sides of throat buffy; eye ring coppery; long loral feathering black with silvery white tips.

2 *P. c. clelandiae* Gilliard, 1961, *Amer. Mus. Novit.,* no. 2031, p. 5 [type in AMNH, no. 708171]. Type locality Telefomin, 5000 feet, Victor Emanuel Mountains. Known only from the type locality. Like *carolae* but with the wing and occipital wires longer and with the upperparts darker, more jet black, less brownish black.

3 *P. c. meeki* Rothschild, 1910, *Bull. Brit. Orn. Club,* vol. 27, p. 35 [type in AMNH, no. 678161]. Type locality Setekwa River, west New Guinea. Known from the Nassau and Oranje mountains. Like *carolae* but chin and sides of throat blackish, not buffy.

4 *P. c. chalcothorax* Stresemann, 1934, *Orn. Monatsb.,* vol. 42, p. 145. Type locality Doormanpaad, upper Mamberamo (Idenburg) River. Known only from the type locality. Like *carolae* but upperparts with a coppery sheen.

5 *P. c. berlepschi* Kleinschmidt, 1897, *Orn. Monatsb.,* vol. 5, p. 46. Type locality 'New Guinea.' Range unknown but possibly the Van Rees Mountains. Like *carolae* but upperparts heavily bronzed, no eye ring, and with the throat black.

6 *P. c. chrysenia* Stresemann, 1934, *Orn. Monatsb.,* vol. 42, p. 147. Type locality Lordberg, Sepik Mountains. Known from the Sepik Mountains (Lordberg and Hunsteinspitze) and the Jimmi River region of the Bismarck Mountains. Like *carolae* but differing by

having the long loral feathering copper-coloured like the eye ring, not black as in all other races.

Lawes' Six-wired Bird of Paradise

Parotia lawesi Ramsay
Male 10¼ in.

Range: Mountains of eastern New Guinea from 3200 to 7500 feet. (See Map 9.7, page 179.)

Adult Male: A thrush-sized black bird with six flag-tipped head wires, a short white or gold tipped fore crest, and with iridescent nape and breast plumage. In more detail, generally black, upperparts velvet black tinged bronze; an erectile fore crest silvery white to dark brown (or gold to dark brown in one subspecies) coming to a point at base of maxilla; a narrow nape patch iridescent blue to purple; on each side of crown behind eye a tuft of three long erectile wire-shafted plumes (up to 163 mm. long) with paddle-shaped black tips. Upper breast to lower neck with a highly reflective feather shield iridescent golden green (pinkish purple in certain lights); rest of underparts including elongated plumes at sides and breast black with a slight gloss. Iris cobalt blue; bill black; feet dark brown.

Wing 150–156; tail 77–85; exposed culmen 14–19; tarsus 51 mm.

Adult Female: Very different from male. Top and sides of head and neck blackish with a narrow line from gape to beneath eye grey flecked black; rest of upperparts dark rufous brown; wings blackish brown with exposed edges paler; tail dark brown; underparts, wing linings and axillaries ochraceous, paler, more grey on throat and richer, more chestnut on wing linings and under tail coverts. Iris pale yellow; bill black; feet dark grey. Wing 141–144; tail 94–102; exposed culmen 18–21; tarsus 48 mm.

Immature: First year plumage much like adult female. Male intermediate plumages or stages of dress: (a) like adult female plumage but iris greenish yellow with an inner ring of cobalt blue, or iris uniform cobalt blue; head all around and hind neck black; fore crest, nape and head wires as in adult male; a few upper breast plumes iridescent copper to ruby; some narrow black exposed edging on wing quills and a few velvet black plumes in upperparts; (b) like (a) but more velvet black in upperparts, wings, and tail, and with iridescent breast plumes generally more uniform copper green, less ruby red; (c) like (a) but upper breast broadly ruby red to copper red with a few green plumes; wings and tail mostly solid velvet black; (d) like adult male but scapulars, lesser upper wing coverts, lower back, breast, and abdomen as in adult female.

Remarks: This species was named for the Reverend W.G. Lawes, a pioneer missionary, from trade skins. The first to discover its home grounds was Carl Hunstein who, in 1884, collected both sexes on Horseshoe Mountain behind Port Moresby. Six years later Sir William Macgregor's expedition met with Lawes' Six-wired Bird of Paradise on Mt Belford in the Owen Stanley Mountains between 3600 and 7000 feet, and one of the expedition naturalists, A.P. Goodwin (1890 : 151) was the first to describe its terrestrial playground.

Lawes' Six-wired Bird of Paradise is apparently fairly common in the Owen Stanley Mountains and scarce or very local in the western part of its range. In recent years Hobart Van Deusen got two specimens in the Kraetke Mountains (4500–5800 feet), N.B. Blood got specimens in the Mt Hagen district, and Bulmer observed the species on the north slopes of Mt Hagen in '. . . garden fallow near forest edge at about 5,800 feet.' Bulmer also got it near Tari (south watershed near Mt Giluwe, 5200–5500 feet) 'in and near tall timber' (MS₂), and the Schoddes (MS) obtained a female at 6600 feet on Mt Giluwe.

Voice: The call is 'a short sharp cry' (Simson, 1907: 387).

Food: Stomach analyses indicate that fruit and seeds are the chief food.

Breeding Behaviour: This species builds and maintains a ground bower which is very similar to that of the other parotias. One that Simson (*op. cit.,* 386) saw in the Owen Stanley Mountains ' . . . consisted of a piece of ground about four yards in width, cleared of moss and dead leaves, and situated on a ridge. Across this cleared space were three thin branches, about one foot from the ground and bare of leaves.' Crandall (1931: 99) observed the courtship dance of a captive bird which was probably very like the dance in the wild: 'Drawing itself erect, the dancer spreads the long, velvety feathers of its back and raises them, fan-shaped, at right angles to the body. The feathers of the lower breast and abdomen are similarly erected to complete the circle, so that the bird of paradise resembles a rather short man, with his head poked through a large, spread umbrella. The dance begins, in slow, short hops, two feet right, two feet left, and back again. Now the six plumes are seen at their best, for the head moves rapidly from side to side with a rhythmic motion, which causes the little tabs to bob madly . . . As a finale, the body is thrown forward into a horizontal position and the bobbing of the head increases in speed until the movements of the plumes can no longer be followed. There is a flap of wings, the body feathers are lowered and the dance is over.'

Nesting: A. S. Anthony obtained a nest and egg at 6000 feet in the Owen Stanley Mountains (Hartert, 1910: 487). Hartert described the nest: 'The nest is built entirely of the wire-like stems of some climbing plant, and lined only with finer stalks of the same kind and some fine rootlets. Unless pressed out of shape the structure is very flat. The single egg is of a vinaceous red, with dark rufous, sometimes almost black patches and spots, and a few underlying greyish spots. Measurements: 33 × 24 mm.'

Subspecies: Four races which divide into two well differentiated groups, (a) the white-crested *lawesi* group with three very similar races, and (b) the gold-crested *helenae:*

1 *P. l. exhibita* Iredale, 1948, *Australian Zoologists,* vol. 2, p. 162. Type locality Mt Hagen district. Known from (?) Mt Giluwe, Mt Hagen, Bismarck Mountains and (?) Kraetke Mountains. Group (a): male like *lawesi* but sides of head darker, more jet black and female more uniformly barred below.

2 *P. l. fuscior* Greenway, 1934, *Proc. New England Zool. Club,*

o

vol. 14, p. 2. Type locality Mt Misim, Morobe district. Known only from the Herzog Mountains. Group (a): male like *lawesi* but female duller, less chestnut brown above and with a darker head.

3   *P. l. lawesi* Ramsay, 1885, *Proc. Linn. Soc. New South Wales*, vol. 10, p. 243. Type locality Astrolabe Mountains. Known from the southern slopes of the mountains of south-eastern New Guinea (Wharton Range, Owen Stanley Range, Mt Suckling, Mt Maneao, etc.). Group (a); male with fore crown silvery white and sides of head brownish black, female with underparts barred heavily on breast and weakly on abdomen.

4   *P. l. helenae* De Vis, 1891, *Ibis*, p. 390. Type locality Neneba, upper Mambare River. Known only from the northern slopes of the mountains at the headwaters of the Mambare and Waria rivers. Group (b): like *lawesi* but male with fore crown golden brown not silvery white.

Ethology: The meager information available suggests that the bower keepers – the seemingly solitary males – are in auditory contact with other males and are not scattered at random through the forest. For example near Wabag in January, 1956 (7500 feet), Bulmer found two bowers of *Parotia* within 15 yards of each other. One was about seven feet in diameter with small saplings growing in it, and red fruit pulp and seeds on the floor of the clearing. The other was about 3 feet 6 inches in diameter. According to Crandall (1932: 7) the courtship movements of species that are widely separated in the wild are very similar. He could detect no difference between the dances of *P. lawesi* and *P. sefilata* in captivity. And from descriptions and analogies of photographs it seems that the four species of *Parotia* clear bowers that are very similar in form.

King of Saxony Bird of Paradise

Pteridophora alberti Meyer
Male 8¾ in.

Range: Mountains of the trunk of New Guinea from the Weyland and Snow ranges eastward to the Bismarck and Kraetke mountains; from 4800 to 8900 feet. (See Map 9.8, page 192.)

Adult Male: A thrush-sized black and orange bird with two immense, scalloped, enamel blue crown plumes. In more detail, head and neck all around velvet black tinged bronze; upper back with elongated black feathering forming a cape (which in display is expanded laterally over the shoulders); lower back to upper tail coverts sooty grey; on each side of crown behind eye an enormous shaft (up to 480 mm. long) with up to 44 enamel-like sky blue lobes protruding from one edge; wings brownish black except quills largely orange ochraceous on basal halves (forming a prominent ochraceous patch on the folded wing); head and neck to upper breast velvety black; feathers of upper breast with narrow iridescent violet blue tips forming a subobsolete shield; rest of underparts yellowish to buffy, the breast pale egg yellow, the sides and abdomen white tinged yellow; under wing and under tail coverts uniform pale ochraceous. Iris dark brown; bill black; feet dark grey; mouth pale green; wing 121–126; tail 81–87; culmen from base 23; tarsus 32 mm.

Adult Female: Very different from male. Upperparts grey to sooty grey, darkest on lower back, becoming more dark ash grey (with traces of black tipping) on head and neck; often present a long spike-like grey feather springing from crown behind eye; underparts white with broad black often scalloped-shaped bars, becoming darker on neck and throat; under wing and under tail coverts chestnut ochraceous with black markings. Iris and bill as in male, feet bluish grey to greyish brown. Wing 107–123; tail 79–91; culmen 22; tarsus 32 mm.

Juvenal: Nestlings like adult female but underparts mouse brown, very soft, fluffy, and somewhat silky in texture; exposed edges of secondaries mustard brown; underparts fluffy with indistinct dark barring and spotting. A relatively long (14 mm.) spike-like feather

185

on the crown behind eye is present in the only nestling examined (male, Mt Hagen, 7 July 1950, 8200 feet, Gilliard).

Immature: First year plumage like adult female but upperparts, especially head, paler, more uniform brownish grey to grey, less scaled dusky grey due to narrow black tipping; underparts whiter due to reduction of black barring and spotting. The spike-like plume is present on one (male) and absent on one (female) of the two young examined. Male intermediate plumages or stages of dress: (a) like adult female but with nasal tuft black; primaries somewhat darker, with concealed bases orange, not grey; (b) like adult male but with some brownish plumes on occiput, chin, and throat; under wing coverts and abdomen spotted and barred as in female but with much egg yellow plumage; occipital plumes relatively short (in one male, 224 mm.) with the blue flags sometimes much reduced in size; (c) like adult male but chin grey; central occiput with a spot of grey; sides and abdomen retaining some bold black barring.

Remarks: Females and young males are generally common within the narrow altitudinal zone occupied by this species, but adult males are very scarce except in certain hard-to-find areas where they congregate to perform their courtship displays.

The King of Saxony is a bird of the cloud forest. In the Wahgi highlands (Mt Kubor, Mt Wilhelm, Wahgi Divide, Mt Hagen) it is apparently rare or absent below about 6800 feet, and above 8500 feet it is again scarce or absent. In the Snow Mountains, Rand got it between 7000 and 9000 feet. On Mt Giluwe the Schoddes (MS) got a series including three adult males between 7500 and 8400 feet, and the writer obtained 13 specimens, including two adult males, between 7200 and 7600 feet in the Victor Emanuel and Hindenburg mountains.

The long occipital plumes of the adult male are highly prized articles of human adornment throughout the highlands of the trunk of New Guinea. In the Wahgi region the blue enamel-like plumes are inserted in the nose (see pl. IX) and bent to form a facial rim between the nose and the crown. For details of the technique employed by the Papuans to hunt these elusive birds of the forest crown, see p. 37.

Shortly before his death, the widely travelled Swedish ornithologist, Count Nils Gyldenstolpe (1955a : 140), noted that the King

of Saxony Bird of Paradise is '. . . certainly one of the most remarkable wonders among the bird-world' and, according to legend, when
in 1894 the great Bowdler Sharpe read A.B.Meyer's terse description proposing the extraordinary genus *Pteridophora*, he remarked
that even a fool would know that it was an artifact.

Later, Sharpe in the introduction to his magnificent monograph
the Paradisaeidae (1898) chastises collectors in general for not
obtaining more information on nesting habits '. . . for the aim of
every ordinary collector in the present day seems to be, not to
furnish us with details of the nesting-habits of the Birds of Paradise,
but to see how many of these beautiful creatures he can procure
for the decorations of the hats of the women of Europe and America
. . . .' Sharpe then noted that these data are of primary importance
to taxonomists especially '. . . when a wonderful form like *Pteridophora* comes to light. . . .' By this time he had assured himself
(a) that *Pteridophora* was not an artifact and (b) that it was a bird
of paradise. However, as late as 1950 the peculiarly exaggerated
plumage of *Pteridophora* caused one specialist to call the King of
Saxony a false bird of paradise (Iredale, 1950 : 163).

By great good luck in 1950 the writer was fortunate enough to be
able to discover for the first time the arboreal dancing places of this
species and to observe its courtship behaviour in the presence of a
female (see below).

Voice: The call of the male begins as a drawn-out hissing note
(sounding like escaping steam) and terminates in an explosive rasp
that can be heard for almost a mile over the crown of the cloud
forest. *Kiss-sa-ba,* the native name for the male in the Kubor
Mountains (above Kup), is based on the sound of its call.

Food: Stomach analyses indicate that this species feeds on tree
fruits and tree seeds which are usually green in colour and usually
relatively large.

Ecology: In searching for food the females and young males
commonly descend to within 15 feet of the ground in ridge forest
and once I saw an adult male with blue plumes searching for food
only ten feet above my head in such a situation. It moved about on
the smaller limbs 'inside' a tree which was about 40 feet tall growing
on a rounded ridge in open hill forest. The smaller, inner, and
exterior limbs and vines of the middle and upper tier of mountain

187

forest, are the optimum habitat of this bird.

Breeding Behaviour: The isolated areas in which the males gather
to display are often well known but jealously hidden by the native
hunters, especially in the Wahgi Highlands where the occipital
plumes are quite valuable in the native economy. The display area
is usually on a steep, heavily forested mountainside. There for no
apparent reason, in certain small areas the males gather to display
on small limbs 40 to 100 feet up. Within the display area the males
suddenly appear to be rather common whereas elsewhere within
the altitudinal belt occupied by the species, they are rare; so rare
that even such thorough collectors as those of the Archbold team
that surveyed the avifauna of the Snow Mountains could find no
trace of the adult males, although they found the females to be
common and, in fact, collected two breeding females in October,
two breeding females in November and one breeding female in
December (Rand, 1942b: 498).

By good fortune I was able to induce my native assistant to
reveal the locations of displaying males (see below). In summary,
the display is given on high vines and branches in pure forest 60 to
100 feet up. Each of a small group of interacting males occupies a
private display area which may be an exposed spire-like limb, a
high thin horizontal limb under a thin canopy of leaves, usually
overlooking a broad vista, or a high vine. The males are spaced
400 or more yards apart. Each male spends much of the day in
the vicinity of his display perch often calling and periodically
visiting his perch to display or perch nervously. When a female
visits a displaying male his actions suddenly become very different
from those which he employs in solitary display. In brief, he begins
violent bouncing motions, at the same time sweeping the occipital
plumes forward in great bows toward the approaching female. As
he does this he expands and pulsates the cape (back feathers)
laterally over the shoulders. The female approaches, mouth
open, and wings fluttering in the attitude of a juvenal begging for
food.

The actions of the male on his main display perch are illustrated by the following excerpt from my field notes of 19 June 1952.
These were written as I sat under a displaying male in the Kubor
Mountains at 7300 feet: 'At 2.14 p.m. *Pteridophora*, which had been
calling nearby for some time, landed on its primary display limb

[80 feet overhead]. I observed it through 8-power glasses for nine minutes, after which it departed. [At other times in recent days, the male had remained on this perch for twelve minutes, seven minutes ten minutes, and once for more than twenty minutes.] During the nine minutes I made the following observations: Once during a timed interval of 30 seconds it called twice and whipped the head about decisively 31 times. The call was a thrice-repeated gargling *grrrrrreeeaaa* followed immediately by a low *ca-ca-ca* uttered twice. The notes have a hissing quality and are delivered with the green mouth half open and pointing upward, and with the neck stretched. The mouth is not closed between notes. While on the perch the bird preened the left wing twice, stretched the left wing so it "fanned" downward to the feet; picked once at the base of the tail which was also opened to one side; puffed out the neck, picked in contortionist fashion at the feathers of the upper breast; once it expanded and lifted the back feathers which form a kind of cape; it then immediately flexed the long occipital plumes so that they were directed upward and outward on each side of the head. During the nine minutes it turned completely around four times in a clockwise direction. The cock watched everything, and once when a distant tree was felled, it snapped its head around in the direction of the sound. Its departure from the perch was by diving off. Its arrival had been indirect with the cock first landing on a twig several feet below its main dance perch, then hopping almost immediately to its main display perch.'

On 12 June 1952, immediately after watching a cock as it called from this same display perch, I dictated the following description into a tape recorder: 'Again the cock was observed to utter its call. It stands as if on tiptoe, its occipital plumes cast steeply downward. It raises its head toward the sky, opens the bill wide, and after one to three seconds, low intensity gurgling, hissing notes reach the ground observer. This stream of sound seems to continue for seconds and then there is a pause, and the procedure is repeated. At the end of the series the mouth is held open for a short while. Gradually the cock relaxes and begins to shake its head. The chief characteristic of the cock on its display perch is its nervousness.'

Other on-the-spot notes are the following, recorded at 8.15 a.m. on 11 June 1952: 'The bird, on occasion, moved its head backward and forward, rather than from side to side. This caused the long plumes, which are apparently controlled by strong muscles, to spring inward and then outward; each time the head thrusts forward, the long plumes, which are normally curved out around the body (with their tips about 12 inches apart) were made to spring forward so that the tips came together almost touching over the tail. As the head moved back and forth, the enameled plumes sprang in and out, and this action was kept up for many seconds. At other times as the head was constantly moved about, the long plumes appeared clumsy. Much of the time they both drooped to one side, one hanging down sharply over the left ear, the other hanging backward over the left wing, and both with the tips hanging from three to ten inches below the level of the bird's feet. But when excited the male elevated the plumes well above the crown and then let them settle slowly to the sides in an orderly manner. In this display, the egg yellow of the breast was easily seen but the iridescence of the upper breast remained invisible, the feathers of the breast and sides were puffed out, ball-like, over the folded wings.'

On Mt Hagen at about 7800 feet on 25 July 1950, I observed a cock displaying to a female. Shortly before, this or another male had been observed on a high perch, a horizontal limb some 65 feet up, under the canopy of a forest. It had then flown to another high perch some 200 yards distant and called. As I approached the new position the male disappeared and a short while later presumably this same male was heard calling from still another position, this time 50 yards away and only about 50 feet up in thick forest. At the new position the male was discovered displaying very noisily and actively to a female. A camera with telephoto lens was rapidly aimed at the pair and the following sequence was observed and filmed. The male was perched on a very thin nearly horizontal limb or vine on the outer side of a tall forest tree. Its long occipital plumes were elevated steeply over the back. With violent motions of the body it caused the perch to bounce up and down six or more inches. This caused the cock's body to undulate violently up and down although it retained its grip on the perch. As it bounced, it flexed the back feathers so that they expanded and retracted laterally over the shoulders. As the bird bounced, the long plumes were brought forward and the head was repeatedly bowed forward and downward. This bowing was a slow graceful sweeping motion. It was repeated six or more times during the forty or sixty rapid bounces that the bird was seen to execute. As the male bounced and bowed, it kept up an almost constant hissing like escaping steam. A *Pteridophora* in female plumage was now seen to approach the male. The female moved slowly through leaves, approaching at an upward angle. As this female advanced the male bounced, bowed, and hissed loudly and vigorously. When within three feet of the male and facing him, the female had the bill partly open and it appeared to be making slight panting movements. Its wings were held loosely and were fluttered like a nestling begging for food; the male at this point was bowing low and casting the enameled plumes forward. The female advanced to within about 18 inches and at this position the blue enameled plumes were sweeping to a point just below and in front of her. When the female approached a bit closer, the male lost control and let go of its perch on one of its upward bounces; at this time it emitted a harsh gurgling hiss and the display was concluded. At this moment the female fled the scene with the male following her closely. Both birds flew directly over me, 30 feet over my head. The male was only a few feet behind the female. I saw his long occipital plumes trailing over the tail. They appeared to be carried stiffly, straight back, with the irregular edges inward and about an inch apart.

Nothing is known of the nest or eggs of this remarkable species.

Subspecies: Three very similar races are known:

1   P. a. *alberti* Meyer, 1894, *Bull. Brit. Orn. Club,* vol. 4, p. 11. Type locality 'mountains on the Amberno River;' type apparently came from the Weyland Mountains. Known from the Weyland Mountains, the (?) Van Rees Mountains, Oranje, Hindenburg, and Victor Emanuel mountains. Female with underparts white with bold black barring.

2   P. a. *hallstromi* Mayr and Gilliard, 1951, *Amer. Mus. Novit.* no. 1524, p. 12 [type in AMNH, no. 348210]. Type locality forests above Tomba, south slopes of Mt Hagen. Known from Mt Giluwe, Hagen, Bismarck, and Kubor mountains. Like *alberti* but underparts generally lighter owing to narrower black barring.

3   P. a. *bürgersi* Rothschild, 1931, *Novit. Zool.,* vol. 36, p. 253 [type in AMNH, no. 678693]. Type locality Schraderberg, Sepik Mountains. Known from the Sepik Mountains (Schraderberg) east to the north slope of the central highlands (Kraetke Mountains). Like

BIRDS OF PARADISE AND BOWER BIRDS

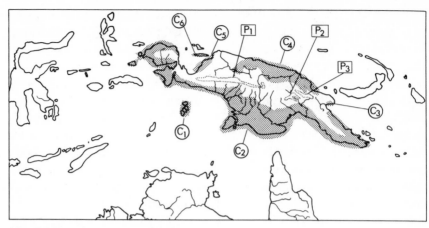

Map 9.8 *Pteridophora* and *Cicinnurus*

Pteridophora alberti (P) 4800–8900 feet)
  Pteridophora alberti alberti (P1)
  Pteridophora alberti hallstromi (P2)
  Pteridophora alberti bürgersi (P3)
Cicinnurus regius (C) sea level–1700 (rarely 2500 feet)
  Cicinnurus regius regius (C1)
  Cicinnurus regius rex (C2)
  Cicinnurus regius gymnorhynchus (C3)
  Cicinnurus regius similis (C4)
  Cicinnurus regius cryptorhynchus (C5)
  Cicinnurus regius coccineifrons (C6)

alberti but with the underparts less whitish, more brownish buff.

Taxonomy: *Pteridophora* appears to me to be closely related to *Lophorina* and *Parotia*. The chief points of similarity are (a) the expandable cape; (b) the complex feathers growing from the back and sides of the crown; and (c) the metallic breast shield. See also annotations under *Lophorina*.

King Bird of Paradise

Cicinnurus regius (Linnaeus)
Male 5–6½ in.

Range: Aru Islands, islands of western New Guinea (Misol,

192

Salawati, Batanta) and all of New Guinea. From sea level to 1700 feet. (See Map 9.8, opposite.)

Adult Male: A starling-sized red and white bird with long twin tail wires tipped with emerald green feather circlets. In more detail, upperparts crimson red glossed silver in some lights; forehead and tail more orange; a spot over eye black glossed emerald green; central pair of rectrices wire-like (up to 170 mm. long) and tipped with coin-like circlets of emerald green feathering; sides of head and chin like back; throat to upper breast purplish crimson followed by buff, then iridescent emerald green pectoral bands; on each side of upper breast an erectile dark grey fan (up to 45 mm. long) broadly tipped emerald green and with grey to brown subterminal bands; rest of underparts and under wing linings white. Iris pale brown; bill

yellow on basal half, pale orange on outer half; mouth pale grass green; feet violet blue. Wing 93–103 (subspecies); tail 29–35; bill 19; tarsus 28 mm.

Adult Female: Very different from male: Upperparts dull olive brown; wing quills and greater upper wing coverts darker and with chestnut external margins; tail olive brown edged with ochraceous; sides of head brown with fine light centre streaking; underparts buffy to pale ochraceous with narrow dark bars; inner margins of wing quills ochraceous. Iris dark brown; bill brownish horn; mouth pale green; feet dark blue. Wing 95–101 (subspecies); tail 53–62; bill from base 19; tarsus 26 mm.

Juvenal: Like adult female but upperparts generally dusky cinnamon brown, not olive; plumage very soft and loose-textured; exposed edges of wing coverts and quills chestnut brown; underparts brownish buff; throat to neck with two narrow black streaks.

Immature: First year plumage like adult female but bill darker and with much chestnut edging on wings. Male intermediate plumages or stages of dress: (a) like adult female but maxilla tuft and fore crown with traces of orange; lores, chin, sides of head, back, upper breast, bend of wing, wing coverts, inner wing quills, with traces of red; exposed edges of wing mustard orange; or, alternately, like adult female but wings with some red, and some inner secondaries solid ochraceous below and red above; (b) like adult female but most upper wing coverts, some wing quills and some upper tail coverts red; (c) like adult female but with a narrow complete collar; central back from collar to upper tail coverts, upper wing coverts, and some secondaries red; under wing quills largely ochraceous; (d) like adult male but head above as in adult female with tinges of yellow; sides of head and throat mostly as in adult female but interspersed with red tipping; upper breast and a large irregular area on mantle as in female; lower breast and abdomen as in male but with traces of barring on sides; axillaries and wing linings buff with dusky bars not uniform white; display fans at side of breast streaked with ochraceous; central pair of rectrices half length and with narrow feather vanes (yellow to orange) extending outward to curled tips, not wire-like as in adult. The fully adult plumage probably is assumed in the fourth or fifth year.

Remarks: The King Bird of Paradise is a widespread, rather common species of the lowland forests from sea level to about 1700 feet, but it is quite difficult to observe unless one knows its calls. The plumes of the male are valuable articles of ornamentation and trade in many parts of New Guinea. Some that I have seen in the headdresses of natives were far removed from areas in which the species lives; for instance, they are used in the Wahgi and Telefomin valleys. In the western part of the island the species is known by its Malay name, *Keping Keping,* which means 'money bird' (Ripley, *in* Mayr and de Schauensee, 1939: 137), a term which, I presume, is based on the resemblance of the round ornamented feathers on the tips of the long tail wires to metallic coins. Or possibly the name is based in part on the fact that for many years (and probably now again in west New Guinea) skins of the adult males carried a high monetary value.

The manner in which primitive Papuans hunt the male with bow and arrow, as well as the way the old-time plume collectors obtained this gorgeous bird, can be inferred from the following notes which I wrote at Lae after an excursion into the Markham River forests with one of the last of the old-time plume collectors: 'Adolph Batze and his son Rae took me through a magnificent original forest in quest of the King Bird of Paradise. In 1952 I had been much impressed when Batze had guided me to an adult male *Cicinnurus* in the same general area some eight miles from Lae. That was in the month of June. Now, in November, we again sought this species. The forest was much more quiet .... Batze would walk a quarter of a mile and then stop and whistle. Usually there was no answer but once in a while a male *Cicinnurus* would answer. Batze's call, which I carefully noted, was a short medium-strength ascending whistle followed by a rapid series of shorter lower notes: WHEN SO-SO-SO-SO-SO-SO. This call seemed to agitate the *Cicinnurus* and his response of course revealed his position, which was always in a tall forest tree. Several times we scanned such big trees trying to sight the *Cicinnurus* but each time we failed, our actions either having scared the male away or caused it to keep quiet and hidden. The singing trees all had thick dark canopies and all were heavily draped with long, thin hanging vines .... I shall never forget the male Batze showed me in 1952. In response to his whistles, it had flown to a perch only 30 feet up on a limblet among small leaves. Its white abdomen and red upperparts were clearly seen, but not until Batze had spent more than a minute trying to point out the bird to me. It was well camouflaged, the white of the underparts blending with light spots penetrating the leaves from the sky.'

Voice: The call in general is much like that of *Paradisaea minor* but higher in pitch (see below).

Food: Tree fruits often relatively large ones. One that I observed feeding ate soft, triangular green tree fruits which were covered with little spines!

Breeding Behaviour: Rand (1938: 7–8), who found the species common on the Fly River, observed males which remained for long periods alone in medium-sized, densely leaved, shrubby forest trees. He wrote 'At one such tree near camp I first recorded a male in it on October 10 and from then to October 31, I visited this tree almost daily, and at various times during the day. Each time the male was in the tree. The presence of a fruiting liana, on the fruit

195

of which many species of birds fed, perhaps even made it unnecessary for the bird of paradise to leave for food, although I did not see it feeding on this fruit.

'Several times I watched this tree for a few hours at a time in the hopes of seeing some sort of display, but in vain. The bird spent long periods sitting quietly in the interior of the tree, frequently calling a harsh "caaar." somewhat drawn out and plaintive.

'When it moved about its actions were quick and active. One of its characteristic actions was to fly down and alight on a small vertical branch or liana, and hop up it, reversing its body at each hop. I saw several other species of passerine birds in this tree and the king bird of paradise paid no attention to these intruding birds. Occasionally I shot a bird in or near this tree. The shot did not frighten the king bird of paradise from the tree; indeed sometimes the sound of the shot stimulated it to call.

'Other males apparently had similar posts nearby, to which they kept, judging by their calls, which I heard day after day when at this one tree. But each male was alone in its tree. . . . Probably this single tree, or sometimes two trees close together, represents the territory held by one male and to which the female comes to mate.'

During the daylight hours of 6 to 10 July 1956, the writer observed a male which spent virtually the whole time sitting and displaying forty feet up in a ninety-foot tree on Mt Tyo in the Finisterre Mountains (1650 feet). The male did not sleep in the display tree but arrived after a feeding expedition at about 7.38 a.m. It then remained in and around the display stage, which was virtually concealed from below by vines and other vegetation and which was overspread by a small, umbrella-like canopy of vines and leaves. Except for a few brief periods when he would dive from the display ground and disappear for a few minutes, the male spent the whole day in the display tree. Once when it returned after an absence of eight minutes, it settled down with the flank plumes fanned outward, the body upright and 'penguin-like,' and the white feathers of the abdomen extending well below the perch; the base of the body seemed to be pressing downward on the gently sloping vine perch in exactly the same spot where this action had been observed a number of times before. Another time, after the male had been gone four minutes it returned and immediately began wiping its bill (about ten times) on a vine above its display perch, at the same time, with the bill held slightly open, it emitted a sound which was low, whirring, and insect-like. It then flexed the display fans to the fullest extent up the sides of the neck, and pulsed them seven times; about then it flexed the wings upward and cried. Half a dozen times during one day the male flew or dove downward from its high perch, once to a perch eight feet from the ground, in a beam of sunlight, where it sat for 45 seconds; once or twice to a hanging vertical vine 20 feet below its display area, where it perched across the vine for 20 seconds, then climbed the vine in a most beautiful manner, going straight up and switching its tail and body from side to side as it climbed. Several times the male suddenly dropped from its display arena like a rock, falling four to ten or more feet before it opened its wings.

Inverted displays were not observed, but many times the male seemed far out of balance as it clung 'drunkenly' to the top of the sloping perch with one foot extended far up the vine, the other lost in its expanded white abdominal plumage. Where the male went during its absences I do not know; but it may be that he flew over the display tree, as Walter Goodfellow suggested in a most interesting observation (*in* Ogilvie-Grant 1915: 21). While watching birds across a river in south-west New Guinea he saw 'a small bird rise from the top of a tree and soar into the air like a Sky-Lark. After it had risen about 30 feet, it suddenly seemed to collapse and dropped back into the tree as though it had been shot.' The bird proved to be a male King Bird of Paradise, and Goodfellow decided that this soaring habit was part of the display.

The male I had under close observation for a full day on 8 July left the display area at about 4.48 p.m. On its display perch during the day it had preened extensively at the base of the back by sliding the bill along a tail wire from its base to the flag; it had opened one wing and lowered the head in a crook for many seconds. It often appeared to yawn, showing the yellow inner mouth parts. During much of the day the gold forehead was the only moving ornament that I could see easily from the ground without binoculars. It danced about a lot under the black umbrella of vines which shaded the main display perch. At other times a curious light like a weak blue fire emanated from the glossy red plumage as the bird sat in the shadows.

Often the male had shaken its body, pressed its wings tightly together over the back and elevated them in the half-closed position. Once when the male disappeared, '. . . very weak grating, churring notes' were heard high overhead. These may have come from the male as it flew above the forest.

Voice: From its display ground the King called frequently: *waa-waa-waa-waa-waa*, much like *P. minor* but with a higher pitch; it also called *kii-kii-kii-kii-kii-kii-kii* much in the manner of *P. minor*, but again higher in pitch. Other calls heard while the male was on the display perches were *quaa-quaa-quaa-qa-qa*, rather deep and raspy, with the wings slightly open and the head bent downward; a single *kee* every 30 to 50 seconds while squatting on the perch; a kingfisher-like *kreea, kreea*; and a drawn-out *kaa, kaa*. Also heard were insect-like buzzing notes and harsh, sharp *quaa* notes. Other males were sometimes heard calling in the distance as Rand had also noted.

In captivity, Sir William Ingram (1907: 224–229, with drawings by G.E. Lodge) observed the display of a solitary male. First the male emitted several short quail-like notes; next he spread the wings, occasionally hiding the head; or he stretched upright and flapped them; then he puffed out the white abdominal plumage and began a warbling song – a low bubbling note. The fan-like side plumes were then spread and opened and closed; the tail was pressed over the back so that the tail wires with their spiral tips were extended over the head; and the body was gently swayed and the small spiral tips made to bounce from one side to the other. Ingram noted that '. . . the swaying body seems to keep time with the song, and at intervals, with a swallowing movement of his throat, the bird raises and lowers his head. Then comes the finale, which lasts only for a few seconds. He suddenly turns right around and shows his back, the white fluffy feathers under the tail bristling in his excitement; he bends down on his perch in the attitude of a fighting cock, his widely opened bill showing distinctly the extraordinary light apple-green colour of the gullet, and sings the same gurgling note without once closing his bill, and with a slow dying away movement of his tail and body. A single drawn-out note is then uttered, the tail wires are lowered, and the dance and song are over.' Ingram noted another rare form of display, the inverted display, when the male dropped under the perch and walked back and forth while suspended with his wings expanded, then closed the wings and stretched the legs so as to resemble a suspended crimson-coloured fruit.

1 Magnificent Rifle Bird (*Ptiloris magnificus*) in display. (Photo: New York Zoological Society)

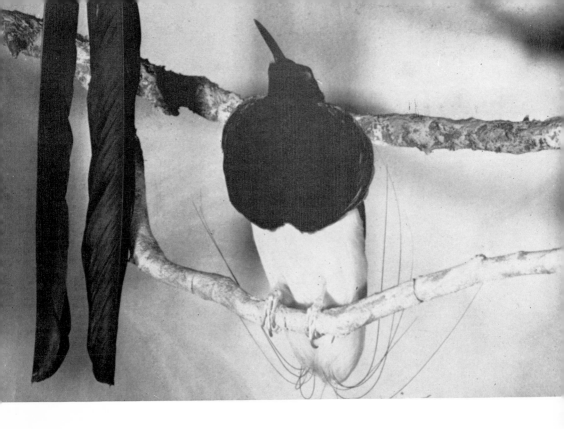

2 Twelve-wired Bird of Paradise (*Seleucidis melanoleuca*). 2a (*above*) Adult male (museum group). 2b (*below*) Female on nest in a pandamus tree.

3 Long-tailed Paradigalla (*Paradigalla carunculata*). Adult male (museum group).

4 Short-tailed Paradigalla (*Paradigalla brevicauda*). Female.

5 Brown Sickle-billed
Bird of Paradise
(*Epimachus meyeri*).
Nest and egg, found
at 8,000 feet in the
Kubor Mountains.

6 Princess Stephanie
Bird of Paradise
(*Astrapia stephaniae*).
6a (*below left*) Male
adult. 6b (*above*)
Female. 6c (*right*)
Looking up into a
display tree. The dark
mass in the centre of
the crown is a blind
(hide) built by natives
and from which they
shoot displaying birds.
A climbing native is
seen on the lower
trunk.

7 Superb Bird of Paradise (*Lophorina superba*). Adult male showing breast shield partly spread.

8 Wahnes' Six-wired Bird of Paradise (*Parotia wahnesi*). Male in display with flag-tipped wires of crown pointing forward and flank tufts spread out like a skirt (photograph of a mounted museum specimen).

9 Queen Carola's Six-wired Bird of Paradise (*Parotia carolae*). Adult male on its bower.

10 Lawes' Six-wired Bird of Paradise (*Parotia lawesi*) Immature male.

11 King of Saxony Bird of Paradise (*Pteridophora alberti*). 11a (*right*) Male perched high in a tree where it displays. Note the elongated head plumes. 11b (*above*) Female. Note small spike plume.

12 Magnificent Bird of Paradise
(*Diphyllodes magnificus*) on
display area. The male (lower)
is displaying to the female.
(From a drawing by B. F.
Chapman)

13 Magnificent Bird of Paradise
(*Diphyllodes magnificus*). 13a (*above*)
Adult male. 13b (*right*) Adult
female.

14 Wilson's Bird of Paradise
(*Diphyllodes respublica*). Adult
male (photographed in the
Honolulu Zoo).

15 Count Raggi's Bird of
Paradise (*Paradisaea raggiana*)
Adult male.

16 Lesser Bird of Paradise (*Paradisaea minor*). Adult male.

17 Emperor of Germany Bird of Paradise (*Paradisaea guilielmi*). Male giving its inverted display (photograph of a mounted museum specimen).

18 Blue Bird of Paradise (*Paradisaea rudolphi*). Male giving its inverted display.
(photograph of a mounted museum specimen).

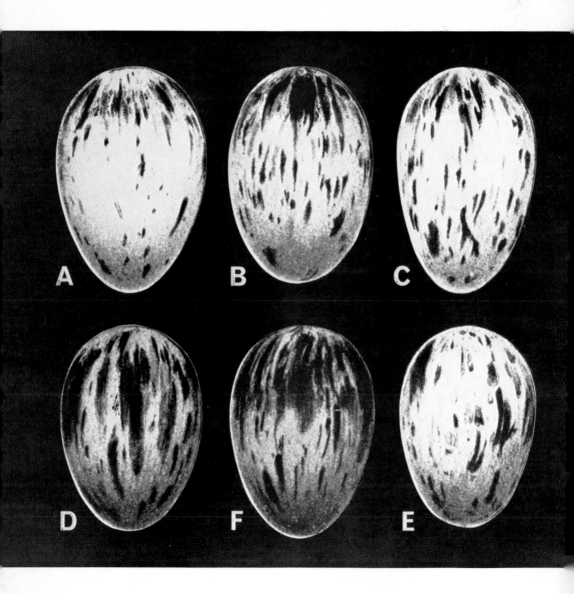

19 Many bird of paradise eggs are mostly buffy to orange streaked with brown. The genera shown here are (A) Twelve-wired Bird of Paradise (*Seleucidis*); (B, C and D) plumed birds of paradise (*Paradisaea*); (E) Rifle Bird (*Ptiloris*); and (F) Astrapia (*Astrapia*).

20 Black-eared Catbird (*Ailuroedus melanotis*). Adult at nest containing young. (Photo: John Warham)

21 Tooth-billed Bower Bird (*Scenopoeetes dentirostris*) on its 'stage'. (Photo: John Warham)

22 Archbold's Bower Bird (*Archboldia papuensis*). Male displaying to female in bower (photograph of a museum group).

23 Macgregor's Gardener Bower Bird (*Amblyornis macgregoriae*). Male (*left*) displaying to female at bower in the Herzog Mountains, New Guinea. (Photo: S. Diczbalis, H. Sielmann production)

24 Golden Bower Bird
(*Prionodura newtoniana*). Male
arranging a twig in its bower.
(Photo: John Warham)

25 The author in camp in the
Adelbert Mountains of north New
Guinea in March 1959, examining
a male (upper) and female specimen
of the rare Adelbert Regent
Bower Bird (*Sericulus bakeri*), and
comparing them with the painting
by Joseph Sibal. (Photo: Mrs E.
T. Gilliard)

26 (*above*) Striped Gardener Bower Bird (*Amblyornis subalaris*). Male (crested)
and female at bower (from a painting by Joseph Sibal).

27 (*above right*) Satin Bower Bird (*Ptilonorhynchus violaceus*). Male (right)
and female at bower. (Photo: John Warham)

28 (*below right*) Spotted Bower Bird (*Chlamydera maculata*). Male at bower, in
forward bowing display. (Photo: John Warham)

29 Great Grey
Bower Bird
(*Chlamydera
nuchalis*). Male in
bower, displaying
to a female.
(Photo: John
Warham)

30 Fawn-breasted
Bower Bird
(*Chlamydera
cerviniventris*). Male
and female at bower;
the female is
squatting in the
bower, and the male
is outside and in
front, twisting to dis-
play his crestless head.

31 Lauterbach's Bower Bird (*Chlamydera lauterbachi*). 31a (*above*) Nest and egg. 31b (*right*) Nestling in nest. 31c (*below right*) Bowers brought in to the author's camp at Kup for study. The unusual concentrations of this species here may represent an exploded breeding arena.

32 Interior of a blind (hide) at a bower of Macgregor's Bower Bird
(*Amblyornis macgregoriae*) on Mt. Kubor, with cameras and tape recorder.

Bergman (1956 : 197), observing a male as it courted a female in captivity, noted that the male began by raising the tail and wires at right angles to the body, then spread the wings and turned to the female while constantly vibrating and spreading the wings to their full extent. Next he suddenly hung upside down with the wings fully extended and vibrating, the bill open, the yellow green gape showing. After ten seconds the wings were closed and the male, still in the hanging position, swung the body from left to right for a few seconds, then released the feet and dropped. Once when the male was singing a song rather like that of the skylark, and as usual when singing, keeping the disks of the tail wires in constant motion, the female flew down and perched beside him. The male then expanded the wings, vibrated them and moved closer to her on the same branch, then he expanded the flank fans, puffed out the white feathers of the underparts till nearly spherical, and swept the tail wires over the back, all the while keeping his head elevated and swaying slightly from side to side. The female, sitting very close to the displaying male, then occasionally picked at his feathers. Later, when the female was ready, the male chased her and she then occasionally assumed the mating position with the body lowered and the tail raised.

Nesting: In the Aru Islands in late March, 1929, Wilfred Frost discovered a nest of this species about seven feet up in a small forest tree. It was in a cavity about 18 inches deep but filled to within a few inches of the lip with palm fibres. Access to the nest was through a hole about one and one half inches in diameter. Two eggs were found, one of which measured 27·5 × 21 mm. These were creamy white tinged with pink and with dark brown streaks on the larger end. A nestling in The American Museum collection was taken by H. Kühn, 10 January 1900, on Misol Island.

Aviculture: Bergman bred this species in captivity in Sweden (1956: 197–205). Two eggs were laid in a nest box a day apart. Incubating began with the laying of the first egg and continued for 17 days. The young were hatched a day apart; their eyes opened on the fifth day. At 12 days the first feathers began to sprout; at 14 days all feathers, both above and below, had sprouted. The young left the nest on the fourteenth day, perhaps prematurely. They flew straight from branch to branch despite the undeveloped tail.

The female alone attended the nest, although the male was

P

present in the enclosure all the while and continued to display to her. Feeding of the young was by regurgitation from the crop; nest sanitation was by swallowing. Insect food was given the nestlings by the female. At 30 days of age the young still begged with fluttering wings and feeble cheeps and were fed by the female. At 50 days of age the young began giving harsh warning cries.

Subspecies: Six subspecies are recognised. All are very similar.

1   *C. r. regius* (Linnaeus), 1758, *Syst. Nat.*, ed. 10, p. 110. Type locality 'East Indies' = Aru Islands. Known only from the Aru Islands.

2   *C. r. rex* (Scopoli), 1786, *Del. Faun. Flor. Insubr.*, pt. 2, p. 88 (based on Sonnerat, 1776, *Voy. Nouv. Guinea*, p. 156, pl. 95). Type locality 'New Guinea' = Sorong district, Vogelkop. [*C. spinturnix* Lesson, 1835, and *C. r. claudii* Ogilvie-Grant, 1915, are synonyms.] Known from Misol, Salawati, Batanta, and New Guinea except between Geelvink Bay and the Huon Gulf.

3   *C. r. gymnorhynchus* Stresemann, 1922, *Journ. f. Orn.*, vol. 70, p. 405. Type locality Heldsbachküste near Finschhafen. Known only from the north-eastern coast of the Huon Gulf.

4   *C. r. similis* Stresemann, 1922, *Journ. f. Orn.*, vol. 70, p. 405. Type locality Stephansort, Astrolabe Bay. Known only from Astrolabe Bay and the upper Ramu west at least to Humboldt Bay and the upper Mamberamo River.

5   *C. r. cryptorhynchus* Stresemann, 1922, *Journ. f. Orn.*, vol. 70, p. 405. Type locality Taua, lower Mamberamo River. Known only from the eastern coast of Geelvink Bay and north New Guinea near the mouth of the Mamberamo River.

6   *C. r. coccineifrons* Rothschild, 1896, *Novit. Zool.*, vol. 3, p. 10 [type in AMNH, no. 678666]. Type locality Jobi Island. Known only from Japen Island.

Evolution and Taxonomy: The close relationship of *Cicinnurus* and *Diphyllodes* is especially apparent when *Cicinnurus* is compared with *D. respublica,* in which the adult male has a scarlet red back with a peculiar silvery gloss exactly as found in *Cicinnurus.* Another factor indicating close relationship is the close similarity in size, pattern, and colouration of the females. In *D. magnificus* the red of the male is of a different hue and much more restricted and the female is of different proportions.

On the basis of morphology then, it would seem that *Cicinnurus* and *Diphyllodes* evolved from a fairly advanced stock of red and metallic green arboreally displaying birds with modified central rectrices – a stock perhaps not too far removed from the ancestral *Paradisaea* with its modified central tail feathers, its iridescent green and shining red markings (the latter now mostly relict on the bases of the ornamental plumes).

On the basis of ethology, the terrestrial displays of *Diphyllodes* appear to be a step ahead of the arboreal displays of *Cicinnurus*, even considering the inverted displays practised by some of the races. This is one reason why I concur with Mayr and Bock in their placement of *Cicinnurus* beneath *Diphyllodes*.

The relationship of *Cicinnuris* and *Paradisaea* is more obscure, but I suspect that it is much closer than is commonly believed. Bock (1963), although noting some minor differences in skull anatomy, wrote: '. . . these differences are minor as the entire construction of the *Cicinnurus* skull is the same as in *Paradisaea*.' But then Bock placed the 'sickle-tails' (*Cicinnurus* and *Diphyllodes*) in a generic group with the flag birds (*Lophorina*, *Parotia*, *Pteridophora*), an interpretation which seems incorrect to me.

On the basis of external morphology (for example, the development of the central pair of rectrices) and call notes (*Cicinnurus* and *P. minor* sound disconcertingly alike), the 'sickle-tails' appear quite different from the flag birds. I would prefer to place them in a distinct group nearer to the plumed birds than to the flag birds. The fact that inverted displays are found in both *Cicinnurus* and *Paradisaea* has not been used to weight this conclusion.

Magnificent Bird of Paradise

Diphyllodes magnificus (Pennant)
Male 7½ in.

Range: Western Papuan islands (Misol, Salawati), Japen Island, and all of New Guinea; from 1900 feet to about 5500, rarely down to 250 feet. (See Map 9.9, page 209.)

Adult Male: A starling-sized, yellow-collared, orange-winged green black bird with long loosely coiled central tail plumes. In more detail, crown and nape with short stubby feathering brownish, tinged orange at sides; spots in front and over eye iridescent green; narrow bare postocular streak pale blue; hind neck to upper back with an erectile glossy golden yellow cape, edged laterally brown to orange brown; back dark red to blackish, somewhat glossy; lower back orange yellow; upper tail coverts and tail (except central rectrices) blackish; central tail feathers greatly elongated (up to 300 mm. long), narrow, loosely coiled, iridescent blue green; median and greater upper wing coverts and

inner secondaries dull mustard yellow to bright orange yellow (subspecies); lesser upper wing coverts dark brown to olive brown; primaries and secondaries blackish with much narrow orange yellow outer edging; cheeks and throat blackish glossed metallic bronze green; underparts from throat to abdomen metallic sea green forming (in display) a flattish shield; midline and lateral fringes of green shield iridescent blue green; rest of underparts sooty black (to deep purplish black, subspecies); under wing coverts sooty to ochraceous brown; inner edges of flight quills ochraceous; under surfaces of elongated central tail plumes grey. Iris blackish brown; bill pale cerulean blue with black edges; feet purplish blue black; naked skin of face and postocular streak pale blue; mouth yellow green. Wing 111–120; tail 35–43; bill from base 21; tarsus 32 mm.

Adult Female: Very different from male. Upperparts dull buffy olive to olive brown, darker on fore half of head, especially around eyes; wings and tail dark brown to olive brown; underparts grey to pale brown narrowly barred black. Iris dark brown; bill pale blue grey; mouth jade green; feet violet blue. Wing 104–115; tail 56–68; bill from base 29; tarsus 31 mm.

Immature: First year plumage much like adult female. Male intermediate plumages or stages of dress: (a) like adult female but lore spots iridescent green; base of bill and chin with some black midline of upper breast with some glossy green feathering; hind neck with variable amounts of yellow; back with traces of red; tail coverts and tail, including central rectrices as in adult male; (b) like adult male except inner secondaries much as in female; much female feathering scattered through green underparts and yellow dorsal plumage. Rand (*in* Mayr and Rand 1937: 201) wrote that the males have at least three immature plumages before reaching the adult: 'The nestling plumage, the first year plumage acquired by an incomplete molt, another immature plumage closely resembling in color that of the adult female, but more olive-yellow on the back and edges of the remiges, acquired by a complete molt.'

Remarks: The Magnificent Bird of Paradise is a fairly common to common species of the rolling mountain forests throughout its broad range. It is chiefly a bird of the midmountains but in a few places it descends almost to sea level, as at Wararuk, near Utu village, at the foot of the Adelbert Mountains, where Father Bernard Johnson (personal communication) recently observed males above their clearings in the floor of original rain forest at an elevation of about 250 feet. It is a difficult bird to observe except in the vicinity of its display grounds, but these are generally well known to the local inhabitants.

Natives of the Kup region in the Wahgi Valley guided me to a series of bowers and, similarly, in the Adelbert Mountains above Maratambu, I was led to a number of bowers by local guides, all of whom seemed to know the dancing behaviour of these birds.

Quite frequently in the Wahgi Valley one encounters men wearing in their hair the spiraling tail plumes and bright plumage of this species.

Ecology: Found chiefly in original and second-growth forests on moderately steep hillsides or on the tops of forested ridges. In the Wahgi region, it is common in riverine forests and gullies bordered by extensive grasslands.

Voice: The calls given by the males in the vicinity of their display courts are varied. Rand described them as mostly loud, harsh calls, *ca cru cru cru,* also a loud, clear *car* or *cre* repeated a number of times, also 'a hoarse or squalling *caaar ca ca ca*.' Some of these calls can be heard more than a quarter mile through the forest.

Food: Apparently chiefly tree fruits. The stomachs of two specimens contained fruit seeds and the flesh of orange fruits.

Breeding Behaviour: The males live apart from the females in special areas where, within earshot of each other, they clear display grounds in the substage of the forest. In 1938 Rand made a series of splendid observations of a male at a bower as it received a visit from a female. In 1952 and again in 1959 the writer spent many days in blinds in the Kubor Mountains and in the Adelbert Mountains in nearly futile attempts to film the remarkable courtship dance that Rand had discovered and described. The individual males make private courts which are 15 to 20 feet in diameter. These courts are attended daily apparently for several months per year and quite possibly for several years in succession. Each male spends many hours per day in and near its court.

The Courtship Area: In the Kup region (5000 feet) of the Wahgi Valley, I found five display grounds in an elongated area of forest about one and one-half miles long. Males were in attendance at three of the courts and their powerful police-whistle calls resounded through the forest. In the Adelbert Mountains two long-established courts, each with an actively displaying male, were studied a half mile apart on a rounded hilltop. One of these I described on the spot as follows:

The Bower: ' . . . The bower consists of about twenty fish-pole-like saplings growing in a carefully cleared, slightly sloping patch of earth in which one blemish occurred – a mound of reddish brown earth some four inches high and six inches in width, the workings of ants, which rises along one edge of the cleared stage and must be a source of unending worry to the bird. All around the edges of the stage are fresh and fairly fresh green leaves, also many brown leaves, and under and back of these there is a mass of forest floor litter. The leaves seem to be the result of trimming activities by the bower owner. Above the bower I note that the sky light shows down strongly. Also I note that the saplings look as though gypsy moths have been working on them. The stripping goes up to a height of 25 feet. One vine-covered, moderately sized tree arches over the bower at a height of eight feet. On its trunk are many leafy vines and all have the broad leaves either mutilated or shorn away. The bower court itself is situated near the trunk of a tall tree fern that for some reason is virtually frondless. This tree fern is sheathed with moss and some of the moss growth is six inches long. This is an indication of the cleaning activities of the Magnificent Bird which has "swept" clean the ground beneath this shaggy plant. Only large immovable roots mar the surface of its stage. The constant cleaning over a long period has graded the earth against these roots in a picturesque way so that it vaguely resembles a contoured rice paddy.'

Rand (1940) described a display ground which he found in the Snow Mountains as follows: 'On the steep forested slopes at these altitudes there are always small areas where the soil is eroding and slipping so fast that forest cannot establish itself. These areas are covered with low forest regrowth. It was in such places that the display grounds were situated. . . . The display area in each case consisted of a more or less circular area on the ground about 15 to 20 feet across from which all leaves, twigs and small plants have been removed. These lay in a windrow at the lower edge of the display ground. Only a few small sticks and logs interrupted the smoothness of the ground. Numbers of saplings mostly dead stood in the display ground. Above the display ground the leaves had been plucked from the saplings and the lower trees, and in places the bark had been plucked from stems so they were frayed. Probably the dead saplings in the display ground were killed in this way by the bird. The result was a clear cone through which light from the sky reached the ground unimpeded. This would be an advantage to the displaying bird in increasing the brilliancy of its colors.'

The Bower Activities: Rand added ' . . . I found that the adult male in attendance spent much time clearing the display ground, picking up leaves and twigs that had fallen and with a flick of his head throwing them down to join the windrow of rotting debris at the bottom edge of the bower. Sometimes when an object did not reach the lower edge of the display ground the first throw the male followed it down, to give it another throw until it reached the bottom. Sometimes when pecking at moss it was removing no object I could see and it really appeared to be grooming or combing the moss carpeting the ground. . . . Less often the male mounted into the saplings and plucked off leaves above and about the edge of the bower. When the leaves fell on the bower they were later thrown away. . . .Sometimes

205

the male pecked off bits of bark from a sapling, worried at the ends of sticks, trying to break them off. Sometimes the sound of its blows on the wood could be plainly heard in the blind where I was hidden ten to fifteen feet away. . . .

'When the male was alone it usually spent most of its time sitting on one or another perch, near the edge of the bower and from two to fifteen feet from the ground. It often sat for long periods, sometimes up to thirty or forty minutes at a time. Much of this time was spent preening its feathers. The body plumage and wing feathers were carefully gone over and the bird frequently stretched, when the wings were carried over the back and the cape shot forward over the head. I never saw it preen or stretch while in the display area. . . . The adult male frequently called from its perch near the edge of the display ground. These loud, far-reaching calls . . . are apparently for the purpose of advertising the bird's presence. They were rarely given while the bird was actually in the displaying ground . . . The scolding notes given when the adult was disturbed at its display area, low spitting and clucking notes and a scolding "chus" I have referred to above. The low soft calls given when a female came to the display area I describe below.'

Rand observed three types of displays in the adult male: (1) a pulsing of the breast shield which was the most common display; this was seen only when the bird was on a perch within a foot or so of the ground display court, and it was used with or without the female being present; (2) a horizontal display which was given while clinging to the side of a sapling – usually a special display sapling – a foot or so above the ground court; it too was given with or without the female being present but, in the latter case, only after a period of active ground clearing; (3) a pecking display with the inside of the mouth displayed; this was done from a normal perching position after copulation. The sequence and effect of these displays can best be understood by reading the following remarkable observations of a male being visited by a female which Rand recorded during a ten-minute period.

'I had been watching the bower from the blind since 1.30 p.m. The adult was about all this period, in and out of the display ground, clearing it and sitting beside it, calling. Three times he gave the horizontal display, each time after visiting the ground for cleaning. At 2.40 the male was on the ground cleaning when I heard another bird fly to a perch close to the blind. The male was all attention at once and flew up and lit on a perpendicular sapling about a foot above the ground. The female, as it proved to be, then came into the display ground and lit on the same sapling about three feet above the male. The male pulsed his breast (display type no. 1) towards the female, and continued to display his shield to her, turning toward her as she moved from sapling to sapling, keeping about four feet above the ground. . . . Once the male followed her to another sapling, and hopped up toward her, with his breast parallel to and close to the trunk, pulsing his shield the while though it was not directly toward her . . . Much of this time the male was calling low, enticing questioning calls of "eek" or "eee." The female sat still and quiet while perched. . . . Then the female flew to another perch about eight feet away, on the edge of the display ground, as though she was going to leave. The male at once turned his back to her and made as if to hop down to the ground and clean. The female at once came back to directly above him and he at once turned toward her pulsing his shield. Again the female flew away to another perch ten feet away and the whole ceremony was repeated. This time, however, while the male was giving his breast pulsing the female began to hop down toward him. He pressed his breast closer to the sapling, pulsing the shield, and gave low, eager, single little calls. The female paused about a foot above the male, who was about that far above the ground. The male then went into the horizontal display, breast shield lengthened and flattened, the iridescent line down the centre visible from where I was, the cape straight out. The tail was in line with the body and was vibrating, possibly from the muscular effort required for the pose, as the dull underside has little ornamental effect. Otherwise the bird was motionless. He held this pose for perhaps thirty seconds. The female hopped down closer. The male then abandoned his pose, and rather deliberately hopped up and mounted her. Copulation ensued. The male then dismounted, hopping to perch just below the female, then display type no. 3 was given. . . . With tail erected at right angles with the back he vigorously pecked the nape of the female. After each peck the male drew back with widely opened mouth, displaying the yellowish green mouth lining so plainly that I could see it. In a few moments the female flew directly from the display ground. This was at about 2.50 p.m.'

Rand reports that on one occasion an immature male visited the display ground while the adult owner was absent. The immature

male then performed display type (3) but without previously cleaning the ground. An immature male that I observed at a display
ground it did not own in the Adelbert Mountains, flew and jumped
around and up and down in the vertical saplings and then edged
down to peck at a stuffed female which had been attached to the
main display perch about two feet above the ground court. An adult
male decoy was placed in a bower about four feet above a ground
court by Rand. The owner cock, when it spied the decoy, flew at it,
lit on it for a moment, momentarily erected its cape and pecked at
the decoy before flying to a perch about ten feet away to sit for some
thirty-five minutes facing the decoy.

Nesting: Bulmer observed three nests *in situ,* all with the female
in attendance, on the north watershed of Mt Hagen. One discovered
24 September 1955, ' . . . was fourteen feet up in a thick cluster of
leaves of a parasitic plant in an elyap tree (soft-wooded tree very
common in garden fallow) in a tree-fallow area lacking undergrowth, at the foot of a steep slope near a cane bed, at 4,500 feet.'
The nest was composed of green moss, plus a little mammal fur, and
was lined with fibres and rootlets. 'External dimensions $6\frac{1}{2}''$ diam,
$\times 4\frac{1}{2}''$ deep; internal $3\frac{1}{4}''$ diam. $\times 1\frac{3}{4}''$ deep.' Two slightly incubated
eggs were collected from this nest. Bulmer's second nest was found
30 September at 4300 feet in a low bush in kunai grass. It was
two feet six inches from the ground and was composed of moss, dry
leaves and weeds, and lined with fine rootlets and plant-like fibres. Its
external dimensions were $6'' \times 4''$ deep; internally it measured
$3'' \times 2\frac{1}{4}''$ deep. It also contained a set of two slightly incubated eggs.
Bulmer's third nest was discovered 24 December at 5200 feet,
twelve feet up in a pandanus tree growing at the edge of a garden.
The female sat lightly on this nest, which contained a set of two eggs.

Eggs: Two, yellowish cream with light brown and grey longitudinal
marks, 29·8–32·8 × 22·0–24·0 mm. (Schönwetter, 1944: 18). Rand
found birds in breeding condition in the Snow Mountains in
February, March, and April and in south-east New Guinea in
September and October. The writer collected a female with an egg
ready for laying on 23 March 1959, in the Adelbert Mountains
(3400 feet).

Subspecies: Four rather similar races are known:

1   *D. m. magnificus* (Pennant), 1781, *Spec. Faun. Ind.,* in Forster's

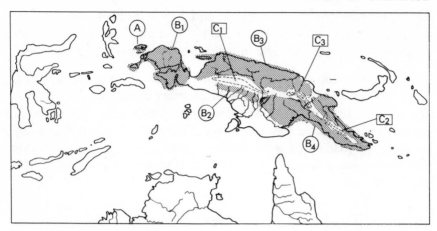

Map 9.9 *Diphyllodes* and *Loria*
Diphyllodes respublica (A) hilly country
Diphyllodes magnificus (B) 250–5500 feet
   Diphyllodes magnificus magnificus (B1)
   Diphyllodes magnificus intermedius (B2)
   Diphyllodes magnificus chrysopterus (B3)
   Diphyllodes magnificus hunsteini (B4)
Loria loriae (C) 5000 to 8500 feet
   Loria loriae inexpecata (C1)
   Loria loriae loriae (C2)
   Loria loriae amethystina (C3)

Indian Zool., p. 40 (based on Daubenton, *Pl. Enlum*, pl. 631). Type locality New Guinea, restricted to the Arfak Mountains. Known from western Papuan islands (Misol, Salawati), Vogelkop, Wandammen District and Onin Peninsula. Scapulars and inner secondaries clay-coloured.

2 *D. m. intermedius* Hartert, 1930, *Novit. Zool.*, vol. 36, p. 36 [type in AMNH, no. 678407]. Type locality Snow Mountains [= upper Setekwa River]. Known from the Weyland Mountains eastward to the southern slopes of the Nassau and Oranje mountains. Like *magnificus* but scapulars and inner secondaries brighter, more dull orange.

3 *D. m. chrysopterus* Elliot, 1873, *Monogr. Birds Parad.*, p. 13. Type locality 'Jobi Island.' Known from Japen Island and north New Guinea from eastern Geelvink Bay and the Mamberamo

Basin eastward to the Telefomin and Sepik highlands and to the north watershed of the Wahgi Divide (Jimmi River region). Like *magnificus* but scapulars and inner secondaries bright golden yellow.

4 *D. m. hunsteini* Meyer, 1885, *Zeitschr. Ges. Orn.*, vol. 2, p. 389, pl. 21. Type locality Hufeisengebirge (near Astrolabe Mountains) [*D. m. extra* Iredale, 1950, Mt Hagen, is a synonym]. Known from eastern New Guinea west to Huon Peninsula, Wahgi Highlands (Kubor, Bismarck, Hagen, Giluwe) and upper Fly River (Mt Mabion). Like *magnificus* but generally lighter on head, back, and wings.

Wilson's Bird of Paradise

Diphyllodes respublica (Bonaparte)
Male $6\frac{1}{2}$ in.
[1850, (Feb.), *Compt. Rend. Acad. Sci. Paris*, vol. 30, p. 131. Type locality 'New Guinea' (=Waigeu Island).]

Range: The western Papuan islands of Waigeu and Batanta. Found only in the hilly interior. (See Map 9.9, page 209.)

Adult Male: A starling-sized red, yellow, cobalt blue, green, and black bird with loosely coiled central tail feathers. In more detail, tuft at base of maxilla, forehead, narrow medial feather line of crown, narrow line crossing crown from region of ears, and narrow line circling hind crown, sides of forehead and throat velvet black; six naked areas on crown and nape cobalt blue; hind neck with a broad erectile yellow cape-fan overhanging back; back, secondaries, outer margins of primaries and upper wing coverts largely glossy crimson red; sides of back, fore back, and a narrow line across lower back velvet black; rump, upper tail coverts, most surfaces of wing quills, and tail (except central pair of rectrices which are much elongated, spiraled, and iridescent violet blue), dark brown to blackish brown; wing quills below with some ochraceous edging; lower throat to upper breast metallic oil green with a sprinkling of small opalescent blue dots on central throat; rest of underparts blackish brown. Iris deep brown; bill black; feet deep ultramarine blue; naked skin of crown and nape bright cobalt blue. Wing 94–98; tail (without central tail feathers) 37–40; bill from base 28; tarsus 28 mm.

Adult Female: Very different from male. Head partially bare as in male, but feathering of crown and nape dark brown, not black; rest of upperparts, including wings and tail, dark brown; somewhat brighter on tail and with the outer margins of the secondaries orange brown; throat and line from gape to ears greyish; rest of underparts buffy ochraceous with narrow dark brown bars; under wing coverts and inner margins of wing quills buffy, the former with chestnut edging. Iris brown; bill black; feet dark cobalt blue. Wing 92–98; tail 54; bill from base 21; tarsus 25 mm.

Immature: First year plumage much like adult female. Male intermediate plumage or stage of dress: like adult male but upperparts chiefly olive brown with traces of crimson red on back and on a few inner secondaries; some pale yellow on hind neck; central tail plumes sickle-shaped, not full-circled, and brown on outer third, not iridescent violet blue; underparts with a scattering of brown feathering on the breast shield and the rest of underparts much as in the adult female.

Remarks: On Waigeu Island in 1931 Georg Stein (1936: 26), collecting for the Berlin Museum, found that this species occurred only in the hilly interior and that the adult males were extremely shy and hard to observe. The home grounds of this wonderful little bird of paradise – one of the tiniest of the family – were first discovered in 1863 on Waigeu Island by Heinrich Agathon Bernstein while collecting for the Leyden Museum. About thirteen years earlier a male trade skin found its way to Europe and was purchased (probably in Paris) by an Englishman, Edward Wilson. Before its shipment to The Academy of Natural Sciences of Philadelphia (to which institution Mr Wilson made many valuable contributions), the wonderful new discovery was briefly examined by a leading ornithologist of that period, Prince Bonaparte, a nephew of Napoleon who, most un-ethically, took it upon himself to formally announce the new dis-covery to science. This was in February, 1850. In August of the same year, the American ornithologist, Cassin having earlier re-ceived the extraordinary new bird by sailing ship from Wilson, described and named it in honour of its donor, saying that he had taken this action ' . . . as a slight acknowledgment of [Wilson's] valuable services to the cause of zoological science in this country.' But the rules of zoological priority seem to have precluded the use of Cassin's technical name.

Prince Bonaparte's action was such that I hesitate to perpetuate his remarks concerning the name which he applied to this wonderful novelty, but his words contain the quintessence and flavour of a bygone era too rich to ignore. His explanation of his name (*respublica*) was that notwithstanding the custom then prevailing of giving the most beautiful bird discoveries the names of princes, he had not the slightest regard for all the rulers in the world and, therefore, had named this most beautiful bird after the Republic: '. . . that Re-public which might have been a Paradise had not the ambitions of Republicans, unworthy of the name they were using, made it by their evil actions more like a Hell (see Iredale, 1950: 113)'. With these words, it appears, Bonaparte torpedoed Wilson and Cassin, an action which purists still remember and resent. Lee Crandall, long the curator of birds at the New York Zoological Society, always called this wonderful bird Wilson's Bird of Paradise and, indeed, most of the American aviculturists keep that name alive. No less than the great European ornithologist, Sclater, after a visit to Phila-delphia to examine the Wilson collection, expressed deep qualms about this matter of nomenclature. He wrote that the Academy was fortunate in possessing the only known specimen of this extra-ordinary bird of paradise, adding: 'America's naturalists were quite unaware when they named this bird that Prince Bonaparte's characters of his *Lophorina* (!) *respublica* were taken from the self-same example. And seeing that even after the correction of this error in the generic appellation the descriptive phrase given by the Prince is positively erroneous, and such as the bird cannot by any possibility be recognised; I must say I think it very questionable whether we ought not to employ Cassin's name *wilsoni* for this species, although certainly subsequent in time of publication to Prince Bonaparte's term *respublica*.'

The Australian ornithologist, Tom Iredale (1950: 113), after a comprehensive study of this question, rejects the name *respublica* in favour of *wilsoni* (*op. cit.*:115). However, Ernst Mayr (*in* Peters, 1962: 199), in his comprehensive revision of the family, continues to recognise the Prince's name, and I have followed Mayr, retaining however the familiar vernacular name.

Very little is known concerning the behaviour of this bird in the wild, although from observations of males in captivity it is known that, like its cousin, the Magnificent Bird of Paradise, it clears a terrestrial bower and displays around a sapling on and near the ground. One can hardly believe that such a fascinating species still remains so little known, particularly in view of the fact that, since Bernstein discovered its home on Waigeu Island in 1863, at least eight bird expeditions with trained observers and collectors in command, have worked on the island. Apparently they all avoided the interior, leaving it to be surveyed by native shoot boys.

The history of a Waigeu megapode, *Aepypodius bruijnii*, recently discovered in the hills of the interior of Waigeu Island (see de Schauensee 1940), reinforces this suspicion. That chicken-sized bird, known from many old native trade skins which were said to have come from Waigeu Island, has never been seen on its home grounds except by native collectors. For this reason its place of origin was doubted. However, one native, Joseph Kokiaij, trained by Dillon Ripley, found it again in the interior of the island in 1938, when he secured a general collection of birds for The Academy of Natural Sciences of Philadelphia.

Habits and Food: Probably similar to those of *Diphyllodes magnificus*, its near relative on the mainland.

Breeding Behaviour: In the Honolulu Zoo in 1953 I photographed (see pl. 14) an adult male which had cleared a court around a sapling in a large cage which it occupied alone. This male frequently clung to the sapling near the ground or moved up and down the shaft near the ground. When debris such as a small twig was dropped on the court, it would become agitated and would work its way down to the very base of the shaft, then with one foot on the shaft above its body and one foot on the shaft at ground level, it would stretch far out over the court to pick up the twig.

Display observed in captivity (from Iredale, 1950:116) is as follows:

'The male jerks the head slightly from side to side, and emits a low, faint, whistling noise. . . . On one occasion the feathers of the neck were raised at this stage. The notes change somewhat and become louder; the jerking of the head ceases and the beak is opened and closed several times (often three). As the beak is opened, the feathers of the head are moved to cause them to assume their normal glossy intense black, which contrasts vividly with the light green of the mouth. Quite suddenly the bird retracts the head and neck, elevating the breast and expanding the "shield", which is now seen to be bright green; in the "bay" at the upper margin of the shield, which is roughly bean-shaped, is the head, the blue crown just showing and two green spots appearing behind and above the base of the bill. The bird remains thus, motionless and silent, for a brief time, and then suddenly thrusts itself forward again almost into the first position, which it frequently resumes forthwith. On two occasions the bird was seen to open and close its beak in this position.'

Nesting: Unknown.

Taxonomy: Series from Batanta and Waigeu islands appear inseparable.

Evolution: This species is about the size of *Cicinnurus regius* and, except for the naked head in *Diphyllodes respublica,* the females are extraordinarily similar for birds of different genera. I wonder if the bare head serves as an isolating mechanism? Only *D. respublica* occurs on Waigeu Island, but both genera occur on Batanta Island. No intergeneric hybrids have yet been discovered between these species, but three hybrids between its cousin *D. magnificus* and *C. regius* have been taken in the wild.

Greater Bird of Paradise

Paradisaea apoda Linnaeus
Male 17–18 in.

Range: Aru Islands and south New Guinea, mostly west of the Fly River. Found in the lowlands, up to 3000 feet. (See Map 9.10, page 220.) Introduced on Little Tobago in the Caribbean; see Appendix 1.

Adult Male: A crow-sized, yellow-crowned, maroon brown bird with a dark throat, immense yellow flank plumes and two elon-

gated central tail wires. In more
detail, forehead, lores, and chin
black glossed green; head and
neck orange yellow; mantle,
wings, and tail maroon brown;
sides of lower head, throat to
upper neck iridescent oil green;
upper breast brownish black (to
dark maroon, subspecies); rest of
underparts maroon brown; an
immense tuft of lace-like plumes
(up to 565 mm. long) on each
side of breast yellow to orange
yellow on basal two-thirds (with
a few glossy maroon feathers at
base), and pale cinnamon on
outer third; central rectrices
wire-like (with narrow dark
maroon vanes on basal 100 mm.),

blackish brown and up to 770 mm. in length. Iris lemon yellow; bill
light grey blue with a pale tip; feet pale dull brown. Wing 204–229
(subspecies); tail 144–172; exposed culmen 36; tarsus 57 mm.

Adult Female: Very different from male. Generally vinaceous
maroon becoming somewhat darker on head and neck all around,
also on upper breast; rest of underparts paler vinaceous maroon.
Iris lemon yellow; bill bluish grey; feet pale brown. Wing 175–187;
tail 134–138; exposed culmen 35; tarsus 48 mm.

Immature: First year plumage much like adult female. Male
intermediate plumages or stages of dress: (a) like adult female but
larger (wing 211 mm.) and with rear half of crown to hind neck
lighter, more vinaceous maroon with a tinge of orange on hind
neck; (b) like (a) but with a chin tuft, also a few scattered feathers
under eye and on throat iridescent green as in adult male; nape and
hind neck with an indistinct dull yellow band; larger (wing 226
mm.); (c) like adult male but hind crown and neck retaining much
brown female feathering; flank plumes absent; upper breast maroon,
not blackish maroon; rest of underparts paler as in female; flank
plumage just beginning to lengthen and pale cinnamon buff; middle
pair of rectrices only a third longer than outer pair; (d) like adult

R

male but abdomen pale vinaceous maroon, not dark maroon brown and with very short (110 mm.) cinnamon buff flank plumes; (e) like adult male but with yellow flank plumes much reduced in length.

Ogilvie–Grant (1915: 16) after studying a large series from the Mimika, Wataika and Utakwa river regions, south-west New Guinea, wrote that '. . . in a wild state the male takes at least five years to assume the adult plumage.'

Remarks: In southwest New Guinea the Greater Bird of Paradise is usually found well inland from the coast in the tropical forests of the floodplains and foothills. In the Aru Islands it is confined to the original forests of the interior. In both regions it is common to abundant and is usually met with in small flocks containing females and young males. Fully adult males appear to be rather scarce.

In 1857, Alfred Russel Wallace, working in the central Aru Islands (on Kobrur Island) became the first naturalist to observe the courtship behaviour of *Paradisaea apoda* in the wild. Stresemann (1954) wrote that 'What (Wallace) saw and heard in six weeks (March to May) and published the same year confirmed many statements made by Helwig (1680), that no one had examined; even the hunting practices of the Aru Islander were exactly as Herbert de Jager had described them about 1682.'

Each year for centuries the Aru Islanders have killed sizeable numbers of adult males for their valuable flank plumes. But they protect the dance trees where groups of males congregate and, of course, the species as a whole, because of its commercial value. Many of the trees have been in use for generations and it was said of the Aru Island plume hunter that he can tell to a bird the number of adult males that can be taken without causing the clan to move or be unduly depleted.

The Greater Bird of Paradise was probably the second species of this extraordinary family of birds to reach Europe. Because the early skins were footless (the Aru Islanders habitually cut off the feet of the trade skins), superstitions sprang up that these birds were extra-terrestrial wanderers, perhaps visitors from Paradise (see page 15) and thus it came about that Carolus Linnaeus, tongue in cheek, named this species *Paradisaea apoda*, the 'footless bird of paradise'.

Shortly after the turn of the century when plume collecting had reached peak activity, an Englishman, Sir William Ingram, became afraid that this beautiful species would be wiped out. He therefore sent an expedition to New Guinea and to the Aru Islands to capture living birds, and he simultaneously searched for and found a safe haven for them in the tropics of the New World. In 1909–1912 he liberated forty-seven Greater Birds of Paradise on Little Tobago, an uninhabited, forested island in the Caribbean. Their descendants still survive on the island in a wild state. In 1958 I observed them during a period of twenty-one days. Two dance trees were studied and I estimated the population to be about thirty-five birds, all of which are believed to be at least third-generation birds. (See Appendix 1.)

Ecology: An active, noisy bird of the upper third of the forest.

Food: Chiefly tree fruits, but probably insects are eaten.

Voice: A.R.Wallace wrote 'Their note is WANK-WANK-WANK-WOK-WOK-WOK-WOK and is so loud and shrill as to be heard a great distance, and to form the most prominent and characteristic animal sound in the Aru Islands.'

Breeding Behaviour: It is important to note (as Wallace did) that Wallace's famous description of the courtship behaviour of the Great Bird of Paradise in the wild was based in part on second-hand information which he was obliged to obtain from his hunters because of illness. 'I had, however, some consolation in the birds my boys brought home daily, more especially the Paradiseas, which they at length obtained in full plumage. It was quite a relief to my mind to get these, for I could hardly have torn myself away from Aru had I not obtained specimens. But what I valued almost as much as the birds themselves was the knowledge of their habits, which I was daily obtaining both from the accounts of my hunters, and from the conversation of the natives. The birds had now commenced what the people here call their "sacaleli", or dancing-parties, in certain trees in the forest, which are not fruit-trees, as I at first imagined, but which have an immense head of spreading branches and large but scattered leaves, giving a clear space for the birds to play and exhibit their plumes. On one of these trees a dozen or twenty full-plumaged male birds assemble together, raise up their wings, stretch out their necks, and elevate their exquisite plumes, keeping them in a continual vibration. Between whiles they fly across from branch to branch in great excitement, so that the whole tree is filled with waving plumes in every variety of attitude and motion. The bird itself is nearly as large as a crow, and is of a rich coffee-brown colour. The head and neck is of a pure straw yellow above, and rich metallic green beneath. The long plumy tufts of golden-orange feathers spring from the sides beneath each wing, and when the bird is in repose are partly concealed by them. At the time of its excitement, however, the wings are raised vertically over the back, the head is bent down and stretched out, and the long plumes are raised up and expanded till they form two magnificent golden fans, striped with deep red at the base, and fading off into the pale brown tint of the finely divided and softly waving points. The whole bird is then overshadowed by them, the crouching body, yellow head, and emerald-green throat forming but the foundation and setting to the golden glory which waves above. When seen in this attitude, the bird of paradise really deserves its name, and must be ranked as one of the most beautiful and most wonderful of living things.'

Later Wallace added the following:

'One day I got under a tree where a number of the Great Paradise Birds were assembled, but they were high up in the thickest of the foliage, and flying and jumping about so continually that I could get no good view of them. At length I shot one, but it was a young specimen, and was entirely of a rich chocolate-brown colour, without either the metallic green throat or yellow plumes of the full-grown bird. All that I had yet seen resembled this, and the natives told me that it would be about two months before any would be found in full plumage. I still hoped, therefore, to get some. Their voice is most extraordinary. At early morn, before the sun has risen, we hear a loud cry of "Wawk-wawk-wawk, wok-wok-wok", which resounds through the forest, changing its direction continually. This is the Great Bird of Paradise going to seek his breakfast. Others soon follow his example; lories and parroquets cry shrilly, cockatoos scream, king-hunters croak and bark, and the various smaller birds chirp and whistle their morning song. As I lie listening to these interesting sounds, I realise my position as the first European who has ever lived for months together in the Aru Islands, a place which I had hoped rather than expected ever to visit. . . .'

Judging from displays which I witnessed on Little Tobago Island (see p. 399) the males can be heard approaching, calling *walk-walk-walk,* shortly before dawn. Soon they fly or dive into the cluster of limbs forming the display arena. The individual males take up positions near each other, some higher, some lower, but usually the male with the longest flank plumes occupies the central perch. In display the wings are held out on either side like oars, the back is arched, and the tail is bent forward under the perch. From time to time the extended wings are spasmodically flapped and the mass of golden plumage is undulated upward like a shaken feather duster. In this way the long, golden flank plumes are spread upward between the out-held wings and the body. As the display mounts, the flank plumes are directed more nearly straight upward and forward until they form a cascade of feathers virtually concealing the back and overhanging the head. The head is now bent far down often below the level of the perch. The posturing male stands frozen or only slightly quivering for many seconds. Next there is often a turning or hopping in short jumps along the perch as the male mounts a knob of wood and appears to copulate with it; or he suddenly delivers harsh calls and charges about the arena limbs. Such jumps, charges, and cries are often synchronised between a number of males all calling and moving in a spasm of displays.

When a female visits the arena, the adult males go to their private limb spaces and, I found, freeze in a most extraordinary manner, each spraying its flank plumes upwards like a fountain, each holding the frozen position with the mouth open, the eyes unblinking, partly closed and appearing glassy. For many seconds to more than a minute each male stands absolutely still like a large golden flower as the female moves about, sometimes very close, sometimes around the periphery of the arena, as though afraid to enter it.

Colour films that I made on Little Tobago Island of such a visit show a bird that I knew to be the 'king' of clan number one (it had the longest plumes), with its immense plumes held statically upward, on the centremost perch, which was always the perch of the 'king' when he was present. Three shorter-plumed males were on perches to the side and above the king and although they were exceptionally quiet, they moved more frequently. The female, during the film sequence, can be seen moving deliberately around the edge of the arena. She moves slowly and covers a considerable distance across the scene, then climbs upward, as all the while the 'king' and two other males can be seen holding their static displays, the 'king' without a motion, the lesser males moving from time to time, but none changing their perch positions.

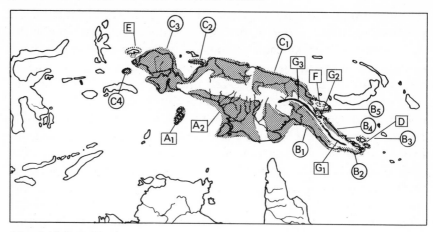

Map 9.10 *Paradisaea.*

Paradisaea apoda (A) Lowlands to 3000 feet
  Paradisaea apoda apoda (A1)
  Paradisaea apoda novaeguinea (A2)
Paradisaea raggiana sea level to 5000 feet
  Paradisaea raggiana salvadorii (B1)
  Paradisaea raggiana raggiana (B2)
  Paradisaea raggiana intermedia (B3)
  Paradisaea raggiana granti (B4)
  Paradisaea raggiana augustaevictoria (B5)
Paradisaea minor (C) sea level to 5000 feet
  Paradisaea minor finschi (C1)
  Paradisaea minor jobiensis (C2)
  Paradisaea minor minor (C3)
  Paradisaea minor pulchra (C4)
Paradisaea decora (D) hill forest, chiefly above 1500 feet
Paradisaea rubra (E) Lowlands
Paradisaea guilielmi (F) 2200–5500 feet
Paradisaea rudolphi (G) 4400–6300 feet
  Paradisaea rudolphi rudolphi (G1)
  Paradisaea rudolphi ampla (G2)
  Paradisaea rudolphi margaritae (G3)

Nesting: The nest apparently remains undescribed. However, according to native collectors, two eggs are laid. These are brownish buff marked with longitudinal streaks of brownish buff, red brown, and blackish brown. An egg in the British Museum from Wokiau

Island in the Aru Islands measures 39·4 × 27·4 mm. (Schönwetter, 1944: 18).

Subspecies: Two similar races are known:

1   *P. a. apoda* Linnaeus, 1758, *Syst. Nat.*, ed. 10, 1, p. 110. Type locality 'India' [= Aru Islands]. Known only from the Aru Islands. Male with upper breast brownish black; male wing 226–231; tail 156–172 mm.

2   *P. a. novaeguineae* D'Albertis and Salvadori, 1879, *Ann. Mus. Civ. Genova*, vol. 14, p. 96. Type locality middle Fly River (300–450 miles upstream). Known from south New Guinea (Mimika River region eastward to a line along political border from coast to the middle Digul and Fly rivers where it hybridizes – '*luptoni*' – with *P. raggiana salvadorii*). Like *apoda* but upper breast paler, more maroon and generally smaller; male wing 203–207; tail 144–154 mm.

Ethology: The pronounced differences between the displays which occur when males only are present in the arena (synchronised charging, etc.) and those which occur when a female visits them (flower display) suggest that perhaps one set is used to establish the breeding rights of the clan of males and the others to attract the females. Since the longest-plumed male occupied the centre perch and the shorter-plumed males the periphery of the courting space, the breeding hierarchy is presumably dictated by the positioning of the males within the arena. The centremost male, I think, is the 'king' of the clan. However, it must be noted that this is only a suggestion. Many field observations will be needed to establish this hypothesis. No observations of mating have yet been made.

I was greatly surprised to discover that the males assumed static flower-like positions on their private display perches when visited by the female since no one had reported this before. My studies of this phenomenon on Little Tobago lead me to believe that it would be very difficult to interpret the patterns of courtship employed by these birds except under natural conditions. This is chiefly because when the female is absent the males are usually in a constant state of agitation, often chasing about or perching away from their private perches, and, on the whole, giving a most confusing picture of their activities.

See notes under *P. raggiana* for a discussion of species limits. The 'rowing' wing position of *P. apoda* in display and the smallness of the arena remind me very much of the courtship behaviour of *Paradisaea minor*.

Count Raggi's Bird of Paradise

Paradisaea raggiana Sclater
Male 13–14 in.

Range: South New Guinea from near the West Irian–Papuan border eastward to Milne Bay, then, in the north, westward to the Markham and upper Ramu Rivers at the neck of the Huon Peninsula and at least to Sattelberg at the top of the Huon Peninsula. Found from sea level to 5000 feet. (See Map 9.10, page 220.)

Adult Male: A crow-sized, yellow-crowned, maroon brown (or yellow) backed, blackish breasted bird with immense red to apricot coloured flank plumes and elongated tail wires. In more detail,

forehead, lores, and chin tufts black glossed green; head and neck orange yellow; a complete collar and greater upper wing coverts yellow; back with varying amounts of yellow or brown depending on the subspecies; wings and tail pale to dark vinaceous brown; sides of lower head, throat to upper neck iridescent oil green; upper breast blackish; rest of underparts pale to dark vinaceous brown; an immense tuft of lace-like plumes (up to 520 mm. long) on each side of breast blood red to apricot orange on basal two-thirds (with a few dark glossy maroon streaks at base), and pale rose cinnamon on outer third; central rectrices wire-like (with narrow dusky maroon vanes at bases), blackish and up to 480 mm. long. Iris yellow; bill blue grey; feet lavender brown; wing 203–231; tail 144–172; exposed culmen 31; tarsus 46 mm.

Adult Female: Very different from male. Forehead and sides of head enclosing eye blackish brown; hind half of crown to neck dull yellow; mantle (including wings) maroon brown (one subspecies) or with varying amounts of yellow; tail maroon brown; throat to upper breast blackish brown to brownish black sometimes with traces of yellow on neck forming an indistinct collar; rest of underparts greyish vinaceous brown. Iris bright yellow, bill chalky blue; feet light brown. Wing 170–180; tail 134–138; exposed culmen 33; tarsus 42 mm.

Immature: First year plumage much like adult female but bird somewhat larger. Male intermediate plumages or stages of dress: (a) like adult female but larger and with a few flecks of iridescent oil green near gape, on chin and on upper throat, or with a cushion of velvety plumes on chin, upper throat, and a tuft at base of maxilla glossy green; (b) like adult female but base of maxilla and chin cushion solid iridescent green and throat to neck blackish brown heavily flecked with iridescent green. (c) like adult male but tail as in adult female and ornamental flank plumes very short (80 mm.), greyish maroon and soft; (d) like adult male, with elongated central tail wires, but with ornamental flank plumes as in (c); (e) like adult male but ornamental flank plumes half-length. The adult male plumage probably requires five to six years to develop.

Remarks: Count Raggi's Bird of Paradise is a common to very common species of the upper half of the forest and forest edge. It also frequents clumps of stunted trees in rocky grasslands and trees in native gardens. I first met with this species in the Laloki River gorge near Rouna Falls about 12 miles inland from Port Moresby. I found females and young males in small bands feeding 15–20 feet up in stunted patches of trees growing on steep mostly grass-covered slopes under the rim of Warirata escarpment. Later I found the species abundant in the Koitaki and Ilolo regions in both tall second growth and original woodlands. I observed perhaps twenty-five females and young males before seeing my first adult male. This bird was encountered just north of Ilolo on the Kokoda trail. It was mid afternoon and the male was solitary. I observed it fly in short stages 20–25 feet up through the forest bordering our path (Gilliard, 1950: 36) as it apparently investigated us. In later years in the Wahgi Valley I found the adult males to be very uncommon except in the vicinity of dancing trees but the females and young males were abundant.

This species was discovered at Orangerie Bay in 1873 by sailors of the corvette *Vettor Risani,* then en route to assist Count Luigi Maria D'Albertis and Odoardo Beccari. D'Albertis recognised that the red-plumed bird of south-eastern New Guinea was quite different from the red-plumed bird of Waigeu and Batanta islands. He sent two examples to Sclater, with the request that, if new, they be named after 'the Marquis Francis Raggi, a great lover of natural history, and especially of ornithology.'

Andrew Goldie, a Scottish bird collector and soldier of fortune who found gold near Port Moresby in 1876 and explored the Astrolabe Mountains in 1877–1878, obtained many examples of this species and he was the first to find its nest and egg. He wrote (*in* Sharpe, 1896): 'This bird inhabits the entire length of British New Guinea towards the east, being often found close to the sea coast. In the Australian Flora district, around Port Moresby, it is more retired, not being found under 1500 feet elevation [but in 1948 the writer found it at 1200 feet at Rouna] probably from not meeting with its ordinary food, as it is very dry in this district at one season of the year. They are most abundant at an elevation of from 2000 to 3000 feet above the sea, but above that altitude are rarely found. In the morning they congregate in the very tallest and largest trees of the district, selecting certain ones about half a mile apart, and here they disport themselves, dancing and strutting with out-stretched plumes till about 8 a.m., when they leave to feed. All day they continue to shout, but do not keep in flocks. They return to the same tree an hour or two before sunset, and continue dancing and shouting often till quite dark. . . . The ornamental plumage is assumed about the end of April and May, and is retained for six or seven months.' D'Albertis in the Fly River region obtained a series including males in fully adult dress. He wrote 'It inhabits dense forest, and is generally found near ravines – perhaps because the trees on the fruit of which it feeds flourish in the neighbourhood of water.'

This is another species which contributed heavily to the plume industry; a traffic which, at its peak, was responsible for the annual slaughter of some 80,000 adult males, mostly of three species of plumed birds, *P. raggiana, P. apoda,* and *P. minor.*

Count Raggi's Bird of Paradise has been hunted since ancient times by the Papuans for reasons of personal adornment. One has only to read A.E.Pratt's observations of a native dance which he witnessed in 1903 at Yule Island, a few miles west of Port Moresby, to realise the magnificence of the feather costumes devised by the Papuans and the great cultural loss that would occur if New Guinea men were prevented from using the plumes of birds of paradise for personal ornamentation.

Ecology: Original and second-growth forests and forest edge, also narrow riverine forests in gorges and small groves of forest in grasslands. Most frequently met with in the middle and upper limbs of tall trees.

Food: Stomach analysis of four specimens: fruits.

Voice: The calls of the male in and near his display area usually begin with a high-pitched weak *kiing*. These notes are often followed by a strong, resonant *kiii-kiii-kiii-kiii-kiii* (each note becoming louder) that ends suddenly with an explosive *waw, woow* (or *what*) that carries perhaps a third of a mile.

Breeding Behaviour: Although this behaviour is still very poorly known, I made observations in 1952 which suggest that the population of adult males in the Kup area of the middle Wahgi Valley (5000 to 5600 feet) splits into small clans during the long breeding season. Each clan takes up a space for its arena in the upper limbs of an isolated grove of trees. The arenas that I studied ranged from 100 to about 400 feet in diameter. The typical arena was in an open grove of tall second-growth trees on a hill or point of land, surrounded by grasslands and native gardens. Each arena was occupied by about three to six adult males, each of which appeared to own a private display space. This was usually centred on a gently sloping limb. These spaces were from 20 to perhaps 50 or more feet apart and were usually situated high up under the canopy of tall, slender trees, one to a tree, but sometimes several males held private spaces in a single wide tree. The males displayed most actively in the early morning, particularly on bright mornings. They quieted down after the sun was well up and some slipped off to feed, sometimes remaining away for hours. However, they spent much of the day in and around the arena, spasmodically calling and occasionally displaying when other males came close. Such displays were to be seen at any time of the day but were uncommon. As a general rule the males sat on their private courts or on semi-hidden perches nearby for many hours per day. They sat quietly except for occasional calling and not infrequently as they sat they would lean backward or to the side so far out of balance they appeared to be dying. On their private spaces they often stropped the bill, then climbed upward, then jumped back down in short hops.

In full display the male of this species makes certain movements which, I think, are unique. For example, after bending forward nearly horizontally to the perch, it elevates the wings upward and forward so that their exterior surfaces come into contact 'back to back' over the upper neck and even, in climax display, over the top of the head. With the body now crouched forward, the male rapidly claps the backs of the wings together and bends the head down to the level of the perch. At the same time the long flank plumes are elevated nearly straight up and expanded. This display is silent and motionless except for the short upstrokes of the wings and the thudding sound of the wing clapping, which is audible seventy feet away.

On several occasions (perhaps at the approach of a strange male or a challenging clan male) I observed a space-owning male as he suddenly became agitated. He would become very noisy and with his plumes raised and nearly concealing his body and head, he would then charge back and forth on his display limb. The commotion he raised caused other space-owning males to leave their private perches and to gather near the agitated male. At such times a confusing assortment of younger birds and females were also present in the arena.

I obtained proof that the display spaces are privately owned when a native plume hunter shot a dominant space-owning male which I had under prolonged observation. Not knowing of the shooting, I sat under its display space – a sloping limb – for three mornings waiting for the distinctively-plumed owner to return. Other adult males in the arena did not visit this limb, but three days after the shooting a young male still in female dress investigated it. It flew in quietly and perched at one end of the limb, then after a few seconds it jumped onto the main display space, crouched, and began thumping its wings overhead, exactly as in the adult male. The film sequence which I made of this dance shows the unique position of the wings during clapping. I took a photograph of the dominant adult which owned this space as it sat on the same perch a day before it was shot.

In December, 1962, at Nondugl, Wahgi Valley, New Guinea,

Fred Shaw Mayer and Jean Delacour (personal communication from Delacour) were surprised to find a nest with young of this species in an aviary containing only females and young males in female plumage. This record answers the old question as to whether young males in female dress can successfully breed.

Nesting: Andrew Goldie was the first to find the nest and egg of this species. He obtained these sometime between 1876 and 1878 in south-eastern New Guinea. A. S. Anthony collected a nest with two eggs in the Owen Stanley Mountains in 1895–1896. The eggs he obtained '. . . are of a beautiful pinkish cream-colour, the markings of a very clear reddish brown with a few underlying violet-grey streaks. Measurements: 38·2 × 24·3 and 37·5 × 25·7 mm.' (Hartert, 1910:489.) Carl Wahnes in August 1908, found a nest with two eggs on Sattelberg, Huon Peninsula, which Hartert described as '. . . a rich, pinkish cream-colour with long rufous brown and deeper grey stripes.' Measurements: 35 × 24·6 and 34·5 × 24·6 mm.

A nest which I obtained in 1958 is a fairly strong cup of vines with some dead leaves in the foundation, lined with brown fibres, mostly from palm leaves. It was 14 feet up in the crotch of a slender croton tree on the edge of tall lowland forests growing in the outskirts of Lae. This nest was lying at the foot of the nest tree when it was shown to me 27 October 1958, by A. L. Malcolm, assistant botanist of the Lae Botanical Gardens. It had been discovered within the botanical gardens on 13 October by one of Malcolm's gardeners. Shortly thereafter Malcolm observed that it contained one well-feathered nestling. The female showed great agitation when Malcolm visited its nest. When he approached, it would fly straight from the nest usually to a tree 30 to 40 feet away. Another nesting record is that of Lawrence Henderson (personal communication), a former Papuan Government officer who found a nest with one young in a sapling in the Koitaki rubber forests in January or February 1938. The nest was discovered when an adult *raggiana* flushed from it. It was fifteen feet up in a sapling fork in the semi-cleared substrata of tall rain forest at an altitude of 1200–1400 feet. For details of the nest, incubating period, and feeding in captivity, see below.

Subspecies: Five well-marked races are recognised:

1   *P. r. salvadorii* Mayr and Rand, 1935, *Amer. Mus. Novit.*, no. 814, p. 11. Type locality Vanumai, Papua. Known from south New Guinea from near the Papuan-West Irian border (Tarara), upper Fly (where it hybridizes with *P. apoda novaeguineae* – '*luptoni*'), and Purari Valley (including the Wahgi, where it hybridizes with *P. minor finschi* at the upper edge of the Baiyer Valley), eastward to the Port Moresby and Cloudy Bay regions. Mantle in both sexes maroon brown; flank plumes scarlet; throat collar broad (yellow).

2   *P. r. raggiana* Sclater, 1873, *Proc. Zool. Soc. London*, p. 559. Type locality Orangerie Bay. Known from south-eastern New Guinea (Orangerie Bay to Milne Bay). Like *salvadorii* but fore back yellow; flank deep scarlet.

3   *P. r. intermedia* De Vis, 1894, *Ann. Rep. Brit. New Guinea, 1893–1894*, p. 105. Type locality Kumusi River. Known from Collingwood Bay (where the flank plumes are a little more reddish) to Holnicote Bay, Kumusi River, and the lower Mambare River. Like *salvadorii* but male and female with the back straw yellow; flank plumes scarlet.

4   *P. r. granti* North, 1906, *Victorian Nat.*, vol. 22, p. 156. Type locality 'German New Guinea.' Exact range unknown but somewhere between the Mambare River and Salamaua. Like *intermedia* but flank plumes reddish orange.

5   *P. r. augustaevictoriae* Cabanis, 1888, *Journ. f. Orn.*, vol. 36, p. 119. Type locality 'Kaiser Wilhelmsland,' restricted to Finsch-hafen. Known from the coast of the Huon Gulf, the Markham River, and the headwaters of the Ramu River (at the Uria River) where it hybridizes with *P. minor finschi* ('*mixta*'). Like *intermedia* but flank plumes apricot orange (throat collar subobsolete).

Taxonomy: Although the Greater and Count Raggi's birds of paradise are considered to represent one species by Ernst Mayr (1941, 1962), I am convinced that they are distinct species because of (a) pronounced difference in display (wing 'rowing' versus 'wrist clapping'); (b) differences in the size of the arena (35 feet as against 400 feet in diameter); (c) differences in plumage characters (chiefly in the female); and (d) the fact that in areas of overlap the Greater and the Raggiana hybridize rather than intergrade.

Aviculture: Prince K. S. Dharmakumarsinhji (1943: 139–144) was the first to breed a bird of paradise in captivity. He accomplished this difficult feat with a race of this species (*augustaevictoriae*) in India in 1940. The birds which he bred came from the Markham River region where they had been obtained a year earlier by the ornithologist-aviculturist Shaw Mayer. His Highness' observations of the courtship and breeding behaviour in captivity are very interesting and should be studied by anyone hoping to rear these birds in captivity. The nest (at which the female was photographed feeding the young) was a cup-shaped structure placed in a secluded spot among casuarina branches 7 feet 4 inches above ground. A single egg was laid. The incubation period was between thirteen and fifteen days. The female fed the young on grasshoppers and locusts which she first stripped of legs and wings, then swallowed, then regurgitated into the mouth of the nestling. In 1963 His Highness told me that she would swallow the insect food, then regurgitate it for the young, even when she was very close to them. 'The salivary liquids,' he thought, 'formed an important part of the feeding.' The juvenal flew out of the nest about one month after hatching.

Lesser Bird of Paradise

Paradisaea minor Shaw
Male $12\frac{1}{2}$–$13\frac{1}{2}$ in.

Range: North New Guinea from the upper Ramu River (where it hybridizes with *P. raggiana*) west to Japen Island, the Vogelkop and the western Papuan islands (Misol Island). Found from sea level to about 5000 feet. (See Map 9.10, page 220.)

Adult Male: A jay-sized dark-throated maroon bird with an orange yellow crown and upper back, and immense yellow flank plumes and elongated tail wires. In more detail, forehead, lores, and chin black glossed green; head, neck, upper half of back and tips of upper wing coverts orange yellow to straw yellow; rest of upperparts maroon brown; sides of lower head, throat to upper neck iridescent oil green; rest of underparts including wings and tail maroon brown, slightly paler, more vinaceous on wings and tail; an immense tuft of lace-like plumes (up to 550 mm. long in one sub-species) on each side of breast pale buffy yellow to canary yellow on basal two-thirds (with a few blood red streaks near base) and generally whitish with traces of pinkish cinnamon on outer third;

229

central rectrices wire-like (with narrow dark maroon vanes on basal 100 mm.), dark maroon and up to 560 mm. in length. Iris pale lime yellow; bill pale bluish grey; mouth pale aqua. Wing 168–198; tail 114–141; exposed culmen 32; tarsus 47 mm.

Adult Female: Very different from male. Entire head, throat, and upper neck all around blackish maroon followed on hind and sides of neck by a dull straw yellow collar; mantle, wings, and tail maroon brown changing to dull yellowish· olive on upper back and edges and tips of some upper wing coverts; underparts white tinged vinaceous maroon on under tail coverts; axillaries, tibia, and under wing largely maroon brown. Iris lime yellow; bill dull blue grey; feet brownish grey. Wing 155–168; tail 109–129; exposed culmen 30; tarsus 40 mm.

Juvenal: Like female but lower neck to upper breast white suffused with variable amounts of vinaceous maroon; plumage of underparts very soft and silky; alula and greater upper wing coverts edged pale rufous.

Immature: First year plumage much like adult female. Male intermediate plumages or stages of dress: (a) like adult female but larger (wing 171–195 mm.) and sometimes with nape and hind neck largely straw to pale orange yellow, or with chin velvety glossed oil green; lores and line from gape with much iridescent green feathering; traces of light feathering on forehead and sides of head and neck, from beneath eye; flank plumes slightly elongated and white; (b) like adult male but flank plumes not developed and lower neck narrowly maroon brown shading to white on midbreast; (c) like (b) but neck to midbreast maroon shading to white on lower breast and abdomen; flank plumes lace-like and buffy to white, but short (110 mm.); (d) an alternate plumage: Like adult male but with entire central breast white and with short orange yellow flank plumes (160 mm. long); (e) like adult male but with flank plumes half length and with midline of lower breast and abdomen vinaceous brown.

Remarks: For centuries the very beautiful Lesser Bird of Paradise was systematically hunted for its plumes. Stresemann has pointed out (1954:263–291) that it is this species which Magellan's men brought home to Spain in 1521 as one of the great discoveries resulting from their historic first circumnavigation of the globe. Helped along by ecclesiastical intrigue plus the footless condition of the trade skins they brought back, the myth that these birds were wanderers from some celestial paradise – birds of paradise – soon spread over Europe (see page 15). Yet, despite the long years of hunting, the Lesser Bird of Paradise is a common to abundant species throughout its extensive range. I found it quite common along the fringes and in the tropical rain forests of the Sepik Valley, in the lowland forests bordering Astrolabe Bay, and in the steep Adelbert Mountains at least to 3500 feet. It is also abundant as high as 4700 feet in the Telefomin Valley near the headwaters of the Sepik, and abundant to about 5000 feet in the Baiyer and Jimmi River regions (Bulmer). Today its calls may be heard in the suburbs of such towns as Madang, Wewak, and Sukarnapura (formerly Hollandia), although the last-mentioned was a centre for a plume industry which concentrated chiefly on this species for more than a century. In the middle Sepik Valley the flank plumes of the Lesser Bird of Paradise are among the most prized of the feather ornaments worn by the Iatmul people. In the midmountain valleys of the Wahgi region the plumes of this species are also highly prized, although they must be obtained through channels of native barter from across the central divide.

Ecology: Tropical rain forests, forest-edge situations, riverine forests, sago swamps, clumps of forest in grassland, trees in native gardens, and in the outskirts of coastal towns. Usually met with in parties in the upper half of the forest.

Voice: This is a very noisy species whose calls are heard from dawn to dark. Calls heard in the Finisterre region: (a) male *wa-wa-wa-wa-wa-waah-wooo wuk*; the first part is rapid and ascending, the notes become more drawn out as they descend, then end in a deep growling note; (b) male calling for attention, *siing-waow*. The first part is a high-pitched, drawn-out cry, the second a raucous, deep derisive *wow*, ending in a growl, which literally seems to explode out of the forest following periods of silence. Especially in early morning and late afternoon the Lesser Bird of Paradise fills the forest with its calls. Perhaps the most frequently heard of its various notes is the whistled, high-pitched *ki-ki-ki-ki-* followed by *waa-waa-waa*; but also frequently heard is the *ka-ka-ka-ka-ka-ka*, which is high pitched, nasal, and rapid. In the *Ficus* rubber forests at Dwai plantation near Bogadjim where the species is abundant, one hears it call every few minutes in the early morning, *wa-we-wee-we-we-we-waaah*, and, less frequently, *whit-whit-whit-whit-whit*, a call which is whip-like.

At Kanganaman, a male recuperating from a broken wing began feeding on grasshoppers within half an hour after undergoing surgery. Within a week it was calling and displaying in a large tree to which it was confined. In late February this male invariably preened and stropped its bill on each side of its perch before delivering a series of clear, penetrating, bugled notes. These, when heard from close at hand, were *gah-ha-ha-waa*, the last note being drawn out and very deep. This series was invariably followed by much shaking (dusting) of the plumage and much sideward hopping, and every four or five seconds the male would emit a low growling *grrr* which was scarcely audible. At other times, particularly after a period of rain, the male would dry its plumage to the accompaniment of short, weak, frequent notes: *gig gig*. At still other times it emitted a plaintive, high-pitched single *quee*, and when another male approached, it called 'angrily,' *ka ga*.

Food: Stomach analyses of a number of specimens indicate that tree and vine fruits, often large and nut-like or small with hard yellow or black pits, and a few insects are the usual fare.

Breeding Behaviour: I have observed and photographed parts of the display of this species, both at Telefomin (4700 feet) and in the Memenga forests of the Adelbert Mountains (1800 to 3800 feet). In the Telefomin region in May, 1954, a clan of males displayed in a small grove of trees which crowned a gently rounded hill in deeply gullied grasslands. Local natives reported that the birds had displayed in the same general area for generations. In the Adelbert Mountains, in late February and March, 1958, I found the Lesser Bird of Paradise displaying near the height of the wet season.

However, the local natives informed me that the chief period of display was in July and August in the latter part of the dry season. In the late afternoon of 14 March, the following calls were recorded. They represent the sounds heard before and during a usual period of display. First a male called 150 yards away; five minutes later another called 75 yards away, and it was answered from very far away. Then other males called in the roof of the forest, none closer than 50 yards away. A typical call was *we wee wa wa wa wa* delivered rapidly, then slowed to drawn-out *was*. Soon a shrill whistling *kii kii kii* was heard, and at 4.30 p.m., with surprising volume, a *ki kwaah ki kwa kwah* blared from the display limbs almost overhead. This was followed by two minutes of silence and then by a high-pitched bugled call, again from the display tree. This call – *kiia kii kiiia kiu ku whuuut* – was a series of shrill, whistled, ascending notes, followed by descending *kis* and ending in a deep, drawn-out *what*. Calls rang forth intermittently from near and far and at 4.49 a shrill but faint cry was heard from overhead. Then I could tell that a male – probably a solitary male – had begun to display alone in the display tree. This I knew from the notes I heard: about ten *kiya kiya kiya* notes followed by a squeaking which was like that of young birds squabbling in a nest (and which I wrote as *gee gee gee kii*), and yet low and hardly audible on the ground. This was followed by silence, then by low churred growls, almost like purring, then some chattering – all noises made by the male as it elevated the plumage and wings and displayed spasmodically in the top of the damp, gloomy forest.

On 27 March, from a blind under another display tree, I observed males jumping about in the upper limbs, emitting choking *kiis* and explosive, high-pitched bugled notes from time to time. One male that I watched through glasses had the flank plumes extended upward between the body and the scapulars at such an angle that they reminded me of hatpins stuck into the upper side of the bird. I also noted that in display the wings are 'held open like oars about to be dipped into the water and then shaken;' and that 'there was a lot of body-shaking and preening of the lower abdomen.' The most interesting observation, however, was of a male '. . . that broke off its display to move six feet to the edge of a limb (60 feet up) to rip off large green leaves and drop them. The bird acted as though it was furious and the leaves dropped for a period of about half a minute.'

The second display area was about 70 feet up near the top of a wild mango tree which rose well above the rest of the forest. It was in an area of many nearly horizontal limbs and many limbs that sloped gently upward. There the displaying males often circled the trunk in their chases, expanding the wings, elevating the flank plumes, preening. Often three males were seen in close proximity to one another. I found that certain limbs were the special stopping places of certain males and that these were so worn that they appeared brown in contrast to the more greyish appearance of the bark of the undisturbed perches. Frequently white-bellied, dark-throated presumably young males were seen with the adult males. These young males shook the body, opened the wings so that they extended forward with the 'palms' down and the 'fingers' open and frozen just as did the adult males. One of the young males was seen to slip to the side and to hang sidewise with the body far off balance as though wounded or in a kind of posturing trance. One of the adult males delivered a deep, resonant *whoo whoo* with its body shaking and its plumes swaying in and out with each note. The tail hung straight down with the wires curved under the body and the neck and head were directed downward as the call was given. During most of the clan display the males were relatively quiet and had I not known the meaning of their muted creaking notes I would have missed the display. After the semi-silence had continued 30 to 50 seconds there would break out a resounding series of sounds somewhat like the ringing of metal – almost a tolling – or at other times, after a period of active display in semi-silence, the birds would break out with loud *caa wooo wooo* calls that sounded vaguely like the calls of a crow. Then would follow the familiar ascending caws ending with a *cawit* that cracked like a whip.

Once in the late afternoon, having emitted a series of calls, a solitary male landed in the crown of the display tree which was then empty of birds. As I watched through eight-power glasses, it suddenly ripped off a leaf or leaves with violent actions of the head and held them in its bill for a few seconds before dropping them.

Male visited by female: on the fifth day of observation under this tree (2 April), the first male of the day arrived at about 7.40 a.m. Half an hour later it began displaying to a presumed female. The female had arrived quietly. It perched beside the male as it elevated the flank plumage, shook vigorously, and then held the wings outward, like oars. The male then held this position for a long time (I was able to film this action). As he did this, he rocked his body, stretching the wings outward in maximum distension as if to soar off. All the while he held the flank plumes high overhead and cascading over the back. Once, while the male held this climax position, the female stood just under him, making abrupt motions with her head. She then moved above him to a somewhat higher perch, then down again and finally reached her bill to the male and pulled several times at the feathers of his neck (or the side of his head. As she did this, the male continued to display stiffly, rocking the body with the yellow plumes directed upward. He did not attempt to mount the female or to drive her away when she pecked at his neck. Rather, he seemed to be in a trance and when she was closest to him he was quite motionless, with the head held far down, much like the males of *Paradisaea apoda* of the Aru Islands in their 'flower' display.

Analysis of Display:　The Lesser Bird of Paradise, like the Greater Bird of the Aru Islands, often performs its arena displays in the top of a single tree with the males dancing close together. Because of this I found it extremely difficult to determine the position and ownership of the key courts within the arena. Peripheral clan members may not hold private courts and dominant males shift about in a confusing manner.

Nesting:　A. E. Pratt (Hartert, 1910: 489) collected a nest (and egg) at Hambitawuria, west New Guinea (1500 feet) which was constructed of twigs and lined with black wire-like fibres or rootlets and, outside, was partially covered with dead leaves. The cup measured 12–13 cm. across and 8 cm. deep. The egg is 'cream-colour, and marked with the characteristically paradiseine long streaks of brown and rufous brown, from the thick end downwards and shorter deeper lying grey ones.' A similar egg from Etna Bay collected by Heinrich Kühn measures 36·1 × 26·4 mm. Two eggs collected by Carl Wahnes in Kaiser Wilhelmsland again are quite similar. They measure 36 × 26 and 35 × 26 mm.

As to the location of the nest, I obtained what I believe to be a reliable native observation of a nest on 'Amil' mountain behind Bogadjim (800 feet) which was built in December, 20 feet up in a slender tree located about 50 feet inside the forest near the edge of a native garden. Also Bulmer reports a nest and single egg from 4000 feet, Baiyer Valley (Mt Hagen area) which his native assistant found very high up in a tree with thick foliage in a garden and fallow zone. He reported that the nest was a flimsy structure of twigs, leaves, and creepers. The nest and egg are now in the Australian Museum.

Subspecies: Four quite similar races are recognised:

1   *P. m. finschi* Meyer, 1885, *Zeitschr. Ges. Orn.,* vol. 2, p. 383. Type locality Karau, between Aitape and the mouth of the Sepik, at long. 142° 30′ E. Known from northern New Guinea from the Aitape region and Sepik Valley eastward to Astrolabe Bay and the upper Ramu River. Flank plumes bright orange yellow, reaching 450 mm. in length; underparts dark maroon. Wing male 173–190; tail 122–131 mm.

2   *P. m. jobiensis* Rothschild, 1897, *Bull. Brit. Orn. Club,* vol. 6, p. 46 (type in AMNH, no. 678912). Type locality Jobi (= Japen) Island. Known only from Japen Island. Like *finschi* but flank plumes paler and much longer (up to 560 mm.); breast somewhat paler; generally larger, wing male 194–198; tail 138–141 mm.

3   *P. m. minor* Shaw, 1809, *Gen. Zool.,* vol. 7, pt. 2. p. 486. Type locality 'New Guinea' restricted to Dorey. Known from west New Guinea eastward in the north to Humboldt Bay and eastward in the south to Etna Bay. Like *finschi* but flank plumes pale as in *jobiensis* (but shorter) and underparts paler, more vinaceous, less maroon.

4   *P. m. pulchra* Mayr and de Schauensee, 1939, *Proc. Acad. Nat. Sci. Philadelphia,* vol. 91, p. 151. Type locality Tip, Misol Island. Known only from Misol Island. Like *minor* but with the brown plumage more purplish, less reddish and with the plumes as in *jobiensis*; generally large as in *jobiensis*; wing male 194 mm. It is curious that the Misol Island population eluded detection until 1939 because both A. R. Wallace and his assistant reported that a species of *Paradisaea* occurred on this island. Allen (*in* Wallace 1862: 156) in fact reported that it occurred only on the north coast of the island and on his second visit to the island in 1860 he succeeded in collecting a skin which Wallace noted (*op. cit.*) '. . . is there finer than in most other places.'

Goldie's Bird of Paradise

Paradisaea decora Salvin and Godman
Male 12–13 in.

[1883 (January), *Ibis*, p. 131. Type locality Fergusson Island.]

Range: D'Entrecasteaux Archipelago (Fergusson and Normanby islands). Found in mountainous areas usually above 1500 feet. (See Map 9.10, page 220.)

Adult Male: A jay-sized dark-throated bird with orange yellow upperparts, lavender grey lower parts and immense red flank plumes. In more detail, forehead (narrowly), lores, chin to neck (very broadly) iridescent green; top of head (from eyes), neck,

mantle, margins of upper wing coverts orange to straw yellow, glossy on mantle; rest of wings and tail above greyish rufous, the wing quills with traces of buffy edging; at lower edge of dark throat, a subobsolete yellow collar succeeded by dark lavender grey on the breast and vinaceous cinnamon grey on the abdomen; tibia, under wing and under tail coverts dull cinnamon grey brown; an immense tuft of lace-like plumes (up to 440 mm. long) on each side of breast mostly bright crimson red with fine greyish buff tipping; at the outer base of each tuft a short tuft (up to 90 mm. long) marked with purplish black on outer half; central rectrices wire-like (with narrow vanes at bases), blackish and up to 410 mm. long. Iris yellow; bill bluish; feet dark slate. Wing 178–181; tail 136–140; exposed culmen 33; tarsus 42 mm.

Adult Female: Very different from male; top and sides of head to neck straw yellow; mantle including wing coverts grey brown strongly tinged with straw yellow; some glossiness on back; wings and tail faded brown; throat to neck blackish brown; rest of underparts pale buff to ochraceous buff with fine black barring on lower neck to upper breast and subobsolete dark barring elsewhere. Iris brown; bill and feet grey. Wing 150–162; tail 123–130; exposed culmen 33; tarsus 38 mm.

237

Immature: First year plumage much like adult female but immature male larger (wing 173–176 mm.). Male intermediate plumages or stages of dress: (a) like adult female but larger and top of head and nape brighter, more orange yellow, less pale buffy yellow; (b) like adult male above and on throat but central tail plumes half length (235 mm.) and with olive brown vanes over entire length (but vanes much narrowed in middle portions); rest of underparts like female; (c) like adult male (including having the black tail wires) but flank plumes short (75 mm.) and cinnamon brown; also with traces of barring on sides of breast, and lower breast to abdomen chestnut brown variably barred as in female.

Remarks: Very little is known about the habits in the wild of Goldie's Bird of Paradise, although the home grounds of this beautiful species were discovered as long ago as 1882. This is doubly surprising because its home islands have been visited by such well-known naturalist-collectors as A. S. Meek, Fred Shaw Mayer, Hannibal Hamlin, L. J. Brass, and R. F. Peterson. Andrew Goldie wrote that he first encountered this species in the mountains of Fergusson Island at a considerable elevation above the sea. Later, A. S. Meek found it not rare, but by no means numerous in the interior of South Fergusson Island from about 1500 feet upwards.

Voice: Goldie wrote that the call is very like that of *Paradisaea raggiana* but with a peculiar shrill whistle added periodically. Stonor (1936), who observed a captive bird in London, wrote that *P. decora* has a greater variety of notes than others of the genus, and may also be described as having a song, even if a somewhat unmusical one.

Breeding Behaviour: It is perhaps significant that Goldie, a veteran bird of paradise collector, noted that the motions of this species while calling are identical with those of *P. raggiana,* but that the males appeared to have no particular tree in which to dance. Stonor wrote (*op. cit.*): 'The display of this species has not been described, but Mr F. Shaw–Mayer, who has seen it frequently [in the D'Entrecasteaux Islands], tells me that it is very similar to the typical *Paradisaea* display, but the plumes are not spread out so much, and are generally not so conspicuously shown.' Stonor added: 'I have also had the opportunity of watching the display of a [male] of this species in the Society's Gardens and find it to be definitely simpler, and although the plumes are spread over the back, as in the rest, the effect is not so striking.'

Nesting: I am unable to find any records of the nest or egg of this species.

Evolution: The discovery of this distinctly marked species living on islands situated within sight of the mainland of New Guinea where another very different species abounds, is highly interesting. *Paradisaea decora* probably has lived for an extended period in the D'Entrecasteaux Islands under refuge-like conditions whereas, on the nearby mainland, its relatives have been under continuous evolutionary pressures from congeneric populations and species. It thus seems likely that the island populations (*P. decora*) have evolved to their present state at a slower rate of evolution. If so, *P. decora* may be considered to be less advanced and more representative of the ancestral New Guinea stocks of *Paradisaea* than the populations inhabiting the mainland lowlands today. In this connection it is interesting to note the similarities of structure that seem to link *P. decora* with *P. rubra* (see below), another island species which also may be less advanced. Yet these two refuge-living species, with their strangely similar displays, inhabit islands situated a thousand miles apart; but each is within sight, or nearly within sight, of the mainland of New Guinea.

Undiscovered Species: The discovery of this well-marked species in the interior mountain forests of the D'Entrecasteaux Islands led and still leads some naturalists to suspect that undiscovered species of birds of paradise hide in the interior mountains of islands situated within sight of New Guinea, for example, New Britain Island. One such believer was Karl Hunstein (see pp. 245, 250). Another was the author, who with his wife, Margaret, ascended the Whiteman Mountains of western New Britain in 1958–1959. Despite extensive collecting and the discovery of two new species and several new subspecies of birds, no trace of birds of paradise (or of bower birds) was found by the Gilliards.

Red Bird of Paradise

Paradisaea rubra Daudin
Male $11\frac{1}{2}$–$12\frac{1}{2}$ in.

[1800, *Traité Orn.*, vol. 2, p. 271. Type locality 'New Guinea' error for Waigeu.]

Range: Western Papuan islands (Waigeu, Batanta, (?) Ghemien, and Saonek). Lowland forests. (See Map 9.10, page 220.)

Adult Male: A jay-sized, orange yellow and maroon bird with a dark (oil green) forehead and throat, very long red flank plumes and greatly elongated ribbon-like tail wires. In more detail, fore half of head (from line behind eyes), sides of head (including auricular region) and throat to upper neck iridescent oil green, with horn-like feather pom poms over each eye; rest of head and neck all around, sides of upper breast, upper back and upper wing coverts orange yellow; middle back bright rufous brown; rump yellow; wings and tail rufous brown; rest of underparts maroon brown becoming dark maroon on breast; a very large tuft of ornamental plumes (up to 300 mm. long) on sides of breast mostly deep glossy crimson red and glossy with decomposed (lace-like) grey tip-

pings; central rectrices narrowly ribbon-like, twisted and very narrow with an enameled texture (up to 585 mm. long). Iris reddish brown; bill greenish yellow; feet dark brown. Wing 171–176; tail 122–124; exposed culmen 30; tarsus 44 mm.

Adult Female: Resembling male but without ornamental plumage. In more detail, fore half of head, throat, and upper neck dark chocolate brown; hind head to upper back and a complete wide neck collar glossy straw yellow; upper back and upper wing coverts glossy yellowish rufous; rest of bird maroon brown, tinged vinaceous below. Iris dark brown; bill olive yellow; feet dark brown. Wing 149–166; tail 110–113; exposed culmen 29; tarsus 39 mm.

Immature: First year plumage much like adult female. Male

intermediate plumages or stages of dress: (a) like adult male but lacking flank plumes and fore back orange brown, not yellow; central rectrices partly elongated (160 to 220 mm.) and maroon brown, not black, with vaning at bases and tips somewhat resembling *P. minor*; lower breast and abdomen like female; (b) like (a) but central rectrices glossy black, not brown, and midbreast dark maroon, not pale maroon.

Remarks: Just over a century ago, on 29 June 1860, Wallace reached Waigeu Island after a hair-raising voyage in a small sailboat from Ceram. His chief reason, he wrote, in visiting this remote island was to observe and collect the Red Bird of Paradise, a wonderful species which first turned up in war plunder in France: 'In the *"Cabinet der Stadhouder"*, which the Revolutionary armies brought from the Hague in 1795,' Stresemann (1954) writes, 'there were several species of Birds of Paradise, including a male of a still undescribed species, the handsome *Paradisaea rubra*.' Wallace found that the Red Bird was heavily hunted by the Papuans for its plumes. Because of such hunting, the Red Bird of Paradise had long been known to science but nothing was known of its habits in the wild: '. . . the very first time I went into the forest I not only heard but saw (*Paradisaea rubra*), and was convinced there were plenty about; but they were very shy, and it was some time before we got any. My hunter first shot a female; and I one day got very close to a fine male . . . . He was quite low down, running along a bough searching for insects, almost like a woodpecker; and the long black riband-like filaments in his tail hung down in the most graceful double curve imaginable . . . another day we saw no less than eight fine males at different times . . . at length the fruit ripened on the fig tree close to my house, and many birds came to feed on it; and one morning . . . a male . . . was seen to settle on its top. . . . I . . . could see it flying across from branch to branch, seizing a fruit here and another there; and then, before I could get a sufficient aim to shoot at such a height (for it was one of the loftiest trees of the tropics), it was away into the forest. They now visited the tree every morning, but they stayed so short a time, their motions were so rapid and it was so difficult to see them owing to the lower trees . . . that it was only after several days' watching, and one or two misses, that I brought down my bird – a male in the most magnificent plumage.'

Abundance, Food: The Red Bird of Paradise apparently remains a common bird in the canopy of the lowland forests and forest edge. Its principal food is fruits and berries, also some insects.

Breeding Behaviour and Voice: Sten Bergman, the Swedish ornithologist-explorer who has worked extensively in West New Guinea, gives the following account (*in* Gyldenstolpe, 1955) of this species on Batanta Island: 'The natives . . . knew where a dancing-tree of *P. rubra* was situated. Before sunrise I left my camp. I had not walked far until I heard a sound resembling the syllables "ah-ah, ah, ah, ah, ah," echoing through the gloom of the forest. Soon I approached the spot where the dancing-tree was supposed to be situated and arrived at a small clearing on which grew a gigantic tree. I soon caught sight of a male which was perched on a branch of that tree although the bird itself was more or less hidden from view by the dense foliage. The bird continuously uttered its call. After a while . . . some other males appeared . . . on the upper tier of some neighbouring trees. Suddenly I caught sight of a beautifully plumaged male who made its presence known by its vociferous calls. The bird moved about on a high, dead limb. Now and then it simultaneously spread out its quivering wings and its wonderful red ornamental plumes while uttering its call. Suddenly several full-plumaged males appeared and settled down on the highest limbs of the huge display-tree in the centre of the clearing. It did not last many minutes until the display was in full swing. I counted up to ten males which were perched in one and the same tree. The birds were continuously on the move from branch to branch quivering with their ornamental plumes and rapidly beating their wings. While displaying they not only uttered their usual calls but also a number of other noises. During the display the males preferred to settle on some dead limbs high up in the canopy of their dancing-tree, particularly such branches which were leafless and where their splendid colours came at their best. In my field-glasses I could see that a few females had also appeared on the display-arena. The sun had now arisen and the sky was almost cloudless, although the rays of the sun could hardly penetrate the canopy of the surrounding dense forests and reach the forest-floor. But the sun-rays had reached the top-most part of the tree chosen for the display so that the wonderful brilliancy of the ornamental plumes beautifully stood out against the green foliage.'

Crandall's valuable close-up observations of the dancing of a male in the New York Zoological Park are as follows: The male ' . . . was standing quietly, his body held stiffly parallel to the perch, with the head plumage fully distended. He then moved his wings slightly away from his body and vibrated them with great rapidity. The body was suddenly jerked to an erect position, and the wings were extended, the vibrating still continuing. The bird then lowered his body and started slowly down the slanting branch. When he reached the tip, the head being lower than the tail, he remained in fixed position for about twenty seconds. During this time the wings were still slightly spread and vibrating. The plumes were very slightly elevated, extending just above the body line, but distinctly not spread. As far as could be determined, their only function was to fill the spaces between tail and quivering wings.

'When this form of frontal display had been completed, the bird turned about and hopped slowly up the branch. He leaped clear of the perch at each jump, alternating the feet in the forward position. This action caused the body to jerk violently from side to side, bringing the red plumes into greater prominence. Reaching the trunk of the cedar, he picked violently at a protruding knot and resumed the normal position.'

Stonor (1936) described the courtship display of a male that he observed in a London zoo as follows: 'It consisted of a very simple dance, with the wings fluttered, and hopping around in small circles; at the same time the curious lappets of green feathers which ornamented the top of the head are stretched out to their fullest extent, as is also the green throat patch. The body is kept almost horizontal. The plumes, which are naturally very conspicuous from their curved nature, are not used; but I have also seen this bird running up a vertical branch in a series of jerks and swaying the body from side to side at the same time, and in this way they are shown to some extent, but the display seems designed to show off the head ornaments rather than the plumes.'

Nesting: Schönwetter's measurements of eggs in the British Museum are 33·5–39·0 × 23·8–25·0 mm.

Geographic Distribution: See remarks under *P. decora* and *P. rudolphi.*

Evolution: See remarks under *P. decora.*

Emperor of Germany Bird of Paradise

Paradisaea guilielmi Cabanis
Male 12½–13 in.
[1888, *Journ. f. Orn.*, vol. 36, p. 119. Type locality 'Kaiser Wilhelm's Land,' restricted to Sattelberg.]

Range: Mountains of the Huon Peninsula; from about 2200 to 4000 feet, occasionally to 5500 feet, rarely to 6000 feet. (See Map 9.10, page 220.)

Adult Male: A jay-sized, dark-capped (oil green), straw yellow backed maroon bird with a dark throat (to upper breast), very large white flank plumes and two very long tail wires. In more detail, entire crown, sides of head (to rear of eye), throat to upper breast metallic oil green; rest of head, neck and back, also lesser upper wing coverts and sides of breast (forming a narrow, in-complete pectoral band) glossy straw yellow; rest of bird deep maroon tinged grey on abdomen and with a light patch on each side of lower breast near bases of ornamental flank plumes; an immense tuft of plumes (up to 360 mm. long) on each side of breast ivory white tinged yellow on basal halves (of some plumes) and much decomposed and lace-like on outer half; central pair of rectrices wire-like (with narrow maroon vanes on basal 100 mm.), maroon and up to 690 mm. long. Iris reddish brown to brown; bill blue grey; feet flesh brown. Wing 169–181; tail 109–119; exposed culmen 36; tarsus 44 mm.

Adult Female: Much like adult male but lacking ornamental plumes. Top and sides of head, throat to upper breast dark chocolate brown; nape to mid-back, also sides of neck and traces on sides of breast (forming a narrow incomplete pectoral collar) glossy straw yellow, darkening to maroon on lower back; rest of bird maroon

244

brown except underparts more pale vinaceous maroon, sometimes with traces of fine barring. Iris yellow. Wing 150–159; tail 102–105; exposed culmen 38; tarsus 40 mm.

Juvenal: Much like adult female but with strong traces of pale barring on breast.

Immature: First year plumage much like adult female. Male intermediate plumages or stages of dress: (a) like female but central pair of rectrices 5–8 mm. longer than rest; (b) like adult male on fore body and back but lacking ornamental flank and tail plumes (the tail as in (a); (c) like (b) but with flank plumes brown and up to 90 mm. long; (d) like adult male but with central tail plumes exceeding rest by about 20 mm. and with ornamental flank plumes very short (140 mm.) and mixed white and vinaceous brown; (e) like adult male with long wire-like central rectrices and white and yellow flank plumes, but latter half length.

Remarks: The Emperor of Germany Bird of Paradise is famous for its habit of hanging upside down during courtship. It was the last bird of paradise discovered by Karl Hunstein, the most successful discoverer of new species of birds of paradise. Hunstein (in company with Stefan von Kotze) found it on Sattelberg in the Rawlinson Mountains in January, 1888. From this mountain, situated at the northern tip of the Huon Peninsula, the mountains of New Britain Island are visible northward across Vitiaz Strait. Less than two months later Hunstein perished by drowning while on his way to New Britain in quest of birds of paradise (see remarks under *Paradisaea decora*).

Between January and April, 1929, the naturalist-collector Rollo H. Beck and Mrs Beck explored the Saruwaged Mountains of the Huon Peninsula for The American Museum of Natural History. In his report of this expedition (1929) Beck wrote that he first met with the Emperor of Germany Bird of Paradise inland from Finschhafen:

'This species begins to make itself heard plentifully at about twenty-two hundred feet, where it replaces a related species [*Paradisaea raggiana augustaevictoriae*] that inhabits the forest of the lower zone. From twenty-two it is heard regularly up to four thousand, where it abruptly stops.' Beck, in making the point that many of the birds of paradise are restricted to narrow altitudinal belts, added:

245

'We spent some time at Zagaheme, which is four thousand feet, and, though we heard and saw [the Emperor of Germany Bird of Paradise] often about the village and below it, when I climbed up a few hundred feet on the ridge behind the settlement, the bird was missing, even though I could hear it calling a thousand feet below. . . .' Shaw Mayer observed and collected this species near Hompua village (2700 feet), Sattelberg Mountains in June, 1931.

Abundance: This wonderful species remains quite common in the mid-mountain forests of the Huon Peninsula.

Food: Chiefly forest fruits (stomach analysis by Shaw Mayer).

Voice: Crandall (1932:79), observing captive birds, noted two types. One, which is very loud and piercing in volume, he wrote, is somewhere between the Raggiana (*Paradisaea raggiana*) and the Lesser (*Paradisaea minor*). This call is delivered with the mouth wide open. Shaw Mayer noted that the native name in the Sattelberg Mountains is *gbau*, based on this call. The other call, Crandall wrote, ' . . . is quite different from anything I have heard before. The bird draws itself erect, expanding the strikingly large green patch on the throat and breast. He then emits a soft, clear *poop, poop, poop,* throwing his head upward with each note and keeping the bill almost closed.'

Breeding Behaviour: Virtually nothing is known of the courtship displays of this species in the wild although there is a questionable report by Detzner (*in* Stresemann, 1924:426) that the males may gather in groups to display. Fortunately, we can turn to Crandall and Stonor for precise observations of the courtship movements of this species in captivity. Crandall wrote that preliminary forms of display were hopping with the body in a stiffly horizontal position, head and neck extended, with the beak turned down and accompanied by slow bobbing up and down from the hips. This was followed by wing spreading in the horizontal plane and rapid vibrating, with the flank plumes slightly spread and somewhat elevated; also by much rapid wing flicking. In the full display, Crandall wrote: 'The bird went through the "bobbing" and "flicking" phases of his display several times. Suddenly he called loudly, and turned *head first* [italics mine] under his perch, which he clutched firmly. The body was drawn up quite close to the perch, in a position nearly horizontal, but with the anterior portion somewhat lower than the posterior. The wings were fully spread and turned well up. The tail, also, was widely spread and turned nearly vertical, so that the long wires extended far above. The head and neck were fully extended and turned upwards. The plumes were erected at an angle of about 45°, those at each side forming a semicircle, overlapping anteriorly and posteriorly to make a complete circle around the inverted abdomen. Each plume now appeared as a separate entity, the widely-spaced barbs being seen to great advantage. Head, wings and tail remained outside the circle, which enclosed only the feet, as they grasped the perch. The body was then moved slowly from side to side, with a slight rotary motion, causing the plumes to wave gracefully but not disturbing the general formation. The display lasted for about five minutes, during which the head, wings and tail were held rigidly in position. The bird made no sound during the period, at the end of which he returned head first to the normal position. After an interval of about ten minutes, devoted to calling loudly and leaping with animation from perch to perch, he repeated the entire performance, including bobbing, wing-flicking, and the inverted climax.'

Stonor (1936) in his studies of the plumed birds of paradise, leaned heavily on ethological evidence. His description of the full display of a male in captivity is as follows: 'In the initial stage the bird starts hopping up and down with the head and neck stretched upwards; it then opens its wings and, jerking the head into the air, calls loudly several times with a clear and not unpleasing and very characteristic note . . . next the wings are fluttered, with the head kept down, and during this part of the performance they are kept open for a few seconds and are then closed suddenly with a snap, this being repeated five or six times; according to my own observations the plumes play no part in the performance . . . The whole time the bird is obviously becoming more and more excited, and seems to be working itself up into a sort of ecstatic state. It suddenly turns upside down, *tail first* [italics mine] and hangs by the feet in a semi-horizontal position. At the same time the wings are half-opened and are kept in this position; the plumes are spread out so that many of them point forward past the head, but others are spread sideways and some point backwards, so that the result is a rosette of plumes covering the underside of the body, which, as Crandall has pointed out, shows the loose structure of the plumes to great effect. Some of the short plumes are coloured yellow, so that while the outer part of the rosette is white, the inside is yellow . . . concurrently with this, the green feathers of the throat, which in this species reach down to the breast, are stretched out to their full extent ventrally, and the brown lower breast and abdomen are also fluffed out . . . this remarkable inverted display is kept up for about a minute or more, and the whole time the bird sways about with increasing speed, until it rights itself as suddenly as it began . . . next follows the third and last part of the display, during which it hops from perch to perch, performing a sort of dance, fluttering the wings and occasionally spinning around in small circles; as in the first stage no use is made of the plumes.'

Nesting: Eggs: Two (or one?), creamy to rose cinnamon, streaked with red brown and grey. Measurements: 36·2–38·5 × 24·6–27·1 mm. (Schönwetter, 1944).

Evolution: Within a space of less than 50 miles, *Paradisaea guilielmi,* a mountain species, interacts with two congeneric species, *P. raggiana* and *P. minor,* and with both it has been known to hybridise in the wild. It seems likely, therefore, that selective forces are operating which favour the development of strong isolating mechanisms between these species and that the inverted displays described above are a part of this development.

Hybridisation: Hybrids are known between the Lesser Bird of Paradise and the Emperor of Germany; also between the Raggiana and the Emperor. They are:

1 *Paradisea duivenbodei* Menegaux, 1913, *Rev. Franc. Orn.,* vol. 5, p. 49. Type locality near Jaur, Geelvink Bay (error), probably back of Astrolabe Bay. = *Paradisaea minor finschi* × *P. guilielmi.*

2 *Paradisea maria* Reichenow, 1894, *Orn. Monatsb.,* vol. 2, p. 22. Type locality Finisterre Mountains, 1500 feet. (Fig. *Jour. f. Orn.,* 1897, pl. 5) = *Paradisaea apoda augustaevictoriae* × *P. guilielmi.*

Blue Bird of Paradise

Paradisaea rudolphi (Finsch)
Male 11½ in.

Range: Mountains of eastern New Guinea; from about 4500 to about 6300 feet. (See Map 9.10, page 220.)

Adult Male: A jay-sized blue-winged black bird with white eye spots, long blue, purple, and cinnamon flank plumes and two very long black tail streamers. In more detail, head to middle back black, somewhat bronzed, but hind crown and nape maroon black; large white spots above and below eye; lower back to upper tail coverts dusky grey blue; throat to upper breast black tinged bronze; lower breast blackish faintly streaked greenish blue with an indistinct cobalt blue band across lower breast; abdomen black; on each side of midbreast a tuft of rust red plumes (up to 65 mm. long) and a greatly elongated tuft of lace-like plumes (up to 260 mm. long), the latter with the basal two-thirds on ventral surfaces opalescent blue to purple; the outer third and upper surfaces reddish cinnamon with ivory shafting on basal halves; wings opalescent blue with the primaries and concealed portions of secondaries largely dark brown; tail blue with some pale edging, except central pair of rectrices greatly elongated (up to 400 mm.) very narrow, black and often with a small subterminal blue spot. Iris blue; bill outer  third grey changing to pale violet blue, then to pale grey green on basal third; mouth pale green; tongue prussian blue at tip; legs dull vinaceous black. Wing 152–157; tail 77–85; exposed culmen 31; tarsus 39 mm.

Adult Female: Upperparts like adult male but lacking ornamental plumes; sides of head including white eye spots as in male; wings as in male; throat to upper breast deep maroon black to rufous brown; rest of underparts, including under wing coverts, rufous brown weakly barred black (subspecies); abdomen tinged pale blue or pale green. Iris light brown; bill bluish white; feet greyish white; wing 155; tail 99–101; exposed culmen 33; tarsus 38 mm.

Juvenal: A nestling observed by Simson (see p. 254) had blue wings and white eye spots much like the adult female. Two nestlings collected by Walter Goodfellow (see p. 254) '. . . looked grotesquely spiny, owing to the abnormally long grey pin-feathers which covered them all over. Each quill ended in a small tuft of grey down . . . The orbital region, and, in fact, the greater part of the head, remained bare long after the rest of the body was covered with feathers.'

Immature: First year plumage much like adult female. Male intermediate plumages or stages of dress: (a) like adult female but central pair of rectrices slightly elongated (5–7 mm. longer); (b) like adult male but central pair of rectrices half length, underparts interspersed with brown, abdomen rufous with dark barring, and with the ornamental flank tufts very short and streaked brown at bases. At least three and perhaps five or more years are required before the fully adult male plumage is acquired.

Remarks: This species, one of the most beautiful birds in the world, was named in honour of Crown Prince Rudolph of Austria, a youthful ornithologist and patron of the sciences whose other memorial is one of poignant tragedy – the tragedy of Mayerling.

The Blue Bird of Paradise was discovered in 1884 by Karl Hunstein in the Owen Stanley Range some sixty trail miles north of Port Moresby. Hunstein had risked his life to reach these highlands, then in the midst of cannibal country. He had ascended the range with only one assistant, a Papuan boy. But he was richly rewarded by discovering four unknown species of birds of paradise, *Epimachus meyeri, Phonygammus keraudrenii, Astrapia stephaniae,* and the Blue Bird of Paradise. He probably first encountered the Blue Bird at about 5000 feet on Mt Maguli. Hunstein sold his wonderful discoveries to Otto Finsch, whom he happened to meet at Cooktown, Australia, in December, 1884. Finsch, having just 'acquired' Kaiser Wilhelm's Land for Germany, must have returned home in great jubilation.

In 1947, at 5000 feet on Mt Maguli, I found it a fairly common species of the tall rain forests. I ascended the mountain by way of an ancient, infamous trail, the 'Kokoda track', which crosses the Owen Stanley Mountains from Port Moresby on the south to Kokoda and Buna on the north.

On Mt Maguli in March I found the females and young males fairly common but adult males rare. Turning eastward on the top of Mt Maguli where the Kokoda begins to descend into a gorge containing a tributary of the upper Brown River, I followed a forested ridge to about 5800 feet. At one place the north face of this ridge is precipitous – too steep for big trees – and from there a magnificent view of Mt Victoria is to be had. In the tall forests crowning this curving ridge, which, I believe, is the original 'Horseshoe Mountain' of Hunstein, I came upon occasional, solitary females that seemed to keep to certain glens in the forest. They usually perched twenty to thirty feet up in the smaller trees. This was in an area containing much water-carrying bamboo (on which for days we depended for drinking water) and many small palms. Unfortunately, I disturbed this area by shooting through it but I strongly suspect that some of the birds I saw were nesting females. Several of them gave short, loud, grating squawks when they saw me approaching.

In the mountains between Mt Yule and the main Owen Stanley ranges in May of 1925 (?) Walter Goodfellow (1926: 59) found the Blue Bird, the Raggiana, the Lawes' Six-wire, the Superb, and the Magnificent birds of paradise all living at 5000 feet. He wrote that the Blue Bird '. . . was by far the least common of them all; not more than three or four specimens were encountered within as many months.'

I encountered the species again in 1950, 1952, and 1956 in the Kubor and Hagen mountains bordering the Wahgi Valley, a region where the species is treasured by the natives for its feathers. In 1952, for weeks I trailed the species, hoping to find and film it in the wild. I failed but succeeded in finding an adult male and in learning some of the reasons for the rarity of this species in the Wahgi region. It is rare because its ecological niche, the midmountain forests, have been largely destroyed by the slash-and-burn farming of primitive man. However, Captain N. B. Blood, a keen field ornithologist, then engaged in obtaining live birds, chiefly birds of paradise, for Sir Edward Hallstrom of Australia and for other aviculturists in Europe and America, knew of areas around and perhaps in the Wahgi Valley where this much-desired species apparently remained fairly common. As for my personal observations in the Wahgi region, I found the Blue Bird of Paradise generally very uncommon or extirpated. I found this species in two places: (a) a small pocket-like gorge at the top fringe of a valley behind Kup in the Kubor Mountains; (b) about sixty miles farther west in the eastern foothills of the south watershed of Mt Hagen at about 6000 feet. On the north watershed of Mt Hagen west of the Baiyer Valley Ralph Bulmer found the species 'fairly common in a narrow zone at forest edge and in garden areas near forest edge at about 6000 feet.' West from Mt Hagen yet another 100 miles (south watershed) at Tari (5200 feet), Bulmer again encountered the species and succeeded in collecting a single specimen. The Blue Bird therefore enjoys a range at least 600 miles in length along both sides (and in the midmountain valleys) of the great cordillera forming the backbone of the eastern half of New Guinea.

The place where I finally found and studied an adult male was in a narrow, small valley at an elevation of 6000–6300 feet, about three miles southeast of the village of Katumbag, Kubor Mountains. I camped in the head of this valley for four days (June 19–June 22) and at other times paid short visits to it. Each day the trees near my tent were visited by a solitary male, but despite my best efforts I failed to track this magnificently plumaged bird to its display grounds.

Some of my journal records follow. June 11: A solitary male was observed and heard in tall trees of the man-made forest edge. It called at irregular intervals as it moved slowly from tree to tree, apparently feeding. The calls, the first syllable descending, the second ascending, were emitted in series of from three to nine, and the male repeated these every four to twenty minutes. For many hours I remained hidden in a blind hoping to discover the display limb of this male by listening to its calls. These came mostly from a line of forest-edge trees 75 to 250 yards distant. When closest to me the calls sounded melodious and song-like, *coo-lee*, and they were quite powerful. My native assistants claimed that the Blue Bird never ascended the Kubor Mountain slopes above an elevation of about 6300 feet.

Food: Fruit, especially orange fruit (stomach analysis by Bulmer) and berries.

Voice: Male: a powerful, melodious *coo-lee*, repeated three to nine times at irregular intervals; during display a low, grating song is emitted. Female: a harsh rasping or scraping call.

Breeding Behaviour: As yet, apparently no European has witnessed the courtship displays of this species in the wild. Crandall (1931, 1936) has described the display of the male in captivity, as has Stoner (1936). Crandall wrote: 'Instead of remaining in an active, upright position [as in most of the other Paradisaeas], he grasps his

252

perch firmly . . . and with legs extended to the utmost, hangs head downwards. During the entire display period of several minutes, the position of the feet never changed, and the firm grip never is relaxed.

'Viewed from the front, the plumes, inconspicuous and rather disappointing when at rest, form a brilliant, inverted triangle, with the raised feathers of the abdomen completing the center. In the middle appears a longitudinal, ovate patch of velvet black, bordered above by a narrow band of dull red, formed by the feathers that ordinarily clothe the abdomen. The long, pendant "wires" rise to half their length, then droop gracefully downward on either side. The wings are held tightly closed and the head is turned upward.

'During the display, the body is moved forward and back, with the hips as a fulcrum and with a violent motion of the body the plumage is frequently spread to its widest expanse. The white lines of feathers which border the eye above and below are conspicuously extended, leaving the bird only a narrow slit through which to peer at the observer. Throughout, the bird sings softly, in a low, grating voice, moving his head slightly by sharp jerks. This habit of singing, in which the Blue Bird of Paradise often indulges when not in full display, seems peculiar to this species.'

Stonor (1936: 1181) who thought that the display of this bird is the most remarkable among the birds of paradise, noted that ' . . . the whole performance is gone through upside-down, the bird hanging almost vertically and swaying rhythmically backwards and forwards, the whole time singing in a curious low, grating voice in time with the swaying movements.' Stonor's description of the major features of the display has particular significance because of his wide knowledge of the displays of conspecific species. He wrote: 'During this performance, the plumes are spread out in the form of a fan, but are not pointed forward to the same extent as in [*Paradisaea guilielmi*]. The colour-effects produced are truly marvellous, slight movements of the plumes causing shimmering waves of blue and violet to pass across the fan, while the patch of red and black short plumes is seen as a black band edged with red at the apex, its shape and position changing at will to an oval area, almost in the centre, and surrounded by blue, through exceedingly dexterous movements of the plumes.'

Nesting: Nest: While crossing the Owen Stanley Range from Port

253

Moresby to Kokoda in November and December of 1905, Colin C. Simson (1907: 385) discovered a nest with one young in it. I strongly suspect that he made his discovery on Mt Maguli where I found solitary females (see p. 250) and where Karl Hunstein probably first discovered the species. Simson wrote: 'The ridge where [the nest] was discovered must have been 5000 feet above sea-level and was in the Eafa district. Dense low scrub and bamboos were growing in the vicinity. The female every day made a harsh scraping noise close to our camp, but we were never able to catch sight of it, and thought that it must be a bower-bird. On the fourth day I crawled into the low thick scrub within a few yards of our camp, and to my surprise the female came flying around my head. The nest was placed on a small tree above the low scrub, which hid it from view. We could never have found it if the bird had not shown us the way to it. A native climbed the tree and brought down a young bird almost resembling the adult female, having the blue wings and white eyelids. I made the native return the bird, which I now regret having done.' In May of 1925 (?) somewhat farther west in ranges running between Mt Yule and the main cordillera of the Owen Stanley Mountains, Walter Goodfellow collected a nest and two nestlings (1926: 59): 'The nest was placed not more than twelve feet from the ground in a low tree of the thick bush near the top of a ridge. It was composed of strips of pandanus-leaves and fibre from the leaves of some palm and with no lining.'

Eggs: An egg, according to Hartert (1910: 489) and Schönwetter (1944), was discovered at 5000 feet in the Owen Stanley Mountains by the collector, A. S. Anthony, the man who guided Colin Simson through these rough mountains when he found the nest of this species. The egg was elongated oval, rich cream colour with longitudinal streaks of red brown and grey. Measurements of egg: 38·5 × 24·3 mm. Herbert Stevens (*in* Greenway, 1935: 87) collected a female in December on Mt Misim in the Herzog Mountains. He noted on the label 'apparently has a nest and is sitting eggs.'

Subspecies: Three similar subspecies are recognised:

1 *P. r. rudolphi* (Finsch), 1885, *Zeitschr. Ges. Orn.*, vol. 2, p. 385, pl. 20. Type locality Hufeisengebirge, south-east New Guinea (probably Mt Maguli, Owen Stanley Mountains). Known from the mountains of south-east New Guinea (Wharton Range, Owen

Stanley Range) westwards in the north as far as the Mambare River. The adult female has the central breast uniform brown and un-barred. The adult male has the head blackish to maroon black on hind crown and nape.

2   *P. r. ampla* Greenway, 1934, *Proc. New England Zool. Club,* vol. 14, p. 1. Type locality Mt Misim, Morobe district. Known from the Herzog Mountains westward to the Kraetke Mountains. Very similar to *rudolphi* but the adult male has the head somewhat lighter, more brownish, less blackish.

3   *P. r. margaritae* Mayr and Gilliard, 1951, *Amer. Mus. Novit.,* no. 1524, p. 11 [type in AMNH, no. 348209]. Type locality Kimil River, 20 miles west-northwest of Nondugl, Wahgi Valley, Central Highlands. Known from east-central New Guinea from the Wahgi and Baiyer Valley highlands (Kubor, Bismarck, Wahgi Divide, and Hagen mountains) westward to the highlands of the Tari region. Like *rudolphi* but the adult female with the breast narrowly barred.

The Ecology of Hybridisation: As noted above, I found an adult male Blue Bird of Paradise perching for prolonged periods in a man-made forest edge. This bird looked out over vast areas of grasslands which in recent times had replaced huge areas of mid-mountain forests – forests that almost certainly had been inhabited by large numbers of blue birds of paradise. When I saw the region, only fragments of the forest remained in a thin ring around the Wahgi Valley. In most places the grasslands have spread upward from the valley floor to more than 6300 feet, the 'cut-off' height for the Blue Bird of Paradise; and in such situations (even though the forest above seems perfectly capable of sustaining the displaced Blues), the species has vanished.

At the spot where I observed my male Blue Bird, a small 'penin-sula' of forest protruded down beneath the 6300-foot 'ceiling' of the species. This was because the land happened to be very steep and poor for farming. But even in this area the few remaining blue birds occupied a hybrid habitat, the fragmented forest edge. And just below them in the broad, mostly grass-covered Wahgi Valley in clumps of trees and other forest-edge situations, the Raggiana Bird of Paradise (*Paradisaea raggiana salvadorii*) was abundant. In this region raggianas were displaying within earshot of the Blue Bird and were clearly increasing in abundance.

The point is that man, by disturbing the forests of the Wahgi region, has apparently shattered ecological isolating mechanisms which normally operate to prevent hybridisation between the Blue and the Raggiana, although from an examination of the morphology and especially of the ethology, one would expect that other barriers would prevent crossbreeding between these very distinct species. That this is not always true was proven by N.B.Blood. In 1947 he collected an adult male hybrid between the Blue and the Raggiana at Minyip, Mt Hagen (north end of Wahgi Valley), which Tom Iredale (1948) named as a new species. In 1950 Iredale kindly showed me this male. It is in full courtship dress and is apparently the only hydrid known between these two well-differentiated species.

Evolution: One is tempted to assume, because *P. rudolpni* and *P. guilielmi* employ inverted displays, that they are more closely related to each other than they are to the other species of the genus *Paradisaea*, since all of the rest display in an upright manner. As in *P. guilielmi* (see comments), *P. rudolphi* interacts with congeneric species in attenuated altitudinal belts or 'fronts'. The zones of possible overlap between high-altitude species and their lowland relatives are very much greater in area (with many more opportunities for interaction and hybridisation) than between lowland species, which generally only come narrowly into contact on the abbreviated coastal plain. Therefore, hybridisation between contiguous lowland species is a relatively minor threat; whereas, in high altitude species it poses a major threat to species integrity. Therefore, it follows that selection pressure in favour of differences (isolating mechanisms) has probably been much greater in altitudinal than in lowland species. The former would quickly merge in the absence of sharp species barriers. This is the basis of my thinking that the ethological and morphological similarities of the two geographically isolated mountain populations, *P. rudolphi* and *P. guilielmi*, may have been independently developed and do not indicate relationships. In other words, I think there is a strong possibility that the similarities of courtship movements (inverted display) and morphology (short flank plumes) in *P. rudolphi* and *P. guilielmi* are due to convergence.

The relationships of *P. rudolphi* are very obscure. However, as in *P. rubra,* the female is barred below and is much like the male above.

The Blue Bird exhibits both these characteristics but their significance is unknown.

Hybridisation: The unique hybrid mentioned above between the Blue Bird of Paradise and the Raggiana was named *Paradisea bloodi* Iredale, 1948, *Australian Zoologist,* vol. 2, p. 161, type locality Minyip, Mt Hagen.

Chapter Ten

Bower Birds

Bower Birds: Species List

Family PTILONORHYNCHIDAE
Ailuroedus buccoides
Ailuroedus crassirostris
Ailuroedus melanotis
Scenopoeetes dentirostris
Archboldia papuensis
Amblyornis flavifrons
Amblyornis macgregoriae
Amblyornis subalaris
Amblyornis inornatus
Prionodura newtoniana
Sericulus aureus
Sericulus bakeri
Sericulus chrysocephalus
Ptilonorhynchus violaceus
Chlamydera maculata
Chlamydera nuchalis
Chlamydera cerviniventris
Chlamydera lauterbachi

White-eared Catbird

Ailuroedus buccoides (Temminck)
Adults 10 in.

Range: New Guinea and the Western Papuan Islands. Found

between sea level and about 2800 feet. (See Map 10.1, page 261.)

Adult Male: A brown-capped, black-collared, emerald green, stocky bird with spotted underparts. In more detail, crown olive brown to dull tan (varies with subspecies); neck buffy with black tips forming a broad blackish collar; rest of upperparts near emerald green; line behind eye, side of lower head and throat chiefly whitish; rest of underparts buffy to ochraceous, sharply contrasted with black tipping particularly on breast (varies with subspecies); under wing coverts buffy to whitish. Iris dark red to crimson, deep red to maroon; bill slate blue to pearl grey; feet bluish grey to grey; skin near eye dark grey. Male wing 128–136; tail 86–95; culmen from base 30–31; tarsus 40 mm.

Adult Female: Slightly smaller and crown usually paler, wing 127–132; tail 80–86; culmen from base 29–30; tarsus 40 mm.

Juvenal: Nestling (upper Fly River, June 17, 1956): natal down sooty brown, iris pale blue, bill brownish black, gape whitish, feet grey (Rand).

General Remarks: The White-eared Catbird was discovered by Salomon Muller at Lobo, Triton Bay, west New Guinea, in 1828. It is a fairly common species of the lowland forests in south-eastern New Guinea and of the lowland and midmountain forests of western New Guinea. Rand (1942a: 499) pointed out '... that the altitudinal range of this species is greater than that of *A.* [*crassirostris*] and includes it. ...'

He added that in south-eastern New Guinea the White-eared Catbird appears to be a lowland species and the Green Catbird a mountain bird, whereas in the south New Guinea lowlands both species occur but are mutually exclusive. In the Adelbert Mountains

I found the White-eared Catbird a common species of the lowland and hill forests up to about 3000 feet and the Green Catbird an uncommon species occurring only above about 3500 feet.

This barbet-like bower bird, although it is a noisy bird, remained little known until recently, probably because of its retiring nature and the denseness of the low shrubbery in which it lives.

Food: Tree fruits and berries.

Voice: The primary calls are oft-repeated series of low, rasping notes, preceded by sharp, scratching sounds.

Breeding Behaviour: Quite by accident in 1958 in the Adelbert Mountains, I discovered the courtship territory of this species. I had erected a blind near the bower of a Magnificent Bird of Paradise located at about 3000 feet on the gently sloping floor of a tall original rain forest. This blind happened to be in an area defended (in late March) by the White-eared Catbird. I discovered this when I sat outside the blind and the catbird darted at me, passing like an arrow close above my head. During four days of observation from this blind I observed the White-eared Catbird to make darting attacks at small birds that passed through its territory. The defended area was a space in the substage of the forest at least twenty feet high and at least forty feet in diameter. This area was thickly cluttered with small moss-covered trees, tree ferns, vines, and brush and the trunks of a few medium and large trees.

The White-eared Catbird called intermittently throughout the day, always from low perches within 100 feet of my blind but often close at hand. Often the calls were delivered at ten to twenty-five second intervals. Not infrequently two white-eared catbirds were in the area. Violent though strangely quiet chasing accompanied by wing rustling always occurred at such times. Often after such semi-silent chasing, the (presumed) territory-owner would suddenly land heavily near the base of a moss-covered sapling, then jump upwards on the trunk and small limbs near the trunk. Once a White-eared Catbird flew to the side of a mossy sapling, then hopped upwards to a perch five feet above ground. In a matter of moments I saw it attacked and chased by another White-eared Catbird. On another occasion one bird, probably the territory owner, perched two and a half feet up on a thin sloping limb and began calling. It stood high on its legs with its tail hanging down steeply. It then bowed pulling the head and neck far downward. As it did this it repeatedly emitted a low rasping sound.

At 9.32 a.m. 28 March as I peered out of my blind I saw two catbirds as they flew directly toward me. One landed in an under-growth bush twelve feet away, the other landed about ten feet up and out of sight. The bird in view then called and bowed in the direction of the other. With each call it first lifted its head and then emitted the rasping sound as the head and neck were depressed to below the level of the perch. The notes were emitted as the head descended and they stopped as soon as the head and neck were jerked up again.

Nesting: C.G. Simson (1907: 384) while travelling in the Owen Stanley Mountains with the great collector A.S.Anthony in November and December, 1905, was shown three nests of the White-eared Catbird. He wrote: 'I saw three myself, situated in low *Pandanus*-trees and easily reached by the hand without climbing. The structure is cup-shaped. It is composed of dry tendrils and

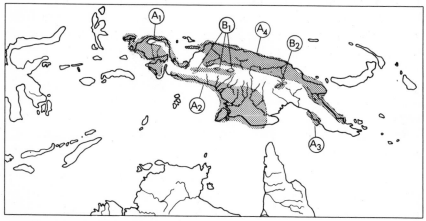

Map 10.1 *Ailuroedus buccoides* and *Archboldia papuensis*

Ailuroedus buccoides sea level to 2800 feet
   Ailuroedus buccoides oorti (A1)
   Ailuroedus buccoides buccoides (A2)
   Ailuroedus buccoides stonii (A3)
   Ailuroedus buccoides geislerorum (A4)
Archboldia papuensis 6700 to 12,000 feet
   Archboldia papuensis papuensis (B1)
   Archboldia papuensis sanfordi (B2)

contains only one egg of a yellowish white colour.' An egg in the British Museum of Natural History (Schönwetter, 1944) from south-eastern New Guinea measures 42·1 × 26·6 mm. Two eggs collected by Carl Wahnes on Sattelberg, Huon Peninsula (1905–1906: November to January) were described by Hartert (1910: 485) as '. . . a rich cream-colour.' Measurements 41·3 × 26·5 and 45 × 29 mm. Rand (1942: 354) collected a laying female in May in the upper Fly River valley.

Subspecies: Four rather similar races are recognis

1 *A. b. oorti* Rothschild and Hartert, 1913, *Novit. Zool.,* vol. 20, p. 526 [type in AMNH, no. 679734]. Type locality Waigeu Island. Known from the western Papuan Islands (Waigeu, Batanta, Salawati) and western New Guinea (Vogelkop and coast of Geelvink Bay to the Siriwo River). Crown dark olive brown, throat white, underparts pale ochraceous buff.

2 *A. b. buccoides* (Temminck), 1835, *Pl. Col.,* livr. 97, p. 575. Type locality Lobo, Triton Bay. Known from south New Guinea from Triton Bay east to the upper Fly River. Like *oorti* but throat tinged brown and underparts darker, more chestnut brown.

3 *A. b. stonii* Sharpe, 1876, *Nature, Lond.,* vol. 14, p. 339. Type locality Laloki River, southeast New Guinea. Known from southeast New Guinea from Hall Sound to the Port Moresby district. Like *oorti* but underparts much darker, and spotting generally smaller on abdomen.

4 *A. b. geislerorum* Meyer, 1891, *Abh. Ber. Mus. Dresden,* vol. 3 (1890–1), no. 4, p. 12. Type locality Astrolabe Bay (restricted by Rothschild and Hartert) and northern coast of Huon Gulf (Lolebu and Bussum). Known from Japen Island and north New Guinea from the Mamberamo River to Collingwood Bay. Like *oorti* but crown much paler, more pale mustard brown.

Evolution: Marshall (1954 : 31) makes the following highly interesting point: 'The catbirds provide a revealing example of how an elaborate terrestrial display . . . can develop in one member of a group while the others retain an arboreal display broadly similar to that of ordinary birds.' It is generally conceded that *Scenopoeetes* and *Ailuroedus* (Tooth-billed Bower Bird, Green Catbird, Spotted

Catbird, White-eared Catbird) comprise the most primitive group of bower birds and that the tree-displaying species (*Ailuroedus*) are less advanced than is the stage-making species (*Scenopoeetes*). However, Bock, on the basis of bower bird skull morphology, observed that the skull of *Ailuroedus* is *not* primitive. He wonders if *Ailuroedus* might have taken up arboreal behaviour secondarily after discarding terrestrial polygynous behaviour such as is still practiced by *Scenopoeetes*. This is an original idea and an interesting possibility. See pp. 42, 46 for a discussion of this subject as regards *Ailuroedus, Manucodia*, and *Sericulus*.

Green Catbird

Ailuroedus crassirostris (Paykull)
Adults 12–13 in.
[*Lanius crassirostris* Paykull, 1815, *Nov. Act. Reg. Soc. Sci. Upsala*, vol. 7, p. 283. Type locality Nova Hollandia [= Sydney, New South Wales.]

Range: Forests of south-eastern and eastern Australia from the Shoalhaven River, New South Wales, northward to the Bunya Mountains, southern Queensland. (See Map 10.2, page 265.)

Adult Male: A light green, pigeon-sized bird with white spotted underparts. In more detail, crown and sides of head yellowish green to olive with variable amounts of blackish tipping, the latter with indistinct dusky bases; nape to upper back olive green with short white centre streaks or spots; rest of upperparts near emerald green; secondaries and secondary coverts on exposed surfaces like back but with small white tips; concealed surfaces of wing quills mostly blackish brown; exposed edges of primaries narrowly pale green to sky blue; central rectrices uniform grass green; rest of tail quills dark usually with green edges and prominent white tips; feathers at sides of upper breast and neck often tipped whitish forming an irregular spot; malar region olive to yellowish green with indistinct black bars; throat mottled greyish, washed green, with short white streaks and spots; breast and sides of abdomen mostly dull grass green often with much white spotting and broad central streaking; abdomen pale often washed yellowish. Iris reddish brown; bill creamy white to horn; feet greyish brown. Wing male 156–167; tail 120–131; culmen 28; tarsus 49 mm. Adult female: slightly

U

smaller: wing 155–170 mm.

Downy Young: Natal down
black.

Remarks: The Green Catbird,
a monotypic species, according
to McGill (1960: 50) is an uncommon inhabitant of the
bushes and heavily timbered
ridges of the coast and adjacent
ranges. In the Sydney district it
is found only in the southern
portions of the county, '. . . principally in the Royal National
Park' (Hindwood and McGill,
1958). Gould observed more than
a century ago that 'This species is
only found in New South Wales,
where it inhabits the luxuriant forests that extend along the eastern
coast between the mountain ranges and the sea.' He added 'Situations
suitable to the Regent and Satin [bower birds] are equally adapted
to the habits of this bird, and I have not infrequently seen them all
three feeding [on wild fruit] together in the same tree.' And
Campbell (1901: 197) who called the species a 'most extraordinary
bird', notes that it is '. . . a denizen of the thick jungle-like scrub
which clothes portions of the coastal regions. . . .' It is generally
agreed that this species is much more easily heard than seen.

Voice: An oft-repeated, cat-like *mew-mew* with a strong accent on
the second *mew*, which can be heard at any time of the day. This
call can be mistaken for a child crying. Also a dawn song which
Marshall (1954b: 150) notes is usually delivered from a low vantage
point in the rain forest. He described this call as a sequence of
sounds beginning with clicking notes and followed by three guttural
cries. The first two are drawn out, the last note is brief.

Food: Chiefly native fruits and berries such as wild figs and
native cherries. Stomachs examined by J.R.Henry in the Bunya
Mountains contained only large and small berries and seeds.

Breeding Behaviour: Gwynne (*in* Marshall, *loc. cit.*) observed a

264

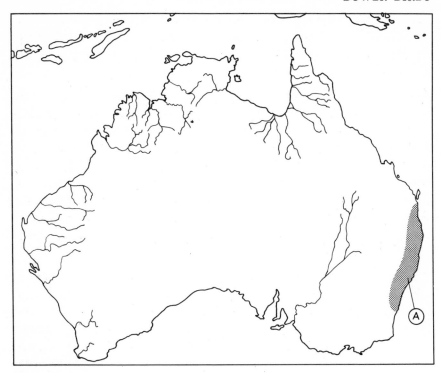

Map 10.2 *Ailuroedus crassirostris* (A)

portion of the courtship display in October just south of Sydney. He discovered one bird chasing another in the rain forest edge. Both birds were emitting their usual cat-like notes. After chasing they perched silently, preened, then resumed their noisy chasing again. Apparently firm pairs are formed with the male assisting at least in the defence of the nest. This may be deduced from Salmon's observation (1953: 263) that both the male and the female performed distraction displays near the nest and young. An additional observation strongly implying that a true pair bond exists in this species of bower bird is W. J. Grime's report of the aggressive activities of 'old birds' in defending their nest and two eggs. He wrote that the '. . . old birds were very savage, flying at us, and fluttering along the ground' (*in* Campbell, 1901 : 197).

Nesting: Nest: A fairly large, thick-walled cupped structure of twigs, tree ferns, and broad leaves, lined with twigs and rootlets (measurements: 9–10 in. wide × 6–7 in. deep; cup 5 in. wide, 3 in.

265

deep). Usually the nest is placed in a forked sapling 4 to 24 feet up in dense forest. Eggs: two to three, near oval, rich cream in colour (measurements: 40·4–45·0 × 28·8–31·6 mm. Schönwetter, 1944, 16).

Evolution: Since nest morphology in *Ailuroedus* seems to be correlated with bower morphology in *Scenopoeetes* (see remarks under *A. melanotis*), I was particularly interested to read Hermann Lau's description of the leafy construction of a nest which he found in November, 1886, in the Bunya Mountains. He wrote (*in* Campbell, 1901: 198) that the nest was an exquisite one placed five feet up in a triple fork of a young tree. Half way up from the bottom it consisted of dry fig leaves, beautifully fastened with twining rootlets, with stronger ones for the rim, and lined with dry grass and roots.

Taxonomy: As pointed out on p. 272, Mayr and Jennings (1952: 2) take the view that because of the 'essential similarity' of the Green Catbird and the Spotted Catbird and 'the agreement of habits' between the two, they 'must be considered as conspecific.' I cannot concur with their conclusion because I find that apparently significant differences exist between the two populations in (a) external morphology and (b) egg colour. In my view in a monomorphic group such as the catbirds, in which subspecies are very similar even when split by pronounced geographic (water) barriers, one has to weigh rather heavily the differences noted above. Therefore I believe these two isolated populations of Australian catbirds represent two biological species.

Spotted or Black-eared Catbird

Ailuroedus melanotis (Gray)
Adults 11–12 in.

Range: North-eastern Australia, the Aru Islands, western Papuan islands and widespread in New Guinea. Usually found in the mid-mountains from 3000 to 5600 feet but in a few areas found near sea level. (See Map 10.3, page 270.)

Adult Male: An emerald green, dark-headed, black-eared, pigeon-sized bird with a variably spotted head, neck, and breast. In more detail, crown to upper back brown to black (subspecies) with brown to white feather centres giving a spotted appearance; ear coverts dark brown to black (in which unique); feathering of upper back grey to rufous with dark margins giving a scalloped appearance; rest of upperparts grass to emerald green; inner secondaries and usually their greater upper coverts tipped white; wing quills dusky with greenish or pale blue outer edges; neck often with an indistinct whitish collar; chin to upper breast dull olive to blackish (subspecies) with medium to large pale centres, palest on throat (which is often whitish with subobsolete dark tipping); underparts buffy to ochraceous (subspecies), the feathers with variable amounts of dark margins, heaviest on upper breast; wing linings whitish; tail on exposed surfaces chiefly emerald green, tipped white, except central pair of rectrices. Male iris brown to blood red; bill light grey to creamy white; feet slate grey. Wing 143–174; tail 109–126; exposed culmen 27–30; tarsus 49 mm.

Adult Female: Like male but slightly smaller, Wing 144–161 mm.

Downy Young and Juvenal: Very young nestling: skin of upperparts blackish, below dusky flesh; natal down grey tinged dark cinnamon on crown, below grey. Nestling (medium sized): head and throat all around covered with dark cinnamon natal down; rest of upperparts emerald green; throat naked, rest of underparts with soft brownish to greyish down on which is a suggestion of dark barring. Nestling (about to leave nest): like adult but sides of head to sides of crown and throat in sheathing, dark collar lacking and below with much soft feathering. Fledgling: like adult but half of feathers of underparts still soft and fluffy.

Remarks: This widespread, polytypic species was discovered by A. R. Wallace near sea level in the Aru Islands in 1857. It is a locally common species of which Claude Grant wrote (*in* Ogilvie-

Grant, 1915: 34) of observations made between 2000 and 3000 feet in the southern watershed of the Nassau Mountains: 'The Barbet-like Cat-bird was a common species inhabiting dense jungle, and was usually seen in pairs. It was generally met with on or near the ground, and was at all times extremely wary and difficult to secure. Its peculiar hissing alarm note, not unlike the spit of an angry cat, was often heard, but the bird was rarely seen.' To the eastward in the Fly River region, Rand met with the Spotted Catbird only near sea level. He wrote (1942a: 352) '. . . I found this species only on the middle Fly River and near the coast, while I found the [White-eared Catbird] only on the upper Fly River where this species did not occur.' Near the coast at Tarara, Rand noted the Catbird as common in the rain forest, but shy. Frequently it was seen 'well up in the lower tree tops.' In Australia the Spotted Catbird is a common species fairly usually found in pairs or flocks within the limited area occupied by the species.

Voice: The call is a loud, drawn-out *eyou-au-au* (Rand, *ibid.*: 352). In Australia the call is recorded as a strong cat-like *yowl*.

Food: Specimens taken in the Fly River region (Rand, *ibid.*: 353) had eaten seeds of a forest tree, seeds of a fan palm, purple fruit pulp, and seeds of a pandanus. Young birds were fed on fruit.

Nesting Behaviour: Rand's observations (*ibid.*: 353) proving that both parents share in the nest duties and in the feeding of the young are highly interesting and important. During three days at a nest near Lake Daviumbu (25–28 September) he first observed both parents as they came to the nest together, then he learned to distinguish their sex (later confirmed by collecting) and was able to make, among many others, the following observations during a two-hour ten-minute period. During this time interval the female visited the nest four times and the male visited it five times:

'11.25 Female came, fed and occupied itself with materials in the nest, apparently picking up things from the bottom of the nest, then began to brood.

11.32 Female left, and immediately male arrived, fed, looked at young a moment and then left.

11.50 Male came to nest, fed, looked at young a moment and then left.

11.52 Female arrived with food in bill (the first time I have been able to see anything in a bird's bill), appeared to feed twice, and then eat what was left in bill, spent a few moments occupied with something in bottom of nest, then started to brood.

11.54 Female left nest.

12.12 Male flew to rim of nest but left without feeding.

12.15 Female came, appeared to feed young, then spent some time in standing on rim of nest, peering down into it, and apparently picking up something from bottom of nest and eating it. Then a large lump of reddish material (fruit pulp?) appeared in bill, was moved about a few times and then deposited in nest. This occupied five minutes, then female began to brood.

12.21 Male appeared in background, female at once left nest and male came directly to nest, carrying something in its bill, quickly fed the young which was giving little hunger calls; male with head on one side watched young for a moment, then left.

12.46 Male came, fed two or three times, watched young for a moment, then left.

1.04 Female lit on edge of nest, peered into nest, appeared to pick up a few scraps from nest but did not feed, then started to brood.

1.10 Female left.'

Nest: Rand described the Lake Daviumbu nest as '. . . a large, loose, bulky structure of slender, dead sticks with a rather neat cup placed in its centre. The outside of this cup was entirely of large dead leaves, mostly of forest trees, laid flat, and inside this was a scanty lining of slender, woody stems which was more substantial about the rim of the nest. A quantity of fresh fruit pulp and seeds was in the bottom of the nest. Outside the triangular nest measured about 475 mm. on each side and 160 mm. deep. The cup measured outside 185 by 100 mm. deep; inside 135 by 85 mm. deep.' This nest was eight feet up in a slender tree fork in rain forest with a dense substage canopy of low palms, pandanus, slender vines, much shade, much fallen moss-covered litter. Another nest found by Rand on 12 December at Tarara was 12 feet up and similarly formed. A nest found in Australia and described by Campbell (1901 : 195) was similarly positioned and of similar construction.

Eggs: Rand found two eggs in his Tarara nest which were unmarked, light olive brown and measured 27 × 40 and 23 × 39 mm. A clutch of two collected by A. S. Meek in North Queensland measured 23 × 42 and 27·8 × 41 mm. (Hartert, 1910 : 485).

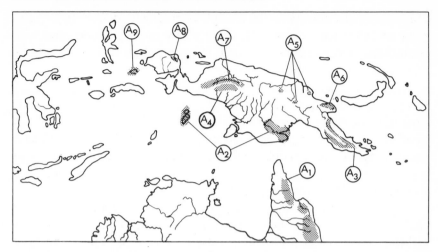

Map 10.3 *Ailuroedus melanotis* (A) (sea level locally), usually 3000 to 5600 feet

    Ailuroedus melanotis maculosus (A1)

    Ailuroedus melanotis melanotis (A2)

    Ailuroedus melanotis melanocephalus (A3)

    Ailuroedus melanotis facialis (A4)

    Ailuroedus melanotis gutaticollis (A5)

    Ailuroedus melanotis astigmaticus (A6)

    Ailuroedus melanotis jobiensis (A7)

    Ailuroedus melanotis arfakianus (A8)

    Ailuroedus melanotis misoliensis (A9)

Subspecies: Nine thinly differentiated races may be recognised:

1   *A. m. maculosus* Ramsay, 1874, *Proc. Zool. Soc. London,* p. 601. Type locality: Cardwell Rockingham Bay. Confined to the Cairns district of Northern Queensland from Cardwell to Kuranda and Cedar Bay [? altitude]. Mathews' *fairfaxi* is a synonym. Head to upper back pale canvas brown with dark brown edges; back dull grass green; underparts dull buffy white with broad olive to brown edges. Male wing 147–159 mm. Female wing 141–152 mm.

    According to Mayr and Jennings (1952: 3) Mathews (1941: 384) described a new subspecies, *blaauwi,* from 'Cape York' (apparently from the Coen area) which is of doubtful validity.

2   *A. m. melanotis* (Gray), 1858, *Proc. Zool. Soc. London,* p. 181. Type locality: Aru Islands. Known from the Aru Islands and south New Guinea (Oriomo River and lower to middle Fly River). Near

sea level. Like *maculosus* but dark areas of head to upper back blackish and dark fringing of upper breast blackish; green of upperparts deeper; ear coverts black, not dark brown. Male wing 169–171 mm. Aru Islands (Lake Daviumbu birds somewhat smaller).

3 *A. m. melanocephalus* Ramsay, 1882, *Proc. Linn. Soc. New South Wales*, vol. 8, p. 25. Type locality: Astrolabe Mountains, south-east New Guinea. Mid mountains of south-eastern New Guinea, west in the south to the Angabunga River and west in the north to Mt Misim, Herzog Mountains. Like *melanotus* but underparts generally more rufous. Male wing 143–155 mm.

4 *A. m. facialis* Mayr, 1936, *Amer. Mus. Novit.*, no. 869, p. 4 [type in AMNH, no. 448982]. Type locality: Snow Mountains (Utakwa River, west New Guinea). Known from the Nassau and Oranje mountains. Like *melanotis* but throat and spotting of upper back more ochraceous, less whitish. Male wing 146 mm.

5 *A. m. guttaticollis* Stresemann, 1922, *Orn. Monatsb.*, vol. 30, p. 35. Type locality Hunsteinspitze, Sepik Mountains. Known only from the Sepik and (subspecies?) Hagen Mountains; Adelbert Mountains (subspecies?). Like *melanotis* but spotting of crown to upper back more rufous, less buffy, throat much darker and underparts generally more deep rufous, less greenish buffy. Male wing 145 mm.

6 *A. m. astigmaticus* Mayr, 1931, *Mitt. Zool. Mus. Berlin*, vol. 17, p. 647. Type locality: Ogeramnang, Saruwaged Mountains. Known only from the mountains of the Huon Peninsula. Like *melanotis* but head more blackish with fewer spots. Male wing 157–160 mm.

7 *A. m. jobiensis* Rothschild, 1895, *Bull. Brit. Orn. Club*, vol. 4, p. 26 [type in AMNH, no. 679724]. Type locality 'Jobi Island,' in error, probably for mainland of New Guinea east of Geelvink Bay. Known from the Weyland Mountains (?) and the mountains on the upper Mamberamo (Idenburg River). Like *guttaticollis* but throat and neck below generally darker due to smaller spots. Male wing 153–161 mm.

8 *A. m. arfakianus* Meyer, 1874, *Sitzungsb. K. Akad. Wiss. Wien*, math-naturwiss, vol. 69 (1), p. 82. Type locality Arfak Mountains. Like *melanotis* but underparts somewhat paler and throat somewhat darker. Male wing 158–161 mm.

9   *A. m. misoliensis* Mayr and de Schauensee, 1939, *Proc. Acad. Nat. Sci. Philadelphia*, vol. 91, p. 152. Type locality Tip, Misol Island, western Papuan islands. Like *arfakianus* but larger. Male wing 174 mm.

Taxonomy: Mayr and Jennings (1952: 1) and Mayr (*in* Peters, 1962) in his latest revision of the Ptilonorhynchidae hold that the Green Catbird of south-eastern Australia is a highly differentiated race of the Spotted Catbird of New Guinea, the Aru Islands, and Cape York. Undoubtedly the green and the spotted catbirds are closely related and form a superspecies, but I cannot accept their view that they are conspecific because, for catbirds, their morphological differences are very pronounced. Indeed they are so great that it seems safe to assume that if the two populations were to come into contact under natural conditions they would be reproductively isolated, or at best they would occasionally hybridise rather than intergrade. The Spotted Catbird is a remarkably uniform polytypic species considering the pressures of geographical isolation to which it has been exposed. It is composed of nine thinly differentiated races, one on Cape York, one in the Aru Islands, one on Misol Island and the rest on the mainland of New Guinea. All have the ear coverts blackish, the head to upper back brown to black with pale feather centres (spotting). The Green Catbird is a monotypic species in which the pattern of the head as well as its colouration is very different from that of the Spotted Catbird. The ear coverts are not black and contrasted with the head colouration, but mostly grass green and similar to the colouration of the head, and the crown to upper neck is not chiefly dark brown to blackish and 'spotted' but generally grass green (with small white spots). In short, although I am strongly in favour of the 'lumping' which Mayr has done so admirably to bring clarity to the great muddled taxonomy of New Guinea and Australian birds, I think the pendulum swung a bit too far in this case. The essential biological truths to be brought out here I think are that the Green Catbird and the Spotted Catbird form a close-knit superspecies and the White-eared Catbird, although more sharply isolated, belongs in this superspecies.

Evolution: Morphologically speaking, the superspecies composed of the three green catbirds, *A. melanotis*, *A. crassirostris* and *A. buccoides*, appears to be closely related to the Stagemaker

(*Scenopoeetes*); but whereas the displays of the catbirds are apparently entirely arboreal and their plumage is generally very brightly coloured (perhaps to fit the needs of protective colouration among green leaves), the display of the Stagemaker is terrestrial and its plumage colouration is generally dark brown (in keeping perhaps with the needs of protective colouration for terrestrial life). Ethologically speaking, in the catbirds the presumably more primitive pair-bond behaviour (with the male helping to build the nest) is adopted, whereas in the Stagemaker polygynous arena behaviour (with the male emancipated and no longer having nest-building duties) is used. With this in mind, it is highly interesting to find that the presumably primitive element of the stock – the green catbirds – uses large tree leaves laid flat in a special manner as a foundation for the nest (see Rand's description above); and the emancipated male Stagemaker also uses large tree leaves laid flat in a particular manner (upside down) as decorations for its bower. Since bower behaviour in arena birds is postulated to be influenced in large part by non-discardable nesting tendencies (see p. 58), the predominant use of leaves in courtship by the male Stagemaker is probably a carry-over from the prominent use of leaves in nest building by the primitive pair-bond stock from which he is apparently descended.

Tooth-billed or Stagemaker Bower Bird

Scenopoeetes dentirostris (Ramsay)

Adults 10½ in.

[1876, *Proc. Zool. Soc. London*, 1875, p. 591. Type locality Bellenden Ker Range (3000–4000 feet), North Queensland]

Range: Australia: North Queensland from the Cairns District (the Endeavour and Bloomfield River regions) south to the Seaview Range near Rollingstone and the Herbert River region. From 2000 to 4800 feet, but seldom at 2000 feet and rarely in lowlands. (See Map 10.4, page 275.)

Adult Male: A stocky bird with heavy, notched bill and striped underparts. In more detail, upperparts brownish olive; sides of lower throat often largely buffy or palest yellowish white forming an indistinct whitish patch; underparts broadly striped whitish and edged olive brown, giving a boldly streaked appearance; axillaries and under wing coverts pale buffy ochraceous often with some dark barring and spotting; flight quills below grey with narrow pale

273

inner edges. Iris dark brown to chocolate brown; bill dark horn to black; feet greenish grey to dark grey. Male wing 145–152 (149); tail 101–105; exposed culmen 21–23; tarsus 35 mm.

Adult Female: Like male: wing 144–150 (147); tail 97–103; exposed culmen 23; tarsus 34 mm.

Downy Young and Juvenal: (Warham, 1962: 29): 'Head still slightly clothed in grey down; neck bare. Iris grey, gape flanged yellow, mouth pale orange, mandible grey tipped dark grey, egg-tooth still present, legs and feet light grey. Breast dull buff with

grey markings, throat brighter buff with grey markings giving a mottled effect . . . mantle dark olive grey. Down still adhering to thighs, rump, and chin.'

Remarks: The Tooth-billed or Stagemaker Bower Bird is restricted to a small area of the Australian hill and mountain forests measuring roughly 200 miles long by about 20 miles wide (Chisholm and Chaffer, 1956). Although discovered in 1874 (by Inspector Robert Johnstone near Cardwell in Queensland) its nest and eggs remained unknown until 1908 when they were found by the oölogist G. Sharp.

The optimum habitat of this curiously behaving species is dense rain forest above about 2000 feet. In this niche it is often one of the commonest of birds and it is likely to be found feeding side by side with its near relative, the Spotted Catbird (*Ailuroedus melanotis*); another close relative, the Golden Bower Bird (*Prionodura*), a much less common species, occupies much the same habitat. Bourke and Austin (1947: 110) found that in spite of the considerable clearing of its rain forest habitat, '. . . the "Tooth-bill" remains very common and most conspicuous. It occurs not only in large tracts of [rain forest], but also wherever small "islands" have been left after clearing. . . . Although we found it on Mt Bartle Frere at altitudes approaching 5000 feet, it seems to prefer lower land. . . . The

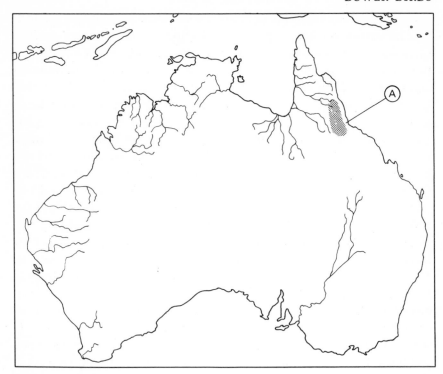

Map 10.4 *Scenopoeetes dentirostris* (A) 2000 to 4800 feet

greatest concentration of the species is near Kairi and at Lake Eacham.'

Food: From stomach analysis the food of this species consists of fruits, berries, and some insects. Warham (1962: 23) noted that a newly fledged juvenal appeared to have been fed red berries.

Warham's (1962) recent observations of dozens of stages on Mt Lewis (3000 to 3500 feet) and on the Atherton tableland (2200–3000 feet) are important additions to Marshall's studies (1954a and b). Warham spent some 44 hours in blinds watching four bowers in an effort to discover the pattern of behaviour employed by this strange bird. I have drawn heavily upon his splendid observations. He informs us that the courts or bowers of the Tooth-bill are easily discovered in spring and early summer '. . . because the males' loud songs are given from close to the bowers and so draw attention to them.'

275

The Bower: The display court is a space near and on the ground, usually under bushes, saplings, spreading palms, in thick jungle. Occasionally it is under pine trees at the edge of pine forests. It is mostly a roughly oval or circular clearing varying from three to eight feet in diameter. The male clears all fallen debris from this space of earth as if with a broom. He then decorates it with fresh green tree leaves of one or more favoured species. Marshall (1954b: 158) notes that the leaves may be up to twice as long as the male which carries them to his bower. These leaves are almost always placed upside down on the 'meticulously clean' court and are replaced with fresh leaves when they wither. The tooth-edged bill (for which this bird is named) serves as a specially modified tool for severing the fresh leaves. Only the male makes use of this tool but both sexes have the specialised bill. Marshall states that about 40 leaves is an average number of bower ornaments, but as many as 103 have been found. Warham (*ibid.*: 24) states that the clearing with its decking of leaves laid upside down constitutes the only ornaments. Snail shells, often white in colour, are sometimes found on one side or on the court but, Warham writes, it is not known if they constitute bower ornaments or are merely natural to the spot and have not been removed. At one bower Warham found 56 leaves. He removed all of them on 5 December in order to study the manner in which the bower owner would refurbish its bower. It was done as follows: almost every day the male carried in from 2 to 10 leaves and placed them carefully on the ground court. By December 12, 25 leaves had been brought in.

Voice: Long ago Kendall Broadbent noted that the Tooth-bill is possessed of an exceptional voice. He wrote (*in* Campbell, 1901: 208): 'It excels all other Bower-Birds as a mimic, and may be fitly termed master mocking bird of Australia'. (See below for an opposing view to this statement.)

Warham (*ibid.*: 24) described the auditory displays of a group of interacting males: 'Toothbills sing in phrases lasting two to four seconds with intervening pauses of from five to ten seconds duration, and from a range of a few feet it was obvious that during the pauses they listened to the outpourings of their neighbours. Not all the birds sing all the time and when a newcomer starts up the others may turn to face his direction and may address their next broadsides towards him. . . . I noted that most songs appeared to contain certain key phrases which recurred again and again, I also found that the songs used by a bird at a particular bower one day were largely different from those it used a day later. . . . In addition to its variability the Toothbill's song is very powerful. . . . Harsh songs come pouring from the singer, which will abruptly switch to quite melodious whistlings. The high pitch of some of the calls make the ears throb. At the peak of his delivery the bird fluffs out his throat and throws back his head with his beak widely opened. The throat pulsates vigorously and the yellowish feathers of that region become rather conspicuous as Marshall figures (*op. cit.*: 160).'

As noted above, this species has long been classed as a first-class mimic (Broadbent, Marshall); but Chaffer (1959b) and Warham hold that the Tooth-bill is not a true mimic, they claim its apparent mimicry is purely the result of accidental similarity in calls. Chaffer points for support to the absence of many very distinctive bird calls in the song repertoire of the Tooth-bill.

Singing Perches: We learn from Warham (*ibid*: 26) that the males may sing for half an hour at a time without shifting their position. Each singer is near its private ground court, usually on a horizontal limb from about one foot above the ground to 20 feet above it. Often the perches are directly above the courts and are heavily worn from repeated long use. They spend far more time on their perches than on their ground courts. Infrequently while on its singing stick the male will emit a continuous and fairly melodious whisper song interspersed with some rapid burring notes. At the same time it will bob from side to side on its perch, rapidly open its wing and appear to examine the ground.

Bower Displays: Marshall, Warham and others have observed males as they sang and displayed alone on their courts, but apparently no positive observations of a male displaying to a female have been made. This may be because such displays are very uncommon, or because, if arena behaviour is the pattern of breeding, peripheral arena males may go through the entire breeding season without a single mating. A. F. Smith, as long ago as 1906, sensed the unusualness of this situation. He wrote: 'There is a mystery about these birds that will take some explaining. How is it that throughout the three hours that I watched him no other bird put in an appearance? If the owner of the playground had a mate, it seems strange that she did not show herself. If his performance is to attract a mate, he is certainly a most persevering but unfortunate suitor, as he has been hard at it for two months to my knowledge. . . .'

Marshall's observation involved a wild male which dropped to its court to display and sing to a decoy (a dead bird) much in the way that *Archboldia* and *Rupicola* are known to seek special spots on the ground when a female wanders through the clan area. He wrote (1954a: 28): 'We have only one brief indication of the possible part played by the leaf-covered stage during the courtship of *Sceno-poeetes*. A dead bird (which on dissection proved to be a male) that had been taken from above one display-ground was placed on a branch a few yards from the singing-stick near another. Within a few seconds the owner of the second stage appeared, but instead of assailing the dead male violently . . . the owner of the stage *flew to the ground at the edge of its leaf-display* [italics mine]. It partly concealed itself from the watcher behind a tree-trunk and called. It seemed that the owner of the stage desired the dead bird (the sexes are identical in external appearance) to come from the low branch towards it and the display-ground.'

Later Warham saw males that appeared to be displaying to females hidden somewhere near their ground courts. On 18 December, near Lake Eacham, after one male had been singing and bringing leaves to its bower for several hours, Warham saw it fly down to its court and alight behind a sapling trunk: 'Here it seemed to be hiding but soon hopped out uttering typical bower-bird cracklings and hissings, quite different from any form of song that I had heard from a Toothbill before. The bird advanced with its beak gaping and the feathers of the upper breast loosened, giving the effect of a broad buff band right across the chest. Its posture was a crouch, back and head were lowered somewhat and as the bird moved forward in a series of jerks its wings were repeatedly flicked out and tail jerked upwards. In this way the bower-bird advanced three or four yards across the [court] and past the hide where the display ended. Throughout this performance I had the impression that the bird was threatening another stationed behind or to one side of my concealed position.'

Warham's observations continue: 'Later this same morning this display was repeated and elaborated. Again the male stood behind the trunk on the ground and started to sing. It switched abruptly to hissings and crackles and began to advance in erratic hops with wings flicking and tail jerking. Then it snatched up a dead leaf in its bill and stood just outside the cleared area for three or four minutes holding this display object. Wings and tail were now only slightly flicked and jerked but every $1\frac{1}{2}$ seconds the head was bobbed up and down twice. A mechanical "drerr, drerr" was made in time with the head movements. In between bursts of these head bobbings the bird maintained a soft continuous whistling completely different from the harsh outpourings usual during song.'

Nesting: The nest is a frail dish-shaped structure (6 to 8 in. wide) of thin sticks, lined with twigs, usually placed in thick vegetation among vines 15 to 80 feet up in wet mountain forest. The eggs, usually two in number, are clear creamy brown in colouration. Measurements: 40·4–44·2 × 27·0–29·4 mm. (after Schönwetter, 1944).

Care of Young and Distraction Display: Warham (*op. cit.,* 29) found a recently fledged juvenal in a patch of rain forest near the Barron River about five miles from Atherton on 22 January. It could fly very weakly and was captured easily. When handled it emitted harsh squawks which soon brought an adult Tooth-bill to the scene. The adult displayed much agitation and '. . . flew hastily to the ground and dashed about there just out of sight and just as described for *Ailuroedus.*'

Analysis of the Display: The curious decorated ground courts, although widely spaced, appear to be clustered as 'clan arenas', in certain parts of the jungle and the owners of the courts appear to interact with one another by means of loud calls and probably to compete for the females that their concentrated voices attract to the arena. I suspect that male tooth-bills live in clans in such arenas, and that the distribution of the courts somehow spells out the breeding hierarchy of the court owners. But this remains to be proved. However, some observations lend support to the arena hypothesis. For example Warham remarked (1962: 24) that 'At all places where this species was studied [by himself] the birds were found in communities where each was in hearing of another.' Marshall found more or less the same thing (see below) and long ago, Smith (1906) made this point: '. . . On 22nd October I seated myself near the bower and watched the bird from ten till twelve. As his cries seemed to be answered by another bird not far away, I then followed the sound and found another playground about 100 yards away, which I watched from twelve till three. Only one bird was at each bower, and, as their antics were the same, one description will do for both. Throughout this time I watched only one bird was at the playground, and he appeared to have no interest in anything but his collection of leaves. He would fly away occasionally for another leaf or some fruit, returning in two or three minutes, when he would place the leaf in position, upside down, have a look at the others to see if they were right, but at no time played with them – and then fly away to a twig about eight feet above the leaves, and there perform; but his repertoire was very limited, his favourite number being the harsh, scolding note of the drongo . . . . Occasionally he would imitate the Rifle-bird and the Little Thrush . . . and he would frequently give a short piercing whistle, which seemed to be his natural call.'

Marshall wrote (1954a: 27) 'In some favoured dense and hilly areas the voices of five or six birds can be heard simultaneously without difficulty by the human ear. The owners of the stages appear to answer each other. Some call almost constantly for more than an hour on end. There is also a low musical soliloquy that can be heard only a few yards away.' A little later in describing the function of display in the Stagemaker, Marshall added (*op. cit.*: 28) 'It is certain that the almost constant babble of noise emitted by the bird enables all rivals and potential mates over a wide area to know where the caller and his stage are located.' This description seems to fit almost perfectly with my definition of an 'exploded' or clan arena (see p. 53) *but with one important difference.* Marshall believes that this species, in fact that all bower birds, practice pair-bond behaviour. This he makes clear (*op. cit.*: 29): 'Avian display – visual, auditory, or a combination of both – is usually associated with conflict and the establishment of territorial domination, the formation of the pair-bond and *the development and synchronization of the sexual processes of the pair* until the environment becomes seasonally appropriate for the female to build her nest and rear her brood . . . . It is the same with bower-birds.' Warham (1962) and Chaffer (1959) in their important contributions on bower bird behaviour, accept Marshall's hypothesis of pair-bond behaviour in these birds. I cannot do so, except to the extent of saying that if pair-bond behaviour does occur in bower-building birds, I would be inclined to believe that it had been secondarily acquired from previously emancipated arena birds.

Taxonomy: Bock (1963) found that this short, heavy-billed genus fits very well with the other genera of bower birds, all of which have a rather distinct skull type.

Archbold's Bower Bird

Archboldia papuensis Rand
Male 14–15 in.

Range: New Guinea: Eastern Highlands at Mt Hagen and Mt Giluwe and in the west, the Snow Mountains, at Lake Habbema and the Bele River west to the Nassau Range (Ilaga) and the Weyland Mountains (Wissel Lakes); between 6700 and 12,000 feet. (See Map 10.1, page 261.)

Adult Male: A jay-sized dark grey to black bird with or without a golden crest. In more detail, generally sooty grey to blackish with narrow black scalloping, sometimes with traces of golden yellow feathering on forehead and hind crown (subspecies), or uniform jet black with a prominent gold crest extending from forehead to nape; flight quills dark grey tinged olive or blackish; bases of primaries and shafts to quills pale yellow; alula sooty brown or jet black. Iris deep brown to reddish brown; bill black; feet grey. Wing 155–170; tail 128–172; bill from base 33; tarsus 41–46 mm.

Adult Female: Like male but smaller and lacking gold crown and crest; alula edged with pale ochraceous, or deep ochraceous with black tip (subspecies). Perishable colours as in male but feet blue grey. Wing 144–153; tail 125–147; bill from base 35; tarsus 37–41 mm.

Remarks: The discovery as recently as 1939 of this very distinct bower bird genus suggests that perhaps other undiscovered species await the explorer in little-known hinterlands of New Guinea. Austin L. Rand, its discoverer, named it in honour of Richard Archbold, one of New Guinea's foremost ornithological explorers. The genus *Archboldia* was erected (Rand, 1940: 9) for the blackish-grey population of the alpine forests of the Oranje Mountains of West New Guinea. In 1950 to my great surprise I found basically similar birds some 400 miles to the east on Mt Hagen (See Mayr and Gilliard, 1954: 363). However, in my series (7♂ [type], 1♂ subad., 2 ♀, 1?) the generally black adult males have the crests

281

elongated and golden in contrast to three males in Rand's series (3 ♂, 3 ♀, 2?), which have no crests and have the plumage of the head blackish like the body. Otherwise, however, my series compared rather closely with all of Rand's specimens, except for differences in colour (much more blackish, less greyish) and size (larger). Excluding the golden crown, these differences appeared to be of advanced racial rather than of specific rank. Furthermore, a careful study of Rand's birds indicated that his three males might not be completely adult, thus perhaps accounting for the absence of the golden crest. For these reasons, Mayr and I described my Mt Hagen series as a new race, *A. p. sanfordi* (Mayr and Gilliard, 1950: 1-3), rather than a new species. [In 1951, Shaw Mayer discovered a population of *sanfordi* on Mt Giluwe, some 20 miles distant from the type locality].

In 1954 I surveyed the Hindenburg and Victor Emanuel Mountains which form major links in the mountain wall connecting the two localities, the Oranje and the Hagen-Giluwe mountains, where *Archboldia* is known to live. I found no trace of this bower bird. This fact, together with information obtained from native woodsmen, convinced me that *Archboldia* does not occur on either the Hindenburg or Victor Emanuel mountains. If so, the two known populations are geographically widely separated. This geographical information, together with the knowledge that in a closely related bower bird, *Amblyornis*, the females of a monomorphic and of two highly dimorphic species are all very similar, leads me to believe that my Mt Hagen bird was in fact a valid biological species. Indeed, if the speciation of *Amblyornis* (in which the females of three species differ hardly at all) is a valid criterion, *Archboldia*, (in which the females of *sanfordi* and *papuensis* differ very appreciably in size and colour) could very well comprise two species, perhaps one highly dimorphic and one monomorphic.

Since our original description of *sanfordi* was based on a study of only four Mt Hagen specimens (which I had brought home in advance of my general collection), it appeared advisable to re-examine the entire series together with specimens collected later by Shaw Mayer, and to compare these with Rand's series of eight from the Snow Mountains. I was able to assemble a series of twelve from Mt Hagen (including 1 ♂, 1 ♂ subad. collected by Shaw Mayer) and four from Mt Giluwe (3 males, 1 ♀ subad. collected by Shaw Mayer agreeing perfectly with the Mt Hagen series). A factor taken into consideration in this study of 'crestless' versus 'crested' populations is that a lone specimen, a *male* in Leiden from Bobare, Wisselmeren, western New Guinea (Rand, 1942b: 498; Junge, 1953: 65) has the head blackish and crestless like the three males in Rand's Oranje Mountain series.

Measurements of the above series (see Table) indicate that the eastern population is distinctly larger and has a different wing-tail ratio (the tail is shorter than the wing in *papuensis*, longer in *sanfordi*).

Table of Measurements of *A. papuensis* and *A. sanfordi* in Millimetres

	Wing	Tail	Tarsus
A. papuensis			
Snow Mts ♂	155, 155, 162	128, 136, 148	41, 42, 43
♀	144, 147, 153	125, 132, 136	37, 38, 41
A. sanfordi			
Mt. Hagen ♂	159, 163, 164	167, 175, 178	43, 43, 44
	166, 166, 166	180, 184	44, 44, 46
	167, 168		
♀	145, 159	141, 147	41, 43
Mt. Giluwe ♂	169, 170	172, 172, 175	

These factors plus differences in colouration and crest form, convinced me that the Mt Hagen – Mt Giluwe birds represented a distinct biological species. This is how the matter stood until recently, when Dillon Ripley (1964) found a population with gold head feathering in the Oranje Mountains (the Ilaga Valley region) just west of the area where Rand got his specimens. Whether Ripley's gold crested birds are the same species as Rand's remains to be determined. It is possible that Rand failed to find the adult crested male because he did not happen to find their arenas. They perhaps live in clans apart from the females and young males (see below), in isolated parts (arenas) of the forest.

History of the discovery of A. papuensis sanfordi *and its bower:* On 12 June 1950, a native trapper arrived at my Mt Hagen base camp (8500 feet) with two birds which he indicated were the male and female of a rare mountain forest bower building bird. His specimens were totally different from anything I had found during four months of collecting in the Kubor, Bismarck and Hagen mountains (5000 and 13,500 feet). At first I took the 'female' to be the rare *Archboldia* which Rand had discovered. However, since the 'male' bore a spectacular golden crown, I soon became convinced (and greatly excited thereby) that the birds represented an unknown species, since Rand's males I knew were crestless.

Food was running short, and I was soon to depart from the highlands; nevertheless I immediately outlined a 'crash' programme to obtain additional specimens. About 100 natives were assembled to view the remarkable birds. I offered them a price in steel, pearl shell, and stick tobacco equivalent to a year's salary for each additional specimen up to the number of ten. I was surprised to note that most of the natives did not know this bird, although on the whole they possessed a remarkably broad knowledge of their avifauna and of many ingenious methods of trapping the various species. This suggested to me that this *Archboldia* probably lived in the alpine forests with which the native is less familiar. My next move was to ask the man who brought in the new birds to lead me to the spot where he had trapped them. To my astonishment he refused to do so. Further to my astonishment, despite the huge bounty, not one *Archboldia* was collected except by the man who had trapped the original birds. This fellow, however, rapidly became a Hagen 'millionaire.' Every day or two he would come rushing into camp with a fresh specimen. His deliveries were as follows: 12 July, ♂ ad., ♀ ad., 15 July, ♂ ad., 17 July, ♂ ad., 18 July (type), ♂ ad., 20 July, ♂ subad. (no crest), 21 July, ♂ ad., ♂ ad., 22 July, ♂ ad., ♀ (?), 12–20 July, ♀ ad.

All of these birds, he said, had come from one 'sing-sing' ground, around which he had his traps. He guarded its location like grim death. However, after much persuasion the trapper finally agreed to take William Lamont and myself to see the 'sing-sing' ground. Thus on 16 June we began our trip by descending to Tomba and then walked some miles south-west on an ancient native trail leading between Tomba and Wabag. Somewhere near the headwaters of the Kaugel River, we crossed a gorge, then mounted a small, rounded ridge and turned roughly southward less than a mile through high forest to the location of the bower. Here the forest was tall and the substage fairly open, although there were many hanging vines, much thin climbing bamboo, and many pandanus trees. The altitude was about 8000 feet. Ferns averaging about two feet tall covered the ground rather uniformly between fallen forest debris. There were no native habitations in the vicinity but a few hunting trails penetrated the area, which, in the bower vicinity, was nearly level without exposed rocks.

We stalked the bower and, as I stood quietly, a female *Cnemophilus macgregorii* was observed feeding about sixty feet up directly over the bower. However, no *Archboldia* was seen. I found three snares set in a rough triangle about the edges of the bower which was a trampled, roughly circular space in the ferns some three and a half feet in diameter. The trampled area looked most unimpressive and brown in contrast to the fern surroundings which were predominantly light green. Interspersed among the ferns were saplings, some woody shrubs, and many strands of golden yellow-shafted climbing bamboo. Three evenly separated runways led into the little trampled area. At the mouths of two of these I found 'set' snares. These consisted of 'wickets' of rattan that bridged the runways. Big loops of fine vine hung to the ground from slots in the tops of the wickets. Above each wicket a bent sapling was set to jerk the loop upwards when the snare trigger was touched. The third runway was bridged by a snare which had been sprung. Caught in it were the easily recognisable yellow-shafted black tail feathers and tail coverts (upper and lower) of a male *Archboldia*. The bird had been snared, but had jerked free, as it was entering the trampled area. The trapper told us that the eleven birds which he brought in between the dates of 12 and 22 July were trapped at this bower.

Bower: The dance ground was little more than a heavy dishevelled matting of dried ferns, grasses, bamboo leaves, and a few sticks. Around the edges it was rather disorderly and seemingly without design, but towards the centre the debris was smaller and more firm and flattened so that the whole presented the appearance of an animal bed.

Secondary Bower Area and Ornaments: Outside one entrance-way (the one with the snare containing *Archboldia* feathers) in another space in the ferns was a disorderly area which I have called the secondary area. This area appeared to be a natural one, in contrast to the dance stage which appeared to have been rather recently fashioned by the birds, presumably by carrying flooring material into the midst of the bed of ferns.

The secondary area was floored with a few plants and a sparse assortment of fallen debris such as leaves and forest debris. In its midst at a distance of about 4–6 feet from the main bower were two elongated heaps of medium-sized land snail shells, each consisting of roughly fifty shells. More than half and perhaps two-thirds of these were broken. The piles were disorderly, and one contained obviously fresher shells. Less conspicuous because of their smallness, but also in definite piles, were two heaps of blackish, longitudinally ridged beetle wing covers and a few body segments and legs of black beetles. Most of these had been stacked in one pile, which consisted of at least twenty-seven wing covers and five body segments. About a foot distant from it was a similar pile, but these were more spread out and rotted so as to be difficult to see. Also scattered about were several hard blue berries about the size of large huckleberries. Also near the piles of shells were the skeletons of two large centipedes.

After photographing the main and secondary bower areas, I collected the following specimens, which constituted most of the paraphernalia which the birds had placed in the secondary area.

1. One hundred and thirty-five snail shells and fragments thereof as follows: (a) 11 intact or nearly intact snail shells ranging in size from 23 (greatest width) to 43 mm.; (b) 10 snail shells which had been broken open, ranging in size from 35 to 44 mm.; (c) 104 snail shell fragments ranging from small chips to segments comprising nearly half of the shell.

These shells ranged in colour from vandyke brown through olive brown and buffy brown with dull yellowish olive markings (these were in the majority) to pale vinaceous grey. Inner surfaces of the shells (seen chiefly on broken shells) were dull whitish to grey with pale vinaceous and pink showing through. Older shells such as were concentrated on one pile were often coated on inner surfaces with patches of grey green lichens.

One intact shell and six fragments, some of which were quite large, were coated with peculiar blue blotches resembling bright watercolour paint which ranged from deep violaceous blue to jay blue, apparently depending on the thickness of the application. The colour was lodged on the exterior of several shells and on the interior of the majority. Its presence is an enigma. One intact shell had the colour only on the inner edge of the lip, as though the colour was applied by a bird with its bill partly open and holding the shell by the lip.

2. Two hard round seeds, one with the seed showing and the other with a covering of shrivelled flesh adhering all round. These were both 12 mm. in greatest diameter.

3. Twenty-seven beetle wing covers ranging in length from 18 to 22 mm. Also 5 large sections of beetle exoskeletons and 3 legs.

The wing covers were all shiny black on the exterior surfaces with fine longitudinal ridges. Inside they were blackish on their outer edges and at both ends and generally brownish amber elsewhere. The other fragments were shining black.

4. Two blue berries the size of large huckleberries (these did not grow overhead) which the natives called *Yombie*. One of the archboldias collected at this bower had its stomach filled with similar blue fruits.

5. Unnoticed at the time and therefore not collected were two large centipedes which were photographed on the secondary area and which were possibly part of the decorations.

Several feet from the secondary area and about five feet from the main bower was a slanting broken tree trunk about four feet tall. A faint trail led from the shell heaps to the base of this trunk. On its rotted top I found a single fresh tree blueberry of the same species described above.

In 1952 I returned to Mt Hagen from America with special photographic equipment designed to obtain photographs of this bower bird on its dance ground. To my great disappointment, the Tomba area (south watershed) was unapproachable because of native warfare. I therefore searched the north-eastern slopes for this species but found no trace of it. Four years later in 1956 I again returned and finally succeeded in rediscovering the bower of this species and in finding out how it is used in courtship.

The five bowers which I found in 1956 (three were in use and two were old) varied from three to eight feet in diameter. All were within an area of about two miles, on the floor of gently sloping mountain forest with a moderately heavy concentration of under-brush, pandanus and tree ferns. All contained fairly large piles of snail shells, piles of black beetle wings, and small piles of honey-coloured resin chips. Draped over low limbs and on the shrubbery surrounding each bower were many strands of living and dead climbing bamboo. The golden yellow colouration of the bamboo was a feature of the bower. Later I saw the male bring such strands, also dead ferns to the bower area. On horizontal limbs, the tops of fallen trunks, and on the ground about the bower I found bits of charcoal, a few green berries, some large dark coloured berries and often large numbers of snail shells (see pl. 22).

Ripley (personal communication) informed me that the bower of the population he discovered in the Ilaga is almost certainly very different from the bowers I had found on Mt Hagen in that stick walls are erected. He described (1964) the Ilaga bower which his trusted assistant found at 12,000 feet and described to him as ' . . . consisting of two walls of interlaced twigs about two feet six inches apart and eighteen inches high. At each end there was a small collection of pieces of charcoal and blackish fruit. The centre space was bare earth. There were no shells or other ornaments. There were no ferns nor vines as described by Gilliard (1959). The whole place was approximately three feet square'.

Behaviour at Bower: On 14 July 1956 (8500 feet) on Mt Hagen I made my first and only observations of a male and female interacting on a bower stage. These observations are unique. They reveal that the pattern of sexual behaviour in this bower bird is different from anything heretofore known in bower birds.

The observations begin at 6.32 a.m.

6.32: Enter blind. Begin second day of observations of Bower no. 2.

7.11: A mighty whistle from *Archboldia*. The loudest noise yet heard in this forest: a long-drawn-out *pheeuw*. Two sets of two notes each with about eight seconds of silence between the pairs and three seconds between the two notes.

7.14: A powerful crow-like call, *kraaaaa*, this again is *Archboldia*.

7.35: Much sound like insects buzzing. Much *kree*-ing and *kraa*-ing. Also notes like *kriii* and *kreeee*. Periodic, usually every three to five seconds. Perhaps two individuals of *Archboldia* are in tree.

7.42 to 7.45: This period was action-packed. First the male *Archboldia* moved to a position six feet over bower. There it *kriii*'d and cawed and vented a deep, hollow growl. It sat with the wings drooped and the tail drawn slightly forwards under the body like a trogon. Next it disappeared for a few seconds and then reappeared on the floor of the bower itself. There it assumed a crouching position over snail

288

shells. With the tail and back nearly horizontal to the ground it moved snail shells with bill. Next it carried a shell to one heap, put it down, picked it up again, then carried it back to original pile. A large grey shell was then picked up and moved a few inches. For perhaps a minute the golden-crested bird dandled the shells. At times the bird moved over the bower mat in a kind of glide or scurry, its head held low. Once it flew up to a low perch beside the bower and delivered a number of *keees*. These were of a ventriloquistic nature. Although the bird sat in plain sight not more than thirty-five feet from my binoculars, I at first could not be sure that the notes were being emitted by the bird I watched. Then I noticed that with each far-sounding *keee* the mouth opened and the tail moved. These ventriloquistic notes were frequent and gave me the impression that three or four individuals of *Archboldia* were in the vicinity. Still, only one male, probably the same individual, has been seen at the bower.

7.58:   *Archboldia* descended to the bower stage to move snail shells again. The bird so far has not remained on the ground more than 20 to 40 seconds.

8.01:   *Archboldia* arrives at perch eight feet over bower carrying a long tendril of vine (at least six inches long) or strip of other vegetation. It paused for several seconds, then dropped steeply and directly on to the bower mat. There it went directly to the heap of blackish snail shells with the strip. It worked quietly close to the ground for some time.

8.05:   The male has been on the bower for quite a few minutes. Most of the time it is nearly or completely out of sight in the 'cave' portion of the bower which I cannot see.

8.06:   The male is now on a perch some eight feet east of the bower.

8.07:   Extremely sharp *kra-kraaa* followed by a snap and a kind of hiss. These notes seem almost deafening. Sun now lights bower stage very brightly. [The male continued to call and visit the bower perches and stage until 9.08.]

9.08:   *Quee* heard 200 feet west, then continues closer and closer around bower to west singing perch. (This oft-repeated call was a little different from the usual notes of *Archboldia*. It had not been heard away from the bower before.

This call may have been emitted by the male as he escorted the female to the bower area.)

9.10: *Archboldia* in vicinity of bower, *kee*-ing.

9.12: Male descends to bower stage and begins a low *churr purr, purr churr, churr.* (Later this churring continued incessantly as the male displayed on the ground.) The female flew into the bower area – a completely black bird which appeared suspicious of everything. It eyed my blind, flew towards it, then back to the bower area, landing on a low horizontal perch. There it fluttered the wings excitedly, looked down at the male which now lay churring on the fern mat. Often the female thrashed its wings loudly. It snapped the head around, bent over with the head dipping to the level of its feet. It raised the tail to the level of the back as it stopped. Often the mouth of the female opened, and I believe it emitted a low, growl-like *churr*. Frequently it changed perches, flying from one edge of the bower to the other. The perches that the female used were about one to three feet above the fern stage on which the male lay displaying. There were at least three such perches. Each was draped with golden bamboo strands and with dried ferns. On one I had seen about five pieces of charcoal, the largest about the size of a golf ball. When the female changed perches, which occured about every minute or two, she frequently flew within a foot of the male. At such times when she passed over the displaying male, she whipped her wings with such rapidity that they sounded as though they would be torn. This ripping, tearing sound, like stiff cardboard being torn, was in part delivered over the male and gave the appearance of whipping. This was the extent of the display of the female. She was never seen to descend to the ground or to touch any ornaments. She was never more than five feet from the male. At least once the female leaned well over her horizontal perch so that her head was perhaps two inches below the level of her feet. Her mouth was open, her back bent, and her tail hung down steeply behind. Her head was almost always pointed at the male. This action occurred late in the long display period. It brought the heads of the male and the female within a foot of each other.

The display of the male appeared submissive and begging in the extreme. A glance at the time annotations shows that it continued unbroken from 9.12 to shortly after 9.35. During this period of more than twenty-two minutes, the male spent all but about one minute lying flat on the fern stage. There it crawled like a wounded animal, body pressed to the ferns, wings half open, their under surfaces against the ferns. The tail was also partly open and pressed to the ferns. So flattened was the bird that it resembled a reptile more than a bird. Only when the bird rose to hop were the legs momentarily visible. The crown was folded flat against the head. The tip lay tightly on the plumage of the neck and upper back. Only the yellow tuft at the fore-head stuck up. The only part of the bird that was elevated was the head and neck. The bill was almost continuously open, and it was usually open wide. The mandibles were continuously flexed as though the bird were gasping. At least half of the time a strand of fern shaft or thin bamboo was held crosswise in the mouth. The movements of the mouth parts gave the appearance of chewing. The direction of the crawl (which resembled a whipped dog crawling towards its master) was always towards the female. Progress was slow. With open, elevated bill the bird crawled perhaps a foot in one or two minutes. The female sat on nearly horizontal perches around the edge of the fern stage, its head usually directed towards the approaching male. Sometimes the male crawled to within a foot of the female before she flew over him, often hovering to whip her wings over his back, then to fly three to five feet across the bower to another low perch. Immediately she flew, the male would turn and slowly crawl towards her again. But every so often (I saw this perhaps ten times) the male would shorten the distance by rising to its feet and hopping from about three inches to about ten inches in the direction of the female. This hop was executed quickly. It was unusual because the bird seemed to execute it from a prostrate position flat on the ground. Except during these jumping periods, the male kept up an incessant churring. In landing on the mat at the end of a jump, the bird slid in on its belly and immediately assumed the 'whipped dog' attitude. It would lie still with the head grovelling for a second or two, then raise the head, open the mouth, and rapidly begin its chewing of the small vine. The male made a complete circuit of the fern stage in about five minutes, following the female as she moved irregularly around its edge. Never did the male touch any of the many shell, insect, or resin ornaments which were in its path. Frequently it crawled among and even over the ornaments. The only ornament used was the strand of vine held in the mouth. This vine was slender and about the length of a match stick. During the crawling display the head was sometimes directed almost straight up.

9.30 : Male still crawling towards moving female. Male is completely 'lost' in display. Female still appears suspicious. Sounds of 'whipping' very loud.

9.37 : Looks like it is over. Both birds flew off silently.

9.43 : Male *Archboldia* flies in. Goes first to horizontal perch at edge of bower (two feet up) used by female. This perch is a cleared area on the top of a horizontal vine. Earlier I had observed it to be deeply scored with claw marks. The cleared area is about eight inches wide. The remaining portion of the vine (about four feet in horizontal length) is thickly covered with a natural covering of moss. A curtain of thin yellowish bamboo shafts and a few dark brown dead ferns are added decorations placed there by the bower owner. The male then jumped to the bower floor. There it stood for a long time, slowly moving its head as it picked at a cluster of greyish and blackish snail shells. Often it raised the head to peer out of the bower. At such times its head resembled that of a lapwing, the fore crest rising steeply, the golden crest lying flat on the crown and extending backwards to a sharp tip which protruded at least half an inch behind the nearly vertical neck. This I would call the 'sentry' position. Aside from these periods when the head bobbed up, the body was held low over the fern mat and ornaments, and the actions were slow and deliberate. The male was absolutely silent during this period.

9.48 : The male is still in the bower. It carried a sixteen inch stalk of some kind of plant into the middle of the fern stage. Next it jumped to another of the perches used by the female, this one two and a half feet up. There it draped the stalk over the perch, stood silently for about ten seconds. Next it jumped to the middle of the bower, picked up a dead fern frond, moved it about three inches, then dropped it.

10.05: Observations close.

Nesting: Three males in breeding condition were taken on Mt Hagen (12–21 July 1956).

Subspecies: Two apparently quite distinct races are known:

1 *A. p. papuensis* Rand, 1940, *Amer. Mus. Novit.*, no. 1072, p. 9. [type in AMNH, no. 305644]. Type locality Bele River (7000 feet), eighteen km. north of Lake Habbema, Snow Mountains. Known only from the Bele River – Lake Habbema region of the Oranje Mountains (6700–9000 feet), the Nassau Range 9400–12,000 feet) and the Weyland Mountains (Wissel Lakes). Greyish black to black above, dark grey below with narrow blackish scalloping; flight quills grey tinged olive (Ilaga Valley: Subspecies ?: some gold feathering on crown and nape [see above]).

2 *A. p. sanfordi* Mayr and Gilliard, 1950, *Amer. Mus. Novit.*, no. 1473, p. 1. [type in AMNH, no. 348448]. Type locality south-western slope of Mt Hagen, four miles west of Tomba, Mandated Territory of New Guinea. Known from the type locality and from Mt Giluwe (8500–9000 feet). Like *papuensis* but generally jet black with a prominent upright golden yellow fore crest and a long narrow depressed golden nape crest; flight quills generally blackish.

Evolution: If it can be confirmed that the Ilaga population builds a stick-walled bower, I will have no hesitation whatever in elevating my Mt Hagen birds to specific rank. Bower form is relatively conservative, witness the twin-walled construction found in *Sericulus*, *Ptilonorhynchus* and *Chlamydera*, and the walled construction described by Ripley is very different from the fern matting with piles of ornaments that I found in six bowers of *Archboldia* on Mt Hagen.

Bock in his studies of skull morphology, was unable to find characters by which *Archboldia* could be separated from the other bower birds. He wrote (1963: 123): 'The skull of the Ptilinorhynchidae is so uniform that it is not possible to suggest generic groups on the basis of the cranial features.'

Vogelkop Gardener Bower Bird

Amblyornis inornatus (Schlegel)
Male 10 in.
[1871, *Ned. Tijdsch. Dierk.*, vol. 4 (1873), p. 51. Type locality interior of Vogelkop (= Arfak Mountains)]

Range: The Vogelkop (Arfak and Tamrau) and Wandammen mountains, from 3800 to 5800 feet. (See Map 10.5, page 310.)

Adult Male: A thrush-sized olive brown bird. In more detail, upperparts brownish olive tinged with amber; crown dark olive brown; sides of head pale brownish olive; underparts buffy to ochraceous, pale on abdomen and darker, more olive brown on sides; wing and tail quills dark brown with somewhat more olive outer margins; and the wing quills with pale greyish inner margins; under wing coverts pale ochraceous to buffy. Iris dark brown; bill blackish, paler on lower mandible; feet dark grey tinged blue. Wing 131–136; tail 92–101; culmen from base 29–32; tarsus 36–38 mm.

Adult Female: Like adult male but slightly smaller: wing 128–134; tail 91–96; culmen from base 30; tarsus 38 mm.

Remarks: The wonderful Vogelkop Gardener Bower Bird remains a fairly common species in the dark interior mountain forests of west New Guinea. It was discovered before 1870 by Papuan collectors in the employ of C. E. H. von Rosenberg and the first naturalist to see its home grounds was Odoardo Beccari who, in September 1872, found it in the Arfak Mountains. High on the range he discovered many new birds and found the courtship house of the Vogelkop Gardener Bower Bird with its astonishing bird-planted garden and artistically arranged decorations. Earlier, on the coast, Beccari had heard native rumours of the extraordinary architectural abilities of a strange mountain bird. When he finally came face to face with it he made on-the-spot colour drawings and descriptions (Beccari, 1877) which still fascinate all who examine them.

Beccari made his discovery on a projecting spur of Mount Arfak at an altitude of about 4800 feet. On the floor of thick virgin forest he found the remarkable bower which he described (1875: 332) as follows:

'The Amblyornis selects a flat even place around the trunk of a small tree that is as thick and as high as a walking-stick of middle size. It begins by constructing at the base of the tree a kind of cone, chiefly of moss, the size of a man's hand. The trunk of the tree becomes the central pillar; another whole building is supported by it. On the top of the central pillar twigs are then methodically placed in a radiating manner, resting on the ground, leaving an aperture for the entrance. Thus is obtained a conical and very regular hut. When the work is complete many other branches are placed transversely in various ways, to make the whole quite firm and impermeable. The whole is nearly three feet in diameter. All of the stems used by the Amblyornis are the thin stems of an orchid (*Dendrobium*), as epiphyte forming large tufts on the mossy branches of great trees, easily bent like straw, and generally about twenty inches long. The stalks had the leaves, which are small and straight, still fresh and living on them – which leads me to conclude that this plant was selected by the bird to prevent rotting and mould in the building, since it keeps alive for a long time.' Beccari then described the garden for which the species is named: 'Before the cottage there is a meadow of moss. This is brought to the spot and kept free from grass, stones, or anything which would offend the eye. On this green flowers and fruits of pretty colour are placed so as to form an elegant little garden. The greater part of the decoration is collected round the entrance to the nest. . . .' Beccari observed some small apple-like fruits, some rosy fruits, some rose-coloured flowers, some fungi and some 'mottled insects' on the turf.

S. Dillon Ripley (*in* Mayr and de Schauensee, 1939) the Secretary of the US National Museum and veteran New Guinea explorer-naturalist, collected birds for the Academy of Natural Sciences in Philadelphia in the Tamrau Mountains of the Vogelkop in 1938 (February to April 1). He ascended to 5200 feet on Mt Bon Kourangen, where he collected for sixteen days. During this period Ripley was fortunate to find many bowers of this remarkable species. He wrote: 'They are extremely neat and well made, the largest I saw measuring eight feet long and the tops of its domes built around two separate saplings were about four and a half feet high. From back to front it measures six feet. The "gardens" on the neatly-cleared terraces in front of the bowers were for the most part elaborately made and carefully segregated as to colour. In the case of a small blue plum-like fruit, however, there were occasionally one or two yellow fruits of the same size mixed in the bed. In the entrance way to one of the bowers, a place of honour usually

w

reserved for large brown decayed fruits or particularly large flowers, I found one most peculiar "bed" white in colour and the consistency of jelly. A few days later I found that it was the sap of a kind of small tree fern that grew in the mountains. How or why it came to be used by the Bower Birds, and what purpose it served, remained a mystery.'

Another bower observed by Ripley (1944) was on gently sloping ground which appeared to have been swept with a broom. This structure, built around a sapling (the fundamental element in the *Amblyornis-Prionodura* group of bower birds) was about three feet high by five feet broad with an opening one foot high. Ripley wrote that this '. . . curious structure fronted on the cleared area. The impression of a front lawn was heightened by several small beds of flowers and fruit. Just under the door there was a neat bed of yellow fruit. Farther out on the lawn there was a bed of blue fruit. At the bottom of the lawn there was a large squarish bed of pieces of charcoal and small black stones. A few brownish fruits lay here also, some of them rather decayed. Off to one side were several big mushrooms in a heap, and near them were ten freshly picked flowers.'

In July and August, 1964, I found a concentration of nine bowers, some old and unused, along about a mile of trail on Mt Bantjiet in the Tamrau Mountains. These bowers differed greatly in proportions and decorations, some with blacks, browns and blues predominating in the piles of ornaments; others with orange or red flowers and red, blue and green tree fruits (see pl. VI). The interior of bower no. 8 was sketched in detail. Its floor was carpeted with moss and the base of the central column was surrounded by a cone of soft moss. The roof was very evenly curved and the ends of the roof sticks were sheared off to form a level ceiling that was even with the top of the doorway. There were, on the mossy floor, a red ornament and a few black beetle exoskeletons.

Bower Display: In 1964 I made what are, to the best of my knowledge, the first observations of the male of this species displaying to a female. On five different occasions, as I watched, a female either appeared at the edge of the cleared area or was present but out of sight, judging from the actions of the male.

On July 28 I made the following notes on the visit by a female: 'At 11.38 grating calls and wing thrashing 35 feet to the left were heard. Now the male rushed into the bower, crouched behind red ornaments, ignored the ornament that I had purposely misplaced, went (apparently) around the column, uttered deep grunts, came to entrance and seemed to be looking at the female (which I could not see but felt sure was nearby). At 11.52 I saw the female. I saw her first when she took flight from a perch about a foot above ground half way between me and the bower. Apparently I scared her for now she leaped from sapling trunk to sapling trunk more or less half way between the blind and the bower. She hung to the vertical perches as did *Chlamydera lauterbachi* at Kup 1950 and Aiome 1964 and peered into the porthole of my blind. Her abdomen appeared brighter yellow than that of the male, otherwise she was identical in coloration. But her actions were very different. She was extremely active and suspicious whereas the male was now seemingly oblivious to all external sounds. I think I could have walked up on him. She looked more at me than at the male who had now come out onto his court and was squatting on his tail. I got no pictures of the female because she did not land on the "lawn" or enter the bower, but I got a few of the frantic male as he performed and "talked" in the most extraordinary manner, almost seeming to be communicating in a complex avian language with the female. Near the height of the display by the male, just as the female arrived, but before I flushed her, the male crouched, almost lying down, in his dark bower house; he then scurried around inside with his back to the center column and appeared to be looking out between the stick bases of the outer wall.

'The calls were recorded during the height of the display, with the female investigating me from perches 10 to 15 feet in front of the male and 3 to 6 feet up, and the male performing at a climax of activity before the female. The male now began emitting loud cat-like *meows* and explosive sounds like the drumming of a grouse – also rapping, ticking sounds and windy creaking noises too numerous and varied to describe. It also emitted calls of other birds, and "other" birds seemed to be everywhere in a forest which at other times is noteworthy for its relative silence. I think nearly all of the "birds" heard at the time were notes emitted by *Amblyornis*. . . . The female left. The male continued to cry for about a minute, then he leaped from his "lawn" to a vertical sapling shaft two feet up and emitted three very loud grating cries, quite different from anything I have yet heard from him. That was it. He now stood still for a while, then leaped back to his court and began yanking at large sticks, pulling some which were very heavy out of place. . . .'

Voice: Beccari noted that, according to his native guides, the Vogelkop Gardener Bower Bird is called *Buruk Guria* (Master Bird) because of its exceptional powers of vocal mimicry. Ripley heard males at or near the bower which emitted 'soft growling, churring noises'; harsh calls, now long and chattering, now loud, almost like a barking dog.

My 1964 notes on this species record·a bewildering number of calls made by the male at the bower. In addition to the calls recorded above, one was a seemingly distant rapping sound which I had thought might perhaps be the rattle of an *Epimachus* but which proved to be a ventriloquistic call of *A. inornatus* delivered when the bird was perched just inside the bower opening. Other calls were emitted later, some from the limbs over the bower and a series of calls from a stump four feet in front of the bower which sounded for all the world like a screen-door being slammed shut and followed by the scratchy vibrations of the screen. This sudden call with metallic reverberations was only heard from this one perch. Some of the many additional calls I recorded were a high wavering whistle; a chugging sound; wheezing, spitting sounds; a sharp click like metal being struck; ratchetting sounds like a stick drawn along a picket fence rapidly; a non-ventriloquial *kah kah* given repeatedly at intervals with the head held up and the bill open; and a series of *keu keu keu keu* calls with the head held high.

Nesting: Nothing is known of the nest or egg of this species. An egg identified as this species by Nehrkorn (1910: 356) also by Schönwetter (1944: 17) was apparently collected in 'British New Guinea' (see Hartert, 1910: 487) and thus is incorrectly identified.

Evolution: Generally speaking sexual dimorphism is fairly pronounced in the bower-building bower birds. The males have bright plumes or patches of colour, usually on their heads or forebodies, which range from red, gold, yellow, shining lavender to halations of glowing pearl. The females, however, are sombrely dressed. But in a few of the bower-building bower birds the male is as sombrely dressed as the female. Some years ago I was struck by the fact that the better 'architects' and 'artists' among the male bower-builders are the species with the least ornamental feathering. In other words I noticed what appeared to be an inverse ratio between the development of the bower and the development of the nuptial plumage. From this beginning I eventually postulated that such unadorned males had come to depend largely upon their elaborate bower ornamentation rather than on their nuptial plumage for the optical stimulation of the female. I further postulated that when external objects become engraved as secondary sexual characters in the courtship pattern, the bright male plumage – the colourful crests for example – are no longer important and they may then be gradually lost through natural selection. This is because display with colourful objects is less of a liability to a ground-displaying bird than display with bright plumage. This hypothetical phenomenon I named the 'transferral effect' (1956: 451).

The species under discussion here, the Vogelkop Gardener Bower Bird (*Amblyornis inornatus*), with its astonishing bower and ornaments, first led me to suspect this correlation. It belongs to a group of three species in which the females are extremely similar and so closely related that, even during the era of taxonomic 'splitting,' they were regarded as races, not species. In fact, so similar are they that ornithologists of the stature of Ernst Hartert virtually refused to believe that in one group [a good species] the male exactly matched its sombre coloured mate, yet in the other two groups [both good species] the males wear brilliant orange erectile crests! Listen, for example, to Hartert in his analysis of specimens from the Vogelkop (1930: 30): 'Both Dr Ernst Mayr and Mr Shaw-Mayer were emphatically told that crested males never occurred in the Arfak or thereabouts, and both failed to ever see one. Yet *some-where they must be common* [italics mine].' So wrote Hartert even though he had for study no less than twenty-three skins collected by Mayr from the Vogelkop (Siwi, Mountains near Ditschi, Gunong Mundi near Ditschi, Lehuma) and the Wandammen Mountains, none of which showed a trace of the crest; and he knew that Salvadori (1880–2: 667) enumerated twenty-six skins from the Vogelkop region, none of which had a sign of a crest.

My transferral hypothesis was developed after I found that: (a) the population with a short, more variable golden crest, (*A. subalaris*) built a less fancy maypole and lawn bower; and (b) the population (*A. macgregoriae*) with a long, spectacular golden crest built a simple, poorly ornamented maypole and lawn bower.

Evidence reinforcing this hypothesis has since been found (see p. 384; *Chlamydera cerviniventris*) in another group of bower birds.

299

Macgregor's Gardener Bower Bird

Amblyornis macgregoriae De Vis
Male $10\frac{1}{3}$ in.

Range: Mountain forests almost throughout New Guinea (except the Wandammen and Vogelkop regions); from 3800 to about 9000 feet. (See Map 10.5, page 310.)

Adult Male: A stocky, thrush-sized, olive brown bird (see illustration below, upper right) with a very large yellowish orange crown. In more detail, upperparts generally olive brown tinged amber; mid to hind crown with long, somewhat glossy, yellowish orange crest plumes composed of narrow decomposed feathers 43 to 78 mm. in length each finely tipped brown; some of the lateral crest plumes nearly solid olive brown; underparts dull olive rufous to ochraceous brown, often with some (mostly concealed) narrow whitish streaking on the throat and upper breast; axillaries, under wing coverts and inner margins of wing quills ochraceous to pale orange yellow; flight quills dark olive brown. Iris dark brown; upper mandible black, lower light horn; feet dark grey. Wing 127–142 (subspecies); tail 80–92; culmen from base 27–29; tarsus 38 mm.

Adult Female: Like adult male but lacking bright crown; upperparts averaging slightly more olive brown, less warm olive brown and underparts averaging slightly paler. Slightly smaller than male, wing 125–132; (subspecies); tail 78–87 mm.

Juvenal: Upperparts largely dark mouse brown (with a faint maroon cast) and plumage very soft; underparts mouse grey, darker on sides, palest on abdomen, and very soft (description of a fledgling, perhaps ten days out of nest).

Immature: First year plumage much like adult female. Male

intermediate plumage or stages of dress: (a) like adult female but plumage generally somewhat more richly saturated with pigment resulting in upperparts being slightly richer rufous; under wing coverts and axillaries slightly deeper orange; underparts slightly more rust brown, less ochraceous buff; (b) like (a) but general body pigmentation averaging somewhat darker and with a very few long orange crest plumes projecting like hatpins from the crown from insertions midway between the eyes; the short brown plumage of insertion region streaked narrowly on concealed halves.

Remarks: For centuries Macgregor's Gardener Bower Bird has been treasured by the Papuans for its spectacular crest plumage. The first record of the plumes being used for adornment is that of Simson (1907: 383), who wrote of it as a rare native curiosity in the Owen Stanley Mountains of south-eastern New Guinea where it is used as a headdress. The next record is that of Stein (1936: 22) from the other end of New Guinea who found that the colourful crest plumage of the male is virtually the only feather decoration worn by the natives of the Weyland Mountains. Between these geographical extremes, in the Kubor Mountains at an altitude of 5600 feet, I once bribed fifty-four highly decorated men to halt their dancing and form a line so that I could make a census of the colourful plumes that they were wearing (see Mayr and Gilliard, 1954: 325). Among the assorted treasures I found a native with the bright crest plumes of *Amblyornis macgregoriae* on his head.

The Papuans have devised ingenious ways of trapping this treasure for which they have many local names. In the Owen Stanley Mountains it is called *Larli* by the Koiari natives (Weiske, 1902: 41); in the Kubor Mountains, it is known as the *Kombok*, but I heard natives speak of it as *Kitsie-Kombok* nearby on the south flank of Mt Hagen. In the Telefomin region it is widely known as the *Fagan*. Rand (*in* Mayr and Rand, 1937: 208) found that two methods of killing the males were used by the natives of the Mt Tafa region, south-eastern New Guinea: (1) by shooting with four-pronged arrows from little blinds built near the dancing places of the males; and (2) with 'dead falls' erected beside the dancing spots (see Rand's photograph of a deadfall trap).

Food: Rand (*in* Mayr and Rand, 1937: 208) wrote: 'The birds fed through the forest singly or more often in twos or small parties, eating the small fruits of the second-story trees as well as visiting the

301

tree tops.' Stomachs examined by Shaw Mayer (*in* Marshall, 1954: 133) held fruits, but insects were found in an ovulating female.

This wonderful species and its strange dancing spot – its bower – were discovered by the Macgregor Expedition (Sir William Macgregor, George Belford, Karl Kowald, A.P.Goodwin) in the Musgrave Mountains of south-eastern New Guinea in 1889. De Vis, ornithologist of the Brisbane Museum, Australia, who named the discovery in honour of Lady Macgregor, also published (1890: 61) the first description of the extraordinary bower structure. This was based on the observations of various expedition members. As time passed other naturalists recorded their observations of the wonderful bower (Goodwin, 1890: 154; Simson, 1907: 383; Weiske, 1902: 41; Chaffer, 1949: 24; Stevens, *in* Greenway, 1935: 90; Gilliard, *in* Mayr and Gilliard, 1954: 364; and doubtless others).

From their observations, mostly of the bower, it became clear that the builder, Macgregor's Gardener Bower Bird, although a very shy bird, must be not uncommon to fairly common throughout its extensive mountain-forest range.

I was deeply impressed and mystified by the bowers of this bird which I first found in 1950 in the mountain forests of the Wahgi region. The questions which they generated led me into the long study of bower birds and birds of paradise imparted in this book. One of the early bowers that I found I described in detail (see below). It was discovered June 16, 1952, above Kup, Kubor Mountains, at an altitude of 7800 feet.

The Bower: The structure was on the ground on the top of a ridge in thick mossy forest under trees reaching seventy feet. The ground and surrounding vegetation was saturated with moisture and everything was dripping wet. The bower appeared to be new and my native guides said it was in active use.

The bower was a column of sticks erected around a thin sapling growing in the midst of a saucer-shaped moss-covered clearing or 'parapet.' It was in the midst of a concentration of saplings, vines and bushes. Down hill from the rim of the parapet at distances of two inches, eight inches, one foot and four feet six inches, were slender vertical saplings which, my guides said, were habitually used by the *kombok* in approaching and departing from the bower (later confirmed). On each was a heavily scratched perching area, brownish in colour, about six inches long, and devoid of moss. This perching area contrasted sharply with the greyish bark and moss covered surfaces of the neighbouring saplings. The saucer-shaped parapet was on moderately sloping ground. Much pale greyish green moss, of a sort that I did not see on the ground, had been brought to the spot and leveled out by the bower-builder to form a nearly level circular platform. This was ten inches high on the downhill side, and firmly packed. Some if not all of the parapet moss had been stripped from tree surfaces. Bits of bark still adhering to the moss proved this. Later when I collected a bower for the American Museum I discovered that the mossy parapet was so compressed and intermeshed it could be rolled up like a thick carpet.

The bower dimensions were as follows: diameter of the moss parapet 3 ft 8 in.; width of the elevated parapet rim, 9 in.; height of the rim $1\frac{1}{2}$ in. to 2 in.; width of the stick column at base, 9 in.; height of the sapling forming the central tower support, 38 in.; basal diameter of the central sapling, $\frac{1}{4}$ in.; maximum height of the stick column, 24 in.; width of the widest part of the stick tower (15 in. up), 15 in.

After five hectic days during which I attempted to photograph the male at this bower (it came at least ten times but rain, mechanical difficulties and ill timing frustrated my efforts), the bower was collected. It consisted of 816 dead twigs and thin rootlets. My Papuan guides said the twigs had been collected by the bower builder in the upper portion of the forest. Of the 816 sticks fewer than one per cent were less than 50 mm. in length; about 15 per cent were between 75 mm. and 150 mm. long, about 85 per cent averaged 190 mm. and half of one per cent were about one foot or longer. Of these the longest was 410 mm., five were about 375 mm. and 12 were about 300 mm.

Mixed among the bower sticks were a few fern shafts and slender bamboo leaves, one very small orchid, one thin root and one thicker than average stick which was well covered with leathery white lichens. This last was apparently a bower embellishment. It was found near the top of the column of sticks. It was 220 mm. long, strongly bifurcated, and 3·5 mm. thick. The majority of the bower sticks by contrast were about 2 mm. thick and many had two or three slender short twigs attached. The white lichens covered this un-usual stick like a ringlet for a distance of 42 mm. Another bower which I found on 12 June at a similar altitude and about two miles distant on the same range (see Mayr and Gilliard, 1954: 364) was under construction. It is of interest that two fungus-decorated sticks were also found at that bower. They too were somewhat more stocky than the sticks used in the bower tower. They had been deposited at the outer edge of the mossy parapet. No ornaments were found about the base of these bowers and no tassels of animal silk were seen on either of the stick towers.

A bower which Norman Chaffer observed (1949: 24) on the Wahgi Divide spur of the Bismarck Range near Nondugl was ornamented with 'small bundles of borings of woodboring insects fastened together with spider web or similar material.' I found no such decorations on the two bowers which I observed in the geographically isolated Kubor Range. However, on Mt Hagen I observed and photographed a bower which had many small 'tassels' of animal silk attached to it and Rand (*in* Mayr and Rand: 1937: 207) who saw many bowers of this species on Mt Tafa far to the east in the Wharton Range, observed such decorations (see below).

I have studied eight bowers and I believe Bulmer studied seven. However, as long ago as 1936 Rand observed no fewer than 20 during four months in the high forests of the Wharton Range. Unfortunately, his important description of the major features of these bowers (found by the first Archbold New Guinea Expedition) was overlooked by Marshall (1954):

These bowers were usually on ridge crests, consequently usually on or by native trails which also follow the ridges. Possibly this is because ridge crests are about the only places where comparatively level ground is available, with a clear view about . . . all the bowers were very similar in general structure, though, of course, some were much more elaborate than others. Since De Vis' description is relatively unknown, it may be advisable to redescribe the bower. It consists of a circular, saucer-shaped runway 3–4 ft. across, and more or less built up of moss, around a sapling about which is built a tower of sticks, making a central column or tower. . . . The most elaborate bower I saw had the saucer-shaped platform of moss ten to twelve inches deep on its outer edges, with the track sunk four to six inches in the upper surfaces. Moss was banked up on the central column to about the level of the outer rim of the runway. The central column had been built about a slender sapling about six feet high. For the lower eighteen inches it was densely packed with small twigs placed horizontally, and many of these had the ends decorated with bits of animal silk. Above that for another foot the sapling was more loosely surrounded with larger twigs so that the central column enlarged as it went up and was perhaps eighteen inches across the top . . . on the outer margin of the platform, just outside the runway, were scattered black pieces of vegetables matter (fungus?) and small pieces of charcoal, probably from native camp fires and which the bird must have gone some distance to secure. This and the animal silk were the only decorations.

Ralph Bulmer, a New Zealand anthropologist with strong ornithological leanings, has spent much time in the interior of New Guinea, chiefly in the Mt Hagen region. With great kindness he has permitted me to quote from his valuable unpublished notes on the birds of Mt Hagen. Bulmer spent four days (during the period 21 October 1955, to 15 February 1956) studying seven bowers on the north flank of Mt Hagen, between 6000 and 7000 feet. Most unusually, all were in disturbed forest near the forest edge, and within a mile of each other in the north watershed above the Baiyer River. Bulmer's observations of bower pilfering, presumably by rival males, lends support to my hypothesis that this species is an arena bird. He wrote (MS_2: 15):

A feature which impressed me greatly was the great difference in dimensions and shape of the maypole on different visits to the same bower. It seemed that any occupied bower is being simultaneously built up by its 'owner' (or 'owners') and pillaged and destroyed by other birds [of the same species] which can get near it. I noted little variation in the radius of the ring, though considerable differences in the height and bulk of the maypole. Bower (ii) provided a particularly interesting example of this. The maypole of this was built onto a 5 ft. cordyline sapling which was leaning at an angle of about 75°. On 21 October the sticks rose in a bulky but fairly neat cone to 3 ft. 6 in. above its moss base. By 21 December, although about the same quantity of sticks remained, they had been knocked down into a much shorter squatter pile not more than 2 ft. high. By the 15 February only $11\frac{1}{2}$ in. of sticks remained.

Bulmer's discovery of multiple cone bower building in *Amblyornis macgregoriae* is highly interesting because, as he points out, of the possibility that this characteristic is analogous with multiple cone building in the Australian maypole bower bird, *Prionodura*. He wrote (*loc. cit.*):

The other point of interest concerned subsidiary or abortive maypoles, which were present close to bowers (i), (iii), (iv), and (v). Bower (i) had an additional maypole with 6 in. of twigs, situated 2 ft. outside the parapet on the north-east side. Bower (iii) had 'within a few yards' a sapling of diameter of $1\frac{1}{2}$ in. with a roughly cleared patch of ground around it and

305

all moss and lichen cleaned from the lower 3–4 ft. of its stem, but no sticks around it. I took this to be the remains of a demolished bower. Bower (iv) had, on 21 October, 1955, three very rudimentary maypoles all within 6 ft. of it, each with just a few sticks and a very little moss. By 21 December, 1955, all sticks had been removed from these, but there was a new bower (v) 20 yards away. There were three abortive maypoles, without [stick] cones, 15 ft., 18 ft., and 14 ft., from this bower, respectively. [Bower] (v), as we have seen, had been demolished completely by 15 February, leaving (iv) standing alone and in good condition, with no other maypoles with sticks anywhere near.

Bulmer concluded this series of observations by saying: 'Whether this is truly analogous to the multiple cone building of *Prionodura* it is not possible to say.' His interpretation '. . . was that the subsidiary maypoles were all temporary structures built in the height of building excitement but demolished and their materials worked into the finally chosen bower when this was well established.'

Bower Decorations: In addition to the tower sticks and the pale greyish green platform moss (probably both collected in the crown of the forest), the bower ornaments are variable and sparse. In order of frequency they appear to be (1) tassels of insect silk (Bulmer, MS$_2$: 16, says they are composed of '. . . a glutinous substance with fibrous material and very small seeds suspended in it') frequent and numerous. (2) Small to medium-sized black and white objects (fungus, animal dung, vegetable matter, charcoal) very sparse and often lacking. (3) Small piles of seeds on the mossy parapet (Bulmer found a few clusters of small dry brown or black berries and small orange-coloured seeds on the parapet) rare.

On Mt Hagen in July, 1956, I studied a group of bowers which were located in nearly level-floored forest at about 8300 feet. It was there that I finally succeeded in making a series of still photographs of an adult male in its bower. One bower that I photographed in detail was rather heavily decorated with about 45 tassels of animal silk, some of them up to an inch long. They reminded me of dangling cocoons as they swayed and spun in little eddies of air. (Later I thought of them when I saw the eye-catching fluttering of the long secondary tassels of the Cock-of-the-Rock (*Rupicola rupicola*) as it posed 'frozenly' on its terrestrial display court in British Guiana). The highest insect silk tassels had been attached 26 in. above the parapet, but mostly they were attached within reaching distance of the bird as it stood on the mossy floor. I noted, as did Bulmer, that the tassels are also hung on sticks and low plants at the rim of and just outside the mossy parapet. My bower with some forty-five insect tassels was also relatively heavily decorated with dozens of very small pieces of lichen, mostly ashy white in colour, but some blackish.

Bower Activities: Almost certainly each bower is owned by a single male who, during the peak weeks or months of the breeding season, spends most of the day in its vicinity. He usually sits quietly on a concealed perch fairly high in the forest within sight of the bower. Every so often, he emits an extraordinary variety of calls, many sounding like bird calls and many sounding like mechanical noises. On Mt Hagen the call most often heard was a *krii koo* followed immediately by a dull snapping *kuk kuk,* like tapping on a box. Also there was much subdued sound resembling wing thrashing, plumage rustling, some gurgles, some ripping sounds, some insect buzzing sounds, some loud limb-rubbing screeches and some tearing sounds. I found this extraordinary orchestration highly confusing as I sat in my dark blind, camera trigger in hand, attempting to outwit this wary bird. The notes are highly ventriloquistic and seem to emanate from many parts of the forest instead of from a concealed perch 20 to 30 feet above and 20 to 50 feet away from me. Several times I heard mixed waves of birds making a noisy approach and once, after hours of tedious waiting, I was infuriated to hear the voices of a band of natives walking right up to my blind. Each time it was the *Kitzie Kombok* that had fooled me. The time the 'natives' approached I was so misled I made noisy movements in my blind and probably revealed my presence to the bower bird!

But after many attempts I managed to observe and photograph the male as he worked in his bower. To reach it he flew down in a series of stages, landing successively lower and lower on the sides of slender, vertical saplings (to which he clung like a reed warbler), until he landed a foot from the ground near the edge of the parapet. He then jumped to the mossy parapet encircling the tower of sticks, stood motionless for a few seconds, then began picking at something at the base of the stick column. I now made five photographs of him as he slowly and silently worked his way (with many long pauses) around the mossy circle. A root projecting from the moss was picked at a number of times.

Another male 1000 feet higher on the same slope of Mt Hagen (in July 1950) had briefly erected its golden, almost cockatoo-like crest when, after flying to the edge of its bower, it had spied a study skin of a male that I had laid out on the mossy parapet. My 1956 male was silent when on its court and it approached the bower so quietly I suspect it made some visits undetected. On the bower parapet it kept the crest folded and flattened against the neck and back. I never saw more than a single bird at a bower.

Rand (*in* Mayr and Rand, 1937: 208), after days of fruitless waiting, saw two birds momentarily in a bower: 'Confused shapes darted about in the runway for a moment, then the birds paused, one with its breast against the central column.'

Once again Bulmer's observations are wonderfully helpful in deciphering the pattern of courtship in this extremely wary species. He writes (MS$_2$: 17–18):

On 22 October 1955 I spent from 9 a.m. to 12 noon in a well built hide, constructed the previous day, overlooking Bower (ii) from a distance of about 12 ft. At 9:35 a.m. a bird with a very small crest visible came down to the bowl of the bower and walked around adjusting the moss base of the maypole with its beak. It worked right round the base, doing this, four or five times. It then started a little dance, hopping from side to side and moving its head from side to side, all the time facing in towards the maypole, sticking its beak backwards and forwards into the moss of the base. When nearest to the hide it looked straight in at me, but showed no obvious sign of anxiety – not at all like the Chlamydera. This activity lasted about a minute. Then the bird hopped out of the bower and broke something off which was hanging from a nearby twig. This it carried back in and worked into the fabric of the base of the maypole. It did this a second time, then hopped again out of the bower, from twig to twig up some nearby bushes and flew off out of sight. The whole time it was at or about the bower was about four minutes.

At about 10:20 after a few minutes of noisy calling by an invisible bird or birds nearby, a bird sat on a branch above the maypole and sang loudly, one of the most extraordinary songs I have ever heard. I can only liken it to a piece of stiff grease-proof paper being vigourously crumpled and torn, as a background to a whole variety of whistles and screams. It began with a low wavering whistle. I thought three birds were present, but I could only see two, one with a very large crest, the other dark and uncrested. The crested bird descended to the bowl of the bower and sang there, generally more quietly and internally than up on the perch, all the time with the neck stretched up and pointing at the maypole, sometimes standing still for a couple of minutes, sometimes moving round, generally clockwise, but always facing the maypole. The uncrested bird hopped about in the branches a few feet above the bower, whistling plaintively. Three times it descended into the bowl, and, each time the crested bird chased it, briefly and violently displayed its crest, thrusting its head forward and flashing the crest over it.

The crested bird left the bower and sang very noisily on a nearby branch, once opening its crest while doing so. Then it returned to the bower, but soon finally left it, singing nearby for a little and then flying away. The uncrested bird had apparently gone off a few minutes earlier. The whole performance lasted about twenty minutes. It might be worth noting that before this performance started there were two or three birds making a 'purring' noise in branches fairly high above, as this ceased when the display and singing proper started, I thought it was made by the bower birds – though it could conceivably have come from some other species, possibly a pigeon.

On 21 December Bulmer returned to the same bower and found it much altered and partly demolished. At 9:15 a.m. he secluded himself in the same blind and almost immediately the bower owner perched close by and called *chack chack*, then began intermittent singing for 15–20 minutes. Once it sang loudly for 2–3 minutes. It did not descend to the bower but at 9:45 Bulmer observed '. . . a dark bird with about half an inch of very red crest . . . approached silently, perched on top of the maypole, and violently tugged out and scattered about a dozen twigs, before suddenly flying off, without as far as I could see, taking anything with him.' At 10:15 a.m. Bulmer saw an uncrested *Ambylornis* sneak to the bower and land briefly on the top of the maypole.

Nesting: Nest (9 July 1950; Mt Hagen, Gilliard): a fairly deep firm cup (exterior measurements 165 × 100 mm.; interior, 100 × 60 mm.) of bark strips and rootlets with many large leaves, including some palm leaves, in the foundation, lined with a firm mesh of black wire-like rootlets (or thin vines). This nest was collected by a native who said it was taken from a small tree in deep forest about 7 feet above ground. Egg: one (9 July, incubation well advanced), oval, buffy white, slightly granulated (egg damaged, measurements approximate: 45 × 28·5 mm.). An egg from 'British New Guinea,' probably the Owen Stanley Mountains (Hartert, 1910 : 487), described by Nehrkorn as uniform yellowish white, measured 40 × 29 mm. Bulmer obtained two females on Mt Hagen at 5600 and 6000 feet, both of which were caught by his natives at their nests on 25 October and 7 January, respectively. Rollo Beck collected a fledgling 10 March 1929, at Sevia, Huon Peninsula.

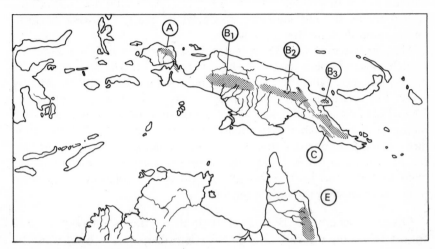

Map 10.5 *Amblyornis* and *Prionodura.*
Amblyornis inornatus (A) 3800 to 5800 feet
Amblyornis macgregoriae (B) 3800 to 9000 feet
   Amblyornis macgregoriae mayri (B1)
     Amblyornis macgregoriae macgregoriae (B2)
     Amblyornis macgregoriae germanus (B3)
Amblyornis subalaris (C) 2200 to 3600 feet
Prionodura newtoniana (E) 1500 to 5400 feet

Subspecies: Three, two fairly similar, one well differentiated:

1   *A. m. mayri* Hartert, 1930, *Novit. Zool.,* vol. 36, p. 30 [type in AMNH, no. 679526]. Type locality 'probably Karon, northern Vogelkop;' error for Weyland Mountains. Known from the Weyland, Tabi, Nassau, and Oranje mountains [*longirostris* is a synonym]. Crest and tail longer than in any other subspecies: males, Weyland Mountains: crest 71, 71, 71·5, 73 (72) mm.; wing 135–142 mm.; tail 87–97 mm.

2   *A. m. macgregoriae* De Vis, 1890 (22 February), *Ann. Rep. Brit. New Guinea,* 1888–1889, p. 61. Type locality Musgrave Range. Known from the Hindenburg Mountains, Schraderberg, Mt Hagen, Mt Kubor, Wahgi Divide, Herzog Mountains, and the mountains of

south-eastern New Guinea [*musgravii* Goodwin and *aedificans* Mayr are synonyms]. Like *mayri* but crest and tail shorter: males, Mt Hagen: crest 51, 53, 56, 60, 62, 62, 65, 66 (60·1) mm.; wing 129–142 mm.; tail 80–93 mm.

3 *A. m. germanus* Rothschild, 1910, *Bull. Brit. Orn. Club*, vol. 27, p. 13 [type in AMNH, no. 679570]. Type locality Rawlinson Mountains. Known only from the mountains of the Huon Peninsula (Saruwaged Range). Like *mayri* but crest and wing much shorter and tail somewhat shorter than in any other subspecies: males: crest 43–48; wing 127–133; tail 84–91 mm.

Analysis of Behaviour: The breeding behaviour of this species remains poorly known but it seems safe to say that the basic pattern is that of arena behaviour with the males living in loose clans, claiming courts, and building bower structures on these courts in certain preferred areas of the forest.

How breeding rights within such clans of bower-building males is established, is unknown. Agonistic displays may play a part, but it is likely that the bower structure (since it is a bundle of secondary sex characters) is also involved. Bower vandalism and abortive bower building, I suspect, function in this process. The concentrating of bowers in certain areas, many being small structures, some being very large and variable, some constantly changing shape and some apparently suffering complete displacement, represents a biological problem which cries out for study.

Evolution: The bowers built by the Mt Hagen populations of *Amblyornis* appeared to me to be more ornate than those built by the semi-isolated but phenotypically indistinguishable Kubor Mountain birds. (The latter are isolated on the south side of the Wahgi Valley.) The bower differences may be correlated with the need for stronger isolating mechanisms on Mt Hagen because of the presence there (in the same forests at the same altitude) of two groups of forest-loving, bower-building birds (*Amblyornis* and *Archboldia*), whereas in the isolated Kubor Mountains only *Amblyornis* occurs. Isolating mechanisms involving character divergence of the bowers rather than of the birds themselves between competing bower bird genera is only a possibility. Between congeneric species (such as the two species of *Amblyornis* in south-eastern New Guinea) it seems irrefutable.

Striped Gardener Bower Bird

Amblyornis subalaris Sharpe
Male 9 in.
[1884, *Journ. Linn. Soc. London*, Zool., vol. 17, p. 408. Type locality Astrolabe Mountains, British New Guinea.]

Range: Known only from the south watershed of the mountains of south-eastern New Guinea between the elevations of 2200 and about 3600 feet. (See Map 10.5, page 310.)

Adult Male: An orange-crested, starling-sized, dark brown bird with lightly striped underparts. In more detail, entire upperparts, forehead, sides of head and neck dark olive brown to chocolate brown on forehead; inserted in central crown a tuft of long slender (shining and somewhat hair-like at tips) golden orange feathers with variable, usually sparse, dark brown tipping and lateral streaking, forming a broad erectile crest; the crest very variable both in size and colouration, ranging from 34 to 47 mm. in length and from deep orange to yellowish orange (and sometimes with so much dark brown feathering that the bright colours are concealed in the folded position); underparts generally olive to ochraceous brown, palest ·on central breast, and with pale centre streaks (for which the  species is named) on the throat to upper breast; under wing coverts and axillaries pale apricot; inner basal margins of wing quills buffy; shafts of flight quills yellowish ivory. Iris brown, bill blackish, feet slate tinged olive. Wing 123–129; tail 88; culmen from base 23; tarsus 37 mm.

Adult Female: Like adult male but lacking bright crest and paler, more olive, less chocolate brown above and below. Wing 121 mm.

Immature: First year dress much like adult female. Male inter-mediate plumages or stages of dress: (a) like adult female but head somewhat darker, more chocolate brown and with traces of orange at bases of several central crown plumes; (b) like adult male but with only a few slender orange crest plumes.

Remarks: The Striped Gardener Bower Bird has long been coveted as an article of personal adornment by the Koari natives inhabiting the southern foothills of the Owen Stanley Mountains. The colourful crest feathers of the male are spaced out and attached to a band to form a headdress (Simson, 1907: 383). It is quite possible that Andrew Goldie, who first discovered this species (a female) in the Astrolabe Mountains in 1884, had seen such a native headdress and recognised that the plumes came from a species unknown to science. Whatever the case, he missed finding the colourfully crested male and it remained for Karl Hunstein to discover it the same year in the Owen Stanley Mountains (probably in the foothills of Mt Maguli).

The Striped Gardener Bower Bird is a fairly common species in the Wharton and Owen Stanley Mountains in an altitudinal zone lying just below that of *A. macgregoriae*. This we know because on the Wharton Range behind Yule Island (near Iola and Deva Deva) Hannibal Hamlin collected seven adult males between 31 May and 15 June 1929, all at an altitude of about 2400 feet. On the other hand, Rand (*in* Mayr and Rand, 1937: 207) working higher in the same range (on Mt Tafa, between 31 May and 23 August 1934) never collected *A. subalaris*, but he observed between twenty and thirty bowers of *A. macgregoriae* (between about 6400 and 8900 feet) and collected a series of males and females.

Colin Simson, the first to call attention to the altitudinal zona-tion in these two very similar species, found pretty much the same situation in the Eafa and Moroka districts during the course of his round trip over the Owen Stanley Mountains in November and December of 1905 (1907: 380). He accompanied the veteran collector A. S. Anthony and his team of hunters, and obtained much valuable information. Anthony, an extraordinarily keen collector and the discoverer of many new species of bird of paradise, pointed out to Simson the differences in the bowers built by the two species: (a) *A. subalaris,* the bower-builder of the lower regions, has a stick tower in an ornamented garden built around a small sapling, topped with a tepee-like roof of sticks; and (b) *A. macgregoriae*, the bower-builder of the higher regions, has merely an unadorned stick tower built around a small sapling. Simson carried a primitive camera with which he managed to photograph both types of bowers. He described the ecology and bower of *A. subalaris* as follows:

Bower: 'I have seen six playgrounds . . . all of them were situated on the slope of a hill on ground well shaded by trees, and usually a little below the summit of a ridge. They were met with at an elevation, I think, of from 3000 to 6000 [probably not above 5000] feet. . . . Each playground consisted of a dome-shaped mass of twigs, about two feet in height and three in width. In this mass of twigs are two rounded openings communicating within and facing the yard in front. Situated between the two openings is an almost black flower-bed, composed of fibre taken from the stems of tree-ferns. Into this bed the bird sticks flowers [some bright yellow], berries [many scarlet, many bright blue], bright coloured leaves [many yellowish green], and beetles [mauve-coloured]. In front of this structure is a yard enclosed with twigs, and over this yard in every playground that I saw were strewn brilliant scarlet fruits, and sometimes a few flowers.' Regarding the distribution of these ornaments Simson wrote: 'In some of the playgrounds the contents of the garden were arranged in a definite order. In one there were yellow flowers on one side and blue berries on the other. It is very common to see a mass of scarlet fruits in a rotting condition lying a yard or two from the playground, where they have been thrown by the birds.'

Bower Behaviour: Simson, like later observers, found it very difficult to observe the birds in their bowers. Indeed he apparently failed to do so but, he wrote, 'After watching a playground without success, I have visited it the next morning and found fresh flowers placed in position.'

In 1889 Sir William Macgregor, the Administrator of 'British New Guinea' (accompanied by the collectors George Belford, Karl Kowald and A.P. Goodwin), ascended the Musgrave Mountains of south-eastern New Guinea. The party made comprehensive collections and many new observations of birds during its ascent of the summit (Mt Knudsford). A.P. Goodwin (1890: 150) described a bower, undoubtedly of *A. subalaris,* which he saw on Mt Belford: 'At a short distance off, the bower from the back looks like a cart-load of sticks rounded on the top. On going round to the front I saw the most beautiful building ever constructed by a bird . . . the edifice was dome-like, only half covered over, and exposed to view, inside a ring or circus. In the centre of this was built a bank of moss, decorated with flowers and seed, out of which grew a small tree interlaced with sticks.'

Except for the bower structures, nothing whatever is known of the courtship behaviour of this marvellous bower bird.

Nesting: Emil Weiske, in 1897 and 1898, ascended the Owen Stanley Mountains by way of the Brown River behind Port Moresby. He reached an altitude of at least 4000 feet and at that height found a number of bowers of *A. subalaris*, also a nest and an egg. He described the nest as cup-shaped and the egg as yellowish white; the egg measures 40·6 × 27·7 mm. (after Schönwetter).

Evolution: Apparently the two closely related and very similar appearing mountain species, *Amblyornis subalaris* and *A. macgregoriae*, displace each other altitudinally wherever they come into contact. This is doubtless because they have recently split from a parent stock and still retain similar ecological requirements. One of the species, *A. macgregoriae*, a wide-ranging bird (with a large gene pool), apparently has not suffered much altitudinal displacement or alteration of its bower form in the area of overlap; whereas the other species, *A. subalaris* (with a small and therefore less stable gene pool) has probably suffered considerable downward altitudinal displacement. It is the lowest-dwelling of the New Guinea *Amblyornis* species. This species appears also to have undergone pronounced changes in its pattern of bower courtship. Its bower is much more specialised and is very different from that of *A. macgregoriae*.

I suspect that complicated bowers, like complicated sexual plumage, develop through selection when there is a need for the sharpening of isolating mechanisms between closely related species. In the Owen Stanley Mountains of south-eastern New Guinea, where two phenotypically similar maypole bower-building birds front on each other over a broad altitudinal belt, there is need for such bower divergence if the two species are to be prevented from merging. But then what about the domed, highly specialised bower of presumably solitary *A. inornatus* of the Vogelkop? Can it be that this bird is not solitary after all? Might not the highly specialised bower form and decorations of *A. inornatus* be due to interactions (perhaps at the upper limits of its altitudinal range) with an

315

undiscovered species of *Amblyornis*? On the basis of its bower, I suspect that the 'lost' *A. flavifrons* may be responsible for the specialisation of bower form.

Yellow-fronted Gardener Bower Bird

Amblyornis flavifrons Rothschild
Male 9½ in.
[1895, *Novit. Zool.*, vol. 2, p. 480. (fig. *Novit. Zool.*, vol. 3, pl. 1, figs, 3 and 4; type in AMNH, no. 679120). Type locality 'Dutch New Guinea.']

Range: Unknown, but probably somewhere in the mountain forests of West New Guinea or the western Papuan islands.

Adult Male: A stocky, thrush-sized brown bird (see illustration on p. 300, lower left) with a golden forehead succeeded by an immense golden crest. In more detail, upperparts dark rufous brown; top of head from base of bill to nape golden yellow, the feathers very narrow and somewhat glossy (with ivory shafts), and very elongated on the crown forming a relatively immense crest; some feathering at rear of crest brownish; sides and under surfaces of head, neck, and sides of upper breast rusty brown; rest of under surfaces pale ochraceous to apricot; inner margins of wing quills pale buff; shafts of flight quills ivory. Iris colour unknown; bill (in dried skin) black; feet (in dried skin) dark brown. Wing 134; tail 83; culmen from base 23·5; tarsus 33 mm.

Adult Female: Unknown.

Remarks: The home grounds of this wonderful bower bird have never been discovered despite the persistent searches of trained collectors and naturalists. At least a dozen expeditions, led by such men as F. de Bruijn, Ernst Mayr, Fred Shaw Mayer, ex-King (then Crown Prince) Leopold of Belgium, S. Dillon Ripley, Sten Bergman, Max C. Thompson and Philip Temple, have looked in vain for it. One reason they have pressed their searches is that this bower bird is the last of the 'plume species' to defy discovery of its home grounds. Of all the many species of birds of paradise and bower birds which were first 'discovered' for science in the plume markets of London, Paris, Amsterdam, Singapore, and Ternate, this bird alone has defied detection. It thus poses a great challenge to the naturalist. Not only is it a beautiful, unknown species of one of the most interesting, scientifically intriguing families of birds known, but the biologist suspects that the conditions of isolation and ecology which caused it to split so widely from the parent stock must certainly have affected many other birds and mammals inhabiting the elusive ecological pocket in which it lives. Thus, they suspect, other unknown species may await discovery.

James Greenway in his excellent *Extinct and Vanishing Birds of the World* (1958) does not list this species, probably because he suspects that it remains unknown only because of the forbidding nature of its home grounds. However, in view of its history I think it should be listed. All told in the museums of the world there exist three (perhaps four) specimens. All were probably obtained by native collectors in the employ of the plume merchant Duivenbode. He was probably the son of C.W.R. van Renesse Duivenbode, the plume merchant who helped A.R. Wallace in 1858 to 1860 when Wallace used Ternate in the Moluccas as his base while exploring in the Moluccas and New Guinea. At least three of the specimens were sold to Lord Rothschild. This I learned from a letter in the American Museum of Natural History written by Lord Rothschild 25 November 1934, to Leonard C. Sanford which reads: 'As to your inquiry about *Amblyornis flavifrons*, [R.C.] Murphy's entry in the shipping list is quite correct; he only saw and handled the type and the one I retained. When I originally described this Bower Bird there certainly were 3 but since the war I have only had 2; what became of the 3rd one I do not remember, i.e. I have a hazy recollection I exchanged it with another museum. Old Duivenbode from whom I had these 3 birds assured me about 5 years after he sold the 3 to me that he had sold a fourth 2 or 3 years after the first 3, but there appears to be no record of this, perhaps it is in Leiden.' In September, 1964, I rediscovered the 'lost' third specimen of *A. flavifrons* in the British Museum skin collection marked 'Rothschild Bequest.' It was catalogued 1939: 12: 9–13. It is a fully adult male with a long golden yellow crest.

Hartert took up the question of the home grounds of this species (he also knew of the three specimens): 'There is a rumour that they may occur somewhere inland of the Berau Peninsula, but this requires confirmation. The three skins are rather of the better 'Arfak preparation,' with 'heels' sewn together and filled with 'kapok.'

Marshall in his well-known monograph on the bower birds (1954: 134) has renamed the Yellow-fronted Gardener Bower Bird, calling it the 'Gold-maned Gardener,' because, he writes, it '. . . is essentially brown-fronted in a manner not very different from *A. inornatus.*' He is wrong in this. Rothschild's name should not be changed. Rothschild (1895: 480) described the adult male in these words: 'Top of the head *from the base of the bill* [italics Rothschild's] and crest brilliant golden yellow.' And he added that his new species differs from all other species in that: 'The yellow of the top of the head reaches *to the nostrils* [italics Rothschild's], while in the other two species the entire forehead is brown like the back.' From the sound of all this careful description [and italicising] Rothschild was apparently trying to correct wrong information. I used an adult male skin (not the type) in making my original description of this species.

Golden Bower Bird

Prionodura newtoniana De Vis
Male 9–9½ in.
[1883, *Proc. Linn. Soc. New South Wales*, vol. 7, p. 562. Type locality mountain forests near head of Tully River, North Queensland.]

Range: Mountain forests of the Atherton-Cairns district, North Queensland (from the Atherton tablelands in the Herbert River region to Mt Cook in the Endeavour River region). Usually from about 3000 feet to the tops of the range at about 5400 feet; rarely down to 1500 feet. (See Map 10.5, page 310.)

Adult Male: A thrush-sized, golden olive bird with yellow underparts and yellow on the head, neck, and tail. In more detail, central crown (including a short, erectile crest) and hind neck shining golden yellow to deep orange yellow (individual variation); rest of upperparts, head, chin and sides of neck yellowish olive; wing quills dusky olive brown with pale olive outer vanes and buffy inner margins; underparts including axillaries and under wing coverts pale cadmium yellow to orange yellow; central pair of rectrices dark olive brown; three outermost pairs of rectrices uniform orange yellow; rest of rectrices tipped orange yellow and margined dark olive brown. Iris brown; bill brownish olive green; feet black.

Wing 120–123; tail 106–114; exposed culmen 16; tarsus 31 mm.

Adult female: Very different from male: upperparts dull olive; flight quills dusky brown with slightly brighter exposed edges; underparts including axillaries, inner edges of wing quills and under wing coverts ashy grey. Iris dull yellow; bill blackish; feet blackish. Wing 115–121; tail 85–88; exposed culmen 16; tarsus 32 mm.

Downy Young: Top of head covered with long dull brown natal down; upperparts dark brown with some long down tipping; underparts chiefly naked but sides of breast and much of abdomen greyish brown.

Juvenal: (Nestling) Top of head with long dull brown down with a slight vinaceous cast; feathers of mantle chiefly olive brown and very soft; throat naked; feathers of rest of underparts brownish grey and very soft.

Immature: First year plumage much like adult female. Male intermediate plumages: (a) like adult female but upperparts brighter, more yellowish olive, less dull olive; (b) like adult male but upperparts generally paler, much less heavily saturated with orange and underparts, particuarly breast and abdomen, faded greyish yellow.

Remarks: The Golden Bower Bird is still a fairly common species within the confines of its range – two small pockets of dense tropical rain forest crowning the highlands of the Atherton Tableland and Mt Cook. The first specimen discovered was a drab-coloured bird (a female or immature male) which the pioneer engineer-naturalist Kendall Broadbent collected in 1882 near the head of the Tully River and which the Australian ornithologist De Vis named as a new genus in 1883. Archibald Meston shot the first male in February, 1889 on Mt Bellenden Ker. His bird was so bright in colouration and appeared so different from the female that the same De Vis inadvertently renamed his own *Prionodura newtoniana* as yet another new genus.

Meston's discovery set off a wave of field parties. The same year (March to May) Broadbent visited the Bellenden Ker range near Cairns, obtained a series of adults, and found a number of bowers. He then joined Meston (June to August) and secured many more specimens. Also in the same year E.J.Cairn and Robert Grant

(April to September) visited the Atherton Tableland, obtained a series of golden bower birds, and studied many of their bowers. Following on their heels, in the 1890's (for 9 years), came a general collector, W. S. Day, who settled in the Bellenden Ker region. Day, who made his living from such material, took a shocking number of specimens. However, he also made observations which appear to be of considerable importance in understanding the complex behaviour of this strange species (see below). In 1908 the egg collector George Sharp, with a team of aboriginal helpers, did more or less the same shocking thing, obtaining no less than 30 sets of eggs of *Prionodura*; and the same year Sidney Jackson, collecting on the Atherton Tableland for the oölogist H. L. White, obtained some observations of bowers and purchased from Sharp the bulk of his collection. The details of these and other explorations in search of the Golden Bower Bird are carefully documented in Chisholm and Chaffer's valuable report of this species (1956: 1–38).

Ecology: Chaffer (*in* Chisholm and Chaffer, 1956: 28) gives a vivid first hand picture of the ecology of the mountain forest which this species inhabits on the Atherton Tableland. He wrote that the time was late October as the rains were ending – a season when the Golden Bower Bird was actively displaying on its bower: '. . . the jungle was now moist to wet. Heavy rain had fallen just prior to my arrival . . . on most days a heavy mist settled over the mountains towards evening . . . the jungle was dripping with moisture and was very muddy underfoot, and leeches were . . . numerous.'

Food: Fruits and berries, probably also some insects. Chaffer (*ibid.*: 33) noted males apparently catching insects among tree leaves and in a tree hollow. He also saw them eating fig-like berries.

Voice: At intervals the male, during his long, quiet waits in the trees over his bower, would give '. . . a pulsating buzzing call of no great volume, varied occasionally by clear notes often repeated.' (*ibid.*: 32). Warham (1962: 18) reported that the male chattered harshly but quietly on its bower and that it gave out hissing notes 'not unlike the "tihurring" scolds of some warblers and strongly suggestive of similar sounds emitted by *Chlamydera* bowerbirds. But more usually at the bower a variety of mechanical notes or "ratchettings" was used.' Warham also noted '. . . loud and harsh chatterings [were] often given as the bird watched us moving near the bower. These notes carried a long way through the forest and would often announce a male's approach when we were at the bower.' Warham noted too that although this species is reported to be a good mimic, he was unable to recognise any of the sounds made by it. Bourke and Austin (1947: 112) described its call notes as a wheezy croak preceded by a rattling noise.

The Breeding Territory: The harsh calls noted above suggest that males are able to interact with one another over considerable areas of forest. Day's observations suggest that under normal, undisturbed conditions each adult male probably maintains a private territory within a clan arena located in deep forest. For example, on Bartle Frere (see Chisholm and Chaffer, 1956: 13), in one favoured place, Day found no fewer than fifteen bowers, of varying sizes, within a radius of 100 yards; and he wrote that he shot, from time to time, no fewer than 30 birds at one of the bowers.

Chaffer (*ibid.*: 29) also found bowers grouped together on the Atherton tableland. But, very interestingly, he found the bowers of two other species of bower birds in the same area. He wrote: 'Altogether, seven occupied bowers [of *Prionodura*] were seen. Four of these were grouped along one jungle-clad hillside in a space of little more than half a mile. In the same area I located five [courts] of the Toothbill and one arbour of the Satin Bower-bird. . . .'

Bower: De Vis's description (*in* Mathews, 1925–1927, vol. 12: 362) of the bower, based on Broadbent's and Meston's field notes and sketches, remains one of the best: '. . . the bower is usually built on the ground, between two trees, or between a tree and a bush. It is constructed of small sticks and twigs. These are piled up almost horizontally round one of the trees in the form of a pyramid, which rises to a height varying from four feet to six feet. A similar pile of inferior height – about eighteen inches – is then built around the foot of the other tree. The intervening space is arched over with stems of climbing plants, the piles are decorated with white moss and the arch with similar moss, mingled with clusters of green fruit resembling wild grapes. . . . Scattered immediately around is a number of dwarf, hut-like structures – gunyaks they are called by Broadbent, who says he found five of them in a space of ten feet diameter, and observes that they give the spot exactly the appearance of a miniature black's camp.' Various observers have confirmed the above description and noted that the structures appear to have no symmetry. A bower area measured by Sidney Jackson (1909) measured 14 × 6 feet with a tower that rose to a height of four feet, but bowers reaching more than eight feet high are not uncommon. Marshall (1954 : 137) wrote '. . . most of the twin pyramids are roughly elongated oval at the base, but some of the bigger ones become nearly rounded. During the sexual season the inner wall of the larger pyramid and other parts of the bower fabric in the vicinity of the display stick are decorated with pale moss, lichens, ferns, flowers and odd bunches of berries.' From Chaffer we learn for the first time that the structure of sticks is 'glued'. On the summit of Mt Haig Chaffer, noting an 'especially firm' bower, discovered '. . . that many of the sticks were glued firmly together, and many were glued to supporting trees. Isolated sticks, otherwise un-supported were found fastened in this manner to a tree trunk above the bower.' He added that '. . . close examination indicated that an inconspicuous fungus growth was responsible.'

The arch, walk, connecting bridge, hedge step, ridge pole, or display stick, as it has been variously called, Chaffer wrote, is not installed by the bird. Rather, the Golden Bower Bird must find appropriately placed saplings that are connected by a vine or stick and thus can be made to serve as a bridge 'across the runway.' Chisholm's descriptions (*in* Chisholm and Chaffer, 1956: 18) of such a bower also on Mt Haig (4000 feet), is as follows: 'Contrary to what reports had indicated . . . it was not ragged, nor was one wall higher than the other. Each wall, built with a multitude of sticks was 3 feet 6 inches high and 2 feet wide, and the runway, elevated 10 inches by a kind of bridge, was 17 inches wide. The total width of the bower, from outer wall to outer wall was 4 feet 10 inches. A most imposing structure, and one that probably had been used for several years (so massed were the sticks), it was made more impressive by the addition of grey-green lichens strewn in the runway and four fresh olive-green flowers (not orchids) attached to an inside wall.'

Bowers are generally built on sloping hillsides. Chaffer (*ibid.*: 25) observed one that had the main tower five feet tall connected to a display perch eighteen inches above the ground. This perch was decorated with grey green lichens at each end, and above the lichens on the main tower wall '. . . numerous dried flowers, cream in colour with shiny black seeds attached.'

Chaffer (*ibid.*: 30) found the bowers very variable in size and layout. Of seven occupied bowers, two had paired walls nearly

322

equal in height, two had one wall large and the other very small, one was almost entirely constructed in the branches of a sapling a foot or more above the ground; but Chaffer found that each of the bowers had a more or less horizontal display perch and bower ornaments of two kinds, grey green lichens and melacope flowers. The largest bower reached 7 feet 6 inches above ground and had the main display perch five feet up. This bower appeared to have been in use for a number of years. One of the smaller bowers was $3\frac{1}{2}$ feet tall with the main display perch only eight inches above ground. One of Chaffer's Golden Bower Bird bowers was 30 yards and one was only 5 yards distant from courts of the Toothbill Bower Bird.

Bower Activities: Chaffer (*ibid.*: 32) observed that the male bower owner spent the greater part of the day in the trees over the bower, often sitting quietly for long periods, often preening, giving a pulsating, buzzing call at intervals varied with clear notes. If Chaffer altered the bower decorations the male would become agitated and sometimes he would go immediately to the bower to replace things in their rightful positions. When visiting the bower the male 'almost invariably brought a Melacope flower or piece of lichen. . . .' Chaffer's observations of the male performing a curious hovering display near the bower is unique. He wrote of a male which had been perching in a stooped position on a vine: 'Quite suddenly he leapt from this perch and flew rapidly towards a tree-trunk, where, with bill pointed directly towards the tree and a few inches therefrom, he performed a spectacular hovering. During this manoeuvre the body is held in a vertical position and the tail is repeatedly opened and closed. . . . Flying toward the bower, the hovering was repeated a foot or so above the high wall.' Later Chaffer saw the male hover low down over bushes, hover over a palm, suddenly alight on a tree branch, press its body against it, raise its crest and jerk its head from side to side, then dash to another tree and repeat the performance. At times the bird clung to steep bark surfaces or even to the underside of a sloping branch, its wings fluttering, its head jerking. But never during eight days of vigil did Chaffer see anything to suggest that a female was in the vicinity during these displays! Sometimes the hovering display imme-diately preceded a clash between males with the bower owner driving off the other bird in a violent chase. And once when the bower owner was absent Chaffer saw two strange males visit the bower, one of which alighted on the display perch and one of which stole lichens. Warham (1962: 19) also once observed two strange males in the bower vicinity. Various observers have seen birds in female dress visit the bower. All such visits were very brief and were carried out quietly while the male bower-owner was absent. I suspect that all such visitors were young males. In this connection Bourke and Austin (*in* Marshall, 1954: 24) several times observed birds in female dress that owned and decorated small bowers. Apparently no observer has yet witnessed the male and female simultaneously at the bower and therefore the key displays of this species remain unknown.

Nesting: The nest (width 6–7 in., depth 3–4 in.) is a fairly deep, strong cup (width 3½ in.; depth 2¼ in.) on a platform of large leaves, twigs, and bark, lined with fine twigs and thin rootlets. It is usually placed in a tree, a cleft or a tree fork about three feet (occasionally 10 feet) above ground in the substage of tall mountain rain forest. The eggs, usually two in number and compressed oval in shape, are pale cream colour to white (measurements: 36–37 × 25–26 mm.). Mathews (1925–1927, vol. 12: 361) wrote: 'The small sticks on the outside portion of the nest are often fastened or glued together, and to the structure, by means of a dead and dried-up growth of slimy fungus.' A unique photograph of the nest and female *in situ* has recently been published by Chisholm (1963 : 251).

Analysis of Behaviour: This appears to be a polygynous species with each adult male maintaining a private court and bower within an arena of considerable size in which a clan of males lives apart from the females and young males. It seems likely that the 15 bowers found by Day in a radius of 100 yards constituted a clan arena.

Evolution: Chaffer's recent discovery that the bower sticks are 'glued' (see above) may be correlated with Mathews' observation (see above) that the nest sticks are also 'glued' together. This similarity of construction between the bower, which is built by the male alone, and the nest, which is built by the female alone, reinforces the hypothesis that bower structure originates from non-discardable nesting tendencies in the emancipated males (see p. 57).

Mayr and Jennings (1952: 4) call attention to the curious fact that although there is no geographical variation in the populations of this very restricted species, there is much individual variation with respect to the shades of yellow in adult males. It is possible that this variation is correlated with the pronounced individual variation often found in arena birds, for example in a close relative, the Striped Gardener Bower Bird (*Amblyornis subalaris*) and the Ruff (*Philomachus pugnax*).

Golden Regent Bower Bird

Sericulus aureus (Linnaeus)
Male 10 in.

Range: West and south New Guinea, east in the north to the upper Mamberamo River, and east in the south to the delta and to the upper Fly River. Found from sea level to 4500 feet. (See Map 10.6, page 329.)

Adult Male: A starling-sized, scarlet orange bird with yellow underparts and much black in the wings, tail, and (one race) the lower half of head. In more detail, head and mantle orange scarlet to

scarlet orange with a silky sheen, the feathers of the upper mantle very long (up to 65 mm.), decomposed, forming a broad erectile cape; rest of upperparts chrome yellow; wings chrome yellow except bend of wing, alula, and outer halves of primaries mostly brownish black; secondaries (except innermost) narrowly tipped black; sides of head (encircling eye) and throat to upper breast black (one subspecies: sides of head scarlet and throat to upper breast yellow); rest of underparts yellow; tail blackish narrowly tipped yellow. Iris greenish yellow to yellow; bill blackish to horn colour (in  nostril area); feet greenish grey to dull slate colour. Wing 135–141; tail 66–84; culmen from base 23; tarsus 45 mm.

Adult Female: Very different from male above, but very similar below. Head and mantle mouse brown tinged grey and olive grey on back, with the elongated feathering of upper back and scapulars white-shafted and with pale, semi-concealed, narrow striping; sides of head and throat pale brown tinged ochraceous; throat with traces of barring; upper breast yellow to pale yellow with some narrow brown concentric bars and margins; rest of underparts yellow to orange yellow; wings generally brown with the inner edges of flight quills and linings yellow to orange yellow. Iris brown; bill brown to black; feet dull slate colour. Wing 137–140; tail 89; culmen from base 24; tarsus 42 mm.

Immature: First year plumage probably much like adult female. Male intermediate plumages or stages of dress: (a) like adult female but semi-concealed striping of upper back and scapulars distinctly wider, less whitish, more yellowish; (b) like adult female but darker below and with a few orange red plumes in the mantle; (c) like adult female but semi-concealed mantle striping as in (a), upperparts darker, more rufous, less greyish; forehead tinged red; some patches of black appearing variously on forecrown, lores, around eyes, and ear coverts; (d) like adult male but with the lower back to upper tail coverts and the wings washed with olive as in the adult female.

Probably three or more years are required for the male to assume the fully adult plumage.

Remarks: The Golden Regent Bower Bird, the first bower bird described (Edwards, 1750; Linnaeus, 1758) remains one of the least known. Because of its bright colouration it was long thought to be a bird of paradise, a possibility which has only recently been virtually discarded. One reason for this uncertainty is that the species had never been seen in its bower and, indeed, its bower had never been found for a certainty. Yet this bower bird is locally not uncommon in the hill and mid-mountain forests of the Vogelkop (whence many scientific and trade plume specimens have come); in forests of the north slopes of the Snow Mountains near Mt Wilhelmina (where the Archbold Expedition found it between 2700 and 3900 feet); in the Wataikwa River region of south-west New Guinea (where in 1910 a British Expedition got seven specimens in sixteen days); and in the Fly River region, where it has been found from near the sea coast (at Tarara) to a point more than 500 miles upstream on the Black River.

Although both Lesson in 1824 and Wallace in 1858 obtained

native-made skins of the Golden Regent Bower Bird during their historic trips to New Guinea, Odoardo Beccari in 1872 was the first to observe and collect this bird in the wild. Beccari's observations are still among the best available (Iredale, 1950: 179).

'It was procured by me near Hatam, on the same fig-tree on which D'Albertis obtained the greater number of his birds. It has more or less the habits of a Bird of Paradise, feeding on fruits and particularly on figs. Not more than two or three individuals are found together, generally only a male and a female. It is a very lively and suspicious bird and after I had killed a male bird, a female, accompanied by another bird (probably a young one), came back after a while to feed on the same tree. Although this bird is found up to an altitude of 3,000 feet or more, it seems to be more abundant on the hills near the sea.' Beccari noted that in the Arfak Mountains the native name is *Komicha*.

The elongated plumes of the hind neck and upper back, as Ogilvie-Grant (1915: 32) puts it are '. . . no doubt capable of being erected to form a conspicuous [gleaming orange scarlet] ruff around the head. . . .' A similar ruff is present in the adult female. The pale striping of the feathers of this ruff is very similar to that of the similar 'ruff' found in the female of *Sericulus bakeri*.

Bower: For a long while it has been pretty well accepted that this species at least on occasion builds a walled bower but the evidence has been circumstantial and rather doubtful. As long ago as 1872 Beccari, who shot it at 3000 feet in the Arfak Mountains, was told by his natives that the Golden Regent Bower Bird 'nested' on the ground (see Marshall, 1954:121). And in August, 1928, Shaw Mayer was shown a bower situated at an altitude of about 4000 feet in the Arfak Mountains which his guides claimed belonged to *Sericulus aureus*. Shaw Mayer, in a letter to Iredale (1950: 178), described this bower as follows: 'It resembled the bower of the Australian Regent Bower Bird but [was] a little larger. The walls were straight and there were no decorations. It was built under a stand of high bamboos. As we were at about 4,000 feet it was unlikely that it belonged to the *Chlamydera* found at lower levels.'

Iredale (*loc. cit.*), in commenting on Shaw Mayer's discovery of this walled bower, observed that no avenue-building bower birds were known from lower elevations in the Arfak region [and according to the literature it seems that none were known from anywhere in

Y

the Vogelkop region]; however, Shaw Mayer, in 1928, seems to have been aware (probably from native talk) that another species did in fact live in the lowlands. That species, *Chlamydera cerviniventris*, was finally collected recently in the Kebar Valley.

Another inconclusive record is that of Ernst Mayr who in 1928 on the Vogelkop was shown a bower with walls which he was told belonged to the Golden Regent Bower Bird, but again the bird was not seen at the bower.

In August, 1964, in the Tamrau Mountains of the Vogelkop at an altitude of 3500–4000 feet, by great good fortune I discovered and photographed (see pl. VII) this species in its bower. No display was seen.

The bower measured seven inches along the avenue and extended upward about ten inches from the ground to the top of the highest sticks in the avenue walls. It was situated on the top of a moderately sloping rounded ridge with steep sides, on the north-west face of the highest summit in an area of at least 30 square miles. This area was densely forested without any grassland. The bower was under tall trees in a moderately open canopied area of the forest, and the display tree of *Paradisaea minor* was almost directly over the bower.

On both sides of the avenue entrance there was a cleared area of forest floor, with the area on the east side much smaller than that on the west. Inside the avenue were five oval blue berries, ranging in size from a large tree huckleberry to a cherry, and a black shelf mushroom about one inch in diameter. A day later I noticed that two of the five blue berries had disappeared and that the shelf mushroom had been shifted. I also noticed a snail shell which I am sure was a recent addition.

The nest and eggs of this species remain unknown.

Subspecies: Two very distinct races are known. A measure of their difference is to be had from Ogilvie–Grant's comment (1915: 32) that 'There seems to be no possible reason for regarding this very distinct bird [*Sericulus ardens*] as a subspecies of [*S.*] *aureus*.'

1   *S. a. aureus* (Linnaeus), 1758, *Syst. Nat.*, ed. 10, p. 108. Type locality 'Asia,' error for Vogelkop (restricted type locality). Known from north-western New Guinea (Vogelkop, Wandammen Peninsula), Onin Peninsula (Fakfak), head of Geelvink Bay (Gebroeders Mountains), and the upper Mamberamo River (Idenburg River).

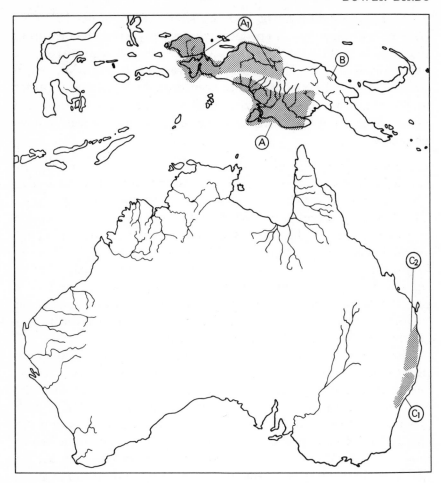

Map 10.6 *Sericulus*

Sericulus aureus (A) sea level to 4500 feet
   Sericulus aureus aureus (A1)
   Sericulus aureus ardens (A2)
Sericulus bakeri (B) 3000 to 4000 feet
Sericulus chrysocephalus (C) lowlands and coastal rain forest
   Sericulus chrysocephalus chrysocephalus (C1)
   Sericulus chrysocephalus rothschildi (C2)

Sides of head (enclosing eye) and throat to upper breast black. Male wing 135–143; tail 81–84; culmen from base 23; tarsus 45 mm. Female wing 137–140; tail 89 mm.

329

2 *S. a. ardens* (D'Albertis and Salvadori), 1879, *Ann. Mus. Civ. Genova*, vol. 14, p. 113. Type locality upper Fly River. Known from southern New Guinea from the Wataikwa River eastward to the upper Fly River and the Wassikussa River [a skin from Mt Hagen (Iredale, 1950: 181) had probably been brought by natives from far to the south-west]. Like *aureus* but with the sides of the head orange scarlet, not black, and with the throat to upper breast yellow, not black.

Evolution: In bower birds that are known to build bowers the female is always protectively coloured (except for the two Australian 'chlamyderas' in which the females may have the lilac nape spot). The Golden Regent Bower Bird is the only consistent exception to this pattern. In this species the adult female is bright orange yellow below (but protectively coloured above) and, in addition to bright colours, it has an erectile ruff which, when elevated, reveals a radial collar of pale white striping. The morphology of the female plus the seeming rarity of the bower leads me to suspect that bower building in this species is of a relict nature (as postulated for its near relative the Australian Regent Bower Bird).

The bower, if it functions as an isolating mechanism, must keep pace with shifting needs; and a mechanism which was effective yesterday might become ineffective today (for example with the enrichment of the avifauna), or its effectiveness might change with geography. Readjustments of the mechanism must accompany changes in selective pressures. In *Sericulus aureus* the readjustment may be in the direction of less specialised courtship such as, for example, the secondary adoption of simple ground courts in place of the bower.

Taxonomy: Bock (1963) has recently found cranial characters which distinguish bower birds from birds of paradise and therefore there is no longer much doubt that the Golden Regent Bower Bird is a true bower bird and not an aberrant bird of paradise.

Adelbert Regent Bower Bird

Sericulus bakeri (Chapin)
Male 10½ in.
[1929, *Amer. Mus. Novit.*, no. 367, p. 1 (type in AMNH, no. 268253). Type locality 'Madang, Astrolabe Bay' = Adelbert Moun-

tains, about 3000 feet, above Maratambu Village.]

Range: Known only from the Adelbert Mountains, 25–35 miles north-west of Madang; from 3000 to at least 4000 feet. (See Map 10.6, page 329.)

Adult Male: A scarlet-crowned, starling-sized, black bird with a massive orange cape and orange wing markings. In more detail, generally black with a faint sheen on throat to upper breast; top of head scarlet (with semi-concealed black feather centres), changing to orange tinged red on nape and hind neck; the red and orange surfaces with a silky texture; the hind neck plumes long (up to 47 mm.), decomposed, forming a broad erectile cape over mantle; flight quills black, the remiges with broad basal portions cadmium yellow (forming a large speculum). Iris pale yellow; bill dark grey with a whitish base; feet blackish; skin behind eye black. Wing 137–140; tail 77–86; culmen from base 23; tarsus 42 mm.

Adult Female: Very different from adult male. Upperparts including head, wing, and tail dark brown sparsely tipped grey on upper back and shoulders, and with a narrow erectile neck ruff, each feather striped whitish (but the white striping is virtually concealed in the folded position); sides of head and neck pale brownish tinged ochraceous; throat whitish with traces of narrow barring; rest of underparts pale buffy grey concentrically barred brown, except on central abdomen. Iris dark brown; bill dark brown; feet brownish to lead grey; gape and mouth orange yellow. Wing 132–142; tail 88–89; culmen from base 24; tarsus 44 mm.

Immature: First year plumage probably much like adult female. Male intermediate plumages or stages of dress: (a) like adult female but sides of lower head and throat less buffy, more ochraceous; (b) like adult male but rump and upper tail coverts with scattered olive brown feathering, also with sides of upper breast, abdomen and under tail coverts largely buffy with some dark barring, especially on sides.

Remarks: The place of origin of this beautiful bower bird was long a scientific enigma. According to the data on the labels of the original specimens, it had been discovered in the very outskirts of a former centre of the paradise plume industry – a gathering spot for professional birdskin collectors. The enigma was best stated by Erwin

Stresemann (1954: 263–91) who commented: 'To the great aston-ishment of the specialists, Rollo H. Beck, an American Museum of Natural History bird collector, totally inexperienced in Papuan ornithology, brought back from his 1928 trip to the Mandated Territory a handsome new bower bird. He had shot three specimens near the coastal town of Madang. As Kaiser Wilhelmshaven, Madang had been for many years the capital of the German Govern-ment of Kaiser Wilhelm Land'. Stresemann then concluded: 'Since then [*Sericulus*] *bakeri* has never been seen again.' Rollo Beck, who died in 1950, was often asked about his find, but was unable to add anything further to the geographical information that he had written on the labels.

In 1956, I set out to solve this mystery. Carrying life-size colour paintings (see pl. 25) of the species, I conducted a methodical search of the 'Madang region,' a large area fronting on Astrolabe Bay. My main searches were (a) in the Bogadjim area (where the town of Madang had been located until tropical fevers forced the government to move it westwards across the bay to its present location); (b) in the foothills of the Finisterre Mountains; (c) in the foothills south of Madang and (d) west of Madang 20 to 40 miles to the foothills of the Adelbert Mountains. During these searches I met with an old native who said he had been a 'shoot-boy' for Mr and Mrs Beck in 1928 in the Adelbert Mountains, but he did not recall the bower bird even when I showed him the paintings. Later in New York, to my great surprise, I learned from Mayr that Mrs Beck had indeed accompanied her husband to New Guinea. What was more, I learned that she still lived in California. I im-mediately wrote to her of my quest and told her of my meeting with her shoot boy 'Winini.' To my surprise Mrs Beck then divulged to me that her husband had shot the rare bower bird in the Adelbert Mountains quite a distance west of Madang.

Thus in 1959 when I went with my wife Margaret to the Adelbert Mountains, we were successful in rediscovering this wonderful bower bird. In all, we collected eleven scientific specimens including the unknown female which is here described for the first time.

Regarding the mystery, I presume that Rollo Beck planned to return to the isolated Adelbert Mountains to make a comprehensive survey of the fauna. He knew that someone would beat him at this if he divulged that the strange new bower bird was restricted to this small 'mountain island.'

The Adelbert Regent is an uncommon resident of forests growing above 3000 feet on the isolated Adelbert Range. I saw it in
the original forests, in tall trees at the forest edge, and flying over
small native garden clearings cut in the forests. It keeps to the middle
and upper limbs of the forest. I never saw it below about thirty-five
feet and my chief recollections of the species are of birds in female
dress perched on thin limbs forty to sixty feet up and of two males
which I saw about a half mile apart on very high perches in the
Memenga forest area (a mountain top above the village of Maratambu).

I camped in the Memenga forests from 16 March to 3 April 1959,
searching constantly for the Adelbert Regent Bower Bird – particularly for its bower – and observing birds in general, especially
birds of paradise. Living side by side with *Sericulus bakeri* I found
Ailuroedus buccoides, Ptiloris magnificus, Diphyllodes magnificus, and
Paradisaea minor.

Voice: Very like the sharp jet and rasping notes of Lauterbach's
Bower Bird. A female in hand uttered a powerful, harsh whistle
with a burr sounding like air blown over a rapidly fluttered
tongue. A male heard in the distance delivered a ratchety *kowwuun,*
somewhat like the voice of *Ailuroedus buccoides* but louder.

Food: Stomach contents (of an adult male): eighteen black ants
averaging about 9 mm. long, also some small hard-shelled insects.
Other specimens had eaten yellow figs.

Bower: Apparently none. I need hardly say that once I finally
found the home forests of the elusive Adelbert Regent, I made
every effort to find its bower. In company with my Sepik hunters,
for weeks I searched in vain. I offered large rewards and consulted
with no fewer than seventy-five local mountain woodsmen. Many
would tell me about *Otidiphaps nobilis* and its terrestrial nest, or give
me details of other ground-nesting birds. Almost all knew the bowers
and many had watched the terrestrial displays of the Magnificent
Bird of Paradise (*Diphyllodes magnificus*). Quite a few even knew of
the walled bowers built in the lowlands by *Chlamydera cerviniventris,* but none of the men had any knowledge of the Adelbert
Regent Bower Bird building a bower or, for that matter, of it even
visiting the ground. Thus when it came time for me to leave the
Adelbert Mountains I was firmly convinced that this bower bird

does not build a bower! However it may be that a bower is occasionally built, as is probably the case in *S. aureus* and *S. chrysocephalus*.

Some excerpts from my field journal are as follows:

19 March 1959; 3300 feet; Memenga Forest. At 7.30 a.m. Rambur [my keenest Sepik hunter and veteran of three of my earlier New Guinea and New Britain expeditions] sighted a male and a female (?) (*Sericulus bakeri*) in tall trees bordering the edge of my camp clearing. They were in the top branches, probably some seventy feet up, but Rambur [who had shot an adult male earlier in the week that was so high he failed to observe its bright colouration] this time could see the red-orange colouration on the head and back of one bird. Rambur raced to get me and within minutes we sprinted back to find the bird had gone. However, Rambur heard the male calling and pointed, and soon I spied it in the top of a very tall tree projecting above the rest of the forest at the lower edge of the little forest garden we stood in. It was some fifty yards off. It sat with its back toward us and its head turned to one side. It rivaled a bird of paradise in the magnificence of its train-like, gleaming red and orange plumage. The red of the crown flowed backward changing to golden orange on the back. As it perched its wings seemed to have an excessively large amount of yellow-gold in them. The tree was about eighty feet tall and sharply pointed with open branches. The male sat on an exposed branch some twelve feet from the top. The branch sloped gently upwards and was about one inch thick. From here *Sericulus* commanded a vast view of the forests below to the north; of the valley of rugged hills to the east, beyond which lies Nobonob Mission, Meganum Village; and Astrolabe Bay, the latter with the Finisterre Mountains fringing its far shores.

At 5.30 p.m. the same day, while hunting in a ridge forest between two small forest gardens located a quarter of a mile apart, Rambur and I observed a different male and a (?) female. One or both had been calling so that Rambur and I were able to go right to them. I watched the bird in female plumage for just a moment. It was about sixty feet up on a limb near the top of a tree overlooking the surrounding forest. Next I saw the male at least seventy feet above ground and appearing black. It sat in the leafy branches just under a dead tree top, with many dead perches on it, that rose above the rest of the forest. This male perched about thirty feet from where the (?) female had perched when first sighted. I watched the male for many minutes as it perched quietly in the fading light.

On 3 April Father Bernard Johnson, who had taken to bird watching while generously helping the expedition, returned from Wama Village (3800 feet, Adelbert Mountains) about eight air miles north of Maratambu Village. He reported that three miles east of Wama he had been shown a tree containing several Adelbert Regent Bower Birds. The tree was about fifty feet tall and on a forested ridge. So sharp was the ridge that Father Johnson had stood hardly twenty feet below a male (which he recognised from having studied scientific study skins several days earlier). He observed this male for about two minutes. It perched near the trunk on a dead limb in the top of the tree. It moved its head so that the red was clearly visible. The rest of the time it perched quietly. Other birds were in the tree lower down. A native with Father Johnson told him they were females of the same species which, near Wama, is called Orrau. Father Johnson, the leading authority on the Adelbert Mountains and a young man of long years and wide travels in these desolate surroundings, did all he could to assist me in finding the bower of *Sericulus*. He questioned many mountain natives but he found no trace of any bower-building birds in the Adelbert Mountains. When I last consulted him (16 September 1963) he still had not found a trace of the bower.

Nesting: Nothing is known.

Evolution: The Australian Regent Bower Bird of south-eastern Australia, the Golden Regent Bower Bird of southern and western New Guinea, and the Adelbert Regent Bower Bird of the Adelbert Mountains of north-eastern New Guinea appear to represent peripheral components of a superspecies. I can find nothing in the behaviour of these stocks that casts any doubt on Mayr's 'sinking' of *Xanthomelus* in *Sericulus*. On the contrary, the 'mysterious' near absence to absence of the bower structure in the three species seems to be a group characteristic.

Australian Regent Bower Bird

Sericulus chrysocephalus (Lewin)
Male 9½–10 in.

Range: Eastern Australia from New South Wales (Gosford) north to southern Queensland (Blackall Range and Bunya Mountains) in the lowland and coastal rain forests. (See Map 10.6, page 329.)

Adult Male: A golden yellow and black thrush-sized bird. In more detail, forehead, crown, nape to upper back golden yellow often strongly washed carmine (subspecies), the forehead and crown with the feathers very short and plush-like; rest of upperparts and tail black with a subtle bluish to purple glossiness; outer two primaries and coverts black; rest of primaries (except usually innermost two pairs) largely golden yellow with broad to narrow black tipping; lores, sides of lower head (including a narrow line over eye), neck and entire underparts black, somewhat glossy. Iris light yellow; bill yellow; feet black. Wing 124–132; tail 82–91 (subspecies); culmen 28–32; tarsus 37 mm.

Adult Female: Very different from adult male. Entire head, throat and hind neck dull brownish to greyish white with small irregular dusky markings; crown dull sooty black; mantle dull olive brown, the feathers of the back often with wide whitish concentric markings, small brown centre spots, and sooty margins; lower back to upper tail coverts olive brown with some pale markings; tail brown with pale outer margins; wings olive brown with paler exposed edges and with the innermost secondaries often narrowly tipped grey; under wing coverts whitish narrowly edged and barred brown; wing quills below dull yellowish grey with paler inner edges; underparts generally dull buffy whitish indistinctly margined and barred with brown especially on upper breast; lower throat with a black central spot. Iris dusky; bill black; feet grey. Wing 134–136; tail 100–103; culmen 30; tarsus 37 mm.

Juvenal: Nestling about to leave nest: like adult female but pale areas generally much lighter, more nearly white and with a softer texture; below the light areas more extensive; throat nearly naked and lacking a dark spot. Wing 113; tail 60 mm.

Immature: First year plumage like adult female. Male intermediate plumages: (a) like adult female but crown spot blacker and with a trace of glossiness; dark margining of back darker and more extensive; throat spot more extensive; hind neck with a few small yellow feathers; (b) like adult male but sides of head and neck retaining a few grey and brown feathers; lower back to upper tail coverts olive brown with spots as in adult female, not jet black; under wing coverts, axillaries and lower breast to under tail coverts as in female, not jet black.

Mayr and Jennings (1952: 6) note that the sequence of plumages is not yet understood, partially because of the lack of accurately sexed specimens, particularly adult females, the great individual variability of the plumages and the fact that some of the sub-adult male plumages are 'progressive', that is, they contain feathers that are partially yellow and partially black. During the course of their studies they discovered that while adult females and immature birds of both sexes have approximately the same measurements of wing and tail, adult males have both the wing and the tail much shorter than the immature (*op. cit.*: 7).

Remarks: The Regent Bird, Australia's most brilliantly coloured bower bird, has been mistaken for an oriole, a honeyeater, and a bird of paradise. It is a shy but not uncommon species of lowland rain forest areas away from cities, but occasionally it ventures into the open lowlands to feed in orchards, gardens, and even suburban houses. An example is the observation in St Lucia near Brisbane (Meggitt and Waddle, 1963: 30) of a male which in June, 1962 '. . . came unannounced into our sitting room . . . and made himself quite at home . . .' flying from chair to chair and helping himself to crumbs from the table. Another example occurred in October, 1947, when a wild male was attracted to an aviary in Taronga Park, Sydney, containing regent bower birds (Hindwood and McGill, 1958: 99). Although not given to extensive wanderings, in the non-breeding season it gathers in flocks composed of ten to twenty birds in the female dress accompanied by one or two brightly coloured adult males (Marshall, 1945b: 117).

For decades the Australian Regent Bower Bird was a popular

cage bird and many were shipped to aviaries overseas. Some built bowers and even bred in captivity.

Regarding the vernacular name, Marshall (1954b: 110) wrote: 'In 1826 the name Regent-bird appeared in a list of Australian animals [Scottowe Esq.] and the bird has been so called ever since.' Scottowe wrote that he named the species in honour of His Royal Highness the Prince Regent.

Food: The Australian Regent Bower Bird, a fruit-eating species, is reported to be rather destructive to cultivated fruit crops. It is especially partial to black, juicy berries of the ink weed, an introduced plant (Campbell, 1901: 211). Chaffer (1932: 8) observed a female 'hawking' on the wing for moths which it then fed to its nestling young. Later this female fed its nestlings on wild raspberries.

The Bower: The rarity of modern observations of the bower of this species is a mystery. Why, in a country with so many top-notch ornithologists and bird photographers, have so few bowers been found? And why have photographs of the bird in the bower not been made? This is peculiar because the Regent lives relatively close to the great city of Brisbane. Because the Australian Regent Bower Bird, a fairly common species, throughout its range lives side by side with the much more common Satin Bower Bird (in which the young male often builds a small variably shaped bower) a possible solution that springs to mind is that the Australian Regent, like the New Guinea Regent, may seldom, if ever, build a bower. And the few bowers that have been attributed to it are perhaps in reality bowers built by young satin bower birds. Concerning this question, Marshall says (1954b: 112) there is in Australia '. . . a widespread supposition that the Regent rarely builds a bower, but this belief is probably without foundation.' In order to satisfy myself on this point I studied the evidence with much care. Some of it is as follows. It leads me to believe that the Australian Regent Bower Bird is discarding its habit of bower building.

The Bower Structure: Ramsay (1876: 456) in the sixties discovered and described a bower which was ' . . . placed upon and supported by a platform of sticks, which, crossing each other in various directions, form a solid foundation upon which the upright twigs are stuck. This platform is about fourteen inches long by ten broad, the upright twigs are some ten to twelve inches high, and the

338

entrance four inches wide. The middle measures four inches across and is filled with land shells of five or six species and several kinds of berries of various colours, blue, red and black, which gave it, when fresh, a very pretty appearance. Besides there were several newly picked leaves and young shoots of a pinkish tint . . . '

A. J. Campbell (accompanied by W. T. Bailey) found a bower in the Richmond River district in November, 1891. He wrote that in a luxuriant forest abounding with regent birds, one evening '. . . we discovered a bower on the ground, underneath thick scrub, and a male bird gaily tripping through. It was perfect, but not so large as those usually built by other bower-building birds being only seven or eight inches high, with walls seven inches broad at the base, and an average width inside of three and a half inches. After much difficulty a photograph was taken of the interesting structure.' Campbell's son subsequently found a similar bower at the same locality but he failed to see the brightly coloured adult male. He wrote (in Campbell, 1901: 210): 'When first seen there were three birds playing in this bower; two were what we took to be males – but they were immature – and the other was a female.'

A fairly recent but very brief observation of the adult male in the bower is that of K. F. Plomley (1935: 199). In August, 1935, near Myall Lakes he made the following observations: 'When the bower was found two fully plumaged males were seen, and four days previously a female or immature male had been observed where the bower was later discovered. One of the males was heard while it was in the bower, but, owing to the obscuring palm leaves, its actions could not be noted.'

Apparently the only definitive modern observations of the male in the bower are those of the able naturalist, M. T. Goddard (1947: 73–74), who discovered and observed an adult male in its bower near Dorrigo on 24 October 1946, and again the next day. Observing the male from a distance of eight feet, Goddard saw it in the central avenue building and painting (see below) and noted that the avenue was decorated with small black berries such as are not used by the Satin Bower Bird. He wrote: ' . . . whilst I was traversing dense brush, my attention was arrested by a *peculiar low chattering*, which was entirely new to my "vocabulary" of bird voices. Investigation revealed a beautiful male Regent Bowerbird . . . in fully adult plumage, attending to his bower. He permitted open observation from a distance of eight feet. . . . The bower was well concealed in a thick growth of fern and lawyer vines and was considerably less than half the size of that constructed by the Satin Bowerbird. . . . It consisted of two parallel, triangular-shaped walls of fine sticks and twigs, placed $3\frac{1}{2}$ inches apart. One wall was 6 inches in height, whilst the opposing one was but half that size. There was no arching effect of the walls and the platform of sticks and twigs upon which adornments are deposited (as seen in bowers of the Satin species) was lacking. The avenue created by the two walls faced east to west. The adornments consisted of twelve black, glossy berries, about twice the size of a pea, together with a single broken shell of a land snail. These were deposited in the avenue between the bower walls.

'I observed the brilliant male for quite some time, during which he moved through the avenue of the bower and toyed with the adornments. Occasionally, he would pick up a twig and place it in one of the walls or re-arrange some of the others. Whilst at the bower, he uttered a characteristic low chattering, which reminded me strongly of that emitted by the acclimatised Starling (*Sturnus vulgaris*) whilst "reminiscing". Later, he flew off into the surrounding brush.'

Bower Painting: 'A careful examination of the walls of the bower revealed a dry, yellowish substance, which adhered to the sticks and twigs and which looked like dried "paint."

'Next morning at nine o'clock the male was again in attendance at the bower. As I approached, a female flew off, but the male was just as trustful as previously. I particularly noticed that he pecked at the sticks of the larger wall, or, rather, that he wiped the extremity of his bill all over the sticks with a pecking action. I could clearly distinguish a small piece of greenish material held between the mandibles towards the extremity of the bill. Later, he picked up a fresh supply of the material from the floor of the avenue and continued operations as previously. Next he turned his attentions to the less robust wall and applied a little of the material. A little later he flew off, apparently to procure a fresh supply of material for further painting.

'Close scrutiny of the walls disclosed that the upper ends of the sticks and twigs were coated with a wet mixture of saliva and a macerated, pea-green vegetable material.'

It is clear from the above five observations in the wild that the Australian Regent Bower Bird, on occasion at least, does build a walled bower. The following observations of captive birds prove that it also builds a walled bower in captivity.

The bower and associated behaviour in captive birds: In 1905, R. Phillipps, a London aviculturist, made a series of remarkable observations of the bower-building activities of immature male regent bower birds. Phillipps identified all birds resembling the adult female as females. This makes his observations difficult to interpret because adult females were also present in his cages. Phillipps' descriptions fit so well with observations that I have made in the wild (in *Chlamydera cerviniventris*) that I make no apology for revising in brackets his text to make it meaningful:

'*These love-parlours, each one built by a female* [immature male] *for her* [his] *sole use* (Phillipps' italics) . . . and each most jealously guarded by its fair owner, were of the shape of a horseshoe but with the sides equidistant throughout their entire length, open only at one end, and inside of about the same length and breadth as the bird, the top of the barricade being about on a level with the back of the squatting female, the sticks woven together, being laid flat, none upright. The female would enter and squat in her [in the immature male's] love-parlour, the tail remaining towards the entrance, whilst a male with every imaginable and unimaginable contortion, accompanied by a continuous discharge of (vocal) fire-arms, would make rushes and furious (feigned) assaults on the front of the breastwork [of the bower], the female sitting in a lump and not moving a muscle.'

Phillipps noted that a second female apparently replaced the first one when it went off to nest. He also observed that ' . . . the rejected females [immature males in adult female dress] . . . built or partly built three love-parlours in different spots.'

Nesting: Nest a fragile saucer-shaped structure (10–12 inches wide × 3–4 inches deep), of sticks, twigs, plant stems with a nest cavity (4–5 inches wide × 1½–2 inches deep) lined with finer twigs and wire-like stems; in dense vegetation, 12 to 40 feet up.

Eggs: Two, sometimes three, broad oval and rather glossy, pale buff to grey, delicately streaked, scrawled, and marbled with brown to black lines and hair-like markings, chiefly about the centre. Measurements 34·3–40 × 22·8–27·9 mm. (after Schönwetter, 1944).

Breeding Season: Early November to January. Gilbert (1910: 44) observed a solitary female constructing the nest. She brought nest material at three-minute intervals.

341

Subspecies: Two rather similar races are recognised:

1 *S. c. chrysocephalus* (Lewin), 1808, *Birds New Holland*, pl. 6, p. 10. Type locality New South Wales. Known from Gosford (near Broken Bay), southern New South Wales, north to southern Queensland (MacPherson Range). Male with light areas of head, neck, and upper back golden yellow, lightly tinged reddish. Wing adult male southern New South Wales 127–129 (128·1); northern New South Wales 126·5–135 (130) (after Mayr and Jennings, 1952:7).

2 *S. c. rothschildi* Mathews, 1912, *Novit. Zool.*, vol. 18, p. 441 [type in AMNH, no. 679359]. Type locality Blackall Range, south Queensland. Known from the Blackall Range and the Bunya Mountains of south Queensland. Male like *chrysocephalus* but light areas of head and neck much more heavily tinged with red. Wing adult males Queensland 125, 126·5, 128, 130 mm. (after Mayr and Jennings, 1952: 7).

Evolution: Phillipps' most significant observation, I believe, is the following, because it offers a possible solution to the mystery of the rarity of the bower, namely that the bower structure is not always necessary to successful courtship. Phillipps wrote (in Marshall, 1954b: 115) '. . . the selected female, *with* or *without* [italics mine] her protective barricade [the bower] squatted lumpily on the ground, on the proposed nesting-site [bower site], and in the nest [bower] itself, while . . . the male sported about her.' In short, Phillipps appears to have observed an adult male courting an adult female which assumed the soliciting position on an unadorned ground court. If this happens in the wild to a part of the population, then I would suspect that bower building is tending towards obsolescence in this species.

An opposite view is expressed by Iredale (1950: 177) who wrote ' . . . it is now concluded that this bird only builds bowers occasionally, and some are quite primitive, as if it were only learning the art, and that it might be a possibly recent habit.' I reject this as a possibility because I believe that a pattern of behaviour as complex as bower-building must have evolved by small steps over a long period of time.

Why the Australian Regent Bower Bird might be discarding bower-building behaviour is an intriguing question. The answer, I think, is linked to the fact that it lives side by side with a close kin, the wide-ranging, abundant Satin Bower Bird (which is also an avenue-builder). The two species, which often flock and feed together, seem to have similar ecological requirements. If they are in competition, sooner or later one will displace the other, or selective forces will reshape the species so that they can regain private niches (Gause's rule). I strongly suspect that this is happening in the Australian Regent Bower Bird (in which the gene pool is relatively small and thus the least resistant to selection pressure) and that part of the reshaping effect is the discarding of the bower.

In this connection a basic factor for consideration is that species of bower birds which build similar types of bowers (i.e. avenues, maypoles, mats) are almost never found living side by side. The only exceptions are the Regent and the Satin avenue builders; but as shown above, in one of these the bower form is probably in process of rapid change. Thus, it seems to me that interspecific competition for unique bower isolating mechanisms lies at the heart of the mystery of the disappearing bower in *Sericulus chrysocephalus*.

Analysis of Behaviour: From Phillipps' observations it is probable that this species is an arena type polygynous bird which may construct a simple bower (especially when young) or may display on a simple ground court. Phillipps' analysis of the plumage and pattern of display in the adult male is very popular, but it compares well with that of other arena birds. He wrote: ' . . . the ordinary bowers are used . . . by the males . . . for the purpose of showing off before one or several females perched close by and above them. Viewed from below, only dense black is exposed to the sight, so [the males] perch high while desiring to conceal themselves. Viewed from above, rich orange and brilliant yellow meet the eye, and so, when the male wants to display before his female, down to the ground he goes and there disports himself. . . . As they go through their extraordinary dances and performances, they constantly look back over their shoulders, backwards and upwards . . . and all the time be it remembered they are clattering and chattering . . . in low subdued tones.'

It is well known in birds of paradise that in the species in which the male descends to the ground to perform its courtship displays, the tail is considerably shorter in the adult male than in the adult females or in the immatures (see *Parotia*). This morphological phenomenon seems to be correlated with the need for a short tail in terrestrial courtship dancing. Therefore it is interesting to learn

z

from Mayr and Jennings (1952:7) that perhaps the same thing happens in *Sericulus chrysocephalus*. They discovered that while the adult female and immatures have approximately the same measurements (of wing and tail), the adult male has both the wing and tail much shorter. And they postulate that the alteration in the shape of the wing [and I would add, the tail] is *presumably correlated with the courtship performance of the adult male.*

Taxonomy: If the bower is in fact disappearing in this species, the deductions of Mayr and Jennings regarding the closeness of the relationship between *Sericulus* and '*Xanthomelus*' will be reinforced. This is because both species of the Regent Bower Bird in New Guinea are apparently also discarding the bower (see pp. 330, 334).

Despite the pronounced differences in morphology between the Regent and the Satin bower birds, the similarity of their bower forms, as Marshall has pointed out, is irrefutable evidence of their close kinship. For further confirmation, we need only look to bower behaviour, nest shape, egg shape and markings, to conclude that Marshall is undoubtedly correct.

Hybridisation: No proven hybrids are known in the Ptilonorhynchidae but there is a good chance that a bird collected and described in 1867 near Brisbane was a hybrid between *Ptilonorhynchus violaceus* and *Sericulus chrysocephalus*. Unfortunately this specimen (named *Ptilonorhynchus rawnsleyi*) is lost. S. Diggles described it as being like *Ptilonorhynchus* but with greenish-blue eyes, olive-black beak and feet, and with a brilliant splash of gold on each wing. Diggles himself suggested that it might be a hybrid between the Satin and the Regent bower birds.

Aviculture: Apparently Reginald Phillipps (1905: 88) and Hirst (1944) are the only ones who have bred this species in captivity. Phillipps' female built a nest and reared one brood in a suspended basket containing straw. The incubation period was about 18 or 19 days. The female, Phillipps reported, disliked mealworms as food for the young but accepted cockroaches, biscuit-sop, and small amounts of egg-flake.

Satin Bower Bird

Ptilonorhynchus violaceus (Vieillot)
Male 11–12½ in.

344

Range: Eastern Australia from northern Queensland (Cairns District) south to the Otway Peninsula, Victoria. From near sea level to about 3500 feet. (See Map 10.7, page 352.)

Adult Male: Generally black with a strong gloss of violet purple (but often appearing lilac blue in sunlight); the plumage of the forehead completely hiding the nostrils (note generic name); flight

quills dull black with some glossy margins and tips. Iris lilac blue to dark blue (becoming rose red in display); bill dull blue with greenish yellow tips; feet dull greenish yellow. Wing 153–176 (subspecies); tail 94–114; exposed culmen 20–23; tarsus 49–53 mm.

Adult Female: Very different from male. Upperparts generally ashy grey green faintly tinged palest blue; wing quills generally dark brown with paler outer edges; inner five secondaries with whitish or buff tips (sometimes framed narrowly with black); inner edges of wing quills with much pale yellow; tail brown; ear coverts dark with greyish to pale buff shaft streaks; underparts grey washed lightly with yellowish buff and palest green, particularly on upper breast; each feather with a pale centre followed by black barring or concentric linations; flight quills below grey brown with pale yellow inner margins; tail rich brown above and greenish brown below. Iris violet; bill dark horn; feet grey. Wing 147–167; tail 98–115; exposed culmen 21–23; tarsus 46–50 mm.

345

Downy Young: Iris brown.

Immatures: First year plumage much like adult female but tail feathers more pointed, wings more brownish and upper wing coverts with rufous edges. Male intermediate plumage or stages of dress: (a) like adult female but ear coverts darker, more dusky brown, less greyish; and lower neck all around and upper breast darker due to decreased pale spotting and increased greyish green 'collar' surfaces; (b) male beginning to change to black stage, like (a) but with some glossy blue black feathers at base of bill, around eye, on crown and in ear coverts [Marshall (1954b:29) writes that sometimes only a few, or even one dark feather appears and then there may be no further change until the next seasonal moult]; (c) male completing change to black stage: like adult male but with some primaries and secondaries, alula, some feathers of back, and lower abdomen as in female.

Males reared in captivity require from about four to seven years to acquire the fully adult blue dress (Marshall, *loc. cit.*).

Remarks: Skins of the Satin Bower Bird – by far the best-known species of the family – reached France by 1816 and John Gould in 1839 was the first to study it in the wild. Marshall (1954b) devotes a major proportion of his fascinating monograph to the Satin Bower Bird, and Norman Chaffer (1959) published a valuable report (with photographs) of his observations during a period of twenty years.

Other naturalists as well have made significant contributions to our knowledge of this species, for example, E. Nubing, P. A. Gilbert, and Ellis McNamara, all of whom studied the Satin Bower Bird for long periods of time.

In the following species write-up I have drawn chiefly on Marshall's and Chaffer's studies.

Ecology and Abundance: The Satin Bower Bird is moderately common to common over most of its 1800-mile-long range. It thrives in damp rain forests and forest edge situations, also tall woodlands with an understory of small trees, from about sea level to about 3500 feet, and is one of the features of the national park areas. It occasionally frequents more open lands and it even occurs in such varied situations as suburban gardens near Sydney and in the deep rain forests crowning the Atherton Tableland near Cairns. It is believed that formerly the species ranged much more widely, and that its forest range has been reduced and split by the advance of xerophilous vegetation. Today, a 600-mile gap exists between the area occupied by the Satin Bower Bird in the north and that which it occupies in the central and southern parts of eastern Australia.

Food: Chiefly fruits and berries. In the non-breeding season the Satin Bower Bird may gather in good-sized nomadic flocks – some numbering as many as 100 – some travelling a hundred or more miles 'right over the Great Dividing Range' (Marshall, 1954b: 30) and occasionally causing considerable damage to fruit growers, but such flocks chiefly seek native forest fruits. Animal food (termites, beetles, moths, and cicadas) is also eaten and the young are fed a large proportion of such foods.

Voice: A flock of feeding birds emits a continuous series of croaking, explosive sounds, also whirring rattles. In display the male emits harsh chattering cries, buzzing notes, creaking notes, ringing cries, and it also engages in a fair amount of vocal mimicry, imitating cat cries, postmen's whistles, and the calls of birds.

The Breeding Territory: Apparently certain large areas of the forest are traditionally used for mating. One such area which Marshall described as an 'abnormally restricted area of about half a mile (1954b: 45)' contains the well-decorated private bowers of four fully adult (blue) males, the two closest of which were only 70 yards apart. That these males interacted is shown by Marshall's evidence of bower robbing and wrecking and the transfer of objects (fragments of marked blue glass) from bower to bower. In other areas Marshall found that the area of interaction between bower-maintaining blue males was larger. For example, he found marked glass 'tracers' were not transferred between bowers located more that 1000 yards apart.

That the display territory or arena is often quite densely packed with private territories (bowers, sub-bowers, simple courts) is suggested by Marshall's 1940 experiment (*op. cit.*: 46) in which 100 marked fragments of blue glass were distributed at night in 18 courts and sub-bowers located along Carrington Drive in the Royal National Park near Sydney. 'Before noon the following day,' Marshall wrote, '76 per cent of the fragments had appeared on the display-grounds of neighbouring blue males.'

347

The Bower: The typical bower of a blue male is a firmly inter-locked mat of twigs and sticks (up to 9 inches long) laid horizontally. It averages two inches in thickness and has two parallel walls of sticks extending upward about 12 inches. These usually arch nearly or completely over the avenue, which is about four to five inches wide. This structure is placed in a clearing three to four feet long and 20 to 30 inches wide. The sub-bowers are usually smaller with fewer twigs and are very variable in shape, with low, thin walls. Sometimes they are mere stick platforms or just clear spaces on the ground. Such bowers are the courts of 'green' males.

Bower Decorations: The bower of a blue male with a full comple-ment of decorations is very colourful. A typical one may contain fifty or so flowers, blue parrot feathers, many blue, violet, and purple flowers and berries, a wide assortment of bluish man–made objects such as glass and paper, and also quite often many small greenish yellow flowers and fruits and assorted straw coloured objects. Included occasionally are aluminium foil, greyish fungi, snakeskins, and often many brownish land snail shells.

Blue (the colour of the adult male) is the preferred colour, yellow green (the colour of the subadult male and adult female) is next in preference. So strong is the Satin Bower Bird's liking for blue that in captivity it has been known to kill small blue birds, apparently to obtain ornaments for its bower (Marshall, *op. cit.*: 61).

Bower Painting: Bower painting was discovered in the Satin Bower Bird in 1930 by G. R. Gannon (1930: 39) who also noted that a 'blue' male seemed to employ a tool – a wad of bark – to apply the paint (which is composed of charcoal dust and saliva). Marshall (1954) considers this remarkable habit to be an extension of and possibly a substitution for the courtship feeding phenomenon that is so widespread in birds. He described the painting process as follows: 'Some – but apparently not all – males collect fragments of fibrous bark, manipulate them with the beak and so manufacture a small oval pellet. . . . This is not a brush. It seems to be a kind of combination sponge, wedge, and stopper which is held almost wholly within the beak. . . . The pellet keeps the beak slightly open as the bird jabs at, and paints, the individual twigs with the sides of its beak. . . . The plaster [jet-black and 2 or 3 mm. thick] soon dries to a gritty charcoal powder that will rub off on a finger. . . .' Marshall added that the paint or plaster is replaced daily during the height of the sexual season and the wads of bark, often still saturated with charcoal and saliva, are often to be found on the avenue floor between the two painted walls where the ornaments are never placed and where fallen leaves are always quickly removed.

Bower Orientation: The Satin Bower Bird (along with the Great Grey Bower Bird) orients its bower across the path of the sun. Marshall took bearings on 66 bowers (1954b: 40) and found that the deviation from 360° was never more than 30°. He shifted a bower in the field from 350° to 50° and found that its owner promptly demolished it and then rebuilt it in its former position (*op. cit.* 42). Laboratory birds did the same, sometimes completing a reorientation job from an east-west direction to a north-south direction in 48 hours! Marshall concluded that the '. . . utility of north-south orientation may be that very early each morning, when energetic display begins, the male can keep the motionless female in view without staring into the rising sun. Likewise, she can watch his flashing display without discomfort.'

Bower Behaviour: (Male alone): Between the months of May through September each bower is carefully maintained by its owner, who usually arrives at dawn, to the accompaniment of 'crackling' sounds. He drops to the ground at the 'rear' of the bower (Warham, 1962: 4), then quietly hops inside to peck at the structure of sticks and also to clear away fallen leaves and shift display objects from place to place in a seemingly haphazard fashion. The male remains in and near the bower much of the day, driving off other blue males and protecting the bower as from time to time the other males attempt to sneak in and wreck the structure and steal the ornaments. Apparently only during brief raids to other bowers or while off on brief food-hunting expeditions, does the male leave the vicinity of his bower.

Bower Courtship and Mating: The adult male apparently displays actively only in the presence of a female. Many observations of a male displaying to a female have been made, but until 1954 (28 September) when Ellis McNamara observed it in the bower, no one had observed copulation and the exact function of the bower had remained obscure. Since then Chaffer has also observed (and photographed) mating in the bower (4 and 28 November). (See analysis of behaviour for a hypothetical reason for the rarity of these observations.)

Some of Chaffer's key observations of satin bower birds at the upper causeway bower near the picnic area in the Royal National Park are as follows (1959: 300):

4 November 1955: 'At 4.45 p.m. the male started "churring" and displaying, and presently the female came to the bower. In contrast to the timidity shown on previous visits, she did not, on this occasion, take any notice of the hide or the camera. She played about for a while in front of the bower and then entered it from the back. The male displayed energetically, and with constant vocal efforts which included many strange churring and scolding notes not at all pleasant to the human ear. The calls often mounted in intensity until they finished with a curious sound like a series of gears running together. He sometimes posed, with very little movement, for minutes with his tail elevated, bill pointed to the ground, and body held high on stiff legs. Occasionally the straw-coloured weed-like material was held in his bill while posturing in the above manner, and once a snail shell was used. These actions were varied by stiff prancing with half-galloping, half-hopping movements. Several times he leapt back and forth across the bower entrance in front of the watching female. During this manoeuvre his wings were outflung in a dazzling flash of colour. Various flash photographs were taken of this display and both birds ignored the flash. For most of the time the female stood quietly in the bower in a rather crouched attitude. Occasionally she would rearrange some of the sticks in the bower wall or perform painting actions. Two or three times she backed out of the bower and, picking up a twig, re-entered and placed it in position in the wall. The male was showing signs of great excitement; his eyes bulged, revealing a lilac edging to the blue of the iris, and at times he rushed right around the bower. Suddenly he dashed up, and quickly mounting the female, copulation occurred. A flash photograph was taken during the brief duration of the act. After the male left her the female stood erect in the bower and rapidly fluttered her wings. He continued to display, although at a reduced tempo, and the female remained quietly in the bower for some time. She then moved to the centre of the bower, where she was seen to be breathing rather heavily. She crouched crosswise in it as though sitting in a nest, and, as the bower walls were spaced only some four inches apart, conditions were rather cramped. Shortly afterwards the male appeared to be attacking her, and he drove her out of the bower several times.

After being driven out she would quickly run around and re-enter the bower. I was fortunate in securing a rather dramatic flash photograph where the male is seen striking the female with his claws as she cowers away from him.

'The display of the male gradually waned, and he sometimes left the bower for short periods. Eventually the female hopped on to a log behind the bower and she was seen to be still breathing heavily, and appeared somewhat distressed. Suddenly to my great surprise she laid an egg, which dropped two feet to the ground. Shortly afterwards she departed, having been at or around the bower for forty-five minutes. I secured the egg, which luckily received only a small fracture in its fall. The egg was quite normal and of a buff ground colour, spotted and blotched with dark brown and slate-grey.' The laying of an egg by the female under such circumstances is surely an abnormal occurrence. But the description of the male's activity merits the inclusion of this data.

According to Australian observers the male continues to attend to his bower for many weeks after his mate leaves him to build the nest and rear the young alone. Polygyny has never been observed and Marshall and Chaffer believe that a strong pair bond develops between a single male and female; and Marshall postulates (1954b: 31) that the pair bonds are begun when the mixed wintering parties break up in spring. He writes 'It is not yet known whether the Satin-birds, like Gannets, Rooks, Ravens, and many other species, pair for life.' He then noted that four 'ringed' blue males were proved to build bowers on the same ridges from 1938 to 1945 but that the females were harder to catch and mark. However, Marshall wrote '. . . in two instances it was proved that the same pair of birds occupied bower-territories in successive years.'

Nesting: Nest: an open, shallow saucer-shaped structure of twigs, lined with leaves (eucalyptus and acacia are often used), placed 5 to 15 feet up; often in a forest tree (or sometimes in a tree standing alone just outside the forest). Eggs: one to three, usually two, dark cream to soiled yellow brown, spotted with cinnamon brown and with underlying purplish grey spots (Hartert, 1910: 484). Measurements (from Schönwetter, 1944): *P. v. violaceus* 42·3–47·0 × 28·7–30·2 mm.; *P. v. minor* 40·5 × 27·5 mm.

Bourke and Austin (1947: 111) in northern Queensland found two nests built within 50 yards of each other. Chaffer (1959: 302)

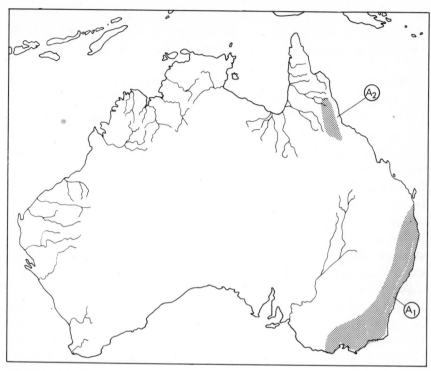

Map 10.7 *Ptilonorhynchus*
Ptilonorhynchus violaceus (A) sea level to 3500 feet
   Ptilonorhynchus violaceus violaceus (A1)
   Ptilonorhynchus violaceus minor (A2)

found a female building her nest in mid-October in the Atherton Tableland forest at an elevation of 3500 feet.

Subspecies: Two size-differentiated races are known:

1 *P. v. violaceus* (Vieillot), 1816, *Nouv. Dist. Hist. Nat.*, nouv. ed., vol. 6, p. 569. Type locality 'Nouvelle Hollande' [= Sydney, New South Wales]. [*dulciae* is a synonym.] Known from southern Queensland south to the forests of the Otway Peninsula, Victoria. New South Wales: male wing 163–174 mm. Southern Queensland: male wing 164–176 mm. Female, breast greyish; white spots of underparts fairly large.

2 *P. v. minor* Campbell, 1912, *Emu*, vol. 12, p. 19. Type locality Herberton, Queensland. Known only from the Cairns District,

northern Queensland. Like *violaceus* but smaller and female differently coloured: male wing 153, 157, 158 mm. Female, breast washed grey green; light spots of underparts smaller.

Analysis of Behaviour: The Satin Bower Bird is probably a polygynous species with the female probably remaining with the males for some few days before departing to shoulder the nesting duties. Marshall suspected this when he wrote (1954b: 69) 'Although each blue male has only one female in attendance at the principal bower once the sexual season is well under way, it is possible that his frequent visits to the sub-bowers and run-ways result, by virtue of his plumage and domineering temperament, in the fertilization of a second or even more females there.' And he noted that each time he removed a blue male from its bower '. . . it and the female were taken over not by a neighbouring bower-building blue bird, but by a male green bird which appeared to be unmated, territorially unattached and therefore free to do so.'

Finally, Marshall comes very close to my conclusions that arena behaviour is the pattern employed by the Satin Bower Bird. He wrote (*loc. cit.*): 'Today we know that sexual selection, as propounded by Darwin, is a rare phenomenon. However, in some gregarious, polygamous species (e.g. European Ruff, Blackcock) it undeniably exists. Darwin hypothesized a struggle between males for mates and the probability of female choice between rivals which, by virtue of their colours, plumes, ruffs, crests, or other special structures of display and/or combat, would succeed in joining their gametes with those of discriminating females. This indeed may occur in the Satin Bower-bird.' But later Marshall seems to have discarded this possibility.

Nowhere does he mention the dichotomy between pairing and non-pairing behaviour, which I consider to be the fundamental factor in the origin and evolution of bower-building. And in his concluding chapter on the evolution of bower-building Marshall states (1954b: 165) that the display habits of the bower birds '. . . are in fact no more than the extraordinary elaboration of the territorial display impulses that are found in other quite common-place birds. Avian display – visual, auditory, or a combination of both – is usually associated with conflict and the establishment of territorial domination (including often the spacing out of the population), the formation of the pair-bond, and the development and

353

synchronization of the sexual processes of the pair until the environment becomes seasonally appropriate for the female to build the nest and to rear her brood. . . . It is the same with the bower-birds in so far as they are known.'

In my opinion, in the rare non-pairing arena birds (such as bower birds, many birds of paradise, many grouse, manakins, the Cock-of-the-Rock, etc.), the territory operates as a sexual mechanism which assists certain males in winning a plurality of mates (sexual selection) amongst a competing clan of emancipated males. It has nothing to do with food, spacing, or nesting. In 'pairing birds' (99 per cent of all birds) territory serves as a mechanism of survival which operates to protect the species in terms of food distribution and space (natural selection).

Spotted Bower Bird

Chlamydera maculata (Gould)
Male 11–11½ in.

Range: Eastern Australia (from mid-Queensland south to New South Wales and Victoria) and south Australia (in the Murray Valley region), also mid-Australia to western Australia. (See Map 10.8, page 361.)

Adult Male: A thrush-sized, blackish brown to buff bird, spotted rufous to buff above, with a vivid lilac pink nuchal patch. In more

354

detail, top half of head to nape buff to rufous, the feathers short with dark margins; hind neck area with a vivid erectile tuft of iridescent lilac pink plumes followed by a dark brown band; rest of upperparts dusky brown to blackish (subspecies) with prominent, buffy, ochre, or rufous spotting; the spotting is vivid on the mantle and upper tail coverts, also on the upper wing coverts, scapulars and secondaries; tail dusky brown with bold buffy to white tips; lower half of head, throat, sides of neck to upper breast ochraceous to buff with some dusky barring especially on upper breast (but throat blackish with ochre or rusty oval spots in one subspecies); flanks buffy to rust-coloured; rest of underparts greyish to buff with subobsolete dusky barring except on central abdomen; under wing coverts buff irregularly tinged ochraceous, with some dusky markings; inner margins of wing quills yellowish white. Iris brown; bill black; feet brown. Wing 146–156; tail 106–115; culmen from base 30; tarsus 42 mm.

Adult Female: Like adult male but often with the lilac pink patch reduced or lacking. Wing 144–149; tail 99–105 mm.

Immature: Plumages incompletely known but apparently first year plumage like adult female except feathering of the upper and lower back paler more greyish to whitish and much softer and loose-textured with narrow mouse brown edges; surprisingly the lilac pink neck plumes may be present but are few in number; lower breast and abdomen paler, more fluffy and more contrasted with narrow dusky fringes.

Remarks: It is not known who first discovered this rather shy, fascinating species, but the Australian literature is replete with fabulous tales about its habits and particularly about its prowess as a camp robber, even a highway robber, for it has stolen everything, it seems, from car keys to a farmer's glass eye. Never having studied this species in the wild, I shall have to lean heavily on Marshall's comprehensive report (1954b: 72–88), also upon Warham's recent field observations (1962: 6–10) and his superb photographic studies (see pl. 28).

The Spotted Bower Bird, an 'avenue-bower' builder and one of the three species which 'paint', is generally uncommon and sparsely distributed although in some areas it is common. Its optimum habitat is in poorly watered inland areas with a thinly dispersed

355

cover of bushy vegetation and spaced-out trees. A favourite spot is in grazing lands, thickets of the prickly bush *Carissa ovata* (beneath which it often builds its bower) and staggered clumps of tall, open trees. But the Spotted Bower Bird also visits orchards and plantings about farmhouses where it may display or even build its bower close to houses.

Voice: A wide variety of sounds, mostly vocal, but some mechanical, have been attributed to this bird. There is even a report of a tinkling sound made by picking up and dropping bower ornaments. Vocal mimicry has been developed to such a degree, Marshall wrote, that the Spotted Bower Bird '. . . is probably the most gifted mocking-bird known.' However, he writes '. . . its original calls are perhaps limited to a ringing, somewhat metallic advertising call, some cat-like cries, and a variety of harsh or hissing notes used in display.' It supplements these with an astounding assortment of mimicked whistles (many perfect imitations of other birds), barks, rachetings, squeaking and chopping notes – a repertoire which apparently includes 'playbacks' of just about any sound the Spotted Bower Bird has ever heard. However, in displaying to a female in the bower (rather than in advertising for one to visit him) the male uses scolding, hissing, sputtering notes, often emitted directly at the female with the crest wide open, or rhythmical mechanical noises.

Food: Chiefly fruits and berries, especially the berries of the white cedar, *Melia azedarock* (Marshall, 1954b: 73) and a fig, *Ficus platypoda*, which thrives in 'periodically waterless' areas. Also, the Spotted Bower Bird feeds on grasshoppers, moths, and caterpillars.

The Bower: The bower is of the avenue type, with two parallel partitions of sticks and grasses set vertically in a foundation mat of horizontal, criss-crossed sticks. The partitions or walls rise 10 to 20 in. above the mat and the avenue is 6 to 9 in. wide and 15 to 30 in. long. The walls facing the avenue are lined with finer material and grass stems. The bower, which occupies a space some six feet long, is usually located in a secluded, shaded place. A favourite location is beneath a thicket of prickly bushes with limbs descending almost to the ground. Bowers are placed near streams, cisterns, or near human habitation, usually near water.

There is no evidence that this species orients the bower across the path of the sun (or in any other direction) as do some of the other avenue builders but like the Satin and the Australian Regent Bower Bird, it 'paints' the inner surfaces of the avenue.

The above description fits the average bower but there are many variations of structure, both in size and choice of building material. One measured seven feet long, another was built entirely of grass, and still another was a collection of sticks without walls.

The Bower Decorations: Often a bushel or more of ornaments are used. By order of abundance these are bones, chiefly bleached white sheep and rabbit bones (sometimes in numbers of more than a thousand); stream-worn pebbles and stones (grey to white); land snail shells (white); seed pods; green berries; pine cones; black stones; and glass (green to amber to white). This species favours white, grey, pale green, amber and mauve, but apparently rejects red, yellow, and blue (Marshall, 1954b: 77). The paint mixed and applied by the Spotted Bower Bird is reddish brown.

Norman Chaffer (1945: 162) observed and photographed a Spotted Bower Bird as it painted the inner walls of its avenue. After preparing a mixture of grass and saliva in its mouth, it worked its bill up and down the grass stems lining the avenue, thus smearing them with the pigmented solution which dribbled out of its bill, but sometimes it 'painted' the grass stems by sliding them between the partially opened mandibles.

Behaviour at the Bower: Mr and Mrs Warham (1962: 7), who watched a bower for some 25 hours, found that bower-building and maintenance is usually done in the morning or after periods of display. Display, they noted, apparently never occurred under solitary conditions. Once five adult spotted bower birds were seen near one bower. Other observers have noted as many as four, five, and seven spotted bower birds near occupied bowers, but the usual observation is of one male displaying to one female, sometimes with a second bird perching passively nearby. A significant variation of this pattern, which, I believe, reveals that this species is not a pair-bond bird but an arena bird, is the observation of Jerrard (*in* Marshall, 1954b: 80) who observed two apparent females that visited, one after the other, the bower of one excited male, who displayed strongly to each in turn.

The mode, sound effects, and intensity of display in this species are very similar to my observations of the Fawn-breasted Bower Bird in New Guinea, even to the extent of becoming so highly excited that he stumbles and falls head over heels! However there is a difference, for chief among the display paraphernalia of the Spotted Bower Bird, as Marshall wrote (1954b: 80), is '. . . the fan-like erection of the coloured nuchal mantle, which gleams silver-lilac as the bird moves in the sunlight.' On the Fawn-breasted Bower Bird there is no trace of crest in either sex, yet I saw again and again the 'crest display motions' described by Warham (1962: 8) for the Spotted Bower Bird. Warham observed that bower activity begins shortly after dawn when the male usually arrives. He announces his approach while still in the bushes and trees nearby with a series of hissing and sputtering notes, then quietly, he descends and unobstrusively enters his bower, usually from the back and begins examining the structure, changing and adding sticks, ornaments, shafts of grass. Warham noted that grass stems are held crosswise in the beak and 'inserted deftly with a downward pushing motion.' I filmed Lauterbach's Bower Bird as it installed the grass stems always with the head perpendicular to the walls and bent so that the throat was parallel to the walls. In this position, monocular vision apparently permitted the exact placement (aiming) of the foundation end of the grass stems, all of which were arranged with extraordinary precision to form the level surface of the vertical partition of grass and sticks.

Warham divided the displays given in the presence of the female into two types: (a) central displays given by the bower owner while standing among the collection of ornaments near the stick walls; and (b) peripheral displays given by the bower owner as it ran in wide circles around the bower, often going outside the bower area for short periods of time. 'Throughout both', Warham wrote, 'the male's crest was more or less expanded and raised.'

Warham's (1962: 8–10) description of key attitudes of central display are given in full below with the kind permission of the author:

Postures during central displays

i.   Upright posture: Standing upright, with feathers rather sleeked, the male looks towards the female and hisses and scolds loudly.

ii.   Raised-wings posture: The male is rather crouched, the folded wings parted and held up slightly from the back, tail more or less horizontal, with the beak wide open. There is much calling and the bird faces the female or stands at a slight angle to her throughout.

iii.   Sideways crest-presentation: The male turns sideways to the

358

bower entrance, picks up an object and holds it in the bill while jerking his head up and down through a very small arc. The nape patch is directed towards the female standing at the far side of the avenue.

iv.   Forward crest-presentation posture: In this attitude the male picks up a display item and, facing the bower and the female with head rather bent, makes five or six rapid jerky movements. These movements are accompanied by rhythmical mechanical noises.

These attitudes might appear in any order with various hissing, crackling and ticking accompaniments, the displaying bird's movements being jerky, erratic, and even violent, its body postures appearing unusual and strained. The bird frequently leapt to its own height in the air, generally alighting some six inches farther from the avenue. It might jump from the upright posture and readopt this on landing, or perhaps take off from the wings-raised posture and alight in the upright one. Sometimes the male would dart forward towards the bower and the female and as quickly dart back again. It would often pick up some bones and shells and shake them from its beak with a sudden angry sideways jerk of the head. The whole attitude of the male was aggressive and he attacked the display things ferociously. In contrast, the female was quiet and watchful, carefully keeping on the far side of the bower or above it, and appearing subdued and timid. She was mostly silent but might hiss a little during peaks in the display. She was seen to stand on the ground at the rear of the bower often half-in and half-out of the avenue with her tail protruding from the entrance. Sometimes she came right down through the tunnel but never did this if the male was in action. Copulation was not seen.

Postures during peripheral displays

In peripheral performances the male raised his head, stiffened his neck, and opened his beak. His tail was cocked up and his wings drooped loosely from the body. The posture was much the same as that of the Great Bower–bird (*C. nuchalis*) in the same circumstances. . . . The bird no longer hopped – the normal gait of the species – but walked or ran as he circled around the bower watching the female. She would then dodge to the other side around the walls to keep these between them. The male's nape was now fully erected and he hissed loudly as he paraded around. This posture seems to be a development of the raised-wings attitude and in one variant the wings are lifted from the back instead of being drooped.

The following description of a portion of central display taken from motion pictures will perhaps give a better idea of the bird's actions:–

Male leaps to the left side of the bower, alighting in upright posture, facing female with bill gaping. Now jerks head forward and downward rapidly and then jumps backwards, still facing female. Remains motionless for a few seconds with closed bill but then hisses and abruptly jumps up to alight with side and tail towards the entrance, then bends stiffly down to pick up bone and attacks it, picking it up and dropping it and jerking the head in sideways crest-presentation. Abruptly jumps round, pecks at ground and facing entrance flicks his wings. Lowers body and wings and jerks the whole body and head up and down. Switches to upright stance, beak open with much hissing and holds attitude for several seconds. Jumps upwards and backwards, alights in upright posture facing female with bill open. Lowers head and jerks up and down several times in forward crest-presentation attitude and then darts forward to the entrance of avenue but recoils at once to stand stiffly to left of entrance in wings-raised posture. Now goes into even more extreme wings-raised posture, body drawn right up and then bent down until head and body horizontal and closed wings raised at 45 degrees from the back. Sidesteps to left of bower turning to face female and then breaks into peripheral run. . . .

Ramsay in 1945 (see Marshall, 1954b: 81) witnessed copulation at the bower. It occurred after a session of intense dancing activity before a passive female. For more than 20 minutes the male flung ornaments about, once hopping completely over the bower, appeared to attack odd sticks and a 'tree-trunk'. Copulation occurred twice, during a five-minute period outside the bower on the ground, then the female entered the bower and crouched there motionless for about ten minutes. She then departed and the male soon '. . . began to tidy up the bower.'

Nesting: The nest is a rather flat, frail, saucer-shaped structure about 10 in. wide by 5 in. deep, composed of thin sticks and twigs and lined with a few leaves. It is placed anywhere from 6 to 50 feet up in a tree or sapling '. . . within a few hundred yards of the bower' (Marshall, 1954b: 85).

Two and rarely three eggs are laid. These are oval in shape, rather glossy, and generally pale greenish yellow, profusely scrawled, lined, and crisscrossed with a labyrinth of dark, twisted hairlike markings. Measurements: 34·0–41·6 × 25·0–28·0 mm. (after Schönwetter, 1944).

The breeding season extends from October through December, sometimes to February.

The female alone builds and protects the nest, feeds and protects the young. Gaukrodger (*in* Marshall, 1954b: 83) observed a female that performed distraction displays near the nest by first giving an outburst of vocal mimicry, then falling almost to the ground where it crept through the grass pretending helplessness.

Analysis of Behaviour: The pattern of courtship behaviour seems to be that of a non-pairing arena bird but experiments with marked birds are sorely needed.

Geographical Variation: Mayr and Jennings (1952: 8) observed that the difference between the eastern (*maculata*) and western (*guttata*) populations of this species is so great that it might be suspected that the level of specific difference has been reached. However, Mayr (*in* Peters, 1962: 179) classifies these very different populations as races of one species and I have followed him. My analysis of patterns of behaviour has turned up no evidence to dictate otherwise.

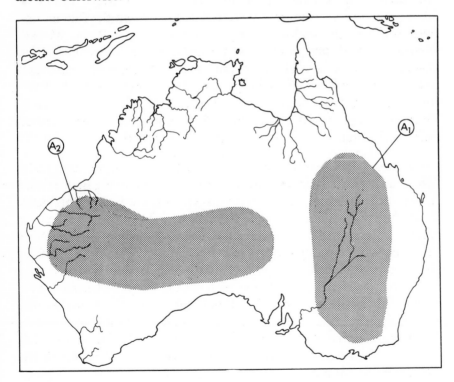

Map 10.8 *Chlamydera maculata.* Lowlands

   Chlamydera maculata maculata (A1)

   Chlamydera maculata guttata (A2)

Subspecies: Two very distinct races are known (see above).

1   *C. m. maculata* (Gould), 1837, *Synops. Birds Australia*, pt. 1, pl. 6. Type locality 'New Holland' [= Liverpool Plains, New South Wales]. Throat ochre with inconspicuous black streaking; upperparts blackish brown with ochre spots; flanks buffy; nape unspotted and usually grey [*occipitalis* Gould, *clelandi* Mathews, and *sedani* Mathews are synonyms]. Known from the drier inland country of Queensland (north almost to Charters Towers), New South Wales, Victoria, and south Australia (lower Murray Valley to Swan Reach) [range after Mayr].

2   *C. m. guttata* Gould, 1862, *Proc. Zool. Soc. London*, p. 162. Type locality 'North-West Australia,' probably upper Fortescue River [*subguttata* Mathews, *macdonaldi* [sic] Mathews, *nova* Mathews, and *carteri* Mathews are synonyms]. According to Mayr (*in* Peters, 1962: 180) known from midwestern Australia, from the Pilbara district south to the middle reaches of the Gascoyne River, Meekatharra, and Malcolm, east to Lake Carnegie; separated by the Gibson Desert from the central Australian range: Macdonnell ranges and Alice Springs area south to the Everard Range, and west to the Rawlinson Range. Like *maculata* but throat black with ochre or rusty oval spots; upperparts black with rufous spots; flanks rust coloured and nape coloured like the back (after Mayr and Jennings, 1952: 8).

Evolution: It is highly interesting that both sexes in this cryptically dressed species should have the bright crest and that the male should make such extensive use of it (by presenting the back of his head, with the crest expanded, to the female). Marshall (1954b: 85) wrote that '. . . the brilliant neckfrill is conspicuous only when it is erected. When it lies flat it has to be looked for carefully or it cannot be seen in the field.' Apparently natural selection has shaped a covering mechanism to hide the crest (in the female it lies flat and is apparently not used) instead of eliminating it entirely. However, the occasional presence of bright neck frill plumes in nestlings contrasts with the absence of any trace of a bright neck frill in some adult females. This suggests that the bright ornament is of no use to the female and is disappearing.

It occurred to me that since the Spotted Bower Bird always lives near the edge of very dry areas and uses great numbers of stones to ornament its bowers, that over the centuries it might have left a series of cairnlike markers which might be used to trace (and date using Carbon 14 methods) the march of deserts across formerly forested areas of Australia. Only one other bird that I know of leaves stone cairns to mark its breeding grounds and that is Bonaparte's Horned Coot (*Fulica cornuta*) of the highlands of Bolivia, Chile, and Argentina, which sometimes builds islands of stones in high Andean lakes on which to nest.

Great Grey Bower Bird

Chlamydera nuchalis (Jardine and Selby)
Male: 13½–15 in.

Range: Far northern Australia from the mouth of the Fitzroy River and Melville Island east to Cape York and the Cairns region. (See Map 10.9, page 371.)

Adult Male: A grey and brown jay-sized bird, usually with a vivid pink to rose lilac nuchal crest. In more detail, head and neck all around ash grey or ash grey tipped white (subspecies), except hind

neck usually with a prominent rose lilac erectile feather tuft (nuchal crest) bordered above and at sides with silver tipping; rest of upperparts pale sooty brown with prominent pale tips; upper wing coverts and flight quills dusky brown with grey outer edges and tips; tail quills dusky brown with prominent whitish tips and some pale margining; underparts including under wing surfaces generally pallid grey sometimes tinged buff and sometimes with traces of barring, becoming more whitish on central abdomen and on inner margins of wing quills; under wing coverts, axillaries and under tail coverts often with traces to moderately defined narrow dusky barring. Iris brown; bill black; feet brown. Wing

363

164–190 (subspecies); tail 124–155; exposed culmen 28–31; tarsus 46–58 mm.

Adult Female: Like adult male but slightly smaller and hind neck ash grey or ash grey with some whitish tipping usually but not always replacing the rose lilac nuchal crest. Crown grey tipped white or uniform grey (subspecies).

Juvenal: Nestling about to fledge: Plumage generally soft and fluffy, crown and upperparts dusky grey to brown with whitish spotting on crown and mantle; some of the nape feathers tinted with rose lilac; throat to upper breast dark grey; rest of underparts pale grey to whitish with narrow dusky barring; central abdomen whitish. Iris brown; feet olive brown; bill dull black (coll. J.P.Rogers, Melville Isl., 11 November 1911).

Immature: First year plumage much like adult female but flight quills somewhat longer and more pointed and underparts, particularly abdomen and flanks, with traces of barring. Male intermediate plumages or stages of dress: (a) like adult male but barred below, particularly on flanks.

Remarks: The Great Grey Bower Bird, the largest species of the family, is a fairly common to abundant species [Warham (1957: 73) calls it plentiful and conspicuous] of the seasonally more humid regions of far northern Australia. Marshall (1954b) reported that it keeps pretty much to regions which receive twenty to sixty inches of rainfall per year and that it is rarely found far from water, fresh or salt, whereas he notes the Spotted Bower Bird is able to get along in much more arid interior areas, even some receiving as little as five inches of rainfall per annum. On the other hand Warham found the Great Grey Bower Bird living in waterless or nearly waterless areas (on Cockatoo Island and in dry country around Derby) and he thinks it can get along without water. One reason for his conclusion is that in the excessively dry areas that he studied, where virtually all passerine birds came readily to watering trays, the Great Grey Bower Bird was never observed to do so.

This species was described in 1830 by the English ornithologists Jardine and Selby shortly after its discovery somewhere in north Australia by the Australian collector, Macleay. For reasons unknown Macleay did not provide an exact locality for his specimens and it remained for John Gould to provide a restricted type locality for it when he discovered that the population of the north-west differed from that of the north-east. Gould received specimens collected by the scientific party aboard HMS *Beagle* (Charles Darwin was aboard as naturalist) in north-west Australia plus other specimens in the British Museum. These compared well with the type. He therefore restricted the type locality of the nominate race and described the Queensland race as new. In 1912, Mathews in a controversial action set aside this fixation. In 1952, after a critical examination of the evidence, Mayr and Jennings found that Mathews had been in error. They wrote (1952:11): 'It is axiomatic in zoological nomenclature, and specifically stated in several opinions, that a name is not to be discarded or the action of the first reviser negated without unequivocal proof. This was not supplied by Mathews, and Gould's restriction of the type locality of *nuchalis* to western Australia will stand.'

Marshall in his comprehensive report (1954b) pointed out that despite the many fragmentary observations, the most essential element of the display of the Great Grey Bower Bird remained little known. Mr and Mrs John Warham, working in western Australia in 1956 (Warham, 1957), then in north-eastern Australia (near Townsville) in 1958 (Warham, 1962), filled many of these gaps. They devoted many days to the study of the bower behaviour of this species and their reports and photographs constitute an outstanding contribution upon which I have been privileged to draw heavily in the following account of the species.

The often abundant Great Grey Bower Bird, sad to relate, is not overly appreciated by country folk because of its liking for soft fruits and its habit of visiting gardens and orchards, sometimes in flocks (during the non-breeding season) in numbers up to thirty or more birds. Marshall (1954b: 99) in a colourful plea for the species, noted that throughout its vast range the Australian aborigines never molest this wonderful bird, with the result that it often builds its bowers close beside native camp-sites, whereas the Australian 'white savages,' in eastern Australia sometimes slaughter great numbers (up to eighty in one week in one small area) because of the birds' minor depredations in homestead gardens. The readiness with which this wonderful bird adopts man and his environs is illustrated by the fact that it often enters houses and has been known to build its magnificent bowers under, in, and on the shaded roofs of houses, also in the abandoned huts of the aborigines. Its habit of stealing shiny ornaments to use as bower decorations is another matter, of course, and the list of its minor crimes, which ranges from spectacles to the stealing of children's toys is legion, and so richly a part of the folklore of Australia that one feels sure the populace would rise up, if need be, to protect this audacious colourful vandal and thief if it were threatened with extinction.

Food: Chiefly wild or rock figs (*Ficus globerosa*), berries and seeds; frequently the seeds of the acacia tree; many kinds of orchard and garden fruits, including paw-paw, guavas, tomatoes, and chilis; also animal food, chiefly insects, which is fed almost exclusively to the very young in the nest. Young about to leave the nest had insects and the seeds of figs (*Ficus globerosa*) in their stomachs (J.P. Rogers, 11 November 1911, Melville Island).

Voice and Mechanical Sounds: Among the calls recorded for this species are the following: cat-like calls (male) and slight hissing sounds (female); explosive hisses (male); chicken-like cackling and chattering, sometimes imitative of children squabbling; mechanical sounds like the crumpling of paper; clinking noises made by picking up and dropping bones, shells, etc. in the bower.

The Breeding Territory: The breeding territory is usually a space well concealed under isolated trees with low-hanging branches or clumps of dense thickets. The presence in this space of a group of one or a few new bowers amidst old bowers (up to nine) is evidence that the same breeding spaces are used for years on end. Marshall suspects that each male builds a new bower each year and, unlike most other avenue builders, that it generally lets the old bower stand. Warham notes that only the male builds and tends the bower.

The Bower: Warham reports (1962: 14) that in the Townsville region Mr and Mrs Millett observed a male displaying to a female (circling her in obvious excitement with a flower in his mouth) that squatted on lawn grass fifteen feet from a bower. This suggests that successful courtship may sometimes be carried out on a simple ground court. The typical bower is remarkably like that of the other avenue builders. It is built of twigs, sticks, and grass stems, or twigs alone. A good example is the one at which the Warhams conducted some of their studies (illustrated in Warham, 1962: 6). It was a mat of sticks laid horizontally into which the male had inserted sticks to form two parallel walls which rose some fourteen inches above the mat and touched near their top forming a kind of avenue tunnel. The avenue was eighteen inches long. Conventional bowers have the mat about 3 inches thick, the walls about 12 inches high, the avenue about (?) 10 inches wide and the outsides of the walls about 22 inches apart. Each bower occupies a space about 6 to 8 feet long and 3 to 5 feet wide.

Bower Ornaments: At the south end or 'rear' of the bower photographed by Warham was an oval area, 17 inches by 20 inches, covered with display objects. A similar but large area covered with display objects was at the 'front' of the bower where the male performed most of his display. Warham wrote that an ' . . . area approximately 7 inches long by 5 inches wide on the floor of the avenue was covered with small white stones and bleached bones.' He noted that similar display objects predominated in the outside oval areas but that man-made objects such as white porcelain, part of a green bottle, etc. were also present.

The number of display objects varies greatly from bower to bower and from place to place. Stones, wallaby bones, land shells, (sometimes up to 800 land shells alone!) predominate in inland areas, whereas near the coast sea-shells and corals predominate.

Green objects (seed pods, berries, leaves, fruits, flowers, glass, cloth, metal) appear very often and are probably of basic importance to the display. Grey, glassy white, silver (leaves and aluminium), and occasionally brass are also used. These are placed on the mat at either end of the avenue and in the avenue and apparently are not hung on the walls as in the Fawn-breasted Bower Bird. The selection of colour and shape and the positioning of the ornaments is done with much discrimination despite the random appearance of the bower. Several observers have noted zoning of ornaments. The male does not add ornaments to the walls but occasionally it stretches upwards to lay twigs horizontally on top of the walls very much in the manner that I have observed the Fawn-breasted to stretch upwards and add a sprig of green berries to the top of the bower walls.

Bower Painting: Warham observed males in the Townsville area which appeared to be engaged in painting their bowers. He wrote (1962: 15): 'Typically the bird worked on the upright inner stems of the avenue walls and, using a peculiar caressing action, wiped its bill up and down each twig. The bird often appeared to be holding a sticky substance in its beak, perhaps pulped fruit, and its mandibles glistened with saliva. However, on none of the bowers

367

inspected after this treatment was there any sign of a band of dis-colouration such as results from similar actions of the Spotted and Satin Bowerbirds.'

Bower Orientation: Marshall (1954b: 93) presented excellent evidence showing that the Great Grey Bower Bird orients its bower across the path of the sun. He wrote as follows of a series of bowers that he examined in the Cape York region: 'Altogether fourteen bowers or their remains were examined and it was found that of those whose orientation could be unquestionably determined, all (no less than thirteen) were pointed within 45° of due north and south. The mean deviation was only 16°, and in the grouped bowers there was a most striking tendency for all within a single assembly to be oriented in a similar way.' Warham confirmed this remarkable tendency which, it would seem, functions as a mechanism to improve the appearance of the display (see below).

Bower Displays: Warham (1962: 11–13) observed that the display of the male in the bower in the presence of females is very similar to that of the Spotted Bower Bird. He divided the displays into 'central' and 'peripheral' types, as follows:

Postures during central displays
   i.   Upright posture: Male faces female and the avenue, draws itself upright, feathers sleeked and beak wide open. As it calls, the tongue frequently flicks out. Bird high-steps forward and may hold display object. This attitude frequently leads to:–
   ii.   Forward stretch posture. Male faces female, body feathers usually sleeked out but sometimes ruffled, neck outstretched, snakelike, and head often turned on one side, sometimes held very low and strained forwards. Bird may or may not hold display object in bill as it stares at female with eyes bulging somewhat. If not holding anything in beak tongue may be repeatedly flicked out. Crest is often only slightly ex-panded and display object is tossed abruptly to one side while this posture is held. By rotation of the head sideways and downwards bird may pass to:–
   iii.   Crest-presentation posture. Beak is lowered and head turned so that nape-crest is directed towards the female. If standing to the left of the avenue entrance head is turned to the left and *vice versa*. Display object is usually picked up from collection underfoot. Head is jerked abruptly and a ticking sound accompanies the movements. Meanwhile, crest may be partly or fully expanded and again bird usually tosses the display object away at conclusion of movement. Body feathers may be

sleeked or ruffled. For an example of a sleeked attitude see photograph in Gilliard (1959a).

Postures during peripheral display

During this part of the display the male circles the arena in a peculiar strutting walk or run while the female manoeuvres to avoid him, keeping the avenue-walls between them. The male may hold his body feathers sleeked with his wings raised and tail horizontal, but more often the body feathers are somewhat ruffled with the wings drooped till they almost touch the ground, and they may be partly spread. In either event the buff tips of the primary and secondary feathers form a rather prominent series of bands across the wings. The tail is cocked up and the crest fully expanded. Some display thing is often held in the bill and as the bird parades around it hisses and ticks loudly.

All these posturings are directed at the female, who watches silently from the other side of the bower, ducking and dodging to avoid the male. His attitudes tend at times to become lopsided as he tilts wings and tail slightly in her direction. With his bill open and empty the yellow buccal cavity is noticeable to the human watcher and is presumably more so to the female.

When the male is unusually excited he may circle the bower in a hopping version of the peripheral display; one male was seen to cover about eighteen inches at each bound in one such episode.

There was no rigid sequence in which these various attitudes featured, and peripheral runs might be preceded or followed by displays of the central type. Usually, in the latter, the forward-stretch posture led to crest-presentation, after which the forward-stretch might be re-assumed, and so on. These clearly-defined attitudes were separated by a variety of jumps and side-stepping movements.

At the bowers females were heard to use only slight hissing sounds. At first they often stood to the rear or above the bower, but as display progressed would generally drop down to the end of the avenue opposite to that near which the male was performing. This was normally the south end because most males displayed at the northern ends of the bowers, where the larger collections of bones and other objects were placed. Only one female was seen at the bower at a time. When inside the avenue the females might move right in between the walls and might probe at them in a rather pre-occupied manner. On several occasions a female – or immature male? – removed a twig and dropped or replaced it, but this was only in the absence of the bower-owner. At the peak of one male's display the female perched on top of one of the walls, staring down at the displaying bird and giving the impression of being both repelled and attracted by his violent performance.

Warham (*ibid.*: 13) then includes some of his on-the-spot (Townsville) observations which illustrate how these posturings are incorporated in the complete display:

(a) Male runs in from left with wings raised in peripheral display, stops in front of avenue. Leaps high with sudden flexing of legs and flick of wings and re-alights in same position. Peers down avenue in forward-stretch posture, bill empty. Lifts head a little, jerks and flicks out tongue. Lowers head and adopts crest-presentation attitude but crest only partly erected. Jerks head and ticks. Grabs large piece of white tape but throws it down again; continues ticking sounds. Raises head and stares at female, tongue flicking out several times. Peers hard in forward-stretch posture, head vertical, crest slightly opened, tongue flicking as he calls. Bends down to pick up red plastic thread, adopts forward-stretch posture with body very attenuated, holds this attitude and then jerks thread away to right. Draws body up into a more erect attitude still looking down avenue at female, tongue flicks out, lowers head into forward-stretch posture and crouches very low as he peers forward. Jerks back, then bends down and picks up fragment of green cloth. Lifts head and, peering forward, jerks head several times and then tosses cloth away to the right. Bows down to present crest, picks up red plastic thread, jerks, ticks and again tosses thread away. . . .

(b) Male performs peripheral run with ruffled plumage and large dead leaf in bill. Travels anti-clockwise in a circle of about four-feet radius around bower, tail raised at 30 degrees to horizontal, wings drooped. Female drops down from bower to right foreground then jumps into cover behind the bower but hastily backs out, apparently finding herself too close to the parading male for safety. Female leaps up to re-alight about three feet to right of bower. Hops further to right and then starts to circle bower in anti-clockwise direction. Male re-appears to left of bower but now has feathers sleeked, neck outstretched, beak gaping and wings spread and almost horizontal. Both birds then disappear to rear of bower. Female reappears left of bower, jumps and hops to right foreground and male comes round to left of bower. The two eye each other. Male bows down and female moves forward and pops into the avenue from the front. Male lifts head and opens beak. . . .

Nesting: Nest: a bulky, shallow cup-shaped and loosely built structure (eggs sometimes can be seen through bottom) composed of slender sticks and twigs with a cup lined with fine twigs and a few leaves (measurements: 10 or so inches wide, 5 to 10 inches deep, with an egg cup some 6 inches wide by $2\frac{1}{2}$ inches deep); placed 1 to 30 feet up in open vegetation where it is easily discovered. Eggs: usually one, sometimes two, oval, ground colour pale grey green or olive green or creamy white with a labyrinth maze of hairlike to spot-like markings, brown to purplish to blackish, mostly concentrated in centre of egg, zigzagging and often encircling egg. Measurements (from Schönwetter, 1944) 38·6–45·8 × 27·7–30·3 mm. (41·4 × 29·1 mm.).

Breeding Season: September to February during the period of rains.

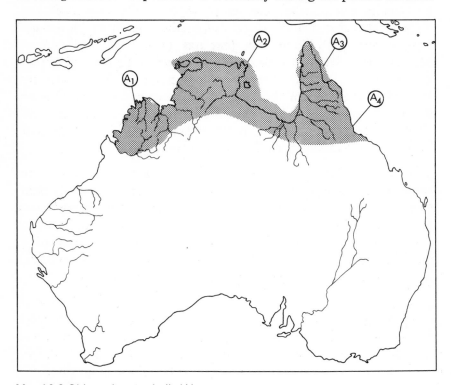

Map 10.9 *Chlamydera nuchalis* (A)

  Chlamydera nuchalis oweni (A1)
  Chlamydera nuchalis nuchalis (A2)
  Chlamydera nuchalis yorki (A3)
  Chlamydera nuchalis orientalis (A4)

Subspecies: Four, which divide into two very well-differentiated groups, each consisting of two similar races (see Mayr and Jennings, 1952: 12).

1 *C. n. oweni* Mathews, 1912, *Novit. Zool.*, vol. 18, p. 440 [type in AMNH, no. 679244]. Type locality Point Torment, north-

western Australia. Known from north-western Australia (west and east Kimberley Districts), south to the Fitzroy River and Halls Creek (Mayr, *in* Peters, 1962: 180). Upperparts rather uniform and greyish; female below generally unicolour greyish like males. Wing male (east Kimberley) 186, 187, 187; west Kimberley, 190–198 mm.

2 *C. n. nuchalis* (Jardine and Selby), 1830, *Ill. Orn.*, vol. 2, pl. 103. Type locality Port Darwin district of northern territory [designated type locality by Mayr and Jennings (1952: 11)]. [*melvillensis* Mathews is a synonym.] According to Mayr (*in* Peters, 1962: 180), known from '. . . Northern Territory north of Mataranka and Birdum to the head of the Gulf of Carpentaria (west of Flinders River); Groote Eylandt and Melville Island. Like *oweni* but somewhat smaller: wing male, Groote Eylandt, 171·5, 173; Melville Island, 172–181; Northern Territory, 175–185 mm.

3 *C. n. yorki* Mayr and Jennings, 1952, *Amer. Mus. Novit.*, no. 1602, p. 14 [type in AMNH, no. 679231]. Type locality Utingu, Cape York; known from Cape York and neighbouring regions of north Queensland as far south as the Cooktown area. Very different from *oweni* and *nuchalis* in having the upperparts more contrasting, more variegated blackish and whitish; also females less unicolour below, more inclined to barring and differing from males.

4 *C. n. orientalis* Gould, 1879, *Ann. Mag. Nat. Hist.*, ser. 5, vol. 4, p. 74. Type locality Port Denison, Queensland. Known from north Queensland (exclusive of Cape York) from Cairns to Bowen and inland to Charters Towers and west to Burketown (Mayr, *in* Peters, 1962). Like *yorki* but smaller and generally lighter in all plumages particularly below. Wing male, Cape York, 164–172 mm.

Analysis of Behaviour: I can find no evidence of pair-bond behaviour in this species but no concrete observations have been made which prove without doubt that it is polygynous.

Evolution: The rose lilac, erectile nuchal crest is of much evolutionary interest (a) because it is the kind of structure which must certainly have a long evolutionary history and (b) because it appears to play an important role in successful courtship in two species of *Chlamydera*. It occurs in the two purely Australian species and is lacking in the two primarily New Guinea species. In one of the

Australian species, the Spotted Bower Bird, it occurs in both sexes (and no bower orientation is employed); in the other, the Great Grey Bower Bird, it occurs usually in the male and usually does not occur in the female (and bower orientation is very precise). In both species display movements causing the back of the head to be turned towards the female, with the bright nuchal feathers expanded, are commonly components of the bower behaviour. In at least one of the crestless New Guinea species (*C. cerviniventris*) similar movements are made but there is no crest.

My hypothesis (1959) from a comparative analysis of the courtship movements in *Chlamydera*, is that the crestless New Guinea species lost its crest (but not the movements associated with it) through a transferral of the forces of sexual selection from bright plumage to display objects (see p. 384).

My analysis was between the Great Grey Bower Bird and the Fawn-breasted Bower Bird. I did not consider the Spotted Bower Bird, in which both sexes have the crest. Reviewing the question now and trying to fit the Spotted Bower Bird into it, I suspect that the reason that both sexes usually have the bright crest in the Spotted Bower Bird is that the crest is becoming less and less important to successful courtship. My reasoning is as follows: bower orientation (as pointed out by Marshall and others) has probably been developed as a mechanism for enhancing the displays of bright plumage (the male thus need not look into the sun and the sun striking him laterally makes his crest plumage stand out etc.). Since bower orientation is practised in other avenue builders but not in the Spotted Bower Bird, which may or may not have crests in both sexes, I suspect that the bright crest is in the process of being discarded. In the Great Grey Bower Bird, however, the crest remains important, and thus that species remains sexually dimorphic.

A very different aspect of this question is based on the observation (without interpretation) of Mayr and Jennings (1952: 14) that possession of a crest in the eastern group of *Chlamydera nuchalis* is much more frequent than in the western group. I suspect that this is correlated with the fact that the eastern group interacts with a crestless species, the Fawn-breasted Bower Bird, and the crest has importance as an isolating mechanism whereas it is no longer needed for this purpose in the western group which is geographically isolated from all other chlamyderas.

Fawn-breasted Bower Bird

Chlamydera cerviniventris Gould
Adults 11–11½ in.
[1850, Jardine's *Contr. Orn.*, p. 100 (*Proc. Zool. Soc. London*, 1850, p. 201). Type locality Cape York, north Queensland. (*nova* is a synonym)].

Range: Cape York peninsula, islands of Torres Straits and eastern New Guinea westward in the south to the Wassikussa River, in the north as far as the Humboldt Bay region, and the Kebar Valley region of the Vogelkop. From sea level to about 1700 feet. Also an old record from Sudest Island (see De Vis, 1892: 9). (See Map 10.10, page 377.)

Adults (Male and Female): A dusky brown (with pale spots) backed, ochraceous breasted, thrush-sized bird. In more detail, upperparts dusky grey brown with pale shaft streaking and pale spotting (on feather centres and tips); crown generally ash grey brown; forehead, lores, sides of head and neck irregularly marked with pale streaking and tipping; flight quills dusky brown with bold whitish tipping and pale narrow margins; chin to upper breast with broad dusky brown central streaking, most prominent on upper breast (where there is often a trace of barring); rest of underparts including under wing coverts and axillaries ochraceous fawn (tawny buff), brighter on abdomen, with traces of dark barring on sides and flanks; inner margins of flight quills

buff. Iris dark brown; bill black; feet greenish brown to grey; mouth deep yellow. Male wing Cape York 139–150 (145·4); south-east New Guinea 143–151 (147·8); north New Guinea 145–152 (149·0) (measurements from Mayr and Jennings, 1952: 15). Tail 110; culmen from base 31; tarsus 42 mm. Female slightly smaller.

Juvenal: Nestling about to fledge: like adult but hind neck naked; plumage generally soft and fluffy; pale dorsal streaking more extensive; throat and neck greyish without bold margins; rest of underparts pale greyish fawn with traces of dusky barring.

Immature: First year dress much like adults but forehead more extensively streaked greyish; upper back retaining a few soft fluffy feathers with broad whitish central streaks.

Remarks: The Fawn-breasted Bower Bird is fairly common in Cape York, Northern Australia, generally common in south New Guinea, but on the north drainage of New Guinea it is very local and uncommon.

It lives in the lowlands, never far from the coast, and often close to beaches, swamplands and mangrove swamps. Its optimum habitat is in grasslands spotted with clumps of trees and fringed with low, open forests. Sometimes, as in the Rouṇa Falls region and in the Vogelkop in suitable ecological areas it goes inland to elevations as high as 1700 feet. In New Guinea over a large proportion of its range the Fawn-breasted Bower Bird is isolated from other avenue-building bower birds. In Australia it appears to be in competition with the Great Grey Bower Bird over much of its restricted range. This point is made clear by Bernard's observations (*in* Mathews, 1925–27: 347). He wrote 'I have now proved that two species are living in close proximity [on Cape York], but that [*C. nuchalis*] is the more generally distributed. A low range of hills, running generally east to west, cuts off a strip of country roughly about 10 miles long by 2 miles wide, at the northern extremity of Cape York Peninsula. The strip is fringed by mangroves, along the coast line, the back land being mostly low, and covered with white tea-trees (*Melaleuca*) rising rather abruptly into the range. Here [*Chlamydera*] *cerviniventris* makes its home, and I did not succeed in finding a single specimen to the south of the range. I noted the bird upon many occasions, securing both skins and eggs. I found *C.* [*nuchalis*] in open forest country only, while I saw *C. cerviniventris* only in the mangroves or tea-trees bordering same.'

Naturalists viewing the marvellous houses and jewellery employed by bower birds have long since come to regard them as a thing apart from other birds. But nothing that the naturalist has found can rival the mythical fire-fighting abilities that the New Guinea natives ascribe to the Fawn-breasted Bower Bird. Emil Weiske in 1902 reported that the natives of the southern watershed of the Owen Stanley Mountains have a legend that the bower will not burn because when threatened by fire the bower owner wets his feathers in a nearby stream and then waters down the stick structure to prevent it from burning. When I read this I was reminded of a strangely similar native story which I once heard in a far distant part of New Guinea. In June 1956 (in the north foothills of the Finisterre Mountains facing Astrolabe Bay) I was told the following story of fire-fighting by the Fawn-breasted Bower Bird. My notes were written at Bom Village, June 19: 'Alis, an older man, described a two-walled bower which he had seen many years before near Bowa. . . . He said that only one bird in the region [*Chlamydera cerviniventris*] displayed in a bower on the ground. His father, a very old man, then told me that many years before there were many birds of this species but that now all were gone. He said that natives killed them by putting a saucer of water beside the bower, then lighting the bower with a match. The bower bird would then dive into the water and after wetting himself would leap at the fire. In this manner the birds were tricked into killing themselves in the flames. Myth? I suppose someone will have to make this test someday. The old man called the bower bird *swari-mani*.

This species – the last bower bird discovered in Australia – together with its bower was found in 1849 near the tip of Cape York by John MacGillivray (1852) who wrote that he had never encountered a more wary bird. MacGillivray had attempted to observe the species in its bower, which he found near the sea coast in bushes some ten feet high. Finally catching a fleeting glimpse of the bird, he shot it in the bower. As a measure of its sustained wariness, Marshall (1954b: 103), writing more than a century later, referred to Rand's (1942a: 351) sighting of a bird in its bower and remarked that apart from Rand's notes, 'little is known about what may take place at the bower.' Rand, after seeing one bird, placed a stuffed female in the bower. When the male returned, it attempted copulation with the mounted bird. Minutes later, it again attempted copulation, and after that it retired to watch the bower and artifact for hours.

Food: Chiefly small vine and tree fruits, also berries and occasionally insects. At Lake Daviumbu Rand collected a specimen which had the stomach crammed with large green ants. At Rouna he found the fruit of a grape (*Tetrastigma*) in the stomach of a specimen.

Voice: Loud churring notes; weak but harsh grasshopper-like notes; a harsh scolding alarm call. Ventriloquial notes of various other birds, including the leather-head (*Philemon novaeguineae*). My notes of sounds which I heard in and around a bower are: a humming and a hissing rasp delivered with the mouth wide open; a sharp rattle or rasping note delivered near the bower; a rasping

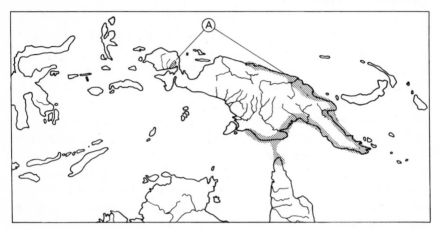

Map 10.10 *Chlamydera cerviniventris* (A)

hissing note; sharp chunks or rasping clicks (24 in 15 seconds); an insect-like hissing; explosive notes; *wick, wick* notes; drawn-out sawing *quaaaa* notes; sputtering rasping notes interspersed with whistled notes; an explosive *kaa-kaa-ka*; a cat-like whine in trees over bower; explosive pumping on ground in cadence with bowing by the male as he displays to a female crouching in his bower.

Bower: The bower is very similar to that of other twin-walled avenue builders of Australia, the Spotted and the Great Grey bower birds, being a mat of sticks laid horizontally and tightly meshed, with two upright, parallel partitions formed by the insertion of 12 to 16 inch long, unbranched twigs into the platform. At the north foot of the Finisterre Mountains a bower (at which I observed a male courting a female) had a platform three feet long and about twenty inches wide. The twin walls were only about 10–12 inches high and short so that the avenue between them was hardly a foot long, and the passage between was narrow. This bower was oriented east and west. Typical of the species, it was in a grove of short, slender second-growth trees about 30 feet inside the forest

377

edge but within sight of (and receiving much lighting from) a large, rolling field of *kunai* grassland about 50 feet above sea level. A stream flowed through the grassfield. The foundation mat of sticks was 2 to 3 inches thick and the walls arched only slightly over the narrow 'avenue.' This bower is now on exhibit in the Rouna Falls Habitat Group in the Whitney Memorial Hall of the American Museum of Natural History.

Rand (*ibid*: 351) gave the measurements of a large, well-formed bower as follows: total length $47\frac{1}{4}$ inches; passageway $21\frac{5}{8}$ inches long, $11\frac{7}{8}$ inches high inside, and $19\frac{3}{4}$ inches high outside; one platform measured $23\frac{5}{8}$ inches across by $5\frac{7}{8}$ inches thick; the other platform measured $19\frac{3}{4}$ inches across by 4 inches thick. It is to be noted, however, that the Fawn-breasted Bower Bird frequently builds much thicker platforms than this, some of them being 14 or more inches in depth (see Crandall, 1931). Since the species often builds in areas which are subject to occasional flooding, the raising of the bower platform may be correlated with flooding. In Australia, bowers have been found to have walls about 14 inches long, 12 to 15 inches high, and 3 to 5 inches thick. These are separated by avenues 3 to 5 inches wide.

Bower Ornaments: Although there are early reports of bowers in Australia being decorated with bleached bones, stones, glass, and the like, these are almost certainly erroneous and due to confusion with *Chlamydera nuchalis*. Rand (1942a), Crandall (1931), and I (MS.) found that the ornaments in New Guinea are almost invariably fresh green berries, or seed pods and green leaves. These are placed on the bower platform, chiefly on the larger platform usually found at one end of the avenue but also in the avenue itself. Sprays of small green berries are hung precariously on the top of the avenue walls, usually over the avenue. When they wither the green ornaments are removed to a heap beyond the edge of the stick platform. In northern Australia, MacGillivray (*in* Mathews, 1926) examined seven bowers, which contained only green berries, one contained 100.

The ornaments at my Finisterre bower ' . . . consisted of large and small green fruits. The large fruits were oval-shaped, and pea green or a trifle paler, the smaller ornaments were somewhat darker than pea green and the size of small marbles, whereas the larger ornaments were the size of very large cherries. The smaller berries were in clusters of 2, 3, or more. Some of them were on the bower mat at one entrance (west) and several clusters were found hanging from precarious positions on the tops of the walls 8 to 10 inches above the passageway. Single large fruits were on the avenue floor and on the mat outside at what proved to be the main dancing position of the bower owner.'

Behaviour of the Male at the Bower: The following on-the-spot notes (and descriptions based on my films) represent the highlights of my observations in the Finisterre region of the Huon Peninsula in 1956. The highlights, which are unique, include (a) four (and probably more) birds simultaneously around the bower; (b) the male building in his bower and inserting sticks; (c) the male bringing green berries; (d) the male hanging the clusters of berries in the top of the avenue walls; (e) the male dancing in the trees near the bower; (f) the male dancing to a female crouching in the bower; (g) various reptile and bird visitors around and in the bower.

On 21 June between 9:17 a.m. and 5:45 p.m. I observed a male which visited its bower twenty times. Once it remained inside the the bower for 26 minutes without stepping outside; for more than 20 minutes of this period it remained in the narrow confines of the central passageway. The next day this male made twelve visits between the hours of 7:40 a.m. and 5:03 p.m.; on one of these visits it stayed 20 minutes. During the long visits it was unaccompanied and its movements were somewhat furtive. It moved green ornaments to new positions on the walls and picked up and inserted sticks here and there in the bower. Each stick was held crosswise in the bill and the head was tilted, with the throat toward the vertical surface of the wall as the lower end of the stick was inserted in the floor. When not working on the bower, the male spent much time on concealed perches 12 to 15 feet above it. From this position it maintained an alert appearance, turning the head and occasionally flipping the wings, and it sometimes slipped silently to a low perch about a foot from the bower. Once there it would reverse position, stretch and tilt the head to look into the bower avenue, preen the wing, back or abdomen, look into the bower again, then hop to the west entrance platform which was the larger and more highly decorated of the two. There it would pick up or pull sticks, or, more often, would pick up a cluster of green fruits and with a number of different movements, would hang them on the top of a stick wall, stretching the legs and neck to do so. Then it would walk slowly through the passage with the head held very low, its shoulders brushing the sides of the bower. The walk through the passage sometimes took several minutes and if the male found something to do on the way out, it would stay there quietly for many minutes; if not, it would come out on the east platform, stand a while, inspect it, picking up or moving the green ornaments, pulling at sticks, then turn and enter the passageway or go around the outside of the walls to the west platform, perhaps to enter the passage again and even crouch there in its centre (the centre had the look of a nest). Finished, the bird would hop to a low, hidden perch in the trees overhead. All the while it was working on the ground, it was absolutely silent.

During my days of observation, bower birds would infrequently begin calling nearby. This usually happened when the male was on the ground. Sometimes, though, calls would start shortly after the male had flown up from the ground. They would begin with rasping notes, some low, like insect buzzing, some grating and hissing repeated about every four seconds and some sharp, clicking noises. As this concert grew louder, an outbreak of explosive notes would occur: *grrr, kaaaa kuaa, qa, qa, kaa*. These notes were accompanied by some wing fluttering, many short chip notes, and deep, repetitious *quarrrru* notes sounding like wood being sawed in the distance. This curious concert always heralded the arrival of a group of fawn-breasted bower birds; they would suddenly seem to be everywhere in the trees overhead, but since the notes were largely ventriloquial, I could never be sure of the number. There probably were as many as six, but I never saw more than four. Once or twice I saw three, perhaps four in the trees close above the bower and another as he approached the west platform of the bower. The others would follow him to within about eight feet but sometimes to within three feet of the bower. The bower owner would go to the west platform (his main dancing platform) and begin a most unusual twisting motion while facing the bower. His head seemed to turn at funny, grotesque angles, often completely away from the bower, and his tail was often spread at the same time. Variations of this contortion would be repeated a number of times, each sequence requiring approximately one to three seconds to execute. As these strange antics (which reminded me of 'anting' postures) proceeded, a bird, presumably a female, would sometimes slip in to perch on a vine about a foot from the east platform. This would excite the male, who now would increase his activity, posturing often with the back of the head directed at the female and the neck strangely contorted (see pl. 30), or with a spray of green berries in its bill. Next the male would go to one side of the avenue entrance (west platform), and there he would alternately crouch very low then stand up very high in a kind of violent jumping action accompanied by pumping, sputtering sounds like porridge boiling. This series of actions sometimes served to attract the female even closer. She would approach quietly via the east platform, then enter the avenue from the side opposite the male. Her actions were slow and cautious. She would turn her head slowly back and forth, then lower her body as if on a nest. In this position she held the tail against and almost parallel to the floor of the passage, and her shoulders touched the side walls. She held her head up and she generally watched the male who now performed about 6 to 18 inches in front of her head. In actions that I observed and filmed, the female left the bower briefly as many as three times before assuming the soliciting position in the central passageway. During these goings and comings the male continued to dance, usually with a spray of green berries or with a large, olive-sized green palm seed in his bill. He faced the female with the green ornaments, and violently jerked them up and down to the accompaniment of explosive churring sounds. Once a female remained in and around the bower for fifteen minutes but despite the ardent courtship actions of the male, there was no copulation.

The following are some excerpts from my field notes which bear on aspects of the above description:

20 June, 4:45 p.m. '. . . A *Chlamydera cerviniventris* with brown-spotted back, clear dull grey head, and pale cinnamon breast descended a vine, reached to the top of one of the bower walls and picked up a cluster of small green fruits. Next it hopped to the platform and began a lengthy, virtually unbroken session of bower inspection during which it played with green seeds, picked up sticks, walked around the outside of the bower, entered the passage, crouched in the centre passage, and all in all made it amply evident that it was the bower owner! . . . The Fawn-breasted continued its activities in absolute silence for just about fifteen minutes . . . at approximately 5:05 the bower owner left for about a minute. To depart it hopped to a vine and then flew off. Immediately there was a crescendo of rasping notes. It seemed that bower birds were everywhere. At a bare minimum I would estimate four birds. Now the male returned, went along one side ramp of the bower,

worked his way through the centre aisle, played with some small green berries, tried to put same on top of the wall, dropped them, picked them up and succeeded in putting them on the wall after holding them in his bill for about ten seconds. Now a second bird arrived, followed by a third (I saw three birds at one time, two on the bower and one five feet directly over it). The last descended to within five feet of the bower, flirted its wings and tail, then departed to higher limbs to join the others, which could be heard but not seen. The rasping continued overhead but the two birds, who were now in and on the apron of the bower, were absolutely silent and their actions were anything but jerky. In fact, they seemed peculiarly subdued and cautious or relaxed in their activities.'

22 June, visit no. 4, 8:35 a.m.: 'Fawn-breasted came to vine one foot from west exit of bower. There it preened side. Next it heard something in my blind and flew to limb three feet up and eight feet from blind. There it sat spread-legged, swinging its head and body from side to side, at the end of each stretching swing with an eye wide and facing the porthole in my blind it would pause, eye the blind and then deliver a hissing complaint note which reached its peak with the bill wide open. This was a long drawn-out hissing note. Immediately on its completion the bird would swing the body from the same stance and begin the examination again, using the other eye. This is the complaint call I have heard a lot but not seen before.

22 June, visit no. 5, 8:46 to 8:55 a.m. (approximately): 'An excellent series of observations and probably some good films. Presumed male (by actions to be described) arrived on approach vine (two feet up and one foot from west of bower). Two others overhead. One seemed to be following and did not dare to approach bower closer than eight feet (overhead). Male hopped to west ramp and immediately began preening (bending head far to right side along side of wing so that head was usually below line of back) to region of base of tail. The head was turned so top brushed feathers of lower side and tail was spread out or fanned partially around grotesquely positioned head. This action was repeated several times and each session required a second or more – sometimes up to three seconds (approximately). A second bird which I will call the female now approached the vine one foot from bower and one foot above ramp and watched. This caused increased activity; posturing on part of male which now hopped to vine one foot from female and

repeated posturing very actively. Next it hopped to west end of ramp and continued the grotesque posturing (I made films of the action through the twin walls of the bower).

22 June, visit no. 6, 9:07 a.m.: '*Pitta erythrogaster* came to bower again. Although bower owners were in immediate vicinity there was no conflict – this was same as yesterday when *Pitta* hopped along ramp, remained on bower stage for about three minutes, looked into avenue, turned about and stood for a long while flicking tail a little, and acting like an actor while I photographed bower and bird in colour. Now the *Pitta* again appeared on the same route it took before. Again it paused on the bower ramp but this time stayed a much shorter time. Yesterday when finally it decided to leave it took several high bouncing hops and was off. Today it took little bouncing hops. Yesterday within five seconds of its departure a bower bird arrived quietly and began fiddling with the sticks of the west entrance of the bower.'

Nesting: Nest: an open, cup-shaped structure of sticks, twigs, plant stalks, strips of bark (8–10 inches across and 4–5 inches deep with an egg cavity 5–6 inches wide by 2–3 inches deep) 10 to 30 feet up in a fork in a forest edge or savanna tree.

Eggs: one to two; slightly glossy, oval, pale greenish olive to pale cream, marked with a labyrinth of brown, purple, and blackish thread-like lines, marks, zigzags, many often encircling the egg. Measurements of egg from north Queensland (Hartert, 1910: 486): 40·6 × 27·9 mm.

Nesting season in Australia: September to December. In New Guinea the Archbold expeditions found a nest with a half-grown nestling at Penzara on the lower Fly River, 15 December 1936; and a nestling in the Cyclops Mountains area of north New Guinea, 30 November 1938.

Analysis of Behaviour: My observations in the Finisterre region were inconclusive. The bower was certainly the property of one male. I could not tell if one or several females visited the male during the period of my observations. The flocks of four or more (probably up to about seven) which paid noisy visits to the trees and vines near the bower may have been of either sex. Only one or two birds were seen in the bower. I suspect that the noisy ones were males and the quiet ones females. I strongly suspect that this species is polygynous and an arena bird.

Evolution: The peculiar twisting of the head by the male while displaying to the female in the bower may constitute relict crest-display. Warham's description (1957: 75) of a male Great Grey Bower Bird twisting to display its bright nuchal crest to a female at its bower almost exactly matches the movements that I observed in the Fawn-breasted Bower Bird in New Guinea. Therefore I hypothesised that the head-screwing movements in the Fawn-breasted Bower Bird date from a time when the species had such a crest and made such movements to display it. With the later incorporation of the green berries as sexual ornaments I postulated (Gilliard, 1959) that the crest was eclipsed in importance and was lost through natural selection – but the movement associated with it persists. This I consider a strong second line of evidence of the 'transferral effect' (see *Amblyornis inornatus,* p. 299).

If the crest has indeed been secondarily lost, an important evolutionary tool is available. It would mean that the two crestless monomorphic New Guinea chlamyderas (as compared with the two nuchally crested Australian chlamyderas), although phenotypically appearing more generalised (more 'primitive') are in fact evolutionarily more advanced, with many of the mechanisms of sexual selection having been transferred from sexual plumage to objects (the bower and its ornaments).

It also would suggest that the original *Chlamydera* stock was crested, and that the most likely place of origin of the genus was in the sparsely wooded grasslands of Australia, a niche which is widespread in Australia but rare in New Guinea.

I reached my conclusions regarding the secondary loss of the crest quite independently, only to find that Mayr and Jennings, well in advance of me, had reached similar conclusions. They wrote (1952: 8) in their introduction to the genus *Chlamydera:*

'Forest is the typical habitat of bowerbirds. Only a few genera contain species that were able to adapt themselves to more open country. The genus *Chlamydera* is the most advanced in this respect, since all of its four species live in more or less open country. There is an interesting difference between the species in the amount of ornamentation: in *maculata* both male and female have the handsome nuchal crest, in *nuchalis* usually only the male has it, and finally in *cerviniventris* and *lauterbachi* it occurs in neither sex. In view of the general distribution of bright colours in the more primitive species of the family, there is every reason to suspect that we have here a secondary loss of ornamentation in these savanna birds and that *C. cerviniventris* and *lauterbachi* do not represent the primitive condition.'

Lauterbach's Bower Bird

Chlamydera lauterbachi Reichenow
Adults 10½ in.

Range: Locally distributed in the low and mid-mountain grass-lands of the main body of New Guinea from the head of Geelvink Bay (Siriwo River) and south New Guinea (Kamura River), east to the Wahgi Valley, Baiyer Valley, Sepik Valley and Ramu Valley. Found from near sea level (200 feet) to 5800 feet. (See Map 10.11, page 394.)

Adult Male and Female: An olive to brown thrush-sized bird with striped throat and chest and yellow underparts. In more detail, top of head and cheeks brownish olive tinged yellow olive (to crown and cheeks pinkish scarlet in nominate race), the sides of head to neck with narrow pale shaft streaks; rest of upperparts grey brown with slender pale shafting and some pale buff to olive feather fringing; upper wing coverts and flight quills dusky brown with pale margins and much buff tipping; chin to upper breast greyish to pale yellow with the feathers strongly margined dusky grey brown; rest of underparts pale yellow to bright yellow (subspecies) with indistinct pale brown barring on sides of breast to sides of abdomen; under wing and tail coverts, inner margins of remiges and axillaries pale yellow. Iris dark liver brown; bill black; feet olive brown: naked skin behind eye dark grey. Male wing 129–134; tail 106–107; culmen 23; tarsus 38 mm. Female wing 124–130; tail 107–113 mm.

Immature: First year plumage apparently much like adults but generally more pallid yellow.

Remarks: Lauterbach's Bower Bird, the only *Chlamydera* confined to New Guinea, was discovered in 1896 by C. Lauterbach, a German botanist, during the course of his expedition with Kersting and E. Tappenbeck. This venture, the 'I Ramu Expedition', went overland from Stephansort on Astrolabe Bay to the Jagei River, a tributary of the upper Ramu River. In 1956 I tried unsuccessfully to duplicate their trip, which I think was via a trail which later became the 'Japanese secret road' through Aiyau Gorge (near Keku) in the southern Finisterre Mountains. Additional material from the Ramu region was sorely needed in order to solve a long-standing problem which was well explained by Ernst Mayr (*in* Gyldenstolpe, 1955: 147): '. . . the question of this species is very complex because the type [of the race *lauterbachi*] seems to be aberrant. Your Nondugl [Wahgi Valley] specimens agree well with north New Guinea birds, except for the type, which has a peculiar reddish wash on the head. No other northern New Guinea bird that I have seen has this coloration. Furthermore, there is never a subspecific difference between birds from the Ramu River lowlands and those of the Sepik River lowlands. Yet adult males from the lower Sepik River lack the reddish tint of the type of *lauterbachi*. I have seen specimens from at least five different districts of New Guinea and with the exception of the type none shows any indication of the reddish color of the type.'

For more than forty years after its discovery this species remained very rare in collections; then in about 1940 Capt. N. B. Blood, collecting on behalf of the Australian Museum, found it comparatively common in the Mt Hagen region. Prior to his discovery only four specimens were known, the type, a male and female discovered in 1930 by Fred Shaw Mayer on the Siriwo River in west New Guinea, and a female discovered in 1910 on the Kamura River, south New Guinea, by the British Ornithologists' Union Expedition.

In 1950 and 1952, when I had occasion to spend some eight months in the general area where Blood had found Lauterbach's Bower Bird, I spared no effort to study its behaviour. My unpublished studies, together with the splendid studies made in 1955 and 1956 by R. N. H. Bulmer in the northern foothills of Mt Hagen, make it possible for me to present here a fairly comprehensive report on the behaviour and nesting of this species. I am particularly indebted to Bulmer (who collected a series of specimens, recorded many nests, and examined 23 bowers) for permitting me to see his unpublished reports and to extract the material credited to him below.

Although common to abundant in the mid-mountain valleys of the Wahgi and Baiyer rivers, Lauterbach's Bower Bird is uncommon in the Sepik and Ramu valleys. In the Sepik, in the Kanganaman Village region (190 miles upstream; native name, *Ganana*) I collected a small series between December and March, 1953–1954.

There I occasionally saw it flying over tall cane-grass fields between isolated trees. In the Wahgi Valley the species is abundant in native gardens, bushy grassland, pit-pit and cane grass swamps, and in forest edge situations up to an altitude of about 5600 feet. It is apparently absent around Mt Giluwe (where the Schoddes and Shaw Mayer failed to find it) and around Tari (where Bulmer failed to find it). Farther west at Telefomin (where in two months of collecting I found no trace of it) it is apparently absent. Yet in the Baiyer it is common (Bulmer) and it is present but in unknown numbers in the Sau Valley north of the Baiyer (Bulmer). The abundance of this species in the man-made grassland of the mid-mountains is probably correlated with land deforestation by primitive man.

In early March 1964, in Berlin, I examined the type of *Chlamydera l. lauterbachi* and determined that it was not aberrant but that the rose coloured head with some barely discernible glossy gold crown feathering was the normal condition. Professor Erwin Stresemann also was of the opinion that the type 'was a perfectly normal bird.' Therefore as soon as I had completed my survey of the Schrader Mountains (see *Astrapia*) I went to the northern foot of that range to search the middle upper Ramu River region for a second specimen of *C. lauterbachi*. The search was a hard and confusing one, first to find the locality where in 1896 Lauterbach had gotten his bird [his had been a trip of exploration in every sense of the word: the big river (The Ramu) he had found was still unknown. He went down it for some days, was attacked, had to return up river and walk out over many tortuous miles to Astrolabe Bay], and then to find the bird. No bowers of *C. lauterbachi* were found despite much travel and the large bounties I offered. No natives knew the bird for sure but many knew the bower of *C. cerviniventris*. At length I gave up the search and decided to study (and film) a fine *C. cerviniventris* bower with more than 100 fresh green berries in it. The second day I saw for a brief spell a bird I assumed to be *C. cerviniventris*, then a day later I was elated to have two *rose headed* chlamyderas come to the same bower and display in it for eleven minutes while I made detailed colour photographs of them. I thereupon decided that *C. lauterbachi* of the Ramu was specifically distinct from the yellow chlamydera of the Sepik and the Wahgi because its bower was so different. But then, alas, I discovered that it was not the bower owner. For the next 12 days only the grey headed *C. cerviniventris* appeared to build at the bower. It was the owner most definitely. We waited in the hot blind, shot-guns cocked, for 12 days before on May 26 the rose headed chlamy-dera returned once again. On that occasion we promptly shot it, thus obtaining a second rose headed specimen and proving that the Berlin type is not aberrant. There remains the chance that the population of the Sepik mouth and the Ramu mouth overlap and that they represent distinct species. This question will have to await the discovery and study of the bower of the Ramu River population.

In the middle Wahgi near Kup (where it is known as *Sel*), where I made most of my studies, I noted that Lauterbach's Bower Bird often flew to high, exposed limbs, or flew along open streams from exposed perch to exposed perch. The action is deliberate and jay-like. Although quite wary near the bower, it exhibits marked curiosity. At times it flew to a low limb to examine me, and once it flew to a perch just in front of my blind to try to look in on me. Once I observed a Lauterbach's Bower Bird (at Katumbag, 5600 feet) in the upper limbs of a fruit-bearing tree growing in a grove of trees (chiefly casuarinas) which comprised the display arena of a clan of raggiana birds of paradise (*Paradisaea raggiana salvadorina*).

Food: Gyldenstolpe (1955a: 149) observed small parties feeding in isolated fruiting trees near Nondugl. The fruit was small, greyish brown and jelly-like. The birds were always 'shy and watchful.' They appeared at their favourite feeding grounds only in the early morning and a few hours before sunset. 'The greatest part of the day they were conspicuous by their absence,' wrote Gyldenstolpe. Stomach dissections show the following articles of food: remains of insects (Shaw Mayer at Siriwo), large seeds, remains of caterpillars (Gilliard at Kanganaman); orange fruit pulp and seeds; grey and white vegetable pulp and two thin black plant fibres as used on inner walls of bowers; black beetle fragments; insects (Bulmer, north flank Mt Hagen).

Voice: Alarm call like a rap on a cardboard box; sharp *chilp, chilp, chilp* notes; an occasional rattle; rasping and hissing notes (Gilliard, Kup region, 1950–1952; Banz area, 1959).

The Breeding Territory: In June and July, 1952, I examined six-teen bowers in an area of about four square miles in the Kup region of the Wahgi Valley. All were located between 4500 and 5300 feet.

Many were in level kunai and cane-grass fields interspersed with clumps of bushes and small trees, near marshy ground or running water; some were in partially shaded situations under large bushy trees; a few were just within the forest edge, some were on little level areas on dry hillsides under bushes. Many were on small rises but several were in marshy areas where the stick platform at times could serve as an island. One was in the bottom of a forested gorge in a narrow patch of grass mostly overhung with forest trees of considerable size. I examined and photographed about half of these bowers *in situ* but, unfortunately, due to other obligations, I could not see all of the bowers in the field. The ones I did not see were picked up bodily and brought to my camp on stretchers.

I suspect (but do not know for certain) that the bowers were unusually concentrated in the Kup region and that the concentration was part of an exploded breeding arena.

Bulmer, between 5 July 1955 and 26 March 1956, examined twenty-three bowers, all of which were located near the villages of Yaramanda and Trepikama (between 4500 and 5500 feet) in the foothills of Mt Hagen west of the Baiyer River. Again I suspect that Bulmer's specimens were part of a concentration forming a clan arena.

The Bower: The Bower of Lauterbach's Bower Bird is unique (a) in having four walls rather than two as in all of the other avenue-builders, and (b) in almost always having the walls of the main avenue angled outward rather than vertical or arched over the avenue as is usual in the other avenue-builders. It is a platform of twigs and sticks into which the builder has inserted four rows (walls) of sticks. The inner pair of walls are usually the longest and these are lined with fine stems of brown grass. The main passage is bracketed at each end by short cross-passages which when viewed from above give the bower passage the shape of an 'H' with a long crossbar. A bird in the central chamber is usually nearly invisible from the exterior because of the screening effect of the end walls (see pl. 31).

Sixteen bowers measured and weighed by me in the Kup region ranged in length from 28 to 38 in., in height from 14 to 25 in., and in width between 19 and 26 in. The width of the central passage varied from $2\frac{1}{4}$ to $3\frac{1}{4}$ in,. and its length from $6\frac{3}{4}$ to $12\frac{1}{2}$ in. All bowers were well-meshed and could be picked up without falling apart. With ornamentation they weighed from $6\frac{1}{2}$ to $16\frac{1}{2}$ lbs. The chief articles of ornamentation were stones, some of which were quite soft in texture. The heaviest bower contained nearly a thousand pale, slate-coloured stones weighing nearly 10 lbs. This bower was constructed of over 3000 sticks and it was lined with more than 1000 hairlike strands of brownish grass. Most of the bowers were decorated with red berries, some with a few, some with 34. Most of the bowers also had large greenish blue berries, generally five to ten in number, though some had over 50 and one had 131. Three bowers had two to five greenish blue berries in them. The stones and pebbles were placed in two locations: the end passages, where 20 to 40 usually, as many as 600 occasionally, were to be found; and in the centre of the main passageway, where clusters of from two to 99 stones were found. A feature of Lauterbach's bower is the insertion of stones in the inner surfaces of the end walls which face the ends of the main passageway. One bower examined had blue grey pebbles inserted with almost mason-like precision between the up-ended sticks, the highest being $7\frac{1}{2}$ in. above the floor of the passage. So many stones had been inserted that they formed a miniature wall about $2\frac{1}{2}$ in. wide. The opposite end wall in this bower was also lined with stones but, curiously, all of the stones were distinctly smaller. The end passage floors averaged somewhat lower than the central or main passage.

Bower Ornaments: Bulmer (MS$_2$: 27) described the bower ornamentation that he found in twenty-three bowers in the region north of Mt Hagen (northern watershed) as follows: '. . . four kinds of decorations were found in the bowers; the blue or green fruit of the *Eleocarpus,* which are hard and almost round and from 15 to 30 mm. long: the softer red berries of a plant resembling turmeric, which are oval and perhaps 20 mm. long; small uneven pebbles of light bluish-grey rocks, and the blue-grey seed of a wild bean, which are about 17 × 14 × 8 mm.' Bulmer found that all but one (an incomplete one) were decorated with stones (from 2 to over 120); all but two bowers contained blue *Eleocarpus* fruits (from 1 to 53); thirteen out of twenty-two contained red berries (from 1 to 24). The beans were confined to two bowers.

Details of three bowers which I studied near Kup (altitude 5100 feet) in April to July, 1952, are as follows:

14 April. Bower no. 1 was in cane grass five feet from swampy ground, close to a rippling stream and virtually surrounded by

12-foot cane grass (*Saccharum robustum*) interspersed with a few tall bushes and a few woody-shafted ferns ranging from 3 to 6 feet in height. Four trees with trunks 6 to 12 inches thick were within 10 feet of the bower. The bower was shaded during the afternoon, but the morning sun beat directly on it. It was oriented more or less across the sun's path. The construction was typical, being formed of twigs and sticks, mostly set on end in a stick platform to form four fence-like partitions. Describing them on the spot I wrote: 'The partitions are arranged so that the passages between them form an 'H' with a long crossbar. The central chamber [the main avenue] is not visible from the exterior. At its centre is a clutch of round stones and several blue marble-sized berries which are clustered together rather like eggs in a nest. At each end of the long central passage where it intersects the short cross passages there are smaller clusters of stones and coloured berries. These range in colour from dark brown to deep green and bright red. All are fresh and of about the same size.'

This bower had been built against four fern shafts which were quite rigid and tall (one was 7 ft. 4 in. tall with a diameter of $\frac{3}{8}$ in. at the base). These shafts were in two pairs located $8\frac{3}{4}$ in. apart. The shafts of each pair were about $2\frac{1}{2}$ in. distant from each other. Dead sticks had been placed systematically between the vertical shafts of each pair of ferns. All were placed with one end toward the ground and the other pointing upward at a steep angle or vertically. Some of the shorter sticks appeared to have fallen and others, particularly those of the central passage floor, to have been meshed to form a locking foundation. Many of the nearly vertical sticks (some of which were two feet long) leaned outward. They pressed against the side foundation supports formed by the sticks about the fern shafts. Others leaned toward the end walls.

Twelve feet east and ten feet above the bower in an isolated tree was a nest containing young of *Rhipidura leucophrys melaleuca* with the adults in attendance. About 500 feet south-west on somewhat higher ground was a small native house (with half a dozen people) and a garden. Large trees walled this area of native habitation from the cane-grass swamp near which the bower was located. At the house an old man said he was accustomed to hearing the '*sel*' morning and evening.

South-east of bower no. 1 at a distance of fifteen and a half feet was the foundation of another bower [no. 2]. It was firmly built but old. No pebbles remained except for one buried deeply and virtually inextricably in the stick platform which was several inches thick. The bower sticks, which numbered many hundreds, had been broken off fairly evenly near their bases so that the platform was stubbly and appeared to have been sheared with clippers. Bower no. 3 had many small stones inserted with almost mason-like precision between the upended sticks. The highest of these insertions was $7\frac{1}{2}$ in. above the floor. Together they formed a nearly vertical wall over an area approximately $2\frac{1}{2}$ in. wide. The other chamber wall was walled similarly with stones but they were all smaller. This end wall was not as high and was walled only to a height of 6 in. The central chamber was well shaded by hundreds of thin, hairlike strands of grass, twigs, and a few rootlets, some of which arched part-way over the passage, some of which lay on the floor of the passage. Most were as fine as or finer than broomstraws and up to a foot in length. Most were standing nearly vertically like pickets and appeared more brownish in colour than the dark grey to blackish of the twigs forming the rest of the bower. They formed a lining somewhat resembling the lining of a nest. The walls of this passage [the avenue] averaged $12\frac{1}{2}$ in. in height. The passage was about 3 in. wide. By contrast the exterior surfaces and the core of the central walls were constructed of rather coarse sticks averaging about $\frac{1}{8}$ in. in diameter. They contrasted with the delicate interior lining in much the way nest lining contrasts with a nest foundation.

The central passage was 12 in. long at floor level. The central 4 in. was decked with an elongated cluster of blue grey roundish pebbles, all of which were smaller than those used on the flooring of the end chambers.

Although searched for with care, no evidence of bower orientation or trace of bower painting was found. Fred Shaw Mayer was the first to find the bower; he shot a bird in one in the Weyland Mountain region. But he did not describe its diagnostic characters, writing only that the structure was '. . . like that of the Satin Bird of Queensland, but without any decorations.' Norman Chaffer made the first detailed studies (1949: 19) during January of 1948 (at 5600 feet) when he found three bowers, but his efforts '. . . to observe and photograph the birds at play in the bowers were not successful due to their extreme timidity.'

Behaviour at the Bower: I also found the bower owner quite shy and wary, but after many efforts I managed to observe and photograph birds in the bower. Many times I watched a male as it worked in its bower and occasionally I observed his actions when a female visited him. In approaching the bower, the male would suddenly fly in, perch on a nearby limb (or on top of my blind) and emit a sharp rapping sound. Then it would fly to a perch over, or very near, the bower, where it would emit a sharp lisping rattle: *shlip, shlip, shlip.* On 5 May 1952, at 8.25 a.m., I observed two birds at the bower (the afore-mentioned bower no. 1) from a blind thirty feet away. One went to the bower via a tall stalk of cane grass which it descended sidewise. In its bill it carried a red berry. Not thirty seconds later a second bird appeared. It seemed excited and with sideward sliding motions went down the same shaft of cane grass to the bower. It jumped into an end passage opposite the one occupied by the first bird. Now there was complete silence. Although mostly concealed, I could see the first bird lean inward over the ornaments in the central passageway. It stretched and occasionally projected its head sharply upward. Several times through the upper part of the wall I saw a moving spot of red as the bird held a red berry in its bill. Unfortunately, in starting the motor of my camera I frightened the birds. One fled off, the other flew to my blind, perching for about five seconds on the side of a shaft of cane grass, and peered in at me.

At other times in 1952 short observations of the male holding red seeds in its bill were made, but it was not until 26 April 1959, that I confirmed my suspicion that the red berry plays a vital part in successful display. At Banz (5300 feet) in the Wahgi Valley at about 8.00 a.m., I observed and photographed a male as it worked in its bower on the soggy floor of tall cane grass near the edge of the Wahgi Valley. This bower held a single red berry. The bird came three or four times to work, always sneaking in alone and working quietly. Once it came out of the bower, turned, and began picking up long sticks and inserting them in the bower by tilting the head to one side and the throat toward the wall. It then climbed to the top of the central wall of sticks and pulled with much violence at a slender sapling shaft which seemed to offend because of its larger size. After these exertions, the male was joined by a female which arrived quietly from the bushes and cane grass overhead. The female jumped into an end chamber and stood there without moving, looking through the main avenue. The male now entered the bower by the same entrance in which the female stood, passed through the main avenue to the opposite end passage, and then picked up the single red berry. Holding this in its bill it then flew to a sapling about eight feet over the bower. The 'female' quickly followed the male and, at this point, it became impossible for me to follow the actions. I have never seen copulation in this species.

From this and another observation of a male carrying a red berry for a prolonged time as it partially circled its bower, then climbed into cane grass and saplings over the bower (Kup, 1952), I strongly suspect that the red berry is a key component of display of the male.

Nesting: Nest: a fairly large, flimsy cup-shaped structure of coarse sticks, grass stems, a few vines, the nest cup lined with thin brownish twigs and grasses, fine vines and some thin strands of bark (measurements: 8 in. wide × 10 in. deep; cup $4\frac{1}{2}$ in. × 2 in. deep); usually placed among closely growing shafts of pit-pit grass (*Saccharum spontaneum*) or in a sapling fork 4 to 9 feet up in cane-grass swamps or in isolated saplings.

Eggs: One; roundish, oval, pale sea green, densely scrawled and streaked with a labyrinth of brown threadlike lines, some spots. Measurements 43 × 28 mm.

Breeding Season: During the period from April, 1955, to March, 1956, Bulmer offered a standing reward for every *Chlamydera* nest shown to him. As a result of his diligent search he observed

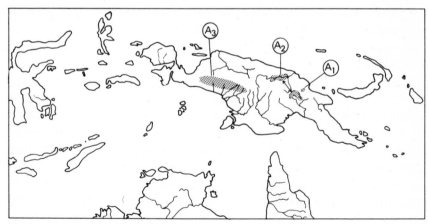

Map 10.11 *Chlamydera lauterbachi* (A) sea level to 5800 feet
  Chlamydera lauterbachi lauterbachi (A1)
  Chlamydera lauterbachi uniformis (A2) and (A3)

394

eggs or young chicks during the months of January (3 nests), August (1 nest), September (2 nests), October (5 nests), November (4 nests), and December (1 nest). The set was always one egg or one chick. In the nearby Wahgi Valley others have found nests or young in January (Chaffer), April (Gilliard), July (Gilliard), and September (Gyldenstolpe). It is evident therefore that Lauterbach's Bower Bird breeds throughout the year.

Subspecies: Two well-marked races are recognised:

1 *C. l. lauterbachi* Reichenow, 1897, *Orn. Monatsb.,* vol. 5, p. 24. Type locality Jagei River, middle upper Ramu (draining from northern foot of Schrader Mountains). Head copper coloured with traces of glossy rose gold on crown as in *Sericulus.* Known only from Aiome and the Jagei River, middle upper Ramu River, near the north foot of Schrader Mountains. Measurements of type (adult male) wing 133, tail 106 mm. (type formerly believed to be aberrant; Mayr, *in* Gyldenstolpe, 1955a: 148).

2 *C. l. uniformis* Rothschild, 1931, *Novit. Zool.,* vol. 36, p. 250. Type locality Siriwo River, head of Geelvink Bay. The range is that of the species except for the range of the nominate form. Birds from the Wahgi, Baiyer and Sau valleys have been previously assigned to the nominate race, mainly because the underparts were somewhat yellower than in *uniformis* and the type of *lauterbachi* was considered aberrant (see Mayr and Gilliard, 1954; Gyldenstolpe, 1955a). Gyldenstolpe, however, expressed doubt as to the subspecific identification and Bulmer has since (Bulmer, MS_2: 1) called attention to the great individual variation in the yellow colour of the underparts, the brightness of the feathers of the crown and nape, and the extent of white spots on the primaries and rectrices. Tail measurements indicate that tail length may increase with increase in altitude: Nondugl, 5200 feet, three males, 106–109; four females, 103–113 (from Gyldenstolpe, 1955a: 146–147); Sepik River, near Kanganaman Village in the lowlands, three males, 99–108; four females, 99–105. The tail of the type of *uniformis*, a male, measures 106 mm. However, these differences are not of subspecific value and in light of the great individual variation in colour it seems best to include in the subspecies *uniformis* all populations of *Chlamydera lauterbachi* except the nominate form from the middle upper Ramu River.

Analysis of Behaviour: No proof has yet been obtained that Lauterbach's Bower Bird is or is not polygynous. However, from the very preliminary investigations reported above, it seems likely that the bowers tend to be concentrated in certain areas. I suspect that this species is polygynous, but with the various mates remaining perhaps for a period of days with the male of their selection.

Evolution: My hypothesis is that Lauterbach's Bower Bird is the most advanced of the avenue-building bower birds (a) because it has added two walls to the basic two-walled bower form found in all other avenue-builders and (b) because it has completed a rare transition from bright plumage to dull plumage (and is now monomorphic) as a result of its substitution of sexual objects in place of sexual plumage in its courtship displays.

The evidence in favour of point (a) is that sometimes an end wall resembles a steeply sloping, stone-decorated end platform (such as is found in other members of the genus *Chlamydera*) rather than an end wall. Also, on the average, the end walls angle outward much more than the walls of the central avenue (see pl. 31), giving the impression that the stone insertion (the masonry wall) in the sloping stick surfaces is a carry-over of horizontal stick platform decorations as adapted to adhere to a steep or vertical surface. How else could the stone decorations have been preserved on a platform that was being tilted upward?

My evidence for point (b) is much less firm. To begin with, as pointed out earlier, the red berry seems to be a key component of the display of the male to a female at the bower and display with ornaments seems to have replaced display with sexual plumage (a bright crest, etc.) in this monomorphic species. Put another way, the bower and its ornaments seem to have assumed the functions of sexual plumage. If this is true, once the forces of sexual selection were transferred from morphological characteristics – the male sexual plumage – to external objects, natural selection might be expected to operate in the direction of protective colouration. Biologically the easiest, quickest way it seems to me, for this colouration to be acquired was for the male to revert to the protective dress of the female by a process of retardation of a plumage phase, the adult male dress. Thus in this species with its remarkably complex bower and display objects, we have, I believe, a crowning example of the 'transferral effect': (1) the proliferation, through externalisation, of the secondary sexual characteristics, in other words the bower, and (2) the altered morphology of the male itself.

In regard to the above it becomes necessary to correct an error. Lauterbach's Bower Bird is not dimorphic as Marshall (1954b: 179) states and his theory concerning secondary dimorphism in this species is rejected. My evidence is based on sight records. Also I inquired of Count Gyldenstolpe who collected nine adults (four males, five females) in the Wahgi Valley (1955a: 147). He confirmed my observations as follows: 'To judge from the series at my disposal there is hardly any difference in colouration between the two sexes. The males perhaps averaging brighter.' Later I discovered added confirmation in Bulmer's unpublished manuscript, 'Notes on the plumage and gonads of bower birds collected in Baiyer Valley, 1955–6.' Bulmer, who 'handled the corpses of fifteen adult and three young specimens' of *C. lauterbachi*, wrote: 'I found it impossible, in the field or with the dead unskinned bird in the hand, to sex the birds without examining the gonads.'

The interactions between the two species of *Chalmydera* found in the Ramu valley at Aiome would well repay intensive study. The male of *C. lauterbachi* which I saw displaying to a female in a *C. cerviniventris* bower had, on his arrival at the bower, begun agressively tearing at the bower structure and only when the female appeared did he suddenly begin displaying. Thus, it would seem that if the bower serves as an isolating mechanism (and I believe that the typical four-walled *Chlamydera lauterbachi* bower will be found in the Ramu valley), then my observations at Aiome indicate that this mechanism can under certain conditions break down. The question remains whether or not components of the display function as isolating mechanisms or whether the species have met so recently in the Ramu area that behavioural isolating mechanisms have not been developed.

The Birds of Paradise of Little Tobago or Ingram Island

NEARLY a century ago the great Alfred Russel Wallace, in his classic report *The Malay Archipelago: the Land of the Orangutan, and the Bird of Paradise,* was the first to describe the extraordinary courtship behaviour of a bird of paradise. He described the strange and fascinating arboreal dances of the Greater Bird of Paradise (*Paradisaea apoda*) of the Aru Islands: '. . . in May when they are in full plumage, the males assemble in the early morning to exhibit themselves . . . in what the people call their "sacaleli", or dancing parties . . .' Wallace stated that these parties were held in certain trees in the deep forest – trees with immense spreading branches. 'In one of these trees a dozen or twenty full-plumaged male birds assemble together, raise up their wings, stretch out their necks, and elevate their exquisite plumes, keeping them in continual vibration. Between whiles they fly across from branch to branch in great excitement so that the whole tree is filled with waving plumes in every variety of attitude and motion.'

Wallace's account was illustrated by a woodcut depicting a tree filled with dancing males. In display each male elevated its immense flank plumes. These were shown fountaining upward while the birds held their wings open as though about to soar off their perches. I had expected to observe similar dances in New Guinea when in 1952 I studied presumably the same species in the Wahgi Valley. However, my Wahgi Valley birds moved quite differently and they never congregated in the manner depicted by Wallace. On the contrary, each adult male appeared to occupy and stoutly defend a solitary tree perch. But each of my males was within earshot, and usually within visual range, of several other males which defended similar dance perches.

In full display my males would bend far over, crook their necks,

399

and then raise their wings over their upper backs and necks. In this position they would 'clap' the outer surface of their wings producing a thumping sound that was audible 40 feet away. Thus, to sum up, the Wahgi Valley males did not congregate closely and they defended solitary display perches and clapped the backs of their wings overhead; whereas from Wallace's observations and from his illustration it is clear that the Aru Island males display close together without clapping the wings. If these differences in courtship behaviour could be confirmed, I thought, there was a good chance that the two populations were specifically rather than racially distinct.

However a possible explanation for these apparent differences suggested itself when I found that Wallace had depended in part on native information in drawing up his report of the *sacaleli* (dancing party) of Aru Island birds. Illness had plagued him and he had written (1869: 466) that to be so afflicted '. . . after so long and tedious a journey . . . to such a rich and unexplored country . . . was a punishment too severe for a naturalist to pass over in silence.' To this he had added: 'I had, however, some consolation in the birds my boys brought home daily, more especially the Paradisaeas, which they at length obtained in full plumage. It was quite a relief to my mind to get these, for I could have hardly torn myself away from Aru had I not obtained specimens. But what I valued as much as the birds themselves was the knowledge of their habits, which *was daily obtaining from the accounts of my hunters, and from the conversations of the natives* [italics added].' My first thought upon discovering these statements was to visit the Aru Islands to make a personal comparison of the behaviour of the Greater Bird of Paradise living there with the presumably conspecific populations that I had studied in New Guinea.

Through a quirk of fate it developed that I did not need to visit the far off Arus to seek the answer: species or subspecies? Instead I could go to nearby Little Tobago Island for there, a long while ago, a wild breeding colony of greater birds of paradise had been established by Sir William Ingram, the founder and first editor of the *Illustrated London News*. Sir William, a dedicated aviculturist and conservationist, had feared for the survival of birds of paradise in their native haunts because slaughter for millinery plumes in his day was reaching unprecedented heights. Deciding to save the birds himself, Sir William commissioned collectors to capture a large number of the Greater Bird of Paradise in the Aru Islands and then to liberate them in the forests of an uninhabited tropical island – Little Tobago Island – which he had acquired in the Caribbean Sea near Venezuela.

Ingram's collectors succeeded in placing 44 greater birds of paradise on Little Tobago in 1909 and by 1912 the total founding stock had been raised to 47 birds, all from the Aru Islands. Today, half a century later, the descendants of these birds still survive in a wild state on the island and a few have escaped to other islands. All are at least third generation birds.

I found that the colony had been left pretty much alone and, surprisingly, that no serious studies had been made of its birds. I was amused to find that the island, which had usually been un-inhabited, was considered to be haunted by the residents of nearby islands. It seems that a whiskey-loving resident of Speyside, marooned on Little Tobago with a dog, chickens and goats had died under mysterious circumstances and the residents of Tobago Island whispered to me that '. . . his ghost walks in the forest.' In another tragedy a jealous lover stole ashore by night and murdered a sleeping man, only to find that someone (the ghost?) had cast off the murderer's boat, marooning him. He promptly went mad and raced through the forests until captured.

According to local records many people have visited the 'haunted' island, presumably to search for birds of paradise, but only one or two had stayed there over night. Other records showed that the first greater birds of paradise (all were in the chocolate brown plumage of the female) had reached Little Tobago in September of 1909 and that some three years later on 2 January 1913, Sir William Ingram and his son Collingwood had visited the island for the first time, staying the night in a wooden shanty. They saw a number of single paradisaeas, some of which were males, and once they saw four birds together. The Ingrams reported that none that they saw had yet acquired the distinctive throat markings of the adult male. Sir William, who died in England on 18 December 1924, did not again visit his island; but his son Collingwood, according to a handwritten entry which I saw in the Little Tobago log book, returned on 6 February 1957 and noted that he was 'pleased to have seen at least six birds of paradise after an absence of 44 years.'

Frederick Truslow and I were amazed to find that the birds we studied and photographed on Little Tobago Island between

24 February and 16 March 1958, had been left so thoroughly to themselves. Little Tobago Island lies about two miles off the north-eastern coast of Tobago Island. It is rather easily reached by small boat through the surf from the village of Speyside three miles distant. It has a single sandy beach about 300 feet long and about 25 feet wide at 'Beach Bay' on the western side of the island. Otherwise rimmed with cliffs, the island is about a mile long and it reaches a height of about 480 feet. Tropical vegetation of the sort that can withstand prolonged periods of drought covers most of the island. The only permanent source of water is a tiny spring just inland from 'Waterhole Bay.' Constantly rustling fan palms comprise 30 per cent of the forest cover, and their large blue black sprays of berries are a primary source of food for the birds of paradise. Next in abundance is the 'Naked Tree' or Plummer Cherry which shades about 25 per cent of the island. At the time of our visit this tree was devoid of leaves but was in fruit. Covering a smaller area – only about five per cent – is the 'Toothbrush Tree', so named because of the Tobagoan's habit of using its fiberous chips for cleaning teeth. Generally slender, with many twisted, nearly horizontal limbs, and with rather small oval leaves, this species and the 'Bananawood Tree' grow to heights of about sixty feet. Both are important in the lives of the birds of paradise.

In many areas gardens containing bananas and papayas have been cut and planted in the forest. These serve as sources of food for the birds of paradise. On the seaward side of the island much of the terrain is covered with short, thorny trees. Apparently this area was not visited by birds of paradise at the time of our visit. At the lower edge of this area, and around most of the island close above the sea in areas sprayed by salt water, there is little shade and here three or more species of cactus occur. One is the Pine Cactus which resembles a series of long fluted pipes standing precariously on end or hanging from cliffs like giant greenish pythons. Another is a many-segmented succulent plant known locally as the *Ratchek* that drapes itself over tree trunks and rocks like anchor chains. A third species is the football-sized *Koptush* or Turk's Head cactus which was in flower at the time of our visit. These plants, together with a large latex-producing tree with thick green leaves called the *Paratapa* and the 'Firewood Tree', a tall shaggy species, comprise most of the vegetation of the island except for an epiphyte that is probably an important component of the ecology. This is the unbelievable

'Broadleaf' which grows wherever there is shade, but mostly on the ground. This plant wraps a strangling anchorage of roots around anything it can reach and in very old plants its entangled roots sometimes form columns up to six feet tall. On top grows a green-leafed plant resembling a great dandelion but with individual leaves that measure up to two feet in width and seven feet in length! I am being factual when I write that a single leaf made a raincoat for me and a half dozen roofed a small house! In the everlastingly damp bases of these plants I found virtually all of the small animals of the island – insects, spiders, lizards, a slender brown snake, crabs, even a small mammal which proved to be new to science (Goodwin, 1961: 16–20).

Jeremiah George, who had been living on the island for some years as Government caretaker, quickly guided us to an inconspicuous tree in the forest of the south-west part of the island and stated that it was the best of about three to five dance trees currently being used by the birds of paradise. In each we were to find a series of nearly horizontal or slightly sloping limbs twenty to forty feet above ground which served as a kind of group dancing stage or arena. If finding the dance trees had been easy, filming, making still pictures and making meaningful observations of the birds was anything but easy! For the next fifteen mornings Truslow and I entered our blinds at or before daylight in our attempts to fulfill our missions. The task was exasperating. The greater birds of paradise would begin calling at dawn, then often they would converge on the dance areas – but one could never be sure which birds or which dance arena would be active that day, and often the males would retire after a few minutes for the rest of the day. Obviously we had not come as planned at the peak of the display season.

We found that the birds displayed at any time from just after dawn to the hottest part of the day and even in the late dusk. Displays may be given once or several times each day in a given area or they may be unaccountably dropped. We found that interactions between two males were usually required for display to occur. Females were seemingly unnecessary and, indeed, only rarely did one appear when the group of males was displaying. Young males were frequently observed as they flew and climbed about the periphery, but they appeared afraid to enter the main display limbs. Other smaller types of birds also attended the dances and they seemed to be stimulated by it. The Crested Oropendola (*Ostinops*

403

decumanus), a large species and the most abundant bird on the island, was never attracted by the dances; but on a number of occasions a male Greater Bird of Paradise, if he happened to be solitary, would begin to dance when an *Ostinops* passed by in the forest crown. The 'chaffing' and bubbling notes of *Ostinops* overlapping with the bugling invitations of *Paradisaea apoda* were pleasant to the human ear.

Displays

The usual regime of display is as follows: the first calls of the males are heard at about 6 a.m. These are quickly answered from near the top of the island and sometimes from down near the sea edge. Soon thereafter a male begins bugling in the half light of the forest near the main display area. At about 6.20 a.m., if his calls have been answered, he flies to a horizontal limb of the display tree. He silently wipes his bill across the perch several times then preens for a minute or two. As he preens the wings are frequently opened an inch or so and then snapped shut. These actions are interrupted when occasionally the male stretches upward to call in a rich bugle-like voice that may carry a quarter of a mile. This usually elicits an answering call and this in turn is frequently followed by rapid shaking of the upper part of the body, particularly of the breast.

The preening and wing flipping may continue for many minutes. The preening involves the under surfaces of the wings (chiefly the under wing coverts), the lower abdomen, the base of the tail, and the tail wires (these are methodically run through the bill to their tips as the male executes long, roundhouse sweeps with its head). Also preened is the upper breast and the neck. In so doing the head and bill assume a 'button hook' twist as the bird reaches high up its neck with its bill. A wing is lowered and a leg is extended over it to permit violent scratching motions. When the bird becomes interested in displaying, he is inclined to stretch. In so doing each wing is stretched separately, and then every minute or so the male extends his body and bill upward, at the same time tightening his body feathers. In this position he emits four or five deep bugled AUK-AUK-AUK notes. With each note he tightens his wings as though to help press out the sound.

If these calls go unanswered, the male gradually abandons his wasp-like wing flipping and moves off, but if there is a reply his vocalizations increase in intensity. Now his bugled calls become high pitched, short and somewhat muted. These may be described as a weak crescendo of *kiis* all run together. These are apt to be interspersed with wing fanning and 'hugging' motions which involve the opening and the holding of the wings in static positions between spasmodic beats in an attitude resembling a beckoning hug. At times the beckoning semi-static 'hug' is held for twenty or more seconds with the head either hidden between the wings or elevated and turned over the shoulder in an oddly contorted manner. During this preliminary display the flank plumes are elevated so that they fountain upwards and backwards. To help raise them the bird frequently rears its body as though preparing to dive. This display is given only when two or more males are near each other. Often it is repeated over and over again as the males work themselves into a state of excitement. Often at this point they suddenly call, then scurry and jump over the display perches in a burst of activity that appears perfectly synchronised. At about this stage the males may appear to lose control of their limbs. They appear crippled as they drag a foot along a perch, shuffling sidewards or crouching deeply. Sometimes two males now perform within a foot of each other.

Such dances take place between two or more males, but they are more animated and prolonged if females are in the vicinity. The climax display had apparently never been described before. I have named it the 'flower display' (1958). This remarkable dance is executed with the head lowered below the level of the perch. In this deep bowing position the bird looks as though it is dying. Its mouth is open wide and its eyes are glassy. The 'dying' bird occasionally executes short, spasmodic movements after each of which it seems to collapse over the perch, but always it presses down on a rounded knob on the top of the limb as though attempting copulation. In this strange position its wings and its long tail wires slope downwards and its immense plumes stand up straight like a golden fountain. Thus it stands frozen and the only motion is a bewitching one, like that of sea ferns, as the thin filaments wave back and forth in the breeze. Like great exotic flowers, the males remain virtually immobile for minutes on end, while the females promenade around, apparently selecting prospective mates. It is probably of more than passing significance that the male with the longest plumes – the king – always seems to occupy the centre or main perch in such 'group' displays.

At the end of each of such displays, if the males do not retire (this was seen once: a male on 'recovering' let out a loud call and flew off rapidly, apparently chasing a female) they settled down in or near the display tree, but not on the rounded limbs where the climax display is executed. Now apparently tired, they assume odd positions, A favourite is with the body squatting, the head turned over the shoulder and the neck pulled back. This may be held for as long as a minute. But sometimes the head is pulled back over the shoulders as though cocked for a forwards lunge. After such movements an odd thing sometimes happens. The bill partly opens and an object resembling a cherry seed comes squirting out. Sometimes three seeds are ejected in quick succession. Examination of the ground under the display limbs showed large concentrations of seeds and many more were seen in spider webbing and in the roots of the 'big leaf' terrestrial plants.

Often wing flipping followed seed spitting, and this often brought on a new round of display which, in subadult males, often continued step by step to the climax display on the rounded limb with the male again crouched in a state of seeming collapse, its plumes again forming a static flower, yellow in the green foliage of the forest subcrown. One young male went through four such cycles in a single afternoon as I watched and filmed him from a blind close by.

The evolution and the biological advantages of these courtship performances is beginning to be understood (see p. 42). Needless to say, Wallace was correct. Sick or not, he penetrated deep into the Aru Island forests and personally witnessed the wonderful *sacaleli* which he described in his classic book on the Malay Archipelago. The differences in display which I found between the birds of the Aru Islands and those of the Wahgi Valley convinced me that two species are involved, the Greater in the Arus and the Raggiana in the Wahgi Valley.

In conclusion I want particularly to call attention to the following little known fact. According to the deed to Little Tobago Island, dated 25 May 1928 which I personally inspected in 1958 in the Government archives in Port-of-Spain, Trinidad, Sir William Ingram's sons, Sir Herbert, Bruce Sterling, and Collingwood inherited the island from their father Sir William Ingram. Later the sons gave it to the State of Trinidad–Tobago on condition that adequate care be given to the birds of paradise and '*with the desire that the said lands should be re-named and henceforth known as Ingram Island*' [italics mine].

406

Excerpts from Field Ledger

For nineteen days (24 February–16 March), in company with Frederick Truslow I watched the Little Tobago birds of paradise usually from about dawn to noon, and sometimes all day. Some of my observations are as follows:

Arena No. 1, *6 March*. Entered blind at 5.30 a.m. First *P. apoda* at 6.01. [We entered the blind so early because it is a slow noisy job to set up the cameras, and it would be risky to do this after daybreak]. Other *Paradisaea* calls were soon heard in many directions, and within minutes it was evident that we were going to get plenty of action. Calls came closer and closer to the dancing area: the bugled ARKs, deep and powerful; the higher-pitched, less powerful ARKs were heard frequently. At 6.08 a.m. a male with shorter than average plumes took up a position on the main display limb. He flipped his wings open and shut, reared up, ('bucked') and called, he opened his wings in the 'bear hug' attitude, he pranced back and forth and elevated his flank plumes, putting on a splendid display. [At about 6.20 I began filming this display at f. 2, using Super Anscochrome]. The male performed all of the phases of the dance that I was then familiar with: a recapitulation of scenes I filmed included: a) the stretching of the body with the head and bill directed upward, and the feathers slimmed down hard to present a slender silhouette (in this position the male appears alert and wary, and, after becoming very slender, he often calls loudly, repeating the notes again and again); b) the male began the wing flipping early in the display, flipping the wings open and shut in vaguely wasp-like wing motions, with the wings never very far open and when closed, pressed to the body; c) the male bent or canted the head, agitated the wings and partly raised the flank plumes; d) the male preened the chest, under wings, scapulars and scratched the head; e) the male spasmodically 'rowed' with the wings held open, 'palm' down and alternately static. After these preliminaries the male moved spasmodically along the top of the display limb, seeming to prance, acting crippled, sometimes dragging a leg, pausing [to assume position D and position E], with the plumes elevated nearly straight up and umbrella-like and the feet constantly shuffling. At this stage of the performance the male often appears to be genuinely injured, and there is no doubt that he has become partially disabled as a result of his sexual excitement. Prior to the beginning of the leg dragging he often stands very 'tall' on his legs and executes a shuffling dance on stiffened legs, next he bends over with the neck stretched out and the body slim and almost parallel to the branch. In this position he remains still for a few seconds, then he suddenly leaps into a series of charges, rapidly bounding to and fro, sometimes entirely circling the main stage on the smaller limbs, and then assuming position D, which is the climax display. In this position the plumes are elevated straight up, the tail is depressed nearly straight down, the head and neck are lowered to the level of, or below, the display perch, as though the bird were looking downward, and the bill is usually held open. Once assumed, this posture is held for varying amounts of time. Often it lasts for only a few seconds and is interrupted as the male makes a quick change to face the opposite direction and then 'freeze' again; but if a female is in the vicinity it may last a full minute or even many minutes, with the male remaining absolutely rigid with only his golden, lace-like display plumes moving in the air currents. When executing this display, the bird resembles a large golden flower and not a bird. When several males assume this same display simultaneously, the tree seems to be decorated with golden flowers. However, all of the males in the display tree do not necessarily assume this pose simultaneously. I filmed a sequence in which one male holds the 'flower' display while others around him are partially 'frozen' but spasmodically flipping the wings in the bear hug display. Still others, presumably young males, are to be seen calling, climbing, flipping their wings in the wasp display in the periphery of the main stage. Cocks with long plumes are the birds which occupy the main stage when a group of cocks is present in the general area, and the young males always keep well back from the stage centre.

This morning two (or perhaps three) all brown, presumably female paradisaeas visited the immediate periphery of the display arena, together with one or two subadult males (which were brown all over but with golden napes). Immediately the three adult males, which were dancing actively together in the main arena, stopped their posturing and assumed the 'flower' or climax display. Some of the males held this pose only for short periods, but the one in the centre of the display stage held it for periods of up to a minute. As he stood contorted and perfectly still, his silhouette was obliterated. The females moved about the edges of the stage, never coming on to the main limb, but keeping up a constant and rather methodical tour of inspection. There was also much plaintive *kii*ing so that the dance party gave off much excited and overlapping sounds. I should judge that the male held the static pose with very few interspersals of movement for no less than three minutes. When it did move, it merely shifted the wings a bit and then immediately assumed the static pose again. During this period I ran 150 feet of film and actually succeeded in reloading the Arriflex camera without disturbing the displaying birds. This provides an indication of their preoccupation, for rapid reloading is impossible to accomplish without making slight noises, such as clicking. [Anscochrome film was used at f. 5 and f. 2 at about 16 frames per second. The f. 2 was the indicated exposure and the

f. 5 telephoto shots were greatly forced. For the latter I slowed the camera motor very much. These films were later processed by the Ansco company at A.S.A. 200].

The entire dance was over in one hour and five minutes or about 7.15 a.m. Immediately afterwards, in the blind, I recorded in my ledger what I had seen, writing at the end: 'The display which I have just described is the finest that I have seen.' It involved at least three adult males and one or perhaps two immature males. Two birds in adult female plumage were observed and a number of other dark birds the size of females or young males were observed flying and jumping about close at hand in the trees bordering the display grounds. [Some of these were photographed through the 300 mm. telephoto lens, which was also used part of the time on the displaying males as they performed about 37 feet from my camera. The bulk of the photography was done with a 200 mm. lens].

I saw no fighting among the adults or young birds, but, nevertheless, the male with the longest and most beautiful flank plumage was usually to be seen nearest the centre of the display arena – a bent limb – and the young males without display plumes kept to the outer edge of the dance arena.

I saw no sign of copulation. The dance seemed to have no definite ending. At the end of a long period of 'flower' display by the long-plumaged male, the party of birds drifted away. The actual end of dancing that I saw was as follows: a number of birds changed position crossing the field of my telephoto finder and suddenly, I noted only a single male remained. It continued to *kii* and then opened its wings in the 'bear hug' display. Finally a bird, which may have been an adult female, flew past this displaying male, crossing behind it in a shallow dive. At this the last male departed, I suspect chasing the brown bird.'

Arena No. 2, *11 March*. Blind located two-thirds of the way up sides of Yellowhead Point (Southwest Hill) and approximately 100 feet higher than blind No. 1. This display area is just within shouting distance of area number one. This area is in a 'bananawood tree' growing in mixed forest with a high crown (approximately 50 feet) with many fan palms and 'nakedwood' trees. The first species is the most abundant tree and the latter is the most obvious tree because its broad, reddish brown leathery trunks rise above the rest of the forest trunks and are of much greater dimensions than the many varieties of spindly trees among which it grows. This location differs from that of arena No. 1 in that, whereas that area is fairly open, or is undergrown with thin palms of several species, this area has a very thick covering of remarkably tall, broad-leaved plants. In fact, the individual leaves often reach a length of six and even seven feet! They rise up so high from the ground that a man can walk among them without being visible, except close at hand.

From its rather continuous, spasmodic calls, I knew a male was preparing to dance and that it was in communication with another male which answered from some 400 feet away. When the short-plumed male raised its head to call – it continuously initiated the vocal exchanges – I observed through high magnification that it compressed the wings tightly to its sides as it expelled each note. I also noted that this fully adult but short-plumed male very frequently peered downward at my blind. It seemed very wary of sounds emanating from the structure, which was located about 35–40 feet from where it sat. Fortunately, this alertness vanished later in the afternoon. This happened after the afore-mentioned intermittent calling, which continued monotonously for a long time. A long-plumed male responded monotonously from various perches fairly far off and showed no inclination to approach close to or to enter the display arena. I took this to mean that it still feared my blind. But about 5 p.m., as I was packing to depart, a series of answering calls was heard from near at hand and shortly the long-plumed male flew into the display arena. It perched immediately above the short-plumed male. The two now began preening very actively and flipping the wings in the wasp motion and in a short while they were dancing together with their wings opened more or less continuously in the 'rowing' position, and with the ornamental plumes cascading upward and backward [the D position]. The short-plumed male performed while standing lengthwise on the display limb. The two birds were observed to perform the same type of displays at the same time. This was very striking during the execution of the shuffling displays for, when one bird ran or scurried along the top of a limb, so did the other; and when one gave a loud series of calls, so did the other. At this point I was astonished at the synchronisation which was achieved both in vocal display and in action. Both males burst forth in a series of bugled notes that so nearly overlapped, they could easily have been mistaken for a series of notes emanating from the throat of a single bird. Almost immediately after witnessing this, I recorded it in my ledger in the blind and not many minutes later I added: this same synchronisation of sound has happened twice again, but since the short-plumed male displayed in the main arena and the long-plumed male was nearby but not in my field of vision, I could not see if the dancing was synchronised again. Once one is familiar with their sounds from close at hand, it is easy to recognise when the calls are synchronised. There is a general increase and a kind of 'bursting' of sound which distinguishes this dual auditory display from that delivered by a single bird.

The dancing of the short-plumed and long-plumed birds that I described just above differed somewhat from that which I had observed at arena No. 1 in that in this arena there was more chasing, the two males flying about and then returning to their perches. The short-plumed bird was particularly active at this, jumping from perch to perch before settling down. Next followed a series of displays which led to the climax display. There were a series of drawn out wing shufflings and tail movements accompanied by relatively weak *Kii*s from both birds. The wings were now thrown forward repeatedly in the 'bear hug' and this position was held for many seconds at a time. Suddenly both birds lowered their heads and wings, depressed their tails and elevated their flank plumes. It was at this time that they appeared to be in near or actual climax display, the position I have earlier called flower-like, and which is to a large extent static. Sometimes this position was assumed while the bird was standing across a limb, and sometimes it was executed while standing parallel to it; but always the long-plumed bird kept to the higher perch and the short-plumed bird kept to the lower perch. As each bird performed on his limb, the displays developed into chases that halted abruptly with each bird standing immobile for 20 to 30 seconds – and sometimes for almost a minute. They stood in the 'flower' pose, although no female was present. This entire dual performance lasted for about an hour. I suspect that they did not hold the 'flower' position any longer because no females were present.

Much of this dance was photographed on still and motion picture film. At the end of the dance the male with the long plumes departed first, perhaps fatigued from the long performance. Within 10 seconds after this 'older' male departed the 'younger' short-plumed male left its lower perch and jumped up to the perch which had been vacated by the long-plumed cock. This was the same perch on which the young male sat when alone in the tree earlier in the afternoon. It was presumably relinquished to the longer-plumed male when he arrived and reoccupied as soon as he left. The young male sat for a while on this, presumably the 'main' perch, then suddenly it dove into the forest and disappeared. It dove to the accompaniment of a higher pitched call – almost a shriek – that differed from all of the *P. apoda* calls that I have heard. The display tree was now deserted for the first time since my arrival at 2.45 p.m. It was at this time that I sent Dandan up the tree with a machete to clear away a number of the smaller peripheral limbs that impeded photography.

I viewed these activities through a 200 mm. lens. This permitted me to confirm the observations of 'chewing' motions that Mr Truslow had reported earlier. These peculiar motions occurred when the short-plumed male appeared to reach a static state in its display: sitting quietly on the display perch, it would preen its scapulars, then open its bill as though chewing with an up and down motion. As I watched this, the cock suddenly spat out two seeds, resembling cherry pips. They emerged one right after the other as though having been flipped out by the tongue. This was quite a surprise because this young male had been occupied continuously for some time with displaying and had not been feeding. The objects were pale yellowish. They struck the large-leaved plants growing some twenty or more feet below with a resounding thump.

13 March. Entered blind at arena No. 2 at 5.50 a.m. Examined the display arena and the limbs around it with great care by using the 200 mm. telephoto lens and the Leica reflex housing while locked on a tripod. In the dim light I was able to make out the limbs by their silhouettes against the sky. In this way I ascertained the display arena limbs are not used for sleeping purposes by *P. apoda*. The calls of males of *P. apoda* as they approached the dance ground reinforced this observation. 'Short-plume' arrived fairly early and remained for about two hours. It 'talked' again with 'long-plume' but the latter still seemed to be frightened by the limb cutting which I had done and it refused to visit the display arena. I left the area between 8.45 a.m. and 2.10 p.m. when I found two males in the vicinity of arena No. 2. Both flew off as Dandan and I sneaked into the blind. At 2.20 p.m. 'short-plume' returned to display on limb No. 2 – the King limb, – then to prance on the rounded top surface of limb No. 2. On the latter it performed with great vigour: with its head down it pirouetted and held still again and again. It worked the bill, squatted, seemed to collapse, then lifted itself in a kind of penguin attitude with its body pressed to the perch. At 2.25 it left the display area in a diving flight which is described below. The departure was accompanied by explosive *Kaws*.

At 2.47 'short-plume' returned to a perch 20 feet from the display arena and, as I write, it is emitting *WAAH-WOOAH* bugles which have a low, ringing quality that is very penetrating. These it delivers usually in series of three followed by 15 to 40 seconds of silence. After a time calls were answered. This event immediately caused 'short-plume' to hop up to the 'king perch' and to begin the chain of displays leading to what appeared to be symbolic copulation on the lower branch. In fact, the actions of this afternoon, because of their sameness in repetition, gave me my first real understanding of the sequence of the behavioural links – the pattern of their complicated series of displays.

The male, after hopping to the 'king perch' in response to the distant calls of another male, began flipping its wings, and by 3.08 p.m. it had gone through the entire display, even descending to go into the climax (the flower display) on the bent top of limb No. 1. At 3.30 p.m. 'short-plume' again went through the entire performance. The beginning of this chain was once again a series of *WAA-WAA-WAA-WAA* notes followed by silence, preening, wing flipping, etc. Answering calls from another male seemed to trigger the dance cycle, which next took the form of the hugging breast display – the spasmodic opening of the wings and holding them open. I hastily recorded this sequence of actions: 'Head over wing and drawn in. Preening. Eject seed; body jerk; bear hug; shake body. Jump down to bent limb (if very excited sometimes first hops rapidly in a kind of frantic chase among nearby branches before going to bent limb). Treads curved limb. Collapses; becomes a flower in silhouette. In ejecting the seeds the male pulls the neck back and spits out pale objects which patter on the big leaves below the perch. This latter action seemed to be a part of the actual display.

To my astonishment, now at 4.35 p.m. 'short-plume' is beginning another series of displays. This is the fourth cycle since my arrival at 2.10 p.m. During this entire period 'short-plume' has had no dancing companions, but he has been interacting vocally with other males. For example, at the present time a male has often come fairly close to arena No. 2 and is answering 'short-plume' from less than 50 feet away.

At 4.38 'short-plume' flew off departing from the curved top of the limb where it had just executed the flower display. The *Kiïing* has now stopped and I cannot hear *P. apoda* calls of any sort. I believe that the birds have gone to feed.

Abundance of *Paradisaea apoda* on Little Tobago

On 15 March after 19 days of continuous observation on Little Tobago Island, I took up the matter of the abundance of *P. apoda* with Mr George, the island caretaker. I informed him that I thought that there were not more than five fully plumed males on the island and that there were probably less than 35 birds of paradise in all. Mr George said that he would agree with this. He said that in 1947–1949 the total of fully plumed males was also about five but that it once got down to one. Mr George informed me that the males that display on the two arenas on north hill near Doublegate garden visit these display arenas when birds are dancing on south hill in arenas one and/or two. Full-plumaged males have often been observed flying across the valley between these hills. This I have seen myself, and it is on this flight that the males seem to be in much danger from hawks. Duck Hawks were observed about five times by us at this spot, and other species, including a large grey hawk which was not a Broadwing, were seen hunting over this area.

My estimates are: a) *Certain:* three long-plumed males, four young males, six females: total population 15 birds. b) *Possible:* five long-plumed males, four short-plumed males, eight young males, twelve females: total population 29 birds. Since writing this I have added a few possible additions, namely young birds in nest and females in hiding, bringing the estimated number to 35 birds at most.

Dispersal of *Paradisaea Apoda* to Other Islands

16 March: Interview with Mr Norbert Augustine of Lucyvale, Tobago Island. 'In the year 1921 we had a storm (?September) and I went to Starwood for about a month of hunting. In hunting I saw one of the birds of paradise. That was in October about a month after the storm. By inquiring about it, I was told it was one of the birds of paradise. A few days afterwards Mr Lubin came and inquired about it. He sent one of his men, which was Wilson, with me to certify. When we went to the spot we saw the bird. And then he (Lubin) himself came over and then we went and about a half hour after we went we saw the bird in the same woods. After seeing the bird, Mr Lubin said: "yes, it is one," and then for my time he paid me four dollars and promised if he should catch it alive he would give me another twenty dollars. And then he camped there for a good time and he never caught it.' Mr Augustine then concluded by saying that ' . . . it was I who told Davidson about the bird. Davidson saw it afterwards.' Mr Charles Corner also remembered the big wind of 1921. He said it blew down trees but not houses.

14 January, 1964: I was informed today by Miss Jocelyn Crane that a hurricane last fall is reported to have driven some birds of paradise to Tobago Island from Little Tobago.

List of Ornithological Explorations in the New Guinea and Moluccan Regions

THE FOLLOWING is a survey of the travels of ornithological explorers who have journeyed to the New Guinea region in quest of birds of paradise and bower birds. I began this survey with a comprehensive study of all of the birds of paradise in the American Museum of Natural History (NEW YORK) collections. The localities and dates found on the specimen labels were plotted on a base map of the South Pacific region. Thus I was able to reconstruct the travels of each collector at least while he was engaged in collecting for Lord Rothschild of The Zoological Museum at TRING, England, or the American Museum of Natural History (whence came the great Rothschild collections in 1932). With this as a start, I then studied much of the literature recorded in the bibliography of this book and some unpublished field journals for additional historical information. Finally I examined the original labels on many specimens of birds of paradise and bower birds at the following sources:

BERLIN   Berlin Museum of Natural History, East Germany
BOGOR   Museum Zoologicum Bogoriense, Indonesia
BRISBANE   Queensland Museum, Australia
CAMBRIDGE   Museum of Comparative Zoology, Mass., USA
CHICAGO   Field Museum of Natural History, Illinois, USA
LONDON   British Museum (Natural History), England
PARIS   Muséum d'Histoire Naturelle, France
PHILADELPHIA   Academy of Natural Sciences, USA

I have not examined several important collections such as the following, though much information concerning them was gleaned from the literature:

BRUSSELS   Musée Royal d'Histoire Naturelle, Belgium

BUDAPEST   Hungarian National Museum, Hungary
DRESDEN   Dresden Zoological Museum, East Germany
GENOA   Museo di Storia Naturale, Italy
HONOLULU   Bernice P. Bishop Museum, Hawaii, USA
LEIDEN   Royal Natural History Museum, Netherlands
NEW HAVEN   Peabody Museum, Yale University, Conn., USA
STOCKHOLM   Swedish State Museum of Natural History, Sweden

Other smaller collections mentioned in the text include the following:

AUCKLAND   War Memorial Museum, New Zealand
BERKELEY   Museum of Vertebrate Zoology, Calif., USA
BRESLAU   Breslau Museum, Poland
CANBERRA   Division of Wildlife Research, Australia
FRANKFURT   Senckenberg Museum, Frankfurt-am-Main, West Germany
HAMBURG   Hamburg Museum, West Germany
ITHACA   Cornell University, N.Y., USA
MUNICH   Munich Museum, West Germany
PITTSBURGH   Carnegie Museum, Pa., USA
SYDNEY   Australian Museum, Australia

List of Subregions for which Chronological Expedition Summaries are Provided

The history of the ornithological explorations of the New Guinea and Moluccan regions is a complicated one. For the purposes of this work, the most meaningful way to present it, I found, was to divide the regions into twenty-seven subregions (See Map A2.1, page 417), and to give a chronological summary of the expeditions that have worked in each subregion. The specific areas where collections were made follow the name of the collector. To this summary I have added certain other information, such as the major discoveries of birds of paradise and bower birds, a listing of the birds of paradise and bower birds collected by each expedition and the present location of the type specimens, and the disposition of the specimens, which is indicated by a brief geographical designation in capital letters (for example, BERLIN for the Berlin Museum of Natural History). The material collected for Lord Rothschild and formerly lodged in his Zoological Museum at Tring is now at The American Museum of Natural History in New York.

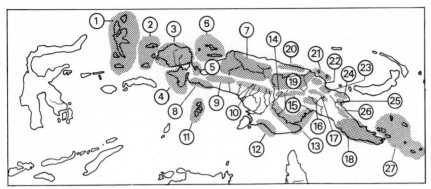

Map A2.1 Subregions for which Expedition Summaries are Provided

1 Moluccan Islands
2 Western Papuan Islands
3 Vogelkop
4 Bombarai Peninsula
5 Wandammen Region
6 Islands of Geelvink Bay
7 North-western Lowlands
8 Triton Bay – Etna Bay Region
9 Nassau – Weyland Mt Region
10 Oranje, Snow and Star Ranges
11 Aru Islands
12 Merauke Region
13 Fly River and Delta Region
14 Dap, Hindenburg, Victor Emanuel Ranges
15 Tari, Giluwe, Hagen Mts
16 Kubor Mts
17 Regenberg, Lordberg, Schraderberg, Wahgi Divide, Bismarck
      and Kratke Mts, and Mt Michael
18 Mountains of South-eastern New Guinea
19 Sepik River Region
20 Torricelli Mts, Wewak, Prince Alexander Mts
21 Islands Bordering Northern Coast
22 Adelbert Mts
23 Astrolabe Bay Region and inland lowlands of Ramu River
24 Mts of Huon Peninsula
25 Lae–Huon Gulf Region
26 Herzog Mt Region
27 Islands of South-eastern New Guinea

1: Moluccan Islands

1858   (8 January 1858 to 1860) Alfred Russel Wallace; LONDON. Wallace used Tidore on the island of Ternate as his head-quarters while collecting in the Moluccas and in the New Guinea region. Half of Tidore, Wallace wrote, was owned by M.D. van Renesse van Duivenbode, a native of Ternate, and scion of an old Dutch family. Duivenbode was educated in England, owned many ships, about 100 slaves, and was called 'King of Ternate'. Duivenbode and his son, both plume merchants, kept an eye out for unusual birds of paradise going through their hands, and diverted these to European museums. Other plume merchants also had their headquarters at Ternate; for example, J. Bensbach, a Dutch-man, who also forwarded select specimens to European museums or to the great plume dealers, such as the Parisian plumassier Mantou, to sell at premium prices to patrons of scientific institutions. Of a slightly more scientific bent was Ternate collector A. A. Bruijn who almost annually, between the years 1875 and 1885, sent teams of collectors to the western Papuan islands and western New Guinea to collect millinery plumes and fair numbers of scientific specimens.

1858   (January–September) A. R. Wallace; Halmahera. LONDON.

1858   (October–April) A. R. Wallace; Batjan. LONDON. Discovered Wallace's Standard Wing (*Semioptera wallacei*) thus extending the range of the Paradisaeidae to the Moluccas.

1858   Charles Allen for A. R. Wallace; Morotai and Halmahera. LONDON. (Undated specimens of *Lycocorax* from Morty Island bearing Wallace's name are in PARIS).

1860   (late in year) A. R. Wallace; Halmahera. LONDON.

1861   (?) Heinrich Agathon Bernstein; Batjan. LEIDEN; PARIS. Spent many months with a team of collectors searching for birds; died 1865.

1862   H. A. Bernstein; Halmahera. LEIDEN. Egg of *Lycocorax*.

1873   and 1874 (June and July, 1873; December, 1874) A.A. Bruijn; Halmahera. LEIDEN.

1876   (December) and 1878: Raffray; Gilolo I. (Dominga). PARIS.

Lycocorax.

1883   A. A. Bruijn collectors; Halmahera I. PARIS. *Lycocorax.*

1883   (October) R. Powell; Obi-Major. TRING.
       Lycocorax.

1883   (October and November) R. Powell; Batjan. TRING.
       Semioptera.

1883   (December) F. H. H. Guillemard; Batjan. TRING; GENOA.
       Semioptera.

1894   (January) W. Kukenthal; Halmahera. TRING.

1894   (April) W. Kukenthal; Batjan. TRING.

1896   (November) W. Doherty; Halmahera (Patani region). TRING.
       Lycocorax, Semioptera.

1897   (August and September) William Doherty; Batjan. TRING.
       Semioptera, Lycocorax.

1897   (September) W. Doherty; Obi–Major. TRING.
       Lycocorax.

1902   (September) Johannes Waterstradt; Halmahera. TRING.
       Lycocorax, Semioptera.

1926   (May and June) Walter Goodfellow; southeast Halmahera.
       LONDON.
       Goodfellow, after a long search, found a clan of *Semioptera*
       which he studied and partly captured.

—?   V. Martom; Batjan I. BERLIN. *Lycocorax.*

1929   (January) Fred Shaw Mayer; Halmahera (Patani Village).
       TRING.
       (24 December) Two nests, each with one egg of *Lycocorax.*

1931   (April–June) Gerd Heinrich; Halmahera I. BERLIN. *Lycocorax,*
       Semioptera.

1931   (June–July) G. Heinrich; Batjan I. BERLIN. *Lycocorax,*
       Semioptera.

1936–39   G. Heinrich; Halmahera and Batjan. Observations of nest
       and egg of *Lycocorax.*

1938   (29 May) G. A. L. DeHahn; Kobe, Halmahera. BOGOR.
       Semioptera.

1951   (9 October) G. A. L. DeHahn. Gunung Biaur, Halmahera
       (600m). BOGOR. *Semioptera.*

1952   (15 January) G. A. L. DeHahn; Ake Wosin, Halmahera.
       BOGOR. *Semioptera.*

1953   (14 June) A. M. R. Wegner; Bira, Obi I. BOGOR. *Semioptera.*

1953   (7 July) A. M. R. Wegner; Labuhon, Babang, Wajana,

419

Batjan I. BOGOR. *Semioptera*.

1954   Dr and Mrs S. Dillon Ripley; western Moluccas (Batjan). NEW HAVEN; BOGOR.

2: Western Papuan Islands

1818–19   (16 December–6 January) J. R. C. Quoy and J. P. Gaimard; Waigeu I. PARIS. Small collection obtained during the exploratory voyage of the *Uranie*.

1823   (6–16 September) R. P. Lesson and P. Garnot; Waigeu (north coast). PARIS. *Paradisaea*.

1860   (21 to 25 June) A. R. Wallace; Misnam Island. LONDON. After being blown ashore during the course of a dangerous voyage in a small sailboat from Ceram to Waigeu, Wallace managed to make a small collection of birds.

1860   A. R. Wallace; Misol I. LONDON.

1860   (29 June–2 October) A. R. Wallace; Waigeu I. LONDON. Wallace collected in the vicinity of Muka and Bessir Villages for about six weeks, obtaining 73 species of birds, 12 of which were new to science. Included were 24 skins of *Paradisaea rubra*. Wallace also visited the Chabui Bay area.

1860   (June and July) C. Allen for A. R. Wallace; Misol Island. LONDON.
A general collection.

1860 (?)   C. E. H. von Rosenberg; Misol I. LONDON.

1860   C. E. H. von Rosenberg; Waigeu I. LEIDEN.
Rosenberg collected mostly in the Mayalibit Bay area. Although on the island at the same time, Rosenberg and Wallace never met.

1863 (?)   H. A. Bernstein; Kofiare I. LEIDEN.

1863   H. A. Bernstein; Waigeu I. LEIDEN; PARIS.
From 1 March to 6 May, Bernstein spent many days collecting on Waigeu Island. He is also reported to have collected on Batanta Island at about this time. He discovered *Diphyllodes respublica*, a species previously known from native trade skins.

1867   (July) Collector?; Sailolo, Salawati I. LONDON. *Ailuroedus buccoides*.

1867   David Hokum; Kofiau I. Destination of specimens?

1868   (11 June) Collector; Misol I. LONDON.

1875 and 1876   (6–14 March 1875; March 1876) Odoardo Beccari; Waigeu. GENOA.

1875   (June) O. Beccari; Batanta I. GENOA.

1875   (25 July) O. Beccari; Salawati I. GENOA; BERLIN. *Diphyllodes*.

1875   (July) O. Beccari; Kofiau I. GENOA.
During thirty hours on this island forty specimens were secured.

1875   (May and November) collectors for A. A. Bruijn; Salawati I. TRING.

1875   collectors for A. A. Bruijn; Kofiau I. Destination of specimens?

1878   Raffray. Waigeu, Salawati and Batanta Is. PARIS. *Diphyllodes respublica.*

1878   M. Laglaize; Waigeu I. PARIS.

1878   (April) M. Laglaize; Batanta I. PARIS. *Diphylodes respublica.*

1879   (July) collectors for A. A. Bruijn; Batanta I. TRING; LONDON; PARIS. *Diphyllodes respublica.*

1879   hunters for A. A. Bruijn; Waigeu I. TRING.
Although chiefly engaged in the plume trade, Bruijn made special efforts to obtain scientific material through his native collectors. One such specimen obtained was an unknown megapode collected about 1879 on Waigeu Island (*Aepypodius bruijnii*). This wonderful new species, although searched for by many expeditions, was not rediscovered until 1938 (see Schauensee, 1940).

1883   J. J. Labillardiere; Waigeu I. TRING.

1883   (24–31 October, probably also November) F. H. H. Guillemard; Waigeu I. (Momos Village area). TRING; GENOA.
Collected birds of paradise and other species during stopover of the voyage of the *Marchesa* (see Guillemard, 1886).

1883 and 1884   (November and February) Carl Platen; Waigeu I. BERLIN.
Birds of paradise were included among the 656 scientific bird skins collected.

1883   (October) R. Powell; Waigeu (Chabiol Bay). TRING.

1883   (November) R. Powell; Salawati I. (Samatee). TRING.

1883   (December) R. Powell; Misol I. TRING.

1900   (January and February) Heinrich Kühn; Misol I. TRING.

1902   (November) F. H. H. Guillemard; Misol and Salawati Is. GENOA; TRING.

1902 to 1903   (26 November–27 January) Johannes Waterstradt; Waigeu I. COPENHAGEN; TRING.

1903   (April) J. Waterstradt; Gebe I. COPENHAGEN; TRING.

1906   (November) W. Goodfellow; Waigeu I. (Sassas). LONDON.

1909   to 1910 (17 December–27 January) L. F. de Beaufort; Waigeu I. (Saonek region).
Observations only. (Beaufort, 1914).

1930   (March) J. C. Frost; Salawati I. TRING.

1931   (6 May–16 June) Mr and Mrs Georg Stein; Waigeu I. BERLIN; TRING.
Secured 110 species of which 7 were described as new sub-species and 14 were new to the known avifauna of this island.

1934   (April) W. J. C. Frost; Batanta I. LONDON.

1934   (May) W. J. C. Frost; Waigeu I. LONDON.

1934   (May) W. J. C. Frost; Salawati I. LONDON.

1936   (25 November) E. Jacobson; Waigeu I. BOGOR. *Paradisaea rubra*.

1937   (19–23 October) S. Dillon Ripley; Schildpad Is. (Lophon, Kam Wa, Marian, and Jef Fa). PHILADELPHIA.

1937   (October–November) S. Dillon Ripley; Misol I. (vicinity of Tip Village on Kassim River). PHILADELPHIA.
Ripley, ornithologist of the Denison–Crockett South Pacific Expedition, made comprehensive collections of birds on this island. Among his discoveries are a new race of bower bird, the Green Catbird (*Ailuroedus crassirostris misolensis*), and a new race of the Lesser Bird of Paradise (*Paradisaea minor pulchra*). Discovery of this species on Misol came as a surprise because Wallace had looked there in vain for it.

1938   S. Dillon Ripley; Salawati and Sagewin Is. PHILADELPHIA.
37 species.

1938   S. Dillon Ripley; Batanta I. PHILADELPHIA.
50 species mostly from Mondok (near Yenanas), Aijem and Mt Behenoe.

1938   (November and December) Joseph Khakiaj; Waigeu I. (Saonek, Nafer Baai, Mt Lapon, Linsok). PHILADELPHIA.
268 study skins of 91 species. Included was the long missing megapode (see above) (*Aepypodius bruijnii*), a rare ground pigeon (*Otidiphaps nobilis*), 3 species of birds of paradise (*Manucodia ater, Diphyllodes respublica, Paradisaea rubra*) and one bower bird (*Ailuroedus buccoides*).

1948 (September and October) Sten Bergman; Waigeu and Saonek Is. STOCKHOLM.

62 species (approximately 168 specimens). Bergman was on Saonek 14–15 September and 11–13 October. On Waigeu, where he found *Paradisaea rubra* and *Diphyllodes respublica*, he remained a month.

1949 (31 May) S. Bergman; Batanta I. BOGOR. *Paradisaea rubra*.

1954 Dr and Mrs S. Dillon Ripley; Misol I. NEW HAVEN.

1955 (25 April–9 May) J. Khakiaj (collector for S. Dillon Ripley); Kofiau I. NEW HAVEN.

1955 (1 September) J. Khakiaj (collector for S. Dillon Ripley); Ajoe I. (25 miles north of Waigeu I.). NEW HAVEN.

1964 (15 June–8 July) E. T. Gilliard and S. Somadikarta with taxidermists Toha and Tojibun (conducting a joint expedition of the American Museum of Natural History and the Museum Zoologicum Bogoriense); Batanta I. (inland from Wailabet village). 230 bird skins of 61 species including *Diphyllodes respublica, Paradisaea rubra, Ailuroedus buccoides, Manucodia ater.*

3: Vogelkop

1824 René P. Lesson; Dorey Bay. PARIS.

Lesson was the first naturalist to observe birds of paradise in the wild. He saw the Lesser Bird of Paradise (*Paradisaea minor*) and the King Bird of Paradise (*Cicinnurus regius*) in the forests bordering Dorey Harbour and in the same region collected from natives a total of 4 species of birds of paradise, *P. minor, C. regius, Phonygammus keraudrenii, Manucodia ater*), and one bower bird (*Sericulus aureus*). Lesson served as general naturalist and ship's apothecary aboard the exploring corvette *Coquille* which encircled the world under command of Duperrey and Dumont d'Urville. Later, in January 1824 in Sydney, Australia, Lesson purchased a skin of the then unknown Paradise Riflebird (*Ptiloris paradiseus*) which came from the northern part of New South Wales (see Stresemann, 1954). He thus extended the range of the family to Australia.

1827 (25 August–6 September): J. R. C. Quoy and J. P. Gaimard; Dorey Bay. PARIS.

Quoy and Gaimard, naturalists aboard the *Astrolabe*, under

the command of Dumont d'Urville, collected birds and other natural history specimens during this period.

1855   Renesse van Duivenbode accompanied by Prince Ali of Tidore; north foothills of Tamrau Mountains via Mega Village; all or nearly all of the birds of paradise collected were for the feather trade (see Mayr and de Schauensee, 1939: 101).

1858   (11 April–29 July) A.R. Wallace; Dorey Bay. LONDON.

Wallace was ill during almost the entire period of his visit to Dorey, being confined to his home for more than a month with an infected foot. Wallace, who wrote of Lesson's splendid observations '40 years earlier' was greatly disappointed by his confinement, which resulted in his being unable to see any birds of paradise himself. His collectors in the Dorey area, however, obtained the Lesser Bird of Paradise (*Paradisaea minor*), the Magnificent Rifle Bird (*Ptiloris magnificus*), and the Golden Bower Bird (*Sericulus aureus*). For much of his stay he was 'the only European resident of the great island of New Guinea.' However, the Dutch warship *Etna* was in the harbour during his stay on the shore. Aboard this vessel was the German naturalist C.E.H. von Rosenberg with two bird skinners. Rosenberg had a specimen of unknown origin of the Black Astrapia Bird of Paradise (*Astrapia nigra*) which he showed to Wallace. Wallace travelled to and from Dorey on trading vessels belonging to Renesse van Duivenbode of Ternate. He began his trip at Ternate on 25 March.

1858   collectors for A.R. Wallace; Amberbaki. LONDON.

While Wallace lay sick at Dorey he dispatched his native collectors on a two-week reconnaissance to hunt for birds of paradise on the northwestern slopes of the Arfak Mountains. They obtained only one species, the King Bird of Paradise (*Cicinnurus regius*).

1861   C. Allen; Sorong area. LONDON.

Collecting for Wallace, Allen worked in this area for about a month searching for birds of paradise known only from trade skins.

1863–68   D.S. Hoedt; Vogelkop and Western Papuan islands. LEIDEN.

1858–70   C.E.H. von Rosenberg; Vogelkop. LEIDEN.

Rosenberg sent Papuan hunters into little-known areas such as the Arfak Mountains. In this way he obtained many rare species including the new genus *Amblyornis inornatus*.

1871–76 hunters for A.A.Bruijn; Manokwari region (January and April, 1875); Sorong region (March and April, 1875); Mansinam Island (May, 1875); mountains behind Andai (June, 1875); Arfak Mts. (February, 1876); Warmendi, Arfak Mts (25 January 1876).

1872 Count Luigi Maria D'Albertis and O.Beccari; western Vogelkop. GENOA.
En route to Manokwari, collected around Sorong and at the Ramoi, the Mariati and the Waron rivers.

1872 Count L.M.D'Albertis and O.Beccari; Amberbaki region. GENOA.
14 species including *Paradisaea minor* and *Ptiloris magnificus*.

1872 Count L.M.D'Albertis and O.Beccari; Arfak Mts. GENOA. The Count, often in company with Beccari, explored in the eastern Vogelkop. Together they found many new birds, including the Black-billed Sickle-billed Bird of Paradise (*Drepanornis albertisii*) and the Golden Regent Bower Bird (*Sericulus aureus*) which, natives told them, 'nested' on the ground.

1872 (September) O.Beccari; highlands of the Arfak Mts. GENOA.
Beccari, the first European to climb these mountains, was richly rewarded by being able to observe in the wild many species of birds theretofore known only from native trade skins. Among these were the Arfak Six-wired Bird of Paradise (*Parotia sefilata*), the Superb Bird of Paradise (*Lophorina superba superba*) and the Black Sickle-billed Bird of Paradise (*Epimachus fastosus fastosus*); but Beccari's most extraordinary discovery was that of the bower of the Vogelkop Gardener Bower Bird (*Amblyornis inornatus*).

1875 O.Beccari; Sorong region; GENOA.
1875 (4–29 February) O.Beccari; mountains near extreme west of Vogelkop. GENOA.
In company with a team of A.A.Bruijn's hunters, Beccari went some 15 miles inland between Dorey Hum Bay and the War Samson River. 67 species.

1875   (April–May) O. Beccari; Arfak Mts. GENOA; BERLIN.
Beccari climbed the Arfak Mountains a second time discovering the home grounds of the Long-tailed Paradigalla (*P. carunculata*), a male with Beccari's original label in Berlin. He also collected a series of *Epimachus fastosus* and *Astrapia nigra*.

1876   (May) Leon Laglaize; Arfak Mts. (Woipirboe). PARIS; LONDON. *Amblyornis inornatus*.

1876   (August) A. A. Bruijn; Arfak Mts. *Amblyornis inornatus*.

1877   (February–March) Raffray; Dorey. PARIS. *Phonygammus, Manucodia, Paradisaea minor*.

1877   (June) Raffray; Amberbaki region (inland 5 miles to 1800 ft near village of Memiaona). PARIS. *Ailuroedus buccoides, Paradigalla, Cicinnurus, Phonygammus, Sericulus, Manucodia, Epimachus fastosus, Parotia*.

1877   (March–May) L. Laglaize; Amberbaki region (inland 10 miles). PARIS. *Parotia* (Karous); *Phonygammus, Ailuroedus buccoides, A. crassirostris, Ptiloris, Epimachus fastosus, Paradisaea minor, Diphyllodes*.

1883   (November) F. H. H. Guillemard; Manokwari. GENOA.

1883   (November) R. Powell; Manokwari. LONDON.

1884   (May) L. Laglaize; Kafou. PARIS. *Ailuroedus buccoides*.

1887   (?) L. Laglaize; Arfak Mts. PARIS. *Lophorina, Seleucidis, Ptiloris*.

[1895   Lord Rothschild described *Ambylornis flavifrons* from a native-made skin from 'Dutch New Guinea'].

1896 and 1897   (October and June) W. Doherty; Manokwari. LONDON; TRING.

1899   (January) J. M. Dumas; Mt Moari. LONDON; TRING; BOGOR.
A collection containing many unusual species, including *Melampitta gigantea* which was long thought to have come from Hollandia region. However, after searching there in vain for rare Dumas collection birds, Ernst Mayr (1930b: 24) discovered that this collection had actually been made in the Arfak Mountains (Mt Moari, near Oransbari, between Andai and Momi).

1904   (?) G. Dehaut; PARIS. *Sericulus*.

1912   (June–July) K. Gjellerup and Feuilletau de Bruijn; Anggi Lakes. BOGOR. *Amblyornis inornatus*.

1921 (14 January) Obdyn; Manokwari region. BOGOR.

1928 (July–August) Fred Shaw Mayer; Arfak Mts. TRING.
At 4000 ft Shaw Mayer was shown a bower which natives said belonged to *Sericulus aureus*.

1928 (7–14 April) Ernst Mayr; Manokwari area. TRING.

1928 (14 April–4 July) E. Mayr; Arfak Mts. TRING.
Comprehensive collections, particularly of mountain species. Mayr went to Momi Village, then inland to Siwi, Ninei, Ditschi, Anggi Gita (lakes), collecting to an altitude of about 7700 ft. Mayr was shown bowers said to belong to *Sericulus aureus*.

1929 Ex–King (then Crown Prince) Leopold of Belgium; Sorong, Manokwari and Anggi Gita in the Arfak Mts. BRUSSELS.
About 21 species.

1930 (February) W. J. C. Frost; N.W. New Guinea. LONDON.

1931 (February) G. Stein; Manokwari. BERLIN.

1931 (July) W. J. C. Frost; N. W. New Guinea near Sorong. LONDON.

1934 (May) W. J. C. Frost. N. W. New Guinea. LONDON.

1937 (15–21 November) S. Dillon Ripley; Manokwari region (Andai, Mansinam Island and Manokwari). PHILADELPHIA.

1938 (22 January–7 February) S. Dillon Ripley; Sorong region (the shore islands of Dom, Tsiof and Efman and the Ramoi and Waron Rivers were collected in 1937). PHILADELPHIA.

1938 (9 February–1 April) S. Dillon Ripley; Tamrau Mts. PHILADELPHIA
Ripley collected in the north watershed of the eastern Tamrau Range to a maximum elevation of 5200 ft on Mt Bon Kourangen (where he collected for 16 days). Access was via the coastal villages of Sausapor, Djokdjeroi and Wejos. He also collected in the south watershed after crossing the divide near Bamoskaboe (2300 ft) to villages at the head-waters of the Kamoendan River.

1938 (May and September) collectors for S. D. Ripley revisited these areas. PHILADELPHIA.

1938 (? May–August) collectors for S. Dillon Ripley of the Denison–Crockett Expedition; Tamrau Mts. PHILADELPHIA.
Collectors 'Joseph' and 'Saban' collected at north coast village of Mega, central Tamrau range, then at various places as far as 60 air miles inland to the headwaters of the Kela

427

Moek River.

1942–44 Yoko-oji; Manokwari area. JAPAN. (see Kuroda, 1958). The entire collection except for 7 skins was destroyed by fire in 1945.

1948–49 S. Bergman with his assistant the Swedish preparator H. Sjoquist (accompanied by two assistants from the Buitenzorg Museum); Sorong region. STOCKHOLM; BOGOR.
A comprehensive survey for birds was carried out in the Sorong region in July, August, November, December, February, and April.

1949 S. Bergman *et. al.*; north watershed of Vogelkop near McCluer Gulf. STOCKHOLM.
The Bergman party made a long trip inland from Inanwatan to Amaru Lakes.

1949 (July, August and September) S. Bergman; Anggi Lakes, Arfak Mts. STOCKHOLM; BOGOR.
Bergman and his collectors travelled from Manokwari to Ransiki, thence inland to Anggi Lakes and higher points. Bergman not only obtained a splendid collection of scientific skins (including *Parotia*, *Amblyornis* and *Lophorina*), but he collected 6 species of birds of paradise alive. He transported these to Sweden where he succeeded in breeding the King Bird of Paradise (*Cicinnurus regius*).

1961 (9 September) R. Versteegh; Kebar Valley (750 m). BOGOR.

1961 (26 October) R. Versteegh. Ransiki, Vogelkop. BOGOR. *Chlamydera cerviniventris.*

1962 (January) R. Versteegh, collecting for L. and S. Quate; Kebar Valley (1700 feet). HONOLULU; NEW YORK.
59 species including *Phonygammus*, *Cicinnurus*, *Paradisaea*, *Chlamydera cerviniventris.*

1963 (19 January–1 March) Max C. Thompson, Larry P. Richards, Philip Temple; Oransbari (50 ft). HONOLULU.
About 150 study skins including 5 species of birds of paradise.

1964 (15 July–15 August) E. T. Gilliard, accompanied by P. Suparlan and taxidermists Toha and Tojibun. Tamrau Mts.

4: Bombarai Peninsula

1860 (?) C. E. H. von Rosenberg; vicinity of Fak Fak. LEIDEN; TRING.

1948–49 (December–January) S. Bergman; Pulu Adi (off south

tip of peninsula). STOCKHOLM.

5: Wandammen Region

1897   W. Doherty; Wandammen Mts. TRING.
1928   (5 July to about 26 July) E. Mayr; Wandammen Mts. TRING.
        Mayr, having entered by way of Wasior and Wondowoi
        villages, ascended to about 4500 ft where he collected many
        birds of paradise and observed many bowers of *Amblyornis
        inornatus*.
1930   (September) F. Shaw Mayer; Wandammen Mts. TRING.
1949   (August and September) S. Bergman; Wandammen Penin-
        sula. STOCKHOLM.
        Bergman *et. al.* entered the peninsula via the west coast
        village of Miei, then walked to the village of Wasior where
        he remained ten days. Here he obtained many living birds of
        paradise, including *Parotia sefilata*.

6: Islands of Geelvink Bay

1869   (19 January–2 March) H. von Rosenberg; Numfor I. LEIDEN.
1869   (12 March–3 April) H. von Rosenberg; Biak I. LEIDEN.
1869   (5 April–6 May) H. von Rosenberg; Japen I. LEIDEN.
1873   (19–22 March) Adolf Bernhard Meyer; Numfor I. DRESDEN.
        Meyer managed to obtain a good collection in this limited
        space of time.
1873   (March and April) A. B. Meyer; Biak I. DRESDEN.
1873   (8–29 April) A. B. Meyer; Japen I. DRESDEN.
        70 species.
1875   (4–14 April and 11–14 December) O. Beccari; Japen I.
        GENOA.
1875   (May) O. Beccari; Biak I. GENOA.
1875   (26 May–1 June) O. Beccari; Numfor I. GENOA.
1875 and 1885   collectors for A. A. Bruijn; Japen I. TRING.
1878 (?)   L. Laglaize; Japen I. PARIS. A series of *Paradisaea minor*.
1879   collectors for A. A. Bruijn; Biak Island ('Kordo'). TRING.
1883   (November) F. H. H. Guillemard; Japen I. GENOA; TRING.
        A small collection was secured during a short visit of the
        yacht *Marchesa*.
1896   (October) and 1897 W. Doherty; Biak I. TRING; LONDON.

1897 (April and May) W. Doherty; Japen I. TRING; LONDON.

1897 (May and June) W. Doherty; Numfor I. LONDON; TRING.

1897 (July) W. Doherty; 'Ron' I. [= Rani Island?].

1903 (July) L. F. de Beaufort and H. A. Lorentz; Biak I.

1915 F. de Bruijn; Biak I. BOGOR.
A small collection, chiefly from the north coast (Warsa, Wai, Bonnik).

1931 (20 February–26 March) Mr and Mrs G. Stein; Japen I. BERLIN.
A large collection including many birds of paradise.

1931 (10–25 April) Mr and Mrs G. Stein; Numfor I. BERLIN.

1937 (November and December) S. Dillon Ripley; Biak I. PHILADELPHIA. 302 specimens.
Ripley worked chiefly in the vicinity of Korrido Village and inland to an altitude of about 2200 feet. Some collecting was also done on Rani Island eight miles southwest of Korrido.

1953–54 (July–December) C. Hoogerheide; Biak I. LEIDEN.

1962 (October–November) Nixon Wilson and L. P. Richards; Nabire, Japen I. HONOLULU.
A small collection.

1963 (15–29 March) M. C. Thompson and P. Temple; Biak I. HONOLULU.
About 30 specimens.

7: North-western Lowlands

(Localities between Mamberamo River delta and Humboldt Bay)

1873–78 (?) hunters for A. A. Bruijn; Tarawai I. (Bertrand I.) GENOA; PARIS?
Count Salvadori studied a small collection from this island a few miles west of Hollandia.

1880 (early) L. Laglaize (leader of a party of hunters in the employ of the merchant A. A. Bruijn); Kave (across from Bertrand I.) PARIS, DRESDEN.
Two new species, *Manucodia jobiensis* and *Drepanornis bruijnii*, the latter apparently from the east coast of Geelvink Bay, were discovered. A specimen from 'Tabi' (*D. bruijnii*) is in Paris.

1896 Ludwig Biró; Tarawai Island. BUDAPEST.

430

1896 and 1897 (October–May) W. Doherty; Takar, Kapur, Sarmi, and Waropen. LONDON; TRING.

Doherty collected methodically during this period: Takar, October and November; Kapur, December and January; Sarmi, January and February; Waropen, Mt Kurudy, April and May; in 1897 he also collected along the Witriwai River some 50 miles west of Hollandia.

1902 (?) F. L. de Beaufort; Hollandia region. LONDON.

1904 (June) W. Goodfellow; Sekar, N.W. New Guinea. LONDON.

1906 (July, Aug., Sept.) W. Goodfellow; Humboldt Bay. LONDON.

1910 (April–May) L. Schultze; Tami, Mündung. BERLIN. *Paradisaea, Ptiloris.*

1911 (January, June and October) K. Gjellerup; Sentani Lake and Cyclops Mts. BOGOR. *Diphyllodes.*

1911 (October) K. Gjellerup; Tami River. BOGOR.

1914 (April) Y. G. ; 'Pionierbivak', Mamberamo River. BOGOR.

1920 (July–December) W. C. van Heurn; sea level to 4500 ft. Many birds of paradise including *Drepanornis bruijnii* from Pionierbivak and a new race of Six Wired Bird of Paradise (*Parotia carolae chalcothorax*) from Doormanpad–bivak (1410 m).

1920 (September, November, December). W. C. van Heurn; Mamberamo and Idenburg rivers. BERLIN; BOGOR.

1928 (18 August–14 September) E. Mayr; Cyclops Mountain region. TRING.

Mayr collected to the summit of the Cyclops Mountains (6940 ft).

1928 (August and October) E. Mayr; Humboldt Bay region. TRING.

Mayr collected around Hollandia in August and October. In October his collectors visited the Hol Village area near the mouth of Tami River where they obtained a series of *Drepanornis bruijnii.*

1928 (September and October) E. Mayr; Lake Sentani region. TRING.

Mayr made a comprehensive survey of lowland birds which included the Fawn-breasted Bower Bird (*Chlamydera cerviniventris*).

1938 and 1939 Third Archbold Expedition to New Guinea (Richard Archbold, A. L. Rand, W. B. Richardson, L. J. Brass); Hollandia region and Cyclops Mts. NEW YORK.

Examples of all species collected are at BOGOR.

1938–39 Third Archbold Expedition to New Guinea, Upper Idenburg River. NEW YORK. Examples of all species collected are at BOGOR.

A comprehensive collection.

1939 (July and November) J. P. K. van Eechoud; Pioneer Bivouac, Mamberamo River. BOGOR.

1939 (July–December) Ch. F. van Krieken; Siriwo River (Ta River tributary), east coast of Geelvink Bay. BOGOR.

1939 (November) J. P. K. van Eechoud. 'Pionierbivak', Mamberamo River. BOGOR.

8: Triton Bay—Etna Bay Region

1828 H. C. Macklot and Salomon Muller; Lobo, Triton Bay. LEIDEN.

The White-eared Catbird (*Ailuroedus buccoides*) was discovered.

1896 (July) Captain Cayley Webster; Triton Bay. LONDON; TRING.

1896 (August) Captain C. Webster; Etna Bay. LONDON; TRING.

1896–1900 ? H. Kuhn; Etna Bay. LEIDEN; TRING.

1904 J. W. R. Koch; Etna Bay. LONDON.

1939 (August and November) collectors for H. Boschma; Etna Bay. LEIDEN.

9: Nassau-Weyland Mountain Region

1909–11 B. O. U. Expedition (Walter Goodfellow, Wilfred Stalker, A. F. R. Wollaston, Claude H. B. Grant, G. Chester Shortridge); Nassau Range (south watershed). LONDON.

This expedition climbed the southern slopes of Mt Leonard Darwin by way of the Mimika River. Great difficulties were encountered; Stalker died; comprehensive collections were made but few birds were obtained above 4000 ft.

1911 (March) Geschenk; Eilanden River (1700 m.). BOGOR. *Paradigalla brevicauda*.

1912–13 A. F. R. Wollaston Expedition (A. F. R. Wollaston, C. Boden Kloss, Lieut. Van der Water); Nassau Range (south watershed). LONDON.

This highly successful expedition ascended to Carstensz peak, (15,800 ft) by way of the Utakwa and Setakwa rivers. The expedition team collected near and above snowline (30 January and 1 February 1913); the actual summit (500 ft higher) was not reached; 1300 scientific studyskins of birds were obtained; many represent new races; no new species were discovered.

1920–21 (October–January) Pratt Brothers; Weyland Mts. (north watershed). LONDON (?); TRING.

Mt Kunupi (6000 ft), Weyland Mts. (October–December); Wangger River (January). [1920 A. E. Pratt, at Hambitawuria (1500 ft) obtained the nest and eggs of the Lesser Bird of Paradise, *Paradisaea minor*.] The three Pratt brothers explored Mt Kunupi (which they reached by way of the Wangger River) to an altitude of about 6400 feet; they found the Wattle-billed Bird of Paradise (*Loboparadisea sericea*), the Splendid Astrapia Bird of Paradise (*Astrapia splendidissima*) and the King of Saxony Bird of Paradise (*Pteridophora alberti*).

1920 and 1923 (May and 14–21 September) Thomas Jackson; Eilanden River region, Dutch New Guinea'. BRISBANE, CAMBRIDGE.

A small collection.

1930 (about June) F. Shaw Mayer; Weyland Mts. (north watershed). TRING.

Shaw Mayer explored the Weylands by way of the Siriwo River. He obtained a comprehensive collection, including examples of a new race of Lauterbach's Bower Bird (*Chlamydera lauterbachi uniformis*) which he observed in its bower.

1931 Mr and Mrs G. Stein; Weyland Mts. (north watershed). BERLIN.

The Steins explored the Weyland Mountains while attempting to reach the Snow Mountains. They made a comprehensive collection which included *Astrapia splendidissima*, *Loboparadisea*, *Pteridophora*, *Loria*, and *Amblyornis macgregoriae*.

1938 (October) J. P. K. van Eechoud; Wissel Lake region. LEIDEN.

Included in the small collection (but unrecognised) was a specimen of an unknown genus of bower bird which, two years later, was found elsewhere and described as a new genus and species, *Archboldia papuensis*.

1939 (August–November) H. Boschma. Wissel Lakes region. LEIDEN.

1939 (16 November) C.F. van Krieken; Siriwo River. BOGOR. *Chlamydera lauterbachi* was found at 30 m.

1962 (July) N. Wilson and Horrie Clissold; Enarotali; Wissel Lakes (6200 ft). HONOLULU.

10: Oranje, Snow and Star Ranges

1910–11 (December–March) Albert S. Meek; Mt Goliath. TRING. Meek, aided by a Dutch military patrol, ascended Mt Goliath via the Eilanden River to about 8000–9000 feet. There he discovered one new species of bird of paradise, the Short-tailed Paradigalla (*Paradigalla brevicauda*) and the home grounds of three extraordinary species of birds of paradise which had been known only from vaguely labelled specimens of commercial origin, the Wattle-billed Bird of Paradise (*Loboparadisea sericea*), the Splendid Astrapia Bird of Paradise (*Astrapia splendidissima*) and the extraordinary King of Saxony Bird of Paradise (*Pteridophora alberti*).

1912 (?) J. W. R. Koch and H. A. Lorentz; Snow Mountains (south watershed). LEIDEN.
Koch and Lorentz, via the Lorentz River from Flamingo Bay, ascended to the summit of Mt Wilhelmina – a remarkable feat of exploration. They discovered many new species including an unknown genus and species of mountain quail (*Anurophasis monorthonyx*), but found no unknown species of birds of paradise or bower birds. In all they collected nearly 4000 scientific skins. This was the third of three Dutch expeditions which, since 1907, had attempted to explore Mt Wilhelmina via Flamingo Bay (see E.D. van Oort, 1910).

1938–39 (May–May) Third Archbold Expedition to New Guinea. (R. Archbold, A. L. Rand, W. B. Richardson, L. J. Brass); Snow Mountains (north to south watershed). NEW YORK. Examples of each species collected are at BOGOR.
This expedition made the most comprehensive collection of birds ever obtained in New Guinea. The range was surveyed

434

from near sea level to more than 15,000 ft (just below the summit of Mt Wilhelmina). Of the 380 forms collected, 40 were new sub-species, 4 were new species, and one of the new species was also a new genus, Archbold's Bower Bird (*Archboldia papuensis*). Many important field observations were made including observations of the nesting habits of Macgregor's Bird of Paradise (*Macgregoria pulchra*) and the courtship behaviour of the Magnificent Bird of Paradise (*Diphyllodes magnificus*).

1959 (April–August) and 1962 Robert G. Gardner, Peter Matthiessen, Michael Rockefeller; Snow Mountains. CAMBRIDGE.
In 1962 Michael Rockefeller disappeared at sea in the Eilanden River area.

1959 (April–August) Star Mountains. LEIDEN.
The Royal Netherlands Geographic Society and the Netherlands Association for Research in Natural History in co-operation with the Netherlands Government sent a large party under leadership of L. D. Brongersma and G. F. Venema to explore the Star Mountains via the Sibil Valley. Scientific bird skins and observations were collected by J. J. Staats on Mt Antares, also in the Sibil Valley, and by F. Scharff up to the summit region of Mt Juliana.
(see Brongersma and Venema, 1962).

1960–61 Dr and Mrs S. Dillon Ripley; Snow Mountains (north watershed). NEW HAVEN.

1961 Laurence W. Quate; Star Mountains HONOLULU.
Quate obtained a small collection in the Sibil Valley at Aliemkop (3900 ft).

1963–64 (December–February) Tjendrawasih I Expedition (Mr Boeadi coll.); Nassau to Snow Mts. BOGOR. A small collection from mid mountains (south watershed) between Wisselmeren and Baliem valley. Localities visited: Titigina, Homejo, Beoga (1960 m), Keniri, Komopa (1765 m), Hitalipa (1500 m), Nabire, Baliem.

11 : Aru Islands

1857 (8 January–2 July) A. R. Wallace, Kobrur I. LONDON.
Wallace was at Dobo 8 to 13 January. He then crossed to

the main island and went into the interior where he remained during most of March, April, and May. He then returned ill to Dobo. Wallace observed and collected 2 species of birds of paradise, *Paradisaea apoda apoda* and *Cicinnurus regius regius* and one bower bird, *Ailuroedus crassirostris*.

1870–72 Samuel White (assisted by two collectors, James Cockerill and F.W.Andrews), destination of specimens and journals (which were sold at auction) unknown.

White conducted a two-year expedition to Cape York (Australia), New Guinea and the Aru Islands on the schooner *Elsie*. Mutiny, sickness and disaster dogged White's trail and very few of his specimens were saved for science.

1873 J.Cockerill and son; Aru Is. destination of specimens unknown. Of this expedition Captain John (James) Moresby of H.M.S. *Basilisk* wrote: 'On 18 January [1873] we took up our old anchorage off Somerset [Cape York] . . . whilst here we fell in with a lonely waif of society, named Cockerill, who has betaken himself to live in a tiny vessel of about eight tons, and accompanied only by his son and two natives, cruised about these seas as a naturalist, and seems to be happy enough in his own way. His boat was laden with specimens of beautiful birds; and from the Aru Islands, 500 miles west of Somerset, which he had just left, he had brought some boxes full of the Great Bird of Paradise, and the still more exquisite King Bird of Paradise, of which he kindly gave me a specimen.'

1894 C.G.Forest; Aru Is. *Ailuroedus melanotis*.

1896 (May and June) Captain C.Webster; Dobo. LONDON; TRING.

1897 (February) W.Doherty; Dobo. LONDON; TRING.

1896, 1897, 1900 H.Kühn; Aru Is. LONDON; TRING.

Kühn is known to have worked in the Dobo area in 1896, and in February, May, and November 1897; also in August and September 1900. Specimens presumed to have been collected by him were taken the same year, 1900, at Soenigi Barkai, at Kobror Island in August and September; also at Trangen Island in September. During these years Kühn obtained an egg of the Glossy-mantled Manucode (*Manucodia ater*).

1904 (February–April) W.Goodfellow; Aru Is. (Silbattabatta). LONDON.

1908–09   W. J. C. Frost; Aru I. LONDON. Little Tobago I. (living specimens).

Frost succeeded in capturing many specimens of *Paradisaea apoda*. Some 47 of these survived a long trip via England to America and were released on Little Tobago between the years 1909 and 1912 (see Appendix I). Wild descendants of this stock still survive on Little Tobago Island in the Caribbean Sea near Venezuela.

1914   (May) W. J. C. Frost; Aru I. (Golili). LONDON. Egg of *Paradisaea apoda*.

1925   (August) W. J. C. Frost; Aru I. LONDON. Egg of *Paradisaea apoda*.

1929   (March) W. J. C. Frost; Aru I. (Kobroor). LONDON. One egg of *Cicinnurus regius*.

1930   W. J. C. Frost, Aru Islands; destination of specimens unknown. One studyskin in the American Museum of Natural History of *Otidiphaps nobilis* (AMNH, 616496) was collected alive by Frost in the Aru Islands in 1930. He probably also collected specimens of birds of paradise on this visit.

1935   (January–February) Soekarno Wakoea; Aru I. BOGOR. A large series of *Cicinnurus*.

1964   (25 July–2 August) M. Djajasasmita; Dobo I., Aru I. BOGOR. A small collection.

12: Merauke Region

1902   A. E. Pratt and son Harry (16 years old); Merauke. LONDON. The Pratts reached Merauke (via Thursday Island and Etna Bay) two months after the station was opened, having gone there from England to collect birds. They remained only ten days because the Tugeri tribesmen were so hostile that collecting was impossible.

1910   (May) A. S. Meek; Merauke and points westward. TRING. Meek visited Merauke on his way to join a Dutch military expedition bound for the Oetakwa River.

1920–24   (September–November) T. Jackson; Merauke and points westward. CAMBRIDGE.

Jackson made a small collection in the vicinity of Merauke, the Endrich River, the Mapi River, the upper Digul River and Princess Marianne Straits.

1925   Dr Thierfelder; behind Merauke. BERLIN. *Sericulus aureus.*

1933   (September–October) Hans Nevermann; near Merauke (Toerey; Welbuti). BERLIN. *Sericulus aureus, Paradisaea apoda.*

1960–61   Andries Hoogerwerf; Merauke region. LEIDEN.

13: Fly River and Delta Region

1875–77   Count L. M. D'Albertis; Fly River. GENOA. Count D'Albertis using a steam launch made a comprehensive survey of the Fly River to a point well above the present location of Thompson's Junction. He discovered many new races of birds and a zone on the upper Fly River in which the Greater and the Raggiana birds of paradise hybridise.

1886   (October) W. W. Froggott; Fly River. BRISBANE. *Cicinnurus.*

1889   (December) Sir William Macgregor; Arowanga, Fly River. BRISBANE.

1920–21   John Todd Zimmer; Delta region (Kikori). NEW YORK.

1933–34   First Archbold Expedition to New Guinea (A. L. Rand, G. H. H. Tate, L. J. Brass); South New Guinea. NEW YORK. Comprehensive collections were made at Daru Island and on the mainland opposite Daru (Wuroi, Dogwa and Oriomo River); 14 new subspecies of birds were discovered.

1936–37   (February–January) Second Archbold Expedition to New Guinea) A. L. Rand, G. H. H. Tate, L. J. Brass); south central New Guinea and middle Fly River. NEW YORK. Comprehensive collections were made during a full year of exploration in the Wassi Kussa area (near Daru) and in the lower, middle, and upper Fly River, Palmer River and Black River regions. Rand made many valuable observations of breeding birds, including life history studies of the Glossy-mantled Manucode (*Manucodia ater*).

1961   Mr and Mrs Richard J. Schodde; Lake Kutubu region (2500 to 2700 ft). CANBERRA. 80 species were collected including four birds of paradise and one bower bird.

14: Dap, Hindenburg and Victor Emanuel Ranges

1936–37   Second Archbold Expedition to New Guinea (A. L. Rand, G. H. H. Tate, L. J. Brass); Dap Mts. NEW YORK. Approaching from the south, Tate led a forward element of this expedition into the foothills of the Dap range. As he was nearing the Victor Emanuel Mountains an aircraft was lost and the expedition had to be terminated. Before rafting out, Tate collected two birds of paradise, *Diphyllodes magnificus* and *Manucodia ater*.

1954 (19 March–29 May) E. Thomas and Margaret Gilliard; Hindenburg and Victor Emanuel Mts (4000 to 8200 ft) NEW YORK; CANBERRA.

97 species, including 10 species of birds of paradise and one bower bird. Two of the former were new races: the Splendid Astrapia Bird of Paradise (*Astrapia splendidissima elliott-smithi*) and Queen Carola's Bird of Paradise (*Parotia carolae clelandiae*).

15: Tari, Giluwe, Hagen Mountains

1938 F. Shaw Mayer; Wabag region. LONDON. Shaw Mayer obtained two feathers of an unknown species of bird of paradise which was named for him, *Astrapia mayeri,* the Ribbon-tailed Bird of Paradise (Stoner, 1939).

1945–47 Captain N. B. Blood; Mt Hagen region. SYDNEY.

Blood obtained many birds of paradise, including an adult male hybrid between the Blue Bird of Paradise (*Paradisaea rudolphi*) and the Red Raggiana (*Paradisaea raggiana*). He also discovered a new reddish race of the Sickle-crested Bird of Paradise (*Cnemophilus macgregorii sanguineus*) and obtained many examples of the recently discovered *Astrapia mayeri*.

1946 (October) F. Shaw Mayer; Mt Hagen. LONDON.

Membe (5000 ft). 8 miles east of Hagen range to Yanka and Welya region (10,000 ft). *Chlamydera lauterbachi, Cnemophilus macgregorii*.

1947 (June) F. Shaw Mayer; Tomba region, Mt Hagen. LONDON. *Cnemophilus macgregorii*.

1950 (1 July–30 July) E. T. Gilliard, Robert Doyle, William Lamont; Mt Hagen. NEW YORK; SYDNEY.

A general ornithological survey was made of the southern watershed from 7000 to 12,000 ft via the Tomba region. 591 study skins were collected; of these eight were new subspecies including a new race of Archbold's Bower Bird (*Archboldia papuensis sanfordi*); a new race of the Brown Sickle-billed

Bird of Paradise (*Epimachus meyeri bloodi*); and a new race of the King of Saxony Bird of Paradise (*Pteridophora alberti hallstromi*).

In all 7 species of birds of paradise and two species of bower birds were obtained. The bower of *Archboldia* was discovered for the first time; films were made of the King of Saxony Bird of Paradise displaying to a female; observations were made of Loria's Bird of Paradise (*Loria loriae*) displaying.

1950   F. Shaw Mayer; Wahgi region near Nondugl and neighbouring Wahgi Divide. LONDON

1950–51   (December–March) F. Shaw Mayer; Mt Hagen (Tomba region). LONDON. *Cnemophilus*.

1951   (March–July)   F. Shaw Mayer; Mt Giluwe. LONDON.
A comprehensive collection between about 7500 feet and 11,000 ft. *Archboldia papuensis sanfordi* was obtained.

1952   (11–18 May) E. T. Gilliard and R. Doyle; Mt Hagen (north flank from Baiyer Valley, 4000 to 9000 ft). NEW YORK; SYDNEY.
A small collection of birds of paradise was obtained including hybrids (*Astrapia stephaniae* x *Astrapia mayeri*).

1952   (September and October) F. Shaw Mayer; Loke Wan Tho, Mt Hagen (Tomba region); MALAYA.
Observations and many superb photographs of birds (including the first photograph of a wild bird of paradise at its nest; see Loke, 1957: 105).

1954   Norman Camps, Ellis Troughton; Mt Hagen (south watershed). SYDNEY.
A general survey of birds was made in the Wahgi Valley–Mt Hagen region.

1955–56   (January–March) and 1960 (September–December) Ralph Bulmer; Mt Hagen (north slope, 4000 to 12,000 ft). SYDNEY.
A comprehensive collection including many nests and eggs of birds of paradise and bower birds. Included were the nests and eggs of Princess Stephanie's Bird of Paradise (*Astrapia stephaniae*) the nest and egg of the Short-tailed Paradigalla (*Paradigalla brevicauda*) and many nests and eggs of Lauterbach's Bower Bird (*Chlamydera lauterbachi*).

1956   (24 February–5 March) Ralph N. H. Bulmer; Tari region (on old maps Hogeria). SYDNEY.

A small collection was made within two miles of the airfield. Included was the Blue Bird of Paradise (*Paradisaea rudolphi* subspecies?)

1956 (July) E. T. Gilliard; Mt Hagen (south watershed) 8500 ft. NEW YORK.
Observations were made of birds of paradise and bower birds including the first observations of courtship behaviour of Archbold's Bower Bird *Archboldia* at its bower; also observations of Macgregor's Bower Bird (*Amblyornis macgregoriae*) and of Ribbon-tailed Bird of Paradise (*Astrapia mayeri*).

1961 Mr and Mrs R. J. Schodde; Mt. Giluwe. CANBERRA.
Collections were made between 5900 and 11,000 ft. Of 76 species obtained, one was a bird of paradise and two were bower birds.

16: Kubor Mountains

1950 (16 May–1 June) E. T. Gilliard and R. Doyle; Kubor Mts. NEW YORK.
Omong River and Mt O'mar (5200 to 8500 ft); 89 species (240 study skins), including 8 species of birds of paradise, and two species of bower birds. One of the birds of paradise, the Sickle-crested Bird of Paradise (*Cnemophilus macgregorii kuboriensis*), was a new race. The nest and eggs of the Brown Sickle-billed Bird of Paradise (*Epimachus meyeri bloodi*) were discovered.

1950 (October–November) F. Shaw Mayer; Kubor Mts. LONDON.
Series: *Chlamydera lauterbachi* (Minj).
A general survey to 9000 ft via the Minj River.

1952 (26 March–15 July) E. T. and Margaret Gilliard, R. Doyle, Henry Kaltenthaler. NEW YORK; SYDNEY.
Life history studies were made of the King of Saxony Bird of Paradise (*Pteridophora alberti hallstromi*), the Count Raggi's Bird of Paradise (*Paradisaea raggiana salvadorii*), the Magnificent Bird of Paradise (*Diphyllodes magnificus hunsteini*), the Blue Bird of Paradise (*Paradisaea rudolphi margaritae*), the Superb Bird of Paradise (*Lophorina superba feminina*), Macgregor's Bower Bird (*Amblyornis macgregoria*) and Lauterbach's Bower Bird (*Chlamydera lauterbachi*).

1963 (June–September) Warren B. Hitchcock, W. Vink, R. Pullen;

Kubor Mts. CANBERRA.

According to the magazine *Pacific Islands Monthly* (Sydney, Australia, November 1963), this team ascended the Kubor Range in the Minj – Nona Divide area to an altitude of 13,570 ft (Mt Milyin Kolyin the 'rock finger' which was first climbed by Father Schilling in 1959); 500 birds were collected at camps placed in the moss forest (9600 ft); alpine shrubbery (10,000 ft); and at a higher camp.

17: Regenberg, Lordberg, Schraderberg, Wahgi Divide, Bismarck and Kratke Mountains, and Mt Michael

1912 (20 November–14 December) Joseph Bürgers (with W. Behrmann?), German Sepik Expedition; Lordberg, 'Durchblick' (6000 ft). BERLIN.

1913 J. Bürgers with W. Behrmann (?), German Sepik Expedition; Regenberg (7–14 May), Schraderberg (20 May–24 June). BERLIN.

Important collections of high mountain species were obtained during this dangerous expedition. Many new birds were obtained including a new race of *Astrapia stephaniae,* and many extensions of ranges of mountain birds were discovered.

1932 (May–November) F. Shaw Mayer; Kratke Mts; Buntibasa district, 4000–5000 ft. LONDON.

1948–1954 (?) Capt. N. B. Blood; Wahgi Valley and surrounding mountains (Wahgi Divide, Hagen, Kubor).

With encouragement from Sir Edward Hallstrom, Blood established an aviary station at Nondugl. Many birds of paradise were kept there and many of them were ultimately shipped to foreign zoos. Blood also prepared many scientific specimens of Nondugl region birds which found their way to foreign museums. He was generous with these, giving many to itinerant collectors such as E. T. Gilliard, and Count Nils Gyldenstolpe.

1948 (January) Norman Chaffer; Wahgi Divide and Nondugl region. SYDNEY.

Chaffer studied the bowers and the bower behaviour of Lauterbach's Bower Bird (*Chlamydera lauterbachi*) and Macgregor's Bower Bird (*Amblyornis macgregoriae*); he also collected the nest and eggs of the latter.

442

1949   (June) F. Shaw Mayer; Mt Wilhelm (N. slopes). LONDON.

1950   (March–June) F. Shaw Mayer; Mt Wilhelm (N. and S. watershed). LONDON.
Study skins and living birds were collected. A live New Guinea Eagle (*Harpyopsis novaeguineae*) collected on Mt Wilhelm eventually reached the London Zoo, England.

1950   (17 April–14 May) E. T. Gilliard and R. Doyle; Nondugl region and adjacent parts of Wahgi Divide (5000 to 7000 ft). NEW YORK; SYDNEY.
A general collection was made; also observations of the courtship behaviour of King of Saxony Bird of Paradise (*Pteridophora alberti hallstromi*); 364 bird skins.

1950   (5–20 June): E. T. Gilliard and R. Doyle; Mt Wilhelm, Bismarck Range. NEW YORK; SYDNEY.
The upper portions (9000 ft to summit) of this mountain were thoroughly surveyed for birds; 61 species (204 study skins) were obtained, including one new species (*Melidectes princeps*) and 4 new subspecies of passerine birds, but no new birds of paradise or bower birds were found.

1951   (17 August–November) Count Nils and Lady Gyldenstolpe; Nondugl region and adjacent areas of Wahgi Divide mountains. STOCKHOLM.
A comprehensive collection was made from about 4000 to 9000 ft.

1954 (?)–1963   F. Shaw Mayer; Wahgi Valley and surrounding mountains (Wahgi Divide, Hagen, Kubor).
Shaw Mayer took over the management of the Nondugl aviaries, Wahgi Valley, on a full-time basis. Like Blood he purchased birds, chiefly birds of paradise, from natives who lived in the surrounding mountains. From time to time such collections were sent abroad. The origin of such birds is not always precisely known, some having been brought from as far away as 100 miles to be sold to Shaw Mayer.

1954   N. B. Blood (with Herman G. Slade, N. Camps, E. Troughton and Reginald McFazdean); Wahgi Divide and Jimi Valley. SYDNEY. General collections of birds including *Paradisaea rudolphi*.

1955   (June) R. N. H. Bulmer; South central Jimi Valley, from Wahgi Divide to Jimi River. Collection of 45? skins.

1957   (?) David Attenborough; Wahgi Valley, Jimi R., Bismarck and Schrader Mts. Films of New Guinea birds of paradise. About 20 birds of paradise taken alive for British Zoological Gardens.

1959   (June) E. T. Gilliard; Banz area, central Wahgi Valley. NEW YORK.
Life history studies and films of bower building in Lauterbach's Bower Bird.

1959   (May–June) Sixth Archbold Expedition to New Guinea (L. J. Brass, H. M. Van Deusen, J. D. Collins); Mt Wilhelm (8000 to 15,000 ft). NEW YORK.

1959   (August–September) Sixth Archbold Expedition to New Guinea (L. J. Brass, H. M. Van Deusen, J. D. Collins); Mt Michael (6000 to 12,000 ft). NEW YORK.

1959   (October) Sixth Archbold Expedition to New Guinea (L. J. Brass, H. M. Van Deusen, J. D. Collins); Kratke Mts. NEW YORK.

1960   (February) R. Bulmer; Schrader Mts (Kaironk River Valley, 5000 to 8500 ft).

1963–1964   (September–January, July–August): R. N. H. Bulmer; Kaironk Valley and adjacent spurs of Bismarck and Schrader Ranges. AUCKLAND. 253 specimens, many preserved in formalin, including *Astrapia stephaniae, Epimachus fastosus, E. meyeri, Loria, Cnemophilus* (sight record), *Parotia lawesi, Lophorina, Pteridophora, Amblyornis macgregoriae, Paradisaea minor, Diphyllodes magnificus.*

1964   (21 April–7 May) E. T. Gilliard; Schrader Mts (flank above Simbai Valley, watershed of Ramu River) 5700 ft to Mt Kominjim (8500 ft). 118 study skins; 125 specimens in formalin representing 55 species of birds, 47 of which came from above 7500 ft, plus 5 species sighted but not collected. Included are *Amblyornis macgregoriae, Epimachus meyeri, Astrapia stephaniae feminina* (including two specimens of hitherto unknown adult male); *Pteridophora alberti.*

18: Mountains of South-eastern New Guinea

1873, 1874–75, 1878–79   Kendall Broadbent, south-eastern New Guinea. BRISBANE.

1873   Sailors aboard corvette *Vettor Risani*, Orangerie Bay, GENOA.

444

En route to assist D'Albertis and Beccari, this corvette called here and obtained a new species; the Count Raggi's Bird of Paradise (*Paradisaea raggiana*) for D'Albertis.

1875 (July) Count L. M. D'Albertis; Hall Sound and Yule Island area. GENOA.
Observed *Paradisaea raggiana* in life.

1876–77 onward Andrew Goldie; Port Moresby region. LONDON.
Goldie, a Scottish bird collector and soldier of fortune, found gold in 1876 near Port Moresby; in 1877 he explored the Astrolabe Mountains.

1878 Carl Hunstein joined Andrew Goldie; Astrolabe Mts and mountains to east. Disposition of specimens unknown.
Hunstein, a German adventurer, discovered many new species of birds of paradise before his death by drowning (see page 455).

1881–83 William Denton and sons, Shelley W. and Sherman F.; Owen Stanley Mts. PITTSBURGH.
The Dentons (see Denton, 1889) made a comprehensive survey of the birds in the southern watershed of the Owen Stanley Mountains to about 3000 ft. Their specimens are from Port Moresby (58 specimens), Labitum (7 specimens), 35 miles east of Port Moresby (131 specimens), Laloki River (22 specimens), and the Sogeri region (5 specimens) 35 miles inland. William Denton died of fever far inland in the Owen Stanley Mountains. Koiari natives carried him to the village of Berrigabadi, 15 miles from Sogeri where he, the first American to collect birds in New Guinea, was buried 26 August 1883. His sons, then working nearer the sea coast, were then notified.

1883 C. Hunstein; Astrolabe Mts. GERMANY?
Hunstein discovered Lawes' Six-wired Bird of Paradise (*Parotia lawesi*) in these mountains.

1884 A. Goldie; Astrolabe Mts. LONDON.
Goldie discovered the female of an unknown bower bird which Sharpe, later that year, named *Amblyornis subalaris*.

1884 C. Hunstein; Mt Maguli, Owen Stanley Mts. DRESDEN.
Hunstein, going alone with one native to a point just a bit higher than William Denton a year earlier, discovered a treasure of four unknown species of birds of paradise, and bower birds; the unknown male of the Striped Gardener

445

Bower Bird (*Amblyornis subalaris*), the Brown Sickle-billed Bird of Paradise (*Epimachus meyeri*), the Trumpet Bird (*Phonygammus keraudrenii*), Princess Stephanie's Bird of Paradise (*Astrapia stephaniae*) and the Blue Bird of Paradise (*Paradisaea rudolphi*).

1885 (May) H. O. Forbes; Sogeri; district behind Port Moresby. PARIS. *Manucodia* (Meroka, 5000 ft, December); *Phonygammus*.

1889 Sir William Macgregor (accompanied by the collectors George Belford, Karl Kowald and A. P. Goodwin); Musgrave Mts (Mt Knutsford). BRISBANE.
Comprehensive collections were obtained which included one new species of bird of paradise, the Sickle-crested Bird of Paradise (*Cnemophilus macgregorii*) [type in BRISBANE, April 1964, no. M7126] and one new bower bird, Macgregor's Bower Bird (*Amblyornis macgregoriae*); also, the expedition discovered the bowers of the Striped Gardener Bower Bird (*Amblyornis subalaris*) and Macgregor's Bower Bird (*Amblyornis macgregoriae*).

1891 (26 June–25 July) Sir William Macgregor and R. E. Guise; Collingwood Bay and Mt Suckling. BRISBANE. *Parotia lawesi, Amblyornis subalaris* (4100 ft), *Manucodia ater*.

1892 (10 February) Otto Finsch; Port Moresby, BERLIN. *Chlamydera cerviniventris*.

1893 Lamberto Loria; Owen Stanley Mountains. ITALY.
Loria's Bird of Paradise (*Loria loriae*) was discovered.

1894 R. E. Guise (with W. E. Armit); Mt Dayman (then called Mt Maneao).

1895 R. E. Guise (with W. E. Armit); Mt Dayman (Mt Maneao). BRISBANE.
This expedition, directed by Sir William Macgregor, camped ten days in the alpine grasslands; 200 bird skins were collected.

1895 (July–August) A. S. Anthony; inland from Mailu Island (south watershed). TRING.

1895 (October) A. S. Anthony; Eafa District below Mt Alex and Mt Bellamy, Owen Stanley Mountains. TRING.

1896 (June–July) Sir William Macgregor; Orangerie and Cloudy bays. BRISBANE.

1896 (August–November) Sir William Macgregor; Mambare

River. BRISBANE.

1896 (September–October) Sir William Macgregor; Mt Scratchley. BRISBANE. Many high mountain species.

1896 (July–September) A.S.Anthony; Mt Cameron and Mt Victoria. TRING; PARIS (Gerrard coll.). *Diphyllodes magnificus, Loria loriae, Astrapia stephaniae, Epimachus meyeri, Paradisaea rudolphi* ('Mt Victoria').

1895–96 A.S.Anthony; south-eastern New Guinea. TRING.

During the course of Anthony's expeditions he made many discoveries. For example, he apparently found the nest and eggs of the Sickle-crested Bird of Paradise (*Cnemophilus macgregorii*) in the Musgrave Mountains (on Mt Knutsford) at an altitude of 11,000 feet. However, so strange was this nest and its eggs that the authorities at the Tring Museum refused to accept them as belonging to a bird of paradise. He also found the nest and egg of Lawes' Six-wired Bird of Paradise (*Parotia lawesi*, 6000 ft); the nest and eggs of the Superb Bird of Paradise (*Lophorina superba*); the egg of the Blue Bird of Paradise (*Paradisaea rudolphi*); the egg of Princess Stephanie's Bird of Paradise (*Astrapia stephaniae*); the nest and eggs of the Count Raggi's Bird of Paradise (*Paradisaea raggiana*); and the eggs of the Trumpet Bird (*Phonygammus keraudrenii*).

1896 Amedeo Giulianetti (Loria's former assistant); Wharton Range. BRISBANE.

Another expedition conducted under the direction of Sir William Macgregor. Giulianetti's best find was a new species of bird of paradise, the Macgregor's Bird of Paradise (*Macgregoria pulchra*).

1897 (March) Sir William Macgregor; Vanapa River. BRISBANE.

1897 (June) collector? Collingwood Bay, S.E. New Guinea. BERLIN. Two adult males of '*Paradisaea intermedia*'.

1897 (July and October) Sir William Macgregor; Wharton Range. BRISBANE.

Large series of high mountain birds, for example 9 *Macgregoria pulchra*.

1897–98 Emil Weiske; Owen Stanley Mountains (south watershed). TRING.

Weiske collected at the 'junction of Laloki and Vanapa Rivers' in 1897 and along the Brown River in 1898. He ascended the Owen Stanley Mountains to at least 4000 feet where he observed the bower behaviour of the Striped Gardener Bower Bird (*Amblyornis subalaris*) and collected the first egg and nest of this species.

1899 (27 May) A.S.Anthony; Vanapa River, S.E. New Guinea. Egg of *Seleucidis ignotus*.

1899–1900 E.Weiske; mountains of south-eastern New Guinea (Aroa River to 5000 feet).

1899 (May–June) A.S.Meek; Collingwood Bay and Milne Bay regions. LONDON.

1902 (August) A.E.Pratt; Keba, mountains of S.E. New Guinea (to at least 6000 ft). LONDON. *Paradisaea rudolphi*.

1903 (January–September) A.E.Pratt and son Harry; mountains behind Yule Island (to at least 3000 feet at Babooni and probably to 6000 ft). TRING. A specimen of *Astrapia stephaniae* at BERLIN was collected at 'Maful, 6000 ft' in August, 1903. Of his New Guinea experiences Pratt wrote: 'There is no paradise without its serpent.'

1903 A.S.Meek; Aroa River (south watershed of the Wharton Range). TRING.
In 1903 Meek spent about three months (January through March) some 60 miles inland on 'Manna Manna Mountain'. He wrote that (Meek, 1913: 111) he spent six weeks on the way to Okuma (2000 ft) and three months at Bwoidunna (3000 ft).

1905 (February) A.S.Meek; Angabunga River (Owgarra), base of Wharton Range. TRING.

1905 (April and May) A.S.Meek; Aroa River region (south watershed of Wharton Range). TRING.
On this trip Meek ascended the Wharton Range (via the head of the Aroa River) to more than 7000 ft. Jubilantly he noted that for the first time he was now in the heart of the bird of paradise country, but that his hunters were ill and could not stand the cold; in this setting with his field boxes swelling with new discoveries, he decided to hold on until the bitter end. This he did for another two weeks – 'the most wonderful ever' – and then, when one of his men perished, he withdrew to the coast. Among the bower birds and birds of paradise which Meek saw for the first time on this trip was Macgregor's Bower Bird (*Amblyornis macgregoriae*), the King of

Saxony Bird of Paradise (*Pteridophora alberti*) and Loria's Bird of Paradise (*Loria loriae*).

1905 (September) A. S. Meek; Mt Lamington foothills (Aicora). TRING.

Meek (*op. cit.*: 167) was attacked by natives in the Lamington foothills; his carriers deserted him and his bird skins were stolen.

1905 (November and December) Colin C. Simson; Owen Stanley Mts. LONDON.

Simson, in company with the seasoned collector A. S. Anthony, crossed the Owen Stanley Range from Port Moresby to Kokoda in November and crossed back again in December. During these extraordinary wet-season travels, Anthony showed him the bowers of Macgregor's Bower Bird (*Amblyornis macgregoriae*), the Striped Gardener Bower Bird (*Amblyornis subalaris*), the nest of the Green Catbird (*Ailuroedus crassirostris*) and the nest of the Blue Bird of Paradise (*Paradisaea rudolphi*).

1906 (January–May) A. S. Meek; Mambare River (north watershed of the Wharton Range). TRING.

Meek went inland via the Mambare to at least 5000 ft where he collected extensively in the vicinity of Biagi Village.

1907 (April–June) A. S. Meek; Kumusi River (north watershed of Owen Stanley Mountains a short distance west of Buna). TRING.

Although Meek got to a point some 80 miles inland and 6000 feet high, his men deserted and the venture was an unlucky one.

1908 (February–April) W. Goodfellow; Moroka District (to at least 5000 ft), Owen Stanley Mts. LONDON. *Paradisaea rudolphi*, nest and 2 eggs of *Ptiloris magnificus* (2000 ft, 9 June).

1909 (March) W. Goodfellow; Bagutana Camp (8000 ft), Owen Stanley Mts. LONDON.

1913 Albert F. Eichhorn, Sonbon I. (near Samarai). TRING.

1918 (January–May) Albert and George C. Eichhorn; Hydrographer Range (north watershed). TRING.

1920 and 1921 J. T. Zimmer; south-eastern New Guinea (south watershed). NEW YORK.

Zimmer collected in the Central Division lowlands (Aroa River, Cloudy Bay, Hall Sound, St Joseph River, Port

Moresby), also in the Eastern Division (Orangerie Bay and Doini Island).

1925 (about) W. Goodfellow; Central Division from coast near Yule Island to 9000–10,000 ft in ranges linking Mount Yule and the main Owen Stanley cordillera (Enongi tribal country). LONDON. Some to Zoological Gardens, London, England.

Goodfellow collected (alive) *Epimachus meyeri* and *Astrapia stephaniae* at highest altitudes. At 5000 ft he collected (alive) *Paradisaea raggiana*, *Parotia lawesi*, *Lophorina superba*, *Diphyllodes magnifica* and *Paradisaea rudolphi*. His most significant discovery was of the nest and two young of *Paradisaea rudolphi* (1926: 58–59).

1928 and 1929 Hannibal Hamlin; south-eastern New Guinea (south watershed). NEW YORK.

Hamlin collected in the Eastern Division (Samarai or Dinner, and Sariba islands and on the adjacent mainland at Belesana and Milne Bay), in the Central Division (Rigo, Kapu Kapa, Hall Sound, Yule Island) and in the uplands and mountains inland from Yule Island (Deva Deva, Mafulu, Jola, Fane, Vanumai Delena). In May and June he obtained a series of 7 males of *Amblyornis subalaris* at an elevation of about 2400 ft.

1928 (5 October–9 December) Lee S. Crandall; south-eastern New Guinea (south watershed). New York Zoological Society.

Crandall went into the Wharton Range (to about 4000 ft) via Yule Island. Obtained 40 living birds of paradise and bower birds of 11 species (many of which are now preserved in the American Museum, New York), also a general collection of live birds.

1928 (15–27 February) Rollo H. Beck; south-eastern New Guinea (Samarai Island and adjacent mainland). NEW YORK.

1933 and 1934 First Archbold Expedition to New Guinea (R. Archbold, A. L. Rand, G. H. H. Tate, L. J. Brass); south-eastern New Guinea (southern watershed). NEW YORK.

Comprehensive collections in the Port Moresby region (Rouna, Laloki River, Sogeri, and inland to the foothills of the Owen Stanley Mountains); in the Wharton Range this expedition made a survey to the summit of Mt Albert

Edward via Yule Island, Mafulu and Ononge. 9 new subspecies and one new species of birds discovered and important observations made. Many bowers of *Amblyornis
macgregoriae* were studied.

1948   (7 February–11 April) E. T. Gilliard; south-eastern New
Guinea (southern watershed). NEW YORK.

Gilliard collected in the lowlands near Port Moresby
(Tupusiele area, Laloki River, Motomotu Village on lower
Brown River), in the uplands (Rouna Pass, Warirata and
Hombron escarpments, Illolo, Goldie River, Imiti Ridge);
mid-mountains, Owen Stanley Range (Kokoda track,
Horseshoe or Maguli Mt 6000 ft), 134 species (450 study
skins); 8 species of birds of paradise and 3 species of bower
birds.

1953   Fourth Archbold Expedition to New Guinea (L. J. Brass,
H. M. Van Deusen, Geoffrey M. Tate, K. M. Wynn); Mt
Dayman and Cape Vogel. NEW YORK.

1962   (July–October) Mrs S. Schodde; Port Moresby, Rigo and
Brown River lowlands. CANBERRA. 161 species (445 study
skins); 4 species of bower birds and birds of paradise.

19: Sepik River Region

(including tributaries to elevations of 3000 feet)

1887   C. Hunstein; lower and middle Sepik. BERLIN.

As a member of the first German expedition to the Sepik,
Hunstein ascended some 200 miles to about the present
location of Ambunti; south of that point he ascended an
isolated mountain range now called the Hunstein Range. A
small collection of birds.

1910   L. Schultze-Jena; western Kaiser Wilhelmsland to middle
Sepik River. BERLIN (but many specimens apparently lost).

1912–13   (March–September) J. Bürgers (often with W. Behrmann), German Sepik Expedition, middle Sepik region.
BERLIN.

240 species (3100 specimens) including 3 new species and
some 80 new races. Most from the middle and upper Sepik
but some on excursions into the mountains [see Regenberg,
Schraderberg, Lordberg]. Localities visited: Malu, Zucker-
hut (490 m), Mt Peilungs, Mai River, Gradlager (800 m),

451

April River (75 m), Bambus Mt, Mt Etappe (1100 m), Topfer River, Lehm River, Maeanderberg (1000 m).

1913 (23 February–25 March) J. Bürgers (with W. Behrmann?), German Sepik Expedition; Mt Hunstein. BERLIN.

1929 (13–25 May) Crane Pacific Expedition (W. A. Weber, F. C. Wonder); Marienberg, Ambot, Keram River.
A small collection including 4 species of birds of paradise, 2 species of bower birds. CHICAGO.

1930 (February) G. C. Eichhorn; middle Sepik River region. NEW YORK.
A small collection.

1953–54 (November–March) E. T. and Margaret Gilliard; middle Sepik region. NEW YORK; CANBERRA.
Extensive collection in the middle Sepik area. Specimens from Aibom, Chambri Lake, Kararau, Kanganaman, Yentchan, Palimbai, Malingai, Soatmeri and Gaikarobi. Nests with eggs of two species of birds of paradise, the Glossy-mantled Manucode (*Manucodia ater*) and the Twelve-wired Bird of Paradise (*Seleucidis ignotus*) found. The latter was studied and photographed on the nest.

1955 (12–28 June) Dr and Mrs R. Bulmer; Jimi River region. SYDNEY.

1962 (May and November) W. B. Hitchcock; Sepik District (Maprik, Pagwi, Chambri Lake). CANBERRA.
2 species of birds of paradise; 63 species (107 study skins).

1963 (10 April and continuing) P. Temple; Sepik River. HONOLULU.
This expedition is making a comprehensive survey of the avifauna of the Sepik Valley.

20: Torricelli Mountains, Wewak and Prince Alexander Mountains

1910 Dr Schlaginhaufen; foothills of Torricelli Mountains. DRESDEN.

1953–55 Father Otto Shelly (Shellenberger); Wewak area. NEW YORK.

1954 (March) E. T. and Margaret Gilliard; Wewak region. NEW YORK.

1962 W. B. Hitchcock; Prince Alexander Mountains. CANBERRA.

21 : Islands Bordering Northern Coast

(Tendanye, Valif, Kairiru, Mushu, Blupblup, Bam, Manam, Karkar, Bagabag, etc.; but *not* including Crown, Long, Tolokiwa, Umboi [= Rook], Sakar or Siassi islands, which zoogeographically belong with the Bismarck Archipelago subregion).
1913   A. S. Meek; Manam I. TRING.
1914   A. S. Meek; Karkar I. TRING.

22 : Adelbert Mountains

1928   (August and September) Mr and Mrs R. Beck; uplands behind Madang. NEW YORK.
Beck apparently collected in the foothills of the Adelbert Mountains between 16 August and 10 September 1928, and again between 28 December 1928, and 16 January 1929. He apparently reached fairly high elevations (3000 ft) because he discovered a new bower bird, the Adelbert Regent Bower Bird (*Sericulus bakeri*) which apparently does not occur below that elevation.
1958   (14–18 June) E. T. Gilliard; Adelbert Mts. NEW YORK.
A reconnaissance was made along the north and eastern base of the Adelbert range and in the lowlands near Madang, in a vain search for the Adelbert Regent Bower Bird.
1959   (2 March–22 April) E. T. and Margaret Gilliard; Adelbert Mts. NEW YORK.
The Adelbert Mountains were surveyed for birds between 400 and 4000 ft. *Sericulus bakeri* was rediscovered above 3000 ft. Studies and films of the courtship behaviour of the Lesser Bird of Paradise (*Paradisaea minor*) and the Magnificent Bird of Paradise (*Diphyllodes magnificus*) were made.

23 : Astrolabe Bay Region and inland lowlands of Ramu River

(including Gogol and Ramu river lowlands behind bay)
1871–73   (?) Miklouho Maclay; Bogadjim, Astrolage Bay. RUSSIA.
Maclay spent 18 months in the Bogadjim region before being taken off by the Russian warship *Izumrud*.
1886–87   Fritz Grabowsky; Samoa Harbour, Hatzfeld Harbour and Tscherimotsch Island. BERLIN.

Grabowsky founded the Samoa Harbour station 21 December 1885, and collected a large number of birds in that general area in 1886–87.

1887–88 John S. Kubary; Constantine Harbour. FRANKFURT.

1888–89 Rohde; Kelana and Stephansort; BERLIN.

1890–2 Bruno and Hubert Geisler; Astrolabe Bay and coasts of Kai Peninsula. DRESDEN; BERLIN.

1890 C. Lauterbach; Gogol River to source (70 km inland). BERLIN.

1891 and 1893 (December and March) Samuel Fenichel; Astrolabe Bay region. BUDAPEST.
95 species.

1894 Bernard Hagen; Astrolabe Bay region (chiefly Stephansort). BERLIN; some to Karlsruhe Museum.

1894 Captain Cayley Webster; Stephansort. LONDON.

1894–95 (second visit) J. S. Kubary; Constantine Harbour. PARIS. *Manucodia ater* (5 May 1895), *Chlamydera cerviniventris* (16 December 1894).

1896–97 L. Biro; Berlinhafen, Astrolabe Bay, Erima. BUDAPEST.

1896 (July and August) C. Lauterbach, O. Kersting, Ernst Tappenbeck ('I Ramu Expedition'); Stephansort overland to the Ramu River. BERLIN.
A single specimen of an unknown species, Lauterbach's Bower Bird (*Chlamydera lauterbachi*) was discovered.

1898–99 Erik Nyman; Astrolabe Bay area (chiefly Stephansort). TRING.

1898–99 E. Tappenbeck; Ramu River. BERLIN.

1900–01 O. Heinroth ('I German South Sea Expedition of Br. Mencke'); various harbours. BERLIN.

1905–06 Carl Wahnes; Astrolabe Bay region. TRING.
Nest and eggs of Lesser Bird of Paradise (*Paradisaea minor*), the egg of the Glossy-mantled Manucode (*Manucodia ater*) and the eggs of the Crinkle-collared Manucode (*Manucodia chalybatus*) discovered.

1909 G. Duncker; coastal area. HAMBURG.

1909–10 C. Schoede; coastal areas. BERLIN. *Cicinnurus* (3 June 1910; Braunschweig Hafen).

1909–10 Lothar von Wiedenfeld; Berlinhafen, Heldbach coast, Simbang Sattelberg. Main collection at MUNICH; some at BRESLAU; BERLIN.

454

1928–29 Mr and Mrs R. Beck; Madang-Bogadjim areas. NEW YORK.

The Becks worked in the Madang-Bogadjim lowlands in early August, in late August and in late December 1928, and again from about 18 to 24 January 1929.

1953 (December) E. T. and Margaret Gilliard; lowlands about Madang. NEW YORK.

1956 (14–19 June) E. T. Gilliard; lowlands about Madang. NEW YORK.

Observations along the coast and the Gogol River, also in lowlands about Bogadjim (Dwai, Bom, Garkobok village areas). The courtship in the bower of a male and female Fawn-breasted Bower Bird (*Chlamydera cerviniventris*) was filmed.

1964 (7–25 May) E. T. Gilliard; Aiome region of Upper Ramu River. 85 study skins, 45 formalin specimens representing 58 species including *Chlamydera lauterbachi, Diphyllodes magnificus, Paradisaea minor, Ailuroedus buccoides;* also films and stills in colour of *Chlamydera cerviniventris* building in its bower and stills of *C. lauterbachi* (two birds) displaying in the bower of *C. cerviniventris*!

24: Mountains of the Huon Peninsula

1871–73 (?) M. Maclay; Finisterre Mts (southwest aspect). RUSSIA?

1878 (?) Heynemann; locality? PARIS *Phonygammus.*

1888 (January) C. Hunstein (with Stephan von Kotze); Rawlinson Mts. BERLIN.

At about 4450 ft Hunstein and Kotze discovered a magnificent unknown species, the Emperor of Germany Bird of Paradise (*Paradisaea guilielmi*). The expedition also discovered *Paradisaea raggiana augustaevictoriae* and many other new birds. Soon thereafter Hunstein, the most successful discoverer of new species of birds of paradise, departed for western New Britain where he was drowned 13 March 1888.

1890 C. Lauterbach; vicinity of Finschhafen. BERLIN.

1892 (March) B. Geisler; 'Finsch Harbour'. LONDON.

1893 Schluter; locality? PARIS. *Paradisaea guilielmi, P. raggiana augustaevictoriae.*

GG

455

1898–9   L. Biró; Simbang, Finschhafen, Sattelberg. BUDAPEST.

1898, 1899   (December and December) E. Nyman; Finisterre Mountains? (south-west slopes?). TRING.

1899   (June–September) E. Nyman; Sattelberg and Simbang region. TRING.

1901   van Kaemperr; locality? PARIS. *Paradisaea raggiana augustae-victoriae.*

1904   (February) Captain C. Webster (and Cotton); Finisterre Mountains? (south-west slopes?). TRING.
Simbang is one of the localities.

1905–06   (November–January) C. Wahnes; Sattelberg. LONDON. Collected eggs of White-eared Catbird (*Ailuroedus buccoides*), nest and eggs of the Magnificent Rifle Bird (*Ptiloris magnificus*) and eggs of Count Raggi's Bird of Paradise (*Paradisaea raggiana augustaevictoriae*).

1906   C. Wahnes; Rawlinson Mts and Sattelberg Range. TRING; nest and egg collection LONDON.
Discovered two magnificent new species of birds of paradise in the high ramparts of these mountains, Wahnes' Six-wired Bird of Paradise, *Parotia wahnesi,* and the Huon Astrapia Bird of Paradise, *Astrapia rothschildi.*

1908–09   (December–March) R. Neuhauss (with missionary Christian Keysser); Sattelberg to interior of Kai Peninsula. BERLIN.
Discovered eggs of *Paradisaea guilielmi* on Sattelberg and made a collection of birds of paradise including *Astrapia rothschildi.*

1909   C. Wahnes; Sattelberg. LONDON. Egg of *Parotia apodia.*

1911   (September) C. Keysser; Kai Peninsula to 12,000 ft in the Saruwaged and Rawlinson Mts. TRING.
A number of new discoveries were made including the nest and eggs of the Emperor of Germany Bird of Paradise (*Paradisaea guilielmi*).

1920   (April and May) William Potter. Rawlinson Mts to at least 3000 ft (Singaua; Bulo). LONDON. A series of *Paradisaea guilielmi, Ailuroedus buccoides.*

1928   (19 October–1 December) Mr and Mrs R. H. Beck; Finisterre Mountains (south-west slopes in Keku and Mt Tyo regions to about 3000 ft). NEW YORK.

1928–29   (8 December–27 April) E. Mayr; Saruwaged Mts.

BERLIN.

A general survey (lowlands to about 12,000 ft). Series of *Paradisaea guilielmi* and *Astrapia rothschildi* obtained at Ogeramnang and Tunzaing (January).

1929 (January–April) Mr and Mrs R.H.Beck; Saruwaged Mts. NEW YORK.

High altitude collecting was conducted near the village of Zagaheme (4000 ft).

1931 F.Shaw Mayer; Sattelberg Mts. TRING; NEW YORK (Sanford Collection).

Shaw Mayer observed males of *Paradisaea guilielmi* near Hompua Village (2700 ft) on 25 June.

1944 J.Frank Cassel; Finschhafen lowlands. ITHACA.

A small collection.

1956 E.T.Gilliard; Finisterre Mts (south-western aspect). NEW YORK.

In searching for the Adelbert Regent Bower Bird, Gilliard explored the Keku region and Mt Tyo to about 2000 ft. On Mt Tyo he discovered and observed the courtship of the King Bird of Paradise (*Cicinnurus regius*).

1959 (13–29 November) Sixth Archbold Expedition to New Guinea (H.M. Van Deusen and L.J.Brass); Headwaters (Umi River) of the Markham River in the foothills (475 m) of the Finisterre Mountains just north of the Ramu–Markham Rift Valley. NEW YORK. Van Deusen saved many birds caught in mist nets.

25: Lae-Huon Gulf Region

1892 (April) B.Geisler; Bukawasip, Huon Gulf. LONDON.

1920 (March–April) W.Potter; Musom and Singaua, Huon Gulf. LONDON.

1950 (8 and 9 August) E.T.Gilliard; Markham River forest behind Lae. NEW YORK.

1958 (23 October–3 November) E.T.Gilliard; Lae region and lower Markham River. NEW YORK.

Observations of the nesting of Count Raggi's Bird of Paradise, *Paradisaea raggiana augustaevictoriae*.

1959 (25 March–10 April) Sixth Archbold Expedition to New Guinea.

457

26: Herzog Mountains Region

—? H. Andechser; Herzog Mts (Sudhong). BERLIN. *Paradisaea maria* (= *P. raggiana augustaevictoriae* × *P. guilielmi*).

1910–12 Governor Hahl and prospector 'Klink'; upper Babu River, Batchelor Mt (up to 9000 ft). MUNICH.

1929 (7 May–29 June) E. Mayr; Snake River region to 7000 ft. BERLIN.
Comprehensive collection including a new race of the Wattle-billed Bird of Paradise (*Loboparadisea sericea*), the Blue Bird of Paradise (*Paradisaea rudolphi*) and the Princess Stephanie (*Astrapia stephaniae*).

1932–33 (27 January–5 May) Herbert Stevens; Herzog Mts to 7500 ft on Mt Misim. CAMBRIDGE.
Collected in the Wau region (23 January to 15 May), at Biolowat Camp (22 May to 22 July), on the upper Watut (26 July to 2 September), at Surprise Creek (27 September to 26 October), at Mt Misim (5000 to 7500 feet) approximately late October to 5 May. 207 species and subspecies (1308 study skins), including a new race of the Blue Bird of Paradise (*Paradisaea rudolphi*) and a new race of Lawes' Six-wired Bird of Paradise (*Parotia lawesi*).

1936 (December) F. Shaw Mayer; Upper Waria River (2500 ft). LONDON. *Chlamydera cerviniventris* female taken 'on nest (eggs broken)' at 2500 ft. LONDON.

1959 Sixth Archbold Expedition to New Guinea (L. J. Brass and H. M. Van Deusen); Herzog Mts area (Oomsis Creek: 10–20 April, 24 April–4 May; Gurakor: 4–11 May; Mt Kainoi – Edie Creek area: 12–28 May). NEW YORK.

1962 (24 September–29 October) Alden H. Miller; Herzog Mt and Bulolo basin region. BERKELEY.
Collections between 1900 and 7800 ft at Bulolo, Zenag, Watut River, Kaiapit, Mt Kaindi, Wau, Edie Creek, and Mt Misim. 118 species including 7 species of birds of paradise and bower birds.

1962 (March–May) Horrie Clissold; Herzog Mt region. HONO-LULU.
Collections at Mt Kaindu, 'Mt Mission', Bulolo (2800 ft), Wau (3800 ft), Nanke Mt (2600 ft).

1963 H. Clissold; Wau. BERLIN. *Phonygammus keraudrenii*

27: Islands of South-eastern New Guinea

1846–50   John Macgillivray; Louisiade Archipelago. LONDON.
Macgillivray, naturalist aboard HMS *Rattlesnake* commanded by Captain Owen Stanley, worked in this area and perhaps
in the D'Entrecasteaux Group.

1873–74   R.N. Comrie; Trobriand Is. LONDON.
Dr Comrie, ship's surgeon aboard HMS *Basilisk*, collected a
few birds in these islands, including a new species of bird of
paradise, the Curl-crested Manucode (*Manucodia comrii*).

1882   C. Hunstein and A. Goldie; Fergusson and Normanby Is.
LONDON; PARIS. *Manucodia comrii*.
Exploring for gold and new birds, Hunstein and Goldie
found one of the most beautiful of the birds of paradise, the
Grey-breasted Bird of Paradise (also known as Goldie's Bird
of Paradise) (*Paradisaea decora*), also a new race of the Curl-
crested Manucode (*Manucodia comrii*).

1890   (13–18 January) L. Loria and A. Giulianetti; Goodenough
I. ITALY?
A very small collection of bird skins was obtained.

1891   (July) Rickard; Fergusson I. SYDNEY.
Nest and eggs of the Curl-crested Manucode discovered.

1894   (May and early June) W.E. Armit; Goodenough I. BRISBANE.
Armit obtained at least 11 species (17 study skins) during his
ascent of Mt Oiamadawa, the lowest of the five northern
mountains of the island (Mayr and van Deusen, 1956: 7).

1894   (September–December): A.S. Meek; Fergusson I. TRING.
Meek, who spent 'six weeks' on the island in 1894, obtained
63 species of birds.

1895   (March–July) A.S. Meek; Kiriwini I.; Trobriand I. TRING.
Meek wrote that he passed the winter season in these islands.
He obtained a large collection which included the nest and
egg of the Curl-crested Manucode (3 March).

1896   (November and December) A.S. Meek and W.G. Meek
(brother); Goodenough I. TRING.
Meek spent about six weeks collecting here. In December he
climbed to a 'great height looking for a particular species of
bird of paradise.' He was then threatened by dangerous
natives and had to be removed from the island by a government rescue party [Author's note: Meek and his party had

set out from Samarai in a 20-foot whaleboat presumably
bound for Woodlark Island. Accompanying him was his
brother, recently arrived from Australia. Unable to make
Woodlark, they were 'shipwrecked' on Goodenough, an
island that needed collecting, but for which Meek had no
entry papers].

1897 (17 February, 17 May, 4 June) A. S. Meek; Fergusson I.
BERLIN.

1897 (March) A. S. Meek (accompanied by Gulliver, W. B. Barnard,
Harry Barnard and Tim Barnard); Woodlark and Mura Is.
TRING.

1897 (August) A. S. Meek; Louisiade Archipelago (St. Aignan or
Misima I.). TRING.
Meek spent much of August near Bogoya Harbour collecting
some 65 species of birds. It was on this island that the natives
(who once had about the worst reputation of any in the South
Seas) are said to have captured the crew of a Chinese ship
and then eaten the sailors one by one.

1898 (March–April) A. S. Meek; Louisiade Archipelago (Sudest or
Tagula I.). TRING.
Meek noted that he saw here for the first time pearl divers
with pickle jars filled with pearls. Among his discoveries
was a new race of the Glossy-mantled Manucode (*Manucodia
ater ater*).

1901 (August and September) A. S. Meek; D'Entrecasteaux Group
(Normanby I.). TRING.

1912–13 A. S. Meek; D'Entrecasteaux Group (Goodenough I.,
March to May, and Fergusson I., December 1912 to 10
January 1913). TRING.

1916 (January–April) A. S. Meek; Louisiade Archipelago (Sudest
or Tagula I.). TRING.
Much collecting was done on Mt Riu.

1923 A. and G. Eichhorn (brothers-in-law of A. S. Meek);
Goodenough I. TRING.
Collection of birds obtained during a stay of 'several weeks'
(Mayr and Van Deusen, 1956: 7).

1928 (November) H. Hamlin; Fergusson I. NEW YORK.

1928 (19–23 November) H. Hamlin; Goodenough I. NEW YORK.
About 14 specimens of mountain birds secured during a trip
inland from Mud Bay.

1930?   H. Hamlin; Louisiade Archipelago. (31 July: Panopompom, Deboyne Is.). NEW YORK.

1935   (September) F. Shaw Mayer; D'Entrecasteaux Group (Fergusson I.). LONDON.
Collecting between sea-level and at least 2500 ft, Shaw Mayer discovered the nest and egg of the Curl-crested Manucode (*Manucodia comrii*).

1953   Fourth Archbold Expedition to New Guinea (L. J. Brass, H. M. Van Deusen, K. M. Wynn); D'Entrecasteaux Group (Goodenough I.). NEW YORK.
L. J. Brass reported hearing about a strange species of bird of paradise in the mountain forest. This may be the bird Meek was pursuing.

1956   Fifth Archbold Expedition to New Guinea. (L. J. Brass and R. F. Peterson, L. Evennett) D'Entrecasteaux Group, (Normanby Island, 10 April to 12 May; Fergusson Island, 21 May to 7 July. NEW YORK.

1956   Fifth Archbold Expedition to New Guinea (L. J. Brass and R. F. Peterson); Louisiade Archipelago: Misima (formerly St Aignan) I. (16 July to 13 August); Sudest I. (15 August to 25 September); Rossel I. (26 September to 29 October). NEW YORK.

1956   (1–24 November) Fifth Archbold Expedition to New Guinea (L. J. Brass and R. F. Peterson); Woodlark I.

1956   (9–10 December) Fifth Archbold Expedition to New Guinea (R. F. Peterson); Trobriand Is. (Liluta and Kiriwina).

Bibliography

ANON 1873. (No title.) *Nature, Lond.*, **8**: 151.

ANON 1920. *Dutch New Guinea and the Molucca Islands.* Handbook prepared under direction of the Historical Section of the Foreign Office, London, no. 87.

ANON 1943. *The New Guinea Handbook.* Canberra.

ANON 1958. *Handbook on Netherlands New Guinea,* New Guinea Inst. of Rotterdam.

ANON 1962. *The Territory of New Guinea.* Annual Report 1960–1961. Part I—Introductory descriptive section, pp. 11–21. Australian Dept. External Affairs, Canberra.

ARMSTRONG, E. A. 1947. *Bird display and behaviour.* New York.

AUER, V. 1946. The Pleistocene and postglacial period in Fuego-patagonia. *Acta. Soc. Sci. Fennica,* **2**: 1–20.

BEAUFORT, L. F. DE 1914. Vogelschetsen van Saonek. *Ardea,* **3**: 89–93.

BECCARI, O. 1877. Le capanne ed i giardini dell *Amblyornis inornata. Ann. Mus. Civ. Genova,* ser. 1, **9**: 382–400.

1878. The gardener bird and a new orchid. *Gardener's Chronicle,* 16 March: 332.

BECK, R. H. 1929. A collector in the land of the Birds of Paradise. *Nat. Hist.,* **29,** no. 6: 563–78.

BEEBE, W. 1926. *Pheasants, their lives and homes.* New York, **2**:1–309.

BERGMAN, S. 1956. On the display and breeding of the King Bird of Paradise, *Cicinnurus regius rex* (Scop.) in captivity. *Nova Guinea,* **7,** pt. 2: 197–205.

1957a. *Through primitive New Guinea.* London.

1957b. Om spelet hos strålparadisfågeln, *Parotia sefilata* (Pennant). *Fauna och Flora,* **52,** no. 5: 186–99.

BERNSTEIN, H. A. 1864. Ueber einen neuen Paradiesvogel und einige andere neue Vögel. *Journ. f. Orn.,* **12,**: 401–10.

BOCK, W. J. 1963. Relationships between the birds of paradise and the bower birds. *Condor,* **65,** no. 2: 91–125.

BONAPARTE, C.L. 1850a. Nouvelles espèces ornithologiques. *Compt. Rend. Acad. Sci. Paris,* **30:** 131–39.

1850b. *Conspectus Avium,* vol. 2. Lugduni Batavorum, E.J.Brill.

BOURKE, P.A., and A.F.AUSTIN 1947. The Atherton Tablelands and its avifauna. *Emu,* **47:** 87–116.

BRONGERSMA, L.D., and G.F.VENEMA 1962. *To the mountains of the stars.* London.

BULMER, R.N.H. MS₁. Bulmer collection. Birds of central New Guinea, 1955–6 and 1959–60.

MS₂. 1) Notes on plumages and gonads of Baiyer Region birds (1955–6); 2) Notes on birds of paradise, 1961; 3) Notes on two New Guinea bower birds, *Chlamydera* and *Amblyornis.*

MS₃. Birds of Mount Hagen.

BULMER, R., and SUSAN BULMER 1962. Figurines and other stones of power among the Kyaka of central New Guinea. *Journ. Polynesian Soc.,* **71,** no. 2: 192–208.

CABANIS, J. 1888. Vorläufige Notiz über 2 neue Paradies-Vögel. *Journ. f. Orn.,* **36:** 119.

CAIRN, E.J., and R.GRANT. 1890. Report on a collecting trip to north-eastern Queensland, during April to September, 1889. *Rec Australian Mus.,* **1:** 27–31.

CAMPBELL, A.J. 1901. *Nests and eggs of Australian birds,* pt. I. Sheffield.

1912. New birds for Australia. *Emu,* **12:** 19–20.

CAREY, S.W. 1938. The morphology of New Guinea. *Aust. Geog.,* **3:** 3–31.

CALEY, N.W. 1959. *What bird is that ?* Sydney.

CHAFFER, N. 1932. The regent bird. *Emu,* **32:** 8–11.

1945. Spotted and satin bower-birds: a comparison. *Emu.* **44:** 161–81.

1949. Notes on two New Guinea bower-birds. *Emu,* **49:** 19–25.

1958a. Additional observations on the Golden Bower-bird. *Emu,* **58,** 133–7.

1958b. 'Mimicry' of the 'Stage-maker'. *Emu,* **58,** 53–5.

1959. Bower building and display of the Satin Bower-bird. *Aust. Zool.,* **12:** 295–305.

463

CHAPIN, J.P. 1929. A new Bower-bird of the genus *Xanthomelas*. *Amer. Mus. Novitates*, no. 367 : 1–3.

CHAPMAN, F.M. 1935. The courtship of Gould's Manakin (*Manacus vitellinus vitellinus*) on Barro Colorado Island, Canal Zone. *Bull. Amer. Mus. Nat. Hist.*, **68**: 471–525.

CHISHOLM, A.H. 1963. The Golden Bower-bird at the nest and bower. *Emu*, **62**: 251–6.

CHISHOLM, A.H., and N. CHAFFER 1956. Observations on the Golden Bower-bird. *Emu*, **56**:1–38.

CRANDALL, L.S. 1929. The New York Zoological Society's expedition to New Guinea. *Bull. N.Y. Zool. Soc.*, **32**:215–56.

1931. *Paradise Quest*. New York and London.

1932. Notes on certain birds of paradise. *Zoologica*, **11**, no. 7: 77–87.

1936. Birds of Paradise in display. *Bull. New York Zool. Soc.*, **39**: 87–103.

1937a. Further notes on certain birds of paradise. *Zoologica*, **22**: 193–195.

1937b. Position of wires in the display of the Twelve-wired Bird of Paradise. *Zoologica*, **22**, pt. 4: 307–10.

1940. Notes on the display forms of Wahnes' Six-plumed Bird of Paradise. *Zoologica*, **25**, pt. 2: 257–9.

1946. Further notes on display forms of the Long-tailed Bird of Paradise, *Epimachus meyeri meyeri* Finsch. *Zoologica*, **31**, no. 3: 9–10.

CRANDALL, L.S., and C.W. LEISTER. 1937. Display of the Magnificent Rifle Bird. *Zoologica*, **22**: 311–314.

D'ALBERTIS, L.M., and T. SALVADORI 1879. Catalogo degli uccelli raccolti da L.M. D'Albertis durante la 2ª e 3ª esplorazione del Fiume Fly negli anni 1876 e 1877. *Ann. Mus. Civ. Genova*, **14**, ser. 1: 21–147.

DARLINGTON, P.J., Jr. 1957. *Zoogeography; the geographical distribution of animals*. New York.

DARWIN, CHARLES 1871. *The descent of man and selection in relation to sex*, vol. 2. London.

DAUDIN, 1800. Traité élémentaire et complet d'ornithologie. Paris.

DELACOUR, JEAN. 1963. Notes on Austral and southern Pacific birds. IX. New Guinea. *Avicultural Mag.*, **69**: 231–234.

DENTON, SHERMAN F. 1889. *Incidents of a collector's rambles in*

Australia, New Zealand, and New Guinea. Boston.

DeVis, C.W. 1883. Description of two new birds of Queensland. *Proc. Linn. Soc. New South Wales,* **7,** ser. 1: 561–3.

1890. Report on birds from British New Guinea. *Ann. Rep. British New Guinea, for* 1888–89. App. C: 105–116.

1891. Report on birds from British New Guinea. *Ibis,* **3,** ser. 6, no. 9: 25–41.

1892. Zoology of British New Guinea. *Ann. Queensland Mus.,* no. 2: 4–11.

1894. Report on ornithological specimens collected in British New Guinea. *Ann. Rep. Brit. New Guinea,* 1st July, 1893 to 30 June 1894, pp. 99–105.

1897. Description of a new bird of paradise from British New Guinea, *Ibis,* **3,** ser. 7, no. 10: 250–2.

1898. (in) Annual report on British New Guinea from 1 July 1896 to 30 June 1897, pp. 81–90.

DHARMAKUMARSINHJI, PRINCE K.S. 1943. Notes on the breeding of the Empress of Germany's Bird of Paradise in captivity. *Zoologica,* **28** pt. 3: 139–44.

DOWNHAM, C.F. 1910. *The feather trade: a case for the defence.* London, London Chamber of Commerce.

DOZY, J.J. 1938. Eine Gletschervelt in Niederländisch-Neuguinea. *Zeitschr. f. Gletscherkunde,* **26**: 45–51.

EDWARDS, G. 1750. *A natural history of birds,* vol. 3. London.

ELLIOT, D.G. 1871. Review of the genus *Ptiloris,* Swainson. *Proc. Zool. Soc. London*: 580–4.

1873. *A monograph of the Paradiseidae.* London.

FINSCH, O. and A.B. MEYER. 1886. On some new Paradise-birds (transl. of article, 1885, *Zeitschr. Ges. Orn.*). *Ibis,* **4,** ser. 5, no. 25: 237–58.

FORBES, H.O. 1885. *A naturalist's wanderings in the Eastern Archipelago.* New York.

FRIEDMANN, H. 1934. The display of Wallace's Standard-wing Bird of Paradise in captivity. *The Scientific Monthly,* **39**: 52–5.

GANNON, G.R. 1930. Observations on the Satin Bower Bird with regard to the material used by it in painting its bower. *Emu,* **30**: 39–41.

GESNER, CONRADI 1555. *Historiae Animalium Liber III,* Tiguri, Froschover.

GILBERT, P. A. 1910. Notes on the Regent-bird (*Sericulus melinus*). *Emu.* **10**: 44–5.

GILLIARD, E. T. MS₁. Notes on the reproductive behavior of three genera of New Guinea bower birds.

MS₂. Wahgi Valley field notes, 1959.

MS₃. Journal and letters. Astrolabe Bay region, 14 June–11 July, 1956, New Guinea.

MS₄. Journal, 1959.

1950. Notes on birds of southeastern Papua. *Amer. Mus. Novitates,* no. 1453: 1–40.

1953a. New Guinea's rare birds and Stone Age men. *Natl. Geogr. Mag.,* **103**: 421–88.

1953b. Exploring New Guinea for birds of paradise. *Nat. Hist.,* **62**: 248–55, 287.

1955. To the land of the head-hunters. *Natl. Geogr. Mag.,* **108**: 437–68.

1956a. Bower ornamentation versus plumage characters in Bower-birds. *Auk,* **73**: 450–1.

1956b. The systematics of the New Guinea Manucode, *Manucodia ater. Amer. Mus. Novitates,* no. 1770: 1–13.

1958. Feathered dancers of Little Tobago. *Natl. Geogr. Mag.,* **114**: 428–440.

1959a. The courtship behavior of Sanford's Bowerbird (*Archboldia sanfordi*). *Amer. Mus. Novitates,* no. 1935: 1–18.

1959b. A comparative analysis of courtship movements in closely allied bower-birds of the genus *Chlamydera. Amer. Mus. Novitates,* no. 1936: 1–8.

1959c. Notes on the courtship behavior of the Blue-backed Manakin (*Chiroxiphia pareola*). *Amer. Mus. Novitates,* no. 1942: 1–19.

1961. Four new birds from the mountains of central New Guinea. *Amer. Mus. Novitates,* no. 2031: 1–7.

1962. On the breeding behavior of the Cock-of-the-Rock (Aves, *Rupicola rupicola*). *Bull. Amer. Mus. Nat. Hist.,* **124**, no. 2: 31–68.

1963. The evolution of Bowerbirds. *Sci. Amer.,* **209**: 38–46.

GILLIARD, E. T., and M. LeCROY. 1961. Birds of the Victor Emanuel and Hindenburg Mountains, New Guinea. Results of the American Museum of Natural History expedition to New Guinea in 1954. *Bull. Amer. Mus. Nat. Hist.,* **123**: 1–86.

1966. Birds of the middle Sepik region, New Guinea. Results of the American Museum of Natural History expedition to New Guinea in 1953–1954. *Bull. Amer. Mus. Nat. Hist.*, **132**: 245–276.

1967. Annotated list of birds of the Adelbert Mountains, New Guinea. Results of the 1959 Gilliard Expedition. *Bull. Amer. Mus. Nat. Hist.*, **138**: 51–82.

1968. Birds of the Schrader Mountain region, New Guinea. Results of the American Museum of Natural History Expedition to New Guinea in 1964. *Amer. Mus. Novitates*, no. 2343: 1–41.

GODDARD, M.T. 1947. Bower-painting by the Regent Bower-bird. *Emu*, **47**: 73–74.

GOODFELLOW, W. 1926. (Remarks). *Bull. Brit. Orn. Club*, **46**: 58–9.

1927. Wallace's Bird of Paradise (*Semioptera wallacei*). *Avic. Mag.*, ser. 4, **5**: 57–65.

GOODWIN, A.P. 1890. Notes on the paradise-birds of British New Guinea. *Ibis*, **2**, ser. 6, no. 6: 150–6.

GOODWIN, GEORGE G. 1961. The murine opossums (genus *Marmosa*) of the West Indies, and the description of a new subspecies of *Rhipidomys* from Little Tobago. *Amer. Mus. Novitates*, no. 2070: 1–20.

GOULD, J. 1837. *A synopsis of the Birds of Australia, and the adjacent islands.* London.

1849. On new species of Mammalia and birds from Australia. *Proc. Zool. Soc. London*: 109–12.

1850. A brief account of the researches in natural history of John McGillivray, Esq., the naturalist attached to H.M. surveying ship the *Rattlesnake*, on the north-eastern coast of Australia, New Guinea, etc., sect. D, pp. 92–105. (In) Jardine, Sir Wm., *Contributions to ornithology*, 1848–52. London.

1862. On a new species of Chlamydera, or Bower-bird. *Proc. Zool. Soc. London*, **11**: 161–2.

1869. *The birds of Australia*, supplement. London.

1879. Observations on the *Chlamydoderae* or bower-birds with description of a new species. *Ann. Mag. Nat. Hist.*, ser. 5, **4**: 73–4.

GRAY, G.R. 1858. A list of birds with descriptions of new species obtained by Mr Alfred R. Wallace in the Aru and Ké Islands. *Proc. Zool. Soc. London*: 169–98.

1859. List of the birds lately sent by Mr A. R. Wallace from Dorey or Dorery, New Guinea. *Proc. Zool. Soc. London*: 153–9.

GREENWAY, J. C.   1934. Description of four new subspecies of birds from the Huon Gulf region, New Guinea. *Proc. New England Zool. Club*, **14**: 1–3.

1935. Birds from the coastal range between the Markham and the Waria rivers, northeastern New Guinea. *Proc. New Eng. Zool. Club*, **14**: 15–106.

1942. A new manucode bird of paradise. *Proc. New Eng. Zool. Club*, **19**: 51–2.

1958. *Extinct and vanishing birds of the world.* Cambridge, Mass.

GUILLEMARD, F. H. H.   1886. *The cruise of the* Marchesa *to Kamschatka and New Guinea with notices of Formosa, Liu-Kiu, and various islands of the Malay Archipelago.* Vols. 1 and 2. London.

GYLDENSTOLPE, N.   1955a. Notes on a collection of birds made in the western highlands, central New Guinea, 1951. *Arkiv. f. Zool.*, ser. 2, **8**, no. 1.

1955b. Birds collected by Dr Sten Bergman during his expedition to Dutch New Guinea 1948–1949. *Arkiv. f. Zool.*, ser. 2, **8**, no 2.

HARTERT, E.   1910. On the eggs of the Paradiseidae. *Novit. Zool.*, **17**: 484–91.

1930. List of birds collected by Ernst Mayr. *Novit. Zool.*, **36**: 27–128.

HARTERT, E., K. PALUDAN, LORD ROTHSCHILD, and E. STRESEMANN. 1936. Die Vögel des Weyland-Gebirges und seines Vorlandes. *Mitt. Zool. Mus. Berlin*, **21**, no. 2: 166–240.

HEINRICH, G.   1956. Biologische Aufzeichnungen über Vögel von Halmahera und Batjan. *Journ. f. Orn.*, **97**: 31–40.

HEINROTH, O.   1902. Ornithologische Ergebnisse der "I. Deutschen Südsee Expedition von Br. Mencke." *Jour. f. Orn.*, **50**: 390–457.

1903. Ornithologische Ergebnisse der "I. Deutschen Südsee Expedition von Br. Mencke." *Jour. f. Orn.*, **51**: 65–126.

HEUSSER, CALVIN, J. 1960. Late-Pleistocene environments of the Laguna de San Rafael area, Chile. *Geogr. Rev.*, **50**: 555–77.

HINDWOOD, K.A., and A.R.McGILL. 1958. *The birds of Sydney.* Sydney, Royal Zool. Soc. New South Wales.

HIRST, A. 1944. The Satin Bower Bird. *Avic. Mag.*, ser. 5, **9**: 47.

HODGE-SMITH, T. 1943. The geology of New Guinea. *Australian Mus. Mag.*, **8**, no. 3: 91–5.

HORNADAY, WILLIAM T. 1931. *Thirty years war for wild life. Gains and losses in the thankless task.* New York.

HUTCHINSON, G.E. 1952. Bowerbirds. *Amer. Sci.*, **40**, no. 1: 148.

HUXLEY, J.S. 1938. Darwin's theory of sexual selection and the data subsumed by it, in the light of recent research. *Amer. Nat.*, 72: 416–433.

INGRAM, SIR W. 1907. On the display of the King Bird-of-Paradise (*Cicinnurus regius*). *Ibis*, **9**, no. 1: 224–9.

IREDALE, T. 1948. A checklist of the birds of paradise and bower birds. *Australian Zool.*, **2**: 161–89.
1950. *Birds of paradise and bower birds.* Melbourne.

JACKSON, S.W. 1909. In the Barron River Valley, North Queensland. *Emu*, **8**: 233–83.

JARDIN, SIR W., and J.SELBY. 1830. *Illustrations of ornithology*, vol. 2. Edinburgh.

JUNGE, G.C.A. 1939. The birds of south New Guinea, Part II, Passeres. *Nova Guinea*, new ser., **3**: 1–94.

KEAST, A. 1961. Bird speciation on the Australian continent. *Bull. Mus. Comp. Zool.*, **123**, no. 8: 1–495.

KENNEDY, R. 1943. Islands and peoples of the Indies. *Smithsonian Inst. War Background Studies*, no. 14.

KLEINSCHMIDT, O. 1897. Beschreibung eines neuen Paradiesvogels. *Orn. Monatsb.*, **5**: 46–8.

KOOPMAN, K.F. 1957. Evolution in the genus *Myzomela* (Aves: Meliphagidae). Auk, **74**: 49–72.

KRIEGER, H.W. 1943. Island peoples of the Western Pacific, Micronesia, and Melanesia. *Smithsonian Inst. War Background Studies*, no. 16.

KURODA, N. 1958. A collection of birds from west New Guinea. *Tori*, 15: 18–30.

LACK, D. 1947. *Darwin's finches.* Cambridge.

L'ÉCLUSE, C.DE. 1605. *Exoticorum Libri Decem: Quibus Animalium, Plantarum.* Antwerp.

LESSON, R.-P. 1830. *Voyage autour du monde . . . sur . . . la Coquille pendant . . .* 1822–25 *. . . par L.I.Duperrey,* Zool., vol. II.

1834–5. *Histoire naturelle des oiseaux de paradis et des épimaques.* Paris.

LESSON, R.-P., and P.GARNOT. 1826a. Description d'une nouvelle espèce de Cassican (*Barita Keraudrenii*). *Bull. Sci. Nat.* (Férussac), **8**: 110–11.

1826b. *Voyage autour du monde . . . sur . . . la Coquille pendant . . .* 1822–25 *. . . par M.L.I.Duperrey. Zoologie.* Vol. I. Paris.

LIBBY, W.F. 1956. Radiocarbon dating. *Amer. Sci.,* **44**: 98–112.

LINNAEUS, C. 1758. *Systema naturae,* Ed. 10, vol. I.

LOKE, WAN THO. 1957. *A company of birds.* London.

MACGILLIVRAY, J. 1852. *Narrative of the voyage of H.M.S. Rattlesnake, commanded by the late Captain Owen Stanley, during the years* 1846–1850. . . . London.

MARSHALL, A.J.

1954a. Bower-birds. *Biol. Rev.,* **29**: 1–45.

1954b. *Bower-birds: their displays and breeding cycles.* Oxford.

1956. Bower birds. *Sci. Amer.,* **194,** no. 6: 48–52.

MATHEWS, G.M. 1912. A reference-list to the birds of Australia. *Novit. Zool.,* **18**: 171–455.

1915. Additions and corrections to my list of the birds of Australia. *Austral. Avian Rec.,* **2**: 123–33.

1923. Additions and corrections to my lists of the birds of Australia. *Austral. Avian Rec.,* **5**: 33–44.

1925–7. *The birds of Australia,* vol. 12. London.

1941. Two new subspecies of birds collected by Dr Scott at Cape York. *Emu,* **40**: 384.

MAYR, E. 1930a. Die Unterarten des Kragenparadiesvogels (*Lophorina superba*). *Orn. Monatsb,* **38,** no. 6: 178–80.

1930b. My Dutch New Guinea expedition, 1928. *Novitates Zool.,* **36**: 20–26.

1931. Die Vögel des Saruwaged- und Herzog-gebirges (NO-Neuguinea). *Mitt. Zool. Mus. Berlin,* **17**: 639–723.

1935. Bernard Altum and the territory theory. *Proc. Linn. Soc. New York,* 1933–4, nos. 45, 46: 19–38.

1936. New subspecies of birds from the New Guinea region. *Amer. Mus. Novitates,* no. 869: 1–7.

1941. *List of New Guinea birds.* New York, The American Museum of Natural History.

1945. Birds of paradise. *Nat. Hist.*, **54**: 264–76.

1953. Fragments of a Papuan ornithogeography. *Proc 7th Pacific Sci. Congr.* 1949, **4**: 11–19.

1963. *Animal species and evolution.* Cambridge, Mass., Harvard Univ.

MAYR, E., and E. T. GILLIARD. 1950. A new bower bird (*Archboldia*) from Mount Hagen, New Guinea. *Amer. Mus. Novitates*, no. 1473: 1–3.

1951. New species and subspecies of birds from the highlands of New Guinea. *Amer. Mus. Novitates*, no. 1524.

1952a. The Ribbon-tailed Bird of Paradise (*Astrapia mayeri*) and its allies. *Amer. Mus. Novitates*, no. 1551: 1–13.

1952b. Six new subspecies of birds from the highlands of New Guinea. *Amer. Mus. Novitates*, no. 1577: 1–8.

1954. Birds of central New Guinea. Results of the American Museum of Natural History expeditions to New Guinea in 1950 and 1952. *Bull. Amer. Mus. Nat. Hist.*, **103**: 317–74.

MAYR, E., and K. JENNINGS. 1952. Geographic variation and plumages in Australian Bowerbirds. *Amer. Mus. Novitates*, no. 1602: 1–18.

MAYR, E., and A. L. RAND. 1935. Results of the Archbold Expeditions. No. 6. Twenty-four apparently undescribed birds from New Guinea and the D'Entrecasteaux Archipelago. *Amer. Mus. Novitates*, no. 814: 1–17.

1937. Results of the Archbold Expeditions, No. 14. The birds of the 1933–1934 Papuan Expedition. *Bull. Amer. Mus. Nat. Hist.*, **73**: 1–248.

MAYR, E., and R. DE SCHAUENSEE. 1939. Zoological results of the Denison–Crockett expedition to the South Pacific for the Academy of Natural Sciences of Philadelphia, 1937–1938. Part I – The birds of the island of Biak. *Proc. Acad. Nat. Sci. Philadelphia*, **91**: 1–37.

Part IV—Birds from northwest New Guinea. *Ibid.*: 97–144.

MAYR, E., and H. M. VAN DEUSEN. 1956. Results of the Archbold Expeditions. No. 74. The birds of Goodenough Island, Papua. *Amer. Mus. Novitates*, no. 1792: 1–8.

McGILL, A.R. 1960. *A hand list of the birds of New South Wales.* Sydney, The Fauna Protection Panel.

MEEK, A. S. 1913. *A naturalist in cannibal land*. London.

MEGGITT, S., and I.WADDLE. 1963. Regent Bower Bird at St Lucia. *The Queensland Nat.*, **17**: 30.

MENEGAUX, A. 1913. Description de deux nouveaux Paradisiers (*Paradisea duivenbodei et P. ragg. sororia*). *Rev. Franc. Orn.*, **3**: 49–51.

MEYER, A.B. 1874. Uber neue und ungenügend bekannte Vögel von Neu-Guinea und den Inseln der Geelvinksbai. *Sitzungsb. K. Akad. Wiss. Wien, Math- Naturwiss.*, **69** (1): 74–90.

— 1891. Ueber Vögel von Neu Guinea und Neu Britannien. *Abh. Ber. Mus. Dresden*, **3**, no. 4: 1–17.

— 1893. Neuer beitrag zur kenntness der Vogelfauna von Kaiser Wilhelmsland, besonders vom Huongolfe. *Abh. Ber. Mus. Dresden*, **4**: 1–33.

— 1895. *Pteridophora alberti*, gen. et sp. n. *Bull. Brit. Orn. Club*, **4**: 11 and 21.

MORESBY, CAPTAIN J. 1876. *New Guinea and Polynesia: Discoveries and surveys in New Guinea and the D'Entrecasteaux Islands*. London.

NEHRKORN, A. 1910. *Katalog der Eiersammlung nebst Beschreibungen der Aussereuropäischen Eier*. 2. Aufl. Berlin.

NEUMANN, O. 1922. Neue Formen aus dem papuanischen und polynesischen Inselreich. *Ver. Orn. Ges. Bayern*, **15**: 234–7.

— 1932. Lophorina superba spinx nov. subsp. *Orn. Monatsb.*, **40**: 121–2.

NEWTON, A. 1899. *A dictionary of birds*. London.

NORTH, A.J. 1892. Note on the nidification of *Manucodia comrii*, Sclater (Comrie's Manucode). *Rec. Australian Mus.*, **2**, no. 2: 32.

— 1906. Description of a new bird of paradise. *Victorian Nat.*, **22**: 156–8.

OGILVIE-GRANT, W.R. 1915. Report on the birds collected by the British Ornithologists' Union Expedition and the Wollaston Expedition in Dutch New Guinea. *Ibis*, Jubilee Supp. no. 2.

OORT, E.D.VAN 1910. Note VIII. Report on a small collection of birds from Merauke, southern New Guinea. *Notes Leyden Mus.*, **32**: 78–82.

— 1915. On a new bird of paradise from central New Guinea,

Falcinellus meyeri albicans. *Zool. Meded. Leiden,* **1**: 228.

OUSTALET, M.E. 1880. D'une Espèce nouvelle de Paradisier (*Drepanornis bruijnii*). *Ann. Sci. Nat.,* ser. 6, **9**: 1.

PAYKULL, G.DE. 1815. Lanii Crassirostris avis antea ignotae descriptio. *Nov. Act. Reg. Soc. Sci. Upsala,* **7**, ser. 2: 282–5.

PENNANT, T. 1781. Specimen Faunulae Indicae. In Forster, J.R., 1781, *Zoologica Indica Selecta.*

PETERS, J.L. 1962. *Check-list of birds of the world,* vol. 15. Eds. E.Mayr and J.C.Greenway. Cambridge, Mass., Mus. of Comp. Zool.

PHILLIPPS, R. 1905. The Regent Bird (*Sericulus melinus*). *Avic. Mag.,* new ser., **4**: 51–68, 88–96, 123–31.

PLOMLEY, K.F. 1935. Bower of the Regent Bower-bird. *Emu,* **34**: 199.

PRATT, A.E. 1906. *Two years among New Guinea cannibals.* Philadelphia.

RAMSAY, E.P. 1874. Descriptions of five new species of birds from Queensland, and of the egg of *Chlamydodera maculata. Proc. Zool. Soc. London*: 601.

1876. List of birds met with in north-eastern Queensland, chiefly at Rockingham Bay. *Proc. Zool. Soc. London,* 1875: 578–603.

1883. Contributions to the zoology of New Guinea, Part VII. *Proc. Linn. Soc. New South Wales,* **8**: 15–29.

1885. Contributions to the zoology of New Guinea. Notes on birds from Mount Astrolabe, with descriptions of two new species. *Proc. Linn. Soc. New South Wales,* **10**: 242–4.

RAND, A.L. 1936. Results of the Archbold Expeditions. No. 12. Altitudinal variation in New Guinea birds. *Amer. Mus. Novitates,* no. 890: 1–14.

1938. Results of the Archbold Expeditions. No. 22. On the breeding habits of some birds of paradise in the wild. *Amer. Mus. Novitates,* no. 993: 1–8.

1940a. Results of the Archbold Expeditions. No. 25. New birds from the 1938–9 expedition. *Amer. Mus. Novitates,* no. 1072.

1940b. Breeding habits of the birds of paradise *Macgregoria* and *Diphyllodes.* Results of the Archbold Expeditions. No. 26. *Amer. Mus. Novitates,* no. 1073: 1–14.

1942a. Results of the Archbold Expeditions. No. 42. Birds

473

of the 1936–1937 New Guinea expedition. *Bull. Amer. Mus. Nat. Hist.*, **79**: 289–366.

1942b. Results of the Archbold Expeditions. No. 43. Birds of the 1938–1939 New Guinea expedition. *Bull. Amer. Mus. Nat. Hist.*, **79**: 425–516.

REICHENOW, A.   1894. *Paradisea maria n. sp. Orn. Monatsb.*, **2**: 22–3.

1897. Neue Vogelarten von Kaiser-Wilhelms-Land. *Orn. Monatsb.*, **5**: 24–6.

1918. (Deutsche Ornithologische Gesellschaft.) *Journ. f. Orn.*, **66**: 437–9.

REINER, E.   1960. The glaciation of Mount Wilhelm, Australian New Guinea. *Geogr. Rev.*, **50**: 491–503.

RIPLEY, D.   1947. *Trail of the money bird.* New York and London.

1950. Strange courtship of birds of paradise. *Nat. Geogr. Mag.*, **97**: 247–78.

1957. The display of the Sickle-billed Bird of Paradise. *Condor*, **59**: 207.

1964. A systematic and ecological study of birds of New Guinea. *Bull. Peabody Mus. Nat. Hist.*, no. 19: 1–87.

ROSENBERG, H. VON.   1878. *Der Malayische Archipel.* Leipzig.

ROTHSCHILD, LORD W.   1895a. A new bird of paradise. *Novit. Zool.* **2**: 59–60.

1895b. *Aeluroedus jobiensis*, sp. n. *Bull. Brit. Orn. Club*, **4**: 26.

1897a. Loboparadisea sericea, gen. et sp. n. *Bull. Brit. Orn. Club*, **6**: 15–16, 24.

1897b. Exhibition of skins of *Paradisea minor* and allies, *P. finschi*, and *P. minor jobiensis*, subsp. n. *Bull. Brit. Orn. Club*, **6**: 45–6.

1898. *Fam. Paradiseidae. Das Tierreich, Aves,* vol. **2**: 1–52. Berlin.

1899. Egg of *Seleucides ignotus. Bull. Brit. Orn. Club*, **8**: 13–14.

1907a. Exhibition and remarks on the types of *Astrapia rothschildi* and *Parotia wahnesi. Bull. Brit. Orn. Club*, **19**: 7–8.

1907b. Description of new bird-of-paradise (*Lophorina minor latipennis*). *Bull. Brit. Orn. Club*, **19**: 92.

1910. (No title.) *Bull. Brit. Orn. Club*, **27**: 13–14.

1930. Exhibition of eggs of the Paradise-Crow (*Lycocorax pyrrhopterus pyrrhopterus*) and *Phonygammus keraudrenii keraudrenii*. *Bull. Brit. Orn. Club*, **51**: 9.

1931. On a collection of birds made by Mr F. Shaw Mayer in the Weyland Mountains, Dutch New Guinea, in 1930. *Novit. Zool.*, **36**: 250–76.

ROTHSCHILD, LORD W., and E. HARTERT. 1896. Contributions to the ornithology of the Papuan Islands. *Novitates Zool.*, **3**: 8–20.

1903. Notes on Papuan birds. VII. Paradiseidae. *Novit. Zool.*, **10**: 65–89.

1911. Preliminary descriptions of some new birds from central New Guinea. *Novit. Zool.*, **18**: 159–61.

1913. List of the collections of birds made by Albert S. Meek in the lower ranges of the Snow Mountains, on the Eilanden River, and on Mount Goliath during the years 1910 and 1911. *Novit. Zool.*, **20**: 473–527.

1929. (No title, note to editor.) *Bull. Brit. Orn. Club*, **49**: 109–10.

ROTHSCHILD, LORD W., W. R. OGILVIE-GRANT, and H. F. WITHERBY. 1913. [Note on the Wollaston-Kloss collection from Carstensz Peak.] *Bull. Brit. Orn. Club*, **31**: 101–106.

SALMON, H. A. 1953. 'Injury feigning' by catbirds. *Emu*, **53**: 263–4.

SALVADORI, T. 1875. Descrizione de ciquantotto nuove specie di uccelli, ed osservazioni interne ad altre poco note, della Nuova Guinea e di altre Isole Papuane, raccolte del Dr Odoardo Beccari e dai cacciatori del Sig. A. A. Bruijn. *Ann. Mus. Civ. Genova*, **7**, ser. 1: 896–976.

1880–2. *Ornitologia della Papuasia e delle Molucche*, vols. 1–3. Torino.

1894. Viaggio di Lamberto Loria nella Papuasia Orientale. XII. Caratteri de cinque specie nuove di uccelli della Nuova Guinea Orientale-meridionale raccolti da L. Loria. *Ann. Mus. Civ. Genova*, ser. 2, **14**: 150–2.

SALVIN, O., and F. D. GODMAN. 1883. Discovery of a new bird of paradise. *Ibis*, ser. 5, **1**: 131.

SCHAUENSEE, R. M. de. 1940. Rediscovery of the Megapode, *Aepypodius bruijnii*. *Auk*, **57**: 83–4.

SCHLEGEL. 1863. (No title.) *Ibis*, **5**: 119.

SCHLÜTER, W. 1911. Seleucides ignotus auripennis Schlüt., Subsp. nov. aus Deutsch-Neuguinea. *Falco*, **7**: 2–4.

SCHODDE, R. MS. Birds of Mount Giluwe and Lake Kutubu. June–October, 1961.

SCHÖNWETTER, M. 1944. Die Eier der Paradiesvögel. *Beitr. zur Fortpflanzungsbiologie der Vögel*, **20**, no. 1: 1–18.

SCLATER, P.L. 1873. (Notes concerning birds collected by D'Albertis). *Proc. Zool. Soc. London*: 557–60.

1876. On the birds collected by Dr Comrie on the south-east coast of New Guinea during the survey of HMS *Basilisk*. *Proc. Zool. Soc. London*: 459–61.

1883. (Note on *Drepanornis*.) *Proc. Zool. Soc. London*: 578.

SCOPOLI, G.A. 1786. *Deliciae florae et faunae in subricae*. Pt. 2. Ticini, Monasterii S. Salvatoris.

SCOTT, J.W. 1942. Mating behavior of the Sage Grouse. *Auk*, **59**: 477–98.

SHARPE, R.B. 1876. Mr O.C. Stone's expedition to New Guinea. *Nature, Lond.*, **14**: 338–9.

1877. *Catalogue of the Birds in the British Museum*, Vol. 3, Passeriformes. London.

1882. Contributions to the ornithology of New Guinea, Part viii. *Journ. Linn. Soc. London*, Zool., **16**: 422–47.

1884. Contributions to the ornithology of New Guinea, Part ix. *Journ. Linn. Soc. London*, Zool., **17**: 405–8.

1891–8. *Monograph of the Paradiseidae, or Birds of Paradise, and Ptilonorhynchidae, or Bower-Birds*. Parts 1–8. London.

1894. (No title.) *Bull. Brit. Orn. Club*, **4**: 12–15.

SHAW, G. 1809. *General Zoology*, vol. 7, pt. 2. London.

SICK, H. 1959. Die Balze der Schmuckvögel (Pipridae). *Journ. f. Orn.*, **100**: 269–302.

SIMPSON, G.G. 1961. Historical zoogeography of Australian mammals. *Evol.*, **15**: 431–46.

SIMS, R.W. 1956. Birds collected by Mr F. Shaw-Mayer in the central highlands of New Guinea 1950–1951. *Bull. Brit. Mus. (Nat. Hist.)*, Zool., **3**, no. 10.

SIMSON, C.C. 1907. On the habits of the birds-of-paradise and bower-birds of British New Guinea. *Ibis*, **1**: 380–7.

SMITH, A.F. 1906. Cairns (N.Q.) notes. *Emu*, **5**: 210–11.

SNOW, D.W. 1962. A field study of the Black and White Manakin, *Manacus manacus*, in Trinidad. *Zoologica*, vol. 47: 65–104.

1963. The Evolution of Manakin Displays. *Proc. XIII Int. Congress*, **1**: 552–61.

STEIN, G.H.W. 1936. Beiträge zur Biologie papuanischer Vögel. *Journ. f. Orn.*, **84**: 21–57.

STONOR, C.R. 1936. The evolution and mutual relationships of some members of the Paradiseidae. *Proc. Zool. Soc. London*: 1177–85.

1937. On the systematic position of the Ptilonorhynchidae. *Proc. Zool. Soc. London*, ser. B, **107**: 475–490.

1939. A new species of paradise bird of the genus *Astrapia*. *Bull. Brit. Orn. Club*, **59**: 57–61.

1940. *Courtship and display among birds*. London.

STRESEMANN, E. 1922a. Neue Formen aus Neuguinea. *Orn. Monatsb.*, **30**: 35.

1922b. Neue Formen aus dem papuanischen Gebiet. *Journ. f. Orn.*, **70**: 405–8.

1923. Dr Bürgers' Ornithologische Ausbeute im Stromgebiet des Sepik. *Arch. f. Natur.*, **89**, no. 7: 1–96; no. 8: 1–92.

1924. Neue Beiträge zur Ornithologie Deutsch-Neuguineas. *Journ. f. Orn.*, **72**: 424–8.

1930. Welche Paradiesvogelarten der Literatur sind hybriden Ursprings *Novitates Zool.*, **36**: 6–15.

1934. Vier neue Unterarten von Paradiesvögeln. *Orn. Monatsb.*, **42**: 144–7.

1953. Laube und Balz der Laubenvögel (Ptilonorhynchidae). *Die Vogelwarte*, **16**: 148–54.

1954. Die Entdeckungsgeschichte der Paradiesvögel. *Journ. f. Orn.*, **95**: 263–91.

WALLACE, A.R. 1862. Narrative of search after birds of paradise. *Proc. Zool. Soc. London*: 153–66.

1869. *The Malay Archipelago*. New York.

WARHAM, J. 1957. Notes on the display and behaviour of the Great Bower-bird. *Emu*, **57**: 73–8.

1962. Field notes on Australian bower-birds and cat-birds. *Emu*, **62**: 1–30.

WEISKE, E. 1902. Ein Beitrag zur Naturgeschichte der Laubenvögel. *Orn. Monatsschr.*, **27**: 41–5.

WILLUGHBY. 1676. *Ornithologiae libri* III, London. (Eng. trans. ed. by John Ray, 1678, London.)

ZEUNER, F.E. 1942. Studies in the systematics of *Troides* Hubner

(Lepidoptera, Papilionidae) and its allies; distribution and phylogeny in relation to the geological history of the Australian Archipelago. *Trans. Zool. Soc. London*, **25**: 107–84.

Index

(Numbers in bold type refer to plates)

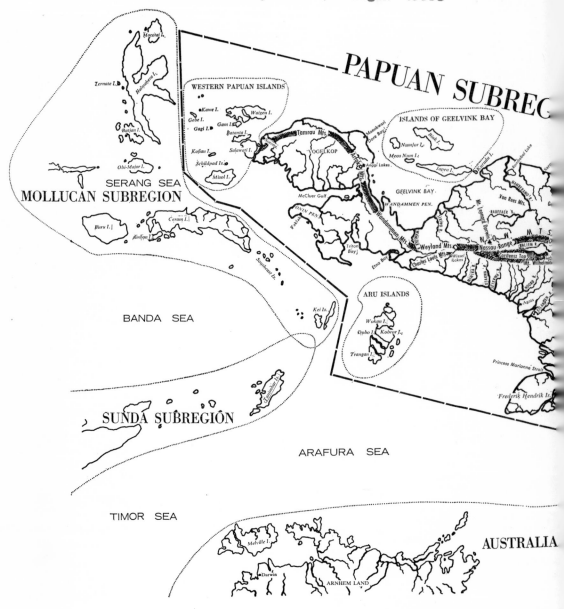

PAPUAN SUBREG

WESTERN PAPUAN ISLANDS

ISLANDS OF GEELVINK BAY

MOLLUCAN SUBREGION

SERANG SEA

BANDA SEA

SUNDA SUBREGION

ARU ISLANDS

ARAFURA SEA

TIMOR SEA

AUSTRALIA